The Legacies of Law

This highly original book examines the function of legal norms and institutions in the transition to – and from – apartheid. It sheds light on the neglected relationship between path dependence and the law. *The Legacies of Law* demonstrates that legal norms and institutions, even illiberal ones, can have an important – and hitherto undertheorized – structuring effect on democratic transitions. Focusing on South Africa during the period 1652–2000, Jens Meierhenrich finds that under certain conditions, law reduces uncertainty in democratization by invoking common cultural backgrounds and experiences. Synthesizing insights from law, political science, economics, sociology, history, and philosophy, he offers an innovative "redescription" of both apartheid *and* apartheid's endgame.

The Legacies of Law demonstrates that in instances in which interacting adversaries share qua law reasonably convergent mental models, transitions from authoritarian rule are less intractable. Meierhenrich's careful longitudinal analysis of the evolution of law – and its effects – in South Africa, compared with a short study of Chile from 1830 to 1990, shows how, and when, legal norms and institutions serve as historical parameters to *both* democratic and undemocratic rule. By so doing, *The Legacies of Law* contributes new and unexpected insights – both theoretical and applied – to contemporary debates about democracy and the rule of law. Among other things, Meierhenrich significantly advances our understanding of "hybrid regimes" in the international system and generates important policy-relevant insights into the functioning of law and courts in authoritarian regimes.

Jens Meierhenrich is Assistant Professor of Government and of Social Studies at Harvard University.

The Legacies of Law

Long-Run Consequences of Legal Development in South Africa, 1652–2000

JENS MEIERHENRICH

Harvard University

CAMBRIDGE
UNIVERSITY PRESS

CAMBRIDGE UNIVERSITY PRESS
Cambridge, New York, Melbourne, Madrid, Cape Town,
Singapore, São Paulo, Delhi, Tokyo, Mexico City

Cambridge University Press
The Edinburgh Building, Cambridge CB2 8RU, UK

Published in the United States of America by Cambridge University Press, New York

www.cambridge.org
Information on this title: www.cambridge.org/9780521156998

First published 2008

A catalogue record for this publication is available from the British Library

Library of Congress Cataloguing in Publication Data
Meierhenrich, Jens.
    The legacies of law: long-run consequences of legal development in South Africa, 1652–2000 /
Jens Meierhenrich.
        p.   cm.
    Includes bibliographical references and index.
    ISBN 978-0-521-89873-7 (hardback)
    1. Rule of law – South Africa – History.   2. Apartheid – South Africa.   3. Democracy – South
Africa.   4. Justice, Administration of – South Africa – History.   5. South Africa – Politics and
government.   I. Title.
    KTL470.M45 2008
    347.68–dc22   2008000099

ISBN 978-0-521-89873-7 Hardback
ISBN 978-0-521-15699-8 Paperback

Contents

List of Figures

List of Tables

List of Cases

Administrator, Transvaal v. Traub 1989 (4) SA 731 (A)
Apleni v. Minister of Law and Order and others 1989 (1) SA 195 (A)
AZAPO and others v. President of the Republic and others 1996 (4) SA 671 (CC)
Bank of Lisbon and SA Ltd v. De Ornelas 1988 (3) SA 580 (A)
Bill v. State President 1987 (1) SA 265 (W)
Bloem v. State President of the Republic of South Africa 1986 (4) SA 1064 (O)
Buthelezi v. Attorney General, Natal 1986 (4) SA 371 (D)
Dempsey v. Minister of Law and Order 1986 (4) SA 530 (C)
Dlamini v. Minister of Law and Order 1986 (4) SA 342 (D)
During NO v. Boesak 1990 (3) SA 661 (A)
Ex parte Chairperson of the Constitutional Assembly in Re: Certification of the Constitution of the Republic of South Africa 1996 1996 (4) SA 744 (CC)
Ex parte Chairperson of the Constitutional Assembly in Re: Certification of the Amended Text of the Constitution of the Republic of South Africa 1996 1997 (2) SA 97 (CC)
Ex parte Moseneke 1979 (4) SA 884
Fani v. Minister of Law and Order (ECD Case No. 1840/1985, unreported)
Gibson Thlokwe Mathebe and others v. KwaNdebele Commissioner of Police and another, TPD Case No. 14181/1987
Government of Lebowa v. Government of the Republic of South Africa and another 1988 (1) SA 344 (A)
Government of the Republic of South Africa and another v. Government of KwaZulu and another 1983 (1) SA 164 (A)
Green v. Fitzgerald 1914 AD 88
Harris v. Minister of the Interior 1952 (2) SA 428 (A)
Henderson v. Hanekom 1903 (20) SC 513
Incorporated Law Society v. Mandela 1954 (3) SA 102 (T)
Jaffer v. Minister of Law and Order 1986 (4) SA 1027 (C)
Komani v. Bantu Affairs Administration Board, Peninsula Area 1979 (1) SA 508 (C)
Krohn v. Minister of Defence 1915 AD 191
Mandela v. Minister of Prisons 1983 (1) SA 938 (A)

Mathebe v. Regering van die Republiek van Suid-Afrika en andere 1988 (3)
    SA 667 (A)
Metal and Allied Workers' Union v. State President 1986 (4) SA 358 (D)
Minister of Law and Order and another v. Dempsey 1988 (3) SA 19 (A)
Minister of Law and Order and another v. Swart 1989 (1) SA 295 (A)
Minister of Law and Order and others v. Hurley and another 1986 (3) SA 568 (A)
Minister of Posts and Telegraphs v. Rasool 1934 AD 167
Minister of the Interior v. Harris 1952 (4) SA 769 (A)
Minister van Wet en Orde v. Matshoba 1990 (1) SA 280 (A)
Mokoena v. Minister of Law and Order 1986 (4) SA 42 (W)
Mokwena v. State President 1988 (2) SA 91 (T)
More v. Minister of Co-operation and Development 1986 (1) SA 102 (A)
Mthiya v. Black Administration Board, Western Cape, and another 1983 (3)
    SA 455 (C)
Natal Indian Congress v. State President NPD (Case No. 3864/1988)
Natal Newspapers (Pty) Limited v. State President 1986 (4) SA 1109 (N)
Ndlwana v. Hofmeyr N.O. 1937 AD 229
Nkwentsha v. Minister of Law and Order and another 1988 (3) SA 99 (A)
Nqumba [sic] v. State President 1987 (1) SA 456 (E)
Ngqumba v. Staatspresident 1988 (4) SA 224 (A)
Nkondo and Gumede v. Minister of Law and Order 1986 (2) SA 756 (A)
Nkwinti v. Commissioner of Police 1986 (2) SA 421 (E)
Omar v. Minister of Law and Order 1986 (3) SA 306 (C)
Omar v. Minister of Law and Order 1987 (3) SA 859 (A)
Powell v. National Director of Public Prosecutions 2005 (5) SA 62 (SCA)
R. v. Abdurahman 1950 (3) SA 136 (A)
R. v. Adams and others 1959 (3) SA 753 (A)
R. v. Lusu 1953 (2) SA 484 (A)
R. v. Pretoria Timber Co (Pty) Ltd 1950 (3) SA 163 (A)
R. v. Sisulu and others 1953 (3) SA 276 (A)
Radebe v. Minister of Law and Order 1987 (1) SA 586 (W)
Release Mandela Campaign v. State President 1988 (1) SA 201 (N)
Rex v. Abdurahman 1950 (3) SA 136 (A)
Rikhoto v. East Rand Administration Board and Municipal Labour Officer,
    Germiston 1983 (4) SA 278 (W)
Roussouw v. Sachs 1964 (2) SA 551 (A)
S. v. Alexander (2) 1965 (2) SA 818 (C)
S. v. Alexander (1) 1965 (2) SA 796 (A)
S. v. Cooper and others 1977 (3) SA 475 (T)
S. v. Gwala and others Reference AD 2021 (Case CC 108/1976)
S. v. Hassim and others 1972 (1) SA 200 (N)
S. v. Mbhele 1980 (1) SA 295 (N)
S. v. Molobi Reference AD 2021 (Case WLD 652/1975)
S. v. Molokeng and others Reference AD 1901 (Case WLD 30/1976)
S. v. Mothopeng and others Reference AD 2021

Preface and Acknowledgments

I happened upon the subject matter of this book – the function of law in times of transition – about a decade ago. I was rereading at the time, for no particular reason at all, Ernst Fraenkel's *The Dual State: A Contribution to the Theory of Dictatorship* (New York: Oxford University Press, 1941), a highly original yet largely forgotten study of the law of the "Third Reich." Written by a German labor lawyer of Jewish faith, *The Dual State* remains one of the most absorbing books – drafted clandestinely in the mid-1930s – ever published in the public law tradition. It was this rereading of *The Dual State* that inspired my "redescription," to borrow Ian Shapiro's term, of apartheid and apartheid's endgame.

I had first encountered Fraenkel – alongside Max Weber and Carl Schmitt – in the early 1990s, as a first-year student of law as well as political science and sociology in my native Germany. I was intrigued by the provocative argument contained in *The Dual State* and its lucid elaboration. I marveled at the effortless blend of insights from numerous disciplines and its deep grounding in the jurisprudence of Weimar Germany. At the time, however, I was preoccupied with comprehending the minutiae of constitutional law in the Federal Republic of Germany rather than the discredited legal theory and practice of the regimes – authoritarian and totalitarian – that had preceded it. It was not until several years later that I began to realize the significance of *The Dual State* for making sense not only of dictatorship then but also of democracy now. This realization had a great deal to do with South Africa, where I had just spent a considerable amount of time witnessing the country's transition from apartheid.

I lived and loved in South Africa for the better part of two years and, as such, learned a fair amount about the country and its people. Johannesburg in particular held my attention. There I met Paul van Zyl, then at the Centre for the Study of Violence and Reconciliation (CSVR). He would go on to become the Executive Director of the Truth and Reconciliation Commission of South Africa (TRC) and is now with the International Center for Transitional Justice in New York. It was Paul who, in 1995, involved me not only in the Centre's work on the TRC (an institution that had not yet been created, let alone heralded and transplanted the world over), but also for allowing me to work, together with two other staff, over an extended period of time in Alexandra, then one of the most densely populated – and most violently contested – townships in South Africa, located on the northern fringe of Johannesburg. It was in Alexandra that I acquired a "feel" for the convoluted politics of South Africa, notably for the real – and imagined – cleavages that have driven it apart.

In May 1995, the National Peace Accord Trust had commissioned the CSVR to facilitate change in Alexandra. The project's aim was to "empower" about twelve hundred families (including their violent members) and other "stakeholders" from different "constituencies" who had been displaced as a result of collective violence that had torn to shreds the social fabric of Alexandra in 1992. Ultimately, this demanded that the CSVR, and our three-person crew who acted on its behalf, play a central role in attempting to rebuild shattered relationships, facilitate a process of sustainable local-level "reconstruction" and "development," and set into motion a process of "reconciliation." I am not sure what, if any, our contribution was in Alexandra, but I remain truly grateful to the township's hostel dwellers and inhabitants (especially those living in the "Beirut area") for welcoming me into their midst, and for allowing me glimpses into their depleted lives.

A year later, I was fortunate to work with Richard Humphries and Thabo Rapoo as well as Khehla Shubane and Steven Friedman at the Centre for Policy Studies (CPS) in Johannesburg. Our focus was on the institutional dimensions of federalism in Gauteng Province. The countless interviews with policy makers, bureaucrats (incoming and outgoing), politicians, and so forth in Johannesburg and Pretoria that we conducted provided me with precious insights into the organizational structure of the postapartheid state, and the politics of institutional stasis – and change – in times of transition. Although research at CSVR and CPS has had no direct bearing on this book, my exposure – and hopefully attunedness – to various sites of contention in South Africa has invariably influenced my account of the role of legal norms and institutions in the transition to – and from – apartheid. Most important, it has sensitized me to the necessity of adopting a perspective from the *longue durée*, of taking seriously the long-run development of institutions, formal and otherwise, for understanding politics and society.

Then came the law, to me the most interesting of all institutions. Directly responsible for my turn to law, or so I discovered in retrospect, was Dennis Davis's "Constitutional Talk," which during the drafting of South Africa's Interim Constitution aired weekly on television courtesy of the SABC, South Africa's Broadcasting Corporation. The sophisticated manner in which representatives from different political groupings as well as scholars – united (for the most part) by a belief in the centrality of law – aired their disputes and preferences was astonishing. This commitment to law was rather surprising and early on persuaded me that there was something truly remarkable about the country's legal development that required further investigation. My investigation of legalization in South Africa began in earnest in 1998, when, as mentioned, I stumbled across *The Dual State*. Rereading Fraenkel, at this critical juncture, allowed me to lay the groundwork for an integrated, interdisciplinary analysis of legal origins and their path-dependent effects in the period 1650–2000. A few years later, my ideas fully percolated, I reconfigured Fraenkel for use in the theory of democracy. This book is the result. It also includes a tentative discussion – a plausibility probe – of my argument in the case of Chile, 1830–1990.

I could not have mustered the courage of my convictions and finished *The Legacies of Law* had it not been for those who offered wisdom while it was in the making. I am indebted to many scholars who generously read and commented on the manuscript in its entirety, namely, Edwin Cameron, Martin Chanock, Christopher Clapham, John Comaroff, Hugh Corder, John Dugard, David Dyzenhaus, Stephen Ellmann, Hermann Giliomee, Richard Goldstone, Donald Horowitz, Arend Lijphart, Michael Lobban, Frank Michelman, Dunbar Moodie, Laurence Whitehead, and Crawford Young. I shall remain forever grateful for the care that the aforementioned took in scrutinizing my argument and evidence, and for helping me mend the weaker parts. My gratitude also extends to Dikgang Moseneke and Albie Sachs, both sitting Judges of the Constitutional Court of South Africa, for their kind interest in my work. I would be remiss if I did not also acknowledge Lew Bateman, for his belief in the importance of this book, and the three anonymous reviewers for Cambridge University Press (one of whom persuaded me to provide this account of the gestation of the manuscript), whose generous praise and constructive criticism further improved the book. Laura Lawrie carefully copyedited the manuscript, Patrizia Kuriger expertly prepared the index, and Emily Spangler patiently facilitated the production. I am grateful to them all.

For comments and suggestions on the work in progress, I also thank Penelope Andrews, Kader Asmal, Robert Bates, Ursula Bentele, William Beinart, David Collier, Larry Diamond, Ivan Evans, Steven Friedman, Robert Goodin, Peter Hall, Michael Hart, Stanley Hoffmann, Richard Humphries, Andrew Hurrell, Thomas Karis, Desmond King, Roy Licklider, Irving Markovits, Shula Marks, Anthony Marx, Timothy Mitchell, Robert O'Neill, Adam Roberts, Donald Rothchild, Bruce Russett, Nicholas Sambanis, Luc Sindjoun, Jack Snyder, Alfred Stepan, Wilfried Swenden, Stephen Walt, Gavin Williams, Elisabeth Wood, Ngaire Woods, and especially Cindy Skach. Moreover, I am grateful to Rupert Taylor, Neil MacFarlane, and Charles Tilly, who were sources of encouragement in the decade from conception to completion.

Rupert was an always-available mentor and interlocutor in 1995 and 1996, when he tutored me – either at WITS, the University of the Witwatersrand, or, more likely, in a coffee shop nearby – in the vagaries of South African politics and society. Neil supported the project from the very beginning, kept me going with thoughtful advice in the middle, and with gentle pressure steered me toward completion of the dissertation that constitutes the nucleus of this book. Chuck was crucial in the middle and also toward the end of the dissertation phase. He pushed me to clarify what was murky, offered counsel when things got stuck, and made me part of the contentious politics crowd at Columbia University – which I left behind only reluctantly when I moved on to Harvard in the millennial year.

Aside from the attention of colleagues known to me, I benefited greatly from feedback that I received during talks at Columbia University, Harvard University, the University of Oxford, and the University of Stellenbosch as well as numerous conferences and workshops, notably the "Democracy and the Rule of Law" workshop convened by Stephen Elkin under the auspices of the Democracy Collaborative at the University of Maryland in 2004. I am grateful to Steve for extending an invitation and his steadfast support of my career ever since, and to Karol Soltan and Rogers Smith for incisive comments on the occasion. Needless to say, none of the aforementioned is responsible for any errors of fact or judgment on my part.

The Rhodes Trust, Oxford, made much of the field research in South Africa possible. The Trust awarded generous funds for this and a related project, and I am especially grateful to Sir Anthony Kenny, former Warden of Rhodes House, for his support. I also received ample funding from the Centre for International Studies (CIS) at the University of Oxford. Additional funds came from the Graduate Studies Committee and St Antony's College, Oxford. Marga Lyall, Secretary at CIS, and Sally Colgan, former accountant at Rhodes House, aided gently in the administration of life. Nancy and Alfred Stepan provided shelter when a landlord struck. Funding for early field research in South Africa came from the *Deutscher Akademischer Austauschdienst* (DAAD) in Germany as well as CSVR, CPS, and the South African Institute of International Affairs at Jan Smuts House, Johannesburg. I thank Steven Friedman, Greg Mills, and Graeme Simpson, respectively.

I am indebted also to Frederik van Zyl Slabbert, Afrikaner democrat, who went out of his way to discuss, early on, the subject matter of this book with me in both Johannesburg and London, as well as Ibrahim I. Ibrahim, MP for the African National Congress (ANC), for facilitating interviews and access to Parliament in Cape Town in 1997. Helen Suzman shared her experiences with me on a memorable afternoon in Houghton. While I learned a great deal from all of my respondents over the years, only very few of whom are featured in the pages to come, I am especially grateful to those in the Natal Midlands who exposed me to KwaZulu politics, including Inkatha "warlord" David Ntombela who allowed me rare access to his world. I owe special thanks to Duncan Randall for making possible my visit to the countryside and the provincial legislature in Pietermaritzburg. Although only a fraction of the data, ethnographic and otherwise, that I collected in South Africa over the years found its way into the manuscript, it is there nonetheless – the foundation upon which my interpretation rests.

I had the good fortune to write and rewrite several chapters while a Fellow at the Institute for Social and Economic Research and Policy (ISERP) at Columbia University's Paul F. Lazarsfeld Center for the Social Sciences. There, Peter Bearman had established, and I was lucky to join, in 1999 a vibrant and diverse intellectual community in pursuit of scholarly excellence, above all in the area of comparative historical analysis. Peter's belief in my project, and my intellectual abilities more generally, gave me confidence at a time when I had little. His example and innovative scholarship have been an inspiration ever since. Similarly inspiring, in the final stages of the project, was the scholarship and mentorship of John Hagan at Northwestern University and the American Bar Foundation (ABF). Alongside John Comaroff and Terence Halliday, John made my sabbatical at the ABF, in 2006, truly memorable as well as enjoyable and productive.

I also acknowledge a European Recovery Program Fellowship in the Department of Political Science, Columbia University, awarded by the *Studienstiftung des deutschen Volkes*, Germany. Rupert Antes deserves special mention for his assistance in matters large and small. At Harvard, I express my gratitude to the International Security Program at Harvard's Belfer Center for Science and International Affairs, John F. Kennedy School of Government, especially Steven Miller, who invited me to become a Fellow. I also thank Harvard's Committee on Degrees on Social Studies, especially Judy Vichniac and Anya Bernstein; the now defunct Project on Justice in Times of Transition at Harvard Law School, the Kennedy School of Government, and the Weatherhead Center for International Affairs, especially Sara Zucker, Ina Breuer, and Philip Heymann; the University Committee on Human Rights Studies, notably Jacqueline Bhabha and Martha Minow; as well as my principal intellectual home, the Department of Government in the Faculty of Arts and Sciences, especially Robert Bates, Timothy Colton, Jorge Dominguez, Grzegorz Ekiert, Peter Hall, Stanley Hoffmann, Elizabeth Perry, Robert Putnam, and Nancy Rosenblum.

Good friends make extraordinary efforts worthwhile. Sumiko Aoki; Britt Aylor; Henning Beste; Michele Calandrino; Carolyn Chen; Ivor Chipkin; Illeana Georgiou; Hans-Martin Jäger; Melody, Josh, Tairou, Omo, and Stella Komyerov; Alex Krämer; Angelo Pacillo; Anke Rose; Shahana Rasool; Uli Scherr; Malte Stellmann; Oliver and Sylke Simons; Wilfried Swenden; and Tracy Yen as well as Michèle, Natalie, Alex, and Jerry Cohen offered, at one point or another, respite from the isolation of research and writing. Josephine, Pat, Frank, and John Skach were, for a while, a second family. Foundations for my curiosity were laid much earlier, and I gratefully acknowledge the late Roland Stief for helping lay them.

My parents, Christa and Friedel Meierhenrich, accompanied the research and writing from afar, as did my grandmother, Helene Brokmann, who contributed to the making of this book with her generous spirit. All three supported me at critical junctures in my life, and I owe each a tremendous debt. For what it is worth, this book is for them.

The Legacies of Law

I

Introduction

From Afghanistan to Sierra Leone, the international community is promoting democratic norms and institutions. It is for this reason that the investigation of general and specific effects of authoritarian legacies has been identified as a "pressing challenge for political science."[1] Research on this institutional overhang is timely, for surviving institutions have received scant attention in the literature.[2] Moreover, while scholars have written widely on how to make democracy work in changing societies, they have said relatively little about the contribution of law to this endeavor. By taking legal norms and institutions seriously, this book contributes new patterns, significant connections, and improved interpretations to the theory of democracy.

The book constructs the foundations for a theory of democracy that revolves around *rules of law*. It sheds light on the neglected relationship between path dependence and the law. By showing how, and when, legal norms and institutions served as historical causes to contemporary dictatorship and democracy, the book advances unexpected insights about the ever more relevant linkages between law and politics in the international system.[3] As such, the book also contributes to the emerging debate over the legacies of liberalism.[4]

[1] Michael Bratton and Nicolas Van de Walle, *Democratic Experiments in Africa: Regime Transitions in Comparative Perspective* (Cambridge: Cambridge University Press, 1997), p. 275.

[2] Richard Snyder and James Mahoney, "The Missing Variable: Institutions and the Study of Regime Change," *Comparative Politics*, Vol. 32, No. 1 (October 1999), esp. pp. 112–117.

[3] For explorations of this linkage, see José María Maravall and Adam Przeworski, eds., *Democracy and the Rule of Law* (Cambridge: Cambridge University Press, 2003).

[4] For a leading contribution to this debate, see James Mahoney, *The Legacies of Liberalism: Path Dependence and Political Regimes in Central America* (Baltimore: Johns Hopkins University Press, 2001).

QUESTIONS

This book is built around an attempt to answer two central questions: How do legal norms and institutions evolve in response to individual incentives, strategies, and choices; and how, once established, do they influence the responses of individuals to large processes, especially democratization? The central theme is the importance of law in modern politics. The aim is to advance our understanding of exactly *how* law matters, to *whom, when, why,* and with *what* consequences. To this end, I advance analytic narratives of apartheid's endgame, surprisingly one of the least understood transitions from authoritarian rule.

Although the evolution of cooperation among adversaries in apartheid's endgame was impressive, the manner in which it was solved was a surprise to many. In the mid-1980s, the stakes in South Africa were perceived as incredibly high, and the depth of racial divisions too deep. The end of apartheid was an outcome expected neither by actors nor scholars. Nelson Mandela, F. W. de Klerk, and most others intimately involved in the process, did not anticipate the advent of democracy. Desmond Tutu, Archbishop Emeritus, remembers it thus:

Nearly everybody made the most dire predictions about where South Africa was headed. They believed that that beautiful land would be overwhelmed by the most awful bloodbath, that as sure as anything, a catastrophic race war would devastate that country. These predictions seemed well on the way to fulfilment when violence broke out at the time of the negotiations for a transition from repression to freedom, from totalitarian rule to democracy.[5]

Scholars echoed this view. For Arend Lijphart, writing in the late 1970s, it was an established fact that in South Africa, "the outlook for democracy of any kind is extremely poor."[6] In the late 1980s, apartheid's endgame had just begun, David Laitin cautioned scholars and practitioners alike: "That democracy, stability, and economic justice can occur in South Africa without being induced by the threat of armed upheaval appears to me to be a dream in the guise of science."[7] Looking back on apartheid's endgame, the eminent historian Leonard Thompson observed, "The odds against a successful outcome seemed insuperable, in part because South Africa was the scene of pervasive and escalating violence."[8] Most recently, Mahmood Mamdani

[5] Desmond M. Tutu, "Foreword," in Greg Marinovich and Joao Silva, *The Bang-Bang Club: Snapshots from a Hidden War* (New York: Basic Books, 2000), p. ix.

[6] Arend Lijphart, *Democracy in Plural Societies: A Comparative Exploration* (New Haven: Yale University Press, 1977), p. 236.

[7] David D. Laitin, "South Africa: Violence, Myths, and Democratic Reform," *World Politics,* Vol. 39, No. 2 (January 1987), p. 279

[8] Leonard Thompson, *A History of South Africa,* Revised Edition (New Haven: Yale University Press, 1995), p. 245.

maintained, "If Rwanda was the genocide that happened, then South Africa was the genocide that didn't."[9] Or, as *The Economist* put it:

Cassandra would have been stumped by South Africa. How easy it was, in the long, dark days of apartheid, to predict catastrophe, only to be assured by South African boosters that all was well. ... The voices of complacency were wrong. Yet so too were those that foretold a bloodbath. Of all of the horrors of the 20th century, South Africa's was unique: it did not happen.[10]

For as Courtney Jung and Ian Shapiro remind us, "[d]espite considerable violence there was no civil war, no military coup, and the cooperation among the players whose cooperation was needed was impressive."[11] This begs explanation. Thus far, the literature has pondered the *wrong* puzzle. The puzzle is *not*, as most of the literature assumes, why cooperation between democracy-demanding and democracy-resisting forces ensued. Rather, the puzzle is why cooperation – despite great uncertainty – spawned commitments that remained credible over time, and that inaugurated one of the most admired democratic experiments in the twentieth century.

ARGUMENTS

The arguments developed in this book to explain the *real* puzzle of apartheid's endgame are counterintuitive. The empirical argument suggests that apartheid law was, in an important respect, necessary for making democracy work.[12] In pursuit of this argument, I analyze the function of legal norms and institutions in the transition *to* and *from* apartheid. The theoretical argument purports that the legal norms and institutions, even illiberal ones, at t have an important – and hitherto undertheorized – structuring effect on democratic outcomes at t_1.

In furtherance of this argument I revisit Ernst Fraenkel's forgotten concept of the dual state. Fraenkel, a German labor lawyer and social democrat, fled the Nazi dictatorship in 1938. From his exile in the United States, he published *The Dual State: A Contribution to the Theory of Dictatorship* (New York: Oxford University Press, 1941). *The Dual State* remains one of the most erudite books on the origins of dictatorship. It provided the first comprehensive analysis of the rise and nature of National Socialism, and was the only such analysis written from within Hitler's Germany. Although widely received on publication in the United States in the 1940s, the concept of the dual state, with its two

[9] Mahmood Mamdani, *When Victims Become Killers: Colonialism, Nativism, and the Genocide in Rwanda* (Princeton: Princeton University Press, 2001), p. 185.
[10] "Africa's Great Black Hope: A Survey of South Africa," *The Economist*, February 27, 2001, p. 1.
[11] Courtney Jung and Ian Shapiro, "South Africa's Negotiated Transition: Democracy, Opposition, and the New Constitutional Order," in Ian Shapiro, *Democracy's Place* (Ithaca, NY: Cornell University Press, 1996), p. 175.
[12] This book, to be sure, does not, in any way, attempt to exonerate or justify the apartheid regime, its policies, or rights violating practices.

halves – the *prerogative state* and the *normative state* – has received only scant
attention ever since. This is unfortunate, for as this book demonstrates, the dual
state is of immediate relevance for the theory of democracy.

Employing Fraenkel, I demonstrate that from colonialism to apartheid,
South Africa was ruled by an ever-changing dual state. This dual state served
what Juan Linz termed a "racial democracy." According to Linz, the paradox
of racial democracy was "reflected in the ranking of South Africa among 114
countries, according to eligibility to participate in elections and degree of
opportunity for public opposition, in scale type 14 (when the least opportunity
ranks 30), far above most authoritarian regimes in the world."[13] This paradox
was the result of the juxtaposition of two societies and political systems. This
strange juxtaposition had unintended consequences for democratic outcomes,
and is the subject of this book. Mine is an analytically driven and empirically
grounded argument for taking the concept of the dual state out of its original
context, and for increasing its extension. The book, in short, establishes the
concept's relevance for the comparative historical analysis of democracy.

As I demonstrate in Chapters 4 and 5, the law of apartheid was a blend of
formally rational law and substantially irrational law. Figure 1.1 represents
this blend. Box "A" represents formally rational law. Government was only
weakly constrained by this law, yet it regulated white commercial activity, as
well as other domains, including parts of black society. Box "B" represents
substantively irrational law. Box "A" is synonymous with the normative state
in Fraenkel's model. Box "B" is synonymous with the prerogative state. Law
affecting the disenfranchised majority under apartheid was for the most part
substantively irrational. At times, however, even substantive law took on a
rational character. Such was the structure of the dual apartheid state.

I show in Chapters 6 and 7 that in apartheid's endgame, the memory of
formally rational law – and agents' confidence in its past and future utility in
the transition from authoritarian rule – created the conditions for the emergence of trust between democracy-demanding and democracy-resisting elites.
Iterative interaction strengthened this reservoir of trust in apartheid's endgame. Adversaries at the elite level found "faith in judicial decision-making as
a source of legitimacy in the governance of a post-apartheid South Africa."[14]
This faith in law produced remarkable, democratic outcomes. In terms of the
Freedom House index of political rights and civil liberties, postapartheid South
Africa achieved a consistent score of 1 for political rights and 2 for civil
liberties in the period 1995–2002. Even as early as 1994, the tumultuous year
of the country's first free parliamentary elections, the scores were 2 and 3,
respectively. What is more, South Africa's apartheid-era ratings are indicative

[13] Juan J. Linz, "Totalitarian and Authoritarian Regimes," in Fred I. Greenstein and Nelson
W. Polsby, eds., *Handbook of Political Science, Volume 3: Macropolitical Theory* (Reading,
MA: Addison-Wesley, 1975), pp. 326–327.
[14] Heinz Klug, *Constituting Democracy: Law, Globalism and South Africa's Political
Reconstruction* (Cambridge: Cambridge University Press, 2000), p. 180.

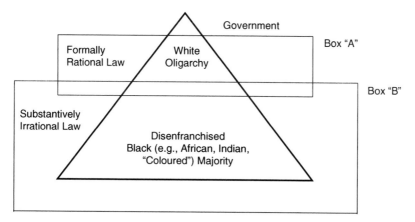

FIGURE 1.1. The Structure of Apartheid Law

of the limits the normative state was able to place on the prerogative state in select periods. The country ratings for the period 1973–1993 average an outcome of "partly free" (with annual scores ranging from 4 to 6 for both political rights and civil liberties).

EXPLANATIONS

Alternative explanations of these democratic outcomes have proved inadequate. The existing literature on apartheid's endgame suffers from three major problems: empiricism, individualism, and determinism.

Empiricism

Empiricism, the practice of describing without theorizing, is characteristic of most writings on apartheid's endgame.[15] Although descriptive narratives of apartheid's ending abound, innovative nomothetic interpretations are rare.[16]

---

[15] Prominent examples are Allister Sparks, *Tomorrow is Another Country: The Inside Story of South Africa's Negotiated Revolution* (Johannesburg: Struik Book Distributors, 1994); Patti Waldmeir, *Anatomy of a Miracle: The End of Apartheid and the Birth of the New South Africa* (London: Viking, 1997); and Steven Friedman, ed., *The Long Journey: South Africa's Quest for a Negotiated Settlement* (Johannesburg: Ravan Press, 1993).

[16] Three partial exceptions are Timothy D. Sisk, *Democratization in South Africa: The Elusive Social Contract* (Princeton: Princeton University Press, 1995); Heribert Adam and Kogila Moodley, *The Opening of the Apartheid Mind: Options for the New South Africa* (Berkeley: University of California Press, 1993), published in South Africa as *South Africa's Negotiated Revolution* (Johannesburg: Jonathan Ball, 1993); and, more recently, Elisabeth Jean Wood, *Forging Democracy From Below: Insurgent Transitions in South Africa and El Salvador* (Cambridge: Cambridge University Press, 2000). Three other important nomothetic studies with even earlier cut-off dates (1989 and 1985, respectively) are Donald L. Horowitz, *A*

Empirical narratives are useful for cutting deeply into a real life setting. They provide an indispensable backdrop for theoretical explanation. But empirical narratives are problematic from the perspective of explanation if pursued in isolation. A serious drawback is that most empirical narratives embody explanations without making explicit the assumptions, tenets, and propositions that underlie explanation. Social scientists have "found it difficult to extract defensible propositions" from empirical narratives because they "often mobilize the mythology and hagiography of their times, mixing literary tropes, notions of morality, and causal reasoning in efforts both to justify and to explain."[17]

With respect to apartheid's endgame, most explanations of its negotiated settlement claim that a mutually hurting stalemate between democracy-demanding and democracy-resisting coalitions made cooperation possible, and thus democracy inevitable. The stalemate hypothesis, however, although pervasive in journalistic and scholarly accounts, cannot explain why apartheid fell and democracy won. It is useful for understanding the *origins* of commitments, but inadequate for explaining the *credibility* of commitments among adversaries, and their *stability* throughout the endgame. Although the thesis of a political stalemate may explain why bargaining occurred in South Africa (a military stalemate never materialized), it fails to illuminate why, and how, bargaining produced sustainable cooperation. In other words, this line of argument cannot answer how domestic adversaries managed to construct credible commitments that prevented political, economic, and social conflict from turning (more) violent, and from derailing democratization.[18] Although the stalemate hypothesis may be able to explain why negotiations ensue in democratization, it cannot explain when, and why, these negotiations produce sustainable, self-enforcing outcomes.

Individualism

Contingent explanations of apartheid's endgame are the norm. Essentially all empiricist analyses are also grounded in methodological individualism. In

Democratic South Africa? Constitutional Engineering in a Divided Society (Berkeley: University of California Press, 1991); Heribert Adam and Kogila Moodley, *South Africa Without Apartheid: Dismantling Racial Domination* (Berkeley: University of California Press, 1986); and Arend Lijphart, *Power-Sharing in South Africa* (Berkeley: Institute of International Studies, University of California, Berkeley, 1985).

[17] Robert H. Bates, Avner Greif, Margaret Levi, Jean-Laurent Rosenthal, and Barry R. Weingast, *Analytic Narratives* (Princeton: Princeton University Press, 1998), p. 12. For a more extensive discussion of empiricism and its pitfalls, see Terry Johnson, Christopher Dandeker, and Clive Ashworth, *The Structure of Social Theory: Strategies, Dilemmas, and Projects* (New York: St. Martin's Press, 1984), pp. 29–74. For a trenchant critique of the analytic narratives approach, in turn, see Jon Elster, "Rational-Choice History: A Case of Excessive Ambition," *American Political Science Review*, Vol. 94, No. 3 (September 2000), pp. 685–695.

[18] For a conventional account of apartheid's endgame, relying on the stalemate hypothesis, see Sisk, *Democratization in South Africa*, esp. pp. 67–75, 86–87. To be sure, the stalemate hypothesis is not an inadequate, merely an insufficient, explanatory tool.

general terms, such analyses are "primarily interested in actors' manipulation of their own and their adversaries' cognitive and normative frames."[19] The most influential individualistic account of apartheid's endgame is Patti Waldmeir's *Anatomy of a Miracle*.[20] Waldmeir, a former *Financial Times* correspondent in South Africa, offers an insightful, comprehensive, and ultimately important account of the interactions between key agents, and the games between these agents and their constituencies. Yet anecdotes belie systematic analysis. What is even more problematic is the neglect of structural variables. Allister Spark's illuminating (and early) account of the hidden negotiations among incumbents and insurgents, likewise, suffers from a "myopia of the moment," favoring a contingent interpretation over a structural perspective.[21]

Determinism

Retrospective determinism refers to the scholarly belief in the inevitability of outcomes.[22] Most available analyses of apartheid's endgame are deterministic in this sense. As indicated a moment ago, with a few exceptions, South Africa's path to democracy is portrayed as an inevitable process that had to unfold the way it did, yielding inevitable outcomes that were bound to result the way they have. Yet seasoned observers viewed the country as a "tinderbox" in the 1980s with an undeclared internal war that had the potential of producing a "bloodbath."[23]

Very convincing reasons existed at the time to believe that a new order (whether democratic or otherwise) would not be negotiated, but imposed; especially because violence had become the modal way with which both democracy-demanding and democracy-resisting forces responded to the problem of social order in the 1980s. F. W. de Klerk put it thus:

---

[19] Herbert Kitschelt, "Political Regime Change: Structure and Process-Driven Explanations," *American Political Science Review*, Vol. 86, No. 4 (December 1992), p. 1028. The contingent study of democratization originated with the four-volume work Guillermo O'Donnell, Philippe C. Schmitter, and Laurence Whitehead, eds., *Transitions from Authoritarian Rule: Prospects for Democracy* (Baltimore: Johns Hopkins University Press, 1986).

[20] Waldmeir, *Anatomy of a Miracle*.

[21] The more recent *Comrades in Business: Post-Liberation Politics in South Africa* (Cape Town: Tafelberg, 1997) by seasoned political sociologists Adam, Moodley, and Frederik van Zyl Slabbert, while evading the problems of empiricism, does not contain a distinct theoretical argument, but reflects on a series of existing views in the literature. The book concerns itself foremost with problems of democratic consolidation, not the immediate endgame (the transition game) that lasted from one critical juncture to another: approximately from the transition in leadership at the helm of the National Party and the government from P. W. Botha to Frederik de Klerk in 1989, to the adoption of the final constitution in 1996.

[22] For a valuable discussion of retrospective determinism in the context of postcommunist transitions, see Stathis N. Kalyvas, "The Decay and Breakdown of Communist One-Party Systems," *Annual Review of Political Science*, Vol. 2 (1999), pp. 323–43.

[23] As quoted in Lijphart, *Power-Sharing in South Africa*, p. 2.

Anyone who would have predicted then that we would be able to bring the IFP and the Freedom Front into the elections; that we would be able to defuse the threat of right-wing violence; that we would be able to hold the elections with reasonable success; that the ANC-led government would adopt responsible economic policies and that the country would be broadly at peace with itself four years after the transformation, would have been accused of hopeless optimism.[24]

De Klerk conveniently leaves out the prerogative state that stood in the way of a resolution of apartheid's endgame. Michael Clough estimated in 1985 that "the white state's coercive capabilities are more than sufficient to avoid negotiated capitulation."[25] The late Joe Slovo, a key negotiator and revered leader of the South African Communist Party (SACP), conceded in 1992 that "we [the democracy-demanding forces] were clearly not dealing with a defeated enemy."[26] And what was more, the apartheid government under de Klerk did not believe in the historical inevitability of black majority rule. Even in hindsight, de Klerk does not accept the argument that the outcome of apartheid's endgame was preordained.[27]

Leading actors in the resistance movement were equally committed to confrontation rather than cooperation. The ANC's declared goal, as evidenced in many manifestos and speeches, was a violent, revolutionary overthrow of racial domination. The historian George Fredrickson reminds us that the ANC slogan "Apartheid cannot be reformed," which so successfully mobilized township resistance in the 1980s, must be understood at face value.[28] In June 1985, the ANC's "council-of-war" conference at Kabwe, Zambia, clearly preferred confrontation to cooperation in dealing with the enemy. The delegates concluded that "we cannot even consider the issue of a negotiated settlement of the South African question while our leaders are in prison."[29] The harbingers of confrontation in the townships were civic associations, the so-called civics. Some

---

[24] F. W. de Klerk, *The Last Trek – A New Beginning: The Autobiography* (New York: St. Martin's Press, 1998), p. 389.

[25] Michael Clough, "Beyond Constructive Engagement," *Foreign Policy*, No. 61, (Winter 1985–86), p. 22, cited in Laitin, "South Africa," p. 277.

[26] Joe Slovo, as quoted in John Saul, "Globalism, Socialism, and Democracy in the South African Transition," *Socialist Register* 1994, p. 178.

[27] Waldmeir, *Anatomy of a Miracle*, p. 149.

[28] George M. Fredrickson, *The Comparative Imagination: On the History of Racism, Nationalism, and Social Movements* (Berkeley: University of California Press, 1997), p. 143.

[29] African National Congress, "Communiqué of the Second National Consultative Conference of the African National Congress, presented by Oliver Tambo at a Press Conference, Lusaka, Zambia, June 25, 1985," reprinted in idem., ed., *Documents of the Second National Consultative Conference of the African National Congress, Zambia, 16–23 June, 1985* (Lusaka: ANC, 1985), as quoted in Klug, *Constituting Democracy*, p. 77. Waldmeir shows that the ANC remained divided throughout the endgame on the choice of confrontation or cooperation as bargaining strategies. "In May 1990, when the Groote Schuur talks took place, the lobby in favor of compromise was frighteningly small." Waldmeir, *Anatomy of a Miracle*, p. 163.

saw the civics as expressions of "people's power" and potential seeds of a revolutionary state.[30] Nelson Mandela remarked this:

Oliver Tambo and the ANC had called for the people of South Africa to render the country ungovernable, and the people were obliging. The state of unrest and political violence was reaching new heights. The anger of the masses was unrestrained; the townships were in upheaval.[31]

In fact, "the idea of negotiation with an undefeated enemy was ruled out as a sellout" within the ANC.[32] Despite conciliatory overtones, both the National Party and the ANC adopted "hegemonic models of bargaining" where democratic, inclusive rhetoric only masked a desire for total control.[33]

Only in hindsight is apartheid's endgame an "easy" case for analysis in which democracy was inevitable. The problem with hindsight, notes Baruch Fischhoff, is that "people consistently exaggerate what could have been anticipated in foresight."[34] The cooperative solution of apartheid's endgame – this so-called negotiated revolution – was neither expected by participants nor predicted by analysts. Apartheid's endgame could have ended differently at various critical junctures. A series of alternative outcomes come to mind, including intensified repression, modernized segregation, violent revolution, and all-out civil war. What the psychology literature calls "outcome knowledge" has clouded much of the existing literature. This outcome knowledge substantially hampers our understanding of apartheid's endgame:

By tracing the path that appears to have led to a known outcome, we diminish our sensitivity to alternative paths and outcomes. We may fail to recognize the uncertainty under which actors operated and the possibility that they could have made different choices that might have led to different outcomes.[35]

To address the problem of outcome knowledge, but also the problems of empiricism and individualism, this book traces the behavior of particular agents, clarifies sequences, describes structures, and explores patterns of interaction employing the theoretical model developed in Chapters 2 and 3. It contains analytic narratives of apartheid's endgame. Paying explicit

---

[30] Khehla Shubane and Peter Madiba, *The Struggle Continues? Civic Associations in the Transition* (Johannesburg: Centre for Policy Studies, 1992).

[31] Nelson Mandela, *Long Walk to Freedom: The Autobiography of Nelson Mandela* (Randburg: Macdonald Purnell, 1994), p. 518.

[32] Adam and Moodley, *The Opening of the Apartheid Mind*, p. 45.

[33] Pierre du Toit and Willie Esterhuyse, eds., *The Mythmakers: The Elusive Bargain for South Africa's Future* (Johannesburg: Southern Books, 1990), as quoted in Adam and Moodley, *The Opening of the Apartheid Mind*, p. 159.

[34] Baruch Fischhoff, "For Those Condemned to Study the Past: Heuristics and Biases in Hindsight," in Daniel Kahneman, Paul Slovic, and Amos Tversky, eds., *Judgment Under Uncertainty: Heuristics and Biases* (Cambridge: Cambridge University Press, 1982), p. 341.

[35] Richard Ned Lebow, "What's So Different about a Counterfactual?," *World Politics*, Vol. 52, No. 4 (July 2000), p. 559.

attention to theory, these narratives examine critical episodes in the endgame. In doing so, they shed light on real and alternative paths open to agents, and the reasons why the former were traveled, and the latter were not.

METHODS

The counterintuitive argument advanced in this book – that apartheid law was necessary for making democracy work – offers a "redescription" of apartheid's endgame. Shapiro recently defended redescription as a methodological approach: "The recent emphases in political science on modeling for its own sake and on decisive predictive tests both give short shrift to the value of problematizing redescription in the study of politics. It is intrinsically worthwhile to unmask an accepted depiction as inadequate, and to make a convincing case for an alternative as more apt."[36] For the purpose of constructing such an alternative, this book synthesizes insights from law, political science, sociology, economics, philosophy, and history. Locating an inquiry "at the boundary or intersection of various established fields has obvious dangers because it may satisfy none of the respective specialists and draw the ire of all of them."[37]

This book's contribution, or so I hope, lies in the fact that it uses the interdisciplinary approach to discern new patterns, significant connections, and improved interpretations about the demise of apartheid and the resurgence of liberalism. The foundation is a synthetic methodology in which nomothetic reasoning converges with ideographic reasoning. The analysis moves back and forth between theoretical and historical levels, using one to amplify and illuminate the other. For, as recent scholarship has shown, "[b]y promoting intimate dialogue between ideas and evidence, the joint construction of history and theory can improve our knowledge of both."[38]

The analysis combines insights from rational choice institutionalism and historical institutionalism, advancing a deep, interpretive analysis that recognizes the interplay between rationality and culture.[39] For the purpose of the analysis, I assume that agents "are partly pushed by internal predispositions

[36] Ian Shapiro, "Problems, Methods, and Theories in the Study of Politics, or: What's Wrong with Political Science and What to Do About It," in Ian Shapiro, Rogers S. Smith, and Tarek E. Masoud, eds., *Problems and Methods in the Study of Politics* (Cambridge: Cambridge University Press, 2004), p. 39.

[37] Friedrich Kratochwil, *Rules, Norms, and Decisions: On the Conditions of Practical and Legal Reasoning in International Relations and Domestic Affairs* (Cambridge: Cambridge University Press, 1989), p. 1.

[38] Nicholas Pedriana, "Rational Choice, Structural Context, and Increasing Returns: A Strategy for Analytic Narrative in Historical Sociology," *Sociological Methods and Research*, Vol. 33, No. 3 (February 2005), p. 350.

[39] For a discussion, see Robert H. Bates, Rui J. P. de Figueiredo, Jr., and Barry R. Weingast, "The Politics of Interpretation: Rationality, Culture, and Transition," *Politics and Society*, Vol. 26, No. 4 (December 1998), pp. 603–642.

and partly pulled by the cost and benefits of the options they face."[40] I further assume that agents "can be narrowly egoistic or ethical, but they are rational in that they act instrumentally consistently within the limits of constraints to produce the most benefit at the least cost. The variation in choice reflects the variation in constraints, often in the form of resources or institutions that delimit or enable action, promote certain beliefs over others, and provide or hide information."[41] In this book, I show not only that the formulation of preferences matters, but also, that legal norms and institutions are critical in the formulation of these preferences.[42]

The remainder of this book is organized into eight chapters. Chapter 2 elaborates the book's substantive concerns – the function of law in transitions to and from authoritarian rule. To this end, it theorizes the concept of law and the dynamics of contention in democratization. Chapter 3 introduces Ernst Fraenkel's concept of the dual state as a structural parameter to choice, making it usable for comparative historical analysis, notably by taking the concept out of its original context and by increasing its extension. Chapters 4 and 5 turn from the *theory* of law to the *history* of law. They chronicle the formation and deformation of law in South Africa. The period under investigation stretches from the days of the Cape Colony to the reform of apartheid, from 1652 to the early 1980s. From this vantage point, the chapters trace the evolution of legal norms and institutions – and explicate their effects – in the making of separate development and apartheid. They are concerned with the explanation of institutions. Although I take the apartheid state as the object to be explained in these chapters, the apartheid state becomes the thing that *does* the explaining in the next. Chapters 6 and 7 demonstrate a path-dependent relationship between law and politics. More specifically, I detail, in three analytic narratives, how apartheid's endgame was structured by the conflicting imperatives of the dual state, and its two halves – the prerogative state and the normative state. Chapter 8 extends this argument by way of a plausibility probe. By offering an individualizing comparison, revolving around Chile's transition to and from authoritarian rule, I inquire into the relevance of my findings for the comparative historical analysis of democracy more generally. Chapter 9 concludes and considers implications. I discuss implications for the study of institutions, reflecting on the contending new institutionalisms in law and the social sciences, and then turn to the practical import of my findings.

---

[40] Dennis Chong, *Rational Lives: Norms and Values in Politics and Society* (Chicago: University of Chicago Press, 2000), p. 7.

[41] Margaret Levi, *Consent, Dissent, and Patriotism* (Cambridge: Cambridge University Press, 1997), p. 9.

[42] For a more comprehensive discussion of agents and preferences, and strategies and outcomes, see Chapter 6. See also Geoffrey Brennan and Alan Hamlin, *Democratic Devices and Desires* (Cambridge: Cambridge University Press, 2000).

IMPLICATIONS

Notwithstanding the fact that the institutional evolution of apartheid features centrally in the analysis, the theoretical – and practical – concerns raised in the book go well beyond the case of South Africa. They are of immediate relevance for the promotion of democratic norms and institutions, which is among the most important humanitarian challenges facing the international community in the twenty-first century.[43] From Bosnia and Herzegovina to Iraq, the international community has been seeking to establish democracy through the rule of law. More often than not, the imposition of legal norms and institutions has failed, as the case of Kosovo attests. The lessons of apartheid are relevant for safeguarding and sustaining democracy in times of transition. Although the lessons derived in this book offer no panacea, it is my hope that they might aid scholars and practitioners in facing uncomfortable facts about the relationship between authoritarianism and democracy – and the legacies of law therein.

[43] For leading commentary, see Thomas M. Franck, "The Emerging Right to Democratic Governance," *American Journal of International Law*, Vol. 86, No. 1 (January 1992), pp. 46–91; W. Michael Reisman, "Why Regime Change Is (Almost Always) a Bad Idea," *American Journal of International Law*, Vol. 98, No. 3 (July 2004); and the contributions in Gregory H. Fox and Brad R. Roth, eds., *Democratic Governance and International Law* (Cambridge: Cambridge University Press, 2000).

PART I

A THEORY OF LAW

2

A Typology of Law

In this chapter and the next, I develop the theoretical argument of this book. This chapter introduces a typology of law, which is indispensable for understanding the social function of law in ordinary times, and reflects on the strategy of conflict in democratization, which is necessary for understanding the social function of law *in times of transition*. The chapter provides the intellectual foundations for my theoretical argument about the legal origins of democracy. Building on these foundations, the next chapter advances a *theory of law*, incorporating insights from the literature on path dependence and increasing returns in economics and the social sciences. In conjunction, the chapters lay the groundwork for the history of law, that is, the comparative historical analysis of apartheid (Chapters 4 and 5) and apartheid's endgame (Chapters 6 and 7) respectively.

FOUR IDEAL TYPES

Throughout this book I take law to refer to a set of norms held by citizens, encapsulated in institutions, and enforced by officials.[1] In this I follow Philip Allott who describes the social function of law thus: "(1) Law carries the structures and systems of society through time. (2) Law inserts the common interest of society into the behavior of society-members. (3) Law establishes possible futures for society, in accordance with society's theories, values, and purposes."[2] This conceptualization of law is grounded in Max Weber's contribution to conceptual jurisprudence (*Begriffsjurisprudenz*). In his attempt

---

[1] On the relationship between law and norms more generally, see Eric Posner, *Law and Social Norms* (Cambridge, MA: Harvard University Press, 2000). For a most important overview of contending conceptualizations of law, see Roger Cotterrell, *Law's Community: Legal Theory in Sociological Perspective* (Oxford: Clarendon Press, 1995). For a distinct (albeit controversial) perspective, see also Brian Tamanaha, *A General Jurisprudence of Law and Society* (New York: Oxford University Press, 2001), and William Twining's review article, "A Post-Westphalian Conception of Law," *Law and Society Review*, Vol. 37, No. 1 (March 2003), pp. 199–258.

[2] Philip Allott, "The Concept of International Law," in Michael Byers, ed., *The Role of Law in International Politics: Essays in International Relations and International Law* (Oxford: Oxford

	Rational	Irrational
Formal	Formally rational	Formally irrational
Substantive	Substantively rational	Substantively irrational

FIGURE 2.1. Four Ideal Types of Law

to understand law comparatively, Weber formed ideal types of law.[3] (See Figure 2.1.) These ideal types are important for analyzing the dual state, especially for making sense of the prerogative state and the normative state, and the contribution of each to the political economy of law (see Chapter 3).

Weber uses two attributes to construct his ideal types. The first attribute concerns the distinction between formal and substantive law. The second concerns the distinction between rational and irrational law. In other words, the ideal types of law are "constituted by the binary oppositions of form and substance (content) as well as rationality and non-rationality (affect, tradition)."[4] In Weber's classificatory scheme, the cross-tabulation of these dichotomous attributes yields four ideal types.

Legal systems rarely fall squarely within one of these types. Historical reality entails "combinations, mixtures, adaptations, or modifications of these pure types."[5] Notwithstanding the complexity of historical reality, Weber considered *formally rational law* to be the most advanced of the four ideal types.[6] It is

University Press, 2000), p. 69. It is important to appreciate that Allott's is an attempt at capturing the concept of law *per se*, not just the concept of international law.

[3] Max Weber, *Wirtschaft und Gesellschaft: Grundriß der Verstehenden Soziologie*, Fifth Edition (Tübingen: J. C. B. Mohr, [1921] 1972), pp. 396–397. For a more comprehensive discussion of these ideal types ("Kategorien des Rechtsdenkens"), see Weber, *Wirtschaft und Gesellschaft*, pp. 395–513. Weber's ideal types are not "a simple dichotomy between the rational justice of the modern West and the kadi justice of much of the non-Western world," as some scholars erroneously claim. See Philip C. Huang, *Civil Justice in China* (Stanford: Stanford University Press, 1996), p. 229. The discussion here draws partially on Robert Marsh, "Weber's Misunderstanding of Traditional Chinese Law," *American Journal of Sociology*, Vol. 106, No. 2 (September 2000), pp. 281–302. Note, however, that Marsh offers a simplified version of Weber's ideal types.

[4] Wolf Heydebrand, "Process Rationality as Legal Governance: A Comparative Perspective," *International Sociology*, Vol. 18, No. 2 (June 2003), p. 331.

[5] Max Weber, *Max Weber on Law in Economics and Society*, edited by Max Rheinstein (Cambridge, MA: Harvard University Press, 1954), pp. 336–337.

[6] Weber writes that "the peculiarly professional, legalistic, and abstract approach to law in the modern sense is possible only in the measure that the law is formal in character." In this passage, Weber associates formally rational law with both professionalism and modernity. Max Weber, *Economy and Society: An Outline of Interpretive Sociology*, edited by Guenther Roth and Claus Wittich (Berkeley: University of California Press, [1921] 1978), p. 657.

important to appreciate, however, that in Weber's typology of law "rationality is not primarily the attribute of a thinking and acting individual subject, but the characteristic of a structure, an institutional sphere, a normative order, or a collectivity."[7] This complements my conceptualization of the state as an institutional structure around which actors' expectations converge.[8]

Weber's typology provides a yardstick for comparative historical analysis. It is useful for making sense of legal systems generally, but especially for understanding legal systems governed by the conflicting imperatives of a dual state.[9] Weber's typology of law generates tentative answers to the question of whether, and how, law matters in a given society.[10] The next section discusses his four ideal types in more detail.

In general terms, *formal law* is internally legitimate because it is technically generalized and consistent, and *substantive law* is driven by extralegal motivations; and whereas *rational law* is controlled by the intellect, *irrational law* is governed by emotion.[11] Law is *formally irrational* (upper right quadrant in Figure 2.1) when the adjudication of law is inspired by ordeals, oracles, or other prophetic revelations. The rigor with which these methods are applied may, however, exhibit formalism, and thus irrational law may nevertheless be formal. Law is *substantively irrational* (lower right quadrant) when enforcement officials make arbitrary decisions from case to case without recourse to general rules. The result of personal discretion, whether informed by political, moral, or other concerns, is unpredictable law. Weber chiefly used the example of qadi justice (*Kadijustiz*) to illustrate the point.[12] Another lesser-known example of which Weber was fond is that of China. There, he was certain, Chinese magistrates without legal technical training reached judicial decisions arbitrarily, that is, in an unpredictable manner with no recourse to written

---

[7] Heydebrand, "Process Rationality as Legal Governance," pp. 331–332.

[8] For a comprehensive discussion, see Chapter 3.

[9] For a most important treatment of the nature and role of legal systems in domestic society, see Joseph Raz, *The Concept of a Legal System: An Introduction to the Theory of Legal System* (Oxford: Clarendon Press, 1970).

[10] Weber's conceptual jurisprudence is not without its critics. For more than a century, lawyers have objected to positivism's emphasis on logically consistent, rational propositions of law. Roscoe Pound disputed the assumption that a correct legal decision can always be derived from existing statutory texts by a process of legal deduction. See Roscoe Pound, *Interpretations of Legal History* (New York: Macmillan, 1923), p. 121. In the social sciences, scholars critical of Weber's transhistorical legal comparisons have legitimately asked how far any given society can deviate "from the 'formally rational' type of law without undercutting the utility of the concept?" See Marsh, "Weber's Misunderstanding of Traditional Chinese Law," pp. 300–301.

[11] For an empirically grounded analysis, see Weber, *Wirtschaft und Gesellschaft*, pp. 468–482.

[12] According to Weber, judgments of the qadi, the judge in the Islamic *sharia* court, take the form of pure arbitrariness. See Weber, *Wirtschaft und Gesellschaft*, pp. 563–564. Weber also considered the introduction of popular elements into criminal law, such as lay justice and forms of today's jury trials, as a form of qadi justice. See Weber, *Wirtschaft und Gesellschaft*, p. 511.

codes or precedents. Adjudication was undertaken on a case-by-case basis by generalists.

Interestingly, one scholar recently found that Weber miscategorized China: "Ch'ing dynasty legal decisions were not 'formally rational,' since they were not based on purely formal, abstract legal reasoning. *But* neither was Chinese law primarily of the 'substantively irrational' type. The general principles upon which Chinese legal decisions were based were drawn from Confucian and legalist philosophy, which though extrinsic to 'purely legal reasoning,' precisely fit Weber's definition of 'substantively rational' law."[13]

Law is *substantively rational* (lower left quadrant) when it is driven by, or the vehicle of, an extralegal moral, religious, or political ideology. Islamic law therefore qualifies as substantively rational, as it is infused with commands of the prophet Mohammed. The rationality of Islamic law – which Weber appreciated despite the law's religious underpinnings – has been elucidated in careful studies by Lawrence Rosen and other leading scholars of legal reasoning in Islam.[14] By contrast, substantively irrational qadi justice constituted a perverted form of Islamic law according to Weber. It represented the exception rather than the norm in Islamic law. *Kadijustiz* was a pejorative (rather than a merely descriptive) term for Weber. It is important to appreciate, however, the bias in Weber's interpretation of qadi justice. For as Patrick Glenn notes, "The qadi, or judge, is the most internationally known figure of [I]slamic law, and this is due largely to disparaging remarks made by common law judges on the allegedly discretionary character of the qadi's function."[15] It is therefore important not to confuse the theory of qadi justice with the history of qadi justice, thus recognizing Weber's misunderstanding of one of the most important institutions of Islamic law. This notwithstanding, Weber's interpretation of Islamic law as substantively rational remains accurate. This is so because "[q]adi dispute resolution takes place in what has been described in the west as a 'law-finding trial' (*Rechtsfindungsverfahren*), so the notion of simple application of pre-existing norms, or simple subsumption of facts under norms, is notably absent from the overall understanding of the judicial process."[16] This difference in the understanding of the judicial process accounts for the lack of formality in the law. The workings of the law in the Islamic legal tradition are dynamic. In contrast to the civil law and the common law, the judicial process in Islamic law is one "in which all cases may be

---

[13] Marsh, "Weber's Misunderstanding of Traditional Chinese Law," p. 298.

[14] On the sophistication of Islamic law, which Lawrence Rosen has linked to the common law, see the latter's *The Justice of Islam* (Oxford: Oxford University Press, 2000); idem., *The Anthropology of Justice: Law as Culture in Islamic Society* (Cambridge: Cambridge University Press, 1989); and Wael B. Hallaq, *The Origins and Evolution of Islamic Law* (Cambridge: Cambridge University Press, 2004). For an excellent introduction to the study of legal traditions, see H. Patrick Glenn, *Legal Traditions of the World: Sustainable Diversity in Law* (Oxford: Oxford University Press, 2000).

[15] Glenn, *Legal Traditions of the World*, p. 163.

[16] Glenn, *Legal Traditions of the World*, p. 163. Emphasis added.

seen as different and particular, and for each of which the precisely appropriate law must be carefully sought out. The law of each case is thus different from the law of every other case, and all parties, and the qadi, are under an obligation of service to God to bring together the objectively determined circumstances of the case and the appropriate principles of the shari'a."[17] The foregoing captures the conflicting imperatives of substantively rational law: the reliance on substance (i.e., the commands of the prophet) on the one hand, and reason (i.e., the systematic quest for justice) on the other. As Weber writes, substantive rationality

means that the decision of legal problems is influenced by norms different from those obtained through logical generalization of abstract interpretations of meaning. The norms to which substantive rationality accords prominence include ethical imperatives, utilitarian, and other expediential rules, and political maxims, all of which diverge from the formalism of [formally rational law and from the] uses [of] logical abstraction.[18]

Other historical examples of substantively rational law – aside from Islamic law – include early Nazi law, or Soviet and Chinese law under communism, but also law derivative of moral considerations like welfare or justice.[19] The systematized nature of these ideologies accounts for the rational character of this substantive law. As logical generalizations, such legal norms are rational; they lose their formal character because of their extralegal source.[20] Law is *formally rational* (upper left quadrant), finally, when it forms a gapless system

---

[17] Glenn, *Legal Traditions of the World*, p. 163.

[18] Weber, *Economy and Society*, p. 657.

[19] Weber, *Wirtschaft und Gesellschaft*, pp. 397, 468–482. Substantively rational law refers to what Weber called *"materielle Rationalität"* in German.

[20] On systematization, see Weber, *Wirtschaft und Gesellschaft*, pp. 396–397. "To a youthful law," Weber writes, "it [systematization] is unknown." Weber, *Economy and Society*, p. 656. The passage in the original German reads as follows: "Sie [Systematisierung] ist in jeder Form ein Spätprodukt. Das urwüchsige 'Recht' kennt sie nicht." Weber, *Wirtschaft und Gesellschaft*, p. 396. For an insightful and sophisticated discussion of the effects of legal systematization and legal differentiation on the social function of law that has influenced my analysis, see Niklas Luhmann, *Ausdifferenzierung des Rechts: Beiträge zur Rechtssoziologie und Rechtstheorie* (Frankfurt am Main: Suhrkamp, 1981); and idem, *Legitimation durch Verfahren* (Frankfurt am Main: Suhrkamp, [1969] 1983). From within positivism, Luhmann, like this book, emphasizes law's contribution to the reduction of uncertainty, and the stabilization of agents' expectations in strategic interaction. See, for example, Luhmann, *Ausdifferenzierung des Rechts*, pp. 92–153. Elsewhere, Luhmann argues that law solves "the problem of time" in social interaction and communication. This contention is closely related to the argument developed here, which emphasizes the ability of legal norms and institutions to lengthen, under certain circumstances, the shadow of the future for interacting agents in democratization. Luhmann called this mechanism the "dearbitrarization of relations." See Niklas Luhmann, *Das Recht der Gesellschaft* (Frankfurt am Main: Suhrkamp, 1993), pp. 124–125, 129. Law's function, according to Luhmann, is this: "Konkret geht es um die Funktion der Stabilisierung normativer Erwartungen durch Regulierung ihrer zeitlichen, sachlichen und sozialen Generalisierung." See Luhmann, *Das Recht der Gesellschaft*, p. 131. ("Concretely, [law] is concerned with the stabilization of normative expectations through a regulation of their temporal, functional and social generalization.") Translation by the author.

of abstract rules.[21] For law to be formally rational it is necessary that in "both substantive and procedural matters, only unambiguous general characteristics of the facts of the case are taken into account."[22] Legal decisions in this type result from the application of a general rule of law – which is comprised of abstract legal concepts – to the particular facts of a case. Formally rational law, thus defined, explains the particular by recourse to the general in abstract form.[23]

Yet formally rational law rarely exists in empirically pure form. Weber believed that only Western Europe's civil law systems fulfilled the requirements of formally rational law. What separated the continental European legal systems from other legal systems, Weber argued, was the great systematization that these civil law systems had achieved.[24] He described all other systems of law derogatively as "empirical justice."[25] Indeed, Weber hypothesized that the

[21] The German passage reads as follows: "daß also das geltende objektive Recht ein 'lückenloses System' von Rechtssätzen darstellen oder latent in sich enthalten oder doch als ein solches für die Zwecke der Rechtsanwendung behandelt werden müsse." Weber, *Wirtschaft und Gesellschaft*, p. 397. Weber further distinguishes two subtypes of formally rational law. These subtypes shall not concern us here. See Weber, *Wirtschaft und Gesellschaft*, p. 396.

[22] Weber, *Economy and Society*, pp. 656–657.

[23] Within formally rational law, Weber distinguishes between two faces of execution: lawmaking ("Rechtsschöpfung") and lawfinding ("Rechtsfindung"). *Lawmaking* refers to the construction of general, rational norms. *Lawfinding* describes the adjudication of these norms – and the legal propositions deduced from these – in the context of specific cases. See Weber, *Wirtschaft und Gesellschaft*, p. 396. In English, see Weber, *Economy and Society*, pp. 653–654.

[24] Civil law systems, per definition, reject the doctrine of precedent, which is the defining characteristic of the common law. Instead civil law relies on codification and the interpretation of these codes by judges. As René David and John Brierley write, "The rejection of the doctrine of precedent, whereby judges must abide by the rules previously applied in an earlier decision, is no accident. The doctrine of precedent has been contrary to the tradition of the Romano-Germanic system ever since the Middle Ages when instead of confiding the creation of a new system of law to judges the ready-made model of Roman law was accepted. Since then it has always been considered necessary that the legal rule be doctrinal or legislative in origin; it must be thought out so as to cover a series of typical cases reaching beyond the limits and free from contingencies of a particular trial." René David and John E. C. Brierley, *Major Legal Systems in the World Today: An Introduction to the Comparative Study of Law*, Second Edition (New York: Free Press, 1978), p. 124. For a comparison of the two systems, see Weber, *Wirtschaft und Gesellschaft*, p. 511. Weber believed that any departure from legal specialization ("Herrschaft des Fachmenschentums") would result in a decline of judicial precision, and, concomitantly, lead to an increase in uncertainty. See Weber, *Wirtschaft und Gesellschaft*, p. 512.

[25] Weber, *Economy and Society*, p. 976. Weber's low respect for the common law was shared by a famous Englishman, Jeremy Bentham. See, for example, Bentham's extensive contribution to institutional design, notably his proposal for the codification of English law. As Gerald J. Postema, a leading commentator on Bentham, writes, "Bentham frequently called attention to the barbarity, inhumanity, and inefficiency of contemporary English law, especially criminal law, but he saved his severest criticism for the system of Common Law which spawned and nurtured these laws. [. . .] Following the continental pattern, Bentham's social criticism and call for law reform [therefore] took shape as a proposal for a fully rational, systematic science of legislation." Gerald J. Postema, *Bentham and the Common Law Tradition* (Oxford: Clarendon Press, 1986), pp. 267–268, 263.

rationalization of law – the process by which legal systems move from the lower left quadrant (substantively rational law) to the upper left quadrant (formally rational law) in Figure 2.1 – involved several stages:

> From a theoretical point of view, the general development of law and procedure may be viewed as passing through the following stages: first, charismatic legal revelation through "law prophets"; second, empirical creation and finding of law by legal notables [...]; third, imposition of law by secular or theocratic powers; fourth and finally, systematic elaboration of law and professionalized administration of justice by persons who have received their legal training in a learned and formally logical manner.[26]

Needless to say, Weber's conceptualization and classification of formally rational law was heavily influenced by developments in France and Germany at the time.[27] In France, the introduction of the *Code Civil* under Napoleon I in 1804 popularized the codification of law, which in turn resulted, at least to some extent, in the democratization of law. The *Code Civil* was motivated by a desire to streamline the law, to develop a coherent, comprehensive, and consistent system of legal norms and institutions. Another objective behind the code, although not quite realized in practice, was to make the law more accessible to the masses by reducing it to a publishable handbook – a handbook that would take its place next to the Bible in people's homes.[28] In Germany, Friedrich Carl von Savigny and the historical school of the Pandectists made strides in the development of private law, leading to the adoption of the *Bürgerliches Gesetzbuch* (BGB) in Germany in 1900. These, in many respects momentous, developments reinforced Weber's belief in the supremacy of formally rational law, and the supremacy of the civil law over the common law tradition. Weber's typology of law, as discussed herein, is critical to explaining – and understanding – the function of law in times of transition.

However, here I depart from Weber's interpretation of law. Weber's argument that common law systems are inherently irrational in formal terms is

---

[26] Weber, *Max Weber on Law in Economics and Society*, p. 303. For a discussion, see also Reinhard Bendix, *Max Weber: An Intellectual Portrait* (New York: Doubleday, 1960), pp. 379–411. On "generalization" and "systematization" as types of rationalization, see Cotterrell, *Law's Community*, pp. 143–146.

[27] Max Weber, *Rechtssoziologie*, edited by Johannes Winckelmann (Neuwied: Luchterhand, 1960), pp. 263–265. Interestingly, Weber measures the French *Code Civil* against Bentham's ideal type of law.

[28] Doris Marie Provine, "Courts in the Political Process in France," in Herbert Jacob, Erhard Blankenburg, Herbert M. Kritzer, Doris Marie Provine, and Joseph Sanders, *Courts, Law, and Politics in Comparative Perspective* (New Haven: Yale University Press, 1996), p. 232. René David and Henry de Vries have placed the *Code Civil* in historical perspective: "The Civil Code became in the nineteenth century the symbol of the desirability and effectiveness of creating law exclusively through representative assemblies rather than through the courts." See René David and Henry P. de Vries, *The French Legal System* (New York: Oceana, 1958), p. 15. Yet consider Provine, who remarks that in terms of its overall importance, the "codification of French law is less important as a break with pre-revolutionary norms than the harbinger of a changed attitude toward courts." Provine, "Courts in the Political Process in France," p. 232.

theoretically untenable and was empirically inaccurate *even* during Weber's lifetime. It is an established fact that common law systems can achieve *at least* the same level of formal rationality as civil law systems.[29] For as Arthur Stinchcombe found,

by the time capitalist principles were applied to manufacturing that Weber took to be central to modern development, they were pretty well formalized, looking fairly Germanic even in England. So perhaps there never was a problem of England's industrial revolution; rather the problem was Weber's forgetting that the laws of commerce with Roman roots, systematized by German professors, were developed by autonomous unbureaucratic cities in case law courts in medieval Europe. They were applied to the detailed problem of creating industrial firms, industrial labor relations, and industrial sales of commodities after being preserved by many generations of appellate judges.[30]

The formal rationality of the common law will become even more apparent in the comparative historical analysis of Chapters 4 and 5. For as we shall see, South Africa's legal system evolved at the intersection of civil law and common law, giving rise to a "mixed legal system" or "mixed jurisdiction" of tremendous sophistication.[31]

Notwithstanding this historical record, Weber couched his analysis of the common law in negative terms. He considered Anglo-American common law as merely a continuation of medieval English law, and thus not formally rational. According to Weber, the common law of his time was no more than a hodgepodge of traditional and charismatic elements whose "legal rationality is essentially lower than, and of a type different from, that of continental Europe."[32] Yet, as intimated, Weber misses important progressive elements of the English and American common law of the time. He overlooks, for example, the progressive elements in the doctrine of precedent as well as the

---

[29] For valuable discussions, see P. S. Atiyah and R. S. Summers, *Form and Substance in Anglo-American Law: A Comparative Study of Legal Reasoning, Legal Theory, and Legal Institutions* (Oxford: Clarendon Press, 1987); Arthur R. Hogue, *Origins of the Common Law* (Indianapolis: Liberty Fund, 1986); and Allan C. Hutchinson, *Evolution and the Common Law* (Cambridge: Cambridge University Press, 2005). For a classic account of English law – by one of its key architects – see Sir Matthew Hale, *The History of the Common Law of England*, edited and with an Introduction by Charles M. Gray (Chicago: University of Chicago Press, [1713] 1971). An influential lawyer and jurist, Sir Matthew (1609-1676) retired as Lord Chief Justice of England.

[30] Arthur L. Stinchcombe, *When Formality Works: Authority and Abstraction in Law and Organizations* (Chicago: University of Chicago Press, 2001), p. 97. For a relevant discussion, see also Glenn, *Legal Traditions of the World*, esp. chapters 5 and 7.

[31] For an overview, see Reinhard Zimmermann and Daniel Visser, "Introduction: South African Law as a Mixed Legal System," in idem., eds., *Southern Cross: Civil Law and Common Law in South Africa* (Oxford: Clarendon Press, 1996), pp. 1-30; and Paul Farlam, Reinhard Zimmermann, C. G. van der Merwe, J. E. du Plessis, and M. J. de Waal, "The Republic of South Africa," in Vernon Valentine Palmer, ed., *Mixed Jurisdictions Worldwide: The Third Legal Family* (Cambridge: Cambridge University Press, 2001), pp. 83-200.

[32] Weber, *Economy and Society*, p. 890.

emphasis on analogy in English common law. Especially in the latter, the development of rules through a close comparative analysis of judicial decisions, exhibited traits of formally rational law.[33] Weber also overlooks the commitment to the rights of individuals that became a key feature of the common law, as we shall see later.

Broadening Weber's restrictive definition of what constitutes formally rational law, I therefore take formally rational law to refer to a body of law that *either* constitutes a gapless system of rules *or* follows norms (not necessarily codified) in a consistent manner, as applied in social life and mediated by legal institutions. With this conceptualization of the *nature* of law – inspired by but distinct from Weber's contribution – I now turn to the *function* of law.

The Legality of Law

For analytical reasons, I distinguish between law's *legality* and its *legitimacy*. It is the argument of this book that the function of law centers on its legality.[34] For law to be legal, it need *not* be democratic. Law and democracy are related, not identical, values. I deliberately exclude moral considerations from my conception of law. Some consider a moral consideration like "justice" essential for rules to be called law. By contrast, I reject, with Weber, the inclusion of values such as "justice," "human dignity" and what he termed "emotionally colored ethical postulates" into the concept of law.[35] However, inasmuch as I share Weber's intellectual stance, I do not share his cynicism. Neither do I reject the importance, nor the pursuit, of ethical postulates in social life. I merely exclude morality from the concept of law. In the words of Joseph Raz,

[33] Harold J. Berman and Charles J. Reid, Jr., "Max Weber as Legal Historian," in Stephen Turner, ed., *The Cambridge Companion to Weber* (Cambridge: Cambridge University Press, 2000), p. 230. For a more comprehensive discussion, see also Stephen P. Turner and Regis A. Factor, eds., *Max Weber: The Lawyer as Social Thinker* (London: Routledge, 1994). Contrary to conventional interpretations of Weber's sociology of law, Weber was *generally* well aware of how the use of analogy might contribute to progressive systematization and modern casuistry (*Kasuistik*). For a brief, yet nuanced discussion, see Weber, *Wirtschaft und Gesellschaft*, pp. 395–396. Weber was right in recognizing the ultimate malleability of the common law at the moment of application. However, the stock of opinions that the common law accumulates will over time constitute general prescriptions not unlike the codified rules in the civil law. And "even though one could not pick up an authoritative and canonical set of rules of contract in a way that one could pick up the tax code or the rules of chess," certain justifications recur and certain principles become ossified. Yet "when it appears to the common law judge that application of what was previously thought to be the rule would be silly, or inconsistent with good policy, or inconsistent with the justifications for having that rule, it is open to that judge to modify the previous rule at the moment of application." See Frederick Schauer, *Playing by the Rules: A Philosophical Examination of Rule-Based Decision-Making in Law and in Life* (Oxford: Clarendon Press, 1991), pp. 174–188. The quote is from p. 175.
[34] For a contrary perspective, see David Dyzenhaus, "The Legitimacy of Legality," *Archiv für Rechts- und Sozialphilosophie*, Vol. 82, No. 3 (1996), pp. 324–360.
[35] Weber, *Economy and Society*, p. 886.

It is to be insisted that law is only one of the values that a legal system may possess and by which it is to be judged. It is not to be confused with democracy, justice, equality (before the law or otherwise), human rights of any kind or respect for persons for the dignity of man. A non-democratic legal system, based on the denial of human rights, on extensive poverty, on racial segregation, sexual inequalities, and religious persecution may, in principle, conform to the requirements of the rule of law better than any of the legal systems of the more enlightened Western democracies. This does not mean that it will be better than those Western democracies. It will be an immeasurably worse legal system, but it will excel in one respect: in its conformity to the rule of law.[36]

I therefore consider norms and institutions *legal* when they display functional competence based on reason. Norms and rules are considered legitimate, if and when they provide, *in addition*, a genuine constraint on power. Law, in other words, is not legitimate as such. It must *turn* legitimate. Legitimate law on this understanding is a *synthesis* of morality and legality embodied in the law.[37] Apartheid law, as we shall see, was legal, but for the most part not legitimate. Early Nazi law, in similar fashion, was also legal, but not legitimate.

One way of determining the legality – and legitimacy – of law involves the examination of legal norms and institutions *in time*, with the help of comparative historical analysis. For legal norms and institutions are integral to the organization of social life. They "apportion decision-making authority among various individuals and institutions, reflecting a society's decisions about who will decide what, who is to be trusted and who not, who is to be empowered and who not, whose decisions are to be reviewed and whose are to be final, and who is to give orders and who is to take them."[38] It is a principle argument of this book that democracy is easier to establish if and when decision-making authority in a society has historically been apportioned primarily by way of

---

[36] Joseph Raz, "The Rule of Law and its Virtue," in idem., *The Authority of Law: Essays on Law and Morality* (Oxford: Clarendon Press, 1979), p. 211. Russell Hardin's conception of law shares features with the conception adopted here (although some differences exist): "My general argument is that the one general moral principle in law is the background principle of *mutual advantage*, as in Hobbes and Coase. Moral claims that are far more explicit and more pervasive than this principle are not persuasively requisite for law to work. Indeed, one can make a claim that is nearly the opposite of the usual claim for a necessary connection between law and morality. Any legal system that is heavily infused with morality will work well *only* if its subjects share that morality." See Russell Hardin, "Law and Social Order," *Noûs*, Vol. 35, Supplement 1 (October 2001), p. 64. Emphases added. For a more comprehensive discussion of mutual advantage, see his *Liberalism, Constitutionalism, and Democracy* (Oxford: Oxford University Press, 1999).

[37] As Thomas Würtenberger writes, "Im Gegensatz zur bloßen 'Legalität', der Übereinstimmung des Handelns mit gesatztem Recht, bezeichnet die 'Legitimität' die Rechtfertigung staatlicher Machtentfaltung durch allgemeinverbindliche Prinzipien. Der Legitimitätsbegriff transzendiert das bloß gesatzte Recht, indem er letzte Verbindlichkeitsgründe staatlicher Herrschaft ausdrückt." See his "Legitimität, Legalität," in Otto Brunner, Werner Conze, and Reinhart Koselleck, eds., *Geschichtliche Grundbegriffe: Historisches Lexikon zur politisch-sozialen Sprache in Deutschland*, Volume 3 (Stuttgart: Klett-Cotta, 1982), p. 677.

[38] Schauer, *Playing by the Rules*, p. 173.

formally rational law, regardless of whether or not this law was moral in content. This book, in other words, advances a procedural theory of law.[39]

Friedrich Julius Stahl's influential definition of the *Rechtsstaat* is useful for illustrating the procedural understanding of law: "The *Rechtsstaat* does most definitely not refer to the purpose and content of the state but only to the form and character of their realization."[40] This book is therefore primarily concerned with the regulatory function of law – especially its function in democratization. Yet in order to fully appreciate the function of law – especially formally rational law – in democratization, we must first understand the dynamics of contention in democratization.

A STRATEGY OF CONFLICT

Democratization is a process whereby democratic rules and procedures are applied to a society previously governed, partially or fully, by other principles. It tends to encompass two phases: transition and consolidation. Transition characterizes the interval between political regimes, and typically comprises a period of *extrication* and a subsequent period of democratic *constitution*.[41] Democratization, as a process, is complete once the consolidation of democracy is achieved. Consolidation requires the behavioral, attitudinal, and constitutional entrenchment of democracy as a system of governance.[42] The road to consolidated democracy, however, is mined. Maneuvering the road is an inherently conflictual process, a dramatic manifestation of the problem of social order.[43] In the process, insurgent actors and ideologies challenge the

---

[39] I develop this theory more fully in Chapter 3. For another, albeit substantially different, procedural democracy of law, see Jürgen Habermas, *Between Facts and Norms: Contributions to a Discourse Theory of Law and Democracy*, translated by William Rehg (Cambridge, MA: MIT Press, [1992] 1996).

[40] Friedrich Julius Stahl, *Die Philosophie des Rechts*, Volume 2 (Heidelberg: J. B. C. Mohr, 1846), p. 106, as cited in Dyson, *The State Tradition in Western Europe*, p. 108.

[41] Extrication can come as collapse or defeat or compromise. Constitution concerns the establishment of democratic rules and procedures.

[42] Juan J. Linz and Alfred Stepan, *Problems of Democratic Transition and Consolidation. Southern Europe, South America, and Post-Communist Europe* (Baltimore: Johns Hopkins University Press, 1996), Chapter 1. More specifically, a consolidated democracy is " ... a system in which the politically relevant forces subject their values and interests to the uncertain interplay of democratic institutions and comply with the outcomes of the democratic process. Democracy is consolidated when most conflicts are processed through democratic institutions, when nobody can control the outcomes ex post and the results are not predetermined ex ante, they matter within some predictable limits, and they evoke the compliance of the relevant political forces." For this definition, see Adam Przeworski, *Democracy and the Market: Political and Economic Reforms in Eastern Europe and Latin America* (Cambridge: Cambridge University Press, 1991), p. 51.

[43] Jon Elster, *The Cement of Society: A Study of Social Order* (Cambridge: Cambridge University Press, 1989); Ian Shapiro and Russell Hardin, eds., *Political Order: NOMOS XXXVIII* (New York: New York University Press, 1993); Karol Soltan, Eric M. Uslaner, and Virginia Haufler, eds., *Institutions and Social Order* (Ann Arbor: University of Michigan Press, 1998).

ingrained patterns according to which a society functions as a society and
compete with incumbents over the future of social order. Democratization can
get stuck, collapse, or reverse at any point along the way. At present, fifty or so
new democracies are estimated to exist in a "twilight zone of persistence
without legitimation and institutionalization."[44]

What makes democratization inherently conflictual is the fact that
adversarial agents interact *strategically* against the background of historically
ingrained definitions of group and countergroup membership.[45] Democratization, then, is a set of strategic interactions in which competing
adversaries, be they individuals, groups, or coalitions of both, react strategically to the incentives they face in political, social, and economic bargaining
situations. Democratization resembles, in most instances, an endgame situation.

Endgames

Endgames are a specific subset of strategic games.[46] Endgames are more difficult to resolve than other games, for cooperation among interacting agents is
particularly "difficult to sustain when the game is not repeated (or there is an
endgame), when information about the other players is lacking, and when
there are a larger number of players."[47] Although the hope in democratization
is that the game will be played again (what else is democracy but a repetition
of cooperation), the fear is that it might not. Under these circumstances,

---

Social order is either transformed, replaced, or transplaced in democratization. See Samuel P.
Huntington, *The Third Wave: Democratization in the Late Twentieth Century* (Norman:
University of Oklahoma Press, 1991), p. 114. Different conceptualizations of modes of
democratization exist. Huntington's conceptualization is the clearest and most user-friendly, and
is hence adopted here. For a similar conceptualization, employing different terminology, see
Terry Lynn Karl and Philippe C. Schmitter, "Modes of Transition in Latin America, Southern and
Eastern Europe," *International Social Science Journal*, Vol. 43, No. 128 (1991), pp. 269–284. For
a perceptive discussion of contrasting images, dimensions, episodes, and patterns of
democratization, see Ruth Berins Collier, *Paths Toward Democracy: The Working Class and
Elites in Western Europe and South America* (Cambridge: Cambridge University Press, 1999),
Introduction and Chapter 5.

[44] Larry Diamond, *Developing Democracy: Toward Consolidation* (Baltimore: Johns Hopkins
University Press, 1999), p. 22.

[45] See Russell Hardin, *One for All: The Logic of Group Conflict* (Princeton: Princeton University
Press, 1995), p. 142. The principal dividing line in democratization is initially between
democracy-demanding and democracy-resisting coalitions. Of course, neither camp is
monolithic. Usually cleavages exist within each camp.

[46] For a further distinction between "inclusion games" and "regime games," see Berins Collier,
Paths Toward Democracy, Chapter 5, esp. p. 189, Figure 5.2.

[47] Douglass C. North, "Autobiographical Lecture," reprinted in William Breit and Roger W.
Spencer, eds., *Lives of the Laureates: Thirteen Nobel Economists*, Third Edition (Cambridge,
MA: MIT Press, 1995), p. 265.

"individuals must choose strategically by incorporating the expectations of the actions of others into their own decision-making."[48]

What complicates strategic choice is the fact that reliable information is usually hard to come by in transitions from authoritarian rule. Furthermore, democratization involves a plethora of players. Although apartheid's endgame, as we shall see in Chapters 6 and 7, consisted of two major coalitions – the incumbent government and the insurgent, ANC-led resistance – smaller players complicated strategic interaction. Consider, for example, the permanent threat that Mangosuthu Buthelezi's Inkatha Freedom Party (IFP) and the Afrikaner Weerstandsbeweging (AWB) on the far right posed throughout the transition, especially in the lead-up to the first national democratic elections in 1994. Multiple players, in other words, complicate strategic interaction.

Processes of democratization are "deadly serious contests for extremely high stakes."[49] They cause changes in societies' balance of three essential commodities: power, wealth, and security. Democratization's principal change agents are, by assumption, power-, wealth-, and security-maximizers. Invariably, processes of democratization create winners and losers; therefore they generate supporters and opponents.[50] Imbalances in power, wealth, and security are important contributing causes of contentious politics. The danger of large-scale confrontation in democratization increases when relevant domestic actors fear political, economic, or physical victimhood.[51] These fears, of course, frequently overlap: power considerations, for example, are often also about wealth; and security fears almost always also involve concerns about power differentials. Let us consider these contested commodities in more detail.

Power

During democratization, incumbents and insurgents compete over power. According to traditional conceptions of power, the commodity refers to "the probability that one actor within a social relationship will be in a position to carry out his own will despite resistance, regardless of the basis on which this probability

---

[48] Jack Knight, *Institutions and Social Conflict* (Cambridge: Cambridge University Press, 1992), p. 17.

[49] Stephen M. Walt, *Revolution and War* (Ithaca, NY: Cornell University Press, 1996), p. 21

[50] The two adversarial groups can be further subdivided into extremists (radicals in the democracy-demanding camp and hardliners in the democracy-resisting camp) and centrists (moderates in the democracy-demanding camp and reformers in the democracy-resisting camp). This classic exposition can be found in Przeworski, *Democracy and the Market*, pp. 67–79. Resistance to democracy on the part of extremists influences centrists generally committed to moderation and accommodation, and vice versa. Some of these interaction effects are discussed in the empirical chapters.

[51] The tripartite distinction between political, economic, and physical fears of victimhood advances existing scholarship. While previous studies have analyzed power imbalances and security imbalances, none has explored the linkages between different *types* of fear. All types of fear can arise at both the elite and mass levels.

rests."[52] Social exchange theorists in the 1960s and 1970s challenged traditional conceptions of power, conceiving of power as dependence rather than domination. Richard Emerson's "power-dependence theory" was of particular significance in this regard.[53] To appreciate the contribution of power-dependence theory, imagine two agents A and B. The assumption in social exchange theory is that the power of A over B is the amount of resistance on the part of B that can be potentially overcome by A. The relationship between A and B is power-dependent in the sense that A's power resides in B's dependence. To the extent that B is more dependent on A than A is on B, A has more power over B, than B has over A. This conception of power is of immediate relevance for making sense of democratization. Linda Molm summarized the key tenets of the exchange theorists' conception of power:

First, *power is an attribute of a relation*, not an actor, derived from an actor's control over resources that are valued by another actor. Because the value of resources is relation-specific, and because some actors have more alternatives for acquiring valued resources than others, it is meaningless to speak of "powerful persons." A may have power over B, but not over C. Second, *power is a potential*, inherent in the structure of mutual dependencies created by the differential access that actors have to others who control resources they value. The definition of power as a potential is essential to a structural theory of power; only by defining power as a potential can it be treated as an attribute of an actor's position in a structure of dependence relations. [...] Third, *power is nonzero-sum*. Because each actor's power is defined by the other's dependence, an increase in one actor's power does not imply a decrease in the other actor's power. There is no a priori relation between the two. Both actors might increase their power over each other, both decrease their power over each other, one increase while the other remains constant, and so forth. As a result, it is both possible and necessary to distinguish between the *average power* and *power imbalance* in a relation.[54]

Let us consider the social function of power in democratization. Democracy-demanding insurgents and democracy-resisting incumbents are regularly offensive positionalists: they each are concerned with relative gains and seek to maximize power vis-à-vis the opponent. Insurgents' motivation for power maximization in democratization stems from their desire to widen political participation. Incumbents, in turn, will try to hinder the redistribution of power as long as possible. Because both incumbents and insurgents generally value power more than security, the process of strategic interaction

[52] Weber, *Economy and Society*, p. 53.
[53] See, for example, Richard M. Emerson, "Power-Dependence Relations," *American Sociological Review*, Vol. 27, No. 1 (February 1962), pp. 31–41; and idem., "Social Exchange Theory," in Morris Rosenberg and Ralph H. Turner, eds., *Social Psychology: Sociological Perspectives* (New York: Basic Books, 1981), pp. 30–65. See also Peter M. Blau, *Exchange and Power in Social Life* (New York: Wiley, 1964); and George C. Homans, *Social Behavior: Its Elementary Forms* (New York: Harcourt, Brace, 1961). The most useful compendium on power remains Steven Lukes, ed., *Power* (Oxford: Blackwell, 1986).
[54] Linda D. Molm, *Coercive Power in Social Exchange* (Cambridge: Cambridge University Press, 1997), p. 30.

in democratization is, at least in its incipient stage, inherently conflictual. Fears of political victimhood may arise among three sets of actors: (1) those associated with the incumbent regime who stand to lose from power changes; (2) those associated with insurgents who anticipate a reversal of democratization; and (3) those previously associated with either incumbents or insurgents who stand to be marginalized in the new order. Social exchange theory therefore captures the social function of power in democratization in important ways. Alongside more traditional conceptions of power, the notion of power-dependence is useful for understanding the essence of strategic interaction in democratization.

Wealth

Democratization also changes the societal distribution of resources. Resources that matter in democratization include employment, education, goods and services, subsidies, property rights, and also natural resources such as oil, water, timber, and diamonds.[55] Prior to democratization, these resources will generally have been allocated unequally and unfairly across society. Democratization therefore demands and often involves a redistribution of wealth.[56] For insurgents, the prospect of redistribution spells hope, among incumbents it usually creates fear. Democratization can be endangered when the balance of wealth changes either too swiftly or too slowly. If it changes too swiftly, yesterday's winners might seek to derail democratization in order to divert the actual or anticipated threat to their wealth. If it changes too slowly, yesterday's losers might mobilize for a radical, revolutionary break with the past, purge yesterday's winners, and seize their assets. Fears of economic victimhood thus raise the specter of confrontation in two important ways: first, by prompting resistance from yesterday's winners who fear to become tomorrow's losers; and, second, by prompting the seizure of wealth by yesterday's losers who are anxious to become tomorrow's winners.

Security

In democratization, fears of political and economic victimhood often combine with fears of physical survival. In fact, impending or imagined imbalances in power and wealth make security a principal concern in democratization. As a result of the difficulty of accurately assessing the intentions and possible reactions of opponents, agents in democratization frequently exaggerate threats to their power and wealth, and also to their physical security.

---

[55] For an excellent analysis, see, for example, Michael L. Ross, *Timber Booms and Institutional Breakdown in Southeast Asia* (Cambridge: Cambridge University Press, 2001).

[56] What matters in this regard is *not* whether wealth is actually redistributed in democratization, but whether agents *fear* that redistribution might be impending.

Two broad types of security fears can be distinguished. First, present or former members of an outgoing regime may fear the real or anticipated "backward looking justice of retribution and restitution."[57] Means to attenuate this type of security fear include, most important, the concession of "golden parachutes." Security fears are generally less likely to trigger confrontation when old elites see "a reasonably bright future for themselves in the new social order."[58] However, negotiating the line between retribution and resolution is not always easy.[59] Golden parachutes can also have unintended consequences. Although amnesty provisions in democratization, for example, may placate the fears of incumbents, they may also provoke the anger of insurgents. If such anger explodes into winner-driven revenge attacks, democratization becomes seriously endangered. In apartheid's endgame, which is examined in greater detail in Chapters 6 and 7, an ostensible compromise was reached: amnesty on a case-by-case basis, in return for perpetrators' full disclosure of the human wrongs they committed under apartheid. In essence, the victims of apartheid were asked to put aside their demand for *retribution* – for punishment and vengeance – in return for a supply of *truth*.[60]

Security fears can also revolve around problems of citizenship. As democratization processes occur more frequently in multinational or multicultural settings, extreme fears of physical victimhood become more salient. Democratization invariably creates pressures for assimilation that can spur fears of survival among minorities, especially if these minorities have been associated with the previous, nondemocratic regime. In South Africa, fears of survival were felt intensely among the Afrikaner and Zulu segments of society, members of both of whom had, although to different degrees and in different ways, supported and substantially profited from "separate development."[61]

In sum, the real, imagined, or anticipated loss of power, wealth, or security in democratization can induce interacting actors, be they elites or masses, to consider war against adversaries. For as Thomas Schelling reminds us, in a highly uncertain environment, "the power to hurt – to destroy things that somebody treasures, to inflict pain and grief – is a kind of bargaining power, not easy to use but used often."[62] The strategy of conflict in democratization can be further elucidated by recourse to Albert Hirschman's hydraulic model.

[57] Jon Elster, "On Doing What One Can," *East European Constitutional Review*, Vol. 1 (1992), pp. 15–17.
[58] Edward D. Mansfield and Jack Snyder, "Democratization and War," *Foreign Affairs*, Vol. 74, No. 3 (May/June 1995), p. 96.
[59] See, for example, Martha Minow, *Between Vengeance and Forgiveness: Facing History After Genocide and Mass Violence* (Boston: Beacon Press, 1998); Robert I. Rotberg and Dennis Thompson, eds., *Truth v. Justice: The Morality of Truth Commissions* (Princeton: Princeton University Press, 2000); Ruti G. Teitel, *Transitional Justice* (Oxford: Oxford University Press, 2000).
[60] For a more comprehensive analysis of transitional justice in South Africa, see Chapters 6 and 7 below.
[61] See, for example, Kate Manzo and Pat McGowan, "Afrikaner Fears and the Politics of Despair," *International Studies Quarterly*, Vol. 36, No. 1 (March 1992), pp. 1–24.
[62] Thomas C. Schelling, *Arms and Influence* (New Haven: Yale University Press, 1966), p. v.

A Hydraulic Model

In *Exit, Voice, and Loyalty*, Hirschman investigated agents' responses to the decline in firms, organizations, and states.[63] In democratization, interacting agents also face decline. However – and this has not yet been appreciated in the existing literature – they face *different* incentives and thus react *differently* than agents in consolidated settings.[64] Unfortunately, Hirschman's hydraulic model only takes into account the responses of customers and members to decline. The responses of management and government lay outside the framework. Here a reconfiguration of the hydraulic model is in order. My chief concern is with Hirschman's definition of "exit."[65]

Extending Hirschman, I posit that "exit" can have at least two meanings. In his seminal contribution, Hirschman analyzed voluntary, especially economic relationships. In voluntary relationships agents can pick and leave partners, as well as interactions, at any point in time. In such relationships, "exit" simply means the termination of interaction – not dealing with one another. Accordingly, whenever rational agents can choose with whom to interact, and on what terms, this will "reduce the chance of exploitation by individuals who do not reciprocate or who are less likely to do so."[66] Yet, agents cannot always avoid dealing with one another.[67] In compulsory relationships interactions are impossible to shirk. They are mandatory. It is compulsory relationships that sustain authoritarian rule. While some agents may withdraw and exit internally under nondemocratic rule (e.g., "internal emigration"), leaving the country – or the authoritarian regime that controls it – is generally not a viable option.[68] When exit is foreclosed, voice becomes a residual, says Hirschman: "with exit

---

[63] Albert O. Hirschman, *Exit, Voice, and Loyalty: Responses to Decline in Firms, Organizations, and States* (Cambridge, MA: Harvard University Press, 1970). See also idem., "Exit, Voice, and the State," *World Politics*, Vol. 31, No. 1 (October 1978), pp. 90–107; idem., "Exit, Voice, and the Fate of the German Democratic Republic;" and Rogers Brubaker, "Frontier Theses: Exit, Voice, and Loyalty in East Germany," *Migration World*, Vol. 18, No. 3/4 (1990), pp. 12–17.

[64] In addition, *more* actors matter in democratization.

[65] See also Anton D. Lowenberg and Ben T. Yu, "Efficient Constitution Formation and Maintenance: The Role of 'Exit'," *Constitutional Political Economy*, Vol. 3, No. 1 (Winter 1992), pp. 51–72.

[66] Bernd Lahno, "Trust, Reputation, and Exit in Exchange Relationships," *Journal of Conflict Resolution*, Vol. 39, No. 3 (September 1995), p. 497. More generally, see also Barry, Brian, "Review Article: Exit, Voice, and Loyalty," *British Journal of Political Science*, Vol. 4, No. 1 (January 1974), pp. 79–107; and Dowding, Keith, Peter John, Thanos Mergoupis, and Mark van Vugt, "Exit, Voice and Loyalty: Analytic and Empirical Developments," *European Journal of Political Research*, Vol. 37 (2000), pp. 469–495.

[67] See Paul Pierson's discussion of the differences between politics and economics. Pierson, "Increasing Returns, Path Dependence, and the Study of Politics," *American Political Science Review*, Vol. 94, No. 2 (June 2000), pp. 257–262.

[68] Exit as leaving may be an option for persons who are no primary targets of authoritarian control. In South Africa, for example, whites could, and did, "leave" apartheid by way of emigration, prompting serious concerns domestically about brain drain.

wholly unavailable, voice must carry the entire burden of alerting management of its failings."[69] I propose, by contrast, that the meaning of exit *changes* where exit is unavailable. Even though the option of leaving is foreclosed in compulsory relationships, the impulse to do so will still arise on the part of unhappy agents. The action to which this impulse gives rise in a compulsory setting is likely to be *stronger* than in a voluntary one. The reason: agents will invariably feel great frustration if leaving, walking away, is not a strategy available to them. They are unlikely to merely want to "alert" management of its failings, as Hirschman assumes. In compulsory relationships, exit is more likely to comprise actions more drastic than terminating interaction. What is more, it is important to recognize that not only customers and members can seek to exit a declining order, but also management and government. For the purposes of this book, "exit" therefore refers to agents' choice of *confrontation over cooperation*, and "voice" to the choice of *cooperation over confrontation*.[70] These definitions refine the ordinary Prisoner's Dilemma.

The ordinary Prisoner's Dilemma says that two interacting agents will reap mutual benefits from cooperation, but will be unable to achieve cooperation on mutual advantage if they are required to act simultaneously. The menu of choices available to agents offers two strategies: cooperation and defection. The intensified Prisoner's Dilemma, as I call it, is identical to the ordinary Prisoner's Dilemma *except* for the fact that the menu of choices is altered. Instead of cooperation and defection, the choices are cooperation and confrontation. The intensified Prisoner's Dilemma captures the dynamics of contention in endgames such as democratization more accurately than the ordinary Prisoner's Dilemma.

In this context, I take confrontation to refer to "goal-seeking behavior that strives to reduce the gains available to others or to impede their want-satisfaction."[71] Pure confrontational interactions are zero-sum: one party can

---

[69] Hirschman, *Exit, Voice, and Loyalty*, p. 34.

[70] The distinction between cooperation and confrontation is superior to other distinctions such as "deliberation/negotiation vs. mobilization/protest," as proposed by Collier, *Paths Toward Democracy*, pp. 19–21. Collier unnecessarily excludes expressive and coercive action from the realm of bargaining. This seems empirically problematic, for what most democratization processes show is that intimidation and violence *are* bargaining tools.

[71] Helen Milner, *Interests, Institutions, and Information: Domestic Politics and International Relations* (Princeton: Princeton University Press, 1997), p. 8. Note that Milner reserves this definition for both conflict and competition. However, I believe that neither of the two notions is the real opposite of cooperation. Drawing on Russell Hardin, I believe that cooperative interactions involve elements of both conflict and coordination. Coordination takes place because all interacting parties are made better off by exchanging, conflict arises because all have to give up something in order for the others to gain. If it is true that conflict is indeed an element of cooperation, it cannot serve as its logical opposite. See Russell Hardin, "The Social Evolution of Cooperation," in Karen Schweers Cook and Margaret Levi, eds., *The Limits of Rationality* (Chicago: University of Chicago Press, 1990), pp. 359–360. Next, competition is something that characterizes *any* bargaining situation. Even processes of cooperation are, at some level, about the resolution of competing interests.

TABLE 2.1. *The Intensified Prisoner's Dilemma*

	Cooperation	Confrontation
Cooperation	2, 2	0, 3
Confrontation	3, 0	1, 1

only gain if another loses.[72] Cooperation, by contrast, refers to a process of exchange in which "actors adjust their behavior to the actual or anticipated preferences of others, through a process of policy coordination."[73] In cooperation, the achievement of want-satisfaction of one party is dependent upon the achievement of some form of want-satisfaction of all interacting parties.[74] Table 2.1 displays the payoffs of a typical endgame situation, what I have termed an intensified Prisoner's Dilemma.[75]

I suggest that a predominance of cooperative bargaining – even if interspersed with instances of cooperation deadlock or cooperation breakdown – will sustain the inherently conflictual democratization process, in particular by allowing the negotiation of more inclusive reform packages and the construction of broader-based support coalitions than would otherwise be possible.[76] This can alleviate democratization's uncertainty predicament, potentially placating fears of victimhood. Cooperation may also lower the salience of groupness,

---

[72] Hardin, "The Social Evolution of Cooperation," p. 359. Non-zero-sum games permit parties to win or lose simultaneously.

[73] Robert Keohane, *After Hegemony: Cooperation and Discord in the World Political Economy* (Princeton: Princeton University Press, 1984), pp. 51–52. Thus for an interaction to count as cooperation two elements need to be present: goal-directed behavior and mutual gains through policy adjustment. See also Milner, *Interests, Institutions, and Information*, p. 8.

[74] A cooperative arrangement then is "any outcome (a) that is better for everybody than the state of anarchy, (b) in which there are no exploiters, defined as noncooperators whose cooperation would cost them less than it would benefit them and others, and (c) in which nobody ends up being exploited, that is, as a cooperator whose cooperation costs him more than it benefits himself and others." See Elster, *The Cement of Society*, p. 50. For a discussion of *types* of cooperation (externalities, helping, conventions, joint ventures, and private ordering), see Elster, *The Cement of Society*, pp. 11–15. On the problem of cooperation, see also Douglass C. North, *Institutions, Institutional Change and Economic Performance* (Cambridge: Cambridge University Press, 1990), chapter 2.

[75] Needless to say, game theory can only approximate empirical reality. As mentioned, most transitional settings are populated with more than two actors. Note that while the payoffs of the intensified Prisoner's Dilemma are identical to the ones in the ordinary Prisoner's Dilemma, the available choices, and the potential consequences of these choices, are not. For a discussion of transition games with more than two sets of players, see Josep M. Colomer, *Strategic Transitions: Game Theory and Democratization* (Baltimore: Johns Hopkins University Press, 2000), esp. pp. 46–71.

[76] Inclusive reforms often include the crafting of fair and representative institutions, often modeled along consociational lines, and "golden parachutes."

potentially easing democratization's bargaining predicament.[77] Conversely, confrontational bargaining, if predominant, impedes the crafting of democracy. Confrontational interactions generally exaggerate assessments of threat, thereby spurring fears of victimhood. In democratization, as in other types of compulsory relationships, acts of confrontation can vary in intensity. Their intensity can range from the nonviolent to the violent.[78] "Exit," here, comprises acts ranging from suppression to resistance to sabotage to secession. Irrespective of their intensity, all confrontational actions seek to reduce gains available to others.

The principal strategic interactions in democratization develop between democracy-demanding and democracy-resisting coalitions. The former coalition usually comprises moderates and radicals, the latter hardliners and reformers.[79] Bargaining is about the redistribution of societies' essential commodities: the process can either aggravate or ameliorate fears of victimhood. Bargaining may take place in the extrication phase, the constitution phase, the consolidation phase, or all of these phases of democratization.[80] Getting adversaries to talk to each other and cobble together agreements about democracy's form and future is frequently problematic. Competing actors are forced to make instantaneous calculations about the likely payoffs of accepting the uncertainties of democratization. Multiple assessment problems, including offense-defense similarity, lack of time, lack of experience, and pervasive distrust, complicate strategic interaction.[81] These assessment problems are a function of several dilemmas germane to democratization.

Strategic Dilemmas

Democratization may produce two dilemmas, each of which has the potential to complicate the achievement of cooperative bargaining: information failures and commitment problems. If either of these dilemmas ensues, assessment problems are likely to cascade. In turn, suspicion among interacting agents may heighten and lead to a third dilemma: the security dilemma. Large-scale social violence becomes more likely when these strategic dilemmas arise and

[77] Barry Weingast, "Constructing Trust: The Political and Economic Roots of Ethnic and Regional Conflict," in Soltan, Uslaner, and Haufler, eds., *Institutions and Social Order*.

[78] For a typology of collective violence, see Charles Tilly, *The Politics of Collective Violence* (Cambridge: Cambridge University Press, 2003).

[79] On the principal political players in democratization, see Przeworski, *Democracy and the Market*, pp. 67–95.

[80] In game theoretical terms, bargaining refers to a game "in which two or more players stand to gain by cooperating, but they must negotiate an acceptable procedure for sharing the gains from cooperation." Herbert Gintis, *Game Theory Evolving: A Problem-Centered Introduction to Modeling Strategic Interaction* (Princeton: Princeton University Press, 2000), p. 345.

[81] For a brief overview, see Barbara F. Walter, "Conclusion," in Barbara F. Walter and Jack Snyder, eds., *Civil Wars, Insecurity, and Intervention* (New York: Columbia University Press, 1999), pp. 304–305.

remain unameliorated and when, as a consequence, agents' assessment of their vulnerability vis- à-vis adversaries rises above a critical, empirically determined threshold.[82] Then, confrontation may reach a point of no return, in which one side decides to bear the costs of collective violence in order to avoid real or imagined victimization.

Information Failures

When there is a lack of accurate information about the principal goals, preferences, and strategies of interacting parties in democratization, cooperation between adversaries will be hampered. As Helen Milner writes, "Incomplete information leads to inefficient outcomes."[83] Information failures can be a direct function of the general uncertainty predicament in democratization, or, interacting agents may have incentives to misrepresent information in order to achieve a bargaining advantage.[84] In both cases, information failures can impede the making of cooperation. This is so because bargaining situations in democratization have a broad scope for opportunism.

This leads to the issue of transaction costs. The possession of private information can confer political advantages in democratization, by lowering transaction costs, and tilting strategic interaction toward confrontation. If groups become suspicious of the intentions of others, fears of victimhood are likely to spiral. This may drive actors to elect confrontational bargaining strategies, thereby potentially causing adversaries to also shun cooperation in favor of confrontation. As the next section explains, security spirals are the

---

[82] Weingast, "Constructing Trust," pp. 163–200. See also Rui J. P. de Figueiredo Jr. and Barry Weingast, "The Rationality of Fear: Political Opportunism and Ethnic Conflict," in Barbara F. Walter and Jack Snyder, eds., *Civil Wars, Insecurity, and Intervention* (New York: Columbia University Press, 1999), pp. 261–302.

[83] Milner, *Interests, Institutions, and Information*, p. 20.

[84] According to constitutional political economists uncertainty, generally speaking, has two sources:

> The first is very close to a statistical problem and comes from the tenuous connection between policy (which governments can change) and outcomes (which citizens care about). It is difficult to predict the effects of policies on outcomes, because (a) causal relations are complex, and (b) there are large stochastic elements in the process of generating outcomes. The other sources of uncertainty is strategic. Strategic uncertainty comes from not knowing the actions of other members of society. We are never certain about the actions other individuals will take. This is problematic because the actions we would want to take often depend upon our calculation of what others will do. If we are uncertain about what others will do, it will be hard for us to determine what course of action we should pursue. In particular, this uncertainty about the actions of others is a problem when we believe that others will take actions that increase their own welfare but will have hurt the rest of society. Thus, as Mancur Olson and others have noted, the fundamental dilemma for a society (or the collective action problem) is how to create a context where self-interested actors have reasons to cooperate.

See Michael J. Ensley and Michael C. Munger, "Ideological Competition and Institutions: Why 'Cultural' Explanations of Development Patterns Are Not Nonsense," in Ram Mudambi, Pietro Navarra, and Giuseppe Sobbrio, eds., *Rules and Reason: Perspectives on Constitutional Political Economy* (Cambridge: Cambridge University Press, 2001), pp. 114–115.

likely result. Democratization thus produces a paradox: achieving and sustaining cooperation in the process necessitates accurate information, yet the availability of accurate information depends on the achievement of cooperative interaction. Therefore, a *veil of ignorance*, will, contra John Rawls, always have *debilitating* effects on the construction of cooperation in democratization. Incomplete information is an incentive to defect, *not* to cooperate.[85] In situations of great uncertainty, payoffs expected to accumulate from cooperation are seriously discounted by bargaining actors if these actors cannot be sure that the other contracting parties will comply with the commitments that are reached.[86] To further illuminate this point, let us imagine the bargaining predicament in democratization as a typical Prisoner's Dilemma.

In the simple Prisoner's Dilemma, noncooperation is frequently the outcome of unintended consequences, even when actors were conditionally predisposed to cooperate at the onset of the game. In the common PD game,

the mere expectation that the second player might choose to defect can lead the first player to do so, if only in self-defence. The first players' anticipation of the second's defection may be based simply on the belief that the second player is unconditionally uncooperative. But more tragically, it may also be based on the fear that the second player will not trust him to cooperate, and will defect as a direct result of this lack of *trust*.[87]

[85] John Rawls' notion of the "veil of ignorance" holds that the less information about likely outcomes of choices is known to self-interested players in a bargaining game, the greater the chances that negotiated rules will be fair and enduring. John Rawls, *A Theory of Justice* (Cambridge, MA: The Belknap Press of Harvard University Press, 1971), esp. pp. 136–142. Rawls writes that, "[a] veil of ignorance prevents anyone from being advantaged or disadvantaged by the contingencies of social class and fortune; and hence the bargaining problems which arise in everyday life from the possession of this knowledge do not affect the choice of principles." Applied to democratization, Rawls' proposition suggests that the chances of crafting democracy cooperatively will increase with the degree of uncertainty. See Rawls, as cited in Robert Paul Wolff, *Understanding Rawls: A Reconstruction and Critique of "A Theory of Justice"* (Princeton: Princeton University Press, 1977), pp. 60–61. This, however, is doubtful. For if a "transition is to produce sustainable democratic outcomes, it may be essential for negotiating partners to enjoy access to accurate information not only about the likely winners and losers once democracy is introduced but on the bargaining latitude of their partners and on the likely effects of particular institutional proposals." Steven Friedman, "Too Little Knowledge is a Dangerous Thing: South Africa's Bargained Transition, Democratic Prospects and John Rawls' 'Veil of Ignorance'," *Politikon*, Vol. 25, No. 2 (June 1998), pp. 75–76. For the argument that uncertainty is desirable in democratization, see also Michael D. Ward and Kristian S. Gleditsch, "Democratizing for Peace," *American Political Science Review*, Vol. 92, No. 1 (March 1998), p. 53.

[86] As Barbara Geddes writes, "[u]ncertainty reduces the expected payoff for cooperation relative to the payoffs associated with other choices and thus reduces the incentive to cooperate." See her *Politician's Dilemma: Building State Capacity in Latin America* (Berkeley: University of California Press, 1994), p. 30. In general terms, decisions under uncertainty imply that agents may be able to imagine possible futures, but are unable to estimate the probabilities with which these futures are likely to occur. See Jon Elster, *Explaining Technical Change* (Cambridge: Cambridge University Press, 1983), p. 185.

[87] Diego Gambetta, "Can We Trust Trust?," in Idem., ed., *Trust: Making and Breaking Cooperative Relations* (Oxford: Basil Blackwell, 1988), p. 216. Emphasis added.

In democratization, uncertainty, created by insufficient, incomplete or asymmetric information, is very likely to produce outcomes that lead to suboptimal levels of exchange.[88] This can exacerbate the *already* conflictual nature of democratization and make confrontation (and therefore collective violence) appear as attractive escape routes in seemingly zero-sum games.[89] For, "[u]ncertainty is what they [authoritarian elites] abhor ideologically, psychologically, and politically."[90]

The problem of insufficient information and miscommunication is pronounced in democratization's reform games, where actors' predisposition toward cooperation will be low given the historical background against which strategic interaction takes place. Incomplete information makes incumbents more wary of entering into commitments with insurgents, and *vice versa*. Incomplete information also increases the chances that either side (or any other relevant parties) defects from struck commitments to form jingoistic coalitions with domestic or international allies. In democratization, incomplete information can potentially transform strategic interaction from a Prisoner's Dilemma situation, in which at least some possibilities for cooperation exist, into a game of Deadlock, in which confrontation is preferred to cooperation.[91]

Commitment Problems

Information failures in democratization can cause commitment problems, "situations in which mutually preferable bargains are unattainable" because actors hold conflicting preferences over a substantive bargaining issue.[92] Contentious bargaining issues frequently arise during political and economic reform. The essence of *political reform* is to get key players, former enemies, to consider, construct, and credibly commit to new rules of the political game. Three subarenas of political reform can be distinguished: constitutional

---

[88] "Only if a set of rules, institutions, and expectations about the actions of other individuals is known to the actor can the actor make utility-maximizing calculations with a reasonable expectation that his or her strategic decisions will lead to success." See Thomas A. Koelble, "The New Institutionalism in Political Science and Sociology," *Comparative Politics*, Vol. 27, No. 2 (January 1995), p. 242.

[89] For a discussion of how the *presence* and *absence* of history – past experience stemming from prior interactions – affects strategic games, especially the Prisoner's Dilemma, see Thomas Gautschi, "History Effects in Social Dilemma Situations," *Rationality and Society*, Vol. 12, No. 2 (May 2000), pp. 131–62.

[90] Adam Przeworski, "Some Problems in the Study of the Transition to Democracy," in Guillermo O'Donnell, Philippe C. Schmitter and Laurence Whitehead, eds., *Transitions for Authoritarian Rule: Comparative Perspectives* (Baltimore: Johns Hopkins University Press, 1986), p. 59.

[91] See Jack Snyder and Robert Jervis, "Civil War and the Security Dilemma," in Walter and Snyder, eds., *Civil Wars, Insecurity, and Intervention*, p. 22.

[92] For this definition of commitment problems, see James D. Fearon, "Rationalist Explanations for War," *International Organization*, Vol. 49, No. 3 (Summer 1995), p. 381. For foundational work on commitment problems, see Oliver E. Williamson, " Credible Commitments: Using Hostages to Support Exchange," *American Economic Review*, Vol. 73 (September 1983), pp. 519–40; and idem., *The Economic Institutions of Capitalism*, Chapters 7 and 8.

reform, electoral reform, and party system reform. The essence of *economic reform* is to "organize an economy that rationally allocates resources and in which the state is financially solvent."[93] Three subarenas of economic reform can be distinguished: stabilization, efficient resource allocation, and, in most cases, some form of privatization.[94] Political and economic reforms are interdependent: success in one arena is likely to feed into the other arena and can help sustain a new democracy.[95] Conversely, failure in one arena may have negative spillover effects into the other arena, increasing instability in a polity. Developments in either arena can function as tipping factors; they can escalate or placate the uncertainty predicament in democratization and heighten or reduce fears of victimhood.[96] Painful adaptations to changing political or economic circumstances often produce widespread resistance by actors, be they elites or masses. If reservoirs of discontent surface, they can be tapped for violent mobilization by extremist actors who stand to be marginalized in democratization.

Credible commitments are difficult to achieve in political and economic reform because of the possibility of opportunism – self-interested behavior such as cheating or free-riding that can have socially harmful consequences.[97] Actors' choices in the strategic interactions of democratization rest not so much on the static situation of the present, but rather, on the dynamic expectations for the future. What makes strategic interactions in democratization liable to opportunistic behavior is the fact that interacting agents base their judgment of others on these actors' past behavior. The motivation for opportunism is

---

[93] Przeworski, *Democracy and the Market*, p. 136.

[94] Adam Przeworski, *Sustainable Democracy* (Cambridge: Cambridge University Press, 1995), pp. 67–68.

[95] On the linkages between political and economic reform, see José María Maravall, *Regimes, Politics, and Markets: Democratization and Economic Change in Southern and Eastern Europe* (Oxford: Oxford University Press, 1997), esp. Chapter 1; Barry R. Weingast, "Constitutions as Governance Structures: The Political Foundations of Secure Markets," *Journal of Institutional and Theoretical Economics*, Vol. 149, No. 1 (May 1993), pp. 286–311; and Joan M. Nelson, "Linkages between Politics and Economics," *Journal of Democracy*, Vol. 5, No. 4 (October 1994), pp. 49–62.

[96] One historic example is Weimar Germany's ill-fated experiment with democracy and the Republic's chronic inability to tackle the economic malaise of the 1920s.

[97] Opportunism is commonly defined as "the ability of one party to an exchange to benefit at the expense of the other party by violating the agreement in his or her post-contractual behavior." See Douglass North, "A Framework for Analyzing Economic Organization in History," in idem., *Structure and Change in Economic History* (New York: W.W. Norton, 1981), p. 36. Opportunism is characteristic of most human interactions but is especially pronounced in democratization due to the uncertainty predicament and the legacy of general societal distrust that is commonly a consequence of sustained non-democratic rule. Oliver Williamson remarks that transactions "that are the subject of ex post opportunism will benefit if appropriate safeguards can be devised ex ante." As examples, he mentions the realignment of incentives and the construction of superior governance structures within which transactions could be structured. See Williamson, *The Economic Institutions of Capitalism*, pp. 48–49.

further heightened when information failures are frequent and serious. Information failures can open or widen a substantive bargaining gap between interacting agents, aggravating the task of constructing credible commitments. Insufficient information works against iterative interaction, and unilateralism (and defection) become more rational strategies. This, in turn, promotes confrontation over cooperation.

If commitment problems persist in newly emergent social orders, the specter of collective violence arises. Two mechanisms are conceivable: first, collective violence as the direct result of specific, substantive commitment problems. In this case, violence may result, for example, from an indivisibility of stakes. Or, second, collective violence may ensue as a consequence of spiraling security dilemmas. In this case, collective violence results chiefly from uncertainty and insecurity, not substantive commitment problems. Frequently, both mechanisms overlap: specific commitment problems *exacerbate* the already precarious level of uncertainty present between interacting actors, launching security dilemmas. Illustrating the compatibility between fears of commitment (the commitment problem) and fears of uncertainty (the security dilemma), the formulation offered here synthesizes these two rationalist explanations for collective violence.

Security Dilemmas

Security dilemmas are likely to appear in democratization, most frequently during extrication and constitution.[98] Once the transition to democracy is complete, the risk of collective violence typically declines.[99] What is it about the transition phase that is conducive to the rise of security dilemmas? Contrary to the consolidation phase in which uncertainty takes on what Adam Przeworski terms an organized character, the transition phase is typically clouded in *absolute uncertainty*.[100] See Table 2.2. Everything is at stake and up

[98] On the security dilemma, see Robert Jervis, *Perception and Misperception in International Politics* (Princeton: Princeton University Press, 1976), chapter 3; and idem., "Cooperation under the Security Dilemma," *World Politics*, Vol. 30, No. 2 (January 1978), pp. 167–214. For the usage of the concept to explain ethnic war, see Barry R. Posen, "The Security Dilemma and Ethnic Conflict," in Michael E. Brown, ed., *Ethnic Conflict and International Security* (Princeton: Princeton University Press, 1993), pp. 103–24. For a critique of the application of the security dilemma to ethnic war, see James D. Fearon, "Commitment Problems and the Spread of Ethnic Conflict," in David A. Lake and Donald Rothchild, eds., *The International Spread of Ethnic Conflict: Fear, Diffussion, and Escalation* (Princeton: Princeton University Press, 1998).

[99] Edward D. Mansfield and Jack Snyder, "Democratization and the Danger of War," *International Security*, Vol. 20, No. 1 (Summer 1995), reprinted in Michael E. Brown, Sean M. Lynn-Jones, Steven E. Miller, eds., *Debating the Democratic Peace* (Cambridge, MA: MIT Press, 1996), pp. 309; 315.

[100] As Karl writes, "Indeed, the dynamics of the transition revolve around strategic interactions and tentative arrangements between actors with uncertain power resources aimed at defining who will legitimately be entitled to play in the political game, what criteria will determine the winners and losers, and what limits will be placed on the issues at stake." See her

TABLE 2.2. *Types of Uncertainty*

	Organized Uncertainty	Absolute Uncertainty
Rules	Certain	Uncertain
Outcomes	Uncertain	Uncertain

for grabs.[101] Whereas in consolidated democracies the *rules* of democracy are generally beyond dispute, and relative uncertainty exists only over democratic *outcomes*, in democratization uncertainty exists over *both*. The situation is further aggravated in so-called war transitions, where uncertainty among adversaries can be expected to be higher, and the need for reducing uncertainty therefore is greater.

The contentious nature of politics and economics in democratization causes actors to worry about their vulnerability vis-à-vis their competitors. In these calculations, agents are aware that interaction may not continue. One or the other agent may die, defect, or the relationship may end for another reason. Because these outcomes cannot be predicted with certainty, "the next move is not as important as the current one. There may be no next move."[102] This dynamic makes democratization dangerous because agents also "prefer to get a given [or presumed] benefit today, rather than having to wait for the same benefit until tomorrow."[103] Tomorrow's benefit may even be less than today's benefit. But even if we leave the desire for power or wealth aside, some agents may mobilize power to achieve security.

The quest for power maximization, in turn, often exacerbates the perception of insecurity on the part of other agents. This is the security dilemma. The principal characteristic of the security dilemma is an action-reaction spiral. Security dilemmas can be so severe that "[e]ven when parties are willing to compromise on their political goals, their fear of being vulnerable may prevent them from reaching a settlement."[104]

"Dilemmas of Democratization in Latin America," *Comparative Politics*, Vol. 23, No. 1 (October 1990), p. 6.

[101] Weingast, "Constructing Trust," p. 191. Mary McAuley concurs, noting that processes of democratization are "periods of social and political turmoil and even less turbulent transition periods are often chaotic, and collective action is fragmented and changeable." See her *Russia's Politics of Uncertainty* (Cambridge: Cambridge University Press, 1997), p. 6.

[102] Robert Axelrod, *The Evolution of Cooperation* (New York: Basic Books, 1984), p. 126. Interestingly, the part of the book from which the quote is taken is entitled "Advice for Participants and Reformers."

[103] Axelrod, *The Evolution of Cooperation*.

[104] Stephen John Stedman, "Negotiation and Mediation in Internal Conflict," in Michael E. Brown, ed., *The International Dimensions of Internal Conflict* (Cambridge, MA: MIT Press, 1996), pp. 341–376. However, the notion that the security dilemma *per se* causes war in democratizing societies is misleading. In many democratizing societies, security dilemmas

Having established the uncertainty predicament of democratization, and the consequences thereof for the bargaining predicament, I am now in a position to clarify the relationship between the intensified Prisoner's Dilemma, as theorized here for the first time, and the conventional Prisoner's Dilemma. The ordinary Prisoner's Dilemma is a Prisoner's Dilemma with *organized uncertainty*. The intensified Prisoner's Dilemma, the typical endgame situation, is a Prisoner's Dilemma where *absolute uncertainty* obtains. See again Table 2.2. Although the payoffs are identical, the threshold to cooperation is higher in the intensified version of the Prisoner's Dilemma. Such then is the strategy of conflict in democratization.

Having elucidated the concept of law and the dynamics of contention in democratization, we can now consider the importance of surviving institutions for making democracy work. The subfield of constitutional political economy maintains that institutions are well suited to combating uncertainty. Institutions are said to help societies overcome the uncertainty predicament by

providing a structure or an arena for human interaction. In particular institutions provide structure by establishing formal rules, much as [James] Buchanan has expressed in a variety of his writings. Institutions prevent chaos by establishing a set of rules that will determine how the game will be played or, in terms of politics, how collective choices will be made. That is, institutions provide a structure or framework under which different players and groups can interact. It would be wasteful, and even dangerous, constantly to place people in a game that they had never seen before. These potential players would need to be given rules to guide or coordinate their actions. By formalizing the rules governing collective choice, institutions allow decision makers to gain greater certainty about the political process.[105]

The question arises as to whether some institutions are more suitable than others for overcoming the uncertainty predicament – and the concomitant bargaining predicament – in democratization. It is to this question that I now turn.

abound. Yet, only some of these dilemmas ever spiral out of control. Even when security dilemmas spiral into war, the incidence of violence is mostly in concentrated time periods; it is typically episodic. As De Figueiredo Jr. and Weingast note, "The security dilemma is not sufficient in and of itself to explain the conditions under which hawkish leaders in subgroups succeed in garnering the support of an often reticent public audience that typically prefers peace to violence." See their "The Rationality of Fear," p. 262.

[105] Ensley and Munger, "Ideological Competition and Institutions," p. 115. Related, see also Bates, de Figueiredo Jr., and Weingast, "The Politics of Interpretation."

3

Path Dependence and the Law

> Law is a presence of the social past. Law is an organizing of the social present.
> Law is a conditioning of the social future.
>
> Philip Allott[1]

On September 20, 1938, Ernst Fraenkel, a German labor lawyer and social democrat, fled the Nazi dictatorship. From his exile in the United States, he published *The Dual State: A Contribution to the Theory of Dictatorship* in 1941.[2] *The Dual State* remains one of the most important books on the origins of authoritarianism and totalitarianism. It constitutes the first comprehensive analysis of the rise and nature of National Socialism, and remains the only such analysis completed within the belly of the behemoth.[3]

Ernst Fraenkel conceived, and secretly wrote, most of what became *The Dual State* in the Berlin of the mid- and late 1930s. The concept of the dual state first found its way into print in 1937 in a series of articles that Fraenkel wrote under the pseudonym "Conrad Jürgens" for the *Sozialistische Warte*, the periodical of the *Internationaler Sozialistischer Kampfbund*.[4] The articles

---

[1] Allott, "The Concept of International Law," p. 69. Again, it is important to appreciate that Allott's is an attempt at capturing the concept of law *per se*, not just the concept of international law. See also Chapter 2.

[2] Ernst Fraenkel, *The Dual State: A Contribution to the Theory of Dictatorship*, translated from the German by E. A. Shils, in collaboration with Edith Lowenstein and Klaus Knorr (New York: Oxford University Press, 1941). The original manuscript was composed in Germany between 1936 and 1938. This so-called *Urdoppelstaat* was only recently discovered. See Ernst Fraenkel, *Gesammelte Schriften, Band 2: Nationalsozialismus und Widerstand*, edited by Alexander von Brünneck (Baden-Baden: Nomos, 1999). The first version published in Germany was *Der Doppelstaat* (Frankfurt am Main: Europäische Verlagsanstalt, 1974).

[3] Alexander von Brünneck, "Vorwort zu diesem Band," in Fraenkel, *Gesammelte Schriften, Band 2*, p. 22. Franz Neumann wrote *Behemoth: The Structure and Practice of National Socialism* (New York: Oxford University Press, 1942) exiled in England and the United States.

[4] The series was published in the *Sozialistische Warte* in 1937 as "Das Dritte Reich als Doppelstaat." See Ernst C. Stiefel and Frank Mecklenburg, *Deutsche Juristen im amerikanischen*

chronicled the breakdown of democracy and the rise of dictatorship in Weimar Germany. The articles quickly turned into a clandestine manuscript. The draft book, written in German, found its way to the United States via France by way of a French embassy official. The official hid this *Urdoppelstaat* in his luggage upon leaving Germany in the late 1930s – thus securing the work's survival. In the United States, Fraenkel rewrote the saved manuscript for American and English readers, and secured a contract with Oxford University Press for its publication.

Throughout his life, Fraenkel remarked that the beginnings of the dual state concept lay in his personal encounters with the Hitler regime – as a lawyer, a social democrat, and a Jew. While allowed to practice law as a veteran of World War I, Fraenkel was simultaneously subjected to official and unofficial discrimination and intimidation. This schizophrenic experience prompted the idea of the dual state as a metaphor and concept – a state consisting of two halves, with conflicting imperatives. The resulting manuscript, translated into English by Edward Shils, combined in a compelling way an astute analysis of ethnographic data with a penchant for theoretical reasoning. It was a powerful analytic narrative of its time.

The Dual State found immediate acclaim in the English-speaking world, where it was widely reviewed in scholarly journals and newspapers alike. Along with Franz Neumann's *Behemoth: The Structure and Practice of National Socialism*, published in 1942, *The Dual State* amounted to a path-breaking study of modern dictatorship.[5] This fond reception notwithstanding, the concept of the dual state, with its two halves – the *prerogative state* and the *normative state* – has received only scant attention ever since.[6] The book, and its crucially important twin concepts, are rarely mentioned in the social sciences, and few political scientists consider *The Dual State* part of the discipline's canon. Even among historians of the "Third Reich," the book is

---

Exil (1933–1950) (Tübingen: J. C. B. Mohr, 1991), pp. 89–90. The *Internationaler Sozialistischer Kampfbund* (ISK), despite its name, was committed to social-democratic – rather than revolutionary – ideals. Involved in the resistance against Hitler, the ISK began operating from the Parisian exile in 1937. Fraenkel is believed to have had very close ties with the ISK. See Brünneck, "Vorwort zu diesem Band," p. 23. The series from the *Sozialistische Warte* is reprinted in Ernst Fraenkel, *Reformismus und Pluralismus: Materialien zu einer ungeschriebenen politischen Autobiographie*, edited by Falk Esche and Frank Grube (Hamburg: Hoffmann und Campe, 1973), pp. 225–239; and in the aforementioned edition of Fraenkel's collected works, *Gesammelte Schriften, Band 2*.

[5] Neumann, *Behemoth*. Interestingly, Neumann rejected the argument and findings of *The Dual State*.

[6] The book has been out of print for many years. The last available edition in English, published by Octagon Books, New York, dates back to 1969. Among the last books to acknowledge the dual state is Carl J. Friedrich and Zbigniew K. Brzezinski, *Totalitarian Dictatorship and Autocracy* (New York: Praeger, 1963), p. 35. Robert J. Barros, *Constitutionalism and Dictatorship: Pinochet, the Junta, and the 1980 Constitution* (Cambridge: Cambridge University Press, 2002), recently referred to Fraenkel's classic, but only in passing.

"seldom read and is then misunderstood."[7] This is unfortunate, for the concept of the dual state is of immediate relevance for the theory of democracy. This chapter argues that the concept of the dual state – with its unique perspective on legal norms and institutions – is ideally suited for rethinking the role of the state in democratization.[8]

Whereas the previous chapter discussed the concept of law and the dynamics of contention in democratization, this chapter introduces the dual state as a conceptual variable. It builds a path-dependent argument around the forgotten concept, thereby completing the theoretical framework of this book. The chapter contributes to the theory of institutional design by introducing new foci for studying the legacies of law, namely, (1) the *long-run development* of legal norms and institutions and (2) the *long-run consequences* thereof.

RETHINKING THE STATE

The concept of the dual state is elegantly simple and straightforward.[9] Fraenkel established the concept inspired by Max Weber's ideal type analysis. The metaphor of a dual natured state, however, had previously been used by Emil Lederer. In 1915, Lederer had described the Wilhelmine state as a two-pronged state, inspiring Fraenkel's subsequent conceptualization. Fraenkel credits Lederer as the first person to "depict the co-existence of the Normative State and the Prerogative State."[10] The combination of the two notions – the prerogative state and the normative state – in one concept sets up a dynamic tension between these elements. Fraenkel's concept of the dual state has built into it what Reinhard Bendix called "conflicting imperatives."[11] The following analysis illuminates these conflicting imperatives. The discussion revisits key arguments from the forgotten classic, and demonstrates their relevance for the theory of democracy.

In *The Dual State*, Fraenkel meticulously recorded the legal origins of *dictatorship*, recognizing the importance of the interdisciplinary study of law. Fraenkel provided a "first-hand description of the National-Socialist legal

[7] Ingo Müller, *Hitler's Justice: The Courts of the Third Reich* (Cambridge, MA: Harvard University Press, 1991), p. 293.

[8] On recent contributions to state theory, see generally Shannon Stimson, "Rethinking the State: Perspectives on the Legibility and Reproduction of Political Societies," *Political Theory*, Vol. 28, No. 6 (December 2000), pp. 822–834.

[9] Ernst Fraenkel, "Anstatt einer Vorrede," in idem., *Reformismus und Pluralismus*, p. 20.

[10] Fraenkel, *The Dual State*, p. 168. Note that Fraenkel was apparently also influenced by Ferdinand Tönnies, *Gemeinschaft und Gesellschaft: Grundbegriffe der reinen Soziologie* (Berlin: Curtius, [1887] 1922); and Werner Sombart, *Das Wirtschaftsleben im Zeitalter des Hochkapitalismus* (München: Duncker und Humblot, 1928), both of which deemed the dual nature of the modern state (*Zwieschlächtigkeit*) its defining attribute. See Fraenkel, *The Dual State*, p. 154.

[11] See, for example, Reinhard Bendix, *Nation-Building and Citizenship*, Enlarged edition (Berkeley: University of California Press, 1977). Note that Bendix uses varying terms to refer to these conflicting imperatives.

system, seen from the point of view of an anti-National-Socialist participating observer."[12] Thanks to his scholarship we know a great deal about the culture of Nazi law, as it developed in the 1930s. But the concept of the dual state can also help us understand the legal origins of *democracy*. Countries served by dual states face, or so I shall argue, fewer challenges in transitions from authoritarian rule than countries that lack such a tradition, for the survival of normative state fragments creates reassurance in transition games.[13] This reassurance stabilizes expectations about the size and shape of democratic outcomes. It is in this sense that mine is a contribution to the theory of democracy.

Path Dependence

My argument about the dual state incorporates insights about increasing returns processes.[14] The argument is path-dependent in this sense. That is to say that the binding quality of choices at one point in time matters for choices at another.[15] However, by emphasizing structured contingency, I suggest that dual states provide "a template that predisposes, but does not fully determine, particular results."[16] Douglass North's observation is apt: at every step along the way, choices exist that provide real alternatives. "Path dependence is a way to narrow conceptually the choice set and link decision making through time.

---

[12] Fraenkel, *The Dual State*, p. xvi.

[13] See Steffen Huck, "Trust, Treason, and Trials: An Example of How the Evolution of Preferences Can Be Driven by Legal Institutions," *Journal of Law, Economics, and Organization*, Vol. 14, No. 1 (1998), pp. 44–60. Huck demonstrates that law, in addition to producing "short-run effects on behavior by changing the incentives of rational players, ... also has long-run effects by driving the evolution of preferences which in turn dictates how players will react to different legal institutions." Huck, "Trust, Treason, and Trials," p. 46. See also Colomer, *Strategic Transitions*, pp. 124–131.

[14] Foundational analyses include Paul A. David, "Clio and the Economics of QWERTY," *American Economic Review*, Vol. 75, No. 2 (May 1985), pp. 332–337; W. Brian Arthur, "Self-Reinforcing Mechanisms in Economics," in Philip W. Anderson, Kenneth J. Arrow, and David Pines, eds., *The Economy as an Evolving Complex System* (Redwood City, CA: Addison-Wesley, 1988), pp. 9–31; W. Brian Arthur, "Competing Technologies, Increasing Returns, and Lock-In by Historical Events," *Economic Journal*, Vol. 99, No. 394 (March 1989), pp. 116–131; Jack A. Goldstone, "Initial Conditions, General Laws, Path Dependence, and Explanation in Historical Sociology," *American Journal of Sociology*, Vol. 104, No. 3 (November 1998), pp. 829–845; James Mahoney, "Path Dependence in Historical Sociology," *Theory and Society*, Vol. 29, No. 4 (August 2000), pp. 507–548; and Pierson, "Increasing Returns, Path Dependence, and the Study of Politics." For comprehensive treatments, see, most important, W. Brian Arthur, *Increasing Returns and Path Dependence in the Economy* (Ann Arbor: University of Michigan Press, 1994); and Pierson, *Politics in Time*. For an exemplary application to comparative historical development, see James Mahoney, "Long-Run Development and the Legacy of Colonialism in Spanish America," *American Journal of Sociology*, Vol. 109, No. 1 (July 2003), pp. 50–106.

[15] Stathis N. Kalyvas, *The Rise of Christian Democracy in Europe* (Ithaca, NY: Cornell University Press, 1996), p. 16.

[16] Michael Bratton and Nicolas Van de Walle, "Neopatrimonial Regimes and Political Transitions in Africa," *World Politics*, Vol. 46, No. 4 (July 1994), p. 489.

It is not a story of inevitability in which the past nearly predicts the future."[17]

By relating structural constraints to contingent choice, we can better understand the ways in which choices are structured by the institutional environment in which they are made, focusing in particular on the structuring effects of legal norms and institutions.[18] I retain the contingency assumption of methodological individualism – according to which social, political, and economic outcomes emanate from interaction and bargaining – yet I bound this assumption by introducing the dual state as a structural parameter to choice.[19] By so doing, I offer a theory of structure. I theorize a way "in which structures create incentives that shape individual choices and thereby collective outcomes."[20] Founded on the assumption of structured contingency, I explain how the dual state affects the *range* of choices available to agents. I pretend *neither* that the dual state matters all the time, *nor* that it always matters all the way down to the level of the individual agent. Terry Karl puts it well:

Structured contingency does *not* argue that individual decisions made at particular points in time, or all observable political or economic phenomena, can be specifically and unambiguously linked to the presence of preexisting institutions. Instead it claims that historically created structures, while not determining which one of a limited set of alternatives decision-makers may choose, do in fact demarcate the types of problems that arise and do define alternative solutions, thereby *restricting* or *enhancing* the choices available. Furthermore, institutional structures may combine to produce a

---

[17] North, *Institutions, Institutional Change and Economic Performance*, pp. 98–99.
[18] The structured contingency approach "retains an analytical focus on human agency, conflict, and choice, the elements that distinguish the social from the physical sciences. But it presupposes that patterns of regularity can be discerned within the tumult of historical events that can make human behavior, however fleetingly and conditionally, susceptible to scientific investigation. Attention to a *structured contingency* approach allows, on the one hand, that structural precedents impart shape to current events and, on the other, that today's private decisions change even durable political institutions. To paraphrase a classic statement, it allows that people can make their own history, even if not under conditions of their own choosing." Bratton and Van de Walle, *Democratic Experiments in Africa*, p. 45. Max Weber also emphasizes the interrelationship between agents and structure. See Stephen Kalberg, *Max Weber's Comparative-Historical Sociology* (Cambridge: Polity Press, 1994), chapter 1. On the idea of contingency in comparative historical analysis, see, most recently, Michael Makropoulos, "Kontingenz: Aspekte einer theoretischen Semantik der Moderne," *Archives Européennes de Sociologie*, Vol. 45, No. 3 (December 2004), pp. 369–399.
[19] As Michael Coppedge writes, a "theory of structural causation is a theory, but an incomplete one, just as theory at the individual level is incomplete until it tells us what process determined the identities and number of players, why these players value the ends they pursue rationally and which variety of rationality guides their choices, how the institutional arena for the game evolved, where the payoffs come from, why the rules sometimes change in mid-game, and how the power distribution among actors determines the macro outcome. And both microtheories and macrotheories are incomplete until we understand them in their slowly but constantly evolving historical-structural context." Michael Coppedge, "Thickening Thin Concepts and Theories: Combining Large N and Small in Comparative Politics," *Comparative Politics*, Vol. 31, No. 4 (July 1999), p. 474.
[20] Robert H. Bates, Avner Greif, Margaret Levi, Jean-Laurent Rosenthal, and Barry R. Weingast, "Conclusion," in idem., eds., *Analytic Narratives*, p. 234.

situation in which one part of action becomes far more attractive or far less costly than another, and thus can define preferences by creating overwhelming incentives for decision-makers to choose (or to avoid) a specific set of policies.[21]

Having discussed the ontology of institutional design – the relationship between agents and structures – and having explicated the theory of institutional design, and my envisaged contribution to it, I am now in a position to show how these institutions matter for explaining – and understanding – democratization.[22] The objective of the comparative historical analysis that follows (in Chapters 4–7) is to explain – and understand – the social function of law with the help of a longitudinal study in a telling case.[23] Let me preview the empirical argument in light of the theoretical argument developed thus far.

The longitudinal analysis of law's function in apartheid (Chapters 4 and 5) and apartheid's endgame (Chapters 6 and 7) is in recognition of the fact that there is "remarkably little study of the culture of the rule of law itself as a distinct way of understanding and perceiving meaning in the events of our political and social life."[24] The comparative historical analysis is thus meant to deepen (theoretically) and broaden (historically) our understanding of the social function·of law.[25]

[21] Terry Lynn Karl, *The Paradox of Plenty: Oil Booms and Petro-States* (Berkeley: University of California Press, 1997), pp. 10–11. Emphases added. See also Bratton and Van de Walle, *Democratic Experiments in Africa*, p. 45.

[22] On what might be called the ontology of institutional design, see, for example, Alexander E. Wendt, "The Agent-Structure Problem in International Relations Theory," *International Organization*, Vol. 41, No. 3 (Summer 1987), pp. 335–370; and, more recently, Peter A. Hall, "Aligning Ontology and Methodology in Comparative Politics," in James Mahoney and Dietrich Rueschemeyer, eds., *Comparative Historical Analysis in the Social Sciences* (Cambridge: Cambridge University Press, 2003), pp. 373–406.

[23] Telling cases are those "in which the particular circumstances surrounding a case serve to make previously obscure theoretical relationships sufficiently apparent." J. Clyde Mitchell, "Case Studies," in R. F. Ellen, ed., *Ethnographic Research: A Guide to General Conduct* (Orlando, FL: Academic Press, 1984), quoted in Timothy J. McKeown, "Case Studies and the Statistical Worldview," *International Organization*, Vol. 53, No. 1 (Winter 1999), p. 174.

[24] Paul W. Kahn, *The Cultural Study of Law: Reconstructing Legal Scholarship* (Chicago: University of Chicago Press, 1999), p. 1.

[25] For important contributions to the cultural study of law, see Paul W. Kahn, *The Reign of Law: Marbury v. Madison and the Construction of America* (New Haven: Yale University Press, 1997); John R. Bowen, *Islam, Law and Equality in Indonesia: An Anthropology of Public Reasoning* (Cambridge: Cambridge University Press, 2003); and Jean Comaroff and John L. Comaroff, *Law and Disorder in the Postcolony* (Chicago: University of Chicago Press, 2006). For earlier efforts, see Karl N. Llewellyn and E. Adamson Hoebel, *The Cheyenne Way: Conflict and Case Law in Primitive Jurisprudence* (Norman: University of Oklahoma Press, 1941); Max Gluckman, *The Judicial Process among the Barotse of Northern Rhodesia* (Glencoe, IL: Free Press, 1955); Paul Bohannan, *Justice and Judgment Among the Tiv* (London: Oxford University Press, 1957); Clifford Geertz, "Local Knowledge: Fact and Law in Comparative Perspective," in idem., *Local Knowledge: Further Essays in Interpretive Anthropology* (New York: Basic Books, 1983), pp. 167–234; Martin Chanock, *Law, Custom and Social Order: The Colonial Experience in Malawi and Zambia* (Cambridge: Cambridge University Press, 1985); Gerald Strauss, *Law, Resistance, and the State: The*

The concept of path dependence is relevant in this context because it highlights the idea that history is "an irreversible branching process."[26] It is founded on the belief that "crucial choice points may establish certain directions of change and foreclose others in a way that shapes development over long periods of time."[27] (See Figure 3.1.) In what follows, I elaborate this idea toward the goal of developing a new explanation of apartheid's endgame. The theoretical contribution of this book lies in integrating the literatures on path dependence and the law.

The concept of path dependence entered the law in the mid-1990s, when scholars working in law and economics and constitutional law began to explore the lock-in effects of *stare decisis*, the doctrine of precedent in the common law.[28] Supplementing this literature with insights from the social sciences, I demonstrate that the evolution of law has profound effects on the evolution of politics. I show that remnants of the normative state – what I call the common knowledge of formally rational law – can provide a modicum of certainty in times of transition. I maintain that law's common knowledge produces, under certain circumstances, behavioral regularities that can vastly reduce the uncertainty predicament in democratization (see Chapter 2). Such are the legacies of law.

The formalization and rationalization of strategic interaction is an important first step toward resolving commitment problems, especially in democratization. The legalization of commitments (e.g., in the area of constitutional design) is an important *next* step. For as Kenneth Abbot writes, "Legalization entails a specific form of discourse, requiring justification and persuasion in terms of applicable rules and pertinent facts, and emphasizing factors such as

Opposition to Roman Law in Reformation Germany (Princeton: Princeton University Press, 1986); Sally Falk Moore, *Social Facts and Fabrications: "Customary" Law on Kilimanjaro, 1880–1980* (Cambridge: Cambridge University Press, 1986); Kim Lane Scheppele, *Legal Secrets: Equality and Efficiency in the Common Law* (Chicago: University of Chicago Press, 1988); Sally Engle Merry, *Colonizing Hawai'i: The Cultural Power of Law* (Princeton: Princeton University Press, 1999); and Lauren Benton, *Law and Colonial Cultures: Legal Regimes in World History, 1400–1900* (Cambridge: Cambridge University Press, 2002). Yet contrary to most of the aforementioned works – and their pronounced historical frameworks – this book is, in addition, decidedly theoretical in approach. Instead of emphasizing one at the expense of the other, the book endeavors to *integrate* ideographic reasoning and nomothetic reasoning in its effort to understand the legacies of law.

[26] Paul David, "Path Dependence, Its Critics, and the Quest for 'Historical Economics,'" in Pierre Garrouste and Stavros Ioannides, eds., *Evolution and Path Dependence in Economic Ideas: Past and Present* (Cheltenham, UK: Edward Elgar, 2000), p. 8.

[27] Mahoney, *The Legacies of Liberalism*, p. 264.

[28] See, for example, Mark J. Roe, "Chaos and Evolution in Law and Economics," *Harvard Law Review*, Vol. 109, No. 3 (January 1996), pp. 641–668; Lucian Arye Bebchuk, "A Theory of Path Dependence in Corporate Ownership and Governance," *Stanford Law Review*, Vol. 52, No. 1 (October 1999), pp. 127–170; Oona A. Hathaway, "Path Dependence in the Law: The Course and Pattern of Legal Change in a Common Law System," *Iowa Law Review*, Vol. 86, No. 2 (January 2001), pp. 601–665; and Richard A. Posner, *Frontier of Legal Theory* (Cambridge, MA: Harvard University Press, 2001), pp. 145–169.

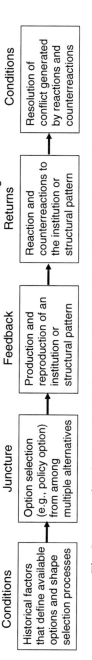

FIGURE 3.1. The Structure of Path-Dependent Explanation. *Source:* Adapted from Mahoney, *The Legacies of Liberalism,* p. 5.

text, precedents, analogies, and practice. Legal discourse largely disqualifies arguments based solely on interests and preferences."[29] My findings suggest that the long-run consequences of legal development – in particular of formally rational law – are twofold. The first effect is *behavioral* (legal norms and institutions affect the actions people take); the second effect is *hermeneutic* (legal norms and institutions affect the beliefs people have).[30] In order to be able to trace the behavioral and hermeneutic effects of law, the remainder theorizes the interplay between *legal structures* (notably legal norms and institutions) and *social preferences* in the context of contentious politics, with particular reference to democratization.[31] The emphasis is on the political economy of law. This is in recognition of the fact that "positive theorists have taken too much politics out of the politics of structural choice."[32]

A THEORY OF LAW

Thus far, I have treated democratization as a process of strategic interactions in which competing adversaries make contingent choices about the future of democracy (see Chapter 2). I now bound this contingency assumption with a discussion of how actors' choices are structured by the context in which they are made, focusing in particular on the legacies of law. The following analysis ties this and the previous chapter together. It configures the dual state as a structural parameter to choice. (See also Figure 3.1.)

In recent years, explanations emphasizing historically specific conditions, or *initial conditions*, have gained ascendance in comparative historical analysis. Such explanations have given pride of place to the dynamics – the mechanisms and processes – of social life. The relational explanations that result, however, have not always centered on initial conditions in the conventional sense of the word. *Contra* the conventional wisdom in historical sociology, Jack Goldstone has shown that in instances of path dependence, "The outcome over a period of time is *not determined* by any particular set of initial conditions. Rather, a system that exhibits path dependency is one in which outcomes are related *stochastically* to initial conditions, and the particular outcomes that obtain in any given 'run' of the system depends on the choices or outcomes of inter-mediate events between the initial conditions and the outcome."[33] *Pars pro*

---

[29] Kenneth W. Abbott and Duncan Snidal, "Hard Law and Soft Law in International Governance," *International Organization*, Vol. 54, No. 3 (Summer 2000), p. 429.

[30] The distinction between behavioral and hermeneutic effects of law originated with Posner, *Law and Social Norms*, p. 33.

[31] For a treatment of democratization as contentious politics, see also Doug McAdam, Sidney Tarrow, and Charles Tilly, *Dynamics of Contention* (Cambridge: Cambridge University Press, 2001), esp. Chapter 9. For a book-length treatment, see Charles Tilly, *Contention and Democracy in Europe, 1650–2000* (Cambridge: Cambridge University Press, 2004).

[32] Terry M. Moe, "Political Institutions: The Neglected Side of the Story," *Journal of Law, Economics, and Organization*, Vol. 6, Special Issue (April 1990), p. 218.

[33] Goldstone, "Initial Conditions, General Laws, Path Dependence, and Explanation in Historical Sociology," p. 834. Second emphasis added. Peyton Young makes a similar point, noting that

toto, Goldstone recently faulted Margaret Somers for misrepresenting her argument about the contribution of fourteenth-century legal institutions to nineteenth-century democratic institutions in England.[34] Somers' argument, says Goldstone, "seems to invoke general laws, does not specify mechanisms, and discusses what is clearly *not* a path dependent process."[35] This illustrates the difficulties in building increasing returns arguments. I find especially convincing in this context Goldstone's contention that

> [t]racing the evolution of a path-dependent system can tell us why certain phenomena and not others finally emerged. But only a *determinate* or *causal* system governed by general laws can tell us why certain phenomena and not others became possible *in the first place.* Only general laws would create a situation in which [as in Somers argument] 14th-century initial conditions have to affect 19th-century outcomes. In a path-dependent system, a wide variety of outcomes are by definition possible *in the first place.* One can eliminate certain of those outcomes at the outset by causal laws, or one can eliminate certain of those outcomes in the process of system change in response to subsequent events, but one cannot explain why anything had to happen in the first place solely by reference to the operation of a path-dependent system. It is for this reason that the study of evolution, although certainly the study of a path-dependent process, *does* utilize invariant laws, as well as allowing for the contingent role of key but undetermined events.[36]

What, then, constitutes a path-dependent explanation? In a path-dependent pattern, "distant historical events set countries on long-run trajectories of development."[37] By examining the legacies of law, in both theoretical and empirical terms, this book advances the debate over the legacies of liberalism, namely, by extending the debate, for the first time, into unchartered terrain.[38] For discussions of liberalism's legacies have thus far failed to consider the function of law in time.[39] This is particularly surprising in view of law's centrality in modern society.[40]

---

in processes of path dependence, "[o]ne can therefore speak of the probability of reaching various outcomes from some initial state, without knowing which one will in fact materialize. Such processes are sometimes said to be 'path-dependent.' Of course, any nontrivial stochastic process is path-dependent in the sense that different paths will be followed depending on the outcome of chance events. A more telling definition of path dependency is that, with positive probability, the process follows paths that have different long-run characteristics (the process is 'nonergodic')." See H. Peyton Young, *Individual Strategy and Social Structure: An Evolutionary Theory of Institutions* (Princeton: Princeton University Press, 1998), p. 8.

[34] Goldstone, "Initial Conditions, General Laws, Path Dependence, and Explanation in Historical Sociology," esp. pp. 834–836.

[35] Goldstone, "Initial Conditions, General Laws, Path Dependence, and Explanation in Historical Sociology," p. 835.

[36] Goldstone, "Initial Conditions, General Laws, Path Dependence, and Explanation in Historical Sociology," pp. 835–836.

[37] Mahoney, "Long-Run Development and the Legacy of Colonialism in Spanish America," p. 85.

[38] Mahoney, *The Legacies of Liberalism.*

[39] Compare, for example, Pierson, *Politics in Time.*

[40] Roberto M. Unger, *Law in Modern Society: Toward a Criticism of Social Theory* (New York: Free Press, 1976).

Let me situate my theoretical argument within the three "core claims" of path dependence.[41] My operationalization of the first core claim of path dependence – which holds that an initial set of conditions leads countries (or other units of analysis) to move in a particular direction – sheds light on the function of law in the transition *to* authoritarian rule in South Africa. I demonstrate in Chapters 4 and 5 that the demands of colonialism and segregation, respectively, led to the emergence of a dual state. The dual state that emerged, consisted, as conceptualized in this chapter, of two halves – a normative state and a prerogative state – and was subject to conflicting imperatives. The second core claim of path dependence holds that countries' movement in a particular direction generates increasing returns, which, in turn, induces further movement in the same direction due to sunk costs. Or, as Mahoney writes, "Increasing returns are often generated when large setup or fixed costs make it difficult for units to change direction."[42] In my empirical argument, this second core claim is illustrated by a discussion of the consolidation of the dual state during apartheid – notwithstanding temporal fluctuations in the relative significance of the prerogative and normative halves of the dual state for political outcomes in this era. The third core claim of path dependence, as theorized by Mahoney and Pierson, holds that "units eventually stabilize around enduring equilibrium points. Once these equilibrium points are reached, the units may be subject to small fluctuations in their development trajectories, but their basic position is 'locked in.'"[43] This third core claim is embodied in an argument about the legacies of the dual state – in particular the normative state – in apartheid's endgame. For I argue that the legacies of the normative state facilitated the resolution of important commitment problems in this endgame, notably by encouraging cooperation over confrontation (see Chapters 2 and 6). My operationalization of the third claim of path dependence, in other words, sheds light on the function of law in the transition *from* authoritarian rule in South Africa. Such, in a nutshell, is my explanation of apartheid's endgame. (See also Figure 3.5.)

Let me develop this path-dependent explanation in more detail. I begin with the assumption that agents have two principal choices in democratization vis-à-vis their behavior toward the existing state: stealing the state and preserving the state.[44] Generally speaking, "[c]itizens have realized that the costs of exiting a *protective state* are quite high (if exit is not explicitly allowed by the rulers)."[45] In democratization, of course, it is not always clear whether an existing state will function as a protective state or as a *punitive state*. This is

[41] Mahoney, "Long-Run Development and the Legacy of Colonialism in Spanish America," p. 53. See also Pierson, "Increasing Returns, Path Dependence, and the Study of Politics;" and Mahoney, "Path Dependence in Historical Sociology."

[42] Mahoney, "Long-Run Development and the Legacy of Colonialism in Spanish America," p. 53.

[43] Mahoney, "Long-Run Development and the Legacy of Colonialism in Spanish America," p. 53.

[44] For the distinction, see Meierhenrich, "Forming States after Failure," esp. pp. 154–155.

[45] C. Mantzavinos, Douglass C. North, and Syed Shariq, "Learning, Institutions, and Economic Performance," *Perspectives on Politics*, Vol. 2, No. 1 (March 2004), p. 78.

reminiscent of the problem of social order (see Chapter 2). "The problem of social order," writes Robert Bates, "is a classic one, and it has been posed in many forms. In political science, it is sometimes cast as a tension between private interests and the public good, between rights and obligations, or between the individual and the collectivity."[46] In general form, the problem of social order asks under what conditions maximizing behavior by self-regarding agents can "lead to allocational decisions that are consistent with a social optimum."[47] This question is at the heart of democratization.

The objective of democratization, as we have seen in the previous chapter, is the transformation of conflict into cooperation rather than confrontation. Whether cooperation or confrontation result from strategic interaction is contingent on the incentives produced by the institutional structure of the state. If the institutional structure rewards opportunism, then confrontation is likely to become the norm. If, by contrast, the institutional structure of the state sanctions opportunism, and rewards productive activities, then cooperation is likely to materialize. Whereas stolen states are likely to aid in the *production* of opportunism, preserved states (what I have elsewhere called *usable states*) are more prone to aid in the *punishment* of opportunism.[48] In the event of the latter, democracy is more likely to become self-enforcing, to use Przeworski's phrase.

Under what conditions, then, do agents preserve states? When, and why, do they steal them? Some agents have an interest in the destruction of states. William Reno observes that a key reason why leaders "prefer weak formal and informal institutions, not only in the sense of straying from rule-based principles but also from the provision of public goods, lies in their fear that enterprising rivals could use control over successful institutions" to challenge their rule.[49] A similar story can be told for Russia. There, "the atmosphere of a collapsed state directly influenced elite attitudes and behavior such that they preferred to pursue short-term private interests rather than to adopt long-term goals involving the provision of public goods."[50] Democratization will falter if, and when, powerful agents perceive more expected utility from

---

[46] Robert H. Bates, *Essays on the Political Economy of Africa* (Berkeley: University of California Press, 1983), p. 19.

[47] Bates, *Essays on the Political Economy of* Africa, p. 19. See also Randall L. Calvert, "Explaining Social Order: Internalization, External Enforcement, or Equilibrium?," in Soltan, Uslaner, and Haufler, eds., *Institutions and Social Order*, p. 131.

[48] On the concept of the usable state, see Meierhenrich, "Forming States after Failure." For a comprehensive analysis, see Jens Meierhenrich "Apartheid's Endgame and the State," D.Phil. thesis, University of Oxford, 2002.

[49] William Reno, "Shadow States and the Political Economy of Civil Wars," in Mats Berdal and David M. Malone, eds., *Greed and Grievance: Economic Agendas in Civil Wars* (Boulder, CO: Lynne Rienner, 2000), p. 53.

[50] Pauline Jones Luong, "The 'Use and Abuse' of Russia's Energy Resources: Implications for State-Society Relations," in Valerie Sperling, ed., *Building the Russian State: Institutional Crisis and the Quest for Democratic Governance* (Boulder, CO: Westview Press, 2000), p. 31.

the *absence* of the state, rather than from its presence.[51] States survive when agents have a stake in their perpetuation. One way to achieve this is through the creation of *stakes*, by which I mean deep interests held in the state:

These stakes can revolve around property, rights, representation, influence, power, or other commodities deemed valuable by interacting agents bargaining over the state's future. Stakes need to engage people living in the state's shadow. The process of creating stakes should lead [interacting adversaries] and other stakeholders to accept the idea that the state is an important, if not foremost, public good. In other words, agents must develop confidence in the state as a primary institutional structure. The state must be seen as an institution that creates opportunities for the acquisition of power, wealth, and security.[52]

An example from Russia illustrates the argument: "By allowing regional and municipal actors to hold a stake in emerging regional 'holding companies,' Russian officials may at least reduce these actors' incentives to undermine the authority and property rights of central authorities."[53] States will function, and survive, as long as agents have a stake in their perpetuation. Given the crucial role of stakes, I submit that it is the *idea* of the state that matters more than previously thought. "The idea of the state forms part of the considerations which groups have in mind when determining where their interests lie and what types of conduct will appeal to decision-makers and the public."[54] My argument is therefore grounded in ideas about the state's expected utility, *not* its coercive power:

Members acquire incentives to preserve institutions. The test of the power of an institution is thus its *utility*, not its coercive force. Institutions serve a purpose for their members. To withhold compliance, thus to weaken them, means losing something valuable. Members have an incentive to care about institutional preservation and, as a result, institutions have force.[55]

Bo Rothstein reasoned similarly: "[I]t is probably not the formal institution as such that people evaluate, but its historically established reputation in regard to fairness and efficiency."[56] In order to construct credible commitments about constitutional design, electoral design, federal design, or any

---

[51] In *Foundations of Social Theory*, James Coleman described the idea of expected utility in the following terms: "The theory of rationality under risk entails the assumption that the individual's preference between two risky alternatives is based on the expected utility of each, where the expected utility of an alternative is the sum of the utilities of the possible outcomes, each weighted by its probability." See James S. Coleman, *Foundations of Social Theory* (Cambridge, MA: Belknap Press of Harvard University Press, 1990), p. 778. The same applies to the theory of rationality under uncertainty.

[52] Meierhenrich, "Forming States after Failure," p. 154.

[53] Solnick, *Stealing the State*, p. 252.

[54] Dyson, *The State Tradition in Western Europe*, p. 3. See also Peter J. Steinberger, *The Idea of the State* (Cambridge: Cambridge University Press, 2004).

[55] Gourevitch, "The Governance Problem in International Relations," pp. 138–139. See also Meierhenrich, "Forming States after Failure," p. 155.

[56] Bo Rothstein, "Trust, Social Dilemmas and Collective Memories," *Journal of Theoretical Politics*, Vol. 12, No. 4 (October 2000), p. 493.

other instance of institutional design, a historically established reputation in regard to efficiency is crucial.

Legacies of efficiency – often associated with formally rational law – are an important factor in the supply of reassurance in transition games. The supply of reassurance, in turn, is indispensable given the uncertainty predicament in democratization. The supply of reassurance can come from within – or from without – a democratizing society. Generally speaking, the supply of reassurance from without (*qua* international agents) is relatively easy to achieve, but generally difficult to sustain. The supply of reassurance from within (*qua* domestic agents), by contrast, is generally difficult to attain, but once achieved, relatively easy to sustain. For the reasons outlined earlier, the supply of reassurance is dependent on the institutional structure of the state – particularly its legal framework, as the remaining sections demonstrate.

The remainder theorizes the role of legal norms and institutions, ascertaining their role in the strategy of conflict (see Chapter 2). The argument operates chiefly at the level of perception.[57] It stresses the fundamental psychological character of stateness, and its relation to the critical role of stakes. Drawing on insights from the cognitive turn in new institutional economics, I submit that the meaning of the state is inherently observer-determined: "A state exists chiefly in the hearts and minds of its people; if they do not believe it is there, no logical exercise will bring it to life."[58]

I argue that the legality of law can "lock-in" stakes for those who stand to lose from democratization. It can facilitate the gradual construction of trust among adversaries, thus accelerating regime formation and government formation. Once legality is routinized, secondary institutions can be introduced. This routinization is crucial, because the construction of secondary institutions can pose serious commitment problems in democratization. For example, a majoritarian electoral system or a presidential constitutional framework can induce fears of zero-sum outcomes.[59] Interacting agents might then value confrontation over cooperation. The presumed zero-sum nature of political

---

[57] As Christopher Clapham writes, states "must be 'constructed' in the minds of at least some of those who form them, including minimally those who run them." See Clapham, *Africa and the International System: The Politics of State Survival* (Cambridge: Cambridge University Press, 1996), p. 9. Of course, states are not only constructed in the minds of those who form them, but, very importantly, also in the minds of those who live within their reach. In changing societies, contending "ideas of the state" may surface and, when they do, need to be reconciled to ensure state survival. On the notion of the "idea of the state," see also Kalevi J. Holsti, *The State, War, and the State of War* (Cambridge: Cambridge University Press, 1996), pp. 82–98. Holsti claims that it "is in the realm of ideas and sentiment that the fate of states is primarily determined." See Holsti, *The State, War, and the State of War*, p. 84.

[58] Joseph R. Strayer, *On the Medieval Origins of the Modern State* (Princeton: Princeton University Press, 1970), p. 5.

[59] Alfred Stepan and Cindy Skach, "Constitutional Frameworks and Democratic Consolidation: Parliamentarianism versus Presidentialism," *World Politics*, Vol. 46, No. 1 (October 1993), pp. 1–22; Skach, *Borrowing Constitutional Designs*.

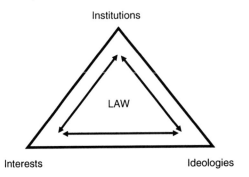

FIGURE 3.2. The Constitution of Law

outcomes may cause some agents to defect from democratization due to fears of victimhood.

Robert Axelrod distinguishes three strategies to promote cooperation on mutual advantage: (1) making the future more important relative to the present; (2) changing the payoffs of interacting agents of the four possible outcomes in the Prisoner's Dilemma; and (3) teaching agents values, facts, and skills that will promote cooperation.[60] In terms of these strategies, and particularly in terms of enlarging the shadow of the future, two modes exist: (a) making interactions more durable, and (b) making them more frequent. A *preserved* state, rather than a *stolen* state, is likely to contribute to both. A preserved state, if endowed with the requisite legal attributes (to be discussed in a moment), can lengthen the shadow of the future for interacting agents, thereby decreasing the chances of defection of either party. Of particular significance in this regard is the institution of law. (See Figure 3.2.)

A Cognitive Manifesto

For the purpose of developing the argument of this book, it is useful to deepen the conception of law with which I began (see Chapter 2). Hereinafter, I assume that law, properly understood, is a manifestation of three interlocking elements: (1) interests, (2) institutions, and (3) ideologies. *Interests* must be part of any conception of law on account of the fact that law is a purposive activity. This assumption is at the heart of consequentialist conceptions of law.[61] *Institutions* such as courts shape the articulation and adjudication of law, and affect the performance of law. *Ideologies*, lastly, refer to the

---

[60] Axelrod, *The Evolution of Cooperation*, p. 126.

[61] See, for example, Joseph Raz, *The Morality of Freedom* (Oxford: Oxford University Press, 1986). For, as Hardin writes, "if law is to work it must serve people well. This is the minimal moral content of law not by definition but by causal requirement if law is to work well." See Hardin, "Law and Social Order," p. 80.

normative underpinnings of the law, that is, the universe of beliefs associated with the meaning of law – law's real and imagined place in society. The mutually constitutive relationship among interests, institutions, and ideologies is captured in the following account: "From an external point of view, institutions are shared behavioral regularities or shared routines within a population. From an internal point of view, they are nothing more than shared mental models or shared solutions to recurrent problems of social interaction. Only because institutions are anchored in people's minds do they ever become behaviorally relevant. The elucidation of the internal aspect," to which this book is committed, "is the crucial aspect in *adequately* explaining the emergence, evolution, and effects of institutions."[62] In this context, constitutional political economists have recently defined ideologies in this sense as "the shared framework of mental models that groups of individuals possess that provide both an interpretation of the environment and a prescription as to how that environment should be structured."[63]

Law is constituted by *interests* because it facilitates the solution of recurrent problems of social interaction. Law is constituted by *institutions* because institutions, as humanly devised constraints, structure incentives in social interaction.[64] Law is constituted by *ideologies* because it is cause – and consequence – of shared mental models as defined herein.

This focus on the ideological underpinnings of the law relates to recent advances in new institutional economics, where the cognitive dimensions of institutions have moved to the forefront of theories of institutional design. Inquiries into beliefs and the way their maintenance and change affects the operation of institutions – their emergence, evolution, and effects – have come to represent the cutting edge of the new institutionalism. Douglass North has been among the trailblazers of this cognitive turn.[65] It is worth quoting at length from his cognitive manifesto:

Beliefs and the way they evolve are the heart of the theoretical issues of this book. For the most part, economists, with a few important exceptions such as Friedrich Hayek, have ignored the role of ideas in making choices. The rationality assumption has served economists (and other social scientists) well for a limited range of issues in micro theory but is a shortcoming in dealing with the issues central to this study. Indeed the uncritical acceptance of the rationality assumption is devastating for most of the major

---

[62] Mantzavinos, North, and Shariq, "Learning, Institutions, and Economic Performance," p. 77. Emphasis added.

[63] Arthur T. Denzau and Douglass C. North, "Shared Mental Models: Ideologies and Institutions," *Kyklos*, Vol. 47, No. 1 (1994), p. 4.

[64] The relationship between interests and institutions is straightforward: "Institutions [including legal institutions] are not necessarily or even usually created to be socially efficient; rather they, or at least the formal rules, are created to serve the interests of those with the bargaining power to devise new rules." North, *Institutions, Institutional Change and Economic Performance*, p. 16. For an empirical instantiation of this argument, see Chapter 4.

[65] For a sustained analysis, see Douglass C. North, *Understanding the Process of Economic Change* (Princeton: Princeton University Press, 2005).

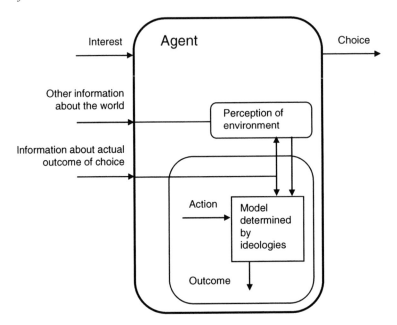

FIGURE 3.3. The Denzau/North Learning Model. *Source*: Adapted from Denzau and North, "Shared Mental Models: Idealogies and Institutions," p. 18.

issues confronting social scientists and is a major stumbling block in the path of future progress. The rationality assumption is not wrong, but such an acceptance forecloses a deeper understanding of the decision-making process in confronting the uncertainties of the complex world we have created.[66]

Such is North's diagnosis. Thus is his prescription:

The way we perceive the world [including the institutions within it] and construct our explanations about that world [and the institutions within it] requires that we delve into how the mind and brain work – the subject matter of cognitive science. This field is still in its infancy but already enough progress has been made to suggest important implications for exploring social phenomena.[67]

Among those who made progress in this emergent field was North himself. Together with Arthur Denzau, North introduced a framework for the study of ideologies and institutions.[68]

Based on preliminary research, Denzau and North developed a model for theorizing the role of ideas in institutional development and political and economic performance. (See Figure 3.3.) The relevance of this research for the

---

[66] North, *Understanding the Process of Economic Change*, p. 5.
[67] North, *Understanding the Process of Economic Change*, p. 5.
[68] Denzau and North, "Shared Mental Models," pp. 3–31.

argument of this book is significant. Consider the following discussion by Denzau and North:

Ideas matter; and the way that ideas are communicated among people is crucial to theories that will enable us to deal with strong uncertainty problems at the individual level [such as the ones encountered in democratization]. For most of the interesting issues in political and economic markets, uncertainty, not risk, characterizes choice-making. Under conditions of uncertainty, individuals' interpretation of their environment will reflect their learning. Individuals with common cultural backgrounds and experiences will share reasonably convergent mental models, ideologies, and institutions; and individuals with different learning experiences (both cultural and environmental) will have different theories (models, ideologies) to interpret their environment.[69]

What is the relevance of this for my argument about the legacies of law? Law, like institutions more generally, is about the stabilization of expectations of those within its reach.[70] Under the right conditions (specified below), law can reduce uncertainty in democratization by invoking common cultural backgrounds and experiences. This speaks to the role of common knowledge in strategic interaction. In instances where interacting adversaries share *qua law* reasonably convergent mental models, the resolution of the bargaining and uncertainty predicaments in democratization (see Chapter 2) are likely to be less intractable.

This resonates with the learning model of Denzau and North, in which shared mental models provide "a set of concepts and language which makes communication easier. Better communication links would lead to the evolution of linked individuals' mental models converging rather than diverging as they continue to learn directly from the world."[71] The learning that results has been referred to as *cultural learning* in the new institutionalism. The term connotes that whenever the solution to a specific problem is obtained in the learning model, the norms and institutions that facilitated the solution will be strengthened. (See Figure 3.3.) Recent scholarship believes that "[a] series of successful solutions to the same problem create what we call a *routine*. The essential characteristic of a routine," in institutional parlance, "is that it is

---

[69] Denzau and North, "Shared Mental Models," pp. 3–4.

[70] Luhmann, *Das Recht der Gesellschaft*, p. 136.

[71] Denzau and North, "Shared Mental Models," p. 18. Mantzavinos defines a mental model as "a coherent but transitory set of rules that enables the organism to form predictions of the environment based on the available knowledge." See C. Mantzavinos, *Individuals, Institutions, and Markets* (Cambridge: Cambridge University Press, 2001), p. 26. Mantzavinos, North, and Shariq further elaborated the nature of mental models: "Depending on whether the expectation formed is validated by the environmental feedback, the mental model can be revised, refined, or rejected altogether. Learning is the complex modification of the mental models according to the feedback received from the environment." See Mantzavinos, North, and Shariq, "Learning, Institutions, and Economic Performance," p. 76. However, it is important to appreciate in this context that mental models are "not ready-made recipes employed every time the individual faces a problem in his environment. *They are, moreover, flexible knowledge structures created anew every time from the ready-made material of the rules.* They are to be understood as the final prediction or expectation that the organism makes about the environment before getting feedback from it." Mantzavinos, *Individuals, Institutions, and Markets*, p. 27.

employed to solve a problem without any prior reflection."[72] If we believe
Denzau and North, the process of learning contributes to human interaction,
in both ancient and modern societies, "the categories and concepts which
enable members of that society to organize their experiences and be able to
communicate with others about them," thereby creating the conditions for the
emergence of routines.[73] Once norms and institutions – which economists
lump together as rules – are employed repeatedly, and successfully so, for the
solution of a problem, "they are successively strengthened and stored by the
organism, and after a time they take the form of unconscious routines."[74]

The Denzau/North learning model is useful for understanding the process of
political change, not least the dynamics of democratization. To paraphrase the
model's inventors: The performance of changing societies is a consequence of
the incentive structures put into place; that is, the institutional framework of
the polity, especially the institutional structure of the state. These incentive
structures are in turn a function of the shared mental models and ideologies of
the agents operating within the institutional framework.[75]

Law is the institutional framework at the heart of this study. I maintain that
law – especially formally rational law – has cultural value in democratization, and
that this value – the ideology of law – has been neglected in the existing literature.
In instances in which formally rational law is instrumental during authoritarian
rule, it will likely become common knowledge. "This common knowledge basis
may help discourage self-interested behavior that is harmful to the general welfare
of society."[76] It is in this sense that ideologies of law can "help individuals frame
complex and unfamiliar problems."[77] Framing can enable interacting adversaries
to face strategic interaction with more ease. Law in democratization may work as
a supplement to the formal and informal enforcement of commitments.[78] If agents
have confidence in the law, they can afford to take larger risks – believe despite
uncertainty – in strategic interaction.[79] If agents have reasonable confidence in the
law, they have more reason to believe despite uncertainty. The formality of law is
what appears to make it useful in democratization. This is so because "[l]egal rules
do more than provide incentives, they change people."[80] As Oren Bar-Gill and
Chaim Fershtman write,

[72] Mantzavinos, *Individuals, Institutions, and Markets*, p. 29.
[73] Denzau and North, "Shared Mental Models," p. 15.
[74] Mantzavinos, *Individuals, Institutions, and Markets*, pp. 29–30.
[75] Denzau and North, "Shared Mental Models," p. 27.
[76] Ensley and Munger, "Ideological Competition and Institutions," p. 116. See also Norman Schofield, "Anarchy, Altruism, and Cooperation: A Review," *Social Choice and Welfare*, Vol. 2, No. 1 (November 1985), pp. 207–219; and Chapter 7.
[77] Ensley and Munger, "Ideological Competition and Institutions," p. 116.
[78] For a brief discussion, see Robert Axelrod, *The Complexity of Cooperation: Agent-Based Models of Competition and Collaboration* (Princeton: Princeton University Press, 1997), pp. 60–61.
[79] Luhmann, *Das Recht der Gesellschaft*, p. 132.
[80] Oren Bar-Gill and Chaim Fershtman, "Law and Preferences," *Journal of Law, Economics, and Organization*, Vol. 20, No. 2 (October 2004), p. 331.

different legal systems may affect not just the behavior of individuals, but who they are. And since who you are also affects how you choose to behave, a new indirect influence on behavior is introduced. Such an approach expands the boundaries of law and economics, introducing the endogenous formation of preferences as part of the analysis.[81]

A habit of legality – not unlike "soft law" in the international realm – provides a *reliable* basis for the construction of credible commitments among adversaries. This is beneficial in democratization because humans *generally* long for reassurance:

Humans attempt to use their perceptions about the world to structure their environment in order to reduce uncertainty in human interaction. But whose perceptions matter and how they get translated into transforming the human environment are consequences of the institutional structure, which is a combination of formal rules, informal constraints, and their enforcement characteristics. This structure of human interaction determines who are the entrepreneurs whose choices matter and how such choices get implemented by the decision rules of that structure. Institutional constraints cumulate through time, and the culture of a society is the cumulative structure of rules and norms (and beliefs) that we inherit from the past that shape our present and influence our future.[82]

The logic of transaction costs completes the argument as laid out thus far. Transaction costs condition what choices agents are likely to make. Transaction costs refer to an agent's opportunity costs in strategic interaction. Such opportunity costs arise for agents because strategic interaction involves the acquisition of three services: (1) the provision of information about the opportunities for interaction, (2) the negotiation of the terms of interaction, and the (3) determination of procedures for enforcing a struck agreement, or contract of interaction. The costs involved in the acquisition of the first service are frequently referred to as *search costs*; the costs involved in the acquisition of the second service as *negotiation costs*, and the costs involved in the acquisition of the third service as *enforcement costs*. The costs of providing all three services are called *transaction costs*. Transaction costs accrue to agents in strategic interaction for social, political, and economic advantage.[83] Transaction costs are subject to the performance of institutions. Institutions can reduce transactions costs and improve human interaction. The question of transaction costs occupies a central place in endgame situations – especially democratization.

---

[81] Bar-Gill and Fershtman, "Law and Preferences," p. 332. For a related argument from law and the social sciences, see Peter Goodrich, *Languages of Law: From Logics of Memory to Nomadic Masks* (Cambridge: Cambridge University Press, 1990). On the question of endogeneity raised by Bar-Gill and Fershtman, see Avner Greif and David D. Laitin, "A Theory of Endogenous Institutional Change," *American Political Science Review*, Vol. 98, No. 4 (November 2004), pp. 633–652.

[82] North, *Understanding the Process of Economic Change*, p. 6.

[83] For a seminal analysis of transaction costs in history, see Douglass C. North and Robert Paul Thomas, *The Rise of the Western World: A New Economic History* (Cambridge: Cambridge University Press, 1973), esp. p. 93.

The increasing returns from formally rational law can be considerable in the calculation of transaction costs, especially in democratization. When adversaries in strategic interaction believe that the other side will commit – and credibly so – to commitments reached, the prospects for cooperation and thus sustainable democracy are increased. This is regularly the case in instances where a rule-governed way of doing things – a habit of legality – survives the worst excesses of authoritarian rule. A habit of legality strengthens the credibility, and thereby the viability, of democratic commitments.[84] If a polity in the past maintained a general fidelity to the law, by which I mean a fidelity to organizing social life (including politics and economics) by legal means, the collective memory of formally rational law is likely to be strong. When these conditions are present, *backward legality* raises the chances of democracy's *forward legitimacy* by providing *forward legality*. In instances in which legality – understood here in the sense of doing things in a formally rational way – has become a *habit*, a state deserves the adjective "normative" – even if this habit suffers interruptions.[85] To paraphrase Mantzavinos, North, and Shariq, cognitive and institutional path dependence will ultimately lead to *political path dependence*. The intuitively formulated proposition that "history matters" designates the importance of the phenomenon of path dependence, starting at the cognitive level, going through the institutional level, and culminating at the political level.[86]

In order to ascertain the path-dependent effects of law – the legacies of law – in democratization, I turn to the cultural study of law, which helps me to relate the theory of law to the history of law.[87] Here we encounter once again the dual state.

THE DUAL STATE

For Fraenkel, the dual state was the joint product of a prerogative state and a normative state. "The complete abolition of the inviolability of law is the chief characteristic of the Prerogative State," claimed Fraenkel in *The Dual State*.[88] "This repudiation carries with it the elimination of the fundamental

---

[84] Joel Migdal, "Studying the State," in Mark Irving Lichbach and Alan S. Zuckerman, eds., *Comparative Politics. Rationality, Culture, and Structure* (Cambridge: Cambridge University Press, 1997), p. 223.

[85] The term is borrowed from Francis A. Allen, *The Habits of Legality: Criminal Justice and the Rule of Law* (New York: Oxford University Press, 1996).

[86] The original reads as follows, "Thus, cognitive and institutional path dependence will ultimately lead to *economic path dependence*. The intuitively formulated proposition that 'history matters' designates the importance of the phenomenon of path dependence, starting at the cognitive level, going through the institutional level, and culminating at the economic level." See Mantzavinos, North, and Shariq, "Learning, Institutions, and Economic Performance," p. 81.

[87] Kahn, *The Cultural Study of Law*.

[88] Fraenkel, *The Dual State*, p. 107.

principle of the inviolability of law from the entire legal order. If inviolability within the sphere of the Normative State exists only under certain circumstances, then it does not hold true as a principle, and conditional inviolability is necessarily the opposite of inviolability."[89] The repudiation of the principle of the inviolability of law in Nazi Germany – its actual as well as its potential abrogation – for Fraenkel raised "the general question of the significance of law."[90]

The Prerogative State

The hallmark of the prerogative state for Fraenkel was government by decree.[91] Drawing on John Locke's *Second Treatise of Government*, Fraenkel defined governance by prerogative as governance without law.[92] Or, as John Locke put it,

This Power to act according to discretion, for the publick good, without the prescription of Law, and sometimes even against it, *is* that which is called *Prerogative*. For since in some governments the Law-making Power is not always in being, and is usually too numerous, and so too slow, for the dispatch requisite to Execution: and because also it is impossible to foresee, and so by laws to provide for, all Accidents and Necessities, that may concern the publick; or to make such Laws, as will do no harm, if they are Executed with an inflexible rigour, on all occasions, and upon all Persons, that may come in their way, therefore there is a latitude left to the Executive power, to do many things of choice, which Laws do not prescribe.[93]

Locke, unlike Fraenkel, conceived of the prerogative state as an arbiter in times of crisis. The idea of the prerogative was representative of what he called *paternal power* ("nothing but that, which Parents have over their Children, to govern for the Childrens good, till they come to the use of Reason, or a state of Knowledge, wherein they may be supposed capable to understand that Rule, whether it be the Law of Nature, or the municipal Law of their Country they are to govern themselves by") rather than *despotical power* ("an Absolute, Arbitrary Power one Man has over another, to take away his Life, whenever he pleases").[94]

In *The Dual State*, Fraenkel stood Locke on his head, equating the prerogative state with *despotical power* rather than *paternal power*. Whereas Locke deemed the prerogative state desirable in some circumstances, Fraenkel

---

[89] Fraenkel, *The Dual State*, p. 107.

[90] Fraenkel, *The Dual State*, p. 107.

[91] Fraenkel, *The Dual State*, p. 30.

[92] Fraenkel, *The Dual State*, p. 66.

[93] John Locke, "The Second Treatise of Government," in John Locke, *Two Treatises of Government*, edited with an Introduction and Notes by Peter Laslett (Cambridge: Cambridge University Press, 1970), p. 375. For a useful discussion, see also Pasquale Pasquino, "Locke on King's Prerogative," *Political Theory*, Vol. 26, No. 2 (April 1998), pp. 198–208.

[94] On the distinction in his writings, see Locke, "The Second Treatise of Government," pp. 380–384. The quotes are from pages 381 and 382, respectively.

judged it objectionable in all circumstances. Under the auspices of a prerogative state, wrote Fraenkel, the government "exercises unlimited arbitrariness
and violence, unchecked by any legal guarantees."[95] The essence of the prerogative state is its "refusal to accept legal restraint, i.e., any 'formal'
bonds."[96] The prerogative state "claims that it represents material justice and
that it can therefore dispense with formal justice."[97]

   This conception is reminiscent of Locke's formulation (which Fraenkel
accepts) that the "*Prerogative* is nothing but the Power of doing publick good
without a Rule."[98] For the command theory of law – despite its emphasis on
rules – amounts to a defense of the King's prerogative.[99] Rules in this conception are epiphenomenal: they are contingent upon, and secondary to, the
imperative of sovereignty.[100] This is immediately apparent in Fraenkel's conceptualization of the prerogative state:

the *presumption of jurisdiction* rests with the Normative State. The *jurisdiction over
jurisdiction* rests with the Prerogative State. The limits of the Prerogative State are not
imposed upon it; there is not a single issue in which the Prerogative State cannot claim
jurisdiction.[...] Where the Prerogative State does not require jurisdiction, the Normative State is allowed to function. The limits of the Prerogative State are *not* imposed
from the outside; they are imposed by the Prerogative State itself. These self-imposed
restraints of the Prerogative State are of cardinal importance for the understanding of
the Dual State.[101]

   One of Fraenkel's contemporaries underscored the point. Carl Schmitt, the
infamous constitutional lawyer, illustrated the influence of this conception in
the jurisprudence of Weimar Germany, noting in 1927 that the *Rechtsstaat*,
"despite its legalism and normativism, is essentially a state and hence always
contains, in addition to its legalistic and normative elements, certain special
political elements."[102]

   But Fraenkel's understanding of the prerogative state was not merely influenced by the *theory* of institutional design. It also reflected the *practice* of
institutional design, as painstakingly catalogued by the labor lawyer in the early
years of Nazi Germany. In conceptualizing the prerogative half of the dual

---

[95] Fraenkel, *The Dual State*, p. xiii.
[96] Fraenkel, *The Dual State*, p. 46.
[97] Fraenkel, *The Dual State*, p. 46.
[98] Locke, "The Second Treatise of Government," p. 378.
[99] See once again Pasquino, "Locke on King's Prerogative."
[100] See also Weingast, "The Political Foundations of Democracy and the Rule of Law."
[101] Fraenkel, *The Dual State*, pp. 57; 58. Emphases added.
[102] As quoted in Fraenkel, *The Dual State*, p. 68. See also Carl Schmitt, *Verfassungslehre*, Eighth
   Edition (Berlin: Duncker und Humblot, [1928] 1993), p. 134, where Schmitt elaborates the
   point, discussing the relationship between law (*Recht*) and state (*Staat*): "Der Staat ist nicht nur
   Justizorganisation; er ist auch etwas anderes als ein bloß neutraler Schiedsrichter oder
   Schlichter. Sein Wesen liegt darin, daß er die *politische Entscheidung* trifft." ["The state is not
   merely a judicial organization; it is something other than a mere referee or mediator. Its nature
   lies in taking the *political decision*."]. Translation by the author.

state, Fraenkel drew on his daily observations of the NSDAP, the party of National Socialism, in Germany. Organizations of terror operating under the auspices of the prerogative state included the S.S. (*Schutzstaffel*), the S.A. (*Sturmabteilung*), and the Secret State Police (*Gestapo*). The prerogative state, Fraenkel believed, grew organically out of the excessive use of Article 48 of the Weimar Constitution. The infamous provision, in Schmitt's even more infamous interpretation, endowed the reluctant last President of the Republic, Paul von Hindenburg, with "dictatorial authority." Fraenkel, a former student of Schmitt, regarded the pronouncements of his former teacher as an exploitation of "the practical possibilities of Art. 48 of the Weimar Constitution" that moved the polity – in theory as well as practice – away from the normative state and into the exclusive domain of the prerogative state.[103] But what was the normative state?

The Normative State

For Fraenkel, the hallmark of the normative state was government by law.[104] The normative state represents a contending view of the rule of law. This view revolves around the idea of law as *constraint*.

In contrast to the prerogative state, the normative state for Fraenkel was "an administrative body endowed with elaborate powers for safeguarding the legal order as expressed in statutes, decisions of the courts, and activities of the administrative agencies."[105] The expansion of discretionary power on the part of the prerogative state did not *per se* invalidate the significance of the normative state during the Nazi regime, according to Fraenkel. Consider this example from administrative law. "A decisive distinction between the administrative agencies of the Normative State and the organs of the Prerogative State rests on the differences between their respective spheres of jurisdiction and is *not* a problem of varying degrees of discretionary power. However extensive the discretion of an administrative agency – such as the Foreign Exchange Control Office – its discretion can be exercised only within the limits of its clearly defined jurisdiction. Were the Foreign Exchange Control Office to exceed its jurisdiction, its acts could be declared null and void in a proceeding before the ordinary courts."[106]

[103] Fraenkel, *The Dual State*, p. 141. Carl Schmitt, "Die Diktatur des Reichspräsidenten nach Art. 48 der Reichsverfassung," *Veröffentlichungen der Vereinigung der deutschen Staatsrechtslehrer*, No. 1 (Berlin, 1924), reprinted in idem., *Die Diktatur: Von den Anfängen des modernen Souveränitätsgedankens* (Berlin: Duncker und Humblot, [1921] 1989).
[104] Fraenkel, *The Dual State*, pp. 69–103. The normative state, as defined by Fraenkel, is *not* identical with either the idea of the *Rechtsstaat* in the civil law tradition or the rule of law in the common law tradition. See Fraenkel, *The Dual State*, esp. p. 71. For a discussion of the *Rechtsstaat* concept, see Böckenförde, "Entstehung und Wandels des Rechtsstaatsbegriffs," pp. 143–169.
[105] Fraenkel, *The Dual State*, p. xiii.
[106] Fraenkel, *The Dual State*, pp. 69–70. Emphasis added.

However, Fraenkel conceded at the same time that "since the jurisdiction of the organs of the Prerogative State is unlimited, a certain tendency exists among the agencies of the Normative State to imitate this example and to enlarge the scope of their own discretion."[107]

Several guardians of law were at work in Fraenkel's normative state, ranging from civil servants to appellate courts.[108] It is worth considering the function of these legal guardians, as Fraenkel saw them, and their contribution to everyday life under the Nazi dictatorship.[109]

---

[107] Fraenkel, *The Dual State*, p. 70.

[108] It is important to state – unequivocally – that German Jews benefited little from the imprint of the normative state on the racial order. As Fraenkel remarked,

Inasmuch as the legal protection of the Normative State is reserved only for the 'constructive forces of the nation' (Best), and inasmuch as the Jews are not considered a part of the German nation but rather regarded as enemies, all questions in which Jews are involved fall within the Jurisdiction of the Prerogative State. Although this was at first only a theoretical principle of National-Socialism, it has now become the regular practice of the Third Reich. The completion of the subjugation of the Jews to the Prerogative State was realized as the moment it was resolved to extirpate the Jews from economic life.

See Fraenkel, *The Dual State*, p. 89. The Nazi official referred to by Fraenkel as "Best" in the above quotation was Werner Best, the legal counsel of the Gestapo. What role for courts in the context of the racial state? Fraenkel had no illusions about the distribution of power between institutions of the prerogative state and the normative state:

The courts capitulated to the political authorities. It has become pointless for Jews to appeal to them for the protection of their rights. In 1937 the [Federal] Supreme Labor Court (*Reichsarbeitsgericht*) justified the denial of all legal protection to the Jews by saying that "the racial principles expounded by the National-Socialist Party have been accepted by the broad mass of the population, even by those who do not belong to the party." If the higher court is supine before the terror of the street, it is not surprising that the lower courts fail to resist the anti-Semitic measures of the Prerogative State. [...] The absolute withdrawal of legal guarantees from one group in the population has serious consequences for the functioning of the Normative State. This is clear to any observer who is capable of perceiving the deeper significance of these developments. [...] In 1920 the National-Socialist Program demanded that the Jews be dealt with according to laws regulating the behavior of foreigners. Since 1938, the Jews are no longer protected by a law for aliens. They are outlawed, *hors la loi*.

See Fraenkel, *The Dual State*, pp. 92; 94; 96. These developments first led to the *social death* and subsequently to the *physical death* of the Jewish population in Germany; the latter brought about in concentration camps and extermination camps throughout Europe. See Fraenkel, *The Dual State*, pp. 95–96. On the dimensions of the Holocaust, see, most recently, Wolfgang Benz, *Dimension des Völkermords* (München: dtv, 1996).

[109] The following discussion is episodic rather than comprehensive. The leading treatments of Nazi law, in both scope and depth, remain Lothar Gruchmann, *Justiz im Dritten Reich 1933–1940: Anpassung und Unterwerfung in der Ära Gürtner*, Third Edition (München: Oldenbourg, 2001); Michael Stolleis, *Recht im Unrecht: Studien zur Rechtsgeschichte des Nationalsozialismus* (Frankfurt am Main: Suhrkamp, 1994); and Ralf Dreier and Wolfgang Sellert, eds., *Recht und Justiz im "Dritten Reich"* (Frankfurt am Main: Suhrkamp, 1989). Noteworthy in this context are the critiques of the dual state concept offered by Karl Dietrich Bracher and Gerhard Schulz. The respected historians contend that the dual state only captures empirical developments in Germany until 1938, when the prerogative state effectively won out over the normative state. See Karl Dietrich Bracher, "Stufen der

Economic Liberty

One of the legal guardians that Fraenkel singled out for analysis was the Prussian Supreme Administrative Court (*Preußisches Oberverwaltungsgericht*). The court earned Fraenkel's admiration for a 1936 decision in which it upheld the principles of the normative state – and withstood the pressures of the prerogative state. The case revolved around the institution of the Economic Enterprise Law (*Gewerbeordnung*), cutting to the heart of the economic foundations of social order. The *Gewerbeordnung*, which preceded the National Socialist order, was founded on the principle of entrepreneurial freedom, or economic liberty. In the early 1930s, "[e]xtreme National-Socialist circles tried to destroy this principle. They tried to brand entrepreneurial freedom as a holdover from the liberal epoch and, accordingly, antiquated and automatically rendered inoperative by National-Socialism. They asserted that restrictions on entrepreneurial liberty should be introduced not only when specially required by statute, but whenever desirable in the light of the general principles of National-Socialism."[110] Thus was the onslaught to which the Prussian Supreme Administrative Court responded. In its decision of August 10, 1936, the court,

declared itself in favor of the Normative State. The court referred to the fact that "it has recently been claimed that in consequence of the revolution in legal conceptions associated with the triumph of National-Socialism, the fundamental principles of entrepreneurial freedom no longer obtain." As early as 1934 the Prussian Admin-

Machtergreifung," in Karl Dietrich Bracher, Wolfgang Sauer, and Gerhard Schulz, eds., *Die Nationalsozialistische Machtergreifung: Studien zur Errichtung des totalitären Herrschaftssystems in Deutschland 1933/34* (Köln: Westdeutscher Verlag, 1960), p. 175; and Gerhard Schulz, "Die Anfänge des totalitären Maßnahmenstaates," in Bracher, Sauer, and Schulz, *Die Nationalsozialistische Machtergreifung*, pp. 373–374. Franz Neumann, Fraenkel's contemporary, was not convinced by the argument either. "I do not agree with the theoretical analysis of Fraenkel, as can readily be seen." See Neumann, *Behemoth*, p. 516, Fn. 63. *Contra* Fraenkel, Neumann held that the centralization and radicalization of social life was all encompassing in the "Third Reich." It reached so far that law had no constraining effects whatever. This argument implies that Fraenkel's emphasis on the normative state is historically untenable. In Neumann's interpretation, National Socialism was a totalitarian regime relying *solely* on a prerogative state. For Neumann, National Socialism was "a non-state, a chaos, a rule of lawlessness and anarchy, which has 'swallowed' the rights and dignity of man." Neumann, *Behemoth*, pp. 47–61; viii. Contemporary evidence underwriting this line of criticism was recently presented in a careful study of the inhumane treatment of prisoner's in the "Third Reich." See Nikolaus Wachsmann, "'Annihilation through Labor': The Killing of State Prisoners in the Third Reich," *Journal of Modern History*, Vol. 71, No. 3 (September 1999), pp. 624–659. A related line of criticism concedes, *contra* Neumann, that law mattered in the "Third Reich." However, by emphasizing the purely repressive character of law, this line of criticism denies the salience of the normative state that Fraenkel found in operation. An example is Alexander von Brünneck, "Die Justiz im deutschen Faschismus," *Kritische Justiz*, No. 1 (1970), reprinted in Redaktion Kritische Justiz, ed., *Der Unrechts-Staat: Recht und Justiz im Nationalsozialismus* (Frankfurt am Main: Europäische Verlagsanstalt, 1979), pp. 108–122.
[110] Fraenkel, *The Dual State*, p. 75.

istrative Court had rejected this contention although other courts accepted it. Despite vigorous criticism, the Supreme Administrative Court held its ground; although, as the court said: "It is true that National-Socialist law had added new legal regulations to those which were already in existence. As yet, entrepreneurial freedom had not been legally abolished. Further restraints and regulations may be imposed only through a new law."[111]

The gauntlet thrown down before the prerogative state was formidable, as the court's opinion was delivered in no uncertain terms. Commented Fraenkel: "[T]he court emphatically refused to renounce the basic principles of the traditional legal and economic order," thus defying the prerogative state, and the further encroachment of the "Third Reich."[112] The judicial behavior of the Prussian Supreme Administrative Court was in line with Fraenkel's characterization of the legal foundations of the Nazi economy more generally:

In spite of the existing legal possibilities for intervention by the Prerogative State where and whenever its desires, the legal foundations of the capitalist economic order have been maintained. If one picks at random a volume of the decisions of a German civil court and examines it systematically, this conception will find complete corroboration. [Roland] Freissler, Secretary of the Ministry of Justice [and between 1942–1945 President of Nazi Germany's notorious People's Court (*Volksgerichtshof*)], has clearly realized that economic law in a narrower sense (the National-Socialists call it "community law") was left relatively untouched by the revolution of 1933.[113] Even Freissler recognizes that the *mores* of the "ethnic community" did not affect it. As late as 1937 Dr. Freissler said in his article "*Der Heimweg des Rechts in die völkische Sittenordnung*" ["The Homecoming of Law in the Racial Order"] that although "Penal Law has not oriented itself towards the *mores* of the ethnic community, economic law has not in any legally effective way appreciated the biological position of the individual as a cell in the German ethnic organism."[114]

Pacta sunt servanda

The principle of the sanctity of contract (*pacta sunt servanda*) was another legal norm in conflict with the ideology of the NSDAP. As early as 1930, Carl Schmitt referred to the principle "as a tendency of 'loan shark' ethics."[115] And

---

[111] Fraenkel, *The Dual State*, p. 75.

[112] Fraenkel, *The Dual State*, p. 76.

[113] Note that the historical literature adopted a different spelling of "Freissler," using "Freisler" instead. See, for example, Gruchmann, *Justiz im Dritten Reich 1933–1940*; Ralph Angermund, *Deutsche Richterschaft 1919–1945: Krisenerfahrung, Illusion, politische Rechtsprechung* (Frankfurt am Main: Fischer, 1990). See also Hermann Weiß, ed., *Biographisches Lexikon zum Dritten Reich* (Frankfurt am Main: Fischer, 2002), pp. 130–132.

[114] Fraenkel, *The Dual State*, pp. 72–73. In describing the workings of the dual state, Fraenkel blurred the distinction between agents and structures, and glossed over the independent contribution of each to the outcomes in question. By so doing, Fraenkel anthropomorphized the state (e.g., "the Prerogative State where and whenever its desires"), introducing analytic imprecision along the lines discussed earlier in this chapter.

[115] Fraenkel, *The Dual State*, p. 76.

yet the Hitler regime did not immediately abolish the principle, not least because of resistance from Germany's courts. Fraenkel pointed to the jurisprudence of an important state court to illustrate the point:

The Bavarian Administrative Court (*Verwaltungsgerichtshof*) had to decide whether a specific National-Socialist *clausula rebus sic stantibus* [a clause allowing the termination of a contract] was valid in the internal legal order of the Third Reich. In 1882 a Bavarian municipality contracted with the Catholic congregation of the town to contribute to the living of the Catholic priest. When the National-Socialists came to power the municipality sought to terminate the contract, arguing that it was entered into under very different political circumstances and could not be considered binding after the National-Socialist revolution.[116]

Yet, as Fraenkel reports,

[t]he attempt of the municipality to evade its contractual responsibilities by appealing to general National-Socialist principles was blocked by the court, which held that "the sanctity of contract is the foundation of the existing legal order. The sanctity of contract is an ethical value and an ethical imperative with which no legal order can dispense." The court characterized the sanctity of contract as "the basis of economic life and of the orderly existence of the ethnic community" and declared that formal rationality had priority over National-Socialist ideas by proclaiming the following principles: "A realistic attitude must be taken towards the objection basing itself on National-Socialist principles. This attitude must be grounded in the positive norms of the existing legal order which is the emanation of the ethical principles accepted as binding by the ethnic community. The court does not exclude all possibility of applying the *clausula rebus sic stantibus* but reserves its right to do so for especially exceptional cases.[117]

Private Property

The institution of private property was upheld by Germany's courts until late into the dictatorship, despite the fact that Nazi land law held that public use (*Gemeinnutz*) trumped private use (*Eigennutz*). As Fraenkel noted sometime in the mid-1930s:

The property system of Germany has not been transformed by the Nationalist-Socialist catchwords. Private property still enjoys the protection of the courts from official interference, except where political considerations are involved. The Rule of Law as it bears on the protection of property is especially relevant to the question of assessment of taxes. Rational calculation as part of the conduct of a business enterprise is impossible if tax assessments are unpredictable. The Third Reich therefore upholds the rule of the Normative State in regard to tax administration.

Related in this regard is Fraenkel's discussion of copyright law, what he calls the law of nontangible property. "The law of non-tangible property

---

[116] Fraenkel, *The Dual State*, pp. 76–77.

[117] Fraenkel, *The Dual State*, p. 77. For the decision, see *Bayerischer Verwaltungsgerichtshof*, June 5, 1936, as published in Nazi Germany's *Reichsverwaltungsblatt* (1938), p. 17.

(copyright, patents, rights of publication, trade-marks etc.) raises a crucial point in our theory of the Dual State, since it is here that the capitalistic system can least easily submit to interference with the existing system of private law."[118] The adjudication of copyright disputes underscores the conflicting imperatives inherent in the racial state. Although Fraenkel's jurisprudential analysis of copyright and other litigation is selective rather than systematic, it lends credence to his argument, *contra* his critics, that the Nazi dictatorship was served by a dual state.[119] Consider the civil suit of a record manufacturer against the German Broadcasting Company (*Reichsrundfunkgesellschaft*), a case of David v. Goliath. The former sought to prevent the latter from broadcasting his records without compensation. Fraenkel interpreted the case, which he described as "perhaps the most important civil case in Germany in recent years," thus:

Two lower courts sustained the Broadcasting Company but the *Reichsgericht* [Federal Supreme Court of the Reich] on November 14, 1936, decided against it. The company had claimed that the courts had no jurisdiction in the case, since radio stations supplying vital political information were therefore an integral part of national policy. The court refused to accept this argument and, furthermore, denied that the radio station was entitled to use records without charge, because they were used in the interest of national welfare. The court held that, even though the activities of the radio station were largely public, the obtaining of material for broadcasting purposes fell within private law since "the broadcasting of a work without the consent of its author or owner, merely on the ground of the public position of the radio station, would amount practically to expropriation." This decision was all the more significant in view of the fact that during the course of the trial the press took an attitude *conflicting* with that of the court.[120]

By defending the idea of private property, the *Reichsgericht* also defended the normative state. And it did so in no uncertain terms, as relayed by Fraenkel:

In the course of reevaluation proceedings, the *Reichsgericht* formulated the principle that "economic considerations [e.g., revolving around public use] cannot induce a court to render a decision clearly in conflict with the law." The *Reichsgericht* emphasized in this decision that "the old principle which guaranteed the stability of the law, i.e., the preamble to the Code of Court Procedure which stated that the judge must obey the law, is still in force and that Art. 336 of the Penal Code, which punishes anyone who tampers with the law with penitentiary sentences up to five years is still valid.[121]

[118] Fraenkel, *The Dual State*, p. 82.
[119] Fraenkel reviewed a total of 106 first instance and appellate decisions. The jurisprudence was culled, for example, from the Federal Supreme Court of the Reich (*Reichsgericht*), 29 cases; the Federal Supreme Labor Court of the Reich (*Reichsarbeitsgericht*), six cases; the Appellate Courts (*Oberlandesgerichte*) of Berlin (five cases), Hamburg (five cases), and Munich (four cases); and fifteen cases from the Prussian Supreme Administrative Court (*Preußisches Oberverwaltungsgericht*), the country's most visible administrative court. For a complete listing of the jurisprudence, see Fraenkel, *The Dual State*, pp. 242–244.
[120] Fraenkel, *The Dual State*, p. 82. Emphasis added.
[121] Fraenkel, *The Dual State*, p. 84.

Bernd Rüthers, in a seminal analysis of private law in the "Third Reich," has confirmed many of Fraenkel's findings.[122] Like Fraenkel, Rüthers is neither an apologist for Nazi dictatorship, nor a revisionist. A liberal legal scholar and judge, his untarnished reputation stems from a life devoted to the investigation of legal perversions in the Nazi judiciary and legal community (including perversions in legal scholarship and higher education). Having meticulously traced the erosion of previously sacrosanct legal institutions such as the law of property and the law of contract in Nazi Germany, Rüthers acknowledges how the institutions of the normative state were fundamental in constraining some of the worst excesses committed under the guise of the prerogative state, at least in the early years of dictatorial rule. As far as the Nazi transformation of property relations was concerned, Rüthers found that the courts of the "Third Reich" were indeed reluctant to acquiesce in the suspension of the constitutional guarantee of property by presidential decree in 1933.[123] With the benefit of hindsight, Rüthers verified the principal validity of the ideas contained in the concept of the dual state as developed by Fraenkel.[124] Otto Kirchheimer, like Neumann a contemporary of Fraenkel, also confirmed the existence of the normative state. Kirchheimer described how this normative state was hollowed out in Nazi Germany: "Auxiliary legal means (*juristische Hilfsmittel*) were supposed to enable the generous use of vague legal standards (*Generalklauseln*), in accordance with the principle of 'good faith' (*Treu und Glauben*)."[125] Yet these vague legal standards created "the possibility of stripping the whole law of its normative and obligatory character without requiring the alteration of a single positive legal statute."[126] *Generalklauseln*, or wide and vague legal standards, gradually replaced surviving remnants of formally rational law.[127] Retroactivity further undermined law's rule. Michael

---

[122] Bernd Rüthers, *Die Unbegrenzte Auslegung: Zum Wandel der Privatrechtsordnung im Nationalsozialismus*, Fifth Edition (Heidelberg: C. F. Müller, [1967] 1997).

[123] Rüthers, *Die Unbegrenzte Auslegung*, pp. 356–360. See also idem., *Entartetes Recht: Rechtslehren und Kronjuristen im Dritten Reich*, Second Edition (München: C. H. Beck, 1989), p. 215. Rüthers takes particular issue with Ingo Müller's selective and one-sided use of evidence. See Ingo Müller, *Furchtbare Juristen: Die unbewältigte Vergangenheit unserer Justiz* (Munich: Kindler, 1987), published in English as *Hitler's Justice*.

[124] The fifth, enlarged edition of Rüthers's *Die Unbegrenzte Auslegung* was published in 1997. This is an indication that the argument and evidence withstood the test of time, and the challenges posed by new scholarship.

[125] Otto Kirchheimer, "State Structure and Law in the Third Reich," in William E. Scheuerman, ed., *The Rule of Law under Siege: Selected Essays of Franz L. Neumann and Otto Kirchheimer* (Berkeley: University of California Press, 1996), p. 144. Kirchheimer's essay was originally published in 1935 under the pseudonym of "Dr. Hermann Seitz," and smuggled into Nazi Germany.

[126] Kirchheimer, "State Structure and Law in the Third Reich," p. 144.

[127] On *Generalklauseln* and judges' expanding role in their interpretation, see also Rüthers, *Die Unbegrenzte Auslegung*. For an economic explanation of their expanding use, see Franz Neumann, "Der Funktionswandel des Gesetzes im Recht der bürgerlichen Gesellschaft," in idem., *Demokratischer und autoritärer Staat: Beiträge zur Soziologie der Politik* (Frankfurt am Main: Europäische Verlagsanstalt, [1957] 1967), esp. pp. 39–51. Carl Schmitt, the most

Stolleis, a leading historian of National Socialist law, therefore speaks of a
transition from dual state to unified state – from a dictatorship-of-law to a
dictatorship-of-terror – in Nazi Germany.[128]

Fair Competition

This brings me to a final domain in which the courts as legal guardians
defended the ideals of the normative state in the midst of Nazi
dictatorship. Based on the analysis of case law from different appellate courts,
Fraenkel concluded that "the previously prevailing law regulating unfair
competition among business enterprises" was upheld despite attempts to usher
the country into the new order.[129] Even though the Nazi-created Board of
Trade and the Trustees of Labor had granted permission to circumvent
the 1909 law regulating unfair competition (*Gesetz betreffend unlauteren
Wettbewerb*) in a number of instances, several appellate courts (*Oberlandesgerichte*) counteracted these attacks by the prerogative state on formally
rational law.

In a case revolving around the fixing of gas prices, the Appellate Court of
Cologne (*Kölner Oberlandesgericht*) on February 1, 1935, found it
"irrelevant" that the price fixing had been approved by the Trustee of Labor of
Düsseldorf and of the Board of Trustee and Industry of Cologne because
neither was "legally empowered to fix prices in a binding way."[130] In a related
case, adjudicated three years later, the Appellate Court of Hamburg (*Ham-
burger Oberlandesgericht*) similarly upheld the law regulating unfair competition, declaring in its decision that competition in the marketplace was "even
now determined by the conditions of supply and demand, that is, the price is
determined in the last analysis in accordance with the interest of the consumer
[rather than the state]. So long as the conduct of the business is in accord with
the other requirements of fair trade practice there is no restriction on the prices
it sets for its products."[131] The findings of the court rendered a defeat for the

important legal theorist of National Socialism, motivates the political necessity of
Generalklauseln in the rarely cited *Fünf Leitsätze für die Rechtspraxis* (Berlin, 1933), as
quoted in Neumann, *Die Herrschaft des Gesetzes: Eine Untersuchung zum Verhältnis von
politischer Theorie und Rechtssystem in der Konkurrenzgesellschaft*, übersetzt und mit einem
Nachwort von Alfons Söllner (Frankfurt am Main: Suhrkamp, 1980), p. 352.
[128] Stolleis, *Recht im Unrecht*, esp. pp. 7–35. For a similar interpretation, see also the former
Fraenkel student Lothar Gruchmann, especially his "Die 'rechtsprechende Gewalt' im
nationalsozialistischen Herschaftssytem: Eine rechtspolitisch–historische Betrachtung," in
Wolfgang Benz, Hans Buchheim, and Hans Mommsen, eds., *Der Nationalsozialismus:
Studien zur Ideologie und Herrschaft* (Frankfurt: Fischer, 1994), pp. 78–103.
[129] Fraenkel, *The Dual State*, p. 79.
[130] For the decision, see *Oberlandesgericht Köln*, February 1, 1935, as published in *Juristische
Wochenschrift* (1935), p. 1106. See also Fraenkel, *The Dual State*, p. 79.
[131] *Oberlandesgericht Hamburg*, May 12, 1937, as published in *Deutsche Justiz* (1937), p. 1712.
See Fraenkel, *The Dual State*, p. 80.

1	Laws must be general
2	Laws must be promulgated
3	Laws must *not* be retroactive
4	Laws must be clear
5	Laws must *not* be contradictory
6	Laws must *not* demand the impossible
7	Laws must remain relatively constant
8	Action must be congruent with laws

FIGURE 3.4. Fuller's Procedural Theory of Law. *Source*: Fuller, *The Morality of Law*, pp. 33–94

doctrine of *justum pretium* – the principle of Nazism which held that exorbitant prices were immoral.[132]

But let us turn from legal practice to legal theory – in particular the theory of democracy – to consider other influences on the conceptualization of the dual state. Earlier in this chapter, I proposed that the concept of the prerogative state owes to John Austin's command theory of law. The concept of the normative state, by contrast, appears to have been inspired by natural law theory. It is worth contemplating these influences on Fraenkel's work. Interestingly, the episodic evidence that Fraenkel marshaled in support of his argument that the Nazi dictatorship was served by a dual state is commensurable with the procedural theory of law which Lon Fuller, H. L. A. Hart's greatest interlocutor, developed some thirty years later. (See Figure 3.4.) With his discussion of the "inner morality of law," Fuller effectively put forth a procedural theory of law, consisting of eight principles of legality. Fuller's theory is not as antithetical to legal positivism as many (including Fuller himself) have claimed over the years.[133] Fuller's theory is relevant for elucidating the influence of the natural law tradition on the conceptualization of the dual state. For the idea of the normative state embodies attributes advocated by natural lawyers, Fuller included. As Fraenkel pointed out, "The flat rejection of the rationalistic traditions of Natural Law [which can be contrasted

---

[132] Fraenkel, *The Dual State*, p. 80.

[133] Space constraints disallow a discussion of the intellectual standoff between legal positivism and natural law over the centuries. For primary texts relevant to this analysis, see Hart, "Positivism and the Separation of Law and Morals;" Fuller, "Positivism and Fidelity to Law;" Hart, *The Concept of Law*; and Lon L. Fuller, *The Morality of Law*, Revised Edition (New Haven: Yale University Press, 1969).

with the moralistic traditions thereof] resulted in a conflict between National-Socialism and the proponents of Natural Law traditions."[134]

Given the enormous standing of Fuller's procedural theory in law and the social sciences, and the purpose of this analysis, I do not propose to enter into the minutiae of Fuller's contribution to legal theory. Suffice to say that Fuller, influenced by the natural law tradition, emphasized the contribution of formally rational law to social order. Elaborating the point, Fuller remarked that "the existence of a relatively stable reciprocity of expectations between lawgiver and subject is part of the very idea of a functioning legal order."[135] This insight from Fuller's procedural theory of law speaks to the essence of the normative state. The philosophical assumptions underlying each are identical. Consider another parallel between the natural law and the normative state in general, and between Fuller and Fraenkel in particular. Writes Fuller:

> Surely the very essence of the Rule of Law is that in acting upon the citizen (by putting him in jail, for example, or declaring invalid a deed under which he claims title to property) a government will faithfully apply rules previously declared as those to be followed by the citizen and as being determinative of his rights and duties. If the Rule of Law does not mean this, it means nothing.[136]

This observation perfectly captures the essence of the normative state, as conceived in *The Dual State*. In his conceptualization of the normative state, however, Fraenkel may have been influenced even more strongly by the *history* of institutional design than by the *theory* of institutional design, especially by the rule of Frederick the Great (1740–1786) whose enlightened despotism appears to have influenced the conceptualization of the normative state – attributes that Fraenkel maintained were at work in the early years of the "Third Reich."

In this context Fraenkel approvingly invokes the interpretation of the eighteenth century state by a leading contemporary: "Otto Hintze views the activities of the enlightened despotism as the beginning of the Rechtsstaat (Rule of Law state), the characteristic system of the nineteenth century."[137] As Fraenkel explained,

---

[134] Fraenkel, *The Dual State*, p. 115. I should point out that a tension exists between Fraenkel's conception of law and the conception of law adopted herein. For reasons outlined earlier, I embrace a separation of law and morals, distinguishing sharply between the legality of law and the legitimacy of law (see Chapter 2). Fraenkel, by contrast, appears to have leaned, in the final analysis, toward a unification of law and morals. Consider the following discussion toward the end of *The Dual State*: "In rejecting belief in the validity of all universal ideas of justice, National-Socialism substitutes a national restricted idea of utility for the humanistic values of Natural Law." See Fraenkel, *The Dual State*, p. 121. This statement is indicative of a tension in Fraenkel's work between a commitment to the rationalistic and moralistic traditions of natural law. Because this tension has no bearing on the argument of this book, I will not dwell on it here.

[135] Fuller, *The Morality of Law*, p. 209.

[136] Fuller, *The Morality of Law*, pp. 209–210.

[137] Fraenkel, *The Dual State*, p. 159.

Guided by the Enlightenment, the strengthened monarchical absolutism tended to impose the doctrines of Natural Law on those spheres which had been regarded as the proper domain of *raison d' état*, and which were, therefore, outside the legal order. ... Enlightened despotism, represented in its purest form by Joseph II of Austria (1765–90) and, to a lesser degree, by Frederic the Great of Prussia, involved an attempt to eliminate completely the two-sidedness of the state. Its aim was the absolute supremacy of the monarchy as the exclusive bearer of political authority and, concurrently, its subjection to Natural Law. The program of the absolute monarchy required not only the centralization of authority but a universally valid legal system as well.[138]

Fraenkel made particular mention of the Prussian *Allgemeine Landrecht* in Prussia, which had revolutionized the function of police powers under the influence of the Enlightenment. Among other things, the progressive code defined the tasks of the police in liberal terms as (1) the protection of citizens from danger, and (2) the maintenance of order.[139] The concept of the normative state, conceived under the influence of the natural law tradition, was grounded in formally rational law (see also the discussion in Chapter 2). A discussion of the issue of the inviolability of law, mentioned earlier, sheds further light on the matter:

Shortly before the National-Socialists' accession to power in 1933, Gustav Radbruch discussed the principle of the inviolability of law as defined by Otto Mayer, a well-known German authority on administrative law. According to Radbruch, the principle grew out of Natural Law and was later incorporated into the system of positive law. The principle is that, once the sovereign has promulgated a law, he may not violate it at his discretion. Thus the principle that legislative power is vested in the sovereign because he is sovereign is restricted by Natural Law [in contradistinction to the command theory of law around which Schmitt's theory of sovereignty revolved].[140]

The principle of the inviolability of law, of course, is also at the heart of Fuller's procedural theory of law, as discussed a moment ago. (See also Figure 3.4.) The preceding discussion has shown that the dual state as a whole existed in permanent tension with itself. It was under pressure from conflicting imperatives. Fraenkel illustrated these conflicting imperatives memorably, reporting the case of a prisoner in a concentration camp who successfully filed his tax

---

[138] Fraenkel, *The Dual State*, pp. 159–160.

[139] The Prussian monarch introduced limits to his absolute prerogative, drawing on doctrines of natural law. As we have seen, another constitutional monarchy that introduced normative and regulative elements into politics and society was Austria under emperor Joseph II. Otto Hintze located the origins of the *Rechtsstaat* in this period. See his "Preußens Entwicklung zum Rechtsstaat," in idem., *Regierung und Verwaltung: Gesammelte Abhandlungen zur Staats-, Rechts- und Sozialgeschichte*, edited by Gerhard Oestreich (Göttingen: Vandenhock und Ruprecht, 1967), esp. pp. 99–123.

[140] Fraenkel, *The Dual State*, p. 107. On Schmitt's theory of sovereignty, see John P. McCormick, *Carl Schmitt's Critique of Liberalism: Against Politics as Technology* (Cambridge: Cambridge University Press, 1997).

return.[141] In this instance, the prerogative state demanded the man's unlawful detention, while the normative state processed his taxes. The latter treated the man as citizen, the former as subject. The anecdote illustrates Fraenkel's observation that, "[o]ne reservation always lurks in the background of the Normative State: considerations of political expediency."[142] But the case of the concentration camp prisoner suggests that the converse is true as well: one reservation always lurks in the background of the prerogative state: considerations of legal formality. The dual state, in other words, contained a "rational core within an irrational shell."[143]

RULES OF LAW

How and why does the dual state matter for explaining and understanding contentious politics, especially democratization? Figure 3.5 provides a schematic and simplified overview of the argument as it is developed in the following chapters.

The previous chapter has shown that establishing sustainable democracy requires the resolution of commitment problems, situations in which mutually preferable bargains are unattainable because actors hold conflicting preferences over a substantive bargaining issue. Commitment problems are frequently related to the design of *secondary institutions*. Legacies of the normative state can ease such problems and encourage their resolution. The causal logic is simple. Credible commitments demand trust.[144] Yet trust is anathema to authoritarian rule. It will thus be in short supply in democratic transitions. Agents must therefore accept vulnerability. They must learn to believe despite uncertainty. I argue that the legacies of a dual state – given adequate normative reserves – induce "an increased ability to face adversaries."[145]

Trust in institutions, however, is *not* analogous to trust in persons.[146] Trust, as a commodity, is epistemologically demanding. As Russell Hardin writes,

---

[141] Ernst Fraenkel, "Das Dritte Reich als Doppelstaat," in idem., *Reformismus und Pluralismus*, p. 234.
[142] Fraenkel, *The Dual State*, p. 65.
[143] Fraenkel, *The Dual State*, p. 206.
[144] On the problem of trust, see Niklas Luhmann, *Vertrauen: Ein Mechanismus der Reduktion sozialer Komplexität* (Stuttgart: Ferdinand Enke Verlag, 1973); Barbara A. Misztal, *Trust in Modern Societies: The Search for the Bases of Social Order* (Cambridge: Polity Press, 1996); Martin Hollis, *Trust Within Reason* (Cambridge: Cambridge University Press, 1998); Valerie Braithwaite and Margaret Levi, eds., *Trust and Governance* (New York: Russell Sage Foundation, 1998); Mark E. Warren, ed., *Democracy and Trust* (Cambridge: Cambridge University Press, 1999); Russell Hardin, *Trust and Trustworthiness* (New York: Russell Sage Foundation, 2002).
[145] Barzel, *A Theory of the State*, p. 357.
[146] Russell Hardin, "The Public Trust," in Susan J. Pharr and Robert D. Putnam, eds., *Disaffected Democracies: What's Troubling the Trilateral Countries?* (Princeton: Princeton University Press, 2000), pp. 31–32.

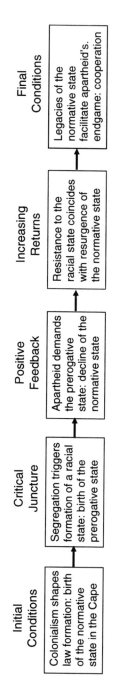

Initial Conditions	Critical Juncture	Positive Feedback	Increasing Returns	Final Conditions
Colonialism shapes law formation: birth of the normative state in the Cape	Segregation triggers formation of a racial state: birth of the prerogative state	Apartheid demands the prerogative state: decline of the normative state	Resistance to the racial state coincides with resurgence of the normative state	Legacies of the normative state facilitate apartheid's. endgame: cooperation

FIGURE 3.5. The Logic of Path-Dependent Explanation

"For me to trust you I must believe your motivations toward me are to serve my interests, broadly conceived, with respect to the issues at stake."[147] Put differently, "a personal relationship involving trust is far richer and more directly reciprocal than a citizen's relationship to government."[148] To trust persons, then, is more demanding – involves more risk – than to trust institutions. I shall henceforth speak of "trust" in persons and "confidence" in institutions. The more confidence adversaries can, and do, vest in the remnants of a normative state, the more reason they have – and the more likely they are – to trust one another. Why should adversaries vest confidence in a dual state? The answer is straightforward. "Almost any set of rules," observes North, "is better than none."[149] Although my argument suggests, *pace* North, that some sets of rules are more important for understanding the process of political change than other remnants of a preexisting normative state assume particular value in democratization.

A culture of law provides common knowledge for interacting adversaries.[150] Such knowledge will obtain whenever agents share a *general* belief in the significance of law for the creation and maintenance of social order. In the context of European integration, shared beliefs about the appropriateness of institutions are also known as *policy ideas*.[151] A culture of law can provide a modicum of certainty (in the form of formality and rationality) in times of uncertainty. The formalization and rationalization of strategic interaction is an important (albeit not sufficient) first step toward resolving commitment problems. The legalization of negotiated agreements (about, say, constitutional design) is a useful second step. For "[l]egalization entails a specific form of discourse, requiring justification and persuasion in terms of applicable rules and pertinent facts, and emphasizing factors such as text, precedents, analogies, and practice. Legal discourse largely disqualifies arguments based solely on interests and preferences."[152] Trust in democracy "results when institutions make it far less likely that one group will be able to capture the state and take advantage of the other."[153] Given their normative reserves, dual states are intimately intertwined with the legal origins of democracy.[154]

---

[147] Hardin, "The Public Trust," p. 34.

[148] Hardin, "The Public Trust," p. 31. Although confidence is a partial analogue to trust, it generally requires less familiarity between sender and receiver.

[149] Douglass C. North, *Structure and Change in Economic History* (New York: W. W. Norton, 1981), p. 24.

[150] Michael Suk-Young Chwe, *Rational Ritual: Culture, Coordination, and Common Knowledge* (Princeton: Princeton University Press, 2001).

[151] Johannes Lindner and Berthold Rittberger, "The Creation, Interpretation and Contestation of Institutions – Revisiting Historical Institutionalism," *Journal of Common Market Studies*, Vol. 41, No. 3 (June 2003), p. 450.

[152] Abbott and Snidal, "Hard Law and Soft Law in International Governance," p. 429.

[153] Weingast, "Constructing Trust," p. 165.

[154] For a related argument, see Weingast, "The Political Foundations of Democracy and the Rule of Law," pp. 245–263. See also Barzel, *A Theory of the State.*

The longitudinal analysis of law's function in apartheid (Chapters 4 and 5) and apartheid's endgame (Chapters 6 and 7) is in response to the fact that there is "remarkably little study of the culture of the rule of law itself as a distinct way of understanding and perceiving meaning in the events of our political and social life."[155] The comparative historical analysis that follows therefore serves to deepen (theoretically) and broaden (historically) our understanding of the rules of law. The focus is on rules of law constitutive of the state. The focus on rules of law – rather than a singular conception of the rule of law – is in recognition of the *multiple* and frequently *contending* structures of law by which costs and benefits are defined and within the framework of which preferences are constructed in any society. Not unlike Allan Hutchinson's recent account of the evolution of the common law, my theoretical argument assumes that law is a meaningful activity that can only be properly understood in its historical and political context.[156]

More specifically, the comparative historical analysis herein considers rules of law a subset of the proverbial rules of the game, which I discussed in the previous chapter.[157] I depart from "vigorous recent claims that firmly associated democracy with the rule of law and authoritarian rule with the 'rule of men' – that is, which treat rule of law features as both definitional and exclusive to democracy."[158] For as Cass Sunstein observes, "The rule of law has many virtues, but we should not overstate what it entails," for "the virtues of rules are inseparable from the vices of rules."[159] Or, as Michel Foucault reminds us, "Rules are empty in themselves, violent and unfinalized; they are impersonal and can be bent to any purpose."[160] The history of the dual state substantiates this observation. For Fraenkel formed the concept of the dual state in response to the multiple and frequently contending structures of law and their coexistence within one sovereign state – the state of Nazi Germany. Given this intellectual history, the concept of the dual state is immediately relevant for explaining – and understanding – the legacies of law.

---

[155] Kahn, *The Cultural Study of Law*, p. 1.

[156] Hutchinson, *Evolution and the Common Law*.

[157] On rules of the game, see North, *Institutions, Institutional Change and Economic Performance*; and Knight, *Institutions and Social Conflict*.

[158] Gerard Alexander, "Institutionalized Uncertainty, the Rule of Law, and the Sources of Democratic Stability," *Comparative Political Studies*, Vol. 35, No. 10 (December 2002), p. 1148. Or, as Andrei Marmor notes, "The most common mistake about the rule of law is to confuse it with the ideal of the rule of the good law, the kind of law, for instance, that respects freedom and human dignity." See his "The Rule of Law and Its Limits," *Law and Philosophy*, Vol. 23, No. 1 (January 2004), p. 1.

[159] Cass R. Sunstein, *Legal Reasoning and Political Conflict* (New York: Oxford University Press, 1996), p. 120.

[160] Michel Foucault, "Nietzsche, Genealogy, History," in idem., *Language, Counter-Memory, Practice: Selected Essays and Interviews*, edited with an Introduction by Donald F. Bouchard, translated from the French by Donald F. Bouchard and Sherry Simon (Ithaca, NY: Cornell University Press, 1977), p. 151.

PART II

A HISTORY OF LAW

4

Apartheid and the Law I

To understand apartheid's endgame, we first need to understand apartheid. As William Riker remarked, at "any point in institutional development, humans start with some pre-existing customs that influence new departures."[1] Following Riker, this chapter revisits the pre-history of apartheid's endgame. It investigates the institutional foundations of the apartheid state, with particular reference to legal norms and institutions. It analyzes state formation and state transformation, and its relationship to race, class, and nationalism in South Africa.[2] The period under investigation stretches from colonial times to the reform of apartheid, from 1652 to the early 1980s. From this longitudinal perspective, the chapter reconstructs the evolution of legal norms and institutions, and explicates their effects, in the making of apartheid. It is concerned with the explanation of institutions. While the book takes the apartheid state as the object to be explained in the next two chapters (the dependent variable), the state will become the thing that *does* the explaining (the independent variable) in the following two chapters.

The discussion in this chapter is organized around critical junctures of state formation in South Africa.[3] The discussion is episodic rather than

[1] William H. Riker, "The Experience of Creating Institutions: The Framing of the United States Constitution," in Jack Knight and Itai Sened, eds., *Explaining Social Institutions* (Ann Arbor: University of Michigan Press, 1995), p. 122.

[2] For an overview, see Shula Marks and Stanley Trapido, "The Politics of Race, Class and Nationalism," in idem., eds., *The Politics of Race, Class and Nationalism in Twentieth Century South Africa* (London: Longman, 1987), pp. 1–70.

[3] In their path-breaking analysis of long-run development in Latin America, Ruth Berins Collier and David Collier defined a critical juncture as "a period of significant change, which typically occurs in distinct ways in different countries (or in other units of analysis) and which is hypothesized to produce distinct legacies." See Ruth Berins Collier and David Collier, *Shaping the Political Arena: Critical Junctures, the Labor Movement, and Regime Dynamics in Latin America* (Princeton: Princeton University Press, 1991), p. 29. The principal argument of this book, couched in these terms, is that the demands of colonialism, segregation, and apartheid, respectively, gave birth to a dual state in South Africa, the legacies of which had an important structuring effect in apartheid's endgame. See also Figure 3.5.

comprehensive. It begins with a brief historical overview of South Africa's strong-state path to democracy. The chapter then returns to some crucial moments of state formation and transformation. It illustrates how, and why, Dutch-descended Afrikaners and British-descended English-speakers converged on the idea of a "racial state," and what it took to turn this racial state into the apartheid state. Focusing on seven stages of state formation, it offers a redescription of the apartheid state as a dual state. The next chapter traces the genealogy of this dual state, and provides an in-depth analysis of how the normative and the prerogative halves of this state emerged, the tensions that their conflicting imperatives produced, and the roles that they played in the construction of white supremacy. Together, this and the next chapter set the stage for the second part of the examination, the analysis of apartheid's end-game and the law.

A HISTORY OF THE SOUTH AFRICAN STATE

A strong-state path, as mapped by Doug McAdam, Sidney Tarrow, and Charles Tilly, has the following stages:

(1) early expansion of governmental capacity
(2) entry into the zone of authoritarianism
(3) expansion of protected consultation through authoritarian citizenship
(4) a less authoritarian, more democratic, but still high-capacity regime.[4]

This four-staged scheme is useful as a heuristic device for introducing the subject of this chapter. (See Figure 4.1.)

An Historical Overview

South Africa traversed the strong-state path identified by McAdam, Tarrow, and Tilly. The emergence of the diamond and gold industries in the late nineteenth century gave rise to rapid industrialization and urbanization. Capitalist forms of production developed in many commercial sectors, turning large numbers of the country's indigenous inhabitants into wage laborers. Capital accumulation in the labor-intensive mining industry, as well as in emerging capitalist agriculture, demanded, above all else, cheap labor. Thus the competing state forms and the various states that existed at the time were centralized to serve a bureaucratic authoritarian regime, albeit one with some constitutional leanings, of which more later. This bureaucratic authoritarian regime served the demands of an emerging capitalist class that had grown prosperous in the wake of the discovery of gold and diamonds in Kimberly and the Transvaal.

---

[4] "Governmental capacity" is defined by McAdam, Tarrow, and Tilly as "the extent of the control governmental agents have over changes in the condition of persons, activities, and resources within the territory over which the government exercises jurisdiction." McAdam, Tarrow, and Tilly, *Dynamics of Contention*, p. 269.

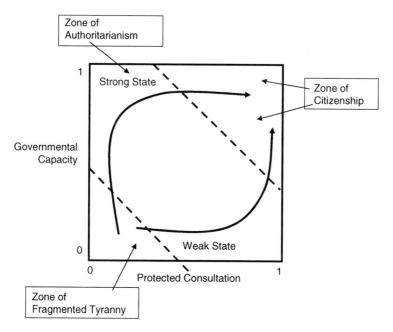

FIGURE 4.1. Strong-State versus Weak-State Paths to Democracy. *Source*: Adapted from McAdam, Tarrow, and Tilly, *Dynamics of Contention*, p. 270.

As in Early Modern Europe, the sovereign state in South Africa won out over its competitors. It ultimately proved superior to the existing sprawling units in that it provided, for the first time, an integrated measure of regularity and predictability for the entire territory, serving a profitable and rapidly expanding market. Interacting colonialists at the turn of the twentieth century had good reason to believe that a centralized state of one unified, white nation would serve capitalism better than a patchwork of competing units. The centralized state won out because it provided superior market predictability and regularity than existing forms of state, as perceived by emerging industrial capitalists and commercial farmers. "The English mining magnates believed that a unified modern state was required to police labor, end internal tariffs, develop railroads to transport minerals, and reduce costly competition among the mining houses."[5] The interaction of markets and hierarchy promised to be the most desirable form of institutional organization for competing colonialists. For the competition between and among crown colonies and republics, as well as different institutional forms, "stood in the way of coherent development."[6]

[5] Anthony W. Marx, *Making Race and Nation: A Comparison of the United States, South Africa, and Brazil* (Cambridge: Cambridge University Press, 1998), p. 85.
[6] Marx, *Making Race and Nation*, p. 85. The dynamics of confrontation between the British and Afrikaner settlers, including the rise of dueling nationalisms and war, are discussed later.

State formation in South Africa can be viewed as the convergence of agents on the centralized institutional structure of the state. The preferences underlying colonialist choices were informed by considerations of efficiency and rational administration.[7] State centralization was desirable because it promised to reduce institutional, especially legal, uncertainty and reduce transaction costs under conditions of industrialization and the rise of commercial society.[8]

Another, equally important motivation for state centralization was the fear of black insurgency. This fear was especially deeply felt among Afrikaners, and was met with the response of racial domination. In the making of segregation, and later apartheid, a plethora of institutions were welded into a single state. The emergent state helped to achieve, and cement, white unity and racial domination. Thus demands of industrialization and modernization, and the desire for a segregated racial order, went hand in hand with a rapid bureaucratization of the state. The systematic bureaucratization of the apartheid state began in earnest in the early 1950s and lasted until the mid-1960s. It was the hub for administering "separate development," Hendrik Verwoerd's vision of South African social order. The Native Affairs Department (NAD) oversaw influx control policy in this apartheid phase. The National Party (NP) expanded the NAD bureaucracy and purged English-speakers within it. "Relying heavily on the services of the Broederbond, the Nationalist government therefore pursued a vigorous programme of 'Afrikanerisation' within all state institutions, transforming the bureaucracy increasingly into an organ of Afrikaner nationalism generally and the Broederbond in particular. This restructuring was one of the Nationalists' major successes of the 1950s, without which the ambitious social engineering policies of the 1960s would not have been possible."[9] This period thus saw the expansion of governmental capacity in South Africa, and the growth of bureaucracy (see Figure 4.1).

---

[7] Capitalist production in South Africa required contractual obligations, coordination, and cheap labor. The four competing institutional forms, serving the two colonies and the two republics respectively, lacked the institutional reach, as well as development, to compete with the centralized, racial state. State centralization streamlined the administration of capitalist development. The government also administered through the racial state an array of controls and coercive measures aimed at disciplining the labor force. For the relationship between capitalism and the development of the state, see North and Thomas, *The Rise of the Western World*. For a useful analysis of state centralization in another case, see Karen Barkey, *Bandits and Bureaucrats: The Ottoman Route to State Centralization* (Ithaca, NY: Cornell University Press, 1994).

[8] For a comprehensive discussion of transaction costs in economic exchange, see Williamson, *The Economic Institutions of Capitalism*, esp. chapters 1, 3 and 15. See also idem., *Markets and Hierarchies: Analysis and Antitrust Implications* (New York: The Free Press, 1975).

[9] Deborah Posel, *The Making of Apartheid, 1948–1961: Conflict and Compromise* (Oxford: Clarendon Press, 1991), pp. 270–271. See also idem., "Whiteness and Power in the South African Civil Service: Paradoxes of the Apartheid State," *Journal of Southern African Studies*, Vol. 25, No. 1 (March 1999), pp. 99–119. On the ideas behind, and strategies of, "Afrikanerization," see also Ivor Wilkins and Hans Strydom, *The Super-Afrikaners: Inside the Afrikaner Broederbond* (Johannesburg: Jonathan Ball, 1978).

The period between 1948 and 1961 signifies the country's entry into authoritarianism. This entry was facilitated by way of law. Separate development became an independent, conservative ideology, a drastic program of social engineering.[10] The most notorious laws of apartheid included the Prohibition of Mixed Marriages Act (1949),[11] which banned marriage between whites and all so-called non-whites; the Group Areas Act (1950, reenacted in Consolidation Acts of 1957 and 1966),[12] which racially segregated urban areas, creating zones for exclusive white occupation; the Suppression of Communism Act (1950),[13] which, in addition to outlawing the Communist Party and the promotion of "communist" doctrines, empowered the Minister of Justice to ban, and remove from certain offices, persons suspected of subscribing to communist ideas, and being involved in communist causes; the Bantu Authorities Act (1951)[14] and the Promotion of Bantu Self-Government Act (1959),[15] which, respectively, created traditional authorities and declared the black population of South Africa was not one homogenous people, but formed eight separate "Bantu national units;" the Terrorism Act (1967),[16] which substantially enhanced the powers of the police, *de facto* allowing for arbitrary arrests; and the Internal Security Amendment Act (1976),[17] which provided for "preventive detention" of persons considered to be "engaging in activities which endangered or were calculated to endanger the security of the State or the maintenance of public order."[18]

Eventually, resistance against apartheid intensified dramatically in the late 1970s and early 1980s. This caused a relative weakening of the state, and marked the beginning of apartheid's endgame. Such was South Africa's strong-state path to democracy. With this overview of state formation in South Africa, let us now review some of the historical stages in more detail. The chapter distinguishes seven stages of state formation. Although most of these stages overlap, peculiar characteristics make them distinct. Table 4.1 summarizes these stages.

---

[10] Leonard Thompson, *The Political Mythology of Apartheid* (New Haven: Yale University Press, 1985), p. 241.
[11] Act 55 of 1949.
[12] Act 41 of 1950; Act 77 of 1957; and Act 66 of 1966.
[13] Act 44 of 1950, amended by Acts 24 of 1967 and 2 of 1972.
[14] Act 68 of 1951.
[15] Act 46 of 1959.
[16] Act 83 of 1967.
[17] Act 79 of 1976.
[18] The information on the Internal Security Amendment Act of 1976 is gleaned from Rob Davies, Dan O'Meara, and Sipho Dlamini, *The Struggle for South Africa: A Reference Guide to Movements, Organizations, and Institutions*, Volume 1 (London: Zed Books, 1984), p. 177.

TABLE 4.1. *Stages of State Formation in South Africa*

Stages	Time Period
Stage I: European Settlers and African Chiefdoms	c. 1652–1910
Stage II: The Unification of South Africa	c. 1902–1910
Stage III: Reasons of State	c. 1910–1930
Stage IV: The Racial State	c. 1920–1948
Stage V: From Segregation to Apartheid	c. 1948–1961
Stage VI: Native Administration and State Formation	c. 1959–1994
Stage VII: The Garrison State	c. 1978–1994

Stage I: European Settlers and African Chiefdoms

In the early 1870s, competing institutional forms covered the territory of what was to become the Union of South Africa in 1910.[19] The idea of the sovereign state had competitors. Dutch-descended Afrikaners and British-descended English-speakers had organized themselves in four autonomous units. The Afrikaners had formed the South African Republic in the Transvaal and the Orange Free State in the heart of the country. The republics had received independence from Great Britain in 1852 and 1854. The English-speaking settlers had formed colonies with representative parliamentary institutions in the Cape of Good Hope and Natal.[20] The European units coexisted with a substantial number of African chiefdoms and autonomous communities. The most important of these indigenous institutional arrangements at the time included the Xhosa, Zulu, Swazi, Tswana, Pedi, Venda, and Griqua chiefdoms, and the southern Sotho Kingdom. Boundaries, the first markings of states, existed between the African and European territorial units, yet the claims to the territories did not always coincide. This gave a first impetus to state formation in South Africa.

[19] Space constraints disallow an in-depth coverage of South Africa's pre-colonial and early colonial history. For expert analyses, see the contributions in Monica Wilson and Leonard Thompson, eds., *The Oxford History of South Africa, Volume I: South Africa to 1870* (Oxford: Clarendon Press, 1971); and Richard Elphick and Hermann Giliomee, eds., *The Shaping of South African Society, 1652–1840* (Cape Town: Maskew Miller Longman, [1979] 1989). Most recently, see Hermann Giliomee, *The Afrikaners: Biography of a People* (Charlottesville: University of Virginia Press, 2003), esp. chapters 1–8. For a critical review of the controversial work, see Christoph Marx, "'The Afrikaners': Disposal of History or a New Beginning," *Politikon*, Vol. 32, No. 1 (May 2005), pp. 139–147. Marx accuses Giliomee for having produced a revisionist, whitewashed history of the Afrikaner people: "The future will show if with this book Giliomee really did Afrikaners a service, because there is not much to be learnt for the future when most things in the past were not that bad." Ibid., p. 147.

[20] Once a *Voortrekker* republic, Natal was incorporated into the Cape Colony in 1844. It became a separate colony in 1856. Zululand was attached to the colony in 1897.

The Sovereign State and its Competitors

But South Africa's colonial history had already begun two hundred years earlier, in 1652, with the arrival of Jan van Rieebeck and the Dutch East India Company at the Cape of Good Hope. Dutch colonialism ended at the end of the eighteenth century when the British seized the Cape to secure its vital overseas trade with India. British colonialism in turn lasted until 1910. The Dutch and British attitudes to colonial state formation differed. Dutch colonialism was based on mercantile plunder, in particular of the East Indies. The dictates of metropolitan accumulation therefore shaped institutional development in the Cape. Dutch colonialism was notable for three things in particular: "firstly the rapid dispossession of the indigenous colonized population; secondly, the largely corrupt and inefficient rule of the Dutch East India Company; and thirdly, the establishment of a stratified settler population."[21] All the while, the Dutch colonial state remained feeble. Neither law nor bureaucracy mattered a great deal in the maintenance of the colony. To the contrary, "Dutch colonial authorities constantly sought to reduce their administrative costs at the Cape."[22] Local officials (*landdrosts* and *heemraden*) were in charge of the administration of justice. Their training was minimal, "and they often lacked the finesse required to handle the frequently conflicting demands" placed upon them.[23] The Cape Dutch colonial administration, in short, was understaffed, overworked, and underpaid. The consequence was a fledgling state, captured by the British in 1795.

Frustrated by liberal British rule in the Cape, the Boers left the Cape Colony in the 1830s in an exodus known as the Great Trek. These *voortrekkers* migrated north to form a separate state on land not yet colonized. The South African Republic and the Orange Free State were the fruits of their quest. Yet Boer state formation differed in important respects from the path taken by the British in the Cape. Whereas British colonialism in the 1860s paved the way for significant capitalist farming in the Western and Eastern Cape and in Natal, Afrikaner colonialism remained wedded to brutal exploitation of the conquered population.

Whereas the British colonies approximated "capitalist states," and relied on commercial capitalism to foster state growth, the Boer republics resembled "rentier states," and relied on the extraction of surplus from rents. These rents, in labor and in kind, were collected from peasants and squatters on their colonized landholdings. The rentier state was both precapitalist and preliberal. The precapitalist form of *economic* development explains why the building of a bureaucracy was not an immediate priority. The preliberal form of *political* development explains why the law did not play a major role in the Boer

---

[21] Davies, O'Meara, and Dlamini, *The Struggle for South Africa*, Vol. 1, p. 4.

[22] Davies, O'Meara, and Dlamini, *The Struggle for South Africa*, Vol. 1, p. 4. See also Albert Venter, *South African Government and Politics: An Introduction to its Institutions, Processes, and Policies* (Johannesburg: Southern Book Publishers, 1989), p. 25.

[23] Albie Sachs, *Justice in South Africa* (Berkeley: University of California Press, 1973), p. 50.

republics. This was to change with the transformation of colonialist landlords
into capitalist farmers only a few years later. Yet this transformation, which
came to the Boer republics belatedly, "was only possible through an intensification and consolidation of the national dispossession and oppression of the
entire African population."[24] State formation in the British colonies was an
entirely different affair. There, commercial agriculture developed under the
auspices of the colonial authorities. The development of institutions was
facilitated by the arrival of missionaries and liberal norms and institutions.
This gave an impetus to the development of law and the rationalization of law.
To be sure, the British authorities used the colonial state to retain tight control
over the black labor force. But the parliamentary and legal institutions
established by the British in the Cape and Natal laid the seeds of a normative
state.

The Origins of the Normative State

The normative state has its roots in the parliamentary institutions that Great
Britain established in the Cape Colony in 1853, and in Natal in 1856.
Although neither colony was a hallmark of democracy, the seeds for institutional development were laid in this period. "[L]egalism fitted well with 'the
conservative, antirevolutionary, middle class culture of the British colonists
who began arriving in 1820."[25] The Dutch-speaking whites in the Cape were
exposed to progressive, liberal ideologies imported from Great Britain.[26]
Humanitarian values and norms, rooted in the Anglo-American Protestantism
of the late eighteenth and early nineteenth centuries, underpinned calls for the
abolition of regressive labor systems and the adoption of basic human rights
for indigenous populations.[27] Interestingly, as a movement of reform in the
colonial world,

humanitarianism was often far more confrontational and explicitly political than in the
metropole. In close alliance with elements of merchant capital, humanitarians (who
were often merchants themselves) pushed for the restructuring of colonial government
and colonial labour relations, and indeed of Britain's relations with the outside world
generally, in more liberal directions.[28]

[24] Davies, O'Meara, and Dlamini, *The Struggle for South Africa*, Vol. 1, p. 11.
[25] Stephen Ellmann, *In a Time of Trouble: Law and Liberty in South Africa's State of Emergency* (Oxford: Clarendon Press, 1992), p. 187. See also Allister Sparks, who argues that segments of the British population at the Cape "established a liberal tradition that has endured through six generations." See his *The Mind of South Africa* (New York: Knopf, 1990), p. 50.
[26] Adam Smith, for example, published his popular treatise *The Theory of Moral Sentiments* in 1759 when he held the Chair of Moral Philosophy at the University of Glasgow. The sixth edition was published shortly before Smith's death in 1790, indicating the widespread influence of the work in Great Britain. Adam Smith, *The Theory of Moral Sentiments*, edited by D. D. Raphael and A. L. Macfie (Indianapolis: Liberty Fund, [1759] 1979).
[27] George M. Fredrickson, *White Supremacy: A Comparative Study in American and South African History* (Oxford: Oxford University Press, 1981), pp. 162–163.
[28] Timothy Keegan, *Colonial South Africa and the Origins of the Racial Order* (Charlottesville: University Press of Virginia, 1996), p. 78.

In South Africa, "aboriginal rights" were promoted by British missionaries in response to settler oppression, whereby the cause became a part of the humanitarian movement's campaign against "the great wall of slavery." The emancipation of slaves in the Cape between 1834 and 1838, especially the abolition of quasi-serfdom of Khoikhoi contract laborers, planted the seeds of liberalism in the Cape region. Advocates of slave emancipation challenged statutory discrimination based on ascribed categories, especially race. "More fundamentally they abhorred the legal status system which underpinned statutory discrimination and which defied the universalistic values of the Enlightenment and of radical evangelical Christianity."[29] One of the missionaries involved in the campaign for the emancipation of slaves, James Read of the London Missionary Society, went as far as pressing charges against individual slaveholders for brutality and violation of contract, invoking legal rights recently granted to the Khoikhoi. It is noteworthy in this context that the humanitarian influence was most persuasive in the Cape when "humanitarian concerns coincided with those of fiscal prudence," for as Timothy Keegan remarks, "In general the missionary cause was an imperial not an anti-imperial force, concerned with the extension of British influence and control."[30]

The greatest achievement for liberalism (and for the normative state) of the time was the passing of "Ordinance No. 50," issued by the Cape Government in 1828. It liberated the Khoikhoi population from most restrictions on their political and economic freedom. The defense of civil and political rights was steadfast, if not of major consequence for the supposed beneficiaries: "It is revealing that the Khoi themselves, according to their missionary spokesman Read, were not greatly excited by Ordinance 50, for by itself it did not hold out any promise of economic independence or an end to *de facto* discrimination. Without land, their newly won legal equality did not seem of great consequence."[31] Hermann Giliomee, similarly, argues that:

The Khoisan did not benefit much from the new legal framework. A study of the way in which Ordinance 50 operated found that it was largely "inoperable" because of the large distances from the farms to the towns. The British judges were supposed to be free of color prejudice, but they did little to give substance to the principle of equality before the law. It is an illusion that Ordinance 50 in terms of substantial social rehabilitation actually achieved anything of great magnitude.[32]

These blemishes notwithstanding, Reverend John Philip, in 1834, persuaded the British government to disallow a vagrancy law that was designed to restrict the hardly won rights, and restore coercive rule over Khoikhoi and the

---

[29] Richard Elphick and Hermann Giliomee, "The Origins and Entrenchment of European Dominance at the Cape, 1652–c.1840," in idem., *The Shaping of South African Society, 1652–1840*, p. 554.

[30] Keegan, *Colonial South Africa and the Origins of the Racial Order*, p. 82.

[31] Keegan, *Colonial South Africa and the Origins of the Racial Order*, p. 117.

[32] Giliomee, *The Afrikaners*, p. 108.

slaves, which were on the verge of being emancipated.[33] Yet British commitment to liberalism was not total. Although the liberalization of the Cape
franchise in 1854 gave Africans, "Coloureds," and Asians the right to vote in
parliamentary and provincial council elections, property and income qualifi-
cations divided the "non-white" population into eligible and noneligible
voters. Only propertied blacks were allowed to participate, for only they were
thought likely to identify with the white Cape bourgeoisie. As a consequence
of the effects that British liberalism had on politics and economics in the Cape
Colony, the rift between Dutch-speaking and English-speaking settlers
widened. As mentioned, this widening rift was the principal cause of the
Great Trek.[34]

This exit from liberalism was the beginning of the racial state. The analysis
of this period reveals a historical pattern. From the beginning, law featured
prominently in both the construction of, and the struggle against, racial discrimination. This pattern is repeated in the eighteenth, nineteenth, and
twentieth centuries. Before the chapter delves deeper into a discussion of these
patterns, let us take a step back, and in broad strokes continue to trace the
origins and development of South African legal norms and institutions.

An Amalgam of Traditions

South African law is an amalgam with a complicated genealogy, the result of
the interaction between European common law and African customary law.
Yet the common law itself is the product of interacting legal traditions,
namely Roman-Dutch law and English law. Roman-Dutch law (*Roomsch-
Hollandsch Recht*) came to South Africa by way of the Dutch East India
Company. Roman-Dutch law consisted of the Roman laws as modified by the
legislature of Holland, as well as Dutch customs.[35] Until late in the eighteenth
century, the Cape courts were staffed by lay jurists. In 1795, when the
British occupied the Cape, Roman-Dutch and English common law confronted one another after the Roman-Dutch legal tradition had structured
developments in the Cape region for more than a century. In accordance
with British colonial policy, the existing legal tradition was retained. Great
Britain's first governor of the Cape Colony recognized the Roman-Dutch
legal tradition, and placed British-born subjects within its reach. "The
retention of Roman-Dutch law was in accord with settled English policy that
inhabitants of conquered territories should continue to live under their own

[33] Initially, a person's legal status was more important than his or her race for the acquisition of
rights and privileges in the Cape. This was due to the fact that the Dutch East India Company
structured Cape society by way of *law*, creating four legal status groups (Company servants,
freeburghers, slaves, and "Hottentots"). Discrimination among legal status groups was
widespread, ranging from issues revolving around domicile, marriage, taxation, and land
ownership. See Elphick and Giliomee, "The Origins and Entrenchment of European
Dominance at the Cape, 1652–c.1840," pp. 528–530.
[34] Fredrickson, *White Supremacy*, pp. 165–171.
[35] On the formal qualities of Roman law, see Weber, *Rechtslehre*, pp. 207–215.

laws."[36] Yet the gradual modernization of political and economic life in the colony, and increasing tensions between Dutch- and English-speaking colonialists, led to a transformation of South African law.[37] Driving this transformation were political and economic processes.

In terms of politics, English law became more important simply because English ideas and institutions came to dominate life in the colony. Many of the penal provisions of the Roman-Dutch law violated the spirit of English law in that they imposed harsh and cruel penalties. These provisions were abolished by way of legislation. Shortly thereafter, criminal procedure was also reformed. It was modeled after the recently revised criminal procedure in England. The new procedure was introduced in 1819 and finally accepted in 1828. In this process, the English law of evidence, albeit with a few modifications, was introduced.[38] The Dutch court structure was repealed courtesy of the First Charter of Justice, which came into force on January 1, 1828. The old dispensation gave way to a structure akin to the British model. Whereas the *Raad van Justitie* had previously been the highest court at the Cape, the Cape Supreme Court, consisting of a chief justice and two other judges, assumed this place under the new dispensation. In 1864 and 1871, supreme courts were also established in Grahamstown and Kimberly.

Another major reform was the introduction of trial by jury.[39] This led to the reorganization of the legal profession into attorneys and advocates. Beginning in 1813, all trials were public. They took place in court with open doors. With effect from December 1, 1834, slavery was abolished in the Cape (via the 1833 Slavery Abolition Act passed by the British Parliament). Ordinance No. 7 of 1843, finally, established the separation of Church and State.[40]

Economic necessities prompted further reforms. Early capitalist development demanded formally rational law, characteristics that the Roman-Dutch

---

[36] Leslie Rubin, "The Adaptation of Customary Family Law in South Africa," in Hilda Kuper and Leo Kuper, eds., *African Law: Adaptation and Development* (Berkeley: University of California Press, 1965), p. 197. This policy draws on a very important rule of English constitutional law. This rule was expressed by Lord Mansfield in *Campbell v. Hall*: "The laws of a conquered country continue in force until they are altered by the conqueror. ... [T]he King has power to alter the old and to introduce new laws in a conquered country." Quoted in Lourens du Plessis, *An Introduction to Law*, Third Edition (Kenwyn: Juta, 1999), p. 50. In South Africa, this British constitutional rule, together with the capitulation conditions of January 10 and 18, 1806, ensured that Roman-Dutch law survived in the colony.

[37] The most complete discussion of this amalgam of traditions is H. R. Hahlo and Ellison Kahn, *The South African Legal System and its Background* (Cape Town: Juta, 1968), Chapter 27. The authors distinguish between "Thesis" (143 years of Roman-Dutch Law during Company rule), "Antithesis" (115 years of Roman-Dutch Law during British rule), and "Synthesis" (Roman-Dutch Law from 1910 onwards).

[38] Rubin, "The Adaptation of Customary Family Law in South Africa," p. 197.

[39] Trial by jury was of very limited success in South Africa. It was the scorn of conservative settlers who were certain that jury trial led to more lenient verdicts. It was abolished in 1969, largely for political reasons. See John Dugard, *Human Rights and the South African Legal Order* (Princeton: Princeton University Press, 1978), pp. 230–234.

[40] Hahlo and Kahn, *The South African Legal System and its Background*, pp. 576–577.

law, as it had developed in South Africa, was not able to provide.[41] As Leslie Rubin writes, "Economic development in the colony served to show that Roman-Dutch principles were inadequate to satisfy the requirements of a changing society, and the laws relating to such matters as shipping, insurance, insolvency, and companies, in force in England, were introduced (in some instances without modification) in the Cape."[42] The institutionalization of commercial transactions, in particular the legalization of credit, debt, and insolvency relations, absorbed a great deal of time. The rationalization of company law and insurance law, too, illustrates the drive toward the rationalization of the common law, and the desire to bring the latter in line with principles of the market. English mercantile law was another innovation taken over from London. As Martin Chanock writes, "Major commercial interests urged from the beginning of British hegemony that there be developed an effective country-wide legal regime to give creditors security."[43]

The English tradition left yet another imprint on the execution of the law. English doctrines and principles were introduced through the application of the law by courts. The courts in turn were staffed with judges trained in England. Consequently, in their interpretation of the law, these judges relied heavily on judicial precedents set by English courts. The adherence to a doctrine of judicial precedent stemmed from "the need for legal certainty, the protection of vested rights, the satisfaction of legitimate expectations and the upholding of the dignity of the court."[44] English law thus established its influence via the administration of justice. Yet the transplant of English law had its limits. Important tenets of Roman-Dutch law remained in place. This remained true after the British declared victory in the Boer War and annexed the Transvaal and the Orange Free State, and also after the proclamation of the Union of South Africa in 1910 (see Stage II). The result was a synthesis of Roman-Dutch law modified by English law, most notably through such additions as case law, procedure, and the law of evidence.

The Cape pattern, this amalgam of traditions, was subsequently extended to the Natal colony, and the republics of the Transvaal and Orange Free State. "The deeper significance of these reforms was that the class of Afrikaner notables was being ejected as the essential pillar in support of the colonial

---

[41] In the Netherlands, Roman-Dutch law underwent a process of codification in the nineteenth century, imitating a trend that had engulfed Prussia, Bavaria, Austria, and France already in the previous century. This turn to codification never reached the shores of the Cape. The development of Roman-Dutch law in South Africa bypassed the incorporation of statute books.

[42] Rubin, "The Adaptation of Customary Family Law in South Africa," p. 197.

[43] Martin Chanock, *The Making of South African Legal Culture 1902–1936: Fear, Favor, and Prejudice* (Cambridge: Cambridge University Press, 2001), p. 176. On the political economy of segregation and apartheid, see, most recently, Charles H. Feinstein, *An Economic History of South Africa: Conquest, Discrimination and Development* (Cambridge: Cambridge University Press, 2005).

[44] Hahlo and Kahn, *The South African Legal System and its Background*, p. 243. Another important avenue of influence was legislation. Some statutes expressly stipulated that English law, not Roman-Dutch law, was applicable. Examples are insurance law and the law of evidence.

regime. Initially the British administration had been constructed on the foundations of pre-existing institutions, administrative and judicial. Now in 1828 the fiscal and the old colonial judges were being ousted by British-appointed and legally trained officers, and at a local level *landdrosts* and *heemraden* were being replaced with resident magistrates and civil commissioners."[45]

An example from the jurisprudence of the Transvaal Republic underscores the point. There, Chief Justice Kotze gave "several pivotal anti-executive, rule of law decisions."[46] In *Powell v. National Director of Public Prosecutions*, a recent appellate judgment, the Supreme Court of South Africa resurrected one of the Kotze decisions, *Ex parte Hull*:

> *Ex parte Hull* appears to be the first reported South African case in which a search warrant was set aside for vagueness and overbreadth. Kotze CJ (Jorissen L concurring) held that the warrant was "too general and too vague." He said that under a loose and arbitrary exercise of a general power to issue search warrants "no one would be safe": The secrets of private friendship, relationship, trade and politics, communicated under the seal of privacy and confidence would become public, and the greatest trouble, unpleasantness and injury caused to private persons, without furthering the true purposes of Criminal Justice in the slightest degree.[47]

As the remarkable jurist continued:

> The secrecy and sanctity of private dwellings might be violated, and one of the first objects that men have in view in associating themselves in political communities throughout the world would be frustrated, if the private citizen did not feel himself against what may be nothing more than the curious eye of the police agent, sheltering itself behind the authority of a search warrant; except only where the Law, in order to further the interests of justice, and so protect society, allows and directs, under special circumstances, the issue of a search warrant.[48]

South African law was born, and the normative state established. But as important as the normative state was, it was only one half of the dual state.

The Origins of the Prerogative State
White South Africans, although divided on many issues, were united in their emphasis on racial separateness. Neither Afrikaners nor British settlers saw a need to cultivate allies among the African and Asian populations of South Africa. Their white racial identity gave them the confidence to forego ties with the indigenous populations. Except for the Boer War, both communities

[45] Keegan, *Colonial South Africa and the Origins of the Racial Order*, p. 101.
[46] Edwin Cameron, Judge of the Supreme Court of South Africa, Personal communication, May 5, 2007.
[47] *Powell v. National Director of Public Prosecutions* 2005 (5) SA 62 (SCA).
[48] *Powell v. National Director of Public Prosecutions* 2005 (5) SA 62 (SCA). I am very grateful to Edwin Cameron for having brought his Kotze reference in *Powell v. National Director of Public Prosecutions* to my attention. On the centrality of law in Kruger's Republic, see my discussion of the religious foundations of the Calvinist legal tradition in Chapter 7.

refrained from relying on Africans in their wars against one another, carefully avoiding passing guns into the hands of African inhabitants.[49] Herein lie the origins of the prerogative state. The African chiefdoms and autonomous settlements "were undermined from within and overwhelmed from without."[50] The manner in which the European settlers, unified in their racial identity, went about subjugating the country's African populations displays characteristics of wanton rule. It was the beginning of force without reason in South Africa.[51] As one scholar puts it, "The road from the bureaucratic rationality of the nineteenth century to the instrumental rationality of the twentieth century [in South Africa] was paved by the violence of conquest, European fantasies of control, and an intolerance for people who imagined the world differently."[52]

Yet cleavages existed between and within the settler populations. As Leonard Thompson writes,

Having been isolated from Europe for several generations and having adopted a distinctive rural mode of life and developed a new language, Afrikaners were conscious of being a separate people, rooted exclusively in South Africa; while the British community, newer to the country and replenished by fresh recruits from Great Britain, tended to despise Afrikaners and to look to London for protection against them as well as Africans. Furthermore, the Afrikaners were themselves divided. They had no tradition of common political responsibility and since the Great Trek they had lived under different political systems and acquired different loyalties. In the Cape Colony, many of them had made an accommodation with English culture and British overrule; in the republics, the dominant sentiment was uncompromising aversion to British authority.[53]

Stage II: The Unification of South Africa

The unification of South Africa marks the intensification of racial segregation.[54] Segregation emerges as the principal organizing principle of the Union, the linchpin around which the country's social order would revolve until the electoral victory of D. F. Malan's National Party in the late 1940s. Yet before segregation there came white-on-white violence. Cecil Rhodes's attempt to force Paul Kruger's Transvaal into submission, and to establish a provisional

---

[49] Leonard Thompson, "The Subjection of the African Chiefdoms, 1870–1898," in Monica Wilson and Leonard Thompson, eds., *The Oxford History of South Africa, Volume II: South Africa, 1870–1966* (Oxford: Clarendon Press, 1971), p. 246.

[50] Thompson, "The Subjection of the African Chiefdoms, 1870–1898," p. 251. On the conjoined histories of state formation and indigenous culture in South Africa, which lie beyond the purview of this analysis, see Clifton Crais, *The Politics of Evil: Magic, State Power, and the Political Imagination in South Africa* (Cambridge: Cambridge University Press, 2002).

[51] For the best discussion, see Thompson, "The Subjection of the African Chiefdoms, 1870–1898," pp. 245–286.

[52] Crais, *The Politics of Evil*, p. 228.

[53] Thompson, "The Subjection of the African Chiefdoms, 1870–1898," p. 247.

[54] The best analysis of unification remains Leonard M. Thompson, *The Unification of South Africa 1902–1910* (Oxford: Clarendon Press, 1960).

government in Johannesburg in 1895, infamously failed and only intensified intrawhite conflict.[55]

White-on-white violence resulted primarily from a struggle over land, and over ideology. The Afrikaners of the Transvaal resented the British opposition to their racial order. They saw it "as a denial of what they took to be firm biblical sanctions for dominating nonwhites by force and formally excluding them from citizenship."[56] One of the participants of the Great Trek remembered the exit from the Cape as a response to "the shameful and unjust proceedings with reference to the freedom of our slaves, and yet it is not so much their freedom that drive us to such lengths, as their being placed on an equal footing with Christians, contrary to the laws of God and the natural distinction of race and religion."[57]

The white conflict over who would rule South Africa, and how, culminated in 1899, the beginning of a devastating three-year war between the British Empire and the Boer republics. The war, called the Anglo-Boer War in the British Empire, and the Second War of Freedom by Afrikaners, was fueled from London by an imperialist press, a nationalist public, and an insatiable government. It was Britain's greatest war effort since the Napoleonic Wars: 448,000 British forces battled 70,000 Afrikaners for close to three years. And yet victory did not come easy for the British. The Boer War "proved to be the longest, costliest, the bloodiest and the most humiliating war for Britain between 1815 and 1914."[58]

The Boer War, writes George Fredrickson, was "essentially a struggle between benign and oppressive racial ideologies."[59] This struggle foreshadowed the struggle between the normative state and the prerogative state as discussed later. The Treaty of Vereeniging – signed on May 31, 1902 – ended the war, but it did not end white conflict. Feelings of groupness had grown stronger on both sides of the white divide during the war. "Memory of the war, carefully nurtured as it was, did more to unite Afrikanerdom than Kruger had ever succeeded in doing."[60] Britain avoided a punitive peace. The

---

[55] Thompson, *A History of South Africa*, p. 139. On the Jameson Raid, and Rhodes's plans for, and policy of, British expansionism in Southern Africa, see Robert I. Rotberg with Miles F. Shore, *The Founder: Cecil Rhodes and the Pursuit of Power* (New York: Oxford University Press, 1988), Chapters 8, 11, 13, 16, 19, and 20.

[56] Fredrickson, *White Supremacy*, p. 171.

[57] Quoted in Fredrickson, *White Supremacy*, p. 171. On Afrikaner ideology, see also A. S. Mathews, "Security Laws and Social Change in the Republic of South Africa," in Heribert Adam, ed., *South Africa: Sociological Perspectives* (London: Oxford University Press, 1971), esp. p. 233. For the most comprehensive treatments of Afrikaner ideology, see Thompson, *The Political Mythology of Apartheid*; and T. Dunbar Moodie, *The Rise of Afrikanerdom: Power, Apartheid, and the Afrikaner Civil Religion* (Berkeley: University of California Press, 1975).

[58] Thomas Pakenham, *The Boer War* (New York: Random House, 1979), p. xix.

[59] Fredrickson, *White Supremacy*, p. 194. The road to white unity led through concentration camps. Twenty-eight thousand Afrikaners and Africans perished in these camps.

[60] LeMay, *British Supremacy in South Africa, 1899–1907*, p. 213, as quoted in Marx, *Making Race and Nation*, p. 89.

government in London realized that the imperial connection depended on English-Afrikaner reconciliation. To reap the rewards of empire, a union was proposed. The idea was set forth for the first time in the 1906 Shelborne Memorandum, drafted by one of Lord Milner's aides. The idea was embraced, and achieved at the expense of liberal values, especially after the Natal rebellion by former chief Bambatha (and the mounting discontent among blacks there) had left whites in Natal "unsure of their capacity to control a distinct state," and whites elsewhere fearful of "the consequences if Natal was left to its own devices."[61] Fear and greed among competing colonialists, in short, gave rise to racial nationalism.

Elections in 1910 inaugurated the new unified state. And on May 31, 1910, Louis Botha, a former military leader of the Afrikaner republics, became prime minister of the new dominion. The election outcome was ironic.

Before the war, the Afrikaners had been disunited, protecting their interests by retreating into separate republics. The British had forced the Afrikaners together in a newly unified state, and then watched as that state became ruled by leaders of the defeated, who would use state power to further enforce segregation.[62]

The effects of unification on state formation were considerable. The state emerged centralized, supreme over all competitors and local institutions. The centralization of the state intensified segregation, and segregation brought further state centralization. Segregation and state formation thus were mutually constitutive processes. During the years 1910 to 1939, successive South African governments made segregation a leading idea of state.[63] Although some of these governments differed in approach, all of them were "concerned to consolidate white power in the new state."[64]

Stage III: Reasons of State

In 1913, Prime Minister Botha and Jan Smuts lost control of the Reef in the Transvaal where strike action threatened lives and property. In January 1914, the government cracked down on white labor protestors in a clandestine move that made history. After concluding that law had failed, the government responded to the strike with a declaration of martial law, arresting the leaders of the strike extra-judicially and deporting them to calm the flames. The response to the response could not have been more drastic. "The reaction, both in South Africa, and in Britain, was intense and angry. There was real perturbation among the judiciary. [Chief Justice Sir James Rose] Innes was outraged. It was, he later wrote, an 'audacious misuse' of martial law in which the executive had 'sabotaged' its own courts. Not only was the viability of the

---

[61] Thompson, *A History of South Africa*, p. 148.
[62] Marx, *Making Race and Nation*, p. 97.
[63] Thompson, *A History of South Africa*, p. 157.
[64] Thompson, *A History of South Africa*, p. 157.

new state called into question again, but so too was its commitment to govern through law. Merriman thought it 'astounding [. . .] a violent unconstitutional action.' Even the apolitical *South African Law Journal* published a critical comment."[65] The episode illustrates how firm the limits on the prerogative state were at the beginning of the Union. It was Innes, the Chief Justice, who was instrumental in laying the foundations for the survival of the normative state in times of upheaval.[66] "Painstaking, patient, and upright," Innes's serving thirteen years at the helm of the judiciary left an indelible mark on the country's legal tradition.[67] As Albie Sachs writes,

Innes has been honoured by lawyers in South Africa primarily because of his contribution to the development of Roman-Dutch law, and many persons regard him as the greatest judge South Africa ever produced. [. . .] Before his elevation to the bench, Innes had been well known as a liberal in Cape politics, and after his retirement he spoke out strongly against attempts to deprive Africans of their limited franchise rights in the Cape. His dismay at the increasing racism in public life in South Africa was matched by his horror of racism in Nazi Germany, where his grandson, Helmut [Graf] von Moltke, also a lawyer trained in the English tradition, was to play a leading role in the anti-Hitler opposition.[68]

But let us return, for now, to the problems of transition and consolidation in early Union South Africa.

In March 1922, Jan Smuts, now Prime Minister, quelled a contentious uprising of workers, the so-called Rand revolt, by force. The internecine battles between white workers and the white government left 220 dead. It was the moment when Afrikaner nationalism turned against Smuts. In the wake of the Rand revolt, the more radical Barry Hertzog succeeded Smuts as Prime Minister. The year was 1924. Hertzog had run on the platform of racial domination, emphasizing more aggressively than his predecessors the distinctiveness of Afrikaner culture. He made good on his promises as soon as he assumed office. Hertzog imbued the South African state with a distinct Afrikaner flavor. The promotion and protection of Afrikaner nationalism became a principal reason of state. Hertzog laid the institutional foundation for the full-blown "racial state" that was to emerge three decades later.

The idea of the state from thence on revolved around Afrikaner culture. To further Afrikaner nationalism, Hertzog catered to the steadily growing Afrikaner underclass that had emerged in the depression. To this end, the Iron and Steel Corporation, a state-owned company, was created. It became a principal employer for many, especially poor, whites. While poor whites

[65] Chanock, *The Making of South African Legal Culture 1902–1936*, pp. 136–137.
[66] I am grateful to Edwin Cameron for his gentle insistence that I include a short pen picture of the great Innes here.
[67] The quote is from an earlier, pre-unification portrait by W. R. Bischop, "Sir James Rose Innes, K.C.M.G.," *Journal of the Society of Comparative Legislation*, New Series, Vol. 11, No. 1 (1910), p. 11.
[68] Sachs, *Justice in South Africa*, p. 136.

numbered only 106,518 in 1916 (8 percent of the white population), this
number had risen to over 300,000 by 1932 (17.5 percent of the white population). The "poor white problem" always loomed large in the Afrikaner mind.
In 1913, the Select Committee on European Employment and Labour Conditions had summarized the problem in the following terms:

> The magnitude of unemployment among Europeans in South Africa is possibly not
> greater than in other countries, but the danger posed is much greater because of the
> presence of the preponderating native population, and constitutes a real social threat.
> [...] [Among the white unemployed there] is a depressing residue of incompetent and
> apathetic indigents: whose condition constitutes a real danger for society. These are
> persons who have entered into a corrupting and demoralizing intercourse with non-
> Europeans, with harmful effects on both sides of the population.[69]

The poor white problem was especially pronounced in the early decades of
the twentieth century. The existence of unemployed, poor whites interfered
with the Afrikaner project of conservative modernization. Three types of
interference can be observed. First, the poor white problem was seen as slowing
down attempts at inculcating segregation (and the notion of white supremacy)
among the black population. Second, it interfered with the administration of
segregation. To generate modest incomes, poor whites sold liquor to blacks.
This widespread, illegal practice undermined the racial regime, which had
banned the sale of alcohol in an attempt to increase the productivity of African
workers. Third, poor whites were real, and imagined, allies of black workers. A
militant white trade union movement, drawing on radical social-democratic
and socialist ideas, marched against the emerging capitalist state in large-scale
strikes in 1907, 1913, and 1922. In this era, poor whites were feared as an
unpredictable reservoir of discontent that trade unions could mobilize in future
strikes.[70] White-on-white militance, in turn, generated other fears: "strikes by
white wage earners were seen as encouraging African workers also to strike"
and "the large-scale deployment of armed force to control striking whites was
seen as rendering the state vulnerable to an 'uprising' by blacks."[71] The possible
formation of a nonracial working class posed a substantial threat to the
emerging Afrikaner state, and capitalist interests within this state. The resolution of the poor white problem was of critical importance for state survival.

Stage IV: The Racial State

Separate development evolved from to idea to principle to ideology. It became
institutionalized in successive stages, each stage planting the notion deeper into

---

[69] Chanock, *The Making of South African Legal Culture 1902–1936.*

[70] For an important Marxist analysis of segregation, see Dan O'Meara, *Volkskapitalisme: Class, Capital and Ideology in the Development of Afrikaner Nationalism* (Cambridge: Cambridge University Press, 1983).

[71] Rob Davies, Dan O'Meara, and Sipho Dlamini, *The Struggle for South Africa: A Reference Guide to Movements, Organizations, and Institutions, Volume 2* (London: Zed Books, 1984), p. 244.

the Afrikaner mind. In the run-up to the 1948 elections, the National Party published a pamphlet with the title "National Party's Colour Policy." In it, the NP called for the maintenance of a "pure white race" and rejected policies aimed at *gelykstelling* (equalization) of whites and blacks. The pamphlet was organized under the following section headings: "Maintenance of White Race as Highest Goal" and "Welfare of Blacks in Developing Separately."[72] Paradoxically, the same issue – race – that had brought about intrawhite conflict was used to heal it. Racial domination gradually transformed a potential conflict across racial lines into a more manageable dyadic form of 'white power over black."[73] Thus was the birth of "racial oligarchy," of the racial state.[74] Thompson describes this birth in the following terms:

During the years 1910 to 1939, the successive South African administrations were all concerned to consolidate white power in the new state. In spite of a rural uprising by aggrieved Afrikaners during World War I, militant strikes by white workers, one of which escalated into a bloody confrontation on the Witwatersrand, and intermittent resistance by Blacks, the reach of the state increased steadily and scarcely anyone questioned its legitimacy.[75]

The historian William Beinart suggests that "the very solidity of the state provided the stepping-stones for whites, both English and especially Afrikaans-speaking, to take power and entrench a system of racially based dominance that was unique in its rigidity."[76] However, a closer look reveals that Beinart has the causality of state formation backward. The segregationist state was not as strong as intimated by Beinart. While the government attached growing importance to the "rational management of Africans" in the 1940s, "administration in the reserves remained in a state of arrested development and without any foreseeable prospect of significant modification."[77] *Contra* Beinart, race-making, industrialization, and conservative modernization led to the emergence of the strong state in South Africa. Although some sturdy institutions already existed at the time of unification in 1910, the emergence of the racial state was a consequence, not cause, of early apartheid.

[72] Quoted after Herman Giliomee and Lawrence Schlemmer, *From Apartheid to Nation-Building* (Cape Town: Oxford University Press, 1989), pp. 34–35.
[73] Anthony W. Marx, "Race-Making and the Nation-State," *World Politics*, Vol. 48, No. 2 (January 1996), p. 182.
[74] The term was coined by Heribert Adam in *Modernizing Racial Domination: The Dynamics of South African Politics* (Berkeley: University of California Press, 1971), arguably the most influential book on the apartheid regime. On the notion of the racial state, from a comparative perspective, see, recently, David Theo Goldberg, *The Racial State* (Oxford: Blackwell, 2001).
[75] Thompson, *A History of South Africa*, p. 157.
[76] William Beinart, *Twentieth-Century South Africa* (Cape Town: Oxford University Press, 1994), p. 3.
[77] Ivan Evans, *Bureaucracy and Race: Native Administration in South Africa* (Berkeley: University of California Press, 1997), p. 280.

Stage V: From Segregation to Apartheid

In the 1940s and 1950s, segregation became apartheid, the more repressive and institutionalized manifestation of racial domination. The period between 1948 and 1958 saw the idea turn into principle, and eventually into government policy. It was the Verwoerdian version of a social contract. Hendrik Verwoerd, prime minister from 1958 until 1966, turned "separate development" into an Afrikaner ideology, updating Hertzog's principal reason of state.[78] D. F. Malan and J. G. Strijdom furthered the institutional design. Malan was responsible for enshrining traditional racial segregation by way of law. His prescriptions include the Prohibition of Mixed Marriages Act,[79] the Population Registration Act,[80] the Group Areas Act,[81] the Bantu Authorities Act,[82] and the Reservation of Separate Amenities Act.[83] Opposition against these early, fundamental laws of apartheid was quelled with the aforementioned Suppression of Communism Act[84] and the Public Safety Act.[85] Strijdom initiated the removal of "coloured" voters from the voters roll in the Cape (of which more below) and extended the notorious pass laws. His government also passed the Riotous Assemblies Act[86] that forbade meetings of more than twelve people without a permit, and outlawed the multiracial trade unions. But Verwoerd's succession in 1958 marks the real beginning of the state of race.

Verwoerd, who had previously been Minister of Native Affairs, gave the fullest expression to the racial state. Under his leadership, it became a "functional aspect of the social order."[87] This idea of state notwithstanding, the making of apartheid was often haphazard. As Piet Cillié, editor of the *Die Burger* from 1954 to 1978 and leading voice of the Afrikaner nationalist movement, wrote:

A system? An ideology? A coherent blueprint? No, rather a pragmatic and tortuous process aimed at consolidating the leadership of a nationalist movement in order to safeguard the self-determination of the Afrikaner.[88]

Yet the fact that planning had unexpected consequences, does not mean that planning was not driven by reason. Administration was rational in the

---

[78] For a discussion of apartheid as a motivating ideology, see Thompson, *The Political Mythology of Apartheid*.

[79] Act 55 of 1949, amended by Act 21 of 1968.

[80] Act 30 of 1950.

[81] Act 41 of 1950, amended twice, by Act 77 of 1957 and Act 66 of 1966.

[82] Act 68 of 1951.

[83] Act 49 of 1953, amended by Act 10 of 1960.

[84] Act 44 of 1950, amended by Acts 24 of 1967 and 2 of 1972.

[85] Act 3 of 1953.

[86] Act 17 of 1956, amended by Acts 15 of 1954 and 30 of 1974.

[87] Stanley B. Greenberg, *Legitimating the Illegitimate: State, Markets, and Resistance in South Africa* (New Haven: Yale University Press, 1987), p. xvii.

[88] Piet Cillié, "Bestek van apartheid: What Is (Was) Apartheid?," *Die Suid-Afrikaan*, Spring 1988, p. 18, as quoted in Giliomee and Schlemmer, *From Apartheid to Nation-Building*, p. 63.

sense that recruitment into organizations of the state was largely rule-based. The Public Service Commission (transformed into the Commission for Administration by the Commission for Administration Act of 1984) oversaw effective personnel management, service conditions, training, protection against nepotism, performance evaluation, and competitive recruitment, inculcating the idea of professionalism.[89] A sophisticated administrative environment developed in the 1960s and 1970s. In the 1980s, this environment was further enriched with the establishment of a Directorate of Promotion and Training, a Training Institute, as well as a competitive training program for university graduates that involved a five-year internship. By 1986, a total of 865,385 bureaucrats served the apartheid state (including homelands).[90] Yet the independence of the bureaucracy was not always insured. Although the Official Secret Act of (1958) and the Income Tax Act (1962) aimed at the control of the illegal use of privileged public information, the discretion bestowed on civil servants was frequently considerable. The quantity of security legislation put "arbitrary power in the hands of bureaucrats who do not have to make public the reasons for their actions, nor can they be called to defend their actions in a court of law."[91]

Thus after the 1948 elections, the balance between the two sides of the dual state (discussed in more detail later) began slowly to tilt. The transition from Jan Smuts to Verwoerd, from United Party to National Party, and from segregation to apartheid, set off a steadily increasing emphasis on the prerogative rather than the normative state. In the years preceding the watershed election, Afrikaners had become increasingly concerned with race relations. The prevalent view at the time was that the state should be called on "to maintain white supremacy and the 'purity' of the white 'race'."[92] The victorious National Party, which consolidated itself in government through an alliance with (and soon absorption of) the Afrikaner Party, was quick to respond to these concerns.

Stage VI: Native Administration and State Formation

Law and bureaucracy were key pillars of apartheid, and had their roots in the early stages of state formation. They eventually gave institutional expression to the racial state. The "ascendancy of bureaucracy in modern society is based in large part on a general acceptance of its superior efficiency – the belief that bureaucratic organizations can outperform alternative ways of mobilizing human efforts."[93] The expansion of bureaucracy in the apartheid

[89] Albert Venter, "The Central Government: Legislative, Executive, Judicial and Administrative Institutions," in idem., ed., *South African Government and Politics*, pp. 78–79.
[90] Venter, "The Central Government," p. 79.
[91] Venter, "The Central Government," p. 78.
[92] Thompson, *A History of South Africa*, p. 185.
[93] Mark V. Nadel and Francis E. Rourke, "Bureaucracies," in Fred I. Greenstein and Nelson W. Polsby, eds., *Handbook of Political Science, Volume 5: Governmental Institutions and Processes* (Reading, MA: Addison-Wesley, 1975), p. 388.

TABLE 4.2. *Employment in the South African State, 1910–1960*

	Total Employment	Central State Employment	Military	Police	No. of State Departments
1913				5,884	13 (2)
1920	150,718		1,307	10,512	22 (106)
1930	227,408	140,042	2,253	10,707	25 (226)
1940	321,403	177,392	5,322	11,655	26 (382)
1950	481,518	280,310	10,532	20,648	27 (430)
1960	798,545	454,692	17,951	25,724	32 (551)

Source: Annette Seegers, *The Military in the Making of Modern South Africa* (London: I.B. Tauris, 1996), pp. 34 and 88. Bracketed numbers refer to semistate bodies.

state followed a similar pattern. Table 4.2 illustrates the expansion of state employment between 1910 and 1960. Between 1950 and 1979, the percentage of gross fixed investment in the state sector rose from 35 percent to 53 percent.[94]

Like state formation, state consolidation was about the utility of the state as a social institution. What the "state's elite will accept as a method – is calculated by utility."[95] Malan and Verwoerd, as the British settlers before them, realized that people "joined together in complex organizational systems can achieve results that individuals alone could never hope to accomplish – the construction of an atom bomb, the launching of a space vehicle into orbit, or the establishment of an educational system capable of meeting the intellectual needs of all citizens from primary school to postdoctoral training."[96] Segregation and apartheid themselves were results that no individual, or community of persons, could have created and sustained in the absence of bureaucracy. As already mentioned, the ascension of Verwoerd was a defining moment of state formation. He introduced will and vision into government policy, something that was lacking in the era of the segregationist state. Concerted attempts were made to convert the Department of Native Affairs into a "state within the state."[97]

The Expansion of the Prerogative State
Ever since European settlers arrived at the Cape, blacks suffered high governmental coercion. Yet in the 1960s, the expansion of coercion was noteworthy. Of particular significance was the "unprecedented application of

[94] Wood, *Forging Democracy From Below*. For a discussion, see also Merle Lipton, *Capitalism and Apartheid: South Africa, 1910–84* (Gower, Aldershot, UK: 1985).
[95] Annette Seegers, *The Military in the Making of Modern South Africa* (London: I. B. Tauris, 1996), p. 87.
[96] Seegers, *The Military in the Making of Modern South Africa*, p. 87.
[97] Evans, *Bureaucracy and Race*, p. 280.

arbitrary police power to large numbers of blacks."[98] Johannes Balthazar Vorster outflanked Verwoerd on the right. Vorster, the former minister of justice under Verwoerd, had been interned during World War II as assistant chief commandant of the pro-Nazi association *Ossewa-Brandwag* (Ox-Wagon Sentinels) for siding with Nazi Germany.

The most important organizations of the prerogative state in this period were the joint security structures, the South African Police (SAP), the Bureau of State Security (BOSS), and the South African Defence Force (SADF). Each of these security organizations was comprised of further organizations and units.[99] Under President P.W. Botha, BOSS became the Department of National Security (DONS). Shortly thereafter, in 1981, it turned into the National Intelligence Service. The bureaucracy was of great significance in shaping first segregation and subsequently apartheid. Its size and functions increased dramatically after the depression of the 1930s.[100] The expansion of the prerogative state involved a series of actions, many of which were reflected in the decisions of the courts. The formation of the prerogative state made necessary the abolition of constitutional restraints and the abolition of restraints on police power.[101]

The Abolition of Legal Restraints

The repeated declaration of states of emergency facilitated the use of the prerogative state. States of emergency, or martial law, are "characterized by the fact that the state continues to exist while the legal order is inoperative." Carl Schmitt, who originated this definition, elaborates as follows: "The decisions of the state are freed from normative restrictions. The state becomes absolute in the literal sense of the word. In an emergency situation the state suspends the existing legal system in response to the so-called 'higher law of self-preservation.'"[102] Between 1960 and 1990, the apartheid government declared five states of emergency. (See Table 4.3.)

The National Party government ruled with an iron fist in this period. It relied on emergency powers for more than forty-three months between 1960 and 1990,

[98] Evans, *Bureaucracy and Race*, p. 168.
[99] For an overview, see Truth and Reconciliation Commission of South Africa, *Truth and Reconciliation Commission of South Africa Report*, Volumes 2 (London: Macmillan Reference Limited, 1999), pp. 313–324.
[100] Beinart, *Twentieth-Century South Africa*, p. 119.
[101] The organization of the discussion owes to Fraenkel, *The Dual State*, pp. 9–46.
[102] Carl Schmitt, quoted in Fraenkel, *The Dual State*, p. 25. Schmitt's position culminates in the proposition that "Souverän ist, wer über den Ausnahmezustand verfügt" (He is sovereign who decides the exception). See Carl Schmitt, *Politische Theologie*, Seventh Edition (Berlin: Duncker and Humblot, [1922] 1996), p. 13. For a discussion of the use of emergency powers in Weimar Germany, an important historical case, see Skach, *Borrowing Constitutional Designs*; Achim Kurz, *Demokratische Diktatur? Auslegung und Handhabung des Artikels 48 der Weimarer Verfassung 1919–25* (Berlin: Duncker und Humblot, 1992); and Peter Blomeyer, *Der Nostand in den letzten Jahren von Weimar* (Berlin: Duncker und Humblot, 1999).

TABLE 4.3. *States of Emergency under Apartheid, 1960–1990*

Year	Description	Detentions
1960	Partial State of Emergency (March 29–August 31, 1960)	11,727 (official)
1985–1986	Partial State of Emergency (July 21, 1985–March 7, 1986)	7,996 (official)
1986–1987	Total State of Emergency (June 12, 1986–June 11, 1987)	25,000 (estimate)
1987–1988	Total State of Emergency (June 11, 1987–June 10, 1988)	5,000 (estimate)
1988–1989	Total State of Emergency (June 10, 1988–December 1988)	3,000 (estimate)
TOTAL		52,723 (estimate)

Source: David Webster and Maggie Friedman, "Repression and the State of Emergency: June 1987–March 1989," in Glenn Moss and Ingrid Obery, eds, *South African Review 5* (Johannesburg: Ravan Press, 1989), p. 22.

almost four years. During these four years, the normative state was put on hold. The emergency restrictions gave rise to surrogate forces in the shape of vigilantes, "violent, organised and conservative groupings operating within black communities, which, although they receive no official recognition, are politically directed in the sense that they act to neutralise individuals and groupings opposed to the apartheid state and its institutions."[103] Emergency restrictions in particular permitted vigilante activity to go unreported.[104] Furthermore, "the right to use force, including lethal force, is freed from virtually all controls or restraints by a provision of the emergency regulations ..."[105] During the 1985–1986 state of emergency, to mention but one example, the security forces were granted additional powers not specified in the Public Safety Act of 1953. Their actions were no longer subject to judicial oversight. This is the background to the notorious order sent to the Port Elizabeth police prior to the Uitenhage shootings, to "eliminate" troublemakers.[106]

[103] Nicholas Haysom, "Vigilantes and Militarization," in Jacklyn Cock and Laurie Nathan, eds., *War and Society: The Militarization of South Africa* (Cape Town: David Philip, 1989), p. 188. See also Gilbert Marcus, "Civil Liberties Under Emergency Rule," in John Dugard, "The Law of Apartheid," in John Dugard, Nicholas Haysom, Gilbert Marcus, eds., *The Years of Apartheid: Civil Liberties in South Africa* (New York: Ford Foundation, 1992), pp. 32–54.
[104] Jacklyn Cock, "The Role of Violence in Current State Security Strategies," in Mark Swilling, ed., *Views on the South African State* (Pretoria: Human Sciences Research Council, 1990), p. 89.
[105] Anthony S. Mathews, *Freedom, State Security and the Rule of Law: Dilemmas of the Apartheid Society* (Berkeley: University of California Press, 1986), pp. 211–212. See also, idem., *Law, Order and Liberty in South Africa* (Berkeley: University of California Press, 1972).
[106] Reported in Anthony S. Mathews, *Law, Order and Liberty in South Africa*, p. 265. See also Ellmann, *In a Time of Trouble*.

The laws of apartheid were enacted by parliament, an institution entirely unconstrained by judicial review, because of the principle of parliamentary sovereignty inherited from the British. Parliamentary sovereignty allowed the legal construction of racial domination. Yet, as David Dyzenhaus notes, "the law was not self-executing under apartheid. It required administration, application and interpretation by judges, magistrates, prosecutors, officials in the Department of Justice and Law and Order, and lawyers, both in the academy and the legal profession."[107] In other words, it is important to remember agents in the history of the apartheid state. How did these agents fare?

Agents of Apartheid

What remains largely unexamined in the literature is the fact that "apartheid was installed not through military means, but largely through the everyday work of civil administration in the 1950s."[108] Authoritarian administrators within the DNA played an influential role in the regulation of black labor, housing, movement, and employment. "National Party cadres looked to the DNA to stamp out the 'chaos' in the labor market."[109] Interestingly, the 1950s saw a convergence on cooperation between liberal and pro-apartheid bureaucrats. Liberal administrators were dominating the civil service in metropolitan areas. These administrators were slowly won over by the routinized character of racial domination, especially that administered by the DNA. While "liberal officials objected to the moral bases of apartheid," they were "impressed by the DNA's 'modern' administrative competencies."[110] The DNA successfully consolidated the ranks of administrators by "championing 'modern' principles of administration:"[111]

If it amassed extraordinary powers and duties, it also rationalized administration by generating a series of functionally specific subdepartments, commissions, and committees. It sought to implement its programs on the basis of empirical evidence through 'scientific' research. It conformed to parliamentary protocol, and even when it ejected senior officials, it did so with the approval of the Public Service Commission.[112]

---

[107] David Dyzenhaus, *Judging the Judges, Judging Ourselves: Truth, Reconciliation and the Apartheid Legal Order* (Oxford: Hart, 1998), p. 27. H. R. Hahlo and Ellison Kahn discuss the extent of judicial-lawmaking in South Africa, see their *The South African Legal System and its Background*, Chapter 9.

[108] Hahlo and Kahn, *The South African Legal System and its Background*, p. 277. For an in-depth analysis of homeland politics, with particular reference to the two largest reservations, see also Jeffrey Butler, Robert I. Rotberg, and John Adams, *The Black Homelands of South Africa: The Political and Economic Development of Bophuthatswana and KwaZulu* (Berkeley: University of California Press, 1977).

[109] Evans, *Bureaucracy and Race*, p. 282.

[110] Evans, *Bureaucracy and Race*, p. 291. Evans sees a transition from paternalistic administration to authoritarian administration when segregation became apartheid.

[111] Evans, *Bureaucracy and Race*, p. 293.

[112] Evans, *Bureaucracy and Race*, p. 293.

Like Ivan Evans, who traces the early contribution of administration to the making of apartheid, this book argues that it matters a great deal that it was civil servants, and *not* military planners, who orchestrated the formation and transformation of the apartheid state. In the 1950s (maybe more than in any other decade), "laws were enacted, instructions were issued, and papers were signed."[113] Procedures mattered a great deal. Bureaucrats within the normative state "valued predictability, stability, and efficiency as goals in themselves and were genuinely impressed by the technical means" that they could deploy.[114] To the same extent that adherence to rules, norms, and procedures legitimized the state in the eyes of liberal, metropolitan civil servants, "the expansion of the state's bureaucratic juggernaut of the 1950s signaled a development not recognized in the literature on Bantu administration: the transformation of Bantu administration into a 'career' [...]."[115] This career was appealing to members of the Afrikaner nation, but to Africans as well. No other than Nelson Mandela was attracted by a career in the rural administration before becoming a Johannesburg lawyer.[116] "His immediate ambition was to become a court interpreter, a much-esteemed profession in the rural areas, which promised both influence and status."[117] Mandela admired both the law and bureaucracy. His personality and life, of which more in Chapter 7, illustrate both the appealing qualities of the normative state, and the threat of the prerogative state.

It is important to appreciate that Mandela was not the only black South African to whom a career in the administrative apparatus of the apartheid state (or the homeland administrations) was appealing. Justice Bess Nkabinde, currently a member of South Africa's Constitutional Court, for example, began her career as a State Law Advisor in the homeland government of Bophuthatswana. Her colleague in Braamfontein, Justice Yvonne Mokgoro, worked as a clerk in the Department of Justice of the erstwhile Bophuthatswana, subsequently being appointed maintenance officer and public prosecutor in the magistrate's court of Mmabatho. And, finally, there is Justice Pius Langa, the current Chief Justice of South Africa, who between 1957 and 1960 worked as an interpreter in the Department of Justice, thereafter as a prosecutor and magistrate. All the aforementioned, in other words, "peopled and ran," as Edwin Cameron put it, "the apartheid bureaucracy and court system."[118]

---

[113] Evans, *Bureaucracy and Race*, p. 294.
[114] Evans, *Bureaucracy and Race*, p. 295.
[115] Evans, *Bureaucracy and Race*, p. 296.
[116] Nelson Mandela, "Jail Memoir," as quoted in Anthony Sampson, *Mandela: The Authorized Biography* (New York: Knopf, 1999), p. 27.
[117] Sampson, *Mandela*, p. 27.
[118] Edwin Cameron, Judge of the Supreme Court of South Africa, Personal Communication, May 5, 2007.

Stage VII: The Garrison State

In the 1970s, the country moved into a "garrison situation" where "the use of physical force as a means of problem-solving has been popularized to the detriment of more persuasive and non-coercive techniques for managing social conflict."[119] In this situation

institutions associated with the use of force, the "managers of violence" to use Laswell's famous phrase, the military and police experience a unique elevation in status relative to the "soft" organizations of society, the parliamentary bodies, the judiciary and the media, whose operating ethics are altogether more complex, subtle and civil.[120]

The reconfiguration of the apartheid state was dramatic: the organizations of the prerogative state began to liquidate the public sphere. "It is not an exaggeration to say that during the years of the Vorster administration (1966–78), South Africa became a police state, with uncontrolled powers vested in the police force. Organizations were outlawed, political meetings prohibited, individuals banned and detained – all without having access to the courts."[121] For the Afrikaner nation, the 1970s were about surviving the real and imagined onslaught of communism. The key pillar of the state in this period, P. W. Botha's infamous National Security Management System (NSMS), was established in August 1979. It was the backbone of the garrison state. Figure 4.2 depicts the place of the NSMS within the institutional structure of the apartheid state, and its relationship to security legislation (representing the normative state) and vigilantes and death squads (representing the prerogative state).[122]

The influence of the normative state (although not its legacy) receded, while the reach of the prerogative state expanded under the NSMS. The militarization of politics, and of the state, immediately preceded apartheid's endgame.[123]

[119] Philip H. Frankel, *Pretoria's Praetorians: Civil-Military Relations in South Africa* (Cambridge: Cambridge University Press, 1984), p. 31.

[120] Frankel, *Pretoria's Praetorians*, p. 31.

[121] John Dugard, "The Law of Apartheid," in John Dugard, Nicholas Haysom, Gilbert Marcus, eds., *The Years of Apartheid: Civil Liberties in South Africa* (New York: Ford Foundation, 1992), p. 22.

[122] Vigilante groups first emerged on the scene around 1985. They grew out of the largely informal structures surrounding the unpopular homeland authorities and Black Local Authorities (BLAs). For a list of vigilante groups, from "Mbokodo" in the Northern Transvaal to "Amasolomzi" in the Western Cape, see Max Coleman, ed., *A Crime against Humanity: Analysing the Repression of the Apartheid State* (Claremont, CA: David Philip, 1998), p. 117. On the operation of death squads, see, most authoritatively, Jacques Pauw, *In the Heart of the Whore: The Story of Apartheid's Death Squads* (Halfway House: Southern Book Publishers, 1991); and ibid., *Into the Heart of Darkness: Confessions of Apartheid's Assassins* (Johannesburg: Jonathan Ball, 1997). For a list of victims of political assassinations in the period 1974–1989 carried out by hit squads and other covert apartheid agents, see ibid., pp. 247–251.

[123] Kenneth W. Grundy, *The Militarization of South African Politics* (Oxford: Oxford University Press, 1988). To appreciate the extent of this militarization in the aftermath of the collapse of the Portuguese empire, consider the graphs in Robert M. Price, *The Apartheid State In Crisis:*

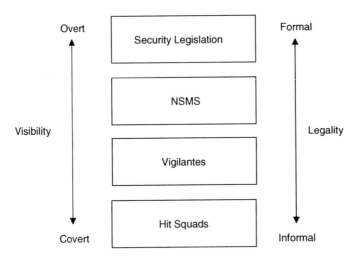

FIGURE 4.2. The Institutional Structure of the Apartheid State: The National Security Management System

It involved increased state centralization, spurred on by a new military-industrial complex at the helm of which stood Armscor, the state-owned Armaments Development and Production Corporation. The NSMS was a device to shorten the bureaucratic chain of command, creating the institutional space for the activities of vigilantes, hit squads, and other covert operations.[124] By the mid-1970s, military planners and business leaders had grown accustomed to working together.[125] Botha, who had presided over Armscor, put military technocrats in charge of reforming apartheid when he became prime minister in 1978. "As first announced in the 1977 Defence White Paper, the SADF generals had evolved their own 'Total National Strategy' to meet the new demands of the time. With P. W. Botha as Prime Minister they were given the chance to implement it."[126] The garrison state was a response to shocks that the government faced in the mid-1970s, in particular the collapse of the Portuguese empire in Southern Africa, the

Political Transformation in South Africa, 1975–1990 (New York: Oxford University Press, 1991), p. 44, figure 2.1. Price reports that defence spending between 1974 and 1980 increased by 454 percent. Defense expenditures consumed twenty percent of total government expenditure by the mid-1980s. Price, *The Apartheid State In Crisis*, p. 43.

124 Annette Seegers, "The Head of Government and the Executive," in Robert Schrire, ed., *Leadership in the Apartheid State: From Malan to de Klerk* (Cape Town: Oxford University Press, 1994), p. 63. More generally, see Harold Lasswell, "The Garrison State," *American Journal of Sociology*, Vol. 46, No. 4 (January 1941), pp. 455–468; and Aaron L. Friedberg, *In the Shadow of the Garrison State: America's Anti-Statism and Its Cold War Grand Strategy* (Princeton: Princeton University Press, 2000).

125 Dan O'Meara, *Forty Lost Years: The Apartheid State and the Politics of the National Party, 1948–1994* (Johannesburg: Ravan Press, 1996), pp. 226–227.

126 O'Meara, *Forty Lost Years*, p. 263.

country's economic malaise, the radicalization of township resistance, and international isolation.[127] A "triumvirate of totalities" conditioned governance: "total onslaught" (the total attack against white South Africa), "total strategy" (the appropriate response to the imagined total onslaught), and "total involvement" (the presumption that the means of total strategy must be all-encompassing).[128]

The might of the garrison state was deployed against opponents of apartheid. Externally, the government authorized military raids on Angola, Botswana, Lesotho, Mozambique, Zambia, and Zimbabwe.[129] Internally, increasing resistance met with new forms of intensified repression.[130] In the insurrection period of the mid-1980s, the SAP and SADF acted in conjunction.[131] The distinction between civil and military functions was virtually erased, strengthening the prerogative state vis-à-vis the normative state. Louis Le Grange, the Minister of Law and Order under Botha, described the unrest in the townships as "war, plain and simple."[132]

Yet reformism and militarization had unintended consequences. Inasmuch as the prerogative state grew, so did the normative state. Two paradoxical and unexpected processes are discernible: whereas reformism aided the prerogative state, militarization aided the normative state. Although the "Total National Strategy" increased the influence of the military in politics, it also increased the efficiency of the administration. A "craze for technocratic rationality" infected the country.[133] "Traditional NP populism now rapidly gave way to a stress on technical rationality and 'scientific' policy-making."[134] Thus although the normative state was curtailed, it was simultaneously replenished.[135]

[127] See Chapter 6 for a comprehensive discussion.
[128] Frankel, *Pretoria's Praetorians*, p. 54. Some reform measures accompanied repression. The most significant of these was constitutional engineering, resulting in the Tricameral Parliament in 1983, which was scorned by many within the emerging alliance of democracy–demanding forces.
[129] For a table of military attacks, see Frankel, *Pretoria's Praetorians*, p. 93.
[130] For an overview of the interaction between repression and resistance, see Price, *The Apartheid State in Crisis*; and Jeremy Seekings, *The UDF: A History of the United Democratic Front 1983–1991* (Cape Town: David Philip, 2000).
[131] The best study of the SAP, its origins and development, is John D. Brewer, *Black and Blue: Policing in South Africa* (Oxford: Clarendon Press, 1994).
[132] Chris Alden, *Apartheid's Last Stand: The Rise and Fall of the South African Security State* (London: Macmillan, 1996), p. 161. On the military's role more generally, see Seegers, *The Military in the Making of Modern South Africa*.
[133] O'Meara, *Forty Lost Years*, p. 269.
[134] Frankel, *Pretoria's Praetorians*, p. 268.
[135] Some military personnel were hesitant to cast aside their "liberal civil-military heritage." Writing in the early 1980s, Frankel finds that "the lingering legacy of liberal institutional socialization is still potent enough" to dissuade the mainstream of the officer corps from the creation of a fully articulated garrison state. Frankel, *Pretoria's Praetorians*, p. 151.

5

Apartheid and the Law II

In the previous chapter, I discussed the seven stages of state formation in South Africa, and their bearing on the evolution of the dual state. This chapter investigates the effects of the dual apartheid state. As the historical overview has demonstrated, successive governments blended legalism and coercion in South Africa, first in the making of segregation, and later in the making of apartheid. These governments used – often concurrently – reason with force, and force without reason.

A DUAL STATE

Dullah Omar, Minister of Justice in the first post-apartheid government, has described the institutional dispensation of the apartheid state as a "dual political system of a parliamentary democracy for whites and a dictatorship for blacks."[1] Legal scholars Kennedy and Schlossberg speak of "executive despotism" in South Africa, which they contend was exercised "side by side" with the "trappings" of parliamentary government.[2] The following discussion traces the institutional effects of this schizophrenic institutional structure – this dual state – for politics and society.

While the normative state occasionally won out over the prerogative state in the years of segregation, the ratio of reason to force began to tilt steadily in favor of the latter when segregation became apartheid. The militarization of politics under President Botha (see discussion of Stage VII in the previous chapter) was the last, and most dramatic, stage of this transformation.

---

[1] Dullah Omar, "An Overview of State Lawlessness in South Africa," in Desiree Hansson and Dirk van Zyl Smit, eds., *Towards Justice? Crime and State Control in South Africa* (Cape Town: Oxford University Press, 1990), p. 19. Omar's characterization requires some qualification. As this chapter makes clear, the "parliamentary democracy for whites" came with restrictions, and the "dictatorship for blacks" was not entirely without rights and freedoms.

[2] W. P. Kennedy and H. J. Schlosberg, *The Law and Customs of the South African Constitution* (London: Oxford University Press, 1935), pp. 459–460.

THE PREROGATIVE STATE

My analysis of the effects of the prerogative apartheid state is organized around four themes: discrimination, fear, destruction, and death. These themes capture the effects that the apartheid state has had on most of South Africa's population for much of the twentieth century.

Discrimination

Some consider the 1920s and 1930s the high point of segregation (see discussion of Stage III).[3] Everyday racial prejudice underpinned official racial discrimination in this period. Allister Sparks writes, "what strikes one today, looking back, is that much of the legislation covered what was already social practice."[4] He recalls that "[e]very town had its separate black quarter of makeshift shacks known simply as a 'location,' as if to emphasize the black man's anonymity, and at night a curfew bell would ring and the blacks would disappear to the 'location' from the white homes and businesses where they worked as housemaids and nursemaids, garden 'boys' and labourers."[5]

The basis of social engineering, during segregation and apartheid, was the annexation of land. The Bantu Land Act,[6] already briefly discussed earlier, and the Bantu Trust and Land Act[7] were key to the institutionalization of discrimination. The two Land Acts of the 1930s allocated 87 percent of agricultural land to whites and only 13 percent to blacks. At the turn of the century, whites had accounted for 21 percent of the population, whereas blacks comprised 67 percent (the latter figure rises to 79 percent of "Coloureds" and Asians are also counted as black, as was common in anti-apartheid discourse).[8] Apartheid, and segregation before it, sustained racial prejudice and achieved racial boundaries through political exclusion, economic marginalization, and social segregation.

Political Exclusion
Favor and prejudice in the political realm were sustained through a whole array of measures. Suffrage was restricted on the basis of race. Only whites were entitled to vote.[9] Even the "multiracial" constitution of 1983 did not do

---

[3] See, for example, Beinart, *Twentieth-Century South Africa*, p. 119.

[4] Sparks, *The Mind of South Africa*, p. 190.

[5] Sparks, *The Mind of South Africa*.

[6] Act 27 of 1913.

[7] Act 18 of 1936.

[8] The figures are reported in Robert A. Schrire, "The Context of South African Politics," in Anthony de Crespigny and Robert Schrire, eds., *The Government and Politics of South Africa* (Cape Town: Juta, 1978), p. xiii. The figures are corroborated by data reported in Thompson, *A History of South Africa*, p. 243.

[9] The 1910 settlement had preserved a qualified franchise in the Cape for male "Coloureds" and blacks in the Cape. The black franchise was abolished in 1936, the "coloured vote" in 1956.

away with exclusion.[10] Other forms of political exclusion included the banning of persons. The banning of persons and organizations was first regulated, as we have seen, in the Suppression of Communism Act. The power was supplemented in the Unlawful Organizations Act, and again strengthened by the Internal Security Act. In terms of duration, banning orders ranged from one to five years. They could be successively applied. The purpose of banning was the removal of politically active persons and organizations from social life. The recent work of the Truth and Reconciliation Commission of South Africa declared banning and banishment orders gross violations of human rights because they imposed severe ill treatment. Banning orders constricted movement and participation in society. The longest banning order lasted twenty-six years.[11] Political exclusion almost always entailed social exclusion as well.

Economic Marginalization

Favor and prejudice in the economic realm were primarily sustained through labor-repressive institutions. Labor repression had dismal consequences across employment sectors, producing one of the most unequal class structures in the world. Francis Wilson and Mamphela Ramphele reported in 1989 that in terms of the Gini coefficient, South Africa had the highest measure of inequality in a set of fifty-seven countries for which data was available.[12]

---

[10] Inasmuch as the constitution extended suffrage to Indians and "Coloureds" in the elections to the 1984 Tricameral Parliament, in an attempt to coopt them into the system, this "sham consociation" (Theodor Hanf) entrenched white supremacy, rather than reform it. The black majority was left entirely out of the new constitutional dispensation. The limits on the participation of the newly included minorities remained significant. The three racially separate and unequal parliaments created for whites, Indians, and "Coloureds" deepened separate development. For an analysis, see L.J. Boulle, *South Africa and the Consociational Option: A Constitutional Analysis* (Cape Town: Juta, 1984). Arend Lijphart, whose theory of consociationalism inspired the making of the constitution, also writes that "the 1983 constitution does not measure up to the basic requirements of consociationalism" and maintained that "the exclusion of the Africans is not only unconsociational but also undemocratic." See Lijphart, *Power-Sharing in South Africa*, p. 56. The distinction between "own" and "general affairs," unfair voting ratios, and the strengthening of the president's decree authority all contributed to continued exclusion. (Note that although the Office of the State President was created in the 1983 constitutional reforms, South Africa remained a parliamentary system.) By also creating a new executive structure, including a powerful President's Council and a strong Office of the President, the government replaced the former Westminster-style cabinet form of government. It "constitutionalizes the government's established policy, makes aspects of apartheid part of the country's basic law." Boulle, *South Africa and the Consociational Option*, p. 211. It turned "reformism into Potemkinism." Sparks, *Tomorrow is Another Country*, p. 6. P.W. Botha's administration "viewed a consociational constitutional arrangement as a 'democratic' means of sharing power while simultaneously guaranteeing white control of the government." Price, *The Apartheid State In Crisis*, p. 288.

[11] *Truth and Reconciliation Commission of South Africa Report*, Vol. 2, pp. 167–69. For an overview of types of banning, its effects, and the relevant security legislation, see Mathews, *Freedom, State Security and the Rule of Law*, Chapter 8.

[12] Francis Wilson and Mamphela Ramphele, *Uprooting Poverty: The South African Challenge* (Cape Town: David Philip, 1989), p. 4.

Labor repression was deployed in agriculture, the mining industry, as well as other commercial sectors.[13] This practice indicates the presence of a dual state under apartheid. For as Fraenkel writes, "the Dual State is characterized by the fact that the ruling class assents to the absolute integration of state power on the following conditions: (1) that those actions which are relevant to its economic situation be regulated in accordance with laws which they consider satisfactory, (2) that the subordinate classes, after having been deprived of the protection of the law, be economically disarmed."[14]

Social Segregation

In terms of social exclusion, the aforementioned Reservation of Separate Amenities Act treated blacks as "separate but unequal," ending a tense constitutional struggle between the judiciary and the legislature. What is interesting here is that the invocation of the seemingly (in the wake of *Brown v. Board of Education* in the United States) illiberal "separate but equal" doctrine had liberal effects in South Africa. The courts questioned the legality of unequal amenities for different races, holding that the common law required an equality of treatment. Consequently, courts struck down all separations that were not in fact substantively equal.

After the courts had struck down discriminatory subordinate legislation by invoking the U.S. Supreme Court's "separate but equal" doctrine, the incensed National Party government revoked the power of the courts to declare such legislation invalid in the 1953 Act.[15] The difference between the two doctrines revolved around the distinction between technical inequality and substantial inequality. Technical inequality, the Appellate Division of the Supreme Court held, was inherent in the regulations establishing separate post office counters for whites and blacks.[16] Although the treatment of blacks and whites was technically unequal, it was deemed substantially equal. In the eyes of the court, "discrimination coupled with equality was not unreasonable."[17] For the courts

---

[13] See Stanley B. Greenberg, *Race and State in Capitalist Development: Comparative Perspectives* (New Haven: Yale University Press, 1980). See also Merle Lipton, *Capitalism and Apartheid*; and Feinstein, *An Economic History of South Africa*.

[14] Fraenkel, *The Dual State*, p. 154.

[15] Dugard, *Human Rights and the South African Legal Order*, pp. 64–65. As Edwin Cameron notes, "the Reservation of Separate Amenities Act disbarred courts from voiding subordinate legislation on the grounds of substantive inequality." Personal Communication, May 5, 2007.

[16] See *Minister of Posts and Telegraphs v. Rasool* 1934 AD 167. For a discussion of the two other key decisions on the principle of equality – *R. v. Abdurahman* 1950 (3) SA 136 (A), and *R. v. Lusu* 1953 (2) SA 484 (A) – see David Dyzenhaus, *Hard Cases in Wicked Legal Systems: South African Law in the Perspective of Legal Philosophy* (Oxford: Clarendon Press, 1991), chapter 3. Interestingly, the three cases cut across the transition from segregation to apartheid. As such, they highlight both important continuities and significant changes in the development of South African law and jurisprudence.

[17] Dugard, *Human Rights and the South African Legal Order*, p. 64. Consider in this context a comparative perspective. Note that the U.S. Supreme Court espoused the constitutionality of "separate but equal" facilities for different racial groups in *Plessy v. Ferguson* (1896), and *rejected* the doctrine in *Brown v. Board of Education of Topeka* (1954). In its 1954 decision, the court ruled that separate facilities are *inherently* unequal with respect to education.

to declare subordinate legislation invalid, substantial inequality was required. Substantial inequality was discrimination coupled with inequality. The 1953 Reservation of Separate Amenities Act ended this niche of judicial independence. It resulted in the establishment of separate and unequal facilities in all areas of social life, ranging from buses to parks to trains and beaches.

Successive apartheid governments, through law and bureaucracy, administered the economics of favor and prejudice. In economic terms, the dual state performed the functions that Stephan Haggard has ascribed to institutions in authoritarianism more generally, particularly with regard to problems of collective action:

Institutions can overcome [...] collective-action dilemmas by restraining the self-interested behavior of groups through sanctions; collective-action problems can be resolved by command. Since authoritarian political arrangements give political elites autonomy from distributionist pressures, they increase the government's ability to extract resources, provide public goods, and impose the short-term costs associated with efficient economic adjustment.[18]

The quotation illustrates the relationship between the state and the regime, a relationship discussed in detail in Chapter 6. The preceding analysis demonstrated the economic utility of the law for whites, especially for those involved in conservative modernization and industrial agriculture. In what follows, the chapter elaborates the mechanisms by which the subordinate classes – Africans, "Coloureds," and Indians – were deprived of the protection of the law.

Fear

The late 1950s inaugurated grand apartheid. The Promotion of the Bantu Self-Government Act created eight, later ten, territorial authorities for blacks. The creation of these "Bantu Homelands" was apartheid's response to decolonization elsewhere on the continent. It represented a tightening of the regime's grip. Verwoerd described the government's Bantustan policy in 1961 as a strategy to buy "the white man his freedom and right to retain domination in what is his country."[19] As mentioned, Verwoerd coined the euphemism "separate development" to disguise the oppressive nature of his grand design. The Bantustan system was maintained by elements working within the prerogative state. "The 'unsophisticated' Bantustan leaders have been used to engage in forms of particularly brutal and sadistic repression which the central apartheid state can no longer afford to be seen to be implementing itself – and for which it can thus disclaim all responsibility."[20]

---

[18] Haggard, *Pathways from the Periphery*, p. 262. The specifically *economic* collective action problems that Haggard has in mind include stabilization, trade liberalization, fiscal reform, tax reform, and the reform of financial markets. See Haggard, *Pathways from the Periphery*, pp. 262–262.

[19] Quoted in Davies, O'Meara, and Dlamini, *The Struggle for South Africa*, Vol. 1, p. 204.

[20] Davies, O'Meara, and Dlamini, *The Struggle for South Africa*, Vol. 1, pp. 210–211.

The security forces of the homelands (both dependent and independent) totaled 32,400 police and military personnel by 1990.[21] Although the normative state constrained apartheid's governing elites, the willing executors assembled under the homeland system perpetrated unlawful repression under the auspices of the prerogative state. The Central Intelligence Service of the Ciskei, for example, launched a bloody campaign against the South African Allied Workers' Union (SAAWU), headquartered in a township just outside East London. The campaign, masterminded by President Lennox Sebe and his brother General Charles Sebe, involved kidnappings, torture, firebombs, and shootings. It was executed by the notorious "green berets," a paramilitary force.[22] Other homelands, run by similarly loyal collaborators, paralleled Ciskei's repressive rule. The armies of Transkei and Bophuthatswana, for example, quelled student unrest and forcefully raided squatter settlements. The army of the Transkei also carried out raids against the neighboring Kingdom of Lesotho, whereas the Bophuthatswana regime under Lucas Mangope fought a proxy war for the apartheid government against ANC operatives near Rustenberg in the late 1970s. Homeland armies were officered by whites, typically army personnel or mercenaries. Homeland governments were often composed partially of white cabinet ministers to ensure that the homelands' policies did not sway from Pretoria's hard line. The fear of repression among black South Africans, many of whom had become subject to population transfers, was thus immense. The culture of fear that apartheid instilled is causally related to the country's still pervasive culture of violence. Both cultures have demonstrated staying power, and, as we will see, both complicated apartheid's endgame.

Destruction

The most consequential form of destruction concerned the destruction of space. Two of the most infamous episodes of forced removals were those involving Sophiatown and Cape Town's District Six. Sophiatown was located in Johannesburg, four miles west of the city center. It was one of the few townships where Africans had successfully purchased landholdings prior to the Urban Areas Act of 1923, which made the purchase of land illegal for blacks. As old photographs from the interracial Drum Magazine show, Sophiatown was the cultural center of black urban life in Johannesburg, housing approximately 60,000.[23] It was a lively, animated, buzzing place:

---

[21] Figure calculated on the basis of Seegers, *The Military in the Making of Modern South Africa*, p. 269. The number of police and military personnel for South Africa at the time was 191,000 plus 16,000 local police (10,000 municipal policemen and 6,000 *kitskonstabels*).

[22] Davies, O'Meara, and Dlamini, *The Struggle for South Africa*, Vol. 1, pp. 210–11; 217–37.

[23] The figure includes the inhabitants for Sophiatown as well as adjacent townships Martindale and Newclare. The three settlements were referred to as the "Western Areas townships." The 60,000 inhabitants broke down into 54,000 Africans, 3,000 "Coloureds," 1,500 Indians, and about 700 Chinese. See Tom Lodge, *Black Politics in South Africa since 1945* (Johannesburg: Ravan Press, 1983), p. 95.

"Sophiatown. That beloved Sophiatown. As students we used to refer to it proudly as 'the center of the metropolis'. And who could dispute it? The most talented African men and women from all walks of life – in spite of the hardships they had to encounter – came from Sophiatown. The best musicians, scholars, educationists, singers, artists, doctors, lawyers, clergymen."[24] In 1955, the government put an end to all this. It moved all of Sophiatown's black inhabitants to Meadowlands, twelve miles outside of the city. It then rezoned and renamed Sophiatown for whites: Sophiatown became Triomf ("Triumph"). The episode also illustrates the limits of the normative state, as the blatant violation of African property rights remained without negative consequences for the perpetrators. District Six had a similar fate. A similarly engaging place, District Six was located in Cape Town's city center and the home of an interracial, yet mainly "coloured" community. Today only a museum reminds of the community that once was. All inhabitants were moved to the Cape Flats, and almost all of the houses razed.[25]

Although not immediately fatal for the residents involved, the governmental destruction of living space, and of communities that surrounded such space, represented a deep invasion of the population's privacy. But forced removals under apartheid also involved the expropriation of land, and the suspension of rights. An official memorandum from the Department of Bantu Administration and Development (DBAD), summarizing the character of and rationale for clearing black land, acknowledges as much:

With the words "clearance of black spots" is understood the suspension of *property rights* vested in [sic] Bantu in land situated in white areas, that is part of the larger policy of the creation of Bantu homelands that has to be *speeded up* [sic].[26]

Forced removals in South Africa exemplify the intersection of the prerogative and the normative state. Whereas population transfers were on the face of it legal, that is, in accordance with the law, notably the amended Group Areas Act, the suspension of one of the most significant private rights, the right to property, of South Africa's majority population indicates the limits of law in South Africa. Between 1960 and 1983, a total of three and a half million forced removals were undertaken. (See Table 5.1.)

The largest single category of removal concerned that from white farms. Between 1960 and 1983, more than one million unwanted farm workers were evicted from their habitat. "Local political and ideological tensions, and the growing security fears of white farmers over the *verswarting* (blackening) of the

---

[24] Miriam Tlali, *Muriel at Metropolitan* (Johannesburg: Ravan Press, 1975), p. 70.
[25] Thompson, *A History of South Africa*, p. 194. For a compelling analysis, see John Western, *Outcast Cape Town* (Berkeley: University of California Press, 1996).
[26] The original memorandum was written in Afrikaans. It was translated by Gerhard Maré and first quoted in his *African Population Relocation in South Africa* (Johannesburg: South African Institute of Race Relations, 1980), p. 2. The above quotation is from Laurine Platzky and Cherryl Walker, *The Surplus People: Forced Removals in South Africa* (Johannesburg: Ravan Press, 1985), p. 115.

TABLE 5.1. *Forced Removals under Apartheid, 1960–1983*

	Eastern Cape	Western Cape	Northern Cape	Orange Free State	Natal	Transvaal	TOTAL
Farms	139,000	—	40,000	250,000	300,000	400,000	1,129,000
Black Spots	19,000*	—	40,000	40,000	115,000	400,000	614,000
Urban Areas	151,100*	32,000	20,000	160,000	17,000	350,000	730,000
Settlements	12,000	—	50,000	50,000*	—	—	112,000
Group Areas	—	409,000[n]	—	14,000	295,000	142,400	860,400
Infrastructural	30,000	—	—	—	18,500	5,000	53,500
Strategic	50,000	—	—	—	—	—	50,000
TOTAL	401,000	441,000	150,000	514,000	745,500	1,297,400	3,548,900

Source: Platzky and Walker, The Surplus People, p. 10. An asterisk means that the reported figure is an estimate. The figure listed for the Western Cape, marked with the symbol "ⁿ," reports forced removals under the Group Areas Act for the entire Cape region. The categories (on the left hand side of the Table) indicate for the most part the type of land from which tenants were removed. "Farms" refers to rented locations on white farms. "Black spots" refer to African freehold land that was acquired before the 1913 Land Act. It typically fell within what was considered white land. "Urban Areas" refers to removal from inner cities. "Settlements" refers to informal shack settlements on the fringes of urban areas. "Group Areas" refers to removals under the Group Areas Act. "Infrastructural" refers to removals with the purpose of infrastructural development including the building of dams, highways, or conservation areas. "Strategic" refers to removals with the purpose of clearing border areas or other plots of land deemed strategically sensitive. See ibid, pp. 30–60.

white countryside, particularly after the rural riots of the 1950s, increased the government's determination to limit and control blacks in non-prescribed white areas."[27]

Another example, illustrating the destructive power wielded under the prerogative state, is the government's bombing of Cosatu House, the national headquarters of the Congress of South African Trade Unions (COSATU), in downtown Johannesburg on May 7, 1987. The bomb blast, ordered after the 1987 general elections had intensified apartheid resistance, is said to have caused the most powerful detonation ever in the Pretoria-Witwatersrand-Vereeniging triangle. The operation was carried out by Eugene de Kock and his infamous *Vlakplaas* unit. Shortly after the Cosatu House incident, Khotso House, the headquarters of the South African Council of Churches (SACC) and the United Democratic Front (UDF), was extensively damaged in Johannesburg on September 1, 1988. Like the Cosatu House bombing, the attack on Khotso House was carried out with the explicit knowledge of P.W. Botha and the State Security Council (SSC). The former state president was implicated in testimonies by Adriaan Vlok, the former Minister of Law and Order, and General Johan van der Merwe, the former head of the SSC, before the Truth and Reconciliation Commission of South Africa. Vlok and van der Merwe, incidentally, were the only former members of government who had applied for amnesty for an unlawful act committed under apartheid. Their testimony confirmed that the government resorted to extrajudicial violence when legal methods proved ineffective in combating the mounting resistance against apartheid. As van der Merwe remarked in his testimony, "We detained about 40,000 people at one specific time and I often said to Vlok this does not lead to anything. We cannot keep them indefinitely."[28] The hope was, van der Merwe notes, that the bombing of Cosatu House "would cause so much disruption that it would give us a breathing space."[29]

Death

The apartheid government used the prerogative state to systematically eliminate regime opponents and potential supporters of banned organizations.

---

[27] Platzky and Walker, *The Surplus People*, p. 31. On the legal foundations, strategies, and implications of forced removals, see also Christina Murray and Catherine O'Regan, eds., *No Place to Rest: Forced Removals and the Law in South Africa* (Cape Town: Oxford University Press, 1990). For an early assessment of the strategic deployment of law by successive apartheid governments, see International Commission of Jurists, *South Africa and the Rule of Law* (Geneva: International Commission of Jurists, 1960).

[28] *Truth and Reconciliation Commission of South Africa Report*, Vol. 2, p. 290.

[29] *Truth and Reconciliation Commission of South Africa Report*, Vol. 2, p. 290. In his testimony, Vlok also summarized a June 1988 interaction with P.W. Botha in which the president, after a regular SSC meeting, returned to the question of how to respond to the Council of Churches and other anti-apartheid organizations: "Mr. Botha [...] told me [...] 'I have tried everything to get them to other insights, nothing helped. We cannot act against the people, you must make that building unusable.'" *Truth and Reconciliation Commission of South Africa Report*, Vol. 2, p. 291.

Elimineer (eliminate), *neutraliseer* (neutralize), *fisiese vernietiging* (physical destruction), *uithaal* (take out), and *aanhouding* (methods other than detention) were among the instructions that its agents received.[30] Fifty pages in the final report of the Truth and Reconciliation Commission are devoted to killings alone. This simple data point is indicative of the extent to which the government relied on elimination proceedings to sustain apartheid. The majority of killings were undertaken extrajudicially.[31] As the Truth and Reconciliation Commission Report states, "[a]s levels of conflict intensified, the security forces came to believe that it was no longer possible to rely on the due process of law and that it was preferable to kill people extra-judicially."[32] The covert operatives and clandestine hit squads were created under the auspices of the prerogative state. The most notorious of these covert units were *Vlakplaas*, segments of the Civil Co-operation Bureau (CCB), and the alleged "Z-squad" of BOSS.

Types of killings ranged from targeted killings (well-known victims include Griffiths and Victoria Mxenge, the PEBCO Three, the Cradock Four, and David Webster); to death after interrogation; killings in ambushes, entrapment killings (the Gugulethu Seven incident was the most publicized of these), and the killing of members of their own forces (e.g., the 1977 murder of the National Party parliamentary candidate, and former government representative at the IMF, Robert Smit and his wife). The planning and administration of the killings was carried out on an ad-hoc-basis by different, separate units within the security forces. Beginning in 1986, the killings were planned, and targets identified, by a structure within the security forces designed particularly for this purpose. This structure, known by its acronym TREWIS, the Counter-Revolutionary Target Centre, initially singled out targets in neighboring countries, but then turned to assisting in the elimination of domestic critics of apartheid.[33] The operation of TREWIS was confirmed in testimonies before the Truth and Reconciliation Commission by the unit's last chairperson, Assistant Commissioner C. J. A. Victor, and General Johan van der Merwe, the head of South Africa's Security Branch in the 1980s.[34]

---

[30] *Truth and Reconciliation Commission of South Africa Report*, Vol. 2, p. 274.
[31] Exceptions include death sentences. Under apartheid, South Africa reportedly had the highest rate of government-sanctioned death in the world.
[32] *Truth and Reconciliation Commission of South Africa Report*, Vol. 2, p. 220.
[33] The acronym reportedly stands for *Teen Rewolusionêre Teiken Sentrum*. Note, however, that a report from the National Intelligence Agency to the Truth Commission disputed the term *teiken* ("target") in the name of the unit. Instead, the report argued, the acronym stood for *Teen Rewolusionêre Inligting Taakspan* ("Counter-Revolutionary Information Taskforce").
[34] *Truth and Reconciliation Commission of South Africa Report*, Vol. 2, p. 275. Note that van der Merwe denies the use of TREWIS outside the country's borders.

Killings at Sharpeville

In a single afternoon on March 21, 1960, 69 Africans died and 186 were wounded in Sharpeville, thirty-five miles outside of Johannesburg.[35] The South African Police were responsible for the dead and the injured, most of them shot in the back. Police had opened fire on demonstrators who had gathered in the Transvaal township.[36] They were casualties of the prerogative state. The victims had gathered for demonstrations as part of a national campaign of defiance for which the Pan Africanist Congress (PAC) under Robert Sobukwe had mobilized, competing with the ANC. The protest had targeted a series of apartheid laws, including the pass laws, the Group Areas Act, and the Separate Representation of Voters Act.

The PAC and the ANC had become rival organizations in the late 1950s. While the ANC eschewed extremism in political action, the PAC promised opportunities to give full and unrestrained vent to political emotion.[37] The "new" defiance campaign planned by the PAC was a response to the premature cessation of the 1952–1953 campaign. The PAC leadership "cherished visions of launching a massive campaign of defiance which would ultimately erupt into a full-scale popular uprising."[38] The apartheid government, relying on the prerogative state, sought to suppress defiance. Paradoxically, the years following the massacre at Sharpeville represented the resurgence of resistance. It was at this time that protest turned to challenge.[39] It was also at this time that the reach of both the normative state and the prerogative state were expanded. In 1953 the Public Safety Act was invoked for the first time, and a state of emergency declared.

Death in Custody

An aspect that only superficially indicates the survival of a normative state was the government's inquest into the death of detainees. Although such inquests were almost always held, they betrayed a serious commitment to legality. "Their results [...] were often inconclusive – generating concern that important evidence had been covered up rather than revealed."[40] The inquest into

---

[35] *Truth and Reconciliation Commission of South Africa Report*, Vol. 3, pp. 528–529. Earlier publications placed the number of deaths at sixty-seven.

[36] For a percipient, classic discussion of the Sharpeville massacre, its causes, course, and consequences, see Gail M. Gerhart, *Black Power in South Africa: The Evolution of an Ideology* (Berkeley: University of California Press, 1978), Chapter 7. More recently, see also Philip Frankel, *An Ordinary Atrocity: Sharpeville and Its Massacre* (New Haven: Yale University Press, 2001).

[37] Gerhart, *Black Power in South Africa*, p. 215.

[38] Gerhart, *Black Power in South Africa*, p. 231.

[39] For the most comprehensive overview of this transformation in the struggle against apartheid, see Thomas G. Karis and Gail M. Gerhart, *From Protest to Challenge: A Documentary History of African Politics in South Africa, 1882–1990, Vol. 5: Nadir and Resurgence, 1964–1979* (Bloomington: Indiana University Press, 1997). The *locus classicus* is Lodge, *Black Politics in South Africa since 1945*. Lodge discusses the massacre at Sharpeville in Chapter 9.

[40] Anthea Jeffery, "The Rule of Law Since 1994," in R. W. Johnson and David Welsh, eds., *Ironic Victory: Liberalism in Post-Liberation South Africa* (Cape Town: Oxford University Press, 1998), p. 75.

Steven Biko's death in detention is a case in point. Biko was detained in the Eastern Cape in September 1977. According to security police, he fell during interrogation in Port Elizabeth and sustained injuries when his head hit a wall. Biko was then driven, naked and unconscious in the back of a police van, to police headquarters in Pretoria, more than one thousand kilometers away. He died soon after his arrival. The hearings of the Truth and Reconciliation Commission revealed that the erstwhile leader of the Black Consciousness Movement did indeed die at the hands of apartheid officials.[41] The example illustrates further the limits of the normative state, and the encroachment of the prerogative state.

The Science of Apartheid
No episode drives home the odious scourge that was the prerogative state as drastically as the case of Dr. Wouter Basson alias "Dr. Death." Basson was the head of South Africa's top-secret program on chemical and biological warfare. An eminent cardiologist and former army brigadier, Basson developed "Project Coast" within the prerogative state. This project constituted one of the most abhorrent aspects of apartheid. Under Basson's leadership, leading scientists at the Project conducted research into such things as a race-specific bacterial weapon, ways to sterilize the black population, and methods to deliberately spread cholera through the water supply.[42] Special hearings before the Truth and Reconciliation Commission in 1998 also revealed that Dr. Death and his scientists had been part of a plot to incapacitate Nelson Mandela before his release from prison. The plot involved the use of thallium, a toxic heavy metal, to permanently impair Mandela's brain function.[43]

Was There a "Third Force"?
The apartheid state showed its prerogative face for the last time in the early 1990s. Escalating levels of violence brought bargaining in apartheid's endgame close to collapse. Yet the violence was qualitatively different from much of the violence in the 1980s. It was no longer targeted, but randomized. Indiscriminate drive-by shootings, massacres in commuter trains, and beer hall attacks generated a general climate of terror, creating extreme fears of victimhood, especially in the townships surrounding Johannesburg. The origins of the violence were not readily apparent. But the increasing number of deaths and the persistent fears threatened to undermine cooperation in apartheid's endgame. This caused some, among them the ANC, the Independent Board of Inquiry, Peace Action (a NGO monitoring human rights), and the Human

---

[41] On Steve Biko and Black Consciousness, see Gerhart, *Black Power in South Africa*.

[42] William Finnegan, "The Poison Keeper," *The New Yorker*, January 15, 2001, pp. 58–75.

[43] Finnegan, "The Poison Keeper," p. 58. For another account of the relationship between bureaucracy and elimination, in another infamous case, see Götz Aly and Karl Heinz Roth, *Die restlose Erfassung: Volkszählen, Identifizieren, Aussondern im Nationalsozialismus* (Frankfurt am Main: Fischer, 2000).

Rights Committee as well as the Johannesburg-based, liberal *Weekly Mail and Guardian* newspaper to ask whether the government was behind the scenes orchestrating a "Third Force" strategy.[44] The government, these sources alleged, was pursuing a two-tier strategy, combining cooperation at the Convention for a Democratic South Africa (CODESA) in Kempton Park with violent confrontation in the townships. Proponents of the "Third Force" theory believed that the apartheid state was clandestinely involved in efforts to derail attempts at solving apartheid's endgame.

Two versions of the theory exist. Adherents of a stronger version believe that the "Third Force" was a continuation of the government's counterinsurgency strategies of the 1980s. They consider the "Third Force" "an integrated network of security force and ex-security operatives, who in conjunction with the IFP, sowed terror in order to undermine the position of the ANC in talks and prepare the way for a victory of a National Party-IFP alliance in the first democratic elections."[45] They believe that the State Security Council, led by de Klerk, was critically involved in overseeing "Third Force" activities. This version of the theory thus lays direct responsibility for the randomized violence in the 1990s at the door of the top echelons of the apartheid regime. It argues that the National Party turned the violence strategically on and off to achieve a bargaining advantage. According to this version of the theory, the objective was to weaken the organizational base of the ANC and interfere with the movement's mobilization for the upcoming elections. Nelson Mandela, an adherent of this version of the "Third Force" theory, talked of an organized and orchestrated strategy of state terrorism. He pulled the ANC out of CODESA in protest shortly after the Boipatong Massacre in the Vaal Triangle in 1993 had led to the death of forty-five ANC supporters.

A weaker version of the theory holds that the government "cultivated an environment where security operatives could act with maximum lawlessness," but that neither de Klerk nor members of his cabinet were involved in the direction of "Third Force" operations.[46] This version of the theory holds that "the clandestine system was consciously designed so ministers could not be held accountable."[47] It sees de Klerk as complicit in fostering violence, but does not indict the former president personally.

Massacre at Boipatong

The linchpin of the "Third Force" theory is the 1992 Boipatong massacre in Sebokeng, which led to the breakdown of bargaining at CODESA. The Truth and Reconciliation Commission found that the massacre had been

---

[44] For an in-depth analysis, see Stephen Ellis, "The Historical Significance of South Africa's Third Force," *Journal of Southern African Studies*, Vol. 24, No. 2 (June 1998), pp. 261–299.

[45] Richard A. Wilson, *The Politics of Truth and Reconciliation in South Africa: Legitimizing the Post-Apartheid State* (Cambridge: Cambridge University Press, 2001), p. 65.

[46] Wilson, *The Politics of Truth and Reconciliation in South Africa*, p. 64.

[47] Wilson, *The Politics of Truth and Reconciliation in South Africa*, p. 64.

executed with the help of police.[48] The massacre revolved around Sebokeng's KwaMadala hostel. On the evening of June 17, 1992, two hundred or so hostel dwellers raped, hacked, stabbed, shot, beat, and disemboweled residents in the near-by Slovo squatter settlement and Boipatong township. Hundreds of homes were looted and destroyed. The rampage left forty-five dead. Most of the perpetrators were identified as Inkatha supporters. In the wake of the massacre, however, eyewitnesses also talked of white men with blackened faces who had been involved in the killing spree. None of these men were identified as policemen, but witnesses, in several statements taken by officials of the Truth and Reconciliation Commission, confirmed the presence of security force vehicles in the area of the attack.[49] Victims of the attacks also confirmed the presence of armed white men during the massacre.[50] Tension in Sebokeng had been building for some time before the massacre. Zulu-speaking residents in the township had begun gravitating toward the Inkatha-stronghold when tensions between the ANC and Buthelezi's Inkatha intensified on the Reef.

In the aftermath of the massacre, several investigations into the killings were undertaken. The first was the Harms Commission ("Commission of Inquiry into Certain Alleged Murders"), chaired by the Hon. L. T. C. Harms. Its report, presented in 1990, found no evidence of "Third Force" activity.[51] It was followed by the Goldstone Commission ("Commission of Inquiry Regarding the Prevention of Public Violence and Intimidation," 1992–1994), led by Justice Richard Goldstone, and, in 1994, a criminal investigation that led to the conviction of seventeen residents of Sebokeng's KwaMadala hostel of murder for their involvement in the killings.

The work of the Goldstone Commission, created by the Prevention of Public Violence and Intimidation Act, constitutes to this day the most thorough *official* investigation into the causes of transitional violence in South Africa.[52] During its three-year tenure, the Commission submitted to the President of South Africa forty-seven substantive reports of varying length (from three to fifty-three pages) into discrete aspects of collective violence, from violence in the Taxi industry to train violence to violence perpetrated in hostels.[53]

---

[48] *Truth and Reconciliation Commission Report*, Vol. 3, pp. 683–689. For a less far-reaching finding, see *Truth and Reconciliation Commission Report*, Vol. 2, pp. 604–605.

[49] *Truth and Reconciliation Commission Report*, Vol. 3, p. 685, Fn. 45.

[50] *Truth and Reconciliation Commission Report*, Vol. 3, p. 686.

[51] However, later hearings of the Truth and Reconciliation Commission established that several witnesses who appeared before the Harms Commission had been instructed by police to lie. See Wilson, *The Politics of Truth and Reconciliation in South Africa*, p. 237, Fn. 8.

[52] Act 139 of 1991.

[53] See, for example, Commission of Inquiry Regarding the Prevention of Public Violence and Intimidation, *Fifth Interim Report on Taxi Violence*, July 26, 1993; idem., *Final Report into [sic] Train Violence*, May 6, 1993; and idem., *Interim Report on the Violence in Hostels*, September 21, 1992. In 2007, all of the Goldstone Commission's 47 reports were made available online by the Human Rights Institute of South Africa. See http://www.hurisa.org.za/Goldstone.htm.

The first concrete evidence of "Third Force" activities surfaced in November 1992 when the Goldstone Commission raided the offices of Africa Risk Analysis Consultants, the Pretoria front company that housed the Directorate Covert Collection of the government's Military Intelligence.[54] At a press conference, Richard Goldstone, the Commission's chairman, announced that the evidence recovered during the raid demonstrated that elements of the SADF were involved in illegal activities. In response, President de Klerk appointed Lieutenant-General Pierre Steyn, the Chief of Defence Staff, to head an investigation into the allegations made by Goldstone and his investigators. The Steyn investigation, as it is commonly known, has been praised for its evenhandedness. In a preliminary oral report to de Klerk on December 18, 1992, Steyn apparently concluded that elements of the SADF "had been involved in, and in certain circumstances were still involved in, illegal and unauthorised activities which could be prejudicial to the security, interests and well-being of the state."[55] The activities of which Steyn spoke reportedly ranged from SADF involvement in train killings to collaboration with the IFP.[56] As far as the orchestration of the violence was concerned, Steyn added that "some members of the senior command structure were largely caught up in the momentum of activities of the past [...] while others were possibly promoting their own agenda."[57] Steyn's findings eventually led to the dismissal of nearly two dozen officers: sixteen SADF staff, including two generals and four brigadiers, were forced into compulsory retirement; seven others were placed on compulsory leave.

Although the Goldstone Commission was careful (some might say timid) in its conclusions – undoubtedly as a result of the limits of its investigative apparatus, and thus data, and the sensitivity of the subject matter – in a subsequent report, dated March 18, 1994, it declared persuasive much of the information furnished by a police officer of the South African Police, referred to as "Q," regarding the orchestration of "Third Force" activities by Unit C1 (later C10) at *Vlakpaas*, commandeered by Colonel Eugene de Kock. Although the Goldstone Commission insisted that "[t]he evidence, much of it strong, remains *prima facie* until proven by normal judicial processes," it acknowledged the existence of a "Third Force" in South Africa.[58]

Then came the Truth and Reconciliation Commission. The TRC concluded its inquiry into the Boipatong Massacre with the following, seemingly incontrovertible finding:

---

[54] I am very grateful to Richard Goldstone for reminding me of his Commission's 1992 raid on military intelligence, and the implications thereof.

[55] As quoted by Dave Stewart, Executive Director of the FW de Klerk Foundation, in a piece entitled "The Steyn Investigation." The piece, published on May 7, 2006, is available for download at www.fwdklerk.org.za.

[56] Stewart, "The Steyn Investigation."

[57] Stewart, "The Steyn Investigation."

[58] Commission of Inquiry Regarding the Prevention of Public Violence and Intimidation, *Interim Report on Criminal Political Violence by Elements within the South African Police, the KwaZulu Police and the Inkatha Freedom Party*, March 18, 1994, paragraph 26.1.

The Commission finds the KwaMadala residents together with the SAP [South African Police Service] responsible for the massacre, which resulted in the deaths of forty-five people and the injury of twenty-two others. The Commission finds the Commissioner of Police, the Minister of Law and Order and the IFP responsible for the Commission of Gross Human Rights Violations.[59]

The Boipatong Massacre has been the cornerstone of the "Third Force" theory. The Truth and Reconciliation Commission presented concrete evidence for "Third Force" involvement in violence. The "Third Force" theory appeared confirmed. Then in November 2000, in an extraordinary turn of events, the Truth and Reconciliation Commission's Amnesty Committee *repudiated* the Commission's findings concerning the Boipatong massacre. In its ruling, the Amnesty Committee found that the Boipatong massacre had been planned and executed *without* any police involvement, dealing a substantial blow to the "Third Force" theory.[60] The Amnesty Committee proceeded to name thirteen amnesty applicants associated with the IFP as the principal perpetrators of the massacre. This extraordinary conclusion supports the findings of earlier investigations that the Truth and Reconciliation Commission had discarded, namely, the findings of the Goldstone Commission and the subsequent criminal investigation leading to the conviction of seventeen residents of Sebokeng's KwaMadala hostel of murder for their involvement in the killings.

What then was the "Third Force"? Answers to this question have relevance for the question of the balance between the prerogative and normative halves of the dual apartheid state. In the 2003 codicil to its report, the TRC attempted to bridge the interpretative divide that had emerged within the organization concerning the massacre at Boipatong, and thus the existence of a "Third Force," suggesting that the Amnesty Committee left "open the possibility of security force complicity: it acknowledged the victims' allegations, while accepting that there was no evidence to connect the amnesty applicants with them."[61] This notwithstanding, at present comparatively little evidence has surfaced regarding the operations and administration of the "Third Force," and may forever lie beyond the reach of scholarship. It has certainly escaped the reach of the TRC: "While the involvement of security force individuals and structures in 'Third Force' violence was to some degree corroborated, the quality and quantity of available evidence, whilst significant, is generally thin. No detailed or focused investigations were initiated; few amnesty applications were received, and lines of command and accountability were not established."[62]

---

[59] *Truth and Reconciliation Commission Report*, Vol. 3, pp. 689–690.

[60] On the ruling of the Truth and Reconciliation Commission's Amnesty Committee, see Anthea Jeffery, "Truth Commission Repudiated by Its Own Amnesty Committee," News Release, South African Institute of Race Relations, November 30, 2000, available at http://www.sairr.org.za/wsc/pstory.htx?storyID=195.

[61] Truth and Reconciliation Commission of South Africa, *Truth and Reconciliation Commission of South Africa Report*, Vol. 6 (Cape Town: Juta, 2003), p. 585.

[62] Truth and Reconciliation Commission of South Africa, *Truth and Reconciliation Commission of South Africa Report*, Vol. 6 (Cape Town: Juta, 2003), pp. 587–588.

The lack of comprehensive evidence concerning "Third Force" activities, however, does not mean that the prerogative state was not underwriting "counterinsurgency strategies" during apartheid's endgame. Notes the TRC,

while little evidence exists of a centrally directed, coherent or formally constituted "Third Force," a network of security and ex-security force operatives, frequently acting in conjunction with right-wing elements and/or sectors of the IFP, was involved in actions that could be construed as fomenting violence and which resulted in gross human rights violations, including random and target killings.[63]

More specifically,

It is now known that President de Klerk approved a Strategic Communication (Stratcom) propaganda project in 1990, which included financial support by the SAP for Inkatha. In July 1991, the existence of a secret police project to fund Inkatha was revealed in the media. ... It is also evident from evidence presented at the Commission that elements in both the police and the IFP continued to collude with one another throughout the negotiation period, and that the police, mainly through Vlakplaas operatives, supplied considerable amounts of weaponry to the IFP during the 1990s.[64]

Aside from what has become known as "Inkathagate," consider also the raid that a parachute brigade of the military Special Forces carried out on Umtata, Transkei, in October 1993. In the raid, five youths were killed. The Truth and Reconciliation Commission found conclusive evidence that the State Security Council had authorized the raid. The meeting at which the order to "neutralize the target" was given was attended by de Klerk, as well as cabinet ministers Kriel, Coetsee, Pik Botha, and Georg Meiring, head of the South African Defense Force (SADF).[65] These, and related, aspects of the apartheid state were subversive of democracy, not supportive of it.[66] Law frequently functioned as a sword in this period, providing the security forces with a *carte blanche*:

The police and military long enjoyed immunity from civil and criminal proceedings when suppressing terrorism or internal disorder, or maintaining public safety. During the state of emergency in the 1980s the area of indemnity was further widened to include any act of a state employee (or with his approval of a private citizen) performed with the intention of maintaining public order. Additional safeguards against civil liability were provided by the Defence and Police Acts, both of which required notice of any civil action against the military or police to be received by the correct official within five months of the alleged misdeed. Legal accountability was

---

[63] Truth and Reconciliation Commission of South Africa, *Truth and Reconciliation Commission of South Africa Report*, Vol. 6 (Cape Town: Juta, 2003), p. 584.

[64] Truth and Reconciliation Commission of South Africa, *Truth and Reconciliation Commission of South Africa Report*, Vol. 6 (Cape Town: Juta, 2003), pp. 582–583.

[65] *Truth and Reconciliation Commission Report*, Vol. 2, pp. 600–602.

[66] On subversive states in democratization, with reference to the former Soviet Union, see Valerie Bunce, *Subversive Institutions: The Design and the Destruction of Socialism and the State* (Cambridge: Cambridge University Press, 1999).

attenuated as much by loosening the controls of law as by exempting people from its operation.[67]

Looking back, this disregard for the law is nowhere more palpable than in the following, revealing exchange between Colonel P. J. Goosen, who subsequently served as Deputy Commissioner of Police, and Sydney Kentridge during the Biko inquest regarding the right of the former to keep a detainee in chains for forty-eight hours:

GOOSEN: I have the full power to do it. Prisoners could attempt suicide or escape.

KENTRIDGE: Let's have an honest answer – where did you get your powers?

GOOSEN: It is my power.

KENTRIDGE: Are you people above the law?

GOOSEN: I have full powers to ensure a man's safety.

KENTRIDGE: I am asking for the statute.

GOOSEN: We don't work under statutes.

KENTRIDGE: Thank you very much. That is what we have always suspected.[68]

Here the tension between the prerogative state and the normative state are powerfully evident. "One of the problems of enduring interest raised by the unhappy history of the South African state in the twentieth century," observes Martin Chanock, "has been the existence of a legal system clearly based on the liberal forms of law at the heart of a racist and oppressive state."[69] The prerogative state half of the dual state has been described above. The analysis now turns to the normative state, the limits that it imposed on wanton rule, and the imprint that it left on the institutional landscape.

THE NORMATIVE STATE

Law was sword *and* shield in South Africa. "Because the regime used legal institutions to construct and administer apartheid, it was vulnerable to legal contestation. All this helps to explain why the opposition might choose law strategically."[70] This section analyzes the limits of the prerogative state and shows under what conditions law was an instrument not merely of oppression, but also of resistance. The discussion focuses on the apartheid state as a normative state. It explores the characteristics of this other, more benign half of the dual state. As

[67] Peter Parker and Joyce Mokhesi-Parker, *In the Shadow of Sharpeville: Apartheid and Criminal Justice* (New York: New York University Press, 1998), p. 56.

[68] As quoted in Hilda Bernstein, *No. 46: Steve Biko* (London: International Defence and Aid Fund, 1978), p. 53.

[69] Chanock, *The Making of South African Legal Culture 1902–1936*, p. 20.

[70] Richard L. Abel, *Politics by Other Means: Law in the Struggle Against Apartheid* (London: Routledge, 1995), p. 3.

two leading lawyers from South Africa once put it: "Law is of the warp and woof of social life, and so far from being concerned with a narrowly circumscribed area, is all pervasive."[71] Where a tradition of it can be discerned, it is "not only concerned with the pathology of society, but with its physiology as well."[72]

Heribert Adam stressed the limits of the prerogative state in the 1970s. While Adam attributed these limits to the regime's physical inability to extend the repressive machinery further across the country's population, he also highlighted the normative constraints placed on the prerogative state.[73] As Adam, together with Kogila Moodley, remarked several years later, "in order to solicit compliance and ensure in-group cohesion, the ethnic state must exercise power legally. Arbitrary terror would increase the costs of coercion and motivate more resistance. Legality thus becomes a substitute for legitimacy. The separation of legality from legitimacy makes it possible to rule illegitimately with the aid of law. Divorced from substantive ideals with universal content, normative regularity becomes a reified faith in procedures . . ."[74]

A turning point was the white response to the killing of Steve Biko, discussed earlier, in particular reactions to it in sections of the Afrikaner press. For the first time, some Afrikaner journalists openly criticized the government on moral grounds. An editorial in *Rapport* exposed something of a rift in Afrikanerdom, caused by Biko's death, more generally: "It is not only opponents of the Government who have grave misgivings about detention without trial and the dimensions it has assumed. . . . [I]t is obvious that one cannot keep on locking up people one after the other."[75] This apparent cleavage cutting through Afrikanerdom underlines how important the legal way of doing things had become in South Africa. Harking back to the beginning of legal culture in the late nineteenth and early twentieth century, Chanock observes that,

even given the extremely high level of intra-white political violence – of strikes, civil war, treason and rebellion – a culture of "constitutionalism" was successfully maintained among and for whites. Limited sanctions in terms of sentences; generous amnesties for political offenders; the maintenance of a very broad arena for freedom of speech and political activity; and the strict patrolling of the limits of the application of statutes which limited freedoms are all features of the polity of the white part of the state. Power was limited to protect white democracy, but not limited where Africans (and Asians) were concerned.[76]

---

[71] Hahlo and Kahn, *The South African Legal System and Its Background*, p. 1.

[72] Hahlo and Kahn, *The South African Legal System and Its Background*, p. 1.

[73] "A mere cynical use of power without the perceptions of a just cause would alienate important sections of Afrikanerdom from the technocrats and ultimately destroy the delicate unity. In this respect, the historical allegiance to a moral heritage of Western values acts as a brake on the unrestrained exercise of coercion in the most ruthless manner." Heribert Adam, "Perspectives in the Literature: A Critical Evaluation," in Heribert Adam and Hermann Giliomee, eds., *The Rise and Crisis of Afrikaner Power* (Cape Town: David Philip, [1979] 1983), p. 29.

[74] Adam and Moodley, *South Africa Without Apartheid*, p. 129.

[75] *Rapport*, February 5, 1978, as cited in Adam, "Perspectives in the Literature," p. 29.

[76] Chanock, *The Making of South African Legal Culture 1902–1936*, p. 41.

The legal way of doing things, the language of law, was indispensable in the cooperative resolution of apartheid's endgame. It proved a *useful* and *usable* legacy of the apartheid state. Let us consider some effects of this legacy in the periods of segregation and apartheid. The discussion that follows draws on empirical examples from different stages of state formation, focusing on important legal cases, beginning with the first stage.[77]

Tsewu v. Registrar of Deeds and the Property of Land 1905

After their exit from the Cape, the *voortrekkers* erected the Transvaal Republic (see Stage I). In the Transvaal, as well as the Orange Free State, sharecropping was widespread in agriculture. Africans resided on land annexed by whites. In the typical sharecropping arrangement, the white farmer relied on the African tenant for the provision of essential supplies. The tenants would provide the oxen for ploughing, and also often the seeds and the plough. White farmers were dependent on black tenants for their labor as well as their resources. The feudal relationship between landlord and peasant was effectively *reversed* in rural South Africa. The individual black sharecropper was able to live a life fairly independent from the landholding farmer. Notwithstanding the crucial economic role of black laborers in agriculture, their entrepreneurial spirit was discouraged. Early republican law prohibited the purchase of land by Africans. Property rights to land were reserved for whites. As Kas Maine, the ordinary hero in Charles van Onselen's masterful account of race relations in rural South Africa, observes: "The seed is mine. The ploughshare is mine. The span of oxen is mine. Everything is mine. Only the land is theirs."[78] Yet African laborers demanded the right to buy land, and to register it in their own names. To break out of their dependent, inferior relationship vis-à-vis white farmers, African sharecroppers mobilized increasing pressure in favor of equal property rights.[79] The case of *Tsewu v.*

[77] Chanock, *The Making of South African Legal Culture 1902–1936*, p. 23. Chanock's definition of a legal culture is similar to my conceptualization provided in Chapter 1: "A legal culture consists of a set of assumptions, a way of doing things, a repertoire of language, of legal forms and institutional practices." Chanock, *The Making of South African Legal Culture 1902–1936*, p. 23. I illustrate the legacies of law, this shared mental model, in some detail in Chapter 7. For the theoretical background, see Chapter 3.

[78] Charles van Onselen, *The Seed is Mine: The Life of Kas Maine, A South African Sharecropper 1894–1985* (New York: Hill and Wang, 1996), p. xvii. Van Onselen creates an immediate, personal sense of the relationship between race and agriculture in twentieth century South Africa. His study opens with these memorable words: "This is a biography of a man, who, if one went by the official record alone, never was. It is the story of a family who have no documentary existence, of farming folk who lived out their lives in a part of South Africa that few people loved, in a century that the country will always want to forget." Van Onselen, *The Seed is Mine*, p. 3.

[79] The analysis of the law of the land, and the dynamics of rural relations, draws heavily on Martin Chanock's comprehensive discussion in *The Making of South African Legal Culture 1902–1936*, pp. 361–405. For a very good discussion of rural agriculture, rural life, and apartheid, see Beinart, *Twentieth-Century South Africa*, Chapters 1 and 2.

Registrar of Deeds revolves around the attempt of an African purchaser to register land in his name.[80] The Registrar of Deeds refused to register the title. In 1905, the case came to be heard by the Transvaal Supreme Court. Departing from Transvaal law, the Court, under the stewardship of Sir James Rose-Innes, invoked the common law and overturned the registrar's refusal. The Court held that Africans were bearers of ordinary economic rights under the common law, establishing a controversial, liberal law of property rights. Politics, and all white political parties, reacted vehemently against the liberal interpretation of the right of property, calling for an ordinance to reverse the court's decision. Britain's Secretary of State vetoed this ordinance. The veto upheld the African right to purchasing landed property – albeit only for a short time.

The impending equality of bargaining power between landlord and laborer raised fears of economic dependency and victimhood among rural whites. Demands for government intervention into rural market relations began mounting in the Transvaal and the Free State.[81] The small victory of the normative state in *Tsewu v. Registrar of Deeds* became void with the adoption of the 1913 Land Act (see Stage III). The Land Act did away with the bargaining power that republican practice had granted African sharecroppers. It stipulated that 77 percent of the country's land was reserved for private ownership by whites (individuals or companies), 13 percent was declared state land, and the remainder demarcated for the sole purpose of black occupation.[82] The Land Act illustrates the limits of the normative state. Unlike its behavior in *Tsewu*, the government this time "refused to give any response or comfort to African representations on the Land Act."[83]

Whittaker v. Roos and Bateman 1912

Shortly after the consummation of the Union by the four colonies, law constrained power. Whittaker and Morant, two workers who had been arrested during unrest on the Reef, stood accused of placing dynamite on tram tracks. For six weeks before their trial, they were held in solitary confinement without access to legal counsel. After their acquittal, the two men brought charges against the Prisons Department. Yet Sir John Wessels, then the Judge President of the Transvaal Supreme Court, dismissed the case. Wessels suggested that the

---

[80] *Tsewu v. Registrar of Deeds* 1905 TS 130.
[81] These demands were also fueled by the speculation for land by local merchants, land companies, and foreign capitalists. Rural indebtedness, for example, was a major factor of white insecurity, and a major cause of loss of land to richer farmers or other agents.
[82] The Land Act stipulated that only whites, but not blacks, could legally lease land. It restructured market relations, and as such political relations between settlers and the indigenous population. A large number of black tenants had to choose between unequal labor tenancy or the surrender of their stock and capital reserves. Prior to the passage of the Land Act, both Botha and Hertzog had lobbied for the replacement of blacks with poor whites in an attempt to solve the poor white problem. Beinart, *Twentieth-Century South Africa*, p. 10.
[83] Chanock, *The Making of South African Legal Culture 1902–1936*, p. 368.

plaintiffs were "not persons with whom we ought to sympathise."[84] In *Whittaker v. Roos and Bateman*, the Appellate Division overturned Wessels' decision, strongly rebuking his judgment as well as the government.[85] Sir James and the five-member court established a case of unlawful abuse of authority on the government's part, and found in favor of the plaintiffs. Punishment and deprivation of rights, the court ruled, was possible only *after* the guilt of a person had been established by a court of law. Martin Chanock, who reports the case, summarizes its significance: "It was the occasion for a very strongly worded attempt to establish a rule of law in a new state by reigning in the abuse of powers by state officials. Its dicta would live on, sometimes invoked, sometimes not."[86]

Miners and Workers 1923

Job reservation laws formed a cornerstone of apartheid. Frequently, these laws were used to appease workers after militant labor strikes. They served as concessions to segments of white labor, particularly those fearful of black competition. In the nineteenth century, statutory color bars were first included in mining regulations to reserve certain jobs for "scheduled persons."[87] Scheduled persons were those in possession of "a certificate of competence." These long-standing, discriminatory regulations were consolidated in an appended schedule to the Mines and Works Act of 1911.[88] This Act specifically barred "coloured persons" from obtaining certificates of competence in the two Afrikaner republics, the Transvaal and the Orange Free State. Yet, to the credit of the normative state, the color bar provisions enshrining job reservation for whites in the Mines and Works Act were ruled invalid by the courts in 1923. Although the Pact government, the ruling coalition government of Nationalist and Labor Party, restored the racial division of labor a few years later under the Mines and Works Amendment Act,[89] the episode illustrates the partial independence of the judiciary in preapartheid South Africa. It lends support to the argument developed in this book that the state in South Africa was of a dual nature. It was repressive, but not only so. At times, legal norms and procedures prevailed over politics and ideology.

Harris v. Minister of the Interior 1952

The National Party government, once in power, dismantled the structures created by Jan Smut's United Party government to cater to Africans, Asians, and "Coloureds." Although the mechanisms for contestation and participation inherent in Smut's unpopular 1946 package deal had been very limited in any

---

[84] Chanock, *The Making of South African Legal Culture 1902–1936*, p. 481.
[85] *Whittaker v. Roos and Bateman* 1912 AD 92.
[86] Chanock, *The Making of South African Legal Culture 1902–1936*, pp. 481–482.
[87] Davies, O'Meara, and Dlamini, *The Struggle for South Africa*, Vol. 1, pp. 174–175.
[88] Act 12 of 1911.
[89] Act 25 of 1926.

event, the Nationalists felt that the inclusion of "blacks" (meaning Africans, Indians, and "Coloureds") on whatever level was detrimental to white supremacy. The government therefore insisted on also removing "coloured" voters in the Cape region from the voters' roll.[90] The importance of law in the making of apartheid is illustrated by the "coloured vote episode," which demonstrates the interaction of the prerogative and normative halves of the dual apartheid state.

In 1951, the NP legislative majority passed an ordinary act of parliament to remove "Coloureds" from South Africa's common voter rolls.[91] A group of "coloured voters" challenged this Separate Representation of Voters Act in a court of law. The Appellate Division of the Supreme Court, South Africa's highest court, ruled that the law was indeed in violation of the Constitution. In *Harris v. Minister of the Interior* (the *Vote* case, 1952), the Appellate Division held that the Constitution demanded that the type of legislation in question be passed with a two-thirds majority in a *joint* sitting of both the lower and upper houses of Parliament.[92] Instead, the NP had passed the bill with simple majorities in the lower and upper house, sitting separately, and the Governor-General had signed the bill. The court held that the earlier decision *Ndlwana v. Hofmeyr*[93] had been wrongly decided. In its unanimous decision, the Appellate Division ruled that "Parliament" had not functioned as "Parliament" within the meaning of the South Africa Constitution Act.[94] In response to the

---

[90] For an overview of the case, and the history surrounding it, see T. R. H. Davenport, *South Africa: A Modern History*, Fourth Edition (London: Macmillan, 1991), pp. 327–332; 342–345.

[91] The original purpose of Sections 35 and 137 of the South Africa Act of 1909 was to guarantee the suffrage of black and "coloured" voters in the Cape Province. Section 152 of the Act required a two-thirds majority in a joint sitting of both houses to amend or repeal the provisions. See, for example, J. D. van der Vyver, "Rigidity and Flexibility in Constitutions: The Judiciary, the Rule of Law and Constitutional Amendment," in John A. Benyon, ed., *Constitutional Change in South Africa* (Pietermaritzburg: University of Natal Press, 1978), p. 64.

[92] *Harris v. Minister of the Interior* 1952 (2) SA 428 (A). For brief commentary, see C. F. Forsyth, *In Danger for their Talents: A Study of the Appellate Division of the Supreme Court of South Africa 1950–80* (Cape Town: Juta, 1985), pp. 63–67.

[93] *Ndlwana v. Hofmeyr N.O.* 1937 AD 229.

[94] To appreciate the importance of the case, *Minister of the Interior v. Harris* (the *High Court of Parliament* case, 1952) must be read in conjunction with *Ndlwana v. Hofmeyr N.O.* 1937 AD 229. In 1936, the Representation of Natives Act had removed Africans from the common voter rolls in the Cape Province. It was a precursor to the legislative action in 1951. After the adoption of the Act of 1936, an African voter challenged its constitutionality before the Supreme Court. The challenge revolved around the claim that the entrenched clauses of the 1909 South Africa Act rendered the use of the unicameral procedure to affect changes to these clauses unlawful. The Appellate Division, however, ruled that the entrenched clauses had *lost* their legal relevance with the passage of the 1931 Statute of Westminster, which provided that no act of British Parliament would extend to a Dominion of the Commonwealth without consent of this dominion. In short, the court ruled that the achievement of sovereign statehood rendered null and void stipulations that had been reached under the Colonial Laws Validity Act, including the agreement entrenched in section 35 of the 1909 Constitution that allowed the Cape to retain the right to vote for Africans and "Coloureds." For an elaboration of the constitutional background, the relevance of the Statute of Westminster of 1931 and its relation to the so-called entrenched sections or clauses of the South African Constitution, see Dugard, *Human Rights and the South African Legal Order*, pp. 25–34.

Supreme Court ruling, the NP majority in Parliament passed, by ordinary procedure, the High Court of Parliament Act.[95] By so doing, it proclaimed itself a High Court, granting itself the power to review and override any judgment of the Appellate Division invalidating an Act of Parliament. Reviewing the passed legislation, the five appellate judges on the Supreme Court ruled that that act, too, was in violation of the Constitution. In *Minister of the Interior v. Harris* (the *High Court of Parliament* case, 1952), the Supreme Court stated (in five separate judgments) that the new High Court was, in essence, Parliament under another name.[96] It further ruled that the entrenched sections of the Constitution envisaged judicial protection by a proper court of law, and that legislation removing this protection could not be passed by ordinary procedure.

In 1955 and 1956, the NP majority in Parliament circumvented the Supreme Court's objections with three key legislative acts. The first act enlarged the Senate by nominating additional members, guaranteeing the NP a two-thirds majority in any future joint sittings of Parliament. The second act increased the number of appellate judges on the Supreme Court from five to eleven.[97] The third act, passed with a two-thirds majority in a joint sitting (thanks to the packed Senate), revalidated the 1951 act to remove "Coloureds" from the voter rolls and, furthermore, denied the courts the power of judicial review. The enlarged Appellate Division of the Supreme Court certified the passed legislation as valid.[98] Only Justice Oliver Schreiner, whose name today appropriately adorns the School of Law at the University of the Witwatersrand, entered a dissent, bravely challenging the eleven members in the majority.

This episode in the formative years of apartheid illustrates well the way in which legal rules, norms, and procedures served the making of apartheid. The episode, however, *also* indicates how legal rules, norms, and procedures constrained the making of apartheid. *Harris v. Minister of the Interior* (the *Vote* case, 1952) and *Minister of the Interior v. Harris* (the *High Court of Parliament* case, 1952) are generally considered landmark decisions in defense of civil liberties. The Appellate Division, under Chief Justice Albert van der Sandt Centlivres (1950–1956), took a principled stand against apartheid. It constrained power by law. Erwin N. Griswold, the former Dean of Harvard Law School, praised the first Harris case (the *Vote* case) as "a great judgment, deserving to rank with the best work of the judges who have contributed to the field of constitutional law."[99] He added that "it would not be well to

---

[95] Act 35 of 1952.

[96] *Minister of the Interior v. Harris* 1952 (4) SA 769 (A). For brief commentary, see Forsyth, *In Danger for their Talents*, pp. 67–70.

[97] The Appellate Division Quorum Act (1955) also provided that *all* eleven judges had to judge cases to determine the validity of a statute.

[98] This paragraph draws on Thompson, *A History of South Africa*, pp. 190–191.

[99] Erwin N. Griswold, "The 'Coloured Vote Case' in South Africa," *Harvard Law Review*, Vol. 65 (1952), p. 1374. See also idem., "The Demise of the High Court of Parliament in South Africa," *Harvard Law Review*, Vol. 66 (1952), pp. 864–875.

underestimate the contribution to history which has been made by the firm wisdom of courageous judges."[100] Griswold in some ways anticipated the principal empirical argument of this book, spelled out fully in the next two chapters, namely that it would be ill advised to underestimate the institutional legacy of the normative state in South Africa. *Harris v. Minister of the Interior* (the *Vote* case, 1952), *Minister of the Interior v. Harris* (the *High Court of Parliament* case, 1952), and other historical traces of the normative state carried unexpected, institutional influence in apartheid's endgame. They held, or so I shall argue, interacting agents back from the brink of confrontation, tying them together in iterated interactions. What the "coloured vote episode" illustrates is that law mattered in white South Africa. The making of apartheid was largely rule-governed. Rules had, for the most part, predictable consequences. But the existence of legal rules, as the next legal case illustrates, was also meaningful to the oppressed in the struggle against apartheid.

R. v. Adams and Others 1959

Nelson Mandela was imprisoned on December 5, 1956. The warrant for his arrest alleged *hoogveraad* (high treason). Mandela was accused along with 156 other leaders of the African resistance, many of them charged with violations under the Suppression of Communism Act. It was the government's attempt to smash the ANC legally, "by linking it with alleged communist designs to overthrow the state."[101] It was the beginning of a marathon trial before a special Criminal Court that ended with an apartheid defeat.

In October 1958 the original indictments against the defendants were withdrawn. In its stead, the prosecution brought charges against thirty of the accused. The remaining men and women were committed to trial in August 1959.[102] This time the indictment spoke of a conspiracy to overthrow the state by violence and the intent to substitute it with a "radically and fundamentally different form of state."[103] After long interactions in court over a period of four and a half years, Judge Frans Lourens Herman Rumpff (who became Chief Justice of the Supreme Court's Appellate Division in 1974) delivered the verdict of the three-judge panel on March 29, 1961. Judge Rumpff found support for several allegations made by the prosecution: that the ANC had been active to replace the government; that it had relied on illegal means of protest in the Defiance Campaign; that certain ANC leaders had advocated violence; and that the ANC was home to left-wing radicalism. Then Rumpff continued with the following words:

On all the evidence presented to this court and on our finding of fact it is impossible for this court to come to the conclusion that the African National Congress had acquired or

---

[100] Griswold, "The 'Coloured Vote Case' in South Africa," p. 1374.
[101] Gerhart, *Black Power in South Africa*, p. 167.
[102] *R. v. Adams and Others* 1959 (3) SA 753 (AD).
[103] The quotation is from the final verdict, as quoted in Mandela, *Long Walk to Freedom*, p. 247.

adopted a policy to overthrow the state by violence, that is, in the sense that the masses had to be prepared or conditioned to commit direct acts of violence against the state.[104]

Mandela's assessment of the judges further illustrates the principal argument of this study. Mandela commended Rumpff, Kennedy, and Bekker as "exemplars of human decency under adversity."[105] In Mandela's view, "in the end an essential fairness dominated" the judgment.[106] Trials in South Africa thus were "not merely show trials with predetermined outcomes, where the intention was merely to discredit the accused regardless of procedures, rules, and facts. Nor were the trials a mere facade masking naked oppression, designed to beguile both the people inside the country and observers beyond South Africa's borders. The South African legal system was one recognizable to the western and common law mind. In a courtroom where a case had to be made out, and where the accused had the right to answer and to cross-examine their accuser before well-trained judges, there was always the chance of an acquittal."[107]

Incorporated Law Society, Transvaal v. Mandela 1954

It was a proud time for the normative state. Just two years before his arrest on treason charges, Mandela had faced disbarment. The South African Law Society had demanded his removal from the roll of attorneys. White lawyers had become suspicious of this illustrious member who just received a suspended sentence for his involvement in the Defiance Campaign. They wanted to be rid off him. Defended by two respected white lawyers, Mandela won the case. Judge Ramsbottom upheld the argument of the defense, and ordered the Law Society to pay costs. It is worthwhile to quote verbatim from Rambottom's principled refusal (Roper J concurring) to allow the plaintiff's counsel to portray Mandela as dishonorable for his resistance to apartheid:

The sole question that the Court has to decide is whether the facts which have been put before us and on which the respondent was convicted show him to be of such character that he is not worthy to remain in the ranks of an honourable profession. To that question there can, in my opinion, be only one answer. Nothing has been put before us which suggests in the slightest degree that the respondent has been guilty of conducts of a dishonest, disgraceful, or dishonourable kind; nothing that he has done reflects upon his character or shows him to be unworthy to remain in the ranks of an honourable profession. In advocating the plan of action, the respondent was obviously motivated by a desire to serve his fellow non-Europeans. The intention was to bring about the repeal of certain laws which the respondent regarded as unjust. The method of producing that result which the respondent advocated is unlawful, and by advocating

---

[104] As quoted in Mandela, *Long Walk to Freedom*, p. 247.
[105] Mandela, *Long Walk to Freedom*, p. 249.
[106] Mandela, *Long Walk to Freedom*, p. 249.
[107] Michael Lobban, *White Man's Justice: South African Political Trials in the Black Consciousness Era* (Oxford: Clarendon Press, 1996), pp. 8–9.

that method the respondent contravened the statute; for that offence he has been punished. But his offence was *not* of a "personally disgraceful character", and there is nothing in his conduct which, in my judgment, renders him unfit to be an attorney.[108]

Ramsbottom's brave *obiter dictum* bespeaks the essence of South Africa's legal tradition. Yet the times were changing. In May 1964, judgment was passed in the Rivonia Trial on six Africans, one Indian, and one white, among them Nelson Mandela. Fifteen months after his acquittal in the Treason Trial, Mandela was back in the dock, this time before the Supreme Court.[109] He and ten others were held under the new ninety-day detention law, enacted in 1963. The charges were sabotage and conspiracy. Throughout the proceedings, at least seven nations were reported to have urged the apartheid government to exercise clemency.[110] The trial is illustrative of the *limits* of the normative state. Nelson Mandela, Walter Sisulu and six other leaders of *Umkhonto we Sizwe* ("the Spear of the Nation") – the recently established, armed wing of the ANC – were sentenced to life imprisonment. The Treason Trial defended the rule of law; the Rivonia Trial marked its limits.

Roussouw v. Sachs 1964

Under Chief Justice L. C. Steyn (1959–1971), the Appellate Division delivered with *Rossouw v. Sachs* one of the most controversial judgments of the 1950s and 1960s.[111] The case was one "in which the freedom of judicial choice was the greatest and the declaration of judicial policy the clearest."[112] The case involved, interestingly, a sitting judge of South Africa's present Constitutional Court, Justice Albie Sachs. Around the time of the decision, Sachs was a Cape Town advocate. He was detained under the government's ninety-day detention law. To pass his time in jail, Sachs requested reading and writing material. This was the beginning of *Rossouw v. Sachs*.

At the heart of the case was the question of whether Act 37 of 1963, the act making detention without trial lawful for ninety days, gives priority to the interest of the executive or individual liberty. Was Sachs entitled to reading and writing material while in jail under the ninety-day detention law? The question cut to the heart of the relationship between the individual and the state under apartheid. Two senior judges of the Cape Provincial Division

---

[108] See *Incorporated Law Society, Transvaal v. Mandela* 1954 (3) SA 102 (T). Emphasis added. See also Sampson, *Mandela*, p. 80. I thank Edwin Cameron for drawing my attention to Ramsbottom's noble words.

[109] For two solid studies of the Treason Trial, see, from the perspective of the social sciences, Thomas G. Karis, "The South African Treason Trial," *Political Science Quarterly*, Vol. 76, No. 2 (June 1961), pp. 217–240; and, from the perspective of law, J. Blom-Cooper, "The South African Treason Trial: R. v. Adams and Others," *International and Comparative Law Quarterly*, Vol. 8, No. 1 (January 1959), pp. 59–72.

[110] Sachs, *Justice in South Africa*, p. 227.

[111] *Roussouw v. Sachs* 1964 (2) SA 551 (A).

[112] Dugard, *Human Rights and the South African Legal Order*, p. 332.

found in favor of Sachs, and ordered that he be supplied with a reasonable amount of reading and writing materials. More important, they emphasized in their judgment that the deprivation of reading and writing material constituted punishment and that "it would be surprising to find that the legislature intended punishment to be meted out to an unconvicted prisoner."[113] With this judgment, the Cape Provincial Division placed visible limits on the expanding prerogative state, emphasizing the importance of rule by law as well as rule of law. The Appellate Division, however, overturned the verdict of the Cape Provincial Division. In *Rossouw*, the Steyn Court found against the individual and for the executive.

The judgment illustrates two things: (1) judicial *restraint* on the part of the Cape Provincial Division, which handed down the first decision, upholding Sachs's right to reading and writing material; and (2) judicial *excess* on the part of the Appellate Division, which overturned the decision, finding against Sachs. Thus, inasmuch as the Cape Provincial Division appeared to be rooted in the normative state, the Appellate Division with *Roussouw* steered the judiciary toward the prerogative state. As Dugard writes,

the court did not "declare" the law in this case, nor was it mechanically guided to the legislative intent by fixed rules of precedent and principle. It exercised a series of choices which, in the result, were seen as favoring the executive as a failure to disapprove of the ninety-day detention law and its departure from accepted principles of justice.[114]

Or, as two other scholars, in what remains the most perceptive analysis of the ninety-day detention law argued forty years ago, "the Court appears to have authorized the neglect of individual rights for as long as one can foresee."[115] Although the excess of *Rossouw* is in retrospect rightly considered legally reprehensible, the restraint shown by the Cape Provincial Division in the first instance supports the argument made herein: parts of the normative state survived the excess of the prerogative state. That the influence of the normative state had limits under apartheid does not diminish its importance, or its utility in apartheid's endgame. The normative apartheid state, as we shall see in more detail, won out over the prerogative state during two prominent phases of apartheid: (1) in the formative years of the regime prior to the 1948 elections,

---

[113] Dugard, *Human Rights and the South African Legal Order*, p. 332.
[114] Dugard, *Human Rights and the South African Legal Order*, p. 336. Unsurprisingly, *Rossouw v. Sachs* assumed an important role in the Legal Hearing of the Truth and Reconciliation Commission of South Africa. The Legal Hearing constituted South Africa's official inquiry into the conduct of the country's legal profession under apartheid. The hearing took place in late October 1997. It lasted three days and heard twenty-five submissions. David Dyzenhaus, one of the participants, has reflected on the hearing in *Judging the Judges, Judging Ourselves*.
[115] A. S. Mathews and R. C. Albino, "The Permanence of the Temporary – An Examination of the 90- and 180-Day Detention Laws," *South African Law Journal*, Vol. 83, No. 1 (February 1966), p. 42.

and (2) in the final years of the regime just prior to apartheid's endgame (i.e., after the 1976 Soweto uprising and before the imposition of the state of emergency in the aftermath of the adoption of the tricameral constitution in 1984).

POLITICS BY OTHER MEANS

In the mid-1970s, law supplemented resistance as an instrument to fight apartheid. Many small, yet important battles were won, for example, before the industrial courts. These newly established courts were empowered to hear industrial disputes. Good legal representation led to several notable developments in the fight against labor repression. Although "[u]sing the law to establish the rule of law is not always easy, especially in a context where so much law has come into being as the result of administrative fiat," several successes were achieved.[116] These included the *Komani* and *Rikhoto* judgments (as well as the *Mthiya* judgment, which is not considered here).[117] Considering their significance in the legal struggle against apartheid, it is worth examining the role of anti-apartheid lawyering in the adjudication of these cases in more detail. But before I do so, it is important to briefly sketch the institutional context from within which the legal struggle was fought.

The 1979 founding of the Legal Resources Centre (LRC) in four major cities, and the establishment of the Centre for Applied Legal Studies (CALS) at the University of the Witwatersrand, initiated a proliferation of legal clinics in the aftermath of the Soweto uprising.[118] Each appealed to the normative half of the apartheid state. Under the auspices of CALS, John Dugard, starting in the early 1980s, convened conferences on the state of law in South Africa, bringing together lawyers from both sides of the racial divide. "The conferences ... probably represented the first time that some judges had met black lawyers and other reformist attorneys outside of court. While the impact of the meetings is difficult to ascertain, Dugard feels that they contributed to progressive decisions by a number of judges who participated. Regardless, they hold instructive value as a model of how an NGO can possibly influence courts without taking a case to trial."[119] In other words, a tradition of judicial

---

[116] Wilson and Ramphele, *Uprooting Poverty*, p. 298.

[117] The three judgments are noteworthy as a set because, as we shall see, they formed a trilogy of appellate decisions that, says Arthur Chaskalson, "opened up the influx control laws and became part of a process which led ultimately to the repeal of those laws." See his "Law in a Changing Society: The Past Ten Years," *South African Journal on Human Rights*, Vol. 5, No. 3 (1989), p. 296.

[118] For a discussion of anti-apartheid lawyering, including the work of the LRC and CALS, see Chapter 7 below. For a defense of anti-apartheid lawyering against its critics, see Stephen Ellmann, "Lawyers against the Emergency," *South African Journal on Human Rights*, Vol. 6, No. 2 (1990), pp. 228–250.

[119] Stephen Golub, "Battling Apartheid, Building a New South Africa," in Mary McClymont and Stephen Golub, eds., *Many Roads to Justice: The Law-Related Work of Ford Foundation Grantees Around the World* (New York: Ford Foundation, 2000), p. 31.

independence survived apartheid, although this independence varied. Even though the courts became prey to political appointments, "the bar – in general – remained loyal to a liberal tradition" with some judges maintaining commitment to the idea of the rule of law.[120] This commitment served "as an important benchmark in debates over the legality and morality of periodic waves of repressive legislation."[121] Another observer had the following to say:

> The court system … was perhaps the only place in South Africa where an African could possibly receive a fair hearing and where the rule of law might still apply. This was particularly true of courts presided over by enlightened judges who had been appointed by the United Party. Many of these men still stood by the rule of law.[122]

Having sketched the institutional terrain, we are now in a position to examine more closely the jurisprudence of the time. The time in question was the late 1970s and early 1980s.

Komani v. Bantu Affairs Administration Board 1979

At the heart of the case of *Komani v. Bantu Affairs Administration Board* was the issue of the extension of residence rights to dependents of migrant workers under the Bantu Urban Areas Consolidation Act.[123] The issue was of some significance because it affected the rights not just of the plaintiff in the case, Veli Willie Komani, a resident of Guguletu township in Cape Town, and his wife, Nonceba Mercy Meriba Komani, but thousands of disenfranchised blacks and their next of kin. As LRC Director Arthur Chaskalson, who would go on to become a member of the Constitutional Court and until recently served as Chief Justice of South Africa, remarked at the time: "This is obviously the sort of case we should do."[124] It became a beacon of hope in the legal struggle against apartheid. It reaffirmed to the resistance movement, at least some members of it, that it could be effective to rely on law – not just war – in pursuing politics by other means. Here is the essence of the case.

Under Section 10(1)(b) Bantu Urban Areas Consolidation Act, Veli Komani had a resident right in Guguletu Township. He was entitled to this right because he had had gainful employment since 1960 and never been convicted. Under Section 10(1)(c) of said Act, Komani then claimed a resident right for his wife, his dependent. In April 1975, the Bantu Affairs Administration Board for the Peninsula Area denied Nonceba Komani a resident right. This denial was confirmed in a court of law three years later. The Board insisted that any resident required a lodger's permit. A renewal of Nonceba Komani's lodger's permit, however, had been denied – an outcome

[120] J. E. Spence, "Opposition in South Africa," *Government and Opposition*, Vol. 32, No. 4 (Autumn 1997), pp. 526–527.
[121] Spence, "Opposition in South Africa," pp. 526–527.
[122] Mandela, *Long Walk to Freedom*, p. 248.
[123] *Komani v. Bantu Affairs Administration Board, Peninsula Area* 1979 (1) SA 508 (C).
[124] As quoted in Abel, *Politics by Other Means*, p. 25.

that led her husband – unsuccessfully at first – to invoke Section 10(1)(c) of the Bantu Urban Areas Consolidation Act.

With the help of the recently established LRC, Veli Komani in 1979 lodged an appeal with the Appellate Division in Bloemfontain. The appeal was heard in 1980. It concerned the limits of prerogative rule in the apartheid state. The question before the court was whether the discretion of the state, as represented by municipal superintendents, trumped the rights of its subjects, as represented by black residents. Extensive evidence was requested and submitted, and oral arguments presented. The proceedings, in many respects, constituted a standoff between the normative state and the prerogative state. Staged on the territory of the former, *Komani* rebuked the excessive use of discretion on the part of Pretoria's Praetorians. In an unanimous opinion, penned by Chief Justice F. L. H. Rumpff, the Appellate Division, in the words of Abel, held that "the government had exceeded its legislative authority in promulgating regulations limiting residence to those with permits. The court acknowledged Mrs. Komani's right to remain in Guguletu."[125]

The responses to the judgment from those with knowledge of the prerogative state are indicative of the contribution that law made in *Komani*. Sheena Duncan, the face of Black Sash, was most exuberant:

This is the most exciting news we've ever had ... The judgment actually makes nonsense of the whole house permit system. It means that no permits will be required except by persons who are not entitled to residence under the law.[126]

The *Christian Science Monitor*, in a hyperbolic moment, declared that "[o]ne of the legal linchpins of apartheid – South Africa's system of racial discrimination – has been sheared by a court decision."[127] More accurately, the *Rand Daily Mail* placed *Komani* in a larger context, observing that "for a decision of our highest court to grant this most elementary of human rights is in itself a commentary on our society."[128] The judgment was indeed a commentary on South African society – but not just in the sense intimated by the journalists at the *Rand Daily Mail*. *Komani*, without a doubt, bespoke the *exclusionary* nature of South African *politics*, illuminating the discriminatory effects of one principal institution of apartheid rule – residential segregation. Yet *Komani also* bespoke the *inclusionary* nature, even though limited, of South African *law*. Black South Africans could not be voters under apartheid, but they could be plaintiffs – and successful plaintiffs at that. Another case made this point.

Rikhoto v. East Rand Administration Board 1983

Where *Komani* helped to improve the situation of dependants of migrant workers, the case of *Rikhoto v. East Rand Administration Board* helped to

125 Abel, *Politics by Other Means*, p. 27.
126 As quoted in Abel, *Politics by Other Means*, p. 27.
127 As quoted in Abel, *Politics by Other Means*, p. 28.
128 As quoted in Abel, *Politics by Other Means*, p. 27.

improve the situation of workers themselves.[129] Even though Section 10(1)(b) of the Bantu Urban Areas Consolidation Act provided that black workers who had held continuous employment with the same employer for ten years were entitled to residence rights, the government routinely argued that contracts were terminated with each annual leave, and acted accordingly. Municipal Labour Officers (MLO) were in a position to reject virtually all applications for residence rights filed by migrant workers.

The instances of rejection piled up quickly, prompting organizations like the LRC and Black Sash to field potential plaintiffs. They found their candidate in Mehlolo Tom Rikhoto. At the time of his application Rikhoto was a lodger in Katlehong, a township located east of Johannesburg and south of Germiston, on the so-called East Rand, adjacent to the townships of Thokoza and Vosloorus. A longtime employee of Hargram Engineering, Rikhoto had applied for a permit under Section 10(1)(b) to gain lawful residence in Germiston. The relevant Labour Bureau denied this application on the grounds that Rikhoto had not been employed by Hargram for ten consecutive years. The Labour Bureau sustained this denial even when Rikhoto's employers furnished a record demonstrating that he had been gainfully employed at the company since 1970. The crux of the matter was that Rikhoto's employment at Hargram had been continuous. However, he had *not* entered into one long-term contract with his employer, but, as was standard for migrant workers, into a series of short-term contracts.

In response to a notice of motion filed in the Supreme Court by the LRC on Rikhoto's behalf, the government insisted that Rikhoto did not qualify under Section 10(1)(b) of the Bantu Urban Areas Consolidation Act because the annual leaves that he had taken as a homeland resident, had broken the continuity of his employment at Hargram. After much legal wrangling in the run-up to the court hearing, the three-judge panel handed down its judgment on September 22, 1983 – *rejecting* the government's case.

The Supreme Court held that the MLO's decision in the case – namely the rejection of Rikhoto's application – "was not reached as a result of valid proceedings, nor was it duly given in terms of any Act. ... [It] was in fact a 'decision' not to perform his functions ..."[130] In particular, the court chided the government for purporting that an employee's temporary absence from work, due to illness or leave, broke the continuity of employment required under Section 10(1)(b) of the Bantu Urban Areas Consolidation Act. In his judgment, Justice J. B. O'Donovan held that "no one could imagine that the useful or satisfactory absorption of a native in an urban community could in any way be affected by occasional departures from the area, not amounting to changes of residence."[131] The judgment further noted that despite the fact that Rikhoto's services to Hargram

---

[129] *Rikhoto v. East Rand Administration Board and Municipal Labour Officer*, Germiston 1983 (4) SA 278 (W).

[130] As quoted in Abel, *Politics by Other Means*, p. 46.

[131] As quoted in Abel, *Politics by Other Means*, p. 47.

were rendered under a series of separate contracts, he and the company had a common and continuing intention that he should remain in employment; ... the arrangements for the renewal of his contract were made each year before he went on paid leave; ... he worked for no one other than the company; and ... his absences from work for other causes have occurred on isolated occasions only. On these facts the Applicant has, in my view, satisfied the requirement of continuity in his work for a period of at least ten years. The question is one of substance, and not of form.[132]

That the impact of *Rikhoto* was not negligible, even though the implementation of the ruling (discussed in the next chapter) left something to be desired, becomes apparent in this, otherwise critical, assessment by Black Sash:

Monday[,] May 30[,] the Appeal Court confirmed the decision of the Transvaal Division of the Supreme Court that Mr. Mehlolo T. Rikhoto was entitled to a qualification in terms of Section 10(1)(b) of the Urban Areas Act. According to a Government statement this meant that an estimated 143,000 migrant workers would immediately qualify to live permanently in the urban areas and would be entitled to bring their wives and children to live with them in terms of Section 10(1)(c) of the Act. It meant that in future all migrant workers would qualify for urban rights after 10 consecutive years with an employer. In the first weeks after the judgement, labour offices throughout the country were inundated by people whose rights had at last been recognized, asking for their 10(1)(b) endorsements.[133]

That the judgment, aside from its real-world ramifications, also made an impression of a symbolic sort was evident in the domestic and international press coverage that *Rikhoto* provoked. The *Sowetan*, although cautious, celebrated the judgments as a "blow at a cornerstone of Government influx policies." The *Sunday Times* believed to have seen displayed "the highest traditions of an unfettered and independent judiciary." Overseas, the *Guardian* dubbed *Rikhoto* "one of the most important judgments ever delivered by South Africa's highest court," and the *New York Times* declared that "[e]ven as it dishonors humanity's basic codes, South Africa worships forms of law."[134]

Although the international press might have slightly exaggerated the significance of *Rikhoto* (as well as the earlier *Komani* judgment), it would be wrong to underestimate the impact of anti-apartheid lawyering, and the contribution of law as both an arena and an instrument in the struggle against apartheid. It was undoubtedly an indirect outcome of the landmark proceedings that the apartheid

---

[132] As quoted in Abel, *Politics by Other Means*, p. 47.

[133] Sheena Duncan, "The Rikhoto Scandal," *Black Sash*, Vol. 26, No. 3 (November 1983), p. 22. On non-compliance by Municipal Labour Officers, see also Abel, *Politics by Other Means*, pp. 63–64. On the economic significance of the judgment, see C. E. W. Simkins, *The Economic Implications of the Rikhoto Judgement*, SALDRU Working Paper 52, Southern Africa Labour and Development Research Unit, January 1983; and Fion de Vletter, "Recent Trends and Prospects of Black Migration to South Africa," *Journal of Modern African Studies*, Vol. 23, No. 4 (December 1985), pp. 667–702.

[134] For the quotations, see Abel, *Politics by Other Means*, p. 53.

regime, *qua* legislation, first partially repealed and then entirely abolished the repressive system of influx control in 1984 and 1986, respectively.[135]

TRIAL AND APPEAL COURTS

What was the overall record of the Appellate Division of the Supreme Court? Did the Appellate Division, the country's highest court, *uphold* the rule of law, as the cases of *Komani* and *Rikhoto* seem to indicate? Or did the court *undermine* the rule of law, as the case of *Omar v. Minister of Law and Order* appears to suggest? Do we have evidence that the Appellate Division, over the course of time, "retreat [ed] from enlightened judicial activism to a conservative judicial activism," as some charge?[136] If so, what difference did this retreat make?

In answer to these questions, I analyze, first, the jurisprudence of the Supreme Court's Appellate Division, from its inception in 1950 until 1990; and, second, juxtapose this jurisprudence with the jurisprudence of South Africa's lower courts, the trial courts. Only a focus on the jurisprudence of *both* trial *and* appeal courts will truly enable us to evaluate the judiciary's commitment to law, for it has been suggested that most abuses of law were perpetrated in the courts of first – rather than last – instance. As Michael Lobban, a foremost voice of this perspective, writes,

[S]cholars have pointed out that the Appellate Division was able to retain its legitimacy and authority even in some of the darkest hours of apartheid. Nevertheless, jurisprudential studies have often overlooked an important way in which South African courts actively assisted the state in fighting its opponents. To understand the workings of the legal system, we must examine not merely the questions of law and legal reasoning which reached the Appellate Division, but also the handling by judges of matters of fact and evidence at trial level.[137]

Lobban's point is valid, of course. Legal scholars of the Appellate Division, however, were generally *aware* that their findings would not necessarily apply to the performance of the trial courts. As Hugh Corder, alongside C. F. Forsyth the

---

[135] Note, however, that not all was well as far as the movement of migrants was concerned, in spite of the repeal of the pass laws in 1986. For as Dugard points out, "[u]nder the guise of denationalization through independence for the homelands, and by a process known as 'orderly urbanization,' a new system of influx control was erected. Through denationalization, all Africans living in South Africa proper after the independence of the homelands would become statutory aliens in the land of their birth and relegated to the status of migrant workers. As such, they would require passports to enter South Africa and permits to seek employment in the same way that actual aliens – say, from Zimbabwe or France – do. Like other aliens, they could be deported to their country of origin, in this case the homelands. For these millions, the passport would replace the pass." Dugard, "The Law of Apartheid," p. 16.

[136] The quote is from Nicholas Haysom and Clive Pasket, "The War against Law: Judicial Activism and the Appellate Division," *South African Journal on Human Rights*, Vol. 4, No. 3 (1988), p. 303.

[137] Lobban, *White Man's Justice*, p. 14. A call for a comparison of lower and higher courts was also issued, several years later, by Klug, *Constituting Democracy*, p. 45.

leading authority on South Africa's appellate courts, conceded in his learned *Judges at Work*, "the slightly rarefied air of appellate proceedings, can act to produce a picture not typical of wider judicial performance. Thus, conclusions arrived at in respect of the AD cannot necessarily be extended to the provincial divisions, though the fact that most judges of appeal had considerable experience at provincial level partially counterbalances this trend to judicial isolation."[138] It is with the provincial level that the next section is concerned.

Trials

One structural feature of South Africa's system of trial courts was the extensive room for "loose legal reasoning – and hence bias – to enter into the judgment. In their interpretation of evidence, and in their attitude to witnesses and defendants, judges drew largely on their own political and social beliefs. They were not merely matching fact to norm: their understandings of the intentions and ambitions of the accused were largely shaped by their prejudices and fears."[139] Even more leverage existed in the country's magistrates' courts, which were "staffed by civil servants from whom no meaningful degree of independence can be expected."[140] In the legal hearings of the Truth and Reconciliation Commission of South Africa, the spokesman of the National Association of Democratic Lawyers (NADEL) accordingly referred to the magistracy disparagingly as "the coal face of apartheid legal system at its worst."[141] In the following, I am primarily concerned with the jurisprudence of first instance courts, although I will make occasional reference to the performance of South Africa's magistrates' courts as well.[142]

Trials in the 1950s and 1960s

With the 1948 elections, the use of trial courts for the purpose of stifling dissent became a regular feature of South Africa's legal order. "When in the 1950s and early 1960s, there had been an upsurge of increasingly radical opposition in response to the development of apartheid, the state perceived that the only way to control it was by an intensive policy of prosecution and

---

[138] Hugh Corder, *Judges at Work: The Role and Attitudes of the South African Appellate Judiciary, 1910–50* (Cape Town: Juta, 1984), p. 216.

[139] Lobban, *White Man's Justice*, p. 15.

[140] Dugard, "The Law of Apartheid," p. 27.

[141] As quoted in Paul Gready and Lazarus Kgalema, "Magistrates under Apartheid: A Case Study of the Politicisation of Justice and Complicity in Human Rights Abuse," *South African Journal on Human Rights*, Vol. 19, No. 2 (2003), p. 144.

[142] The only study of the latter remains Paul Gready and Lazarus Kgalema, "Magistrates under Apartheid: A Case Study of the Politicisation of Justice and Complicity in Human Rights Abuse," *South African Journal on Human Rights*, Vol. 19, No. 2 (2003), pp. 141–188. For another version of this research which is based on a dozen or so interviews with magistrates, see idem., "Magistrates under Apartheid: A Case Study of Professional Ethics and the Politicisation of Justice," Occasional Paper, Centre for the Study of Violence and Reconciliation, August 2000.

detention."[143] Accordingly, political trials became "a regular and, from the Government's point of view, necessary feature of the political process."[144]

For the period under investigation, 1950–1970, Dugard, in his seminal *Human Rights and South African Legal Order*, usefully distinguishes three major phases of trial activity, during each of which apartheid governments sought to quell opposition with the help of the first instance courts. The first trial phase (1952–1953) came in response to the Defiance campaign, which had been launched by the ANC in 1951 and that, by the end of the following year, had resulted in some eight thousand detention cases, a number of which were adjudicated by the courts. The prosecution's strategy involved a focus on a large number of minor cases. The second trial phase (1956–1961) was consumed by the convoluted Treason Trial, which I discussed earlier. The prosecution's strategy in this second phase shifted from a focus on a large number of trials of minor cases to a focus on one trial of major defendants. With the Treason Trial, the government invested substantial resources (R414,078) in a proceeding involving high-profile defendants, which ended in their acquittal. The third trial phase (1960–1966), comprised once again a series of smaller trials arising from unlawful membership in banned organizations, such as the ANC and PAC, ranging from *S. v. Nokwe* (conviction of black conference organizers on account of ostensible ideological affinities with the banned ANC) to *S. v. Alexander* (conviction of Neville Alexander and other "coloured" defendants for acts of sabotage as part of the banned Yu Chi Chan Club) to *S. v. Naidoo* (conviction of an Indian lawyer on account of membership in the banned Communist Party). The examples are meant to give an idea of the types of cases that were politicized in the courts.[145]

Trials in the 1970s

Aside from "trials of harassment" (e.g., the prosecutions of Laurence Gandar and Benjamin Pogrund of the *Rand Daily Mail*; and Barend van Niekerk of the University of Natal), the decade of the 1970s became synonymous with the adjudication of terrorism cases.[146] Ninety-nine such cases – involving 245 defendants – were heard by the lower courts between 1975 and 1979 alone. The trials of the 1970s continued the increased pace of prosecutions of

[143] Lobban, *White Man's Justice*, p. 2.

[144] Dugard, *Human Rights and the South African Legal Order*, p. 212.

[145] *S. v. Nokwe* 1962 (3) SA 71 (T); *S. v. Alexander* (2) 1965 (2) SA 818 (C) and *S. v. Alexander* (1) 1965 (2) SA 796 (A); *S. v. Naidoo* 1966 (4) SA 519 (N). An exception was the much publicized and larger Rivonia Trial, which led initially to the acquittal, but eventually to the conviction, of leaders of *Umkhonto we Sizwe*, the armed wing of the ANC. See *S. v. National High Command* 1964 (1) SA 1 (T); *S. v. National High Command* 1964 (3) SA 462 (T).

[146] High-profile examples of so-called harassment trials are *S. v. South African Associated Newspapers Ltd.* 1970 (1) SA 469 (W); and *S. v. Van Niekerk* 1970 (3) SA 655 (T). For an extensive discussion of the latter case, see Dugard, *Human Rights and the South African Legal Order*, pp. 292–302. The names of all 245 defendants in the ninety-nine terrorist trials of the 1975–1979 period, as well as conviction statistics, are available Lobban, *White Man's Justice*, pp. 265–271. See also Table 7.6.

political opponents, but the 1967 Terrorism Act (effective retroactively from 1962),[147] instead of the Internal Security Act (formerly Suppression of Communism Act)[148] and the Unlawful Organizations Act,[149] which had governed the majority of trials in the previous decade, became the preferred instrument of choice on the part of the apartheid government. As Dugard writes, "Most persons charged with serious political offences since 1967 have been charged under this Act."[150]

In addition to the notorious prosecution of black students – on conspiracy charges – that resulted in the trial of *S. v. Cooper and others*, and involved the South African Students' Organization (SASO) and the Black People's Convention (BPC) as well as two other student organizations, the government set its sights on the dangers of "armed struggle."[151] Whereas in *Cooper* revolutionary *ideas* were on trial (Black Consciousness), the subsequent trials sought to punish (and deter) revolutionary *action*. The trials of "armed and dangerous" revolutionary leaders, real and imagined, focused on the issue of recruitment.[152] For it was the consolidation and cross-fertilization of resistance organizations – banned and otherwise – and their possible militarization that the apartheid state feared the most. Therefore, incumbent law sought to deter insurgent war.

The preoccupation was with the activities of black youth, leading to a prosecutorial focus on both leaders and followers. In a series of minor trials, the apartheid state aimed at preventing black youths – rank-and-file – from leaving South Africa to receive military training in neighboring countries. In several larger trials, the prosecution turned to student leaders of the South African Student's Movement (SASM) and the National Association of Youth Organizations (NAYO), among others. Here the idea was to punish individuals, but perhaps more important, to penetrate what the prosecution saw, not entirely without justification, as conspiracies dedicated to the overthrow of the apartheid regime.

[147] Act 83 of 1967.
[148] Act 44 of 1950, extended and renamed in 1976. See Internal Security Amendment Act 79 of 1976. The amendment broadened the scope of the act to make it applicable to "subverters" in general – turning the legislation into a viable catch-all instrument for the prosecution of any and all opposition, individual and organizational, and of whatever persuasion, liberal or radical. The sweeping authority bestowed by the Act becomes even more apparent if one considers that the term "communism" had *already* been interpreted in the jurisprudence of the courts in extremely broad terms, most important perhaps in *R. v. Sisulu and others* 1953 (3) SA 276 (A), the appellate judgment that led to the conviction of Walter Sisulu and other ANC members – architects of the defiance campaign – for having advocated communism, rather than having defied apartheid.
[149] Act 34 of 1960.
[150] Dugard, *Human Rights and the South African Legal Order*, p. 220.
[151] *S. v. Cooper and others* 1977 (3) SA 475 (T).
[152] To get a sense of this era, see, for example, the colorful autobiography by one (white) participant in the armed struggle, Ronnie Kasrils, *"Armed and Dangerous": My Undercover Struggle against Apartheid* (London: Heinemann, 1993). For a more objective take, see Stephen M. Davis, *Apartheid's Rebels: Inside South Africa's Hidden War* (New Haven: Yale University Press, 1987), which remains the only serious study of its kind.

As for the former, Eric Molobi was one of those who stood trial, and was convicted.[153] *S. v. Molobi*, according to Lobban, who examined the trial records held in the Department of Historical Papers at the University of the Witwatersrand in Johannesburg, demonstrates a number of things, first, the desire on the part of the apartheid government (and thus the prosecution) to show that contentious *ideas*, on the part of young blacks like Molobi, would invariably lead to contentious *acts*, usually terrorism. Molobi was convicted for having incited friends, South African exiles, while he was vacationing in Botswana, to undergo military training. The vexing question, absent any concrete evidence, was whether or not the conversations Molobi had had with his friends on the topic of resisting the apartheid state constituted a conspiracy to commit sabotage, and other crimes, in South Africa, as charged by the prosecution.

The case is interesting because it brings to the fore again the conflicting prerogatives of the apartheid state. On the one hand, as Lobban writes, "The state had no evidence either of *actual* recruitment or of any developed network of recruits: and the case was evidently a pre-emptive strike against disgruntled individuals who might turn to the armed struggle, through personal contacts they had beyond the borders."[154] On the other hand, the trial, while undoubtedly political, exhibited a commitment to the inviolability of legal rules and procedures in court proceedings on the part of Judge V. G. Hiemstra, who presided.

Adopting a somewhat restrictive interpretation of the Terrorism Act, Hiemstra acquitted Molobi of the conspiracy charge, but not without noting, in a rather liberal fashion, that "mere expression of an opinion, however forcefully, can be neither incitement nor encouragement if it does not got further than expression of an opinion. … [T]he Terrorism Act was surely not intended to suppress debate on the problems of the country."[155] (Many, of course, would argue that the suppression of debate on the problems of the country was the Act's intention precisely.) This notwithstanding, Molobi, although there was scant evidence of active recruitment, was, as noted, convicted, for inciting his friends to take part in military training, and sentenced to five years in prison (the minimum sentence under the Terrorism Act).[156] In a more substantial trial, known as the "NAYO case," which revolved around similar charges under the Terrorism Act as *Molobi*, but raised a different set of legal problems, a similar bifurcation between the interests of the government and the interests of the court was visible.[157] The objective of the former was to reveal the operation of a conspiracy among four executive members of NAYO and others; the objective

[153] *S. v. Molobi* Reference AD 2021 (Case WLD 652/1975), as reported in Lobban, *White Man's Justice*, p. 272.

[154] Lobban, *White Man's Justice*, p. 114.

[155] Lobban, *White Man's Justice*, p. 115.

[156] For another recruitment case, this time involving five members of a Grahamstown branch of the SASM, see *S. v. Ndukwana and others* Reference AD 1901 (CASE CC72/1976), as reported in Lobban, *White Man's Justice*, p. 272. For details on the trial, see ibid., pp. 119–123.

[157] *S. v. Molokeng and others* Reference AD 1901 (Case WLD 30/1976), as reported in Lobban, *White Man's Justice*, p. 272. For details on the trial, see ibid., pp. 123–137.

of the latter was to aid the former *within the limits of the law*. In this phase of trials, "the very fact of putting people on trial for precise activities meant that the state," unlike in earlier phases, "had to prove those activities; and the need to construct a convincing and consistent case was thus an important constraint on the state," placed there by the normative state, "which could work to the benefit of activists."[158] This is indeed what transpired on a number of occasions, some of which I presented here briefly. "It was the state's failure to make out a case, and the courts' refusal to act as a rubber stamp to the executive, that allowed the acquittal of Molobi on the conspiracy charge, and that of most of the NAYO defendants. Particularly, in the latter trial, the [government's] ambition was clearly frustrated by the court."[159]

In retrospect, the terrorism trials of the early 1970s, in the years preceding the 1976 Soweto uprising, marked "a clear progression in the state's perception of the threat posed by black consciousness organizations. Instead of seeking to prosecute grand conspiracies involving the long-term aims of large organizations, the state now sought to identify and break into nascent structures of recruitment for military training, particularly for the ANC in exile, set up by those involved in SASM and NAYO."[160] Then came Soweto.

Suddenly, the number of suspected insurgents increased sharply, from several hundreds to many thousands. In response, the legislature expanded the jurisdictions and powers of lower courts by passing in 1977 the Lower Courts Amendment Act and the Criminal Procedure Act.[161] Among several streamlining features of the new legislation, the revised plea procedure stood out. It provided for the conviction (and sentencing) of defendants immediately following a guilty plea, *dispensing* with the requirement of the prosecution to produce *any* evidence in support of such a plea. In the first terrorism trial the use of this plea procedure had the disconcerting effect that the four defendants were convicted twenty-one minutes after they had pleaded guilty to the charge of planning to undergo military training.[162] In an effort to cope with the burgeoning number of cases, accelerated trials became a sign of the times. Inasmuch as this facilitated the prosecution of terrorism cases, it created insurmountable hurdles for the legal representation of defendants by counsel. In this climate, changes in the Criminal Procedure Act put a greater burden on defendants to prove that confessions were extracted under undue influence. In the wake of these changes, as Lobban explains, a presumption as to the admissibility of confessions was enshrined in the criminal law of procedure.[163] The insistence on this assumption by what seems to have been

[158] The presiding judge in *Molokeng*, Judge Irving Steyn, had already previously interpreted the Terrorism Act restrictively, acquitting the defendant Petrus Tshabalala who had been charged with inciting two youths to undergo military training. See Lobban, *White Man's Justice*, p. 133.
[159] Lobban, *White Man's Justice*, p. 138.
[160] Lobban, *White Man's Justice*, p. 137.
[161] Act 91 of 1977; Act 51 of 1977.
[162] *S. v. Mbhele* 1980 (1) SA 295 (N).
[163] Lobban, *White Man's Justice*, p. 151.

the majority of judges in terrorism cases, sets this phase of trials apart from the previous two. The other distinguishing feature of the trials of the 1970s was the widening use of torture (and the concomitant reluctance of many judges to entertain the existence of its use).[164] Throughout this era, legal relief was hard to come by for detainees, largely on account of the complicity of the magistracy in the administration of political trials, for they "performed crucial functions in relation to political detainees, including overseeing a complaints safeguard machinery."[165] As the legal hearings of the TRC made abundantly clear, this machinery failed. Others say, the machinery was set up to fail:

There is voluminous evidence that torture under apartheid was widespread and systematic. It is clear, therefore, that the complaints and safeguard system failed to protect detainees. Criticism of magistrates and the system over which they presided long precedes the TRC. Detainees were totally cut off from family, friends, their lawyers and private doctors. In this context the responsibility of magistrates was immense: they were one of the few outlets detainees had to non-custodial personnel. But when assigned responsibility for overseeing the complaints and safeguard system for detainees they faced the challenge of dual obligations – which is crucial to understanding the attitudes and conduct of magistrates – on the one hand to their employer and colleagues and on the other to the detainee whose well-being they were charged with ensuring. The system of custodial supervision, therefore, was designed to fail because magistrates were deliberately placed in an insidious position.[166]

This, among other things, amounts to an assertion of the prerogative state, indicated by an increased use of arbitrary – rather than legal – procedures for political ends.[167]

---

[164] For a most well-known trial, that of Harry Gwala (one of the few ANC members of the ANC National Executive Committee with influence in Natal), see *S. v. Gwala and others* Reference AD 2021 (Case CC 108/1976), as reported, and discussed comprehensively, in Lobban, *White Man's Justice*, pp. 111; 167–188; 272. On the topic of torture, and the assertion of the prerogative state, Lobban adds that "Even in a liberal court, the gap between correct legality and sinister reality was a great one: for, at least until the inquest on the death of Steve Biko [which was heard at the end of 1977], it seemed impossible to believe that the police and the medical officers who worked with them could make systematically untruthful statements." Ibid., pp. 190–191. This, we know now, is precisely what often happened, of course. This is exemplified in *S. v. Hassim and others* 1972 (1) SA 200 (N). For a first indication of judicial perturbation at allegations of torture, see *Dlamini v. Minister of Law and Order* 1986 (4) SA 342 (D), in which two judges insisted that allegations of torture always be "assiduously investigated." Ibid., at 349.

[165] Gready and Kgalema, "Magistrates under Apartheid," p. 146.

[166] Gready and Kgalema, "Magistrates under Apartheid," p. 164.

[167] On the issues of torture and detention, see also Don Foster and Dennis Davis, *Detention and Torture in South Africa: Psychological, Legal and Historical Studies* (New York: St. Martin's Press, 1987); and Centre for Applied Legal Studies, *A Report on the Rabie Report: An Examination of Security Legislation in South Africa* (Johannesburg: Centre for Applied Legal Studies, 1982). For an earlier account, see United Nations, *Maltreatment and Torture of Prisoners in South Africa: Report of the Special Committee on Apartheid* (New York: United Nations, 1973).

Lobban's finding concerning the trials of the 1970s, that there were "two faces to South African justice – the 'light' side of the courtroom spectacle, and the 'dark' side of the police cells" – reflects, once again, the inherently schizophrenic nature of the apartheid state with its two halves, and their conflicting imperatives. The bifurcation in the jurisprudence of the trial courts – a commitment to the executive coupled with a commitment to the law – continued in the aftermath of Soweto. Although the proceedings against the so-called Pretoria Twelve (featuring as a defendant, among others, Tokyo Sexwale, the savvy post-apartheid Premier of Gauteng) on charges of conspiracy to recruit, train, and arm ANC members, were presided over by a conscientious judge who was discerning in separating fact from fiction as well as following rules and procedures, any assessment of the proceedings against Zephania Mothopeng and others in the so-called Bethal Trial will invariably result in a *diametrically opposed* appraisal.[168] Here the normative state was virtually absent. Lobban, the foremost scholar of legal contention in this period, explains:

In brief, the state's need to use the Bethal trial to crush the PAC and its nascent support in the townships was greater than the state's need to use the Pretoria trial [i.e., *Sexwale*] to crush the ANC. This helps explain both the extremely high level of violence used in the investigation of the case, and the fact that the trial was held *in camera* in a distant town.[169]

Trials in the 1980s

Although the rise of the prerogative state regularly obfuscated the use of and reliance on procedures, especially in the legal realm, a revival of procedural justice was noticeable in the mid-1980s. The balance between the prerogative state and the normative state tilted back – somewhat – in favor of the latter:

By the 1980s, opponents of apartheid no longer saw the courtroom only from the point of view of the defendant facing broad charges under draconian legislation. Now there were more opportunities for the opponents of apartheid to use the law for their own ends. In part, this reflected the fact that there were more lawyers and legal academics in the 1980s working not only in the area of human rights but in a range of areas of law of particular interest to the oppressed. A number of student activists banned in the 1970s had spent their time qualifying as lawyers and were now able to channel their opposition to apartheid into the courtroom. These lawyers were able to shape the meaning of the reforms of apartheid announced in the Wiehahn and Riekert Reports in 1979 in a way that was most favourable to the opponents of the system. The new labour law of the 1980s served to create space for trade unions to operate freely. Similarly, legal challenges helped to undermine the pass laws. ... [T]he state was no longer able to control its enemies through trials.[170]

---

[168] *S. v. Sexwale and others* Reference AD 1901; *S. v. Mothopeng and others* Reference AD 2021. Both as reported in Lobban, *White Man's Justice*, p. 272.
[169] Lobban, *White Man's Justice*, p. 218.
[170] Lobban, *White Man's Justice*, pp. 261–262.

Consider two court cases, *Buthelezi v. Attorney General, Natal* and *Mokoena v. Minister of Law and Order*. In the former, the court in Natal ruled that an attorney general must not deny an accused person the right to bail without affording that person a prior hearing (dissenting from a contrary finding in the Transvaal).[171] In the latter, Judge Richard Goldstone (until recently a Justice of the Constitutional Court) ruled that a "Release Mandela" calendar, which contained excerpts from the Freedom Charter, could *not* be construed as evidence that the accused was furthering the aims of the ANC.[172] In yet another case, *Nkondo and Gumede v. Minister of Law and Order*, the court instituted a tighter review procedure for the banning of persons and organizations.[173] Before this last decision, ministers enjoyed wide discretion to impose security measures. Broad and unspecific reasons were sufficient to detain. The court ruling imposed a limit on the prerogative state, albeit a penetrable one. Henceforth, the Minister of Law and Order was required to give precise and detailed reasons for any ban under the existing security legislation. How does the record of the appellate judiciary, the Appeal Court and the Appellate Division, compare?

Appeals

As indicated, the jurisprudence of the Appellate Division caused resignation on the part of some observers, especially in the late 1960s and 1970s, the years of the Vorster administration. "In this environment of political paranoia, South Africa's highest court, the Appellate Division of the Supreme Court, adopted a policy of judicial restraint or abstention in its interpretation of the security laws. The result was that brutal interrogation of detainees became the rule and suspicious deaths in detention a not uncommon occurrence."[174] According to some observers, the Appellate Division sustained this stance well into the 1980s:

Enough cases involving challenges to the exercise of state power under emergency rule have now reached the Appellate Division to justify the conclusion that earlier judicial endeavours to impose some kind of legal restraint on the executive have, for practical purposes, been in vain. In case after case, the country's highest court has overruled points on which some provincial courts had relied to curb the security establishment during the early days of the current succession of states of emergency ...[175]

What are we to make of this interpretation? What of the appellate jurisprudence? What does the latter say about the meaning of law? Does this jurisprudence invalidate the advances of *Komani* and *Rikhoto*?

---

[171] *Buthelezi v. Attorney General, Natal* 1986 (4) SA 377 (D).

[172] *Mokoena v. Minister of Law and Order* 1986 (4) SA 42 (W).

[173] *Nkondo and Gumede v. Minister of Law and Order* 1986 (2) SA 756 (AD).

[174] Dugard, "The Law of Apartheid," p. 22.

[175] John Grogan, "The Appellate Division and the Emergency: Another Step Backward," *South African Law Journal*, Vol. 106, No. 1 (February 1989), p. 14.

In answer, let us consider the role and attitude of the South African appellate judiciary, circa 1950–1990. To begin, it is important not to think of the Appellate Division as a static institution. It was far from it, transforming and deforming itself (and being transformed and deformed by others) repeatedly. At least three periods of appellate review can be distinguished during the apartheid years: (1) 1950s; (2) 1960–1970s; and (3) 1980s.

Appeals in the 1950s

From 1948 until 1958, the newly incumbent apartheid regime faced stiff opposition from the Appeal Court, as the Appellate Division was still called then. As we have seen above, two judgments in particular constituted this opposition, namely, *Harris v. Minister of the Interior* and *Minister of the Interior v. Harris*.[176]

Many liberal commentators have since attributed great significance to this appellate behavior. Notes Dyzenhaus, "liberal lawyers regard as especially significant the flurry of hostility which took place between the government and the Appellate Division in the period when the court invalidated the government's first two attempts to remove the 'Coloureds' from the common electoral roll."[177] Another observer provides the details:

The Appeal Court, which consisted of a number of the most liberal judges ever to grace it, refused to acquiesce meekly in the new apartheid legal order and challenged the government on two grounds. First, it set aside administrative acts providing for unequal amenities for different races, holding that the common law required an equality of treatment (akin to the "separate but equal" doctrine in the United States). Second, it obstructed the government's attempts to remove Coloured voters from the electoral roll in the Cape Province, holding that Parliament had failed to follow the correct constitutional procedure.[178]

The commitment to procedural regularity and individual liberty was a continuing commitment. It was a legacy from the period 1910–1950, when the Appeal Court, in the estimation of Hugh Corder, "struck a remarkably fine balance between the interests of the individual and those of society with, perhaps, a slight bias in certain areas towards those who were deprived in some way. Certainly, in the spheres of freedom of expression and the proper administration of justice, the court throughout assumed a role staunchly in favour of individual freedom, and restrained unjust action on the part of officialdom."[179]

This found the approbation of many anti-apartheid lawyers, one of whom wrote admiringly, in the mid-1980s, at a time when the Appellate Division was not ruling in accordance with this legal tradition, that the jurisprudential

---

[176] *Harris v. Minister of the Interior* 1952 (2) SA 428 (AD); *Minister of the Interior v. Harris* 1952 (4) SA 769 (AD).
[177] Dyzenhaus, *Hard Cases in Wicked Legal Systems*, p. 50.
[178] Dugard, "The Law of Apartheid," p. 28.
[179] Corder, *Judges at Work*, pp. 68–69.

approach of the 1950s was "consistent with the *inherent principles* of South African law," which to him included freedom from arbitrary arrest and detention without trial; a right to legal representation; freedom from cruel and unusual punishment, and other such rights contained in the International Covenant on Civil and Political Rights.[180]

The independence of the country's highest court was gradually curtailed, however. The court's "obstructionism [in the first years of apartheid had] so angered the government that it increased the size of the Appellate Division and set about systematically appointing lawyers sympathetic to its ideology to the Supreme Court, particularly to the Appeal Court."[181] By 1959, the court-packing had already netted discernable, indeed far-reaching results. "[T]he government had brought the judiciary into line. Thereafter, restraint and abstention were to characterize judicial decisions on race and security. The unequal application of the Group Areas Act by administrative fiat was approved by the Appellate Division, despite the absence of clear statutory authority; and the detention-without-trial laws of the 1960s were made still harsher by judicial interpretation in favor of the executive. The provincial divisions followed the lead of the Appellate Division and likewise refrained from challenging the legal apparatus of apartheid."[182]

Appeals in the 1960s–1970s

As indicated in the previous section, the late 1950s marked the politicization of the judiciary in the sense that the Appellate Division largely abdicated its role as arbiter, or "buttress" (in the words of Justice van den Heever in *R. v. Pretoria Timber Co*), between the state and its subjects.[183] It became, for the

[180] D. J. McQuoid-Mason, "Omar, Fani and Bill – Judicial Restraint Restrained: A New Dark Age?," *South African Journal on Human Rights*," Vol. 3, No. 3 (November 1987), p. 323. Emphases added.

[181] Dugard, "The Law of Apartheid," p. 28. The increase in the court's size was accomplished through the Appellate Division Quorum Act 25 of 1955. Henceforth, eleven instead of five judges heard cases concerning the validity of a statute. The five-member quorum had come into use in 1936. Originally, Section 110 of the South Africa Act 1909, as amended by the Administration of Justice Further Amendment Act 11 of 1927, had stipulated a quorum of four judges. The Supreme Court Act 59 of 1959 authorized the Chief Justice to increase the quorum if he felt that a particular case would benefit from the deliberations of a larger bench. Lastly, it is important to point out that the Appellate Division does not sit en banc, but in panels.

[182] Dugard, "The Law of Apartheid," p. 28. As per the Supreme Court Act 59 of 1959, the Supreme Court of South Africa during the apartheid years consisted of the Appellate Division, with seat in Bloemfontain, as well as seven *provincial divisions* (Natal, NPD; Orange Free State, OPD; Northern Cape, NC; Eastern Cape, ECD; Transvaal TPD; Cape, CPD; and South West Africa/Nambia, SWA) and three *local divisions* (Witwatersrand, WLD; Durban and Coast, DCLD; and South Eastern Cape, SE CLD). The Supreme Court Amendment Act 46 of 1980 stipulated that the Appellate Division comprise a Chief Justice and thirteen judges of appeal. The quorum in cases concerning the validity of legislation was eleven; in criminal and civil appeals, three judges sufficed.

[183] *R. v. Pretoria Timber Co (Pty) Ltd* 1950 (3) SA 163 (A), at 181.

most part, an advocate of the state instead, especially under Chief Justice Steyn. As Corder writes regarding this period, "[a]lthough the courts have seldom associated themselves directly with government policy, their decisions reveal that since the appointment of Steyn as Chief Justice the implementation of government policy has been substantially facilitated by a failure to keep the executive within the law."[184] Edwin (now Judge) Cameron's damning assessment of the Chief Justice is couched in elegant prose:

What is certain is that he was appointed in 1955 to an appeal court which had gained a reputation throughout the Western world for its fearlessness and for championing fundamental rights rather than acquiescing in their impairment. He did not leave it so. In a country which has a legal system abundant in refinement and flexibility and which offered at least the opportunity for preserving the non-statutory fabric of justice vigorous and resilient in its protection of fundamental values, that is epitaph enough.[185]

In this vein, the Supreme Court Act of 1959 laid a solid foundation for a jurisprudence of executive-mindedness that the Appellate Division would only overcome at century's end.

Appeals in the 1980s

The transition from appellate jurisprudence responding to the imperative of state security to appellate jurisprudence predicated on the principle of individual liberty originated with the aforementioned *Rikhoto* judgment. In addition to *Rikhoto*, the 1986 judgments of *Minister of Law and Order and others v. Hurley and another* and *Nkondo and Gumede v. Minister of Law and Order*, both reigning in police excesses in the practice of detention, were indicative of a more fundamental transformation of appellate jurisprudence concerning the Internal Security Act.[186] After fits and starts – and government

---

[184] Corder, *Judges at Work*, p. 236. For a similarly dire assessment of Justice Steyn, see, among many, Edwin Cameron, "Nude Monarchy: The Case of South Africa's Judges," *South African Journal of Human Rights*, Vol. 3, No. 3 (November 1987), esp. pp. 340–341.

[185] Edwin Cameron, "Legal Chauvinism, Executive-Mindedness and Justice: L C Steyn's Impact on South African Law," *South African Law Journal*, Vol. 99, No. 1 (February 1982), p. 75. Adds Cameron, "L C Steyn's impact on South African law has, on the whole, been regrettable. ... L C Steyn presided over a court that did little to fortify fundamental rights and entitlements at a time when these were under increasing attack from executive encroachment. His own judgments provide notable evidence to justify this charge. And in matters involving the disputed application of this country's discriminatory laws in the field of race, he revealed himself to be empathetic to the programme of legislative racialism that was being enacted." Ibid., 74. For an angry (and ultimately unconvincing) critique of apartheid's critics, see Adrienne van Blerk, "The Record of the Judiciary (1)," in Hugh Corder, ed., *Democracy and the Judiciary* (Cape Town: IDASA, 1988), pp. 26–45.

[186] *Minister of Law and Order and others v. Hurley and another* 1986 (3) SA 568 (A); *Nkondo and Gumede v. Minister of Law and Order* 1986 (2) SA 756 (AD). For the most comprehensive account of judicial attitudes toward the security legislation in the Bloemfontain court, from the 1950 Internal Security Act to the 1967 Terrorism Act to the amended Internal Security Act of 1982, and relevant jurisprudence, see Forsyth, *In Danger for their Talents*, pp. 129–181.

interference in the mid-1980s – the transition was completed with the (delayed) appointment of Justice Corbett as Chief Justice of the Appellate Division in 1989. Corbett succeeded Chief Justice Pierre Rabie. When push came to shove, Rabie had typically toed the government line in the adjudication of security-related cases. This is not altogether surprising, for it was Rabie who proclaimed in an 1987 interview with Johannesburg's *Sunday Star* that to him the United States represented "freedom run mad."[187]

One of the last occasions on which the Rabie Court came to the rescue of an apartheid government losing ground was (with the exception of the *Omar* judgment to be discussed later) the 1986 case of *Tsenoli v. State President.*[188] Without rehearsing the technical details of the case (like many in this period, it concerned the question of the legality of the 1986 state of emergency), it is relevant to point out that the Appellate Division ultimately found in favor of the government, holding that a lower court judgment – which had found fault with the manner in which President Botha had issued emergency regulations, and the scope of the powers of arrest and detention that these regulations had conferred on the security forces – was "forced and strained and not supported by the language used by the legislature."[189] By so finding, the Rabie Court slowed down the resurgence of the normative state.

The judgment came on the heels of other Supreme Court cases that had not ended favorably for the government, a development that more than likely influenced the government-friendly judgment of the Rabie court in *Tsenoli*:

> The initial legal challenges to the 1985 emergency regulations, although largely unsuccessful, demonstrated a change in judicial temper. The unwillingness to scrutinize emergency regulations that characterized the approach during the 1960 emergency was jettisoned, with the courts showing a readiness to examine the regulations critically and, if necessary, strike them down. Litigation following the 1986 emergency was more intense. Several decisions struck down regulations on the grounds of vagueness, gross unreasonableness, or exceeding the ambit of the empowering provisions. In other decisions, the court ordered the release of detainees.[190]

It is reasonable to infer that it was for these *political* reasons that the Appellate Division in *Tsenoli* "expressly refused to interpret security legislation restrictively so as to favor individual liberty."[191] Under Rabie's stewardship,

---

[187] As quoted in Dyzenhaus, *Hard Cases in Wicked Legal Systems*, p. 173.

[188] *Tsenoli v. State President* 1986 (4) SA 1150 (A).

[189] Ibid., at 1178.

[190] Marcus, "Civil Liberties Under Emergency Rule," p. 50. For judgments resulting in the release of detainees, see *Dempsey v. Minister of Law and Order* 1986 (4) SA 530 (C), which only two years later, on appeal, would give occasion for another controversial judgment by the Rabie Court; *Jaffer v. Minister of Law and Order* 1986 (4) SA 1027 (C); and *Radebe v. Minister of Law and Order* 1987 (1) SA 586 (W).

[191] Marcus, "Civil Liberties Under Emergency Rule," p. 51. The jurisprudence mentioned in the text included, among others, *Metal and Allied Workers' Union v. State President* 1986 (4) SA 358 (D); *Natal Newspapers (Pty) Limited v. State President* 1986 (4) SA 1109 (N). And yet, as Sarkin insists, judicial options for mitigating features of apartheid were available to judges.

the Appellate Division issued four additional judgments that sought to stem the tide of resistance that was mounting under the banner of the UDF in the mid-1980s. These were *Omar v. Minister of Law and Order*; *Minister of Law and Order v. Dempsey*; *Staatspresident en andere v. United Democratic Front en 'n ander*; and *Ngqumba v. Staatspresident*.[192] The first three deserve particular attention, for they sparked a heated debate among legal scholars and practitioners in South Africa concerning the legal – and moral – performance of the highest court in the land, and the function of law in times of transition.

Of utmost significance is *Omar*, for it led in many opposition quarters to resignation, prompting anti-apartheid lawyers to question the utility of law in the struggle against the state. For some, the judgment of the Appellate Division was a throwback to the jurisprudence of the 1960s. Lawrence Baxter commented thus:

In this decision the court has secured for the government an executive carte blanche that was neither obviously contemplated by the Public Safety Act [which was at the center of the judgment] itself nor justified under the South African constitutional tradition, tattered though this tradition may have become. The decision is a political and legal disaster for South Africa, for South African lawyers and, above all, for the victims of apartheid. Its significance extends far beyond the particular issues that were in dispute before the court.[193]

Or, as Dennis Davis put it, "nothing could be more devastating to the continued belief of the majority of the population in the value of the rule of law."[194] What was at issue in *Omar*, this watershed judgment?

For a list of thirty ostensible options, ranging from dissenting opinions to increased rigidity in the admittance of evidence in political trials, see Jeremy Sarkin, "Judges in South Africa: Black Sheep or Albinos: An Examination of Judicial Responses in the 1980s to Law and Human Rights and the Options Available to Temper the Effects of Apartheid," LL.M Thesis, Harvard Law School, 1988, pp. 93–135.

[192] *Omar v. Minister of Law and Order* 1987 (3) SA 859 (A); *Minister of Law and Order and another v. Dempsey* 1988 (4) SA 19 (A); *Ngqumba v. Staatspresident* 1988 (4) SA 224 (A); and *Staatspresident en andere v. United Democratic Front en 'n ander* 1988 (4) SA 830 (A). On defeated challenges in the courts, see also *Bloem v. State President of the Republic of South Africa* 1986 (4) SA 1064 (O); *Release Mandela Campaign v. State President* 1988 (1) SA 201 (N); and *Mokwena v. State President* 1988 (2) SA 91 (T). A trenchant critique of Bloem can be found in Dennis M. Davis, "Judicial Endorsement of Apartheid Propaganda: An Enquiry into an Acute Case," *South African Journal on Human Rights*," Vol. 3, No. 2 (July 1987), pp. 223–233. A detailed discussion of some of the other cases is available in Dennis Davis and Hugh Corder, "A Long March: Administrative Law in the Appellate Division," *South African Journal on Human Rights*, Vol. 4, No. 3 (1988), pp. 281–302; and Haysom and Plasket, "The War against Law," pp. 303–333. For another example of an ultimately unsuccessful legal challenge, met by the government at the last minute by way of retroactive amendment of the regulation at stake in the case, see the Eastern Cape Provincial Division's judgment in *Nkwinti v. Commissioner of Police* 1986 (2) SA 421 (E).

[193] Lawrence Baxter, "A Judicial Declaration of Martial Law," *South African Journal on Human Rights*," Vol. 3, No. 3 (November 1987), p. 318.

[194] Dennis M. Davis, "*Omar*: A Retreat to the Sixties?," *South African Journal on Human Rights*," Vol. 3, No. 3 (November 1987), p. 331.

The fundamentals of apartheid were at issue, the institutional design of "separate development." A critical plank in this design was Public Safety Act 3 of 1953.[195] It were the provisions of Section 3(1)(a) and Section 3(1)(b) that caused the clash of apartheid and anti-apartheid lawyers in *Omar*, and the Supreme Court jurisprudence that led up to it. The first set of provisions of the Public Safety Act authorized the State President to make regulations that he deems either necessary *or* expedient in the pursuit of public safety or the maintenance of public order, and to retire such regulations at his pleasure. The second set of provisions mentioned earlier empowered the State President to exercise his authority under Section 3(1)(a) *even retrospectively*. It was these provisions of the Public Safety Act that occasioned a flurry of litigation, culminating in the Appellate Division's judgment in *Omar*. The proceedings in *Omar* represented a contest over the distribution of power between the normative state and the prerogative state:

> The *Omar* case had the potential for a showdown between the courts and the executive, involving, as it did, a decision by the highest court of the country on the exercise of power by the supreme executive authority. Moreover, it followed in the wake of recent conflicting decisions involving divisions of the Supreme Court in all four provinces. What was at stake was the purported exclusion through regulations by the State President of two fundamental and universally acknowledged human rights. The stage was set for a decision relating to the ambit of judicial control over administrative action and the extent to which individuals could rely upon the courts for protection against executive excesses.[196]

The "conflicting decisions" referenced in the quote are *Metal and Allied Workers' Union v. State President* 1986 (4) SA 358 (D); *Bill v. State President* 1987 (1) SA 265 (W); and *Nqumba [sic] v. State President* 1987 (1) SA 456 (E), all of which were government-critical; as well as *Omar v. Minister of Law and Order* 1986 (3) SA 306 (C); *Bloem v. State President of the Republic of South Africa* 1986 (4) SA 1064 (O); and *Fani v. Minister of Law and Order* (ECD Case No. 1840/1985, unreported), all of which were government-friendly.[197] Whereas the Appellate Division in its judgment in *Omar* overruled

---

[195] Act 3 of 1953.

[196] André Rabie, "Failure of the Brakes of Justice: *Omar v. Minister of Law and Order* 1987 (3) SA 859 (A)," *South African Journal on Human Rights*, Vol. 3, No. 3 (November 1989), p. 300. For ease of presentation, I have omitted a discussion of the more technical aspects of the case. These are discussed, among other places, in Davis, "*Omar*," pp. 326–331; Grogan, "The Appellate Division and the Emergency," pp. 14–27; Etienne Mureinik, "Pursuing Principle: The Appellate Division and Review under the State of Emergency," *South African Journal of Human Rights*, Vol. 5, No. 1 (1989), pp. 60–72; Rabie, "Failure of the Brakes of Justice," pp. 300–311; and Graham Van der Leeuw, "The *Audi Alteram Partem* Rule and the Validity of Emergency Regulation 3(3)," *South African Journal on Human Rights*, Vol. 3, No. 3 (November 1989), pp. 331–334.

[197] *Metal and Allied Workers' Union v. State President* 1986 (4) SA 358 (D); *Bill v. State President* 1987 (1) SA 265 (W); *Nqumba [sic] v. State President* 1987 (1) SA 456 (E); *Omar v. Minister of Law and Order* 1986 (3) SA 306 (C); *Bloem v. State President of the Republic of*

the former set of cases, it upheld the latter. The overruled cases – *Metal and Allied Workers' Union, Bill,* and *Ngqumba* – were regarded by many in anti-apartheid circles as advances, especially given their origins, in the realm of civil liberties. Their tenor was that persons detained under the emergency regulations of the time were entitled, qua right, to legal representation and to ex post facto ministerial information about the reasons for their detention. *Omar* scaled back these advances. For many this outcome raised the specter of *Rossouw*, which, as we have seen, in 1964 set the pro-executive tone of the trial and appellate divisions of the Supreme Court for the next few decades, until the early 1980s. Accordingly, Anthony Mathews's assessment of *Omar* is reminiscent of his trenchant assessment of *Rossouw*:

> Though the majority judgment [in *Omar*] is quite lengthy, the proposition adopted by the court, and repeated several times, can be boiled down to the simple statement that because wide powers have been conferred by the Public Safety Act 3 of 1953 upon the State President to make emergency regulations, he can legislate to the prejudice of fundamental rights virtually at will so long as he does not act in bad faith or for improper considerations. As a kind of subsidiary premises of its judgment, the appeal court also declared that this same wide language makes the State President, and not the courts, the judge of the reasonableness of his own regulations. Acting on these two premises, Rabie ACJ boldly annihilated the claims of the detainee to a modicum of fundamental rights protection.[198]

This outcome was particularly chilling, given the procedural prehistory of the appellate judgment, where the validity of the emergency regulations had been "considered by at least 16 judges in five divisions of the Supreme Court, with judges fairly evenly divided."[199] Dugard, with justifiable frustration, points out that "[i]n these circumstances one might be forgiven for having expected, first, that the court would have been constituted to include, in addition to the Acting Chief Justice, the most senior judges of appeal; and, secondly, that the court would have delivered a carefully reasoned judgment, with a full consideration of all the relevant authorities and arguments. Both of the expectations were unfulfilled."[200] As some opined at the time, "liberal roots are not the only ones that have grown in South Africa's legal soil."[201]

South Africa 1986 (4) SA 1064 (O); and *Fani v. Minister of Law and Order* (ECD Case No. 1840/1985, unreported).

[198] Anthony S. Mathews, "*Omar* v. the Oumas," *South African Journal on Human Rights*, Vol. 3, No. 3 (November 1989), pp. 313. For his broader critique of South Africa's judiciary, see also Mathews' important *Freedom, State Security and the Rule of Law*; and *Law, Order and Liberty in South Africa*, respectively.

[199] John Dugard, "*Omar*: Support for Wacks's Ideas on the Judicial Process?," *South African Journal on Human Rights*, Vol. 3, No. 3 (November 1989), p. 297.

[200] Dugard, "*Omar*," p. 297. By way of an aside, Rabie's judgment was sixteen pages long. For a discussion of the legal reasoning in *Omar*, see in particular Dyzenhaus, *Hard Cases in Wicked Legal Systems*, pp. 168–171, but also Ellmann, *In a Time of Trouble*, pp. 83–98.

[201] Davis and Corder, "A Long March," p. 300.

Although *Dempsey* and *Staatspresident v. United Democratic Front* did not
stir quite as much emotion as *Omar*, they were cause for concern among anti-
apartheid lawyers nonetheless. *Dempsey* was problematic from the perspective
of individual liberty because it made arrests during the state of emergency
more easily justifiable, requiring only that an arresting officer deem an arrest
necessary for one of the purposes stipulated in the emergency regulations. The
ruling extended the reach of the state, notably into the townships, making it
"virtually impossible to challenge the validity of an arrest under emergency
powers."[202] *Staatspresident v. United Democratic Front*, in turn, removed the
checks on another organ of state – the State President, whom we encounter
here for the second time. The court held that, under the so-called "ouster
clause" in the Public Safety Act, the President of the Republic was empowered
to promulgate vague and uncertain regulations, and that such promulgations
were beyond the purview of judicial review.[203] The case, considered by some
the "nadir" of the Rabie Court's jurisprudence, concerned the scope of the so-
called media emergency regulations.[204]

The feared impact of the Rabie jurisprudence of the mid-1980s was
immense, and largely justified. In this era, "[t]he courts retained their jurisdiction but in large part it was a jurisdiction to pronounce legal what the
executive says is legal."[205] This excerpt from Marcus reflects the mood of the
time:

These decisions caused grave disquiet in legal circles and in the human rights community generally, not only because they tampered with long-standing traditional pre-
cepts, but also because they were largely the product of a disproportionately small
group of judges presided over by Chief Justice Rabie, whose tenure of office was
inexplicably and possibly unlawfully extended [thus delaying the appointment of Justice Corbett to the position of Chief Justice] after he had reached the compulsory
retirement age. Apart from the occasional dissent, the Appellate Division in these cases
showed itself unwilling to assert traditional libertarian values, preferring instead to
allow the executive a free hand.[206]

---

[202] Marcus, "Civil Liberties Under Emergency Rule," p. 52. See *Minister of Law and Order and
another v. Dempsey* 1988 (4) SA 19 (A). For a more extensive analysis of *Dempsey* than can,
due to space constraints, be provided here, see Ellmann, *In a Time of Trouble*, pp. 72–83.

[203] *Staatspresident en andere v. United Democratic Front en 'n ander* 1988 (4) SA 830 (A). It must
be added that in this period, Rabie appointed panels that were dominated by five executive-
minded judges, also known as the "emergency team." "When a nonmember of the team sat on
an emergency case and dissented, he never again sat on an emergency case during Rabie's
tenure." Etienne Mureinik, "Emerging from Emergency: Human Rights in South Africa,"
Michigan Law Review, Vol. 92, No. 6 (May 1994), p. 1977.

[204] Ellmann, *In a Time of Trouble*, p. 98. See also ibid., for a perceptive and exhaustive discussion
of the court's reasoning in the appellate case.

[205] Dyzenhaus, *Hard Cases in Wicked Legal Systems*, p. 172.

[206] Marcus, "Civil Liberties Under Emergency Rule," p. 53. For an interesting and concise
discussion of possible reasons for the controversial extension of Rabie's tenure as Chief Justice
of the Appellate Division, see Cameron, "Nude Monarchy," pp. 343–346.

However, the pendulum swung back only temporarily, from 1985 until 1988, and even then it did not swing as far as some observers claimed. Interestingly, with *Government of Lebowa v. Government of the Republic of South Africa and Another*, the Appellate Division under Rabie handed down a more positively received judgment.[207] The *Evening Post* showered the court with praise: "The country can be truly grateful to the Supreme Court. ... However much its authority has been whittled down by Government statutes, it stands as a beacon of truth and justice."[208] After several years of contention among various constituencies over the incorporation of Moutse, an entity in Northern Transvaal that was home to North Soto and a Ndebele minority, the entity was made part of the Lebowa Territorial Authority in 1962. In the late 1970s, the apartheid government flouted the idea of excising Moutse from Lebowa and incorporating it into the territory of KwaNdebele, which became self-governing in 1981. The incorporation was intended as a precursor to independence of the latter.

A drawn-out struggle over independence ensued, replete with internecine violence, including assassinations. In February 1986, representatives of Lebowa "challenged the excision of Moutse on the grounds that South Africa had failed to consult Lebowa" unsuccessfully in a Pretoria courthouse.[209] The judge in the case found that the government's 1980 excision had been conducted properly, and, in addition, validated retroactively in 1983. After further legal wrangling, the matter of Moutse ended up in the Appellate Division, where it was heard twice, first, in the form of a challenge brought by Lebowa, which the court rejected within three weeks, and, second, in the form of a challenge lodged by Chief Tlokwe Gibson Mathebe, leader of the Moutse community. In *Mathebe*, the court found that the National States Constitution Act, which the government claimed demanded the incorporation of Moutse into KwaNdebele, did *not* oblige the State President to proceed with the formation of national states (i.e., independent homelands like KwaZulu Natal). The court, presided over by Justice E. M. Grosskopf, held that practical considerations – such as administrative complications – were legitimate reasons for not proceeding with the establishment or expansion of a self-governing territory.[210]

[207] *Government of Lebowa v. Government of the Republic of South Africa and Another* 1988 (1) SA 344 (A). See also the earlier appellate case, which came to influence the litigation in *Lebowa, Government of the Republic of South Africa and another v. Government of KwaZulu and another* 1983 (1) SA 164 (A).

[208] As quoted in Abel, *Politics by Other Means*, p. 468.

[209] Abel, *Politics by Other Means*, p. 459.

[210] For the trial court judgment, see *Gibson Thlokwe Mathebe and others v. KwaNdebele Commissioner of Police and another*, TPD Case No. 14181/1987; For the appeal court judgment, see *Mathebe v. Regering van die Republiek van Suid-Afrika en andere* 1988 (3) SA 667 (A). Chief Justice Rabie, I should emphasize, did not serve on the bench when the *Mathebe* judgment was handed down. For the most complete treatment of the Moutse imbroglio available in print, see Abel, *Politics by Other Means*, pp. 435–494.

This did not mean that the apartheid state caved in the Moutse matter – within weeks the Minister of Constitutional Development and Planning, Chris Heunis, pronounced the government's intention to introduce new legislation that would make legal what now was not. It did mean, however, that even the Rabie Court, this executive-minded institution, did not give the government a carte blanche across the board. Furthermore, it can be interpreted to mean that law had not succumbed entirely to the dictates of power. This fact facilitated the *volte face* of the Appellate Division in 1989.

For under Chief Justice Michael Corbett, the times of the law, they were a-changin'. In *During NO v. Boesak*, to name but one important example, Corbett's Appellate Division set aside *Minister of Law and Order v. Dempsey*, putting regard for individual liberty at the forefront of the court's jurisprudence – and returning to the appellate jurisprudence of the pre-apartheid years and the 1950s.[211] The jurisprudence spoke for itself:

> We can measure the difference between the Rabie and Corbett courts, roughly but usefully, simply by asking how many cases of the Corbett court have been decided in favour of those challenging the use of emergency power. As of the end of 1990 there have been six reported emergency decisions by the Appellate Division since Corbett became chief justice, and of those four have granted at least some relief against the state's use of its emergency authority, whereas under Rabie only three of the twelve emergency cases did.[212]

But the jurisprudential changes were not merely substantive, but procedural as well. "Perhaps more significantly, the court took important steps to shift the burden of justifying a detention back onto the authorities and substantially to widen the class of administrative decisions that cannot be taken without prior hearing."[213]

The Appellate Division underwent a behavioral transformation as well, with individual judges more frequently asserting – and airing publicly – independent interpretations of the facts and the law of the cases before them. For as a review of the administration of justice in 1998 revealed, "In Bloemfontein [the seat of the court] tensions within the Appellate Division were given unusual expression. The rate of dissent showed a sharp increase – to

---

[211] *During NO v. Boesak* 1990 (3) SA 661 (A). For a quantitative analysis, measured by concurring and dissenting votes and opinions, of the individual voting patterns of South Africa's appellate judges – and their inferred political leanings – across case types (criminal, civil rights, tort, economic, apartheid) during the 1950–1990 period, see Stacia L. Haynie, *Judging Black and White: Decision Making in the South African Appellate Division, 1950–1990* (New York: Lang, 2003), pp. 62–86. One of several interesting findings is that in apartheid-related trials, "the overall patterns of voting do *not* support the suggestion that Afrikaans-speaking judges were more conservative than their English-speaking brethren." Ibid., p. 80. Emphasis added.

[212] Ellmann, *In a Time of Trouble*, p. 142.

[213] Mureinik, "Emerging from Emergency," p. 1979. For the relevant case law, see *Minister van Wet en Orde v. Matshoba* 1990 (1) SA 280 (A); and *Administrator, Transvaal v. Traub* 1989 (4) SA 731 (A).

nearly 15 per cent of decided cases, reversing a thirty-year decline and up from only one per cent in 1980."[214] What is more, in *Bank of Lisbon and SA Ltd v. De Ornelas*, the members of the court in the majority judgment rebuked one of their colleagues – once again publicly – for his tardiness in preparing a dissenting opinion.[215]

The foregoing amounted to a curtailment, if modest, of the prerogative state. Geoff Budlender came to a similar conclusion via a different route: "What we are now seeing is a deliberate move away from arbitrariness and towards law in one key area [what he terms "black urban law"], while at the same time there is a move away from legal control in another key area [the area of security law]. Each of these trends is the result of deliberate policy decisions."[216] Those are the workings of a dual state in which, according to Fraenkel, "the Normative and Prerogative States constitute an interdependent whole, consideration of the Normative State alone is not permissible."[217]

The uneven appellate jurisprudence of the 1980s shows that "judicial victories are embodied in political struggles; they are neither self-realizing nor self-effectuating; appellate decisions are the beginning of the fight, not the end. A powerful adversary like the South African government does not surrender because of a single legal defeat."[218] Inasmuch as the critique of the Appellate Division and of much of its jurisprudence between 1950 and 1990 is apt, the court's relative contribution to preserving the rule of law cannot be denied:

With rare exceptions, those who faced prosecution in criminal trials did so with the assistance of counsel, likely funded not by the state but rather, quite often, by foreign donors who thus supported the strategy of courtroom resistance to apartheid. Many others, who did not face prosecution, chose to initiate legal action in the hope of securing redress for some of the grievances they experienced as a result of the system of apartheid. The lawyers who represented these clients, moreover, by no means adopted courtroom strategies of total defiance, instead their characteristic approach seems to have been to play within the rules, to press the categories of South African legal argument to their limits but still to remain within those categories. Finally, and perhaps most surprisingly, these lawyers and their clients sometimes won. Ironically, therefore, the same lawyers who most urgently asserted the existence of a crisis of judicial legitimacy were also engaged in litigation that invoked and sometimes demonstrated the capacity of South African law to render just results.[219]

---

[214] Edwin Cameron, Gilbert Marcus, and Dirk Van Zyl Smit, "The Administration of Justice, Law Reform, and Jurisprudence," *Annual Survey of South African Law* (1988), p. 500. Emphases added.

[215] *Bank of Lisbon and SA Ltd v. De Ornelas* 1988 (3) SA 580 (A), at 609.

[216] Geoff Budlender, "Law and Lawlessness in South Africa," *South African Journal on Human Rights*, Vol. 3, No. 2 (1988), p. 145.

[217] Fraenkel, *The Dual State*, p. 71.

[218] Abel, *Politics by Other Means*, pp. 64–65. Emphases added.

[219] Stephen Ellmann, "Law and Legitimacy in South Africa," *Law and Social Inquiry*," Vol. 20, No. 2 (Spring 1995), p. 408.

In fact, elsewhere Ellmann insists that "the Rabie court, as sensitive as it was to the demands of the emergency, should *not* be seen as fecklessly surrendering common-law protections to the whims of the executive."[220] He claims, contrary to much legal scholarship, but I think rightly so, that the Rabie court remained committed to preserving the country's legal tradition. That his argument was counterintuitive was not lost on Ellmann, who had the following to say about his controversial claim in 1992. Considering the provocative nature of his argument, it is worth referencing him verbatim:

> To say that the court was determined to preserve a legal order in South Africa may seem implausible, in light of the extent to which the emergency system was meant precisely to remove legal accountability and of the extent to which the court's decisions protected that system. I am not saying, however, that the court meant to subject emergency powers to close judicial scrutiny, or to preserve the human rights protections embodied in many formulations of the rule of law. I am saying only that the court was determined to maintain that South African governmental power was conferred by law and was confined within boundaries, however wide, that were set by law.[221]

Do we possess any evidence in support of this claim? Yes, says Ellmann, pointing to a number of features in the appellate jurisprudence of the Rabie court, notably the court's "insistence, perhaps most evident in *Swart* and *Apleni*, that the rules of the game be adhered to," and its "retention of so many of the doctrines of interpretation of legislation and of review of official action."[222] *Pars pro toto* of the cases examined (the *toto* runs to about half a dozen), here is a brief portion of Ellmann's argument concerning *Ngqumba v. Staatspresident*, which the author singles out because the Appellate Division accepted the existence of a requirement according to which a person arrested under the emergency regulations was entitled to be informed as soon as reasonably possible of the reasons for his or her arrest.[223]

That Ellmann, an American lawyer who remained an outsider in South Africa, was not all off with his careful analysis of the Appellate Division's jurisprudence in the 1980s demonstrates the admiring review of his book by an insider whom many counted among South Africa's most erudite legal scholars, and most ardent advocates of human rights, Etienne

---

[220] Ellmann, *In a Time of Trouble*, p. 115. Emphasis added.

[221] Ellmann, "Law and Legitimacy in South Africa," p. 135.

[222] See *Minister of Law and Order and another v. Swart* 1989 (1) SA 295 (A) and *Apleni v. Minister of Law and Order and Others* 1989 (1) SA 195 (A) as well as *Nkwentsha v. Minister of Law and Order and another* 1988 (3) SA 99 (A). However, I find unpersuasive Ellmann's "third feature," namely, in his parlance, "the court's decision that when the State President makes emergency regulations he is still subject to judicial review." Ellmann, *In a Time of Trouble*, p. 135. For reasons outlined earlier, the jurisprudence of the Rabie court essentially pushed executive action on the part of the State President *beyond* judicial review. See, most important, *Omar v. Minister of Law and Order* 1987 (3) SA 859 (A).

[223] *Ngqumba v. Staatspresident* 1988 (4) SA 224 (A). Stephen Ellmann, *In a Time of Trouble*, p. 117.

Mureinik.[224] Writes Mureinik: "Ellmann's analysis is based on an encyclopedic reading of the South African literature, legal and other, and his perceptions weave a rich fabric of subtle insight. South African lawyers will learn much about their legal traditions from Ellmann's delicate account; indeed, they will learn much about their country. Most South Africans will be startled to discover that Ellmann has spent weeks rather than years in South Africa itself."[225]

Ellmann, to use the terms employed in this study, put his finger on the conflicting imperatives of the dual state, namely the oscillating relationship between the prerogative state and the normative state in this most unusual type of hybrid regime. Consider the following description, which illustrates once again the inherent tension in – and defining characteristic of – the institutional structure of the apartheid state – what Raymond Suttner once referred to as the "contradictory unity" of law: "South Africa has had its share of state-supported hit squads [which represented the prerogative half of the apartheid state], but the Appellate Division even in its darkest period [i.e., under Chief Justice Rabie] set its face against such truly naked [and arbitrary and unpredictable] power [thus representing the normative half of the apartheid state]. In doing so the court may have helped to slow – though it certainly did not stop – South Africa's descent from authoritarian law to state or vigilante terrorism."[226] This is reminiscent of an observation by Jerome Frank, the venerable American jurist, who once remarked, "Obviously, the courts cannot do the whole job. But, just as obviously, they can sometimes help to arrest evil popular trends in their inception."[227]

---

[224] For the contrary, but insufficiently substantiated, argument that Ellmann's view is "overly optimistic," see Heinz Klug, "Law Under and After Apartheid," *Law and Social Inquiry*, Vol. 25, No. 2 (Spring 2000), p. 661.

[225] Mureinik, "Emerging from Emergency," p. 1981. Mureinik's early death was a serious loss for the legal profession in South Africa. For tributes to his life and work, see the contributions by John Dugard and others to the *South African Journal of Human Rights*, Vol. 12, No. 3 (1996).

[226] Ellmann, "Law and Legitimacy in South Africa," p. 138. On the consequences of this inherent tension – and defining characteristic – of the institutional structure of the apartheid state and its antecedents, see Chapters 6 and 7 below. Suttner apparently coined the notion of South African law's "contradictory unity" in an unpublished 1983 paper, entitled "The Role of the Judiciary in the South African Social Order," as quoted in Hugh Corder, "Crowbars and Cobwebs: Executive Autocracy and the Law in South Africa," *South African Journal on Human Rights*, Vol. 5, No. 1 (1989), p. 3.

[227] Jerome Frank, "Some Reflections on Judge Learned Hand," *University of Chicago Law Review*, Vol. 24, No. 4 (Summer 1957), p. 698. John Dugard, who also used this quote in his influential 1978 treatise, wonders whether Frank might have had the example of South African in mind when he made his remark. Dugard believes that this might have been the case because "in the same address, after making his general observation, Frank commented as follows on the absence of a Bill of Rights and judicial review in South Africa and on the way in which the legislature had 'overruled' decisions of the 'Centlivres court' in the early 1950s: 'whether if supported by a Bill of Rights like ours, the South African court's decisions would have withstood the onslaughts of the regnant majority in the legislature, no one can say with certainty. But who can say that such decisions would not have done much to stem the terrifying growth of tyranny in that troubled land, a growth which, so many intelligent observers believe, may issue before long in a devastating civil war.'" Dugard, *Human Rights and the South African Legal Order*, p. 388. The quote within the quote can be found in Frank,

Based on the jurisprudence in the period 1950–1990, it appears, on balance, that many trials and appeals exhibited fidelity to law. At some times this fidelity was more pronounced than at others; at times it was not in evidence at all. The research undertaken by Lobban into the performance of trial courts (with particular reference to the Black Consciousness era) reveals, contrary to conventional wisdom, that apartheid's lower courts, while not above flagrantly violating rules and procedures, overall retained a core commitment to due process. I have drawn on this important – and insufficiently appreciated – data because it contradicts the conventional wisdom. It calls into question the argument that the disproportionately benign jurisprudence of the Appellate Division is exceptional – not representative – of judicial performance during the apartheid years.

As for the Appellate Division, a quantitative analysis of its jurisprudence between 1950–1990 – a docket of 3,044 reported cases – shows, furthermore, that it

was not ideologically supportive in the whole of [the government's] decision making. If the Court was the legislature's lackey or at least comprised of individuals philosophically sympathetic to the regime, the *support of the government should have been more systematically evidenced*, and one would anticipate this conservative philosophy to have affected private economic decisions as well. That the data do not support this implies that the Court was not pro-executive *in toto*. This analysis, however, does not undermine the damage incurred to rights and liberties by decisions like *Omar*, nor should it lessen the volume of the critics of the Court for those choices.[228]

"Where the government had been evaluated more generously [by the Appellate Division] in the past, the Court's decisions suggest that abruptly changed in the late 1970s."[229] However, as my qualitative analysis has hopefully demonstrated, it would be far too crude and simplistic to speak of an "abrupt" jurisprudential paradigm change in the late 1970s. The jurisprudence of the appellate judiciary was mixed throughout the apartheid years. Early jurisprudence earned the court the distinction of being regarded "a liberal

---

"Some Reflections on Judge Learned Hand," p. 698. Cf. the similar observation by Dennis Davis, "Adjudication and Transformation: Out of the Heart of Darkness," *Cardozo Law Review*, Vol. 22, Nos. 3–4 (March 2001), p. 828: "[W]hile the law has no judicially fixed content, it does constitute a site of important, albeit limited, struggle."

[228] Haynie, *Judging Black and White*, p. 61. First emphases added. For a comment on the methodology of measuring judicial ideology, see ibid., pp. 139–140. As far as the discussed fluctuation in the jurisprudence of the Appellate Division is concerned, Haynie finds that the court "significantly increased and decreased its support of the government in response to key political events;" more specifically it appears that "the Court's sensitivity to those challenging the regime was heightened" as contention between the apartheid government and the resistance movement intensified. Ibid., pp. 102–103.

[229] Haynie, *Judging Black and White*, pp. 102–103. See also Haynie's related claim that the Appellate Division "was becoming increasingly liberal," and according to her regression analysis, "inevitably so *regardless of the tenure of the Chief Justice*." Idem., "Judicial Descision-Making and the Use of Panels in the South African Appellate Division, 1950–1990," *Politikon*, Vol. 29, No. 2 (November 2002), p. 158. Emphases added.

institution in an illiberal community," and yet its record was uneven even then.[230] Subsequent jurisprudence prompted coinage of a label far less complimentary, but the courts' commitment to law was never extinguished entirely. Exemplary in this regard is perhaps the comment appended by Judge G. Friedman to the unreported case of *Natal Indian Congress v. State President*.[231] Although the judge found in favor of the government, his remarks will have left an impression on his Praetorian masters:

In the result I regret that the application must fail. I use the word "regret" advisedly. In general one of the traditional roles of the court is to act as a watch-dog against what I might term executive excesses in the field of subordinate legislation. It fulfills its role by measuring that legislation against long and well-established legal principles. It is therefore a matter of regret that in the field of security legislation, the legislature should have seen fit to remove from the court the role which, as I have said, is traditionally one entrusted to it, of fairly and without favour or prejudice, safeguarding the interest both of the state and its officers on the one hand and those of its citizens on the other.[232]

Nicholas Haysom, an influential advocate of apartheid's victims, and Clive Plasket, based on this and other jurisprudence, state the argument about law's function more forcefully (thus perhaps overstating it):

There is no need to catalogue the cases, notably since 1981, which have served to expose official abuses, temper executive action or reverse government policy: the clearest testament to the fact that the courts have exercised these powers is to be found in the willingness of political organizations and trade unions to approach the courts, even during the state of emergency, in order to establish the boundaries of executive power.[233]

Continue the two lawyers,

One of the peculiar features of South African society is that the courts allow an impoverished black employee to call his or her white employer to account, and a voteless black resident to summon a white cabinet minister before court. Law has been used as an attenuated form of accountability in a country where the majority of citizens are denied the right to exercise a more conventional form of accountability, the franchise.[234]

Against this background, a picture of apartheid jurisprudence emerges in which courts – trial and appeal – did not consistently favor the apartheid government, but frequently remained attuned to the demands of law.

---

[230] Dugard, *Human Rights and the South African Legal Order*, p. 279. The larger point is that the jurisprudence of apartheid – just like the law of apartheid – cannot be presented as a coherent whole. Related, see also Davis, "Adjudication and Transformation," esp. p. 826.

[231] *Natal Indian Congress v. State President* NPD (Case No. 3864/1988).

[232] *Natal Indian Congress v. State President* NPD (Case No. 3864/1988) at 11, as reported in Haysom and Plasket, "The War against Law," p. 330.

[233] Nicholas Haysom and Clive Plasket, "The War against Law: Judicial Activism and the Appellate Division," *South African Journal on Human Rights*, Vol. 4, No. 3 (1988), p. 306.

[234] Haysom and Plasket, "The War against Law," p. 307. We must keep in mind, however, that the magistracy performed *consistently* suboptimally, to put it mildly, from the perspective of political rights and civil liberties.

Intelligent Design

In addition to some of the country's courts, NIS, the National Intelligence Service, surprisingly served the normative state in the run-up to apartheid's endgame. Although the organizational predecessors of the NIS, namely, BOSS and DONS, were constitutive units of the prerogative state, NIS slowly moved into the realm of the normative state. The powers of NIS were curbed in 1981, and NIS distanced itself further from the prerogative state in 1987 when it withdrew from the National Security System. In the late 1980s, NIS was the principal channel of communication between the government and the ANC. Moved from the Department of Justice to the Office of the State President in 1989, NIS assumed a pivotal role in the investigations of "Third Force" activities. Under President F. W. de Klerk, and the leadership of General Pierre Steyn, NIS began penetrating the security forces in this capacity.[235] The emphasis on legal norms and institutions at the height of the insurrection period suggests that some fragments of the normative state had survived the apartheid onslaught, even treading on the turf of the prerogative state.

A WICKED LEGAL SYSTEM

In *Krohn v. Minister of Defence*, Sir James Innes, then South Africa's Chief Justice, remarked "one of the features of the English Constitution, a feature reproduced in the self-governing Dominions, is the absolute supremacy of the law."[236] This conception of the rule of law – the supremacy of the normative state over the prerogative state – dates back to A.V. Dicey's *An Introduction to the Study of the Law of the Constitution*, published in 1885. As a fundamental legal principle, it has underpinned British constitutionalism ever since. Yet the rule of law as an idea never enjoyed the same standing in South Africa. There, statutory and emergency powers violated the spirit of the principle early during British colonial rule. Causally related to the decline of the rule of law were the expansive use of delegated legislation and the granting of wide discretions of a quasi-judicial nature to ministers and bureaucrats.[237] Martin Chanock writes that

[t]hese legal developments which resulted from the growth of the state were not singular to South Africa, and they produced huge challenges for lawyers educated within the Diceyan constitutional world view with its distinctive understanding of the division of powers, and its tendency to deny many of the realities of the new administrative state. Nonetheless there clearly were special characteristics of the growth of the state in

---

[235] *Truth and Reconciliation Commission Report*, Vol. 2, pp. 318–319.
[236] *Krohn v. Minister of Defence* 1915 AD 191, as quoted in Chanock, *The Making of South African Legal Culture 1902–1936*, p. 470.
[237] Chanock, *The Making of South African Legal Culture 1902–1936*, p. 472.

South Africa which were distinctive. While a largely British constitutional and legal imagination governed many of the responses, the new state to which South African lawyers were responding had a significant different focus: race.[238]

The interaction of race-making and state formation was responsible for the limits of the normative state. The liberal institutionalism of the Cape Colony was capped in the first decade of the twentieth century. The British quest for reconciliation with the Afrikaners after the Boer War initiated the path toward racial state formation. The achievement of white unity "took precedence over English liberalism."[239] In the apartheid years, law served to "create, regularize and authorize power, rather than to restrict it."[240] Although the normative state existed, it ultimately served apartheid just like the prerogative state. John Dugard, in his seminal *Human Rights and the South African Legal Order*, describes law's role with these words:

In South Africa the law ... reflects the discriminatory expectations of the least enlightened section of the white community and translates popular prejudice into legal norms. It therefore provides authoritative support for the racist attitudes of those determined not to relent in their devotion to white supremacy. At the same time it restrains those who would otherwise question the prevailing social order by threatening them not only with social ostracism but also with criminal prosecution. The apartheid legal order thus serves both to institutionalize racial discrimination and to obstruct evolutionary social change.[241]

By all accounts, therefore, apartheid was framed by a "wicked legal system" – a legal system that was handmaiden to a repugnant regime. The system may have been wicked, but what mattered, as I hope to demonstrate, was that it remained a system, supported by a number of legal traditions.[242] It is here that we encounter similarities between the law of apartheid and Nazi law, as discussed by Ernst Fraenkel.

The Structure of Apartheid Law

Reflecting on Nazi law, Fraenkel made a simple, yet important observation: "a nation of 80 million people can be controlled by a plan *only* if certain definite rules exist and are enforced according to which the relations between the state and its members, as well as the relations between the citizens themselves, are regulated."[243] As the preceding analysis of state formation and state transformation has tried to show, the same was true for twentieth century South Africa. Smuts, Malan, Strijdom, Verwoerd, Vorster, and Botha,

---

[238] Chanock, *The Making of South African Legal Culture 1902–1936*, pp. 472–473.

[239] Marx, "Race-Making and the Nation-State," p. 194.

[240] Chanock, *The Making of South African Legal Culture 1902–1936*, p. 483. As Elisabeth Wood notes, "from 1948 until 1994, the political regime developed a peculiarly legalistic, antiliberal, and antidemocratic form of rule." Wood, *Forging Democracy from Below*, p. 113.

[241] Dugard, *Human Rights and the South African Social Order*, p. 106.

[242] For an extended discussion of South Africa's legal traditions, see Chapter 7.

[243] Fraenkel, *The Dual State*, p. xv. Emphasis added.

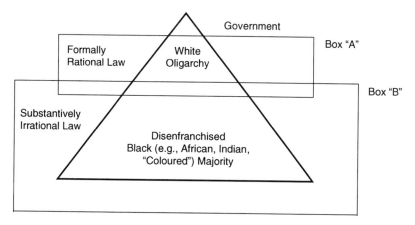

FIGURE 5.1. The Structure of Apartheid Law

successive leaders of successive Afrikaner governments, understood that white supremacy required force without reason as well as reason without force. This was the origin of the dual state. The dual state, above all else, made it possible to hold back a nation of millions. It was critical to ensuring the survival of whites, and the repression of blacks. Accordingly, some have characterized nondemocratic rule in South Africa as a form of legal-bureaucratic domination. Other observers remarked that this form of rule led to congealed injustice. Forged out of an unlikely alliance of English and Afrikaner interests, the apartheid state served the projects of racial domination, segregation, and eventually separate development so well because it was founded on *both* norms *and* institutions, especially legal norms and institutions. Contradictory pulls were at work in this state of law.[244] The law of apartheid was a blend of formally rational law and substantially irrational law (see Figure 5.1). The triangle of the figure represents the structure of apartheid South African society, and law's role in it.

Box "A" represents formally rational law. Government is only weakly constrained by this law, yet it regulates white commercial activity, as well as other domains, including parts of black society. Box "B" represents substantively irrational law. Law affecting the disenfranchised majority under apartheid was for the most part substantively irrational. At times, however, even substantive law took on a rational character. To recall Max Weber's categories, substantive law is driven by extralegal considerations.[245] These considerations, or ideologies,

---

[244] Michael Mann finds "an impeccably liberal society and democratic state for whites" that "coexisted with authoritarian and militaristic rule over blacks." See Michael Mann, "Authoritarian and Liberal Militarism: A Contribution from Comparative and Historical Sociology," in Steve Smith, Ken Booth and Marysia Zalewski, eds., *International Theory: Positivism and Beyond* (Cambridge: Cambridge University Press, 1996), p. 236.

[245] Weber, *Wirtschaft und Gesellschaft*, pp. 468–482. See also Chapter 2.

are the source of substantive law. Law was substantively rational under apartheid in the sense that law, such as discriminatory legislation, served the purpose of racial domination, but often maintained a level of systematic sophistication.

Apartheid law, in this sense, was often procedurally just. Joseph Raz has distinguished eight principles that characterize this procedural understanding of the rule of law:

(1) All laws should be prospective, open, and clear.
(2) Laws should be relatively stable.
(3) The making of particular laws should be guided by open, stable, clear, and general rules.
(4) The independence of the judiciary must be guaranteed.
(5) The principles of natural justice must be preserved.
(6) The courts should have review powers over the implementation of the other principles.
(7) The courts should be easily accessible.
(8) The discretion of the crime-preventing agencies should not be allowed to pervert the law.[246]

The predictable nature of much of apartheid law accounts for its formally rational character (see Box "A"). Apartheid law lost most of its formal character due to its extralegal source (see Box "B"). This side was substantively irrational. The above analysis discussed a select number of cases in which agents working within the apartheid state decided cases arbitrarily without recourse to legal norms and rules. The result of excessive personal discretion, whether informed by political, moral, or other concerns, is always unpredictable law. Apartheid law, in this sense, was frequently unpredictable law; it was substantively irrational law.

Yet apartheid law had another side (see Box "A"). We saw that the attribute *legality* draws on arguments about constitutional tradition. The South African state, as this chapter has shown, has a very long such tradition, although this tradition was distorted and dehumanized under apartheid. Yet institutional remnants and ideas of this normative state survived. As Justice Laurie Ackerman, a former Constitutional Court judge, suggested in an interview: "In South Africa today there exists a deep sense that conflicts need to be settled in *legal* disputes."[247] South Africans, according to Ackerman, have displayed less cynicism about, in particular, the constitution-making process, than he believes citizens do in other newly democratizing countries. Ackerman attributes this to

---

[246] Raz, "The Rule of Law and its Virtue," pp. 214–219. For a discussion of these principles in the apartheid context, see Mathews, *Freedom, State Security, and the Rule of Law*, esp. pp. 23–30.

[247] Laurie L. Ackerman, Justice of the Constitutional Court of South Africa, Interview with the author, Johannesburg: September 25, 1996. For a similar view, see Helen Suzman, former veteran MP for South Africa's Democratic Party and its various predecessors, Interview with the author, Johannesburg: September 26, 1997. Suzman was for many years the sole member of the opposition in Parliament.

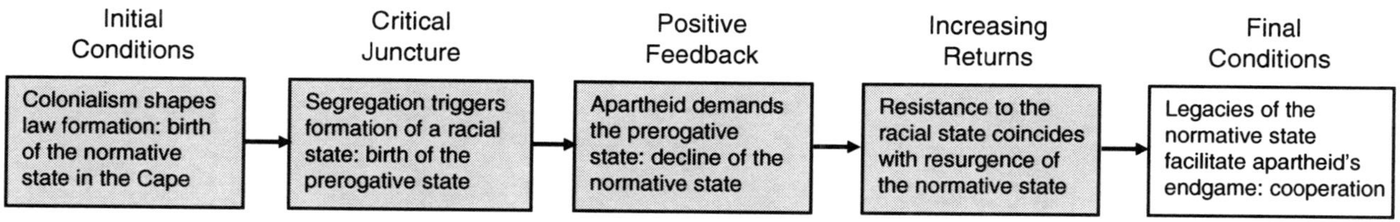
Initial Conditions
Colonialism shapes law formation: birth of the normative state in the Cape
Critical Juncture
Segregation triggers formation of a racial state: birth of the prerogative state
Positive Feedback
Apartheid demands the prerogative state: decline of the normative state
Increasing Returns
Resistance to the racial state coincides with resurgence of the normative state
Final Conditions
Legacies of the normative state facilitate apartheid's endgame: cooperation

FIGURE 5.2. The Logic of Path-Dependent Explanation: The Argument Thus Far

the efficacy and long-standing tradition of constitutionalism and "minority democracy" in South Africa.[248]

What difference this tradition – this shared mental model of law – made in apartheid's endgame is the subject of the next chapters. Figure 5.2 summarizes the argument thus far. Although this and the previous chapter described the evolution of law – from initial conditions to increasing returns – the next and the chapter thereafter turn to the legacies of law, thereby completing my comparative historical analysis of the long-run development of law (Chapters 4 and 5), and the long-run consequences of legal development (Chapters 6 and 7), in this telling case.

---

[248] Laurie L. Ackerman, Interview with the author, Johannesburg: September 25, 1996. For the notion of "minority democracy," see Steven Friedman, "South Africa: Divided in a Special Way," in Larry Diamond, Juan J. Linz, and Seymour Martin Lipset, eds., *Politics in Developing Countries: Comparing Experiences with Democracy*, Second Edition (Boulder, CO: Lynne Rienner, 1995), p. 534. On the related notion of "racial democracy," applied to South Africa and Israel, see Linz, "Totalitarian and Authoritarian Regimes," pp. 175–411.

6

Apartheid's Endgame and the Law I

This chapter shows that the apartheid state was, in an important respect, necessary for making democracy work. The analysis finds a path-dependent relationship between law and politics. I explain why the *dual state* from the past, as explicated in Chapters 4 and 5, was a *usable state* in the present of apartheid's endgame. I show how the ultimate logic of apartheid's endgame was structured by this state. The state mattered both as an idea and an institutional structure. The apartheid state – *qua* law – provided the possibility of, and potential for, the kind of action that could move interacting adversaries away from confrontation, toward cooperation. From the perspective of the *longue durée*, the dual state served apartheid, but it served democracy as well. In what follows, I focus on legal norms and institutions. As we shall see, as specific legacies of liberalism, these legal norms and institutions facilitated – in crucial and unexpected ways – the resolution of apartheid's endgame.

FROM CRISIS TO ENDGAME

Before the endgame there was crisis. Apartheid's government under P. W. Botha experienced a number of serious shocks to the country's racial edifice that together pushed the regime toward exhaustion. Three shocks in particular contributed to apartheid's crisis: (1) the collapse of the Portuguese empire in southern Africa; (2) the economic downturn and the u-turn in investment; and (3) the mounting resistance and insurrection in the country's townships. Interaction effects among these shocks plunged the apartheid regime into disarray.

The Collapse of the Portuguese Empire

In 1974 a coup by the Armed Forces Movement ended the dictatorship of Marcello Caetano, successor to Salazar, in Portugal. The successful overthrow marked the end of the Portuguese overseas empire. As the main motivation behind the coup was to extricate Portugal from entanglements abroad, the new

Lisbon government hastily pulled out of Africa.[1] The new rulers embarked on the task in a fast-track procedure. Ryszard Kapuscinski memorably described Portugal's rapid and chaotic withdrawal from Luanda.[2] Mozambique's quick advance to independence and celebrations of Frelimo's transitional government on September 25, 1974, set off demonstrations of support within South Africa, organized among others by the South African Students' Organization (SASO).[3] In February 1975, the Popular Movement for the Liberation of Angola (MPLA) became the official government of the People's Republic of Angola, legitimated by the Organization of African Unity (OAU).

Within a year of the fall of dictatorship in Portugal, both Mozambique and Angola had become independent. Zimbabwe, formerly Rhodesia, followed suit in 1980. Within a few years, South Africa's *cordon sanitaire* of like-minded governments and regimes was all but decimated. Out of a total of four white minority governments in the region a few years prior, only South Africa remained at the beginning of the 1980s. To Pretoria's great anxiety, the Soviet Union flew thousands of Cuban troops in cargo planes into Angola to aid the new government there, the Popular Movement for the Liberation of Angola, against two Pretoria-backed rebel movements, the National Front for the Liberation of Angola (FNLA) and the National Union for the Total Independence of Angola (UNITA). By the end of 1975, the governing parties in Angola and Mozambique were (1) firmly committed to Marxism-Leninism; (2) vociferously opposed to apartheid; (3) had close ties with the ANC; and (4) received military and other support from the Soviet Union.[4] Robert Mugabe, who became Zimbabwe's first president, developed ties with China, bypassing a connection with the Soviet Union, thus introducing yet another communist force into Southern Africa.

These developments dealt serious blows to apartheid's stand. After Angola's independence, units of the South West African People's Organization (SWAPO), Namibia's foremost independence movement, began launching raids on Namibia from bases in southern Angola, increasing the sense of encirclement felt in Pretoria. A 1975 government white paper warned that the developments in the Southern African region "will undoubtedly encourage the radical elements in revolutionary organizations inside and outside [South Africa] and incite them to greater efforts."[5] In short, the successive transitions from colonial rule to some form of Marxism-Leninism in Southern Africa greatly increased security fears on the part of apartheid's military planners, prompting a steep increase in military spending. The government faced a "fundamental security

---

[1] David B. Abernethy, *The Dynamics of Global Dominance: European Overseas Empires, 1415–1980* (New Haven: Yale University Press, 2000), p. 148.

[2] Ryszard Kapuscinski, *Another Day of Life* (San Diego: Harcourt Brace, 1987).

[3] Gerhart, *Black Power in South Africa*, p. 298.

[4] Price, *The Apartheid State in Crisis*, pp. 40–41.

[5] Quoted in Price, *The Apartheid State in Crisis*, p. 42.

dilemma."[6] The economic malaise that stagnation had produced inside South Africa only exacerbated this dilemma.

Economic Downturn and the U-Turn in Investment

South Africa entered a full-scale recession in 1976. The economic logic of apartheid, with its reliance on labor repressive policies, proved no longer viable, and all industrial sectors reported sharp production declines. "The mid-1970s recession ... went beyond a normal cyclical downsizing to reflect a profound structural crisis for South African capitalism – one which called into question its specific path of development over the past fifty years."[7] It became increasingly evident that apartheid's architects did not appreciate the "medium-term implications for an expanding manufacturing sector of a small and fixed skilled-labor pool and consumer goods market."[8] The limits of economic policies became increasingly evident. "Apartheid, which in the first two decades served the growth interests of a fledgling manufacturing sector, became a fetter on growth as the sector expanded, matured, and developed new imperatives that could not be met within the existing apartheid structures."[9]

P. W. Botha's administration faced severe constraints on productivity and economic growth. Although the political repercussions of this economic downturn were encouraging for South Africa's democracy-demanding forces, they proved devastating for Pretoria. Inflation rose above 10 percent and the increase in GDP was not keeping up with a rapidly growing population.[10] Whites were beginning to suffer financially, causing the poor white problem to return to Afrikaner society, substantially weakening the government's traditional support base. To make matters worse for the apartheid government, the economic malaise acquired a distinctly political dimension. The alliance of maize and gold, which had shaped the economic policies of the National Party in the 1940s and 1950s (and which at the time had steadfastly opposed the economic preferences of the manufacturing sector and the recommendations of the Fagan Commission, convened by the United Party), had become marginalized in politics and society.

Largely as a result of the transformation and diversification of the economy and the modernization of agricultural farming (involving extensive mechanization and capital consolidation), core economic interests within the National Party constituencies shifted in the 1970s and 1980s.[11] Many Afrikaners seized

[6] Robert M. Price, "Security versus Growth: The International Factor in South African Policy," *Annals of the American Society of Political and Social Science*, No. 489 (1987), pp. 103–122, here p. p. 108, as quoted in Sisk, Democratization in South Africa, p. 66.
[7] O'Meara, *Forty Lost Years*, p. 178.
[8] Price, *The Apartheid State in Crisis*, p. 35.
[9] Price, *The Apartheid State in Crisis*, p. 35.
[10] Thompson, *A History of South Africa*, p. 221.
[11] On the diversification of the economy in the 1960s, see Stanley Trapido, "Political Institutions and Afrikaner Social Structures in the Republic of South Africa," *American Political Science Review*, Vol. 57, No. 1 (March 1963), pp. 75–87.

opportunities in business, leaving agriculture behind. For example, the proportion of Afrikaners employed in agriculture dropped by 14 percent in a quarter of a century (from over 30 percent in the 1940s to less than 16 percent in the mid-1960s).[12]

This shook up apartheid's political base. Economic diversification gave way to political diversification among National Party supporters. This in turn strengthened the hand of the English-dominated business community which had for some time demanded more government consideration for the manufacturing sector.[13] Calls for economic liberalization *qua* political liberalization grew more incessant and were increasingly in line with important Afrikaner business interests. Economics, in other words, trumped ethnicity. Paradoxically, apartheid's economic success (the growth and investment boom in the 1960s) turned out to be largely responsible for the adverse political consequences of the economic downturn and decline in investment that engulfed the country in the 1980s. Modernization was associated with an increased demand for democracy.[14] This demand registered with investors, principally causing what Elisabeth Wood calls the "investment u-turn."[15]

Wood demonstrates that the deepening of mobilization by workers and township residents and governmental repression induced a dramatic decline in investor confidence and a corresponding decline in investment, beginning in the mid-1970s.[16] Investors were apparently not convinced that the country's political and economic situation warranted favorable expectations of future rates of return. This situation also had international repercussions. Disinvestment (the removal of financial wealth or resources by foreign corporate investors) was accompanied by divestment (the removal of financial wealth or resources by foreign private investors). There were also government-mandated financial sanctions imposed on South Africa. The largest single divestment effort undertaken in the United States was a 1986 bill signed by California Governor George Deukmejian. It required state pension funds and the University of California "to sell up to $12 billion of shares in firms doing business in South Africa."[17] Disinvestment had its own logic in South Africa. It was intertwined with political developments. Increased mobilization in the country's townships spurred disinvestment in three ways: it depressed present profit rates, dampened expected profit rates, and rendered expectations of the

[12] Price, *The Apartheid State in Crisis*, p. 38.

[13] Wood, *Forging Democracy from Below*, p. 160.

[14] For a review of the theoretical debate, see Adam Przeworski and Fernando Limongi, "Modernization: Theories and Facts," *World Politics*, Vol. 49, No. 2 (January 1997), pp. 155–183.

[15] Wood, *Forging Democracy from Below*, p. 152.

[16] Wood, *Forging Democracy from Below*, p. 152.

[17] William H. Kaempfer, James A. Lehman, and Anton D. Lowenberg, "Divestment, Investment Sanctions, and Disinvestment: An Evaluation of Anti-Apartheid Policy Instruments," *International Organization*, Vol. 41, No. 3 (Summer 1987), p. 461.

future sufficiently uncertain for key investors to suspend investment.[18] The case of Chase Manhattan Bank bears out the third causal path toward disinvestment. Chase Manhattan's decision, in July 1985, to stop extending credit to South Africa came in the immediate aftermath of the apartheid government's imposition of a state of emergency. Investor confidence, thus, fell as resistance and insurrection thrived.

Resistance and Insurrection in the Townships

In June of 1976, some fifteen thousand schoolchildren protested against the introduction of Afrikaans as the language of instruction in secondary schools in Johannesburg's South Western Townships. Soweto, as the townships are called for short, made headlines around the world that day when police fought schoolchildren with tear gas and violence, killing two and injuring others. That single day in June revved up radicalism in the townships. The government's disproportionate use of violence threw the country into the throes of insurrectionary upheaval. In the second half of 1976, between six hundred and one thousand people (depending on who is doing the counting) are estimated to have died in confrontations between forces demanding democracy and those resisting it. More than five thousand were injured.[19] Resistance became insurrection in this period. In the years that followed, more radical and more defiant masses mobilized against apartheid than had ever threatened the regime before. Winnie Mandela's call in 1985 to make the "townships ungovernable" fell on open ears in indigent settlements and overcrowded townships around the country. Thousands of township youth joined the ANC in exile. *Umkhonto we Sizwe* camps in the region became institutions of military education. In these camps, disillusioned township youth received the training necessary to confront apartheid, with violence if necessary.[20] This turn toward confrontation interfered not only with political life, but with economic life as well.

Various indicators show a decline in economic performance in the period between the mid-1970s and mid-1980s. Wood reports that the ratio of private gross domestic investment to capital stock in South Africa fell from 6.2 percent

---

[18] For the general point about the relationship between investment and mobilization, see Wood, *Forging Democracy From Below*, p. 151.

[19] Alan Brooks and Jeremy Brickhill, *Whirlwind Before the Storm* (London: International Defence and Aid Fund for Southern Africa, 1980), pp. 255–256.

[20] Note, however, that the ANC in exile also tried to exert a moderating influence on radicalized township youth. Through the Soweto Students' Representative Council (SSRC), for example, ANC operatives in Mozambique tried to recruit key members of the Soweto student leadership and channel their violent and undirected challenges to apartheid into more organized forms of resistance such as stayaways, demonstrations, and boycotts. Karis and Gerhart, *From Protest to Challenge*, p. 280. More generally, see also Glenn Adler and Jonny Steinberg, eds., *From Comrades to Citizens: The South African Civics Movement and the Transition to Democracy* (London: Macmillan, 2000).

in 1972 to 4.6 percent in 1979, and dropped further to 3.8 percent in 1986 (all data reported by the South African Reserve Bank).[21] The flow of long-term capital investment, another sensitive measure for investor confidence, corroborates the finding. Although the inflow of long-term private capital increased rapidly during the 1960s and remained high during the early 1970s, the inflow turned into an *outflow* of capital after 1977. The massive drain of capital "precipitated a sharp drop in the real effective exchange rate – which declined by thirty-four percent from 1983 to 1985 – and caused a sharp increase in the real price of capital goods as a significant portion is imported."[22] Resistance and insurrection, thus, were causally related to the economic downturn and the u-turn in investment. Stayaways and strikes, frequently organized by trade unions (restrictions on which had been relaxed by the government), imposed direct costs on firms and employers.[23] With every day that workers spent in the streets instead of on the shop floor, the labor-intensive mining industry incurred financial losses. The government's use of repression to contain resistance and insurrection under the auspices of the prerogative state only worsened apartheid's crisis.

"Financial sanctions – imposed as a result of the regime's repressive response to mobilization – led to a decline in the value of the rand prompting a steep increase in the real price of capital goods and the user cost of capital."[24] Financial sanctions targeted capital movement, and included the removal of nonstructural, physical capital, the forced sale of South African subsidiaries and shares in South African firms, bans on new direct foreign investment and new loans to the apartheid government, as well as a ban on the renewal of current debt.[25] Financial sanctions were complemented with other types of sanctions, including trade sanctions. Trade restrictions were applied to both imports and exports. In terms of sanctioned import categories, several products were restricted by one or more countries, including steel, iron, coal, gold, "strategic minerals" (platinum, chromium), diamonds, uranium, textiles, Krugerrand

---

[21] Wood, *Forging Democracy from Below*, pp. 153–154.

[22] Wood, *Forging Democracy from Below*, p. 155.

[23] Anthony W. Marx, *Lessons of Struggle: South African Internal Opposition, 1960–1990* (New York: Oxford University Press, 1992), Chapter 6; Glenn Adler and Eddie Webster, eds., *Trade Unions and Democratization in South Africa, 1985–1997* (London: Macmillan, 2000); Seekings, *The UDF*, pp. 61–64; 202–204; 231–235; Jeremy Baskin, *Striking Back: A History of COSATU* (Johannesburg: Ravan, 1991); Steven Friedman, *Building Tomorrow Today: African Workers in Trade Unions, 1970–1984* (Johannesburg: Ravan, 1987); and Gay W. Seidman, *Manufacturing Militance: Workers' Movements in Brazil and South Africa, 1970–1985* (Berkeley: University of California Press, 1994). For an insider's perspective dealing with the dynamics of contention in Alexandra township, see Mzwanele Mayekiso, *Township Politics: Civic Struggles for a New South Africa* (New York: Monthly Review Press, 1996).

[24] Wood, *Forging Democracy From Below*, p. 168. See also Deon Geldenhuys, *Isolated States: A Comparative Analysis* (Johannesburg: Jonathan Ball Publishers, 1990).

[25] Charles M. Becker, "Economic Sanctions Against South Africa," *World Politics*, Vol. 33, No. 2 (January 1987), p. 156.

coins, and agricultural products.[26] In terms of sanctioned export categories, a number of countries eliminated petroleum products (oil), high technology products (computers, nuclear technology), consumer goods, manufactures, and agricultural products from their trade with South Africa.[27] Sanctions adopted by the U.S. Congress in 1987 (overriding the veto of then President Ronald Reagan) also restricted U.S.-South African airline traffic. The money drain exacerbated the economic downturn. As governor of the South African Reserve Bank, Gerhard de Kock, put it in 1988: "In the present international political climate the capital account remains the Achilles heel of South Africa's balance of payments."[28] The money drain in turn caused a brain drain, a serious hollowing out of white society. The large exit (defined in this context as out-migration) of white South Africans, concerned about their future in South Africa, only compounded the country's skills shortage, which had been one of the causes of the economic downturn in the first place.[29] Next came the transition from crisis to endgame.

From Botha to De Klerk

The transition from crisis to endgame was preceded by a transition in leadership. At the helm of the National Party and the apartheid government, F. W. de Klerk replaced P. W. Botha, the *Groot Krokodil*, assuming the leadership of party and government. De Klerk was to become Nelson Mandela's main interlocutor in the endgame proper. Mangosuthu Buthelezi later joined the adversarial duo, but did not muster the same influence. Mandela and de Klerk were the leaders in the three-cornered bargaining that ensued. Later bargaining turned into a two-cornered affair, leading to the collapse of the Convention for a Democratic South Africa (CODESA).[30] But first came the transformation of the ruling National Party. Early in 1989, Botha suffered a stroke and was forced to resign the NP leadership. When it became clear six months later that his cabinet, other NP functionaries, and many party rank-and-file were supporting de Klerk rather than Botha (there was even a revolt in the cabinet), Botha resigned. De Klerk, while committed

[26] Anton D. Lowenberg and William H. Kaempfer, *The Origins and Demise of South African Apartheid: A Public Choice Analysis* (Ann Arbor: University of Michigan Press, 1998), p. 111. Note that the Lowenberg/Kaempfer list is incomplete. It had to be amended here. See also Audie Klotz, "Norms Reconstituting Interests: Global Racial Equality and U.S. Sanctions Against South Africa," *International Organization*, Vol. 49, No. 3 (Summer 1995), pp. 451–478; Audie Klotz and Neta Crawford, eds., *How Sanctions Work* (London: Macmillan, 2000).
[27] Becker, "Economic Sanctions Against South Africa," pp. 154–155.
[28] Quoted in Thompson, *A History of South Africa*, red. ed., p. 243.
[29] The voluntary exit of white South Africans compounded the demographic decline of the country's white population. Official statistics surveyed at the time showed a drop from 21 percent of the total population in 1960 to 15 percent in 1985. In the same survey, the government calculated that by 2005, the percentage of whites would have dropped to 10 percent. Thompson, *A History of South Africa*, p. 241.
[30] On the inner structure and workings of CODESA, see Friedman, ed., *The Long Journey*.

to apartheid, changed the government's attitude toward anti-apartheid organizations, allowing mass demonstrations in cities around the country. The leadership transition initiated the return of the normative state and the decline of the prerogative state. In his famous speech to parliament on February 2, 1990, de Klerk lifted the ban on the ANC, SACP, PAC and some other thirty proscribed organizations including the UDF and the Congress of South African Trade Unions (COSATU). On February 11, Nelson Mandela, too, walked free.

The End of the Cold War

I have thus far argued that three shocks contributed to apartheid's crisis: (1) the collapse of the Portuguese empire in Southern Africa; (2) the economic downturn and the u-turn in investment; and (3) the mounting resistance and insurrection in the country's townships. It remains for me to consider the international dimensions of democratization in South Africa.

The democratization literature distinguishes three forms of international influence – contagion, control, and consent.[31] I will herein only examine the *contagion* perspective, the only one with any explanatory purchase in the case at hand. According to the logic of contagion, democratization in one country or geographical region spills over into a neighboring state or a different world region by way of demonstration. Laurence Whitehead recently identified five different "regional clusters" where processes of democratization are said to have been contagious. He groups South Africa together with Namibia into a Southern African cluster, suggesting that a demonstration process was at work between the latter country's decolonization and the former's democratization. However, this argument is not particularly helpful for understanding democratization in South Africa, for it overlooks that both of these processes – decolonization and democratization – crucially involved one and the same agent, namely, South Africa's apartheid government.

Namibia's independence in 1990 was facilitated by U.S.-sponsored negotiations that the apartheid government entered into in May 1988. In conjunction with Angola's aforementioned MPLA government and Cuba, South Africa signed the accords on Namibia's independence on December 22, 1988. Neither military stalemate in Angola nor superpower involvement convinced apartheid South Africa to agree to Namibian independence. Instead, the Pretoria government calculated that only improved relations with other African states would help restore South Africa's tainted image in the world.[32] Pretoria's Praetorians

---

[31] Laurence Whitehead, "Three International Dimensions of Democratization," in idem., ed., *The International Dimensions of Democratization: Europe and the Americas* (Oxford: Oxford University Press, 1996), p. 4.

[32] Heribert Adam and Kogila Moodley, *The Negotiated Revolution: Society and Politics in Post-Apartheid South Africa* (Johannesburg: Jonathan Ball Publishers, 1993), p. 47. See also Donald Rothchild and Caroline Hartzell, "Interstate and Intrastate Negotiations in Angola," in I. William Zartman, ed., *Elusive Peace: Negotiating an End to Civil Wars* (Washington, DC: Brookings, 1995), pp. 181–187.

tried to shed its colonial image to pave the way for a readmittance in the comity of nations, and they did so *before* the end of the Cold War. The opening of the apartheid mind transpired not by way of contagion but instead was motivated by a rationally motivated change in preferences that *predated* democratization in the region. Consequently, a process of contagion from within the region never materialized. Could demonstration effects from elsewhere have prompted democratization?

The sequence of democratization immediately preceding South Africa's transition was that taking place on the territory of the former Soviet Union, which had disintegrated in the wake of *perestroika* (economic restructuring) and *glasnost* (transparency). Reference is routinely made to the importance of the end of the Cold War, specifically the dissolution of the Soviet Union, in understanding change in South Africa.[33] One proponent of this perspective maintains that the way to direct negotiations between the apartheid government and the ANC was crucially paved by "normative and structural changes in the international system itself." The "deideologization" of foreign policy that accompanied the collapse of the Soviet Empire, so the author argues, "forced both sides [the democracy-demanding and democracy-resisting forces in South Africa] to rethink their basic positions, particularly with regard to regional and domestic conflict-resolution issues."[34] However, mere synchronicity does not demonstrate an international source of democratization. If we believe Michael Bratton and Nicolas Van de Walle, variation in outcomes across democratization cases in Africa indicate that "major explanatory variables intervene between the international context and transition process[es]."[35] This applies also to the case of South Africa.

Inasmuch as South Africa's interacting adversaries closely followed the democratic experiments in Eastern Europe, the fact remains that steps toward a reform of apartheid had preceded the systemic changes in Europe by several years. In fact, they date as far back as 1986, when secret conversations between government officials and the apartheid state's most prominent prisoner, Nelson Mandela, commenced.[36] In fact, Allister Sparks reports that the SACP's Joe Slovo had already in the spring of 1987 declared a preference for cooperation over confrontation with the NP: "If there were any prospect of settling this thing peacefully tomorrow, we would be the first to say let's do it."[37] This statement was remarkable. For as Sparks points out, "twelve years

---

[33] See, for example, Lawrence Schlemmer, "The Turn in the Road: Emerging Conditions in 1990," in Robin Lee and Lawrence Schlemmer, eds., *Transition to Democracy: Policy Perspectives 1991* (Cape Town: Oxford University Press, 1991); Giliomee, "Democratization in South Africa," pp. 90–92.

[34] Graham Evans, "South Africa in Remission: The Foreign Policy of an Altered State," *Journal of Modern African Studies*, Vol. 34, No. 2 (June 1996), p. 254.

[35] Bratton and van de Walle, *Democratic Experiments in Africa*, p. 30.

[36] Allister Sparks, *Tomorrow is Another Country: The Inside Story of South Africa's Negotiated Revolution* (London: Heinemann, 1995), pp. 21–36.

[37] As quoted in Sparks, *The Mind of South Africa*, p. 366.

before Slovo had written a book entitled *No Middle Road*, in which he
warned against the 'illusion' that there might be a route to democracy in
South Africa other than through the 'seizure of power' by the ANC's guerilla
forces."[38]

Therefore, democratization in East Central Europe is only marginally relevant for explaining the onset and resolution of apartheid's endgame – at least in
terms of the logic of contagion.[39] More relevant are the costs – and benefits –
that the ANC and NP incurred on account of the liberalization and dissolution
of the Soviet Union.

ANC

Some observers have claimed that the apartheid government managed to retain
control over the transition because of Soviet decline. Before I scrutinize this
argument, it is important to recall that during the Cold War the Soviet Union
considered the ANC its most important ally in Southern Africa:

The ANC leadership under Oliver Tambo was trusted by the Soviets, who kept up
a close relationship with the South African leaders [in the resistance struggle]
through Moscow's embassy in Zambia, where the ANC had its exile headquarters.
Perhaps surprisingly, the documents show that Soviet closeness to the ANC developed
in spite of, rather than because of, the South African Communist Party's strong
influence within the Congress. The International Department, which – alongside
the KGB [the Soviet Union's Committee for State Security] – was the key Soviet
institution in developing the links, disliked and mistrusted many of the leading South
African Communists, among them the political head of the ANC military wing, Joe
Slovo, for their emphasis on independence and their suspected fondness for Euro-
Communism.[40]

The latter point is significant, for, surprisingly, it was Slovo, formerly
General-Secretary of the SACP and communist stalwart, who invented the
so-called sunset clause that paved the way for the still to be discussed power-
sharing agreement between the NP and the ANC alliance. Slovo's crucial and
uncharacteristically compromising bargaining behavior becomes more readily
understandable against the background of his run-ins with the KGB and the
International Department – and in the context of *perestroika* and *glasnost*: "As
Moscow's attention was increasingly consumed by domestic problems, no
longer did it welcome foreign 'adventures'. If South Africa featured at all in the
Kremlin's agenda, it had a low priority. No longer was it seen in the context of
a struggle against capitalism; but rather as a long-shot trading partner. Paradoxically, therefore as the West moved towards the ANC, Moscow showed

---

[38] Sparks, *The Mind of South Africa*, p. 366.
[39] Frederik van Zyl Slabbert, *The Quest for Democracy: South Africa in Transition* (London:
Penguin, 1992), p. 35.
[40] Odd Arne Westad, *The Global Cold War: Third World Interventions and the Making of Our
Times* (Cambridge: Cambridge University Press, 2007), pp. 215–216.

signs of sympathy for the white government."[41] This being the case, the SACP quickly adapted to changing circumstances:

In the rapid rush to stay ahead of the collapse of Soviet-bloc communism, the SACP abandoned so much of its ideological canon that some political observers suggested that the Party had become indistinguishable from a European-style and social-democratic party. The Party scrapped the Marxist conception of the dictatorship of the proletariat and questioned Leninist tenets claiming an inherent vanguard role for the Party. The SACP endorsed multiparty democracy and regular elections; independence of the trade unions; freedom of speech, worship and the press; and a mixed economy with a place for private enterprise and foreign investment.[42]

And yet, the dissolution of the Soviet Union – and the end of the Cold War – was probably less significant for developments in late-twentieth-century South Africa than some will have us believe. Adrian Guelke, for example, showed that by the 1990s most of the ANC's strength derived from its domestic – rather than international – supporters. Although there may have been an alteration in the balance of *perceptions*, the end of the Cold War had no significant repercussions for the balance of power between democracy-demanding and democracy-resisting forces in South Africa. In some respects, the end of the Cold War even *strengthened* – rather than weakened – the ANC's bargaining position vis-à-vis the NP-led apartheid government:

In particular, it enabled the ANC in the course of the transition itself to cast off associations that might have weakened its appeal inside the country and generated external opposition to the prospect of an ANC-dominated government. With the demise of the Soviet Union, even the party's continuing close relationship with the SACP lost most of its ideological significance, so that attempts to embarrass the ANC over the relationship by and large fell flat, a reflection of the weakening resonance of anti-communism. In a different ideological context, the pressure on the ANC to break with the SACP would have been far greater. Given the importance of the SACP in the projection of the ANC's policies of non-racialism, it seems probable that the ANC would have resisted the pressure, but at some political cost to the party.[43]

Although the dissolution of the Soviet Union was a double-edged sword for the ANC, I find unpersuasive the argument that the end of the Cold War

[41] James Barber, *Mandela's World: The International Dimension of South Africa's Political Revolution 1990–99* (Oxford: James Currey, 2004), pp. 71–72. Stephen Ellis and Tsepo Sechaba have noted in this context that "Perestroika had had the effect of bringing the Soviet Union and USA closer together, and at the same time it had persuaded Moscow's policy-makers that since there was to be no revolution in South Africa, it was in the Soviet interest to be on good terms with those in power." See their *Comrades against Apartheid: The ANC and the South African Communist Party in Exile* (London: James Currey, 1992), p. 194.
[42] Martin Murray, *The Revolution Deferred: The Painful Birth of Post-Apartheid South Africa* (London: Verso, 1994), p. 127.
[43] Adrian Guelke, "The Impact of the End of the Cold War on the South African Transition," *Journal of Contemporary African Studies*, Vol. 14, No. 1 (January 1996), p. 98. For the contrary view, see Adam and Moodley, *The Negotiated Revolution*, p. 47.

affected the ANC's bargaining position as adversely as is commonly assumed. But let us consider how the NP fared.

NP

F. W. de Klerk, speaking for the apartheid government, remarked in his autobiography that the collapse of the Soviet Union placated "one of our main strategic concerns for decades – the Soviet Union's role in southern Africa and its strong influence on the ANC and the SACP. ... A window had suddenly opened which created an opportunity for a much more adventurous approach than had previously been conceivable."[44] By contrast,

> The rapid thaw in the Cold War almost immediately made it far more difficult for hardliners in South Africa itself to justify their intransigence, at home or abroad, as some kind of last-ditch defense against communism. Developments in Eastern Europe have thus simultaneously forced de Klerk's hand. Democratization was now, dramatically, in the air world-wide while weakening the case of those within his own camp who might oppose any more advanced reform agenda. In addition, the apparent weakening of the Soviet Union (a key ANC ally) on the one hand, and the "idea of socialism" as a global option on the other, may also have moved the powers-that-be to conceive the ANC as freshly available for various "reasonable" and "pragmatic" compromises. In short, the "end of the Cold War" was one factor suggesting the existence of a new window for a successful liberal reformism, one crafted, precisely, to preempt revolution.[45]

The available evidence suggests that the ANC and NP may have benefited in *equal measure* from the end of the Cold War, this momentous shift in the international system. Both incurred costs (the ANC lost an ally; the NP lost a threat) *and* reaped benefits (the ANC became acceptable; the NP faced a weakened adversary). The end of the Cold War may have altered the playing field – but to no party's advantage.

This insight, as important as it is, says nothing, however, about *why* the window of opportunity that the end of the Cold War afforded was seized, or *how* it was possible to preempt revolution.

What, then, are we to make of the end of the Cold War? What consequences, if any, did it have for democratization in South Africa? In the final analysis the international dimensions of democratization of South Africa are not negligible – but neither are they critical – for explaining the resolution of apartheid's endgame. As one observer put it, "the international dimension, while important as a stimulus, bore fruit only after domestic change [had

---

44 De Klerk, F. W. *The Last Trek – A New Beginning: The Autobiography* (New York: St. Martin's Press, 1998), pp. 160–161.

45 John S. Saul, "From Thaw to Flood: The End of the Cold War in Southern Africa," *Review of African Political Economy*, Vol. 18, No. 50 (1991), p. 154. Dan O'Meara puts it thus: "The Soviet Union was retreating from the Third World even before the fall of the Berlin Wall. By the end of 1988 it was placing strong pressure on the ANC to reach a negotiated settlement which guaranteed whites rights. Not even Magnus Malan's most obdurate general could now credibly argue that every strike in South Africa was part of Moscow's grand design." See his *Forty Lost Years*, p. 379. For an almost identical argument, see Giliomee, *The Afrikaners*, p. 629.

begun]."[46] It follows that the dynamics of democratization in South Africa must be explained primarily by reference to domestic politics.

Samuel Huntington once remarked that a democratic regime is not installed by causes but by *causers*. Let us therefore turn from the international dimensions of democratization once again to the internal dimensions thereof. The specific focus is on agents and their preferences.

The previous chapter showed that apartheid, or "separate development," was organized Afrikanerdom's response to the problem of social order (or rather, their understanding of the problem). This response, designed in the 1950s, entailed systematically suppressing the preferences of the country's black majority in the social, political, and economic realms for more than forty years. As a solution, the chosen response was highly coercive. It "aimed at comprehensive communal, economic, and political control of subjugated populations and was engineered in every dimension by relocating selected categories of people."[47] And yet, in apartheid's endgame, bargaining turned from equilibrium confrontation to equilibrium cooperation. Several questions arise:

Why did the NP concede so much in the negotiations, ending up not with power-sharing but majority rule?[48]

Why did its white constituency accept majority rule which more than 90 per cent firmly rejected in polls taken in the late 1980s?[49]

Why did the tripartite alliance make concessions and trust their NP interlocutors?

Why did the white right (Freedom Front) and the black right (Buthelezi's IFP) shift from confrontation to cooperation?

And what convinced interacting adversaries that struck agreements would be honored; what explains the credibility of these commitments?

The next part traces the preferences and interactions of agents to find answers to these and related questions.

AGENTS AND PREFERENCES

Chapter 2 established why, and when, fears of victimhood accompany democratization. In apartheid's endgame, fears of the future were particularly pronounced. Fears revolving around political, social, and economic considerations abounded on all sides of the political divide.

---

[46] Chris Landsberg, "Directing from the Stalls? The International Community and the South African Negotiation Forum," in Steven Friedman and Doreen Atkinson, eds., *South African Review 7: The Small Miracle* (Johannesburg: Ravan Press, 1994), p. 281.

[47] Pierre du Toit, *State Building and Democracy in Southern Africa: Botswana, Zimbabwe, and South Africa* (Washington, DC: United States Institute of Peace Press, 1995), p. 156.

[48] Herman Giliomee, "Surrender Without Defeat: Afrikaners and the South African 'Miracle,'" Unpublished Paper, University of Cape Town, n.d., p. 16.

[49] Giliomee, "Surrender Without Defeat," p. 16.

Fears of the Future

Table 6.1 reports white expectations of impending social change, recorded in 1988. Many members of the Afrikaner *laager* who had supported or otherwise been associated with separate development greatly feared a revolution from below in the dying days of apartheid (*political victimhood*). Certain elements "resist[ed] the consequences of democratization to the extent that they say, 'If this goes on, my interests will be so threatened I cannot survive.'"[50] Fears were political, social, and economic in kind. Another survey reported that 87 percent of prominent Afrikaners feared a decline in white prosperity (*economic victimhood*), 85 percent a decline in safety/security (*physical victimhood*), and 61 percent a decline in employment (*economic victimhood*).[51]

The rapidly increasing brain drain in the course of the 1980s is but one of many indicators of the fears that consumed many Afrikaner minds. It is important to remember in this context that apartheid was a "fort built on fear."[52] Any real or imagined threat to the racial order was bound to upset the Afrikaner sense of self. It is thus not surprising that a majority of whites expected an increase in discrimination (86 percent of those polled), crime (84 percent), and a decrease in living standards and way of life (81 and 83 percent), the safety of property (80 percent), law and order (80 percent), and physical security (75 percent). Impending changes were feared greatly. With regard to fears of economic and physical victimhood, many whites (Boers and Englishmen alike) remembered vividly the crisis in the aftermath of the 1960 Sharpeville massacre. Then the government's reliance on the prerogative state met with an angry and unexpected African response. The response made visible limits of the prerogative state, and of white control. In April 1960, a massive stayaway of black workers brought businesses and industries to a halt in Cape Town. More than thirty thousand protestors marched to downtown Caledon Square. Gail Gerhart reports that "it was in Cape Town that the security of whites appeared to be most threatened by African defiance ... The spontaneous massing of such a large crowd of Africans in the center of a 'white' city was an unprecedented situation."[53] Gun shops in Cape Town and

---

[50] Frederik van Zyl Slabbert, former MP for South Africa's Progressive Party and official Leader of the Opposition, interview with the author, London: October 20, 1997. Slabbert was the principal organiser of the "Dakar Meeting" between the ANC leadership and Afrikaner opinion-makers that paved the way for official negotiations over the end of apartheid. How deeply whites have feared apartheid's endgame, and still fear today, is partially revealed by a new white literature that has emerged in post-apartheid South Africa. Although the authors spearheading this literature, J. M. Coetzee (whose novel *Disgrace* is particularly chilling) and Nadine Gordimer (*House Gun*), are hardly new on the country's literary scene, the tone of their novels is strikingly grim. As Rachel Swarns writes, expressing a sense of uprootedness, the new literature "vents and explores ... fears about the post-apartheid nation." Rachel L. Swarns, "After Apartheid, White Anxiety," *New York Times*, November 14, 1999, p. 1.

[51] Manzo and McGowan, "Afrikaner Fears and the Politics of Despair," p. 17.

[52] The term is Dan O'Meara's. See his *Forty Lost Years*, pp. 17–131.

[53] Gerhart, *Black Power in South Africa*, pp. 244, 242.

TABLE 6.1. *White Expectations of Black Rule in 1988*

Expectations	Percent
1. The lives of whites will not continue as before.	89
2. Whites will be discriminated against.	86
3. Crime will increase.	84
4. The way of life will not be protected.	83
5. Living standards will decline.	81
6. Property will not be safe.	80
7. Law and order will not be maintained.	80
8. The physical safety of whites will be threatened.	75

Source: Based on Robert Schrire, *Adapt or Die: The End of White Politics in South Africa* (Johannesburg: The Ford Foundation, 1991), p. 28. The original figures were adapted from a report compiled by the Human Sciences Research Council of South Africa and published in the *Financial Mail* (Johannesburg), October 7, 1988, p. 30.

the Transvaal within days sold out their stocks to fearful whites. The killings at Sharpeville produced "[a] cycle of violence and counter-violence [that] escalated progressively during the coming decades and created the context in which gross human rights violations became increasingly endemic."[54] Was a similar crisis on the horizon in the 1980s? By then, the black resistance was more organized, more effective, and more radical than in the 1960s. It had matured into a full-blown liberation movement. White fears, accordingly, were immense.

Unsurprisingly, white fears on the far right were more extreme. Fears there led to action. Organized right-wing violence attempted to stem the tide of change. A sizable segment of white extremists mobilized for a "Third Afrikaner War of Freedom." Those involved in the mobilization were not random fringe radicals. Seasoned parliamentary leaders of the Afrikaner nation publicly threatened armed struggle against democracy, including Andries Treurnicht (founder of the Conservative Party), Andries Beyers, Koos van der Merwe, and Corné Mulder.

Johann van Rooyen attributes the rise of extremist right-wing violence to the "perception among the right that the demise of white *baasskap* (domination) was a foregone conclusion and that parliamentary and non-violent resistance would not prevent this."[55] The number of militant right-wing groups rose to two hundred in apartheid's endgame. This landscape of fear is an indication of how difficult a cooperative resolution of apartheid's endgame must have appeared to whites in the late 1980s.[56] Now consider the fears on

---

[54] Truth and Reconciliation Commission of South Africa Report, Volume 5, pp. 528–529.

[55] Johann van Rooyen, *Hard Right: The New White Power in South Africa* (London: I.B. Tauris, 1994), p. 194.

[56] As in Zimbabwe, white fears in the countryside of South Africa were not groundless. Consider in this context the farm killings that have wrecked rural South Africa in the endgame. Between 1992 and 1997, some 350 farmers were killed on their property. Richard Jurgens, "The Civil War That Never Happened," *Leadership*, Vol. 17, No. 2 (1998), pp. 40–47.

the part of democracy-demanding forces. Members of the disparate resistance movement against apartheid, as well as those not associated with the struggle against apartheid, feared repression from above.

Apartheid's Endgame

The insurgent UDF, this coalition of leading liberation movements, anti-apartheid organizations, civic associations, and other nongovernmental groups faced the apartheid government in an endgame situation.[57] Here I chronicle one crucial transformation that occurred in this endgame: the intensified Prisoner's Dilemma gave way to another game, an assurance game. In an assurance game (or coordination problem), each agent, generally speaking, wants to act only if the other agent(s) act(s). Assurance games are less difficult to solve than prisoner's dilemmas, or endgame situations. In endgames, all agents prefer to free-ride – to reap benefits at no cost. For the reasons outlined in Chapter 2, the scope for opportunism is great in endgames.

Interestingly, coordination problems preceded *and* followed apartheid's endgame. Before apartheid's endgame, the question of whether strategic inter-action should be structured by way of law was a coordination problem. "In a coordination problem, each person wants to coordinate with others but there can be considerable disagreement about how to coordinate."[58] In apartheid's endgame, the ANC-coalition within the democracy-demanding coalition, as well as the *verligtes* within the National Party establishment preferred to make law central to bargaining. Needless to say, the ANC-coalition and the NP-*verligtes* wanted to rely on the law *only* if the adversary would also do so. This presented a typical coordination problem, separate from the larger end-game. This particular coordination problem was one subgame of apartheid's endgame. The game *per se* in no way precipitated the outcome of the endgame, the intensified Prisoner's Dilemma about the future of social order. The argu-ment proposed here is that the endgame *was* critically affected by the solution to this first coordination problem. Consider again the coordination problem and its solution: it was solved by common knowledge. Enter the ideology of law, this shared mental model.[59]

Michael Chwe has recently demonstrated the importance of common knowledge for solving coordination problems.[60] The argument advanced here is that the common knowledge necessary for solving this sketched coordina-tion problem was law itself. The history of law, the legacy of the normative state, supplied the common knowledge that was necessary for solving the coordination problem. The particular solution that was found, in turn, made a

---

[57] The standard work is Seekings, *The UDF.*

[58] Chwe, *Rational Ritual,* p. 12.

[59] The theoretical discussion of shared mental models, and the relationship between institutions and ideologies, is contained in Chapter 3.

[60] Chwe, *Rational Ritual,* esp. Chapter 1 and 3.

solution to the intensified Prisoner's Dilemma, apartheid's endgame, conceivable. Convergence on a legal way of doing things was a coordination problem; it was solved by reference to a shared memory, a common knowledge, of doing things in a legal way in the past. This brought agents closer together, making bargaining possible by reducing uncertainty. The intensified prisoner's dilemma (prisoner's dilemma plus absolute uncertainty) was about to turn into an ordinary prisoner's dilemma (prisoner's dilemma plus organized uncertainty).[61] Whereas agents still were willing to choose confrontation (exit) over cooperation (voice) and continued to prefer free-riding, the absolute uncertainty under which agents were operating in the early phase of apartheid's endgame had, at least in the perceptions of key agents, ebbed down somewhat. The institution of the dual apartheid state helped to stabilize expectations about expectations.[62] The next transformation was one where the prisoner's dilemma turned into an assurance game. This is when apartheid's endgame became a "simple" coordination problem: *all* key agents (except for outliers such as the "hard right" and the IFP) wanted to cooperate on mutual advantage. The beginning of this phase was 1994, after the first democratic elections.

Agents and Preferences I

It is generally problematic to treat collective actors, or informal social aggregates, as if they hold preferences because collective desires, beliefs, or preferences do not exist.[63] Yet, the divisions between democracy-demanding forces and democracy-resisting forces were fairly clear cut at the onset of the endgame. The principal agents discussed here can realistically be treated as unitary actors. These agents' *a priori* preferences did not suggest that cooperation on mutual advantage would be possible, or sustainable. On the contrary, as responses to decline, agents seemed to favor confrontation over cooperation. Each side strove to reduce the gains available to the adversary. Both democracy-demanding and democracy-resisting forces viewed strategic interaction as zero-sum.[64] A willingness to adjust behavior to the actual or anticipated preferences of the adversary through a process of policy coordination was missing on all sides. The NP government, for example, used cooperation after the failure of the 1983 constitutional reform process but reverted to confrontation once resistance in the townships mounted. As Jung

---

[61] See Chapter 2, especially Table 2.2.
[62] Luhmann, in his *Ausdifferenzierung des Rechts*, pointed out that in strategic interactions, third, fourth, and *n* levels of reflexivity need to be considered: expectations of expectations of expectations, and expectations of expectations of expectations of expectations, and so on.
[63] Jon Elster, "Introduction," in idem. ed., *Rational Choice* (New York: New York University Press), pp. 3–4. See also Kalyvas, *The Rise of Christian Democracy in Europe*.
[64] A game is zero-sum when interacting agents vie for a finite resource, and the resource is allocated among agents according to their competitive ability, generating winners and losers, but no intermediate category. As spelled out in Chapter 2 of this book, non-zero-sum games permit agents to win or lose simultaneously.

and Shapiro write, the NP's "widespread refusal to cooperate, together with the refusal of any country outside South Africa to recognize the tricameral solution as legitimate, weakened the government's position and was followed by increasingly militant grass roots mobilization, notably among the urban black youth."[65] In the face of apartheid , the ANC alliance, especially township youth, launched a violent campaign to make the country's townships ungovernable.

Neither government nor opposition were initially predisposed to compromise, or even cooperate. For democracy-demanding forces the principal preference was revolution. Internal differences existed within these forces regarding the nature of revolution: the preferences ranged from violent to nonviolent. That violent revolution was indeed a preference held by many in South Africa's townships is illustrated by reference to the so-called Boipatong Massacre in 1992. When Mandela visited the township after the massacre of forty-three ANC supporters there, "the crowd chanted at him: 'We want arms, we want arms'." As O'Meara explains, Mandela responded with language similar to that which he had used in 1961 to proclaim the onset of armed struggle.[66]

For the democracy-resisting coalition, the first preference was segregation. Again, internal differences existed, with preferences ranging from reform apartheid (among *verligtes*) to apartheid repression (among *verkramptes*). Based on these preference orderings, we would expect democracy-demanding and democracy-resisting forces to pursue as their principal strategies confrontation, not cooperation.

STRATEGIES AND OUTCOMES

Agents do not select outcomes, they select strategies. Let us examine whether selected strategies led to desired outcomes in apartheid's endgame. Given the initial preferences, we would expect a predominance of confrontation among interacting agents. We would expect agents' choice of confrontation over cooperation to work against the peaceful resolution of apartheid's endgame.

Strategies and Outcomes I

To some extent, the empirical evidence bears out these predictions. The NP mobilized against democracy as long as it could: "the goal throughout was to prevent, rather than provide a controlled route to, majority rule."[67] The strategy was confrontation, not cooperation. The NP government responded to the popular upsurge in the townships with repression. In mid-1986, then President Botha declared a nationwide state of emergency. Similarly, the ANC showed

[65] Jung and Shapiro, "South Africa's Negotiated Transition," p. 194.
[66] O'Meara, *Forty Lost Years*, p. 411. On the Boipatong Massacre, see also the discussion in the previous chapter.
[67] Friedman, "Too Little Knowledge is a Dangerous Thing," p. 4.

"little interest in starting serious negotiations" up until 1990 and 1991.[68] Thereafter, interactions remained conflictual, but began to evince elements of cooperation. Throughout June 1992, the NP government and the ANC engaged in a "war of letters" over the Boipatong Massacre. Despite attempts to reconvene bilateral talks between the principal players, the negotiation process was reduced to a "vituperative exchange," replete with "mutual recriminations and thinly veiled personal insults."[69]

And yet, we see a gradual move toward strategic cooperation, not confrontation. The turning point in apartheid's endgame was the "Minute of Understanding" of September 1992. In the aftermath of Boipatong and the subsequent shooting of fifty ANC supporters near Bisho, in the Ciskei, both the NP and the ANC had reverted to confrontation. The townships were angry. In April of that year, Chris Hani, Secretary General of the Communist Party, had been assassinated by a group including a former Conservative Party MP. The ANC, in a show of strength, had launched a "Mass Action" campaign of massive strikes and demonstrations in mid-1992. The combined impact of these events, however, steered moderates on all sides away from confrontation. The Minute of Understanding, signed by the ANC and the NP, some believe, "symbolised the end of all NP attempts to outmanoeuvre the ANC" and the beginning of *real* cooperation.[70]

Consider, for example, three critical commitments that were reached thereafter: proportional representation, the creation of a constitutional assembly *after* the first democratic elections, and the idea of a truth commission (all of which are treated in detail below). All three were compromise outcomes. Thus, contrary to their original preferences, democracy-demanding and democracy-resisting forces alike adopted strategies *not* consistent with their *a piori* preferences. "Although consistent with internationally recognised constitutional norms, the constitutional guidelines adopted by the ANC," to give but one example, "were not consistent with the organisation's rhetoric of a 'people's war', 'people's power' and 'ungovernability' which dominated the struggle in South Africa in the 1980s."[71] Surprisingly, the ultimate settlement of apartheid's endgame was founded upon allocational decisions that, given the constraints and cleavages of the case, approximated a social optimum.

The question remains, however, why interacting agents believed that the settlement was, and would remain, credible under uncertainty. In answer, we need to see why, and how, agents' preferences changed, how this affected their strategies, and ultimately, the contours of apartheid's endgame. So how, and why, did strategies and outcomes change?

---

[68] Jung and Shapiro, "South Africa's Negotiated Transition," p. 195.

[69] Sisk, *Democratization in South Africa*, p. 214.

[70] S. J. Terreblanche, "FW de Klerk verspeel sy kans om ware Staatsman te Word," *Vrye Weekblad*, February 1994, quoted in O'Meara, *Forty Lost Years*, p. 412.

[71] Heinz Klug, "Participating in the Design: Constitution-making in South Africa," in Penelope Andrews and Stephen Ellmann, eds., *The Post-Apartheid Constitutions: Perspectives on South Africa's Basic Law* (Johannesburg: Witwatersrand University Press, 2001), p. 137.

Strategies and Outcomes II

Strategies are based on preferences. However, if we examine apartheid's endgame, neither did selected strategies lead to desired outcomes, nor did selected strategies reflect original preferences. If we compare agents' strategies with agents' preferences prior to apartheid's endgame, we find significant divergences. Based on their original preferences, agents should not have found it rational to cooperate in apartheid's endgame. Nevertheless, cooperation occurred. The discrepancy between preferences, strategies, and outcomes, this book submits, is due to a transformation of preferences in apartheid's endgame. Without this transformation in preferences, cooperation on mutual advantage would not have been possible in apartheid's endgame. The transformation occurred in two steps.

First, although agents maintained their first-order preferences (revolution and segregation, respectively), both sides broadened their horizon and also contemplated other acceptable outcomes. The emphasis is here on key, decision-making elites within each camp. The updated preference ordering for the ANC was, in descending order of preference, (1) revolution, (2) compromise, and (3) segregation. The updated preference ordering for the NP was (1) segregation, (2) compromise, and (3) revolution.

Second, the dynamics of contention mentioned earlier (including Boipatong, Bisho, and ANC mass action) moved all players to the brink. As Willie Esterhuyse remarks: "This looking into the abyss played a major role in bringing De Klerk and Mandela together."[72] The NP realized, through the ANC's campaign of mass action, that revolution was possible. The ANC, in turn, realized that without "the cooperation of the National Party, the transition to a postapartheid South Africa would certainly be violent and chaotic. The ANC could make the country ungovernable, but only the National Party could make it governable for the time being."[73] As a consequence, both sides changed their preference orderings. The key ANC strategists began to value compromise over revolution over segregation. The NP *verligtes* began to prefer compromise to segregation to revolution. A significant learning process got underway, moving the country closer to democracy.

As Timothy Sisk writes: "The patterns of politics in South Africa shifted greatly in the process of transition. Political parties transformed themselves to adjust to the political environment unfolding before them. As institutional choices of the political parties converged on a settlement, they developed a common interest in creating a new purpose, which is, implicitly, to create a system that pulls toward moderation rather than polarization."[74] The question remains, however, why was cooperation considered credible? Why did interacting agents trust one another? To account for the variance between

---

[72] As quoted in O'Meara, *Forty Lost Years*, p. 412.
[73] Marina Ottaway, *South Africa: The Struggle for a New Order* (Washington: The Brookings Institution, 1993) p. 163.
[74] Sisk, *Democratization in South Africa*, p. 266.

preferences, strategies, and outcomes, the next section examines the dual state as a conceptual variable, and shows how the normative half of this state – in particular the legacies of formally rational law – helped to reconstitute agents' preferences in key and contentious areas, namely *electoral design, constitutional design,* and *justicial design.*

Agents and Preferences II

Before the 1994 election, many feared that those who stood to lose from democratization, notably the white right and Inkatha, would plunge the country into renewed violence. This did not happen. Law, as an institutional structure, was instrumental. Jack Spence reports a nice piece of anecdotal evidence. He tells of two Black Sash demonstrators who, after the country's first national democratic elections, were seen holding a poster thanking the police for their efforts.[75] The police, in spite of enormous incompetence, bias, and corruption, fulfilled useful functions, deemed valuable even by apartheid's opponents (in this case, two Black Sash demonstrators). The law of apartheid helped democracy survive. Let us examine this claim in more detail in three critical episodes of apartheid's endgame.

Analytic Narratives

All three episodes, or analytic narratives, to be discussed here revolve around the design of secondary institutions. The design of these institutions posed serious commitment problems, situations in which mutually preferable bargains were unattainable because interacting agents held conflicting preferences over a substantive bargaining issue. All three episodes singled out here demonstrate the utility of the state, both as an *idea* and an *institutional structure.* The first episode concerns the design of the country's electoral system (*electoral design*). The substantive bargaining issue dividing interacting adversaries in this episode was the question of whether to adopt a system of majoritarian or proportional representation. The second episode concerns the problem of constitutionalism (*constitutional design*). The substantive bargaining issue at stake in this episode was the question of who would be involved in the design of the new constitution, what the procedure for this process would be, and when it would take place. The third and last episode revolves around the question of retroactive justice, and the establishment of the Truth and Reconciliation Commission of South Africa (*justicial design*). The substantive bargaining issue at stake was the question of whether retribution, restitution, or reparation should be the guiding principle in dealing with the past. Existing accounts of the three episodes have elaborated descriptive rather than analytic narratives. The following analysis revisits the episodes as bargaining

---

[75] J. E. Spence, "Reflections of a First Time Voter," *African Affairs,* Vol. 93, No. 372 (July 1994), p. 341.

dilemmas, reconstructing agents' preferences and strategies, and relating outcomes to the structural context in which strategic interactions took place. Each
of the analytic narratives highlights the function of law in the construction of
credible commitments, gradually moving forward the path-dependent explanation of apartheid's endgame. For as Ellmann observes, "The transitional
agreements the ANC endorsed are the product of compromise rather than a
simple expression of the ANC's preferences. Moreover, they are the product of
a process in which lawyers – whose disposition toward legal arrangements
may not have been shared by those they represented – played a major role."[76]

Narrative 1: Electoral Design

The point "of creating particular institutions is to put obstacles in our way in
order to force us to move along certain paths and not others."[77] Another point
of creating particular institutions is to put obstacles in the way of *others*. Bargaining over South Africa's first electoral system bears out this point. Because of
its power to determine "who governs," conflicting preferences regarding the
design of the electoral system initially divided all interacting adversaries. It was a
commitment problem as defined herein. Furthermore, "speculation on how they
[interacting parties] would possibly fare under various electoral systems was rife
with uncertainty, and the outcome was unpredictable."[78] The situation in short
was clouded in absolute uncertainty, as the term is used herein.

In the 1993 constitutional negotiations, the NP wanted an electoral system
that would produce proportionality in the translation of votes into seats. Such
a system, it was hoped, would generate enough seats to frustrate an anticipated
ANC majority in parliament. The principal ANC preference was to select a
system that would produce solid majorities, and sufficient seats to reflect a
clear transition from apartheid to majority rule. The IFP, like the NP, was in
favor of a system of proportional representation. Substantive differences thus
divided the principal adversaries. What is more, the ANC leadership was in
"demand-escalating mode" at the time.[79] Yet, the choice of the first electoral
system was surprisingly uncontroversial. Cooperation on closed list proportional representation (PR) was reached rather quickly. Both process and
outcome in the bargaining over seats and votes were surprising. The process
stands in stark contrast to the verbal confrontations between Mandela and
de Klerk at the time. The outcome was surprising as well, for closed list PR
was not used during apartheid, and thus not a system that the NP was

[76] Ellmann, "Law and Legitimacy in South Africa," p. 473.
[77] Russell Hardin, "Why a Constitution?," in Bernard Grofman and Donald Wittman, eds., *The
Federalist Papers and the New Institutionalism* (New York: Agathon Press, 1989), p. 116. As
Hardin writes: "Today, one need not 'love it,' but if one wishes to renege, one must 'leave it' or
become criminal." See Hardin, "Why a Constitution?," p. 117.
[78] Sisk, *Democratization in South Africa*, p. 266.
[79] Jung and Shapiro, "South Africa's Negotiated Transition," p. 196.

familiar with.[80] It was neither the outcome preferred by the ANC, namely a majoritarian formula, nor the outcome preferred by the NP. And yet convergence was unproblematic. Let us unpack this outcome.

The ANC had actually shied away from the simplest majoritarian formula – first-past-the post – because of concerns with past gerrymandering of voting districts, a legacy of apartheid settlement patterns. Both the NP and the IFP caved in because each expected more electoral returns under closed list PR than under any other electoral formula.[81] An important backdrop to convergence was the fact that agents had previously invoked the tradition of the normative state. "Perhaps the only clear source of agreement was procedural – an acceptance that parliament would remain sovereign while Codesa talked, but would be bound by the convention's agreement."[82] This agreement is indeed noteworthy. Its credibility stems from an external source. This external source was the normative state. We can now complete our narrative of electoral engineering in apartheid's endgame. The surprising convergence on closed list PR is now much less surprising. The procedural guarantee, apparently recognized by all interacting adversaries (if only tacitly), allowed adversaries to take risks, to choose cooperation over confrontation in bargaining over seats and votes, despite the fact that uncertainty was clouding the bargaining situation. All hoped that strategic compromise might produce rewards in the future. As Friedman shows, all parties except for the ANC miscalculated in their choices for an electoral system. This miscalculation notwithstanding, moderation prevailed even in the aftermath of institutional choice.[83]

Narrative 2: Constitutional Design

Russell Hardin contends that the drafting of a constitution is different from signing a contract. Whereas the latter is a typical prisoner's dilemma situation, the former is not. A constitution, says Hardin, is not a contract. It lies *before* contracting. It *creates* the institution of contracting. "Creating a constitution is itself primarily an act of coordination on one of many possible ways of ordering our lives together, not an act of cooperating in a prisoner's dilemma or exchange."[84] Let us consider these propositions in the context of

---

[80] Friedman, "Too Little Knowledge is a Dangerous Thing," p. 63.

[81] On the calculations of the NP and IFP, see Friedman, "Too Little Knowledge is a Dangerous Thing," pp. 63–70.

[82] Steven Friedman, "From Breakthrough to Breakdown," in idem., ed., *The Long Journey*, p. 26.

[83] For the argument that both the NP and IFP miscalculated in choosing closed list PR, and why the system did not benefit ascriptive groups, see Friedman, "Too Little Knowledge is a Dangerous Thing." On ascriptive groups and identity politics in South Africa, see Courtney Jung, *Then I was Black: South African Political Identities in Transition* (New Haven: Yale University Press, 2000). On the effects of electoral systems in Southern Africa more generally, see Reynolds, *Electoral Systems and Democratization in Southern Africa*.

[84] For discussion of this point, see Hardin, "Why a Constitution?," pp. 101; 102–108; 113–115.

apartheid's endgame. Constitution making in South Africa was in reality two processes. The first process (1991–1993) preceded the country's first democratic elections, the second process (1994–1996) commenced once the votes were tallied and the seats assigned. Following Hardin's typology, constitutionalism in apartheid's endgame was _both_ a problem of contract _and_ of coordination. The first process (1991–1993), concerned with the adoption of an Interim Constitution, was a classical prisoner's dilemma situation. It resembled a contract in the sense that it provided incentives to enter a constitutional agreement and _still_ renege. Put differently, the payoffs from cooperation did not outweigh the payoffs from confrontation. Fears of political victimhood were widespread among agents. Indeed important agents, most important the NP and ANC, believed that they faced a (0,3) payoff in the making of the Interim Constitution, potentially receiving their _least_ preferred outcome. Thus the scope for opportunism was large throughout the making of the Interim Constitution.

The scope for opportunism narrowed dramatically _after_ the elections, and with the beginning of the second phase. The reasons are relatively straightforward. By then, principal agents had a shared history of interaction. Previous commitments had stuck, including the electoral commitment discussed earlier, and the various "ethnic contracts" to be discussed later. Furthermore, other commitment problems, in particular bargaining over how to deal with the apartheid past, showed potential for resolution. The most important empirical signal underlying the cooperative turn was the absence of bloodshed during the elections. These are the principal reasons why the second phase of constitution making was a coordination problem, not a contract.

The shadow of the future in the second game was thus different from the shadow of the future in the first game. Most important, the shadow was _longer_ in the second game. The making of the Interim Constitution thus resembled a prisoner's dilemma, whereas the making of the final constitution became an assurance game. Although the final constitution was self-enforcing, the Interim Constitution was not. The difference can be explained with reference to the "abdication aspect" of constitution-making. In theory, a more or less democratically elected constitutional assembly is dissolved once the constitution is delivered. The constitutional assembly abdicates "in favor of the principles laid down" in the document because it "should not govern, the principles should."[85] In apartheid's endgame, two very different bodies were charged with constitution-making. The first body was a multiparty conference known as the Multiparty Negotiating Process (MPNP), a successor to CODESA. It was more inclusive than CODESA I and II. When the MPNP opened in April 1993, the Conservative Party and the IFP came on board (the IFP left the MPNP in July of that year) and the "centripetal dynamic that brought the

[85] Francis Sejersted, "Democracy and the Rule of Law: Some Historical Experiences of Contradictions in the Striving for Good Government," in Jon Elster and Rune Slagstad, eds., _Constitutionalism and Democracy_ (Cambridge: Cambridge University Press, 1988), p. 135.

government and ANC together was pulling other parties toward the newly consolidated political center as well."[86] Only the right-wing *Afrikaner Weerstandsbeweging* (AWB), the purified Herstigte National Party, and the left-wing Azanian People's Organization (AZAPO) refused to become involved. Notwithstanding the rapprochement between important democracy-demanding and democracy-resisting forces, the assassination of Chris Hani only a few days after the inception of the MPNP, as well as left-wing, right-wing, and "Third Force" violence, strained bargaining over constitutional choice. The MPNP eventually endorsed an Interim Constitution in November 1993.

The interim text was to take effect after the 1994 elections. The old apartheid parliament ratified the Interim Constitution, "thus providing legal continuity between the old regime and the new," as Leonard Thompson notes.[87] It also created an interim government, the Transitional Executive Council (TEC). We already see the relevance of past practices for future outcomes. The interacting adversaries – and adversaries they still were – bound themselves by law. This legal way of doing things, recognized on all sides of the political divide, had its roots in the normative state. The particular process of this first stage of constitution making was path-dependent in this sense. The connection between past and present is also visible in another example. There was also to be legal continuity between the Interim Constitution and the final constitution. No amendment to the interim text would be valid if it violated the thirty-four constitutional principles contained in it. Other amendments had to be passed by a two-thirds majority in the Constitutional Assembly.

The Constitutional Assembly (CA) was the second body charged with constitution-making in apartheid's endgame. The CA was comprised of both houses of parliament and had to pass a new constitution within two years of

---

[86] Sisk, *Democratization in South Africa*, p. 225. While delegates from nineteen political organizations were represented at CODESA in 1991 and 1992, MPNP invited representatives from altogether twenty-three organizations. This number decreased after several defections. For an account focusing on the constitutional law of the period, and the technical legal questions that efforts at restructuring it raised, see Heinz Klug, "Constitutional Law: Constitutional Reform," *Annual Survey of South African Law* (1992), pp. 693–729. The evolution of these efforts, and the provisions of the interim constitution, is ably documented in idem., "Constitutional Law: Towards a New Constitutional Order," *Annual Survey of South African Law* (1993), pp. 1–41; and idem., "Constitutional Law," *Annual Survey of South African Law* (1994), pp. 1–23.

[87] Thompson, *A History of South Africa*, p. 249. For a commentary on the provisions of the Interim Constitution, see Dion Basson, *South Africa's Interim Constitution: Text and Notes*, Revised Edition (Kenwyn: Juta, 1995). For an insightful account of constitution-making in South Africa, with particular reference to constitutional influence and constitutional borrowing from abroad, see Klug, *Constituting Democracy*; and Dennis M. Davis, "Constitutional Borrowing: The Influence of Legal Culture and Local History in the Reconstruction of Comparative Influence: The South African Experience," *International Journal of Constitutional Law*, Vol. 1, No. 2 (April 2003), pp. 181–195. A contemporary classic, with evidence from twentieth-century Europe, is Skach, *Borrowing Constitutional Designs*. An international law perspective on post-apartheid constitutionalism is provided in John Dugard, "International Law and the South African Constitution," *European Journal of International Law*, Vol. 8, No. 1 (1997), pp. 77–92.

the first session of the new parliament. The two-year deadline was enshrined in the Interim Constitution. It found its way into the document upon the insistence of the ANC which did not want to be "stuck" with a government of national unity for any longer than absolutely necessary. The CA consisted of six theme committees, ranging from committees devoted to the character of the state (to discuss such issues as supremacy of the constitution; citizenship; and suffrage) and the structure of the state (viz., separation of powers; relations between national and provincial government; self-determination; electoral system) to committees canvassing issues related to the judiciary and the legal system (viz., structure of the court system; appointment of judicial officers; relationship between the common law and customary law) and fundamental rights (viz., nature of bill of rights, constitutional rights).[88]

The abdication of constitution makers occurred after the adoption, and certification by the Constitutional Court, of the final constitution.[89] Between constitutions, the usable state stabilized expectations among adversaries. The normative state provided a sense of rules.[90] It underwrote *regulative* rules,

---

[88] See "The Making of the Constitution," Special Report, *TransAct*, Vol. 2, No. 8 (September 1995), pp. 1–3; 6–12. TransAct was a publication devoted to the analysis of law-making in South Africa's transitional parliament, published monthly by the Centre for Policy Studies, Johannesburg. For an overview of contentious actors and contentious issues (i.e., the education clause; the property clause; and the labor relations clause) surrounding the CA, see Katharine Savage, "Negotiating South Africa's New Constitution: An Overview of the Key Players and the Negotiation Process," in Andrews and Ellmann, eds., *The Post-Apartheid Constitutions*, pp. 164–193.

[89] The two certification judgments are *Ex parte Chairperson of the Constitutional Assembly: in re Certification of the Constitution of the Republic of South Africa 1996* 1996 (4) SA 744 (CC); and *Ex parte Chairperson of the Constitutional Assembly in Re: Certification of the Amended Text of the Constitution of the Republic of South Africa 1996* 1997 (2) SA 97 (CC). For careful and indispensable technical analyses, see Matthew Chaskalson and Glenda Fick, "Constitutional Law: Constitution of the Republic of South Africa Act 108 of 1996," *Annual Survey of South African Law* (1996), pp. 1–47; and Victoria Bronstein and Kim Robinson, "Constitutional Jurisprudence and the Bill of Rights: The Certification Judgments," *Annual Survey of South African Law* (1996), pp. 48–115. Important commentary on the certification judgments is also provided by Matthew Chaskalson and Dennis Davis, "Constitutionalism, the Rule of Law, and the First Certification Judgment: Ex parte Chairperson of the Constitutional Assembly in Re: Certification of the Constitution of the Republic of South Africa 1996* 1996 (4) SA 744 (CC)," *South African Journal on Human Rights*, Vol. 13, No. 3 (1997), pp. 430–445. In an aside, Davis is particularly well qualified for such commentary seeing that for several years in the mid-1900s he hosted "Constitutional Talk," a sophisticated and often contentious talk show with a changing cast of characters, chiefly scholars and practitioners with a stake in South Africa's constitutional design, that was funded by the Constitutional Assembly and broadcast on public television. My regular viewing of these segments in South Africa was one impetus to embark on this project.

[90] Consider in this context the technical contribution of lawyers to the making of South Africa's constitutions, which illustrates yet another (and very concrete) way in which law mattered in apartheid's endgame. As Hassen Ebrahim, the Executive Director of the Constitutional Assembly, writes: "Technically, it [the Interim Constitution] was drafted by lawyers charged with the responsibility of crafting and constructing the provisions of both the Interim and the final Constitutions. While lawyers played a very small role in authoring the concepts or sense in

making possible the transition to the MPNP. The Interim Constitution then established *constitutive* rules, guiding the MPNP, further embedding cooperation as a bargaining strategy. The constitutive rules that the first phase of constitution-making established were both formal and informal. In terms of formal rules, the constitutional principles of the Interim Constitution were particularly important in making the transition to legitimate law possible. In the second phase of constitution-making, the constitutional principles gained further credibility. They became democracy-reinforcing constraints.[91] In the process of constitution-making, the drafters bound themselves *to* law, accomplishing this feat by way *of* law. As Leon Wessels, the former NP Member of Parliament and Deputy Chair of the Constitutional Assembly, remarks, "[t]he vehicle of judicial interpretation was employed on many occasions to break deadlocks and reach compromises during the negotiation process."[92]

The two constitutions did not only reflect the preferences of the drafters; they *generated* preferences as well (agents and structure worked in unison at this level as well).[93] These *emergent* preferences helped turn law legitimate, and commitments credible.

Overall, however, constitutionalism was fragile. "The uncertain outcome of the transition began to weigh heavily on the white right."[94] This notwithstanding, the most important voice on the white right, General Constant Viljoen, in many ways caved in to the democratic process, while simultaneously achieving most of what he set out to do in the first democratic elections. "He split the 'white right' down the middle, thus mitigating the danger of Afrikaner anti-system violence, bred from exclusion, which certainly was a more pressing possibility before he brought his 'moderates' into the democratic

---

these provisions, their role was nonetheless important and it changed through the different negotiating processes. During the drafting of the Interim Constitution technical committees of lawyers were tasked with considering the various political party submissions. They tried to find agreement by constructing various formulations which were then negotiated multilaterally." Hassen Ebrahim, "The Making of the South African Constitution: Some Influences," in Andrews and Ellmann, eds., *The Post-Apartheid Constitutions*, p. 98.

[91] The previous paragraph draws on Stephen Holmes, "Precommitment and the Paradox of Democracy," in Elster and Slagstad, eds., *Constitutionalism and Democracy*, pp. 225–232. Regarding democracy-reinforcing restraints, Holmes writes: "Rules restricting available options can enable individuals and communities to achieve more of their aims than they could if they were left entirely unconstrained." See Holmes, "Precommitment and the Paradox of Democracy," p. 236.

[92] Leon Wessels, "The End of an Era: The Liberation and Confession of an Afrikaner," in Andrews and Ellmann, eds., *The Post-Apartheid Constitutions*, p. 41.

[93] On endogenous preferences in constitutionalism, see Cass R. Sunstein, "Constitutions and Democracies: An Epilogue," in Jon Elster and Rune Slagstad, eds., *Constitutionalism and Democracy* (Cambridge: Cambridge University Press, 1988), pp. 348–352. The first phase of the new constitutionalism in South Africa in particular involved "facilitative" pre-commitment strategies. These strategies, "designed to solve collective action problems, often in the form of prisoner's dilemmas," facilitated the resolution of apartheid's endgame. Sunstein, *Designing Democracy*, p. 99.

[94] Sisk, *Democratization in South Africa*, p. 207.

process. He put the issue of an Afrikaner *Volkstaat* firmly on the agenda (which many argued is all he wanted to do as, being a rational man, Viljoen realized the concept of a *Volkstaat* was a non-starter, but debating the issue over the following five years reduced the threat of immediate and possibly violent secession by small pockets of white right-wingers in the '*Volkstaat* heartlands' of the Transvaal and Northwest)."[95] Questions, however, remain: Why did Viljoen, who commanded powerful forces in the depths of the Transvaal, sign onto democracy? What made him trust that he and his supporters of the right fringe would not suffer political, economic, and physical victimhood?

It is important to understand that "much of the convergence [on the Interim Constitution] occurred *prior* to formal constitutional negotiation, in the preliminary negotiation phase."[96] Timothy Sisk notes that there was "emerging agreement about what constituted a fair set of common political institutions."[97] How did this emergence come about? Reference to a "mutually hurting stalemate" (Zartman) or a "common destiny" (Sisk) are hardly sufficient to explain, let alone understand, convergence. The preceding analysis has offered an alternative explanation. It established that the usable state played a causal role. It enabled agents to solve these bargaining dilemmas as assurance games, as a way of eventually solving the endgame. The argument advanced herein explains why formal constitutional negotiations were based on cooperation, but did not create it (*contra* Sisk).[98] As per the discussion in the previous chapter, agents' convergence on a mutually acceptable way of doing things prior to formal constitutional negotiations (i.e., cooperation on mutual advantage) had their origins in the normative state. The discussion of constitutionalism in apartheid's endgame (like the earlier discussion of electoral engineering) bears out one of the theoretical arguments developed in the preceding chapters: that a primary institution, a usable state, must be in place before convergence on secondary institutions, such as electoral systems and constitutions, is possible in democratization.

An Excursus on the Bill of Rights

A complicated subset of constitution making was the debate over a bill of rights to protect civil and political rights. The idea of a bill of rights was proposed first by the South African Law Commission in 1989, which had been

---

[95] Reynolds, *Electoral Systems and Democratization in Southern Africa*, pp. 189–90.

[96] Sisk, *Democratization in South Africa*, p. 7. Emphasis added.

[97] Sisk, *Democratization in South Africa*, p. 7.

[98] Other early analyses of constitution-making in South Africa include David Welsh, "The Making of the Constitution," in Hermann Giliomee, Lawrence Schlemmer, and Sarita Hauptfleisch, eds., *The Bold Experiment: South Africa's New Democracy* (Halfway House: Southern Book Publishers, 1994), pp. 81–98; and Bertus de Villiers, ed., *Birth of a Constitution* (Kenwyn: Juta 1994). For a narrative written by an insider, see Hassen Ebrahim, *The Soul of the Nation: Constitution-Making in South Africa* (Cape Town: Oxford University Press, 1998).

established by the Minister of Justice in 1986.[99] Naturally, the NP preferred to protect group rights rather than individual rights. The NP's preference for group rights reflected segregationist ideas as well as a concern for the survival of the white minority in a multiracial democracy. The objective was to avert a possible "tyranny of the majority." The IFP, too, was concerned with group survival. Inasmuch as NP and IFP elites primarily feared the loss of power and wealth, NP and IFP constituencies and rank-and-file primarily feared economic and physical victimhood. As the wealth of IFP supporters was generally speaking very modest, fears of survival outweighed other fears. The organizations that had once made up the UDF, by contrast, favored the protection of individual rights. The ANC won this constitutional battle. Although the Interim Constitution provided for a right to culture, its significance was circumscribed. The interpretation of the clause, which was phrased vaguely, was left to the courts.[100] It was a backhanded way to dispense with the idea of group rights.[101]

But a second issue divided the bargaining partners: the issue of social and economic rights, so-called second- and third-generation rights. Based on provisions in the 1956 Freedom Charter, the ANC, the principal representative organization of the anti-apartheid alliance, advocated the inclusion of far-reaching social and economic rights, including freedom from hunger, right to shelter, and so on, into the constitutional text. The NP rejected this approach, as did the Democratic Party (DP). Apart from political reasons motivating

---

[99] Interestingly, the Law Commission concluded in its report that what the government saw as worthy of constitutional protection in terms of group rights (culture, religion, language, education) was only justiciable in terms of individual rights. See South African Law Commission, Working Paper on Group and Human Rights, No. 25, Project 58 (Pretoria: South African Law Commission, March 1989), as cited in John Dugard, "Human Rights and the Rule of Law in Postapartheid South Africa," in Robert A. Licht and Bertus de Villiers, eds., *South Africa's Crisis of Constitutional Democracy: Can the U.S. Constitution Help?* (Washington: American Enterprise Institute, 1994), p. 125. For an overview of the debate, see also Sisk, *Democratization in South Africa*, pp. 259–264.

[100] Charles Dlamini, "Culture, Education, and Religion," in David van Wyk, John Dugard, Bertus de Villiers, and Dennis Davis, eds., *Rights and Constitutionalism: The New South African Legal Order* (Kenwyn: Juta, 1994), p. 579.

[101] The NP had also changed its preferences regarding the issue of group rights. Minister of Constitutional Development and Planning, Gerrit Viljoen, announced in late 1990 "that the NP intends on negotiating a safeguard to ensure that the Bill of Human Rights cannot be arbitrarily abolished or changed. What the bill cannot however ensure is political group rights and it is to the constitution itself that we look for the safeguards." Mimeo, Office of Constitutional Development and Planning, September 27, 1990, as quoted in Sisk, *Democratization in South Africa*, p. 261. The fact that the NP transformed its preferences from group rights to individual rights suggests a strong belief in institutional design, and in the law as an arbiter of conflict, supporting one of the principal arguments of this book. It is likely that the NP's *volte face* was informed by developments in neighboring countries. In Zimbabwe, the institution of group rights had not had the effects intended by its proponents. In Namibia, by contrast, the white minority had favored interest representation over statutory race group representation. Whites learned that the emergence of interest-based alliances would accord them greater influence in politics than race-based alliances ever could. See Sisk, *Democratization in South Africa*, p. 264.

their objection, the NP and DP were adamant that second-generation rights were nonjusticiable. The final Interim Constitution contained few provisions regarding social and economic rights.[102] The ANC lost this constitutional battle.

What the discussion over the form and shape of the bill of rights in South Africa illustrates is that cooperation had become an equilibrium solution to commitment problems. John Dugard argued that the architects of post-apartheid South Africa brought "to the negotiating table jurisprudential baggage that is likely to hinder rather than to promote the advancement of rights."[103] This claim only seemingly contradicts the argument advanced here. Dugard charged that those responsible for drafting the bill of rights did not share a belief in the inalienability of the rights of the individual. He argued that it is in this sense that jurisprudential traditions were incompatible in apartheid's endgame. Dugard is right in pointing out that the notion of a bill of rights was not an idea immediately embraced by all parties. The parties further interpreted the purpose of a bill of rights quite differently: the ANC saw a future bill of rights as a radical institution of empowerment, the NP instead as a conservative institution of constraint.[104] This book does not suggest that the idea of a bill of rights was embraced by all parties. The claim is rather that key adversaries embraced a *legal way of doing things* in South Africa. What is remarkable in the debate over the bill of rights is that almost all interacting adversaries converged on the idea of legalizing the future. It was an "embrace of constitutional supremacy, institutionalized through the establishment of a Constitutional Court."[105]

In the debate over the bill of rights, the ANC won the debate over individual rights and lost the debate over social and economic rights. Taken together, bargaining over the bill of rights was a cooperative process, yielding cooperative outcomes as defined in Chapter 2. The achievement of want-satisfaction of one party (the ANC) was dependent upon the achievement of some form of want-satisfaction of all interacting parties (here the NP). Furthermore, there were no exploiters, and no cooperator was being exploited, that is, received less benefits than he contributed to costs.[106] In conclusion, if such contentious issues as group rights and socioeconomic rights can be addressed vehemently in deliberation rather than violently in the streets, the future of democracy is bright.[107]

---

[102] Bertus de Villiers, "Social and Economic Rights," in van Wyk et al., eds., *Rights and Constitutionalism*, p. 627. On the (continuing) debate over social and economic rights in South Africa, see also Sunstein, *Designing Democracy*, pp. 221–237.

[103] Dugard, "Human Rights and the Rule of Law in Postapartheid South Africa," p. 124.

[104] See Sisk, *Democratization in South Africa*, p. 263.

[105] Klug, *Constituting Democracy*, p. 119.

[106] Elster, *The Cement of Society*, p. 50.

[107] On deliberative, or discursive, sources of democracy, see Jürgen Habermas, *Faktizität und Geltung: Beiträge zur Diskurstheorie des Rechts und des demokratischen Rechtsstaats* (Frankfurt am Main: Suhrkamp, 1992). For a discussion of contention involving second- and third-generation rights under the Interim Constitution, see Klug, *Constituting Democracy*, pp. 166–177. Klug reports the infamous legal battle over school admissions at the Laerskool Potgietersrus, a state-aided public school in a small town in the Northern Province. Laerskool

The future was made brighter by the usable state. It provided a longer shadow of the future, making possible the evolution of cooperation among adversaries.[108]

Narrative 3: Justicial Design

Let us turn to another episode to illustrate how democracy was stabilized by way of law in apartheid's endgame. For its establishment, the constitution of the Truth and Reconciliation Commission of South Africa depended on legality – on rules and procedures. A contentious institution such as a truth commission needs to be established in a way that all interacting adversaries in democratization feel certain about its intention, design, and reach. In apartheid's endgame, the decision to institutionalize the search for transitional justice was made early in the endgame. It was enshrined in the Interim Constitution as a principle.

The Truth and Reconciliation Commission Act of 1995 authorized the TRC's creation. The Act mandated an inquiry into "the identity of all persons, authorities, institutions and organizations" involved in gross violations of human rights under apartheid and the preparation of a "comprehensive report which sets out its [the commission's] activities and findings."[109] The creation

---

Potgietersrus was an Afrikaans-medium school, with a recently introduced English-medium "stream." The schools' governing body, however, had denied the admission of several black pupils on "ground of culture." Their objective, the governing body claimed in its submission to the Constitutional Court, was to protect Christian Afrikaans culture as it saw permissible under the Interim Constitution. The Court rejected the school's cultural protection argument and found in favor of the black parents who had brought the case, finding four counts of prima facie discrimination in the governing body's actions. Klug, *Constituting Democracy*, p. 167. The case is instructive because it illustrates the legitimacy of law in post-apartheid South Africa. It shows that law turned legitimate in South Africa. This in turn was significant because it has reached rural Transvaal, and has inspired confidence in a legal way of doing things among black families there.

[108] Axelrod, *The Evolution of Cooperation*.

[109] Promotion of National Unity and Reconciliation Act, Act No. 34 of 1995. On the legal framework, see also Truth and Reconciliation Commission of South Africa Report, Volume 5, pp. 589–606. I do not propose to recount the history of the TRC, alternatives to its formation, its day-to-day operations, the work of its specialized committees, nor any of the other dimensions of its existence. Although scholarship on the TRC is burgeoning, much of it is mediocre. Yet some studies buck the trend. For an interesting early analysis, see Stéphane Leman-Langlois, "Constructing a Common Language: The Function of Nuremberg in the Problematization of Postapartheid Justice," *Law and Society Review*, Vol. 27, No. 1 (Winter 2002), pp. 79–100. A careful legal analysis, one of the very few in existence, is Anurima Bhargava, "Defining Political Crimes: A Case Study of the South African Truth and Reconciliation Commission," *Columbia Law Review*, Vol. 102, No. 5 (June 2002), pp. 1304–1339. For insightful analyses from other disciplines, see, most important, Wilson, *The Politics of Truth and Reconciliation in South Africa* the contributions in Rotberg and Thompson, eds., *Truth v. Justice*. Alex Boraine provides an insider's account in *A Country Unmasked: Inside South Africa's Truth and Reconciliation Commission* (Oxford: Oxford University Press, 2000); Fiona C. Ross, *Bearing Witness: Women and the Truth and Reconciliation Commission in South Africa* (London: Pluto Press, 2003); and some of the chapters in Deborah Posel and Graeme Simpson, eds., *Commissioning the Past: Understanding South Africa's Truth and Reconciliation Commission*

of the commission was mandated, although not in these terms, in a postscript (often referred to as the postamble) in the country's Interim Constitution, which was in force from April 27, 1994 until February 7, 1997. The parameters for the commission's work were to be determined through a piece of ordinary legislation. The provision in the Interim Constitution reads as follows:

> The adoption of this Constitution lays the secure foundation for the people of South Africa to transcend the divisions and strife of the past, which generated gross violations of human rights, the transgression of humanitarian principles in violent conflicts and a legacy of hatred, fear, guilt, and revenge. These can now be addressed on the basis that there is a need for understanding but not for vengeance, a need for reparation but not for retaliation, a need for *ubuntu* but not victimisation. In order to advance such reconciliation and reconstruction, amnesty shall be granted in respect of acts, omissions, and offences associated with political objectives and committed in the course of the conflicts of the past. To this end, Parliament under this Constitution shall adopt a law determining a firm cut-off date, which shall be a date after 8 October 1990 and before 6 December 1993, and providing for the mechanisms, criteria, and procedures, including tribunals, if any, through which such amnesty shall be dealt with at any time after the law has been passed.[110]

The only concrete function mandated by the Interim Constitution was that in the spirit of *ubuntu* (humanness) amnesty be granted to perpetrators of gross human rights violations. It was the beginning of what may be called the principle of qualified amnesty for which the TRC is now famous around the world. Four weeks after the Interim Constitution took effect, Dullah Omar, the newly appointed Minister of Justice, announced to parliament the government's decision to set up a commission that would deal with the past, and laid out its terms of reference. He emphasized that the commission would work toward the establishment of both truth and reconciliation, giving concrete meaning to the constitutional postscript contained in the Interim Constitution.[111]

(Johannesburg: Witwatersrand University Press, 2002). For the perspective of a distinguished ANC academic, constitutional negotiator, and cabinet minister, see Kader Asmal, Louise Asmal, and Ronald Suresh Roberts, *Reconciliation Through Truth: A Reckoning of Apartheid's Criminal Governance*, Second Edition (Cape Town: David Philip, 1997). Several years later Kader Asmal looked back in "Truth, Reconciliation and Justice: The South African Experience in Perspective," *Modern Law Review*, Vol. 63, No. 1 (January 2000), pp. 1–24. On the consequences of the TRC, see, above all, the extensive and sophisticated scholarship of James L. Gibson, most important his *Overcoming Apartheid: Can Truth Reconcile a Divided Nation?* (New York: Russell Sage Foundation, 2004); most recently, his "The Contributions of Truth to Reconciliation: Lessons from South Africa," *Journal of Conflict Resolution*, Vol. 50, No. 3 (June 2006), pp. 409–432; and many articles in-between. For a conceptual perspective on reconciliation, see my "Varieties of Reconciliation," *Law and Social Inquiry*, Vol. 33, No. 1 (Winter 2008), pp. 195–231.

[110] Constitution of the Republic of South Africa, 1993, Act 200 of 1993.

[111] Boraine, *A Country Unmasked*, pp. 40–43. Omar's announcement followed an internal debate over the question of retroactive justice within the ANC that had begun in earnest with the decision of the ANC's National Executive Council (NEC) in 1993 to pursue the idea of a truth commission. See Boraine, *A Country Unmasked*, pp. 30–38.

The organization and operation of the TRC reflected a strong – some say exaggerated – belief in the promise of law. Formally rational law, as defined earlier, was the leading principle underlying the process of coming to terms with the apartheid past. Richard Wilson recently offered a critique of this rationalist preoccupation in justicial design. Wilson charged that the TRC's excessive emphasis on legal rules, norms, facts, and procedure undermined its role in apartheid's endgame. Asserts Wilson: "[T]he rationalization of truth production created a dissonance between bureaucratic and popular understandings of the past, the rationalization of justice created new relational discontinuities between institutional and informal justice."[112] He might have added that major agents in apartheid's endgame did not recognize the TRC's legitimacy, including P. W. Botha and Mangosuthu Buthelezi.[113] Yet once one analyzes the TRC as an *intervening variable* in apartheid's endgame, as this book does, none of the aforementioned objections are particularly damaging. For one, Wilson fails to understand the origins of the truth commission. The idea of establishing a truth commission was a compromise solution reached by interacting adversaries at a time in apartheid's endgame when democracy was still in the offing. The idea of an institution administering amnesty for gross human rights violations became the solution to the commitment problem of the Interim Constitution. The TRC became a sustainable solution to a series of dangerous commitment problems. But what is neglected is the fact that the establishment of the TRC was a commitment problem in and of itself.

The establishment of the TRC, in fact, was a cardinal commitment problem. It was a situation in which a mutually preferable bargain was unattainable because the agents in apartheid's endgame held conflicting preferences over the substantive bargaining issue. It was by many accounts the issue least subject to open discussion in the bargaining among interacting adversaries at CODESA I and II. The influence of smaller agents was very limited and the ultimate solution to the commitment problem was the outcome of a direct political deal among the NP and the ANC. The parameters of this deal were set out in the postamble discussed earlier. The deal involved the exchange of amnesty for continued cooperation on mutual advantage. It was struck after all other constitutional negotiations regarding the Interim Constitution had ceased.[114] How did the solution come about?

[112] Wilson, *The Politics of Truth and Reconciliation in South Africa*, p. 227.
[113] Consider in this context also the blunt remark by C. F. Eloff, Judge President of the Transvaal High Court, in his written submission to the TRC regarding its hearing on the judiciary, that "it will be a meaningless exercise." See his "The Role of the Judiciary," reprinted in *South African Law Journal*, Vol. 115, No. 1 (1998), p. 64.
[114] Richard A. Wilson, "Justice and Legitimacy in the South African Transition," in Alexandra Barahona de Brito, Carmen Gonzaléz-Enríquez, and Paloma Aguilar, eds., *The Politics of Memory: Transitional Justice in Democratizing Societies* (Oxford: Oxford University Press, 2001), p. 199.

LAW AS COMMON KNOWLEDGE

Apartheid's endgame was, in some sense, a revolution by law. As Arthur Chaskalson, the former Chief Justice of South Africa and President of the Constitutional Court, writes,

In asking how successful the transition to democracy has been in South Africa, we should understand that South Africa has, in fact, undergone a revolution. Although the revolution was marked by episodes of violence, it has been a revolution which in its final and crucial stages – often the most violent and destructive stages of a revolution – for the most part had been peaceful. The revolution was ultimately effected through law. This has important implications for the type of society that may emerge.[115]

In the previous sections of this chapter, I have described some of the implications of this revolution by law, focusing on the negotiations over the nature of the electoral system, the constitution, and the TRC. It remains for me to uncover the determinants of this revolution: What can account for the function of law in South Africa's transition to democracy?

In South Africa, the law has always been important; it featured prominently in the construction of apartheid and in the struggle against it. In what follows, the discussion shows that legality may, under certain circumstances, breed legitimacy, and that it has done so in South Africa. Law – even when stripped of morality – can be conducive to achieving cooperation under adversity. In Pufendorf's terms, legality can reduce the noise and jarring dissonance of social life, thereby delivering unanimity to deliberations.[116] When agents believe (or their cognitive maps say) that some confidence in the workings of the law, present and future, is warranted, the obstacles to cooperation are reduced. Legality had this effect in South Africa.

Anti-apartheid Lawyering

To be sure, the country's racial oligarchy was created, extended, and secured by way of law. I have sought to demonstrate as much in Chapters 4 and 5. Scholarship and testimony before the Truth and Reconciliation Commission have clearly established the culpability of the law and the judiciary for "separate development."[117] Law, however, also aided the struggle against apartheid. Focusing on the legal profession, Albie Sachs, who was both subject (as a lawyer) and object (as a defendant) of apartheid law, reflected on this bifurcated

---

[115] Arthur Chaskalson, "The Transition to Democracy in South Africa," *New York University Journal of International Law and Politics*, Vol. 29, No. 3 (Spring 1997), p. 297. See also Anthony Lewis, "Revolution by Law," *New York Times*, January 13, 1994, p. A 15.

[116] As discussed in Gerald J. Postema, "Law's Autonomy and Public Practical Reason," in Robert P. George, ed., *The Autonomy of Law: Essays on Legal Positivism* (Oxford: Oxford University Press, 1996), p. 91.

[117] See also Dyzenhaus, *Judging the Judges, Judging Ourselves*.

history of law, echoing David Dyzenhaus's trenchant critique of the profession, but in a less vigorous manner:

[T]he organized profession has shown itself to be notably fearful or even worse, indifferent in the face of repeated invasions by the legislature and the executive of basic rights and liberties relevant to due process – one thinks of areas where legal and judicial functioning are directly affected, such as declarations of states of emergency which go on for years, detention without trial, the bringing of witnesses to court straight from months of solitary confinement, the denial of access to detainees to lawyers and the indirect ouster of judicial review. Happily, there are *other traditions* to which one can point with pride.[118]

Richard Abel, the foremost chronicler of public interest litigation in South Africa, has unearthed one such tradition. He traced ten episodes in which law constrained the prerogative state by appealing to the normative state; ten legal campaigns that illustrate the law as sword and as shield in the struggle against apartheid.[119]

The relative successes in the *Komani* and *Rikhoto* cases are exemplary of this contribution of anti-apartheid lawyering.[120] But the contribution of law did not always revolve around high-profile cases. Throughout the apartheid years, Geoffrey Budlender, working with the LRC, stressed the importance of combining selective "impact" litigation on the appellate level with high-volume "service" litigation on the ground level. Successes of anti-apartheid lawyers on this ground level – where the everyday life of the oppressed was directly affected – account in large measure for the surprisingly favorable views that black South Africans held of the law, a topic to which I will return later. Most important at the ground level were issues surrounding the implementation of legal victories, for favorable jurisprudence alone proved insufficient to battle the consequences of apartheid. Consider in this context once again the landmark judgment of the Appeal Division in *Komani*, which we encountered in the previous chapter:

As hard-won as the "impact victory" was, the "service victory" proved even more elusive. At first the Minister of Co-operation and Development, Piet Koornhof, was recalcitrant and delayed the enforcement of *Komani*. On the ground, bureaucrats the country over, from the West Rand Administration Board to the Western Cape Administration Board, placed exorbitant demands on applicants for residential permits,

---

[118] Albie Sachs, "The Future of Roman Dutch Law in a Non-Racial Democratic South Africa: Some Preliminary Observations," *Social and Legal Studies*, Vol. 1, No. 2 (June 1992), p. 223. Emphasis added.

[119] Space constraints disallow a closer analysis of these episodes. See Abel, *Politics By Other Means*. See also idem., "Legality Without a Constitution: South Africa in the 1980s," in David Dyzenhaus, ed., *Recrafting the Rule of Law: The Limits of Legal Order* (Oxford: Hart, 1999), pp. 66–80. The late Donald Woods, too, used the law as a tool in the struggle against apartheid. The Biko biographer and former editor of the *Daily Dispatch*, a newspaper based in East London, won thirty-seven lawsuits against the apartheid government. He was placed under house arrest after he had forced the government to open an inquiry into the death of Steve Biko. See "Obituary: Donald Woods," *The Economist*, August 25, 2001.

[120] For a detailed discussion of these cases, see Chapter 5.

from irrelevant documentation to the visitation of government offices in many different parts of the metropolitan (or rural) area concerned.

Particularly disheartening in the immediate aftermath of *Komani* was a comment by Labor Director Armand Steenhuizen: "I have nothing to do with the judgment's practical application, but all I can say is that there will be absolutely no change."[121] The implementation of the *Rikhoto* judgment ran into similar snags. As the Black Sash's Sheena Duncan reported at the time:

In the first and second weeks of June people who went to ask for a [Section] 10(1)(b) endorsement to be placed in their Pass Books were asked a great many questions about their families. They were asked for the names of wives and children, where they were living, how many of the children were sons or daughters. A form was filled in and they were told that the application would have to be "sent to Pretoria." This was unlawful. The whereabouts of a man's family have nothing whatsoever to do with his [Section] 10 (1)(b) rights, nor has "Pretoria" anything to do with the obligation of the Labour Officer to endorse a person's identity document with his legal rights.[122]

To further stall compliance with the Appellate Division's judgment in *Rikhoto*, applicants, after having submitted superfluous paperwork,

were told to return to the Labour Bureau in a month's time. When they did so they were told that the form relating to their families had been "cancelled" and they were given a long and detailed form on which their employer was required to list the dates of every contract during the ten year period and the dates of every period of paid leave and every period of unpaid leave. ... Many employers justifiably refused to fill in the form on the grounds that they do not keep their records that way.[123]

Bureaucratic intransigence notwithstanding, anti-apartheid lawyers managed – by threatening litigation, pursuing litigation, and otherwise speaking law to power – to enforce in many instances the letter of *Komani* and *Rikhoto*, bringing relief to many (although by no means all) suffering under the Urban Areas Act. The following case, retrieved by Richard Abel, is worth recounting because it illustrates, once again, certain limits of the prerogative state and its pursuit of residential segregation:

In one instance its flagrant lawlessness hurt the government. Mafiri Maria Mashiane married William Silika Mhlongo in 1959 and came to live with him in Old Pimville, where he had [Section] 10 rights and a lodger's permit. When she sought an endorsement the New Canada office ordered her out of the city ten days after the Komani decision. Phoned by [Geoffrey] Budlender [of the LRC] in January 1981, Pretorius [the Superintendent for the Orlando West part of Soweto] justified the denial on the ground that she had entered Johannesburg without permission (twenty-two years earlier). The LRC sued, and the state defaulted on July 21 before Judge Richard Goldstone, who noted on the brief that the "Court's displeasure [is] to be made known to Minister."[124]

[121] As quoted in Abel, *Politics by Other Means*, p. 29.
[122] Duncan, "The Rikhoto Scandal," p. 22.
[123] Duncan, "The Rikhoto Scandal," pp. 22–23.
[124] Abel, *Politics by Other Means*, pp. 33–34.

It was "service victories" such as these, brought about by lawyers on the ground, that created confidence in the law on the part of those who were black and disenfranchised – a strand of the analysis that I will pick up in the next chapter.

Speaking of lawyers on the ground, Sachs, whom we encountered previously and again a moment ago pointed to the country's venerable tradition of anti-apartheid lawyering:

We do not have to have recourse to Grotius or Coke to find *legal* freedom fighters in our past. Gandhi, Schreiner, Krause, Seme, Mathews, Fischer, Nokwe, Berrange, Kahn, Muller, Mandela, Tambo, Slovo, and Kies; the list is long and can be made much longer, of persons, drawn from every section of our community who saw the pursuit of their legal careers as being inextricably linked up with the pursuit of justice.[125]

Continues Sachs,

The list is even longer of those who, without confronting the system of justice head-on, used their legal talents to defend those dragged before the courts under apartheid or security laws – Pitje, Kentridge, Bizos, Mohamed, Kuhny, Aaron, Cheadle, de Villiers, Richman – the list is being added to by day. Perhaps of special interest is the role played by certain far-sighted and fair-minded judges over the years. Rose-Innes was a judge of whom any country could be proud, *and he is as much part of our patrimony as the hanging judges of today.* An outstanding legal scholar who researched into and adapted RDL [Roman Dutch Law] to modern conditions, he imbued his judgments with as much of the spirit of liberty and equality as he could.[126]

This prodigious talent, operating under the auspices of a dual state, orchestrated a series of legal campaigns – culminating in *Komani* and *Rikhoto* – seeking to address the ills of apartheid. Many of these campaigns (some described earlier, others described later) were in large part underwritten by international funding agencies, including the Ford Foundation and the Carnegie Corporation. In the cases of *Komani* and *Rikhoto*, for example, a substantial portion of the legal fees were underwritten by "American foundations seeking to export the test case strategy pioneered by the NAACP in civil rights and generalized by legal services and public interest lawyers."[127] The Ford Foundation's Stephen Golub, reflecting on the boisterous claim of the Nationalist MP H. M. J. van Rensburg, in a 1985 parliamentary debate, that "the South African administration of justice and the judicature stand out as a symbol of hope and confidence," for example, believes that the apartheid regime's "distorted notion of the rule of law provided limited openings that Ford grantees and their allies eagerly exploited."[128] The analysis of *Komani* and *Rikhoto* in the previous chapter bears out this view.

---

[125] Sachs, "The Future of Roman Dutch Law in a Non-Racial Democratic South Africa," p. 223. Emphasis added.
[126] Sachs, "The Future of Roman Dutch Law in a Non-Racial Democratic South Africa," pp. 223–224. Emphasis added.
[127] Abel, *Politics by Other Means*, pp. 62–62.
[128] Hansard cols. 6747–48 (H. M. J. van Rensburg) (April 6, 1985), as quoted in Abel, *Politics by Other Means*, p. 13; Golub, "Battling Apartheid, Building a New South Africa," p. 22.

It is opportune to consider briefly the international dimensions of anti-apartheid lawyering in this context, for it is doubtful that the legal struggle against apartheid could have been sustained over the course of several decades absent financial injections from abroad. In addition to underwriting legal campaigns, the international network of lawyers associated with anti-apartheid litigation also lent important legitimacy to these efforts, keeping the apartheid regime on its toes. "Both within and outside South Africa, where government or bar opposition looms, the involvement of prestigious legal talent sometimes protects politically controversial groups [and individuals]."[129] This held true for the involvement of domestic as well as international jurists.

The long standing of public interest litigation in South Africa, conveyed in the following quote, is an indication that opportunities *truly* existed for legally challenging – and at times defeating – the apartheid regime:

Though public interest law achieved a kind of critical mass in the 1980s, its roots reach back at least to the 1950s. Before Ford became involved other organizations were actively using the law to oppose apartheid. The Treason Trial Defense Fund enabled attorneys to successfully defend 156 anti-apartheid activists, arrested in 1956 for alleged high treason, in a trial that dragged on until 1961. Established in 1960, the South African Defense and Aid Fund (SADAF) initially focused on explicitly political cases, but later supported other civil and criminal litigation pertaining to apartheid. After the government banned the SADAF in 1966, the London-based International Defense and Aid Fund quietly channeled external assistance to South African lawyers fighting apartheid.[130]

The 1973 conference on "Legal Aid in South Africa," held at the law school of the University of Natal in Durban, was a watershed event for putting anti-apartheid lawyering on a firmer footing. According to one participant, John Dugard, the conference was "the start of the idea of public interest law" in South Africa.[131] In the wake of the gathering, Dugard and others launched the CALS at the University of the Witwatersrand, which we already encountered in the previous chapter in the context of appellate victories over the apartheid regime. The founding of CALS was inspired by Sydney Kentridge's call to arms at the Durban conference. Sir Sydney, today of Brick Court Chambers in London, then insisted that "we do have principles of common law which we can invoke" in the struggle against apartheid.[132] And so he did.

Centrally involved in the process, often coordinating legal responses, was the LRC, which Felicia Kentridge, Sir Sydney's wife, helped get off the ground and Chaskalson later led to national and international prominence. Established in 1979 (see also Chapter 5) and controlled and funded by the Legal

---

[129] Golub, "Battling Apartheid, Building a New South Africa," p. 24.

[130] Golub, "Battling Apartheid, Building a New South Africa," p. 22.

[131] As quoted in Golub, "Battling Apartheid, Building a New South Africa," p. 23.

[132] Legal Aid in South Africa: Proceedings of a Conference held in the Faculty of Law, University of Natal, Durban, from 2nd-6th July, 1973 (Durban: University of Natal Faculty of Law, 1974), p. 265.

Resources Trust, a charitable and educational trust under South Africa's Fundraising Act, the LRC sought, from its inception, to narrow the gap between *law* and *justice* (this formulation illustrates an important point this book is trying to make, namely that even in instances where *justice* is absent, the *law* may be operating as an independent force that influences strategic interaction). As Wallace Mgoqi, an attorney with the LRC's Cape Town office, wrote in the early 1990s:

The Centre's work has been both responsive to the problems experienced by its clientele and pro-active in the sense of finding creative and imaginative ways of dealing with repression. The Appellate Division cases in *Komani, Rikhoto* and *Mthiya* illustrate the point. Here day-to-day problems experienced by black people over the restriction of their movement in urban areas formed the basis for an action which resulted not only in relieving the immediate pressure of the influx control laws but also in a campaign against these laws which ultimately led to their repeal in the late 1980s.[133]

As South Africa's first public interest law firm, the LRC, in conjunction with Black Sash and the support of international donors, assisted black clients in multiple areas, ranging from housing to land, from pensions to workers' compensation, and from delicts to consumer abuse.[134] Anti-apartheid lawyers and the NGOs associated with them celebrated some of their most far-reaching successes in the labor arena. "University-based institutes played particularly wide-ranging roles in assisting black South Africans' most organized and important domestic political force: the labor movement. Seeking to control and regulate illegal and increasingly disruptive black trade unions, Parliament passed the 1979 Labor Relations Act. This allowed unions to organize, register, strike, and take disputes to industrial courts."[135] Following the reports of two crucial commissions of inquiry in 1979 – the reports of the so-called Wiehahn and Riekert Commissions – the government softened apartheid's edges by way of law. Numerous legal restrictions on the vertical and horizontal mobility of black labor were relaxed, some repealed. New industrial legislation accorded the right to organize to independent trade unions.[136] Furthermore, legal provisions regarding job reservation and laws controlling the movement and settlement were partially overhauled. The legal challenges and training made possible under the auspices especially of the CALS, which in 1980 established a Labor Law Project, but also under the auspices of other institutes and organizations around the country (for example, the

---

[133] Wallace Mgoqi, "The Work of the Legal Resources Centre in South Africa in the Area of Human Rights Promotion and Protection," *Journal of African Law*, Vol. 36, No. 1 (Spring 1992), p. 2. Emphases added.

[134] For a succinct overview of the LRC's work, see Mgoqi, "The Work of the Legal Resources Centre in South Africa in the Area of Human Rights Promotion and Protection," pp. 1–10. For an in-depth analysis of LRC legal campaigns, see Abel, *Politics By Other Means*. See also the discussion of *Komani* and *Rikhoto* in Chapter 5.

[135] Golub, "Battling Apartheid, Building a New South Africa," p. 32.

[136] Price, *The Apartheid State in Crisis*, pp. 102–133.

University of Cape Town's Labor Law Unit) facilitated these developments. In the estimation of some,

South Africa's labor scene might have been much more chaotic and counterproductive in the 1990s if union leaders had not worked with reform centers in the 1980s. And the centers' assistance helped unions cut larger slices out of apartheid's inequitable economic and political pies.[137]

Perhaps more important, especially for our purposes, is the fact that the synergetic relationship between lawyers and laborers further ingrained a legal way of doing things in the country's edifice. It demonstrated – in contrast to the confrontation increasingly practiced in the "ungovernable" townships – the value of cooperation. It has been argued that the most significant contribution to labor relations provided by South Africa's leading research centers, like CALS and LRC, were "'the crucial negotiation skills that were imparted to trade unionists.' By helping to build the unionists' skills and legal knowledge through training and advice, the centers enabled them to make use of the law. On the policy level, unions banded together to persuade the government to repeal the controversial 1988 Labor Relations Act. And through a kind of paralegal training, shop stewards learned how to handle day-to-day disputes such as unfair dismissals. The centers also won notable court victories for both unions and individual members, and made labor law an important arena for legal practice and instruction."[138]

The effect on union behavior was remarkable, as this speck of evidence, relayed by Ellmann, indicates: "One South African advocate told me, for example, that he had been struck by union litigants' tendency to obey adverse court orders and appeal them, rather than simply disobey them."[139] This behavior on the part of union litigants, if it was the rule rather than the exception, is even more remarkable given the UDF movement in the 1980s and the strategy of defiance practiced in the resistance movement more generally, most memorably in the 1952 Defiance Campaign. The improvement of working conditions for laborers by way of litigation provides one clue as to why black South Africans had such a surprising amount of confidence in the law of apartheid.[140]

A third commission, the Rabie Commission of Inquiry, reported in February 1982. Its investigation concerned the entire gamut of security legislation, procedures, and practices.[141] Although biased in favor of the government, and

[137] Golub, "Battling Apartheid, Building a New South Africa," p. 33. See also Clive Thompson, "Trade Unions Using the Law," in Hugh Corder, ed., *Essays on Law and Social Practice in South Africa* (Cape Town: 1988), pp. 335–348.
[138] Golub, "Battling Apartheid, Building a New South Africa," p. 32.
[139] Ellmann, "Law and Legitimacy in South Africa," p. 411.
[140] For an extended discussion of survey data concerning South Africans' confidence in the legal system, see Chapter 7.
[141] Davies, O'Meara, and Dlamini, *The Struggle for South Africa*, Volume 1, p. 177. See also the discussion of Nkondo and Gumede v. Minister of Law and Order 1986 (2) SA 756 (AD) below.

intent on maintaining apartheid legislation (especially legislation concerning detention without trial), the Commission devised certain limits for the prerogative state. For example, it recommended review procedures to guarantee the rights of detainees, and narrowed the scope of punishable offences under the label "terrorism." It instead recommended the establishment of new categories, including "subversion" (acts not involving violence) and "intimidation." Legislation based on the Rabie recommendations was passed in the same year.

Inasmuch as arbitrariness generally superseded the principle of due process and other such principles under apartheid, the rule-by-law plank of the state created a modicum of reassurance that ultimately took on cultural significance, at least among elites. Although the Rabie Commission did not put an end to the excesses committed under the prerogative state, it may have averted some of them. The modicum of reassurance that the normative state provided, of course, was principally intended to structure the life of the country's white minority, the government's primary support base. In instrumental terms, the showcasing of the normative state was also intended, of course, to have a signaling effect on the international community because "white South Africans could invoke their adherence to legality as basis for claiming membership in the community of Western nations; as a testament to their own civilization, in contrast to the barbarism they attributed to those whom they ruled; and as a gift to the subjects of apartheid, a gift from which whites could reap gratitude and respect."[142]

This notwithstanding, the normative state, even when circumscribed, instilled a belief in the value of doing things in a *legal* way, affecting white and "coloured"colored and black behavior alike. Although black defendants had generally a cautious, and often a cynical, view of the law, "it is clear," according to Lobban, "that most defendants recognized that arrival in court out of detention meant that an important boundary had been crossed, and that they could seek vindication and even protection from the court. Although not subscribing to the same view of the court's neutrality and fairness as held by whites, most defendants at least sought to defend themselves in a way that involved accepting the court's rules. ... It was only in exceptional circumstances that defendants refused to accept the conventional rules of the courts of their enemies."[143] Or, as Chaskalson, put it, "In political trials, those

---

[142] Ellmann, "Law and Legitimacy in South Africa," p. 409. The instrumental use of law by successive apartheid governments caused many anti-apartheid lawyers to worry that their appearance in the country's courts might lend a measure of legitimacy to the legal system, and thus to a regime that was not deserving of it. For others, this "was no cause for regret. On the contrary, the possibility that anti-apartheid lawyering might have encouraged South Africans to see virtue in the ideals of fearless advocacy, independent judging, and the rule of law offered promise that these same ideals would be honored in postapartheid South Africa." Ibid. The possible "legitimation effect" of anti-apartheid lawyering could, plausibly, help to explain the surprising confidence of black South Africans in the law of apartheid, which is to be discussed below.

[143] Lobban, *White Man's Justice*, pp. 10–11.

charged almost without exception turned to lawyers to defend them."[144]
Continued Chaskalson:

The role of the judiciary within South Africa was a complex one, and it would be oversimplifying to see it as no more than the instrument of a repressive state. It enforced unjust laws – almost invariably without protest – and in so doing helped to legitimate them within the white community. But, at the same time, the South African state was based on structures that had legal form. The courts require the state and its officials to adhere to the forms of law, and, in so doing, imposed some constraint upon the exercise of arbitrary power. Laws could be and were changed in response to adverse court rulings, but there were political costs to such actions, and, in the end, there were constraints that no government and no official was willing to risk breaking, openly.[145]

Moreover, recent survey data confirm that confidence in judicial and law enforcement institutions by both black and white South Africans is indeed statistically significant.[146] Such significance cannot be created over night, as the late Etienne Mureinik recognized. According to Mureinik, a staunch critic of the apartheid regime, judges in South Africa took it for granted

that every racial distinction requires statutory justification, usually express. In the absence of such, they enforce contracts, and remedy delicts, and strike down administrative decisions, and administer companies, and protect property, and enforce statutory duties, and apply rules of court, on the unquestioned premise *that the race of the parties before them is irrelevant.* Routinely they affirm conceptions of the equal treatment of individuals which are quite discordant with the theory underlying apartheid statutes; whether consciously, such as when they strike down by-laws and regulations for partial and unequal treatment, or unconsciously, such, perhaps, as when they apply the doctrine of precedent.[147]

The aforementioned survey data, to be discussed in more detail later, offer further evidence that a relationship between dual state and usable state existed in apartheid's endgame, and that it has had the effects predicted by the theoretical model advanced in Chapters 2 and 3.

The other culturally ingrained and significant way of doing things in South Africa, of course, was (and, unfortunately, still is) the application of violence against adversaries. Although more attention has been paid to the latter, the former has been of significant importance in the ending of apartheid. Paradoxically, then, two "behavioral cultures" existed side by side in South Africa: a culture of violence and a culture of law. Both, in different ways and to different degrees, shaped apartheid's endgame.

[144] Arthur Chaskalson, "From Wickedness to Equality: The Moral Transformation of South African Law," *International Journal of Constitutional Law*, Vol. 1, No. 4 (October 2003), p. 596.

[145] Chaskalson, "From Wickedness to Equality," p. 598.

[146] Richard Morin, "Rainbow's End: Public Support for Democracy in the New South Africa," Working Paper 2000–10, Joan Shorenstein Center on the Press, Politics, and Public Policy, John F. Kennedy School of Government, Harvard University, 2000, p. 21.

[147] Etienne Mureinik, "Dworkin and Apartheid," in Corder, ed., *Essays on Law and Social Practice in South Africa*, pp. 207–208. Emphases added.

The state, however, was not a strong state in apartheid's endgame.[148] Its coercive apparatus, this net of tangled organizations, was not strong enough to stem the tide of millions that the struggle against apartheid had engulfed. What is more, key planks of the state's structure collapsed. The administrative institutions on which the regime had relied in the homelands were crumbling one after the other. Yet the key institutions at the core of its structure remained virtually unchanged. It is therefore misleading to speak of state collapse or even state failure in South Africa.[149] The state proved usable. We can gain a good understanding of the utility of the state in apartheid's endgame by examining an auxiliary indicator (in addition to the state of law). This will help us appreciate why the state was preserved, not stolen.

An Excursus on Taxes

In a comparative analysis of the post-apartheid government's ability to collect taxes, Evan Lieberman writes, "by the late 1990s, the South African state was able to collect approximately 15 percent of its GDP in the form of progressive, direct income taxes while the Brazilian state could barely collect 5 percent of GDP of such revenues."[150] This institutional overhang, among others, accounts for the utility of the state in apartheid's endgame. At that point, "the legacy of the tax state provide[d] some promising prospects. Though absolute and per capita expenditure on whites was always significantly greater than on blacks in apartheid South Africa, within this highly unequal society, blacks still received more on the expenditure side than they contributed in the form of taxes on the revenue side. ... There is good reason to believe that with the eradication of ... racial engineering, the post-apartheid state has better-than-average capacities to ameliorate income and wealth disparities, particularly given the tax state it inherited."[151]

Lieberman's argument and mine are cut from the same cloth, and therefore are commensurate. Both of us focus, albeit in different ways, on the role of institutional structure – law in my case, bureaucracy in his case – in the transition to and from apartheid, and we both analyze the unintended consequences thereof. Although my principal emphasis is on the evolution – and effects – of law, and his on the evolution – and effects – of bureaucracy, we are

---

[148] See Meierhenrich, "Forming States after Failure," pp. 153–169.

[149] For the erroneous view that the South African state collapsed, see Sipho Shezi, "South Africa: State Transition and the Management of Collapse," in I. William Zartman, ed., *Collapsed States: The Disintegration and Restoration of Legitimate Authority* (Boulder, CO: Lynne Rienner, 1995), pp.191–204.

[150] Evan S. Lieberman, "Payment for Privilege? The Politics of Taxation in Brazil and South Africa," Unpublished Paper, University of California, Berkeley, n.d., p. 4.

[151] Evan S. Lieberman, *Race and Regionalism in the Politics of Taxation in Brazil and South Africa* (Cambridge: Cambridge University Press, 2003), pp. 277–278. On the significant and insufficiently appreciated relationship between taxation and liberty, see the important *The Cost of Rights: Why Liberty Depends on Taxes*, by Stephen Holmes and Cass R. Sunstein (New York: Norton, 1999).

in agreement about the institutional centrality of the state, especially in comparative terms, for explaining South African politics and society.[152]

Reasoning backward, it should be apparent why agents had an incentive to *preserve* the state rather than *steal* it in the throes of apartheid's endgame. As Frederik van Zyl Slabbert, an insider and driving force of the early negotiations between government representatives and opposition representatives, remarked:

> They [Mandela and de Klerk] both had the capacity to hurt one another, and they did not want to do that, because in the final analysis what they could gain through compromise was more than they could gain by conflict. And the one thing that was the prize for both was the continuation of the state. There's no question about that. There's no question about de Klerk. De Klerk thought he could control the situation for much longer than it turned out to be. ... He could remain in charge of the state. Now Mandela knew that if he got a foothold in the state, he would get far more power than his movement ever had. So there was something to be gained for both of them.[153]

Apartheid's endgame was a struggle "over the state – who controls it, and toward what end."[154] It was a struggle *against* the regime, and *over* the state, fought on the foundation of an elaborate legal tradition.[155]

---

[152] For a comparative analysis, see Chapter 8. Whereas Lieberman's comparative focus is on Brazil, mine is on Chile.

[153] Frederik van Zyl Slabbert, Interview with the author, London: October 20, 1997.

[154] Sisk, *Democratization in South Africa*, p. 5.

[155] In fact, as I shall show momentarily, the struggle was fought on the foundation of *several* legal traditions. I should emphasize, however, that I am not here referring to the civil law and common law legal traditions.

7

Apartheid's Endgame and the Law II

This chapter picks up where the previous chapter left off. It demonstrates the difference that law, in particular South Africa's legal tradition, made in apartheid's endgame. And yet, as Edwin Cameron, a judge on the South African Supreme Court of Appeal, reminds us, "The survival of law and legal regulation in [South Africa] can by no means simply be assumed."[1]

LAW AS TRADITION

A legal tradition connotes "a set of deeply rooted, historically conditioned attitudes about the nature of law, about the role of law in society and the polity, about the proper organization and operation of a legal system, and about the way law is or should be made, applied, studied, perfected, and taught."[2] South Africa's legal tradition – this ideology of law – is an underappreciated factor in the country's transition to democracy (see also Figure 3.2). I have argued, throughout this book, that choices about cooperation and confrontation in democratization are crucially affected by the presence, or absence, as well as the nature of a legal tradition in newly democratizing countries. I believe that legal traditions, or legal ideologies, provide shared mental models that can, under the conditions specified in this book, help overcome uncertainty and bargaining predicaments. For as we saw Denzau and North claim in Chapter 2,

[u]nder conditions of uncertainty, individuals' interpretation of their environment will reflect their learning. Individuals with common cultural backgrounds and experiences will share reasonably convergent mental models, ideologies, and institutions; and individuals with different learning experiences (both cultural and environmental) will have different theories (models, ideologies) to interpret their environment.[3]

---

[1] Edwin Cameron, "Our Legal System – Precious and Precarious," *South African Law Journal*, Vol. 177, No. 2 (2000), p. 372.
[2] John Henry Merryman, *The Civil Law Tradition: An Introduction to the Legal Systems of Western Europe and Latin America* (Stanford: Stanford University Press, 1969), p. 2.
[3] Denzau and North, "Shared Mental Models," pp. 3–4.

I maintain that South Africa's legal tradition, for reasons already and further to be explicated, served as a shared mental model in this sense, and with the effects thus described. "Even though this tradition was often honored in the breach rather than the observance during the heyday of apartheid, it left institutional traces helpful in holding the National Party government accountable for violence, through such devices as the Goldstone Commission during the transition, and the Truth and Reconciliation Commission afterward."[4] Confidence in these institutional traces was a path-dependent effect of the "self-binding" that the commitment to law of successive governments has affected over the span of several centuries. With an eye to the jurisprudence in the terrorist trials of the 1980s, one analyst reinforces the point: "[I]t is a sign of the political and legal force of *ideas*," what Denzau and North speak of in terms of ideology, "of a right to petition, of a right to religious succor, and of a right to political freedom, that even in the midst of the state of emergency, the government found itself giving its own notice a narrowing interpretation."[5]

Let us examine, in more detail, the contours of South Africa's legal tradition, focusing, to begin with, on survey research undertaken between 1981 and 1993 that measured the confidence of black South Africans ("Coloureds," Asians, and Africans) in the country's legal system.

Survey Data on Confidence in the Legal System

The data demonstrate that black South Africans held significantly more favorable views of the law and its institutions than is commonly assumed, a finding that provides support for the argument advanced herein. I shall briefly examine the data, then evaluate it, then explain it.

Examining the Data

The data reported in the following were collected in 1981, 1990, and 1993, respectively. Markinor, a leading and respected commercial polling agency in South Africa, administered the data collection.[6] Focusing on a dozen or so

---

[4] Ian Shapiro, *Democracy's Place* (Ithaca, NY: Cornell University Press, 1996), p. 98.

[5] Stephen Ellmann, "Legal Text and Lawyers' Culture in South Africa," *New York University Review of Law and Social Change*, Vol. 17, No. 3 (1989/1990), p. 413.

[6] Markinor is presently a member of both the Walker Information Global Network and the Gallup International Association. The 1981 data consists of responses from six hundred whites and six hundred Africans in metropolitan areas as well as responses from two hundred "Coloureds" in Cape Town and two hundred Asians in Durban. The 1990 data consist of responses from 1,236 whites, 600 Africans in metropolitan areas, 500 Africans in rural areas (100 in each of the five homelands), 200 "Coloureds," and 200 Asians. The 1993 data consist of responses from 804 whites, 1,000 Africans (excluding hostel dwellers), 400 "Coloureds," and 400 Asians, all in metropolitan areas. See Markinor, *The Markinor South African Social Value – In Association with Gallup International* (March 1982); Markinor, *The World Social Value Study – South Africa – Urban Written Report* (March 1991); and Markinor, *Markinor Social-political Trends* (May 1993); and related statistical data provided directly to Stephen Ellmann, on whose data reporting in "Law and Legitimacy in South Africa," pp. 407–479, I rely in my analysis.

institutions ranging from the armed forces to the church to the legal system, the question that surveyors put to respondents was the following (this is the formulation used in 1990): "Please indicate, for EACH item listed here, how much confidence you have in them; is it a great deal, quite a lot, not very much, or none at all?"[7] My concern here is solely with the legal system (although comparative data on the police and parliament will appear in some of the graphics).

In the sample, the respondents likely took the term "legal system" to refer to courts and related institutions (other than parliament and the police) that were operating in South Africa at the time; in other words, to courts "as seen within the penumbra of other legal institutions."[8] Although the meaning of "confidence" was similarly ambiguous in the research design (compounded by the imperative of translating concepts into several languages), I propose that it is reasonable to assume that Markinor in all likelihood elicited responses concerning the extent to which individuals – black, white, "coloured," and other South Africans – felt certain that the institution in question – the legal system, police, or parliament – would operate in a manner that was predictable and produce outcomes not categorically adverse to their interests.

The first poll, administered in 1981, reported that 50 percent of black respondents had confidence in the legal system, of which 24 percent had "a great deal" of confidence, and 26 percent "quite a lot" of confidence. It is startling that the percentage of black South Africans expressing "a great deal" of confidence in the legal system was *greater* than the percentage of English-speaking whites who expressed this sentiment, the latter accounting for only 18 percent of the respondents. The display of confidence was even greater among "coloured" (51 percent) and Asian (59 percent) respondents.[9]

The data for 1990 is even more remarkable. As Table 7.1 demonstrates, by then, some 62 percent of black South Africans living in urban areas reported to have confidence in the legal system (27 percent having "a great deal" of confidence; 35 percent "quite a lot" of confidence). Their counterparts in the countryside vested even more confidence in the legal system: 33 percent at the time had "a great deal" of confidence, 46 percent "quite a lot" of confidence. This means that the majority of the black rural population had faith in the law on the eve of apartheid's endgame, possibly as much as 79 percent of this population. This is a striking finding, for as Ellmann writes, "black South Africans showed a level of confidence in their country's legal system quite comparable to that displayed by whites."[10] Although remarkable, there is no

---

[7] Markinor, *The World Social Value Study – South Africa – Urban Written Report* (March 1991), as quoted in Ellmann, "Law and Legitimacy in South Africa," p. 421.

[8] Ellmann addresses these and other methodological concerns expertly in "Law and Legitimacy in South Africa," pp. 420–423.

[9] This section relies heavily on Ellmann, "Law and Legitimacy in South Africa," pp. 407–479. Unless otherwise indicated, Ellmann is the source of all Markinor data.

[10] Ellmann, "Law and Legitimacy in South Africa," p. 426.

TABLE 7.1. *Confidence in the Legal System, 1990*

	Urban Africans	Rural Africans	"Coloureds"	Asians	Whites
A great deal	27.4	32.9	13.1	31.7	28.2
Quite a lot	35.3	45.9	43.1	30.2	47.2
Not very much	21.3	12.8	28.7	21.0	18.0
None at all	10.7	3.6	1.6	7.4	2.9
Don't know	5.3	4.9	13.4	9.6	3.7

Source: Markinor, *The World Social Value Study – South Africa – Urban* Written Report (March 1991) in conjunction with additional data containing more detailed statistical breakdowns. Adapted from Ellmann, "Law and Legitimacy in South Africa," p. 426.

reason to suspect that the responses from black South Africans were anything but genuine:

Though they would not likely have been speaking with an interviewer of a different race, they might still have feared that their answers might be used to their disadvantage by powerful whites. Thus it is conceivable that the levels of confidence that black South Africans expressed in the legal system masked their true, more critical judgments. Conceivable, yes; likely, no. This theory is hard to square with the harsher judgments that the [black South African] poll respondents *did* offer with respect to other institutions.[11]

Already in the first poll, 24 percent of black respondents had stated that the structure of South African society "must be radically changed by revolutionary action," and 13 percent of those polled "had undertaken themselves" or were "prepared to" use "personal violence like fighting with other demonstrators or the police."[12] These and responses like it suggest that black South Africans meant what they said when being polled.

What are we to make of the euphoria surrounding the year 1990, when F. W. de Klerk delivered his February 2 speech, which led to Nelson Mandela's release from prison? Was the confidence of black South Africans buoyant on account of these watershed events? Did the 1990 data offer a false – an amplified rather than accurate – reading of black attitudes? Perhaps, muses Ellmann. However,

the fact that sentiments toward the legal system could improve as a result of hope for the end of apartheid demonstrates that black South African opinion was not irrevocably fixed. Strong as their opposition was to apartheid itself, black South Africans apparently were *not* utterly disenchanted with the institutions through which apartheid operated, and instead were prepared to revise their views of the institutions of South African society if they believed those institutions had become forces against, rather than for, the maintenance of injustice.[13]

[11] Ellmann, "Law and Legitimacy in South Africa," p. 424.
[12] As reported in Ellmann, "Law and Legitimacy in South Africa," p. 425.
[13] Ellmann, "Law and Legitimacy in South Africa," p. 427. Emphasis added.

TABLE 7.2. *"Coloured," Asian, and White Confidence in the Legal System, 1993*

	"Coloureds"	Asians	Whites
A great deal	10.7	6.8	20.5
Quite a lot	26.5	28.3	31.6
Not very much	45.8	49.2	28.8
None at all	9.3	10.9	9.6
Don't know	7.7	4.8	9.4

Source: Markinor, *Markinor Social-political Trends* (May 1993) in conjunction with additional data. Adapted from Ellmann, "Law and Legitimacy in South Africa," p. 477.

But a certain amount of disenchantment materialized. By 1993, and the third Markinor poll, the percentage of black South Africans expressing "a great deal" of confidence had decreased to 6 percent and the percentage of those expressing "quite a lot" of confidence was down to 19 percent. Among black respondents in urban areas, disillusionment was particularly keenly felt: 35 percent let surveyors know that they had "not very much" confidence in the legal system, and 26 percent expressed no confidence at all. The confidence in the legal system of "Coloureds", Asian, and Whites also declined in this period (See Table 7.2).

And yet the picture is not as bleak as it may appear at first sight. "Even at the end of this period," insists Ellmann, quite persuasively,

it is worth remembering that a quarter of the urban African population expressed considerable confidence in South Africa's legal system. Neither the frustrations after 1991, nor the years of the state of emergency before then, nor the thousands of largely unpunished political killings of recent years, had altogether dulled black South Africans' confidence in the nation's legal system.[14]

Additional data regarding the phenomenon of black South African's confidence in the legal system is displayed in Table 7.3, which introduces a within-case comparison. Here respondents' attitudes toward the legal system are contrasted with their attitudes toward the police and parliament – two other institutions of the apartheid state. Across the board it is obvious that black South Africans, urban and rural alike, vested more confidence in the legal system than in either of the two other institutions. Although urban respondents' confidence in the police and parliament was impressive (49 percent and 54 percent, respectively, had either "a great deal" or "quite a lot" of confidence), it does not equal the percentage of city dwellers confident in the legal system (63 percent).

---

[14] Ellmann, "Law and Legitimacy in South Africa," p. 428.

TABLE 7.3. *Urban and Rural African Confidence in the Legal System, Police, and Parliament, 1990*

	Urban Africans			Rural Africans		
	Legal System	Police	Parliament	Legal System	Police	Parliament
A great deal	27.4	21.4	20.9	32.9	34.5	38.0
Quite a lot	35.3	27.2	32.7	45.9	34.7	30.0
Not very much	21.3	26.8	25.5	12.8	19.4	14.3
None at all	10.7	21.8	13.8	3.6	8.7	6.6
Don't know	5.3	2.7	7.2	4.9	2.7	10.2

Source: Markinor, *The World Social Value Study – South Africa – Urban Written Report* (March 1991) in conjunction with additional data containing more detailed statistical breakdowns. Adapted from Ellmann, "Law and Legitimacy in South Africa," p. 429.

The pattern remained stable over time, at least between 1990 and 1993, the early and disquieting phase of apartheid's endgame. Although black South Africans in urban areas were certainly somewhat disillusioned at the time of the third Markinor poll, in 1993, they remained less wary of the legal system – in which, as we have seen, 26 percent placed "a great deal" or "quite a lot" of confidence – than of the police (19 percent) and parliament (18 percent). How significant is this finding?

This finding is significant because it tells us that Africans' assessments of the system of justice are not simply a function of their evaluations of all South African institutions. Instead, we now know not only that Africans (and other blacks) often held surprisingly favorable views of their legal system, and never held entirely unfavorable views of it, but also that those views are, at least in part, the result of Africans' evaluations of the particular features of the system of justice that distinguish it from other South African institutions. It appears that this system – and thus, it would seem, the courts in particular – enjoyed a measure of institutional prestige in African eyes greater than that retained by either Parliament or the police.[15]

Other surveys, albeit smaller in scope, have borne out the Markinor findings. A 1998 interview study conducted by the Human Sciences Research Council (HSRC), South Africa's statutory research agency dedicated to the applied social sciences, revealed that 41 percent of Africans in the infamous Durban area townships of KwaMashu and Umlazi, agreed with the statement that "[i]n this country nobody will be sentenced to prison without good

---

[15] Ellmann, "Law and Legitimacy in South Africa," p. 430. It is noteworthy in this context that, as far as the police were concerned, "Coloureds" and Asians, at least in 1990 and 1993 (not so much in 1981), were less circumspect than Africans. In 1993, for instance, an astonishing 49 percent of Asians and 51 percent of "Coloureds" reported to have "a great deal" or "quite a lot" of confidence in the police. This finding is quickly explained. "Coloureds and Asians were in many respects less acutely victimized by apartheid, particularly in its late years, than were Africans ..." Ibid., p. 432. Ellmann also points, quite plausibly, to a " 'law and order' anxiety" in these groups.

TABLE 7.4. *What Kind of Symbols Represent Justice?*

Symbol	Response (in %)
Courts	72
Police	64
Civic associations	60
Lawyers	54
People's marshals	53
Judges	49
People's courts	37
Tribal authorities	32
Warlords	16
Other	13

Source: Daniel Nina and Stavros Stavrou, *Research on Perceptions of Justice: Interaction between State Justice and Popular Justice* (April 1993). Adapted from Ellmann, "Law and Legitimacy in South Africa," p. 451.

reason." Moreover, 29 percent of those polled agreed that "[i]n the courts all people are treated justly."[16] This, once again, is an astonishing data point, especially in light of the confrontational stance that the apartheid regime had begun to take in the country's townships in an attempt to quell the UDF-led resistance. Some twenty-two hundred respondents in a questionnaire study distributed by the left-leaning Community Agency for Social Inquiry (CASE) in November and December 1992, while not being asked directly about their attitudes toward the legal system, professed opinions about the topic. Aged between sixteen and thirty years, these township youth – which at the time represented the most radical members of black African communities – had surprisingly temperate perceptions of the police – this arm of the law. "51% of African youth disagreed or disagreed strongly with the proposition that 'the police are the enemy'; 62% agreed or strongly agreed that 'the police protect the community'; and 47% agreed or strongly agreed that 'the police can be trusted.'"[17]

Table 7.4 contains data that further illustrate the surprising amount of confidence that black Africans vested in the law, broadly defined. Asked in the early 1990s what kind of symbols represented "justice" in South Africa, 72 percent of those polled felt that courts came closest to presenting justice, 64 percent felt that it was the police, and 54 percent and 49 percent, respectively, thought that lawyers and judges best symbolized justice. Once again, "it

[16] As reported in Ellmann, p. 435. On the political significance of the two townships, especially during apartheid's endgame, see, for example, Paulus Zulu, "Durban Hostels and Political Violence: Case Studies in KwaMashu and Umlazi," *Transformation*, Vol. 21 (1993) pp. 1–23.
[17] Ellmann, "Law and Legitimacy in South Africa," pp. 435–436.

is striking that the respondents felt as disposed as they did to name elements of the current legal system as symbols of the judicial system or justice."[18]

Anecdotal data, focusing on perceptions of lawyers, provide additional evidence. According to Albie Sachs, "Africans throughout South Africa had become accustomed to the use of lawyers, who, if they could not secure rights for them, could at least soften their disabilities. African witnesses complained about pass raids, curfews, rude policemen and unequal laws (the law has only one eye), but they did not disparage the use of lawyers. It might even be argued that the more unfavourably Africans felt towards the laws, the more well-disposed they were towards the lawyers. Racial statutes were so pervasive and the criminal law so extensive that lawyers came increasingly to occupy in relation to African society the position which doctors, moneylenders and priests occupied towards the poor of other lands."[19]

The empirical vignettes, in conjunction with the quantitative data, suggest that the black *masses* vested a considerable amount of confidence in legal norms and institutions. But what are we to make of black *elites* in South Africa? What were their attitudes to law?

Anthony Sampson, for example, reports of being struck at the time by how much of Mandela's optimism depended "on his respect for the law, and his trust in the integrity of another lawyer, President de Klerk."[20] The experiences of other leading lawyers of the resistance – Dikgang Moseneke, Ismail Mahomed, and Dullah Omar – further illustrate this respect for the law, especially among leading cadres of the ANC and its allies. The empirical vignettes that follow are meant to complement – and exemplify – the survey data regarding the confidence of black South Africans in the legal system under apartheid.[21] At the outset it is worth noting that in 1962, Africans accounted for only 6.3 percent of the legal profession. Out of some three thousand attorneys in South Africa, only thirteen were black and none of these was in practice as an advocate.[22] By the 1980s, the number of African attorneys had risen to approximately 650 (out of 6,500 attorneys), and the number of

---

[18] Ellmann, "Law and Legitimacy in South Africa," p. 450. The study, undertaken in November 1992, surveyed 100 Africans from the townships of Umlazi and Clermont, not far from Durban. Ibid., p. 446, Fn. 130. For related scholarship, yet more prospective, see the experimental and survey approach by James L. Gibson and Amanda Gouws, *Overcoming Intolerance in South Africa: Experiments in Democratic Persuasion* (Cambridge: Cambridge University Press, 2003), Chapter 7, which is focused, as far as legal institutions are concerned, solely on the Constitutional Court. Gibson develops a comparable argument in his single-authored *Overcoming Apartheid*, Chapter 8.

[19] Sachs, *Justice in South Africa*, p. 202.

[20] Anthony Sampson, "18 Days: A South African Journal," *New York Times Magazine*, March 18, 1990, p. 44.

[21] For a critical, but tendentious account, see Parker and Mokhesi-Parker, *In the Shadow of Sharpeville*.

[22] Altogether 44 "nonwhite" attorneys were in practice in 1962, in addition to the 13 African attorneys, there were 26 Indians and 5 "coloured" lawyers. Sachs, *Justice in South Africa*, p. 211; Abel, *Politics by Other Means*, p. 19.

African advocates to some 45 (out of 650 advocates).[23] Let us consider the careers of a few of the individuals behind these figures.

Dikgang Moseneke, deputy leader of the Pan Africanist Congress (PAC) between 1990 and 1992, was trained as a lawyer, following imprisonment on Robben Island and Pretoria Central Prison. His admission as an advocate of the Supreme Court culminated in *Ex parte Moseneke*, which undercut the professional resistance he had initially faced.[24] In 1993, after ten years at the bar, Moseneke, who, in addition to being a justice of the Constitutional Court of South Africa, serves as Deputy Chief Justice of South Africa, and Chancellor of the University of the Witwatersrand, became the second black African to ever serve as senior counsel. His respect for the law, and the loopholes that it invariably provided, becomes evident in this recollection:

From 1976 through to 1986 there was no peace in this country. Young people never could take it lying down. There were waves of challenges, rioting, fighting the police, trying to burn down government buildings. So I went into practice in this chaos. We did a lot of administrative law cases; these abounded. There were challenges against executive orders of a wide variety, challenges against government decrees, challenges against directives which emanated from provincial authorities and councils. I did a lot of civil applications to court to challenge the wide variety of governmental action. I would sometimes argue that a particular act was outside the law as it stands; it was wider than what the law provided and was therefore invalid as ultra vires. If the superintendent chucked somebody out of their house, because most of the houses were rented houses owned by the local authorities, I would go and review that in the Supreme Court. Afrikaners have this formalistic sense of justice. If the superintendent did not comply with minor, nonsensical prerequisites, they would in fact set aside the order. They were not liberal judges, but their sense was that rule of law was important.[25]

Reflecting on the case of a black attorney by the name of Richard Ramadipe, who had been detained under the emergency laws, Moseneke offers another illustration of the commitment to formally rational law that, in his opinion, pervaded the administration of justice under apartheid:

The warrant of arrest, which was signed by the minister of justice and which authorized Richard's detention under the emergency laws, directed that he should be kept in a police station in Potgietersrus [a small town north of Pretoria]. He was in fact being kept in a prison – a regular prison, not a police lockup. I said, "A warrant such as this is an instrument which limits liberty and must therefore be restrictively interpreted in favor of the individual." All of those principles were still there in South African law. They never removed them. I argued that the policeman must detain the person at the place where the warrant directs. Otherwise he may detain this guy on his farm, in the boot of his car, at his friend's home, in a shebeen [a township tavern], maybe in a brothel. The judge bought that argument – again, this Afrikaner mentality.[26]

[23] Abel, *Politics by Other Means*, p. 19.

[24] *Ex parte Moseneke* 1979 (4) SA 884.

[25] As quoted in Kenneth S. Broun, *Black Layers, White Courts: The Soul of South African Law* (Athens: Ohio University Press, 2000), p. 99.

[26] As quoted in Broun, *Black Layers, White Courts*, p. 100.

The case of Ismail Mahomed provides additional material. Mahomed was arguably the lawyer with the greatest impact on the adjudication of human rights cases in South Africa. Born in Pretoria in 1931, Mahomed first studied political science, later law, at the University of the Witwatersrand, and began working as an advocate in 1957.[27] From early on involved in anti-apartheid lawyering, he was centrally involved in a Pietermaritzburg trial of the entire leadership of the UDF. Despite regular setbacks, Mahomed remained committed to the legal struggle against apartheid, retaining confidence in the law of apartheid. During the interview for the Chief Justiceship of South Africa – which was held on October 4, 1996 and for which he vied with the more experienced Justice H. J. O. van Heerden of the Appellate Division – he told of his attraction – because of the indignities that he was suffering under apartheid – to "the majesty of the law."[28] Mahomed said he gained confidence in the law's "capacity to provide equal protection for all citizens" and "its ability to build the moral fibre of the nation."[29] The Pietermaritzburg trial sustained this confidence:

There were two massive satisfactions out of that case. The first was in the initial stages of the case. In those days, if the attorney general gave a certificate that he did not consider it in the interest of the security of the state . . ., then the court was precluded from giving bail. You just waited in jail, even if in the end nothing happened to you. While the trial went on for a year or two, you stayed locked up. In that case [the Pietermaritzburg trial of the UDF leadership], we attacked the validity of the certificate and we succeeded and we got bail. It was a very good thing to see the leaders of the United Front get out. The other satisfactory thing was that, after the cross-examination of the expert [a scholar of communism whose textual analysis of UDF documents formed the backbone of the prosecution's case] and the way we managed to portray the trial, every accused was acquitted. That was very satisfying, very satisfying.[30]

On the occasion of his appointment as Chief Justice, in 1996, Mahomed affirmed once again his confidence in the law: "I hope that I will be able to contribute to the urgent need to salvage the image of the law so that it in fact

---

[27] As a result of the restrictions that the Group Areas Act placed on "non-whites," Mahomed practiced in Johannesburg without an office for twelve years. Because as an Indian, he was not entitled to "occupy" an office in the building housing the city's advocates, he became, between 1957 and 1969, a permanent guest in the offices of Bram Fischer, Sydney Kentridge, Arthur Chaskalson, and other lawyers on the sixth floor of the advocate building, occupying their spaces whenever the white lawyers were in court or otherwise engaged. Mahomed was given his own office, in 1969, and, in 1974, when he received silk (became a senior counsel), was finally allowed to use the building's common room. The late Ismail Mahomed relayed this anecdote in Broun, *Black Layers, White Courts*, pp. 162–166.

[28] As quoted in Dennis M. Davis, Gilbert J. Marcus, and Jonathan Klaaren, "The Administration of Justice, Law Reform and Jurisprudence," *Annual Survey of South African Law* (1996), p. 885.

[29] As quoted in Davis et al., "The Administration of Justice, Law Reform and Jurisprudence," p. 885.

[30] As quoted in Broun, *Black Layers, White Courts*, p. 186.

is, and is properly perceived to be, a friend and protector of the people instead of an instrument of racial, gender or political oppression."[31]

Like Mahomed, Dullah Omar, the first post-apartheid Minister of Justice, was born in South Africa, in Cape Town in 1934. Growing up in District Six, he completed his undergraduate and law degree at the University of Cape Town. After articles with a Jewish law firm, Omar opened his own law firm during the 1960 state of emergency. Anecdotal evidence, relayed by Omar, illustrates the pervasive belief within the resistance movement in the importance of legal norms and institutions, albeit this time in an everyday setting: Robben Island.

For some twenty-five years, Omar set out to sea to represent many of the prisoners on the island. He regularly weathered the "Cape of Storms, on a segregated ferry, to defend the likes of Robert Sobukwe, the leader of the PAC, and other members of what would become, over time, the resistance movement. Two vignettes from Omar's time on Robben Island are of relevance for our purposes. Although the prison population on the Island was organized along party political lines, Omar notes that "[t]here was a code of conduct which the parties had among themselves. There was great political tolerance in a sense. Of course, the groups fought each other as well – ANC, PAC, Black Consciousness Movement. I often came there in the midst of some of those battles. But looking back, in general, it was quite remarkable that they were actually able to have rules: for example, how they recruited members; how the parties conducted themselves; how the parties consulted with each other; how they communicated with each other."[32] The rules that Omar speaks of amounted, in a sense, to a prison constitution. This may be said to represent yet another instance of African constitutionalism, a topic to which I will return shortly in the context of a discussion of the religious foundations of legal tradition in South Africa. The second anecdote culled from Omar's reminiscences has to do with the adjudication of criminal matters on the island. This anecdote illustrates the belief of the apartheid state in the sanctity of rules. Recalls Omar,

On occasion, there were charges that involved more than violations of prison regulations, criminal charges such as assaulting a warder, fighting with a warder. Then I would go to the Island to defend people in a normal criminal trial. The trial provided me with much more latitude and scope than where there were mere violations of prison regulations, because in a criminal trial you are presumed innocent until you are found guilty. You have the right to cross-examine properly. You have the right to call witnesses and all sorts of things. So if a chap was charged with assault, they would bring in a magistrate to hear the case. The magistrate would not apply the prison regulations. He would apply the normal rules of criminal procedure. I would decide that, in mitigation, I wanted to call the accused's wife to give evidence. The accused had not seen his wife for a year. Or I might call his father or mother to give evidence. That threw the

---

[31] As quoted in Davis et al.
[32] As quoted in Broun, *Black Layers, White Courts*, pp. 227–228.

prison authorities into a big tantrum. The court, of course, had no way of saying that they were not going to allow it, because the criminal procedure provided that you were entitled to call witnesses.[33]

In Omar's example, we have, in other words, two organizations of the apartheid state working at cross-purposes, the prison authorities representing the prerogative state, and the magistrate representing the normative state. It is the existence of the normative state that accounts, at least in part, for the surprising confidence that black South Africans (and those aligned with them, like Omar) vested in the law. But what are we to make of Mandela's open defiance of the law, especially in the 1960s, when he challenged the legitimacy of a court because he feared that he would "not be given a fair and proper trial."[34] Did Mandela lack confidence in the law? Not according to Jacques Derrida, the French philosopher. A discourse analysis of Mandela's courtroom addresses convinced Derrida that Mandela was a *"man of the law,"* notwithstanding this man's public defiance of the law of apartheid.[35] Derrida discerned on the part of Mandela, even where the latter stood accused, a certain admiration for those who are engaged in the administration of justice. If we believe Derrida, Mandela has always been a man of the law: As the late philosopher writes:

He has always appealed to the law even if, in appearance, he has to oppose himself to such-and-such specific legality, and even if certain judges have made of him, at certain moments, an outlaw. A man of the law, he was this first *by vocation.* On the one hand, he always appeals to law. On the other hand, he has always felt himself attracted by, appealed to by the law before which people have wanted him to appear. He has moreover accepted to appear before it, even if he was also constrained to do so. He seizes the occasion, we don't dare to say the good opportunity. ... So he presents himself in this way. He presents himself in his people, before the law. Before a law he rejects, beyond any doubt, but which he rejects in the name of a superior law, the very one he declares to admire and before which he agrees *to appear.*[36]

---

[33] As quoted in Broun, *Black Layers, White Courts,* pp. 228–229. The mention of this anecdote is not to suggest, of course, that the prison system on Robben Island upheld the standards of a fair trial, least of all in the case of minor infractions. "[I]nsofar as the mere contravention of prison regulations [as opposed to criminal charges] was concerned, those hearings were absolutely farcical. These were kangaroo courts. The warders were the judges, they were the prosecutors, and they were the witnesses. We used to fight, go through the motions of putting up a hell of a fight, knowing that we were going to lose." Ibid., p. 229.

[34] As per Mandela's 1962 courtroom testimony, reprinted as "Black Man in a White Man's Court" in Sheridan Johns and R. Hunt Davis, Jr., eds., *Mandela, Tambo, and the African National Congress: The Struggle Against Apartheid, 1948–1990* (New York: Oxford University Press, 1991), p. 112. For another example of Mandela's defiance rhetoric in the dock, see his "Prosperity Will Prove that I was Innocent," reprinted in Kader Asmal, David Chidester, and Wilmot James, eds., *Nelson Mandela: In His Own Words* (New York: Little, Brown, 2003), pp. 18–26.

[35] Jacques Derrida, "The Laws of Reflection: Nelson Mandela, In Admiration," in Jacques Derrida and Mustapha Tlili, eds., *For Nelson Mandela* (New York: Seaver, 1987), p. 26.

[36] Derrida, "The Laws of Reflection," pp. 26–27.

We might express this thought more simply by saying that Mandela respected the *legality* of apartheid law, its liberal form, but resented the *morality* of apartheid law, its illiberal content. Continues Derrida,

A man of law *by vocation*, then, Mandela was that also by profession. It is known that he first studied jurisprudence on the advice of Walter Sisulu, then the Secretary of the National African Council. It was in particular a question of mastering Western law, this weapon to turn against the oppressors. These do not finally realize, in spite of all their legal ruses, the true force of a law that they manipulate, violate, and betray.[37]

And this, finally, is how Derrida described the force of law in Mandela's hands, finding that the longtime prisoner

does not accuse his judges, not immediately, at least not in the moment when he appears before them. Doubtless he will first have objected to them: on one hand, the Court had as yet no black [member] in its composition and thus offered no guarantees of the necessary impartiality ...; on the other hand, the president [of the court] happens to remain, between sessions, in contact with the political police. But once in front of his judges, these objections having of course not been sustained, Mandela no longer accuses the tribunal. First, he still maintains inside him this respectful admiration for those who exercise a function exemplary in his eyes and for the dignity of a tribunal. Then the respect [for] rules permit him to confirm the ideal legitimacy of an [institution] before which he also needs to *appear*.[38]

Mandela's guarded belief in the legitimacy of law, as we have seen, was not entirely unique and in fact shared by many black South Africans. The data at least indicate as much. As Ellmann puts it, "Africans who saw a great unfairness in their legal system nonetheless still saw that system as linked to justice, both symbolically and in terms of its entitlement (positive or moral) to enforce the law."[39]

Evaluating the Data

What inferences, then, can we draw from the data concerning the function of law in apartheid's endgame? For starters, it is reasonable to conclude, based on the examined data, that there existed "a sizable body of African opinion that accorded more legitimacy to the South African legal system than many observers might have assumed."[40] Overall, the data support my argument that South Africa's legal tradition has influenced the ways in which adversaries – democracy-demanding and democracy-resisting elites – interacted in the dying days of apartheid.[41]

---

[37] Derrida, "The Laws of Reflection," p. 29.

[38] Derrida, "The Laws of Reflection," p. 36.

[39] Ellmann, "Law and Legitimacy in South Africa," p. 451. See also Dennis M. Davis, "Remaking the South African Legal Order," *Social Justice*, Vol. 18 (1991), p. 77, who, in a pilot study of black African attitudes in and around Cape Town, found that "a surprising level of confidence still exists in some legal institutions such as the Supreme Court."

[40] Ellmann, "Law and Legitimacy in South Africa," p. 435.

[41] The formulation of the "dying days of apartheid," an apt reference to the political violence that accompanied South Africa's transition to democracy, was coined by Rupert Taylor. The literature on the topic is vast. For an analysis of this violence, see, for example, Rupert Taylor

It appears that the courts, even under apartheid, had a modest "legitimacy-conferring capacity."[42]

The significance of the presented data, both quantitative and anecdotal, can hardly be overestimated. As far as the latter is concerned, Kenneth Broun's assessment is apt. What is remarkable to him is *not* the fact that black lawyers such as Dikgang Moseneke, Lewis Skweyiya, and Ismail Mahomed represented leading anti-apartheid activists in the courts and won notable victories:

> The importance of these individuals and the many others whose contributions were less visible and dramatic is that they in fact had significant legal careers. By all rights, under the system as it existed, they should not have been in the courtroom at all – except as defendants in criminal cases. The knowledge and experience of these lawyers cannot help but have laid the foundation for [the] operation of a true rule of law in a new South Africa. The lawyers saw how the system worked. On occasion, as in some of the successes reported here, they learned the value of recourse to legal rights. On other occasions, they learned the value of a judiciary untarnished by racial bias simply by observing one that was not. The South African system had legal processes that could provide a fair trial if the judges themselves would rise above their own prejudices and pressure from the executive and legislative branches of government.[43]

This is an argument from the legacies of law, as put forth herein. Irrespective of whether we think that institutions, in order to be deemed legitimate, must inspire a "favorable affective orientation," as Tom Tyler, a foremost scholar of legal compliance, suggests, or insist that they possess "a widely accepted mandate to render judgments for a political community," as James Gibson does, we are forced to conclude, at least based on the survey data examined above, that black South Africans considered the country's legal system under apartheid fairly legitimate.[44] For the data demonstrate that "many or even most black South Africans expressed considerable confidence in the South African legal system."[45] What accounts for this counterintuitive finding?

and Mark Shaw, "The Dying Days of Apartheid," in David R. Howarth and Aletta J. Norval, eds., *South Africa in Transition: New Theoretical Perspectives* (London: Palgrave, 1998).

[42] The term originated in the public law literature in the United States. See Robert A. Dahl's seminal "Decision-Making in a Democracy: The Supreme Court as a National Policy Maker," *Journal of Public Law*, Vol. 6, No. 2 (1957), pp. 279–295. More recently, see Gibson and Gouws, *Overcoming Intolerance in South Africa*, p. 155.

[43] Broun, *Black Layers, White Courts*, pp. 191–192.

[44] Tom R. Tyler, *Why People Obey the Law* (Princeton: Princeton University Press, 2006); Gibson, *Overcoming Apartheid*, pp. 294–295.

[45] Ellmann, "Law and Legitimacy in South Africa," p. 412. Contrariwise, Charles Dlamini and John Dugard, at around the same time, and in separate analyses, claim that "blacks have the least confidence in the legal system of South Africa" (Dlamini) and "it was inevitable that blacks would lose confidence" (Dugard) in the law of apartheid. See Charles Dlamini, "The Influence of Race on the Administration of Justice in South Africa," *South African Journal on Human Rights*, Vol. 4, No. 1 (1988), p. 38; and John Dugard, "Blacks and the Administration of Justice," in Dugard et al., eds., *The Years of Apartheid*, p. 103. Neither study furnishes quantitative data, however. This imbalance in the supporting evidence makes it difficult to generalize the Dugard/Dlamini argument, especially in the context of the exceptionally

Explaining the Data

Ellmann, in an important, yet frequently overlooked, article proposes three explanations, focusing on the role of what he terms *conservatives, speakers,* and *activists* in shaping black perceptions of law's legitimacy in the apartheid era. This analytic distinction is relevant because it helps us to appreciate that "within the parameters of discontent there exists a wide range of ideological orientations."[46] With this in mind, it is reasonable to expect – no hard data exist – that differences in ideological orientations translated into differences in attitudes toward the law. Bill Keller, now the Executive Editor of the *New York Times*, for example, drew our attention to the following:

Obscured by the revolutionary images, the great secret is that the majority of black South Africans are deeply conservative people. It's not that they are content to be governed by white men but that they are wary of sudden change, that they are devoutly religious, that they find solace in land and family and tradition, that they are intensely respectful of authority. The silent majority craves stability as much as opportunity, and more than it craves justice.[47]

This empirical fact, obvious to anyone who has conducted research in South Africa's countryside as well as townships, goes a long way toward explaining the relatively high esteem in which many black South Africans – Nelson Mandela included – held the law and its institutions. Writes Ellmann: "Men and women so moderate are not friends of apartheid. But they may not make the leap of delegitimation that many observers assumed was inevitable, from dislike of apartheid to condemnation of all its institutions."[48] Related, black South Africans, in a survey conducted by Lawrence Schlemmer for the HSRC in the early 1990s, expressed remarkable patience regarding the representation of blacks – as magistrates and judges – in the country's legal system: only 35

---

data-rich study by Ellmann. For another unsubstantiated diagnosis in the Dugard/Dlamini vein, focused on the Natal Supreme Court, see Jeremy Sarkin, "Judges in South Africa: Black Sheep or Albinos: An Examination of Judicial Responses in the 1980s to Law and Human Rights and the Options Available to Tempter the Effects of Apartheid," LL.M Thesis, Harvard Law School, 1988, p. 29. On the question of black representation in the judiciary, see, aside from Dugard, who tackles the issue in passing, also D. D. Mokgatle, "The Exclusion of Blacks from the South African Judicial System," *South African Journal on Human Rights*, Vol. 3, No. 1 (March 1987), pp. 44–51. For a personal account of the humiliation he suffered, see Justice Pius N. Langa's sobering TRC's submission, "Submission to the Truth and Reconciliation Commission on the Role of the Judiciary," reprinted in *South African Law Journal*, Vol. 115, No. 1 (1998), pp. 36–41. Justice Langa was appointed as Justice of the Constitutional Court in 1994, and became Deputy President in 1997. After serving as Deputy Chief Justice from 2001 until 2005, he was appointed President of the Constitutional Court, thus becoming the second black (which I use here in an inclusive sense) Chief Justice of South Africa.

[46] Jeremy Seekings, "Visions of 'Community' in South Africa's Informal Township Courts," Paper presented at the International Sociological Association, Amsterdam, June 1991, p. 7.

[47] Bill Keller, "A Surprising Silent Majority in South Africa," *New York Times Magazine*, April 17, 1994, p. 37.

[48] Ellmann, "Law and Legitimacy in South Africa," p. 441.

234 A History of Law

percent of those polled demanded changes of personnel.[49] This suggests "that many Africans evaluated the need for changes in their legal system with a considerable degree of moderation, and that this evaluation is consistent with the inference that they saw some measure of virtue in the system as it stood."[50] What Ellmann discusses under the rubric of *conservatives*, in other words, captures black South African attitudes toward the law borne out of a penchant for gradual – rather than revolutionary – change and a concomitant attachment to the benefits, for example, of the outreach network of the Legal Resources Centre and other institutions of the "advice center" movement of the 1980s.

With Ellmann's *speakers*, we enter the realm of rights and recognition. Those who might be called speakers, so the reasoning goes, accorded the South African legal system a certain amount of legitimacy to the extent that it created fora, even if limited and circumscribed, for making rights-based appeals, as Mandela famously did during the "Treason Trial." In this sense, then, "[s]ome parts of the legitimacy of the courts in the eyes of speakers may have flowed directly from the speakers' own religious convictions, but to the extent that the speakers saw their words as potentially persuasive the legal system could also have earned legitimacy because it allowed those words to be spoken – by the litigants themselves, or by their lawyers."[51] It is plausible, based on scant and anecdotal data, that a certain portion of black South Africans might well have had confidence in courts insofar as the latter recognized the civility of defendants – and let their voices be heard.

Finally, there are the *activists*. In Ellmann's scheme, these are "men and women who were vividly conscious of the injustices pervading their lives, and who saw their task more as the mobilization of pressure against whites than as the transformation of whites' hearts."[52] These, he says, "seem less likely to have exaggerated any virtues the [South African] legal system might have. Though it is impossible to be certain, I suspect that African 'activists' have not been among those who have affirmed confidence in the country's legal system in polls over the years."[53] And yet, even these least likely believers had reason

[49] As reported in Ellmann, "Law and Legitimacy in South Africa," pp. 443–444.
[50] Ellmann, "Law and Legitimacy in South Africa," p. 444.
[51] Stephen Ellmann, "Law and Legitimacy in South Africa," *Law and Social Inquiry*, Vol. 20, No. 2 (Spring 1995), p. 462.
[52] Ellmann, "Law and Legitimacy in South Africa," p. 463.
[53] Ellmann, "Law and Legitimacy in South Africa," p. 463. Heinz Klug makes the interesting point that the so-called people's courts that sprang up in the townships during the insurrection period, and which are commonly considered to have administered vigilante justice, might, in reality, have been exemplary of a commitment to a functional equivalent of formal law on the part of township youth. Writes Klug: "While rejecting the formal law, the people's courts often adopted procedures and formats that mimicked the formal courts. Despite these acts of denial and the obvious rejection of law, these examples provide yet more evidence of law's autonomy, when even the act of denial is premised on the assertion of an alternative form of law – through the invocation of higher law, in the case of captured guerillas, to the procedures and formats followed by some involved in the people's courts." See his "Law Under and After Apartheid,"

TABLE 7.5. *Political Trial Outcomes, 1986–1993*

	Total No. of Accused	Convictions and Admissions of Guilt	Acquittals and Cases Discharged	Cases Withdrawn	Convictions as % of Total No. of Accused
1986	690	195	N/A	495	28.2
1987	792	229	N/A	563	28.9
1988	574	255	N/A	319	44.4
1989	3,183	493	N/A	2,527	18.2
1990	3,894	710	657	2,527	18.2
1991	3,246	478	418	2,145	14.7
1992	4,298	708	184	3,379	16.5
1993	1,747	251	305	1,145	14.4

Source: Coleman, *A Crime against Humanity*, p. 80; Ellmann, "Law and Legitimacy in South Africa," p. 465. The number of withdrawn cases for the period 1986–1989 includes the number of acquittals and discharged cases.

TABLE 7.6. *Terrorism Trial Outcomes, 1975–1979*

	Total No. of Accused	Convictions and Admissions of Guilt	Acquittals and Cases Discharged	Cases Withdrawn	Convictions as % of Total No. of Accused
1975	5	4	0	1	80.0
1976	42	24	12	6	57.1
1977	64	42	19	2	65.6
1978	74	48	24	2	64.9
1979	60	40	15	1	66.7

Source: Lobban, *White Man's Justice*, p. 266.

to have at least some confidence in the law, as the data in Tables 7.5 and 7.6, make clear.

Anti-apartheid lawyering, discussed earlier, created important grounds for such confidence. Data compiled by the independent Human Rights Commission regarding the conviction rates in political trials between 1986 and 1993, for example, show that apartheid courts have never convicted more than 44 percent of those who stood accused in these trials, and regularly acquitted

p. 666. On South Africa's people's courts, see Jeremy Seekings, "People's Courts and Popular Politics," in Glenn Moss and Ingrid Obery, eds., *South African Review 5* (Johannesburg: Ravan Press, 1989); Winfried Schärf, "The Role of People's Courts in Transitions," in Hugh Corder, ed., *Democracy and the Judiciary* (Cape Town: IDASA, 1988), pp. 167–184; and Sandra Burman, "The Role of Street Committees Continuing South Africa's Practice of Alternative Justice," in Corder, ed., *Democracy and the Judiciary*, pp. 151–166.

more than 80 percent, notably in the period 1989–1993. Government statistics for the period 1992–1993 report a high conviction rate of 78 percent in the trials revolving around crimes against state security, which classify as political trials. Although remarkable when compared with the conviction rates in Table 7.5, this conviction rate still means, however, that nearly 25 percent of defendants in these trials walked free. The same goes for the higher conviction rates in the terrorism trials of the 1970s, as depicted in Table 7.6.[54]

Two general conclusions can be drawn. First, the data "might be taken to suggest that the courts act[ed] with some measure of scrupulousness even in political trials."[55] Second, if the conviction rates in the country's political trials were relatively low (at least when compared to other authoritarian regimes) because the courts respected rules and procedures, "then the accused in these trials – and the members of the public who followed these events – could have come to accord a measure of recognition to the benign aspects of the courts. Since many of the trials appear to have taken place in the magistrates' courts rather than the Supreme Courts, moreover, even these lower courts might have garnered a modicum of respect as a result of these trials."[56]

Against this background, Ellmann is right, I believe, in claiming "that the modest achievements of the South African legal system on this score may have helped to legitimize the *ideals* of impartial adjudication and courageous protection of legal rights, even as radical observers of this system found much reason to say that those ideals were not being realized."[57]

Taking the preceding discussion into account, the law became meaningful to members of the black majority – who, as we have seen, vested confidence in its norms and institutions to a surprising degree – for different reasons. It might be useful to distinguish in this context among different types of *meaningful legal action*, which, inspired by Max Weber's typology of meaningful social action, I take to refer to intentional legal acts of meaning deliberately or consciously taken in relation to and directed toward other people. Examples of meaningful legal action are acts of compliance or obedience. With this in mind, four ideal types of meaningful legal action are conceivable – traditional, affectual, value-oriented, and instrumental legal action (see Figure 7.1). Ellman's explanations

---

[54] For a compilation of documentary material relating to political trials in this period, see Glenn Moss, *Political Trials: South Africa, 1976–1979* (Johannesburg: Development Studies Group, 1979). For a more thorough treatment, see Cathi Albertyn, "A Critical Analysis of Political Trials in South Africa, 1948–88," Ph.D. dissertation, University of Cambridge, 1991.

[55] Ellmann, "Law and Legitimacy in South Africa," p. 464.

[56] Ellmann, "Law and Legitimacy in South Africa," p. 66. On the performance of trial courts in South Africa versus the country's Appellate Division, see the discussion in Chapter 5 above.

[57] Ellmann, "Law and Legitimacy in South Africa," p. 463.

Meaningful Legal Action	
Intentional legal acts of meaning deliberately or consciously taken in relation to and directed toward other people	
Traditional	Automatic reaction to habitual stimuli: actors use the law because they are accustomed to it
Affectual	Action based on, and driven by, emotion: actors use the law because of desires or feelings
Value-oriented	Action oriented toward an ultimate value: actors use the law because it accords with their beliefs
Instrumental	Action based on a calculation of ends and means: actors use the law for strategic gain

FIGURE 7.1. Types of Meaningful Legal Action

can be profitably subsumed under these ideal types, thus making his empirical observations about the attitudes of conservatives, speakers, and activists amenable to comparative historical application. In our case, this subsumption generates further insight into the sources of confidence in the legal system on the part of black South Africans during the apartheid years.

For example, the behavior of conservatives, in Ellmann's parlance, can be further illuminated by thinking of it in terms of either *traditional legal action* or *value-oriented legal action*, or both. For what appears to be the hallmark of the conservative paradigm is legal action oriented to habitual stimuli (actors use the law because they are accustomed to it) or legal action oriented toward an ultimate value (actors use the law because it accords with their beliefs). In other words, the conservative paradigm in South Africa illustrates both the traditional function of law and the value-oriented function of law. It explains why, "even in a 'crisis of legitimacy,' there may still be many people who continue to defend the legitimacy of the imperiled institution," even those who – ultimately – want to bring it down.[58]

The behavior of Ellmann's speakers, next, illustrates what Cass Sunstein in a different context has termed the expressive function of law. This function connotes *emotional legal action* based on, and driven by, feelings. The desire of performing, of speaking in public, "the opportunity to be heard, and heard even with some measure of respect, which the higher South African courts did provide," this desire speaks to an emotional need for communication, often manifesting itself as a need for acknowledgement, as the proceedings of the TRC made abundantly clear.

---

[58] Ellmann, "Law and Legitimacy in South Africa," p. 416.

Finally, the instrumental use of law, or *instrumental legal action*, is oriented toward discrete individuals' objectives and based on a calculation of ends and means, and captures the behavior of Ellmann's activists. Moseneke, whom we encountered previously, provides a relevant insight on this score, commenting on the strategy of anti-apartheid lawyering. By so doing, the Chief Justice throws into sharp relief the essence of the dual state:

We truly and fully exploited the prim and proper rule-of-law approach that Afrikaners have always had. It was always an enigma. They were vicious oppressors and exploiters, but they also believed that they were part of some civilized world where there were civilized norms. As for the judges, they thought that, in fact, they could uphold the principles of the common law in the face of a basic statutory overlay that was going to trample each and every principle. So you had a very strange thing – people who were very meticulous about rules, like most Calvinists all over the world. They were positivists; they believed that the law was sacred. What was law was sacred and had to be observed, even if the law was adopted for the wrong reasons. So we consciously exploited what we saw as a weakness, the soft belly of a very tough animal.[59]

The payoffs of targeting the belly of the behemoth were considerable. Here is once again Moseneke:

We made them play by the rules and I think it paid enormous dividends. But ironically, on the other side, it made us addicted to fairness, to just dispensations, to an independent judiciary. Black lawyers in general honestly believe that the state must not be arbitrary. Executive power must be controlled by law enshrined in a constitution which must serve as supreme law, and the courts must be independent. We believe in democratic political institutions. Those issues were negotiated at Kempton Park [the deliberations that produced the 1993 Interim Constitution]. There was no debate about those issues because we were basically dealing with lawyers who, for the better part of their lives, had fought against the vicious system and had come to appreciate constitutional safeguards and constitutional democracy. ... So out of that lawyering, there has emerged a very rich tradition of fairness, of judicial review, of rule of law, and, I think, of integrity. There are a lot of honest, good South Africans who would like to make the law supersede the whims and fancies of individuals in the executive area of the government. ... That is the upside of the whole era.[60]

In short, the strategic interaction of adversaries (agents) in the context of apartheid's legal norms and institutions (structure) created a self-reinforcing process of legitimation that facilitated the country's peaceful transition to democracy. As argued previously, confidence in the institutional structure of the state made possible, to an important degree, the development of trust among persons, thereby lengthening the shadow of the future for interacting adversaries in apartheid's endgame. It is in this sense that the apartheid state was necessary for making democracy work, for South Africa's legal tradition, this cluster of surviving legal norms and institutions, became an important

---

[59] As quoted in Broun, *Black Layers, White Courts*, pp. 107–108.
[60] Broun, *Black Layers, White Courts*, pp. 108–109.

focal point around which apartheid's endgame unfolded.[61] The question remains, however, what accounts for the confidence of South Africans, especially black South Africans, in the law. The answer, as the next section proposes, has to do with religion.

The Religious Foundations of Legal Tradition in South Africa

Appreciating the religious foundations of South Africa's legal tradition is important for understanding the sources of confidence that different segments of society have placed in the legal system. Absent such an appreciation, our understanding of the meaning of legal norms and institutions in the transition to – and from – apartheid will remain incomplete, for as Harold Berman remarks, "The legal systems of all Western countries, and of all non-Western countries that have come under the influence of Western law, are a secular residue of religious attitudes and assumptions which historically found expression first in the liturgy and rituals and doctrine of the church and thereafter in the institutions and concepts and values of the law. When these historical roots are not understood, many parts of the law appear to lack any underlying source of validity."[62] With this in mind, let us hone in on the religious foundations of legal tradition in South Africa. I distinguish among Calvinist, Anglican, and vernacular traditions of law (see Figure 7.2).[63]

The Calvinist Tradition

An inquiry into the Calvinist tradition, and the preoccupation of the latter with the law, is indispensable because, "according to their creation story, Afrikaners were Calvinists of Western European origin and a nation in their own right before the arrival of the English."[64] This creation story was at the heart of the Calvinist tradition in South Africa. It was President Paul Kruger who first gave form to the invented tradition when, in the nineteenth century, he applied "the doctrine of the national covenant to the people of the South African Republic."[65] A religious transplant, the founding principles of the Calvinist tradition in South Africa are quickly told:

---

[61] Thomas Schelling was the first to discuss the role of focal points as possible solutions to coordination problems. See his *The Strategy of Conflict* (Cambridge, MA: Harvard University Press, 1960).

[62] Berman, *Law and Revolution*, p. 166.

[63] For an overview of South Africa's major theological currents, then and now, see, most important, Richard Elphick and Rodney Davenport, eds., *Christianity in South Africa: A Political, Social, and Cultural History* (Berkeley: University of California Press, 1997). For a survey of the historiography of theology, see Norman Etherington, "Recent Trends in the Historiography of Christianity in Southern Africa," *Journal of Southern African Studies*, Vol. 22, No. 2 (June 1996), pp. 201–219.

[64] Moodie, *The Rise of Afrikanerdom*, p. 2.

[65] Moodie, *The Rise of Afrikanerdom*, p. 26. On invented traditions, see, most important, Eric Hobsbawm and Terence Ranger, eds., *The Invention of Tradition* (Cambridge: Cambridge University Press, 1983).

The Calvinist Tradition
Afrikaner Protestantism and religious legalism in the
nineteenth-century Dutch Reformed Church

The Anglican Tradition
Anglo-American Protestantism and religious legalism
in the nineteenth-century Cape Colony

The Vernacular Tradition
"Bantu Prophets" and religious legalism in the nineteenth-
century evangelical movement

FIGURE 7.2. The Religious Foundations of Legal Tradition in South Africa

According to Kruger's understanding of the sacred history, God chose His People (*volk*) in the Cape Colony and brought them out into the wilderness. There He chastised them, "so that they would ask all help and strength from Him" for "it was necessary that the vine be pruned down to the stem so that it could bear good fruit." God then covenanted with the chastened People, and "the enemies were defeated and the trekkers inhabited the land which God has given them in this rightful manner."[66]

Noteworthy for our purposes in this *religious* narrative are the references to two *legal* notions, the concept of the covenant ("God then covenanted with the chastened People") and the concept of rights ("the land which God has given in this rightful manner").

The concept of the *covenant* was at the heart of Afrikanerdom. "The disciplined community of Christians," Dunbar Moodie writes, "came to be expressed in terms of a voluntary covenant – the social covenant – by which the believing individual willingly submitted to an earthly authority, always remembering, of course, that both ruler and community were finally subject to God. Those in the community who did not believe were simply coerced for the sake of God's honor."[67] This is reminiscent in both style and substance of the contractual tradition of Hobbes's *Leviathan*, which, too, espoused a belief in the instrumental function of law, notably in the function of the covenant as an agreement by which to submit to an authority that disciplines and punishes.

A religious metaphor that subsequently assumed legal significance, the concept of the covenant figured prominently in the creation of the Calvinist tradition in South Africa.[68] On their pilgrimage of martyrdom, the Great Trek,

---

[66] Moodie, *The Rise of Afrikanerdom*, pp. 26–27.
[67] Moodie, *The Rise of Afrikanerdom*, p. 25. On the centrality of the covenant in Afrikaner thought, see also Thompson, *The Political Mythology of Apartheid*, pp. 144–188.
[68] Recall in this context Berman's observation that "basic institutions, concepts, and values of Western legal systems have their sources in religious rituals, liturgies, and doctrines of the eleventh and twelfth centuries, reflecting new attitudes toward death, sin, punishment,

the Afrikaners in the eastern part of the country encountered Zulu resistance (culminating in the murder of the settler Piet Retief on the occasion of his purchasing land from the Zulu king Dingane, the assassin and successor of his half-brother Shaka). Led by Andries Pretorius, a band of avengers, on December 16, 1838, defeated Zulu resistance in the battle of Blood River, paving the way for the solemn declaration of a Boer Republic, Natalia. The story of the subjugation of the Zulu at the hands of the Afrikaners is of immediate relevance for understanding the importance of law in their lives:

> The covenant of Blood River was central to Kruger's civil theology, although he seems to have perceived its essential significance only after his participation in its renewal at Paardekraal in 1880. Kruger then saw the cause of God's wrath – that his People had neglected their *contractual obligations* in failing to celebrate Blood River for over thirty years. For this sin, He had visited them with the oppression of British occupation and had delivered them into the hands of the enemy until, with contrite hearts, they congregated at Paardekraal to renew their vow in humility before Him. Only then did He mercifully save them by His miraculous intervention.[69]

The reference to "contractual obligations" is testament to the fact that the Afrikaner civil religion was founded on a deep-seated respect for legal norms and institutions, both sacred and secular.

Of relevance to the emergence of this respect for the law are the teachings of a Dutchman, Abraham Kuyper, a conservative minister in the *Hervormde Kerk* of Holland who, in 1901, was elected prime minister of his country. Because his doctrine of the state – although it was not without dissenters – became enormously influential in the Dutch Reformed churches in South Africa, it is important to consider briefly its import for the creation of a legal

---

forgiveness, and salvation, as well as new assumptions concerning the relationship of the divine to the human and of faith to reason. Over the intervening centuries, these religious attitudes and assumptions have changed fundamentally, and today their theological sources seem to be in the process of drying up. Yet the legal institutions, concepts, and values that have derived from them still survive, often unchanged. Western legal science is a secular theology, which often makes no sense because its theological presuppositions are no longer accepted." Berman, *Law and Revolution*, p. 165.

[69] Moodie, *The Rise of Afrikanerdom*, p. 27. Emphasis added. The "contractual obligations" refer to the vow that the members of Pretorius commando (later known as the *Wenkommando*) took several days before the Battle of Blood River. According to a firsthand account by a participant, Jan Bantjes, "That Sunday morning, before the service began, the chief Commandant called together the men who would conduct the service, and told them to suggest to the congregation that they should all prey to God fervently in spirit and in truth for his help and assistance in the struggle with the enemy; [he said] that he wanted to make a vow to the Almighty, (if they were all calling), that 'should the Lord give us the victory, we would raise a House to the memory of his Great Name, wherever it shall please Him"; and that they should also invoke the aid and assistance of God to enable them to fulfill this vow." Thompson, *The Political Mythology of Apartheid*, pp. 152–153. The "miraculous intervention" is a reference to the 1881 Afrikaner victory in their "War of Freedom," the reclaiming by armed force of the Transvaal Republic from the British who had annexed the colony in 1877. For a discussion of the British occupation, see Chapter 4 above.

tradition among the Afrikaners. Kuyper's Calvinist doctrine of the state set him apart from the contending currents of his time. As Moodie writes, Kuyper's doctrine was "directly opposed to both the popular sovereignty of radical liberalism and the state sovereignty of German absolutism."[70] For Kuyper, social life existed independent of the state, and therefore should not be unduly constrained by an overzealous executive. The solution for him lay in the law. "Calvinism," wrote Kuyper in 1899,

> just in proportion as it honoured the authority of the magistrate, instituted by God, did it lift up that second sovereignty, which had been implanted by God in the social spheres, in accordance with the ordinances of creation. It demanded for both independence in their own sphere and regulation of the relation between both, not by the executive, but *under the law.*[71]

Returning to South Africa, where Kuyper's doctrine of the state found many adherents in the Afrikaner community, we find traces of the Dutchman's influence. It is telling, for example, that African communities were labeled by Boers "nations without the law."[72] Kruger, perhaps more than his countrymen, also apparently insisted on equality before the law. It is illuminating in this context to contemplate an excerpt from Psalm 89, Kruger's favorite quotation:

> If they violate my *statutes*
>   and do not keep my *commandments*;
> Then I will *punish* their transgression with the rod
>   and their iniquity with scourges;
> but I will not remove from him my steadfast love
>   or be false to my faithfulness.
> I will not violate my *covenant*, or alter the word that went forth from my lips.[73]

The biblical quotation is significant for two reasons. First, it illustrates the role of law in South Africa's Calvinist tradition (from "statutes" to "commandments" and from "punishment" to "covenant"), and vice versa. Second, it illustrates the importance that Kruger, and the Afrikaner community writ large, placed on compliance with the law. Obedience was a religious duty, the immediate outgrowth of orthodox Calvinism, this religious transplant.

Directly relevant for our purposes is the fact that Calvin occasionally likened "godlessness" to "lawlessness."[74] This is indicative of the centrality of law – and order – in the life of Calvinists, especially those of the Afrikaner persuasion. For as one scholar notes,

> Calvin gives the concept of law a major role in his ethics. This is evident in the prominence he gives to the Decalogue and its exposition in a number of his writings.

[70] Moodie, *The Rise of Afrikanerdom*, p. 54.
[71] Abraham Kuyper, *Calvinism* (Amsterdam: Honeker and Wormser, 1899), pp. 120–121.
[72] Moodie, *The Rise of Afrikanerdom*, p. 28.
[73] As quoted in Moodie, *The Rise of Afrikanerdom*, p. 28. Emphases added.
[74] As quoted in David Little, *Religion, Order, and Law: A Study in Pre-Revolutionary England* (Chicago: University of Chicago Press, [1969] 1984), p. 45.

His catechism for the church in Geneva (1545) contains a major section of questions and answers in which the requirements and prohibitions enjoined in the commandments are explained. He devotes two chapters in the *Institutes* [*of the Christian Religion*] to the law, one of which contains a lengthy exposition of the Ten Commandments. ... The law has this importance because it is the "perfect rule of righteousness" that God has given to his people. Because the law reveals the eternal will of God, it is, for Calvin, the ultimate moral norm.[75]

And so it was for the Afrikaners as well, for, as we shall see, the law has been central to their existence. Chief Justice F. L. H. Rumpff, the fourteenth Chief Justice of South Africa, paid homage to the early tradition of law within the Afrikaner community in 1977 on the centenary of the Transvaal Supreme Court: "[T]he Vootrekkers and their descendants in effect brought with them a legacy consisting of a triad of freedom, law, and religion. ... Their interest in the application of law was remarkable."[76]

The Afrikaner commitment to law was further entrenched in the twentieth century under the influence of the so-called jural school. As John Hund and Hendrik W. van der Merwe remark, "The jural school is marked by an excessively legalistic style of scholarship. ... The jural school draws upon an established tradition of *volkekunde* scholarship as well as upon the ideological doctrine of legal positivism. In addition to this, it shows heavy signs of influence by the writings of the Dutch jurist and theologian Herman Dooyeweerd, whose doctrinal teachings pervade much of contemporary South African Roman-Dutch legal scholarship."[77]

In a perceptive study of the relationship between Calvinism and the law, David Little reminds us also that in Calvin's thought the state

is by no means invented by men. Nor does it simply arise from some natural capacity for political order, though man is naturally a political animal. It is first and foremost a theological entity, and it falls squarely under the aegis of Calvin's "passion for order." It is ordained and established by God for the maintenance, at all costs, of his providential design.[78]

In the eyes of several commentators, Calvin's theological thought bespeaks a commitment to formally rational law *à la* Weber.[79] Weber, in *The Protestant Ethic and the Spirit of Capitalism*, memorably maintained that it was "rationalization which gave the Reformed faith [from which Calvinism

---

[75] Guenther H. Haas, "Calvin's Ethics," in Donald K. McKim, ed., *The Cambridge Companion to John Calvin* (Cambridge: Cambridge University Press, 2004), p. 97.

[76] F. L. H. Rumpff, "Centenary of the Transvaal Supreme Court," *De Rebus Procuratoriis* (1977), as quoted in Ellmann, *In a Time of Trouble*, p. 190.

[77] Hund and van der Merwe, *Legal Ideology and Politics in South Africa*, p. 32.

[78] Little, *Religion, Order, and Law*, p. 42. See also I. John Hesselink, *Calvin's Concept of the Law* (Allison Park: Pickwick Publications, 1992); Josef Bohatec, *Calvin und das Recht* (Graz: Boehlaus, 1934).

[79] For analysis of this claim's validity, see Little, *Religion, Order, and Law*.

sprang] its peculiar ascetic tendency."[80] The essence of this asceticism – which has obedience at its core – can be described as follows:

The command of God (the law) is fulfilled in Christ by his voluntary loving obedience, and therefore can become fulfilled by the members of the Body. Christ himself is not only the correct interpreter of the law, by means of his life, death, and teachings, but he *is* the law, insofar as he embodies the end toward which the law points – the free and reverent submission to the sovereignty of God. By constraining themselves increasingly under the "yoke of Christ," by accepting Christ's "pattern" of obedience, Christians come to grasp the real purpose and function of the law. They come progressively to attain "the perfection of righteousness." In other words, they come to affirm the law not as an unavoidable necessity that coerces and restraints them, but as the command of God that sets them free for loving, voluntary response. "When men willingly honor God's glory and acknowledge the world to be ruled by him and themselves to be under his authority, then they give true evidence of religion."[81]

The emphasis on the importance of rule-guided behavior – of legal norms and institutions – in other words is a *sine qua non* of Calvinist theology and practice: "Calvin has too poor an opinion of human nature to leave the Christian to persevere in isolation. He recommends membership in a disciplined community as a guide and mainstay for the conscience."[82] In the context of South Africa, the Calvinism preached by the Dutch Reformed churches (the *Nederduitse Gereformeerde Kerk*, the *Nederduitse Hervormde Kerk van Afrika*, and the *Gereformeerde Kerk*) was founded on a belief in the centrality of the state and compliance with its laws: "Nationalist Afrikaner writing down the years reflects the Calvinistic belief that the State is divinely ordained and created, that it can exist independently of the citizen, over whom it has exclusive powers, and that rulers are finally responsible to God, whose agents they are and in whose name they act."[83] Law, by this token, derived its legitimacy from the divine. Needless to say, this neo-Calvinism "was clearly tailored to fit Nationalist Afrikaner prejudices."[84] This, however, should not distract from the significance accorded to law in the Boer community,

---

[80] Max Weber, *The Protestant Ethic and the Spirit of Capitalism*, Translated by Talcott Parsons with an Introduction by Anthony Giddens (London: Routledge, [1930] 1992), p. 72. For a critical analysis of Weber's interpretation of Calvinism, see Philip Benedict, "The Historiography of Continental Calvinism," in Hartmut Lehmann and Guenther Roth, eds., *Weber's Protestant Ethic: Origins, Evidence, and Contexts* (Cambridge: Cambridge University Press, 1993), pp. 305–325.

[81] Little, *Religion, Order, and Law*, p. 50.

[82] Moodie, *The Rise of Afrikanerdom*, p. 24.

[83] René de Villiers, "Afrikaner Nationalism," in Wilson and Thompson, eds., *The Oxford History of South Africa, Volume II*, p. 371. On the history of the Dutch Reformed churches in South Africa, see Jonathan N. Gerstner, "A Christian Monopoly: The Reformed Church and Colonial Society under Dutch Rule," in Richard Elphick and Rodney Davenport, eds., *Christianity in South Africa: A Political, Social, and Cultural History* (Berkeley: University of California Press, 1997), pp. 16–30. On their role in the twentieth century, see Johann Kinghorn, "Modernization and Apartheid: The Afrikaner Churches," in ibid., pp. 135–154.

[84] De Villiers, "Afrikaner Nationalism," p. 371.

especially by elites. One member of this elite was Chief Justice J. A. Truter, who, on the occasion of the first assembly of the court in the new Court House on January 19, 1815, proclaimed a preference for the rule of law over the rule of men:

It is certain that, dangerous as it is, on the one hand, to leave man to the arbitrary direction of each interested individual, equally dangerous is it, on the other, if the laws prescribed on the establishment of society be not kept sacred and inviolate. Then, says Cicero, everything is uncertain; no citizen is longer safe in his person – his property becomes a prey to avarice and plunder – confidence and tranquility are banished from his mind – happiness is but a visionary illusion – and, in one word, all is uncertainty. Such being the case, it needs no demonstration that it may well be considered as an essential privilege in every society, that the system of the laws and usages, which must form the guide in deciding over the life, honour, and property of a member of the community, is so framed and established, that not only a deviation therefrom is difficult, and a reparation, easy, but also that every individual carries this conviction in his mind; for in this conviction is to be found true contentment, and consequently the unimpeded progress of every man's welfare and prosperity.[85]

It is precisely this "conviction of the mind" with which this part of the analysis is concerned. I propose that this conviction – this mental model – was firmly rooted in the Afrikaner mind.[86] In other words, as André du Toit and

---

[85] As reprinted in André du Toit and Hermann Giliomee, *Afrikaner Political Thought: Analysis and Documents, Vol. 1: 1780–1850* (Berkeley: University of California Press, 1983), p. 101.

[86] The ideology of the rule of law of which Chief Justice Truter speaks, however, was not without dissenters. A principal dividing line was that between officials and colonists. It is worthwhile to briefly inspect this dividing line, for it foreshadows the janus-faced state – the dual state – of later years:

In the final analysis the difference between the officials and the colonists may seem to amount only to a slight difference in emphasis on the importance of law and order in theory and in practice. The colonists seldom directly opposed the idea of an impartial legal order as such. They tended rather to stress the many practical inconveniences and their own insecurity. It follows that if an effective legal administration could have provided them with easy access to the courts and with security of property, or, as they termed it, "with such measures as shall protect us in the legal and peaceable possession of our rights as burghers" which to their minds meant above all effective policing against "vagrants," then their objections would have fallen away. The officials, for their part, also recognized the importance of the practical administration of law enforcement. Thus [Lieutenant-Governor Andries] Stockenström regarded the provision of a local magistrate as removing "the most important obstacle to good order". Nevertheless there are profoundly different set of assumptions involved here. To Stockenström the law appeared as an ideal and as a matter of fundamental moral principle. Once law and justice was recognized as basic to the social order, only the practical task remained of providing "a fair and impartial administration". The colonists, such as the Colesberg memorialists of 1837, agreed on the practical problems of inadequate law and order, but had quite different ideas on its underlying causes. They blamed the increase in crime and insubordination not so much on the local magistrate, as on the law itself: "We attribute it entirely to a multiplicity of contradictory and ineffective laws, which like an old book ought to be revised, corrected and amended." Evidently they did not conceive the law itself in ideal terms but as an all too human creation. Law and justice are not absolute, but instrumental to a particular social order. Two different notions of *order* thus confronted each other, if only implicitly. For the colonists, order

Hermann Giliomee have argued, "an ideology of the *rule of law*" was one of the "main components in the developing political thinking of the Afrikaner officials."[87] And as I have tried to show, the ground from whence this ideology sprang was religion.

Much like the concept of the covenant, the concept of *rights*, next, forces us to consider the religious foundations of the Calvinist tradition of law. For example, during the framing of the country's first constitution, in 1910, both Marthinus Steyn, the President of the Orange Free State, and Barry Hertzog, the leader of the National Party and future Prime Minister, insisted on equal rights for settlers of Dutch and British origins, effectively advocating group rights. Hertzog put it thus in this outline of his infamous "Two Streams Policy":

> Community life in South Africa flows in two streams – the English-speaking stream and the Dutch-speaking stream, each stream with its own language, its own way of life, its own great men, heroic deeds and noble characters. That this is so was the result of history. No one is to be blamed for it and each has the right to prize, to protect and to defend what is his own.[88]

Here Hertzog in all but name advocated for the constitutional protection of group rights. Louis Botha, who would become the first Prime Minister of the Union of South Africa, and Jan Smuts, who with the former founded the South African Party in 1911 and later served two terms as Prime Minister (1919–1924 and 1939–1948), found the stance of Steyn and Hertzog wanting. Rejecting the idea of group rights for a non-dominant ethnic group, Smuts declared,

> The whole meaning of Union in South Africa is this: We are going to create a nation – a nation which will be of a composite character, including Dutch, German, English and Jew, and whatever white nationality seeks refuge in this land – all can combine. All will be welcome.[89]

Smuts, and his ally Botha, in other words, "continued to hold that combination of white racism and egalitarian liberalism which had been earlier propounded by Paul Kruger."[90] Adds another scholar, "In their struggle to free themselves of British imperial control, the Afrikaners became republicans,

---

was defined as the maintenance and proper policing of the prevailing system of labour and property relations, and there was a breakdown of order when their own interests were being threatened instead of upheld. For the officials, on the other hand, order was defined by the rule of law, and the principles of justice and equality might require legal and social reform.

Du Toit and Giliomee, *Afrikaner Political Thought: Analysis and Documents*, Vol. 1, pp. 83–84.

[87] Du Toit and Giliomee, *Afrikaner Political Thought: Analysis and Documents*, Vol. 1, p. 82.

[88] As quoted in T. Dunbar Moodie, *The Rise of Afrikanerdom: Power, Apartheid, and the Afrikaner Civil Religion* (Berkeley: University of California Press, 1975), p. 75.

[89] As quoted in William Keith Hancock, *Smuts: The Fields of Force, 1919–1950* (Cambridge: Cambridge University Press, 1968), p. 36.

[90] Moodie, *The Rise of Afrikanerdom*, p. 76.

and as republicans they showed another form of attentiveness to law: they became constitutionalists."[91]

Despite substantive differences (Botha and Smuts favoring an integrationist pattern of political organization; Steyn and Hertzog opposing it), these agents of Afrikanerdom were united in their appreciation of law as an instrument for the settlement of disputes. Underlying this appreciation were Afrikaners' twin desires: to be ruled by law – but by their *own* law.[92]

On the part of the aforementioned Afrikaner leaders, Botha and Smuts, the appreciation of law, grounded as it was in the Calvinist faith, was honed during years of legal education and practice. Steyn, for instance, received his legal education in the Netherlands as well as in England at the Inner Temple. Called to the English bar in 1882, he returned to South Africa where he initially practiced as a barrister in Bloemfontain before being appointed State Attorney of the Orange Free State. In the early 1890s, Steyn proceeded to become second *puisne* judge and eventually first *puisne* judge of the colony's High Court. Hertzog, like Steyn, came of age as a lawyer in the Netherlands, at the University of Amsterdam, having previously read for a law degree at Victoria College in Stellenbosch (what would subsequently become the University of Stellenbosch). After three years, from 1892 until 1895, of practicing law in Pretoria, Hertzog, like Steyn, was appointed to the Orange Free State High Court. The principal interlocutor of these two was Smuts, the most accomplished lawyer of his generation. After initial study at Victoria College, Smuts left South Africa for England on a scholarship in 1891. Landing two firsts in law at the University of Cambridge, where he was a member of Christ's College, Smuts completed his legal training by finishing first in the Inns of Court honors examination in London. In 1897, appointed by Kruger, Smuts served as State Attorney of the Transvaal.[93]

Farther afield, but not without relevance, are Smuts' efforts at legalization in another domain: international affairs. Aside from having participated in numerous peace conferences, Smuts, of course, was an integral force behind the establishment of the League of Nations and an influential voice at Dumbarton Oaks and San Francisco in the deliberations over the nature of the United Nations. Among other things, Smuts effectively coined much of the language of the United Nations Charter.[94] A version of the "Smuts preamble"

---

[91] Ellmann, *In a Time of Trouble*, p. 190. But even prior to that, Afrikaner constitutionalism had been "an undoubted success." See Dugard, *Human Rights and the South African Legal Order*, p. 19. Going back in colonial time, Ellmann points out that the 1854 Constitution of the Orange Free State, "was heavily influenced by the United States constitution." Ellmann, *In a Time of Trouble*, p. 190. Dugard, who first made this point, adds that some constitutional provisions "were accepted almost verbatim and translated into Dutch." See his *Human Rights and the South African Legal Order*, p. 19.

[92] Ellmann, *In a Time of Trouble*, p. 191.

[93] On his tribulations in this role, see, for example, Davenport, *South Africa*, pp. 85–86.

[94] For a brief discussion, see Peter Marshall, "Smuts and the Preamble of the UN Charter," *The Round Table*, Vol. 358, No. 1 (January 2001), pp. 55–65.

was subsequently included as the third preambular paragraph in the United Nations Declaration of Human Rights.[95] From religious covenant to international charter, such was the panoply of legal tradition of South Africa's Afrikaners before unification.

The Anglican Tradition

Intimately bound up with the missionary movement in the Cape, the ideas of the Enlightenment infused the colonial administration of the colony under the British, constituting another legal tradition in South Africa – what might be called the Anglican tradition.[96] As one scholar writes, "[t]he 'English speaking church' denominations included the Anglican Church of the Province (CPSA), which was the church of the British colonial establishment, and had become a separate province of the Anglican communion in 1870, and the Church of England in South Africa (CESA). Baptist, Congregational, Methodist and Presbyterian churches, which had also arrived in South Africa at the beginning of the nineteenth century to minister to British settlers, also belonged to this group. Associated with each were missionary societies that sought to evangelize the indigenous peoples of the sub-continent. Settler and mission congregations developed along parallel lines; in due course these separated lines would begin to converge, but not until well into the twentieth century."[97] In the early years of the British settlement, "English-speaking communities reproduced the parochial life of Great Britain. ... Church architecture, liturgy, and hymnody reminded the church members of 'home.' The majority of their ministers were trained in Britain until the middle of the twentieth century."[98] So pervasive was the Anglican tradition.

As we have seen in Chapter 4, the discourse of rights emanating from this tradition – which in turn was influenced by the Enlightenment – provided the foundation for the abolition of quasi-serfdom of Khoikhoi contract laborers and the adoption of basic human rights for indigenous populations in the Cape colony.[99] In light of the fact that the Anglican tradition of law has, at least

---

[95] Johannes van Aggelen, "The Preamble of the United Nations Declaration of Human Rights," *Denver Journal of International Law and Policy*, Vol. 28, No. 2 (2003), esp. pp. 133–134.

[96] Interestingly, with their occupation of the Cape, the British brought their *own* varieties of Calvinism to South Africa. "[T]he Dutch were not the only Calvinistic influence on the nation of South Africa. Presbyterian churches were planted by the Scots and English in the nineteenth century, especially among the Bantu people of the eastern Cape." R. Ward Holder, "Calvin's Heritage," in Donald K. McKim, ed., *The Cambridge Companion to John Calvin* (Cambridge: Cambridge University Press, 2004), p. 252.

[97] John W. de Gruchy, "Grappling with a Colonial Heritage: The English-speaking Churches under Imperialism and Apartheid," in Donald K. McKim, ed., *The Cambridge Companion to John Calvin* (Cambridge: Cambridge University Press, 2004), p. 155.

[98] De Gruchy, "Grappling with a Colonial Heritage," p. 155.

[99] This aside, we must bear in mind, however, that the English-speaking churches "generally supported the racially discriminatory constitution of the Union and South Africa" and their "sometimes meagre and almost always wary response to African nationalism provoked considerable cynicism among blacks." De Gruchy, "Grappling with a Colonial Heritage," p. 157.

outside of South Africa, received a fair amount of attention, I refer to this literature and my earlier discussion. It is relevant, however, that the diffusion of English legal transplants, based on the Anglican tradition, resulted in the retrenchment of Boer practitioners. The latter were excluded from the legal profession – notably from juries – on account of, among other things, their insufficient command of English. This was a significant curtailment of Boer influence that, in turn, further heightened the reception for Krueger's covenant. As Moody writes, "[t]he anglicization policy instituted under Lord Charles Somerset, governor at the Cape from 1814 to 1826, struck at the heart of Afrikanerdom."[100] The Anglican Church would strike again, in the next century, when it appointed Desmond Tutu to be the first black Anglican Archbishop of Cape Town in 1986. It is entirely fitting that Tutu, in many respects representing the Anglican tradition of law, would come to stand at the helm of what some consider an exercise in excessive legalism – the TRC.[101]

The Vernacular Tradition

Generally overlooked, but hardly less significant for the development of South Africa's legal tradition than the Calvinist and Anglican traditions is the vernacular tradition of law, the latter being associated with the independent church movement that emerged in the late nineteenth century.

The institution of the church came to South Africa's black population by way of colonial evangelists, the so-called Nonconformists. As John and Jean Comaroff write, "The evangelical movement that cut a swathe through Protestant denominations in the late eighteenth-century – and forged the great mission societies – was driven by a faith that all human beings were potential believers."[102] Although it "had not existed traditionally among San, Khoikoi, and Bantu-speakers," the institution of the church proved contagious in the countryside.[103] "By 1883 the whole Bible appeared in Tswana, Xhosa, Sotho, Zulu, and a New Testament in Nama."[104] This religious transplant, however, was quickly rightsized by Bantu prophets in accordance with the needs of the black population. "'The church' referred to here was not the single hierarchy of medieval Europe. It consisted of a number of 'missions' sent by churches of Europe and America, which worked more or less independently, each of the

---

[100] Moodie, *The Rise of Afrikanerdom*, p. 4.

[101] Writes Wilson, "the South Africa TRC restricted both the narrative form and the content (especially, excluding revenge) of deponents in a process of legal colonization of the realms of personal experience." Wilson, *The Politics of Truth and Reconciliation in South Africa*, p. 225. For my discussion of the TRC, see above and below.

[102] John L. Comaroff and Jean Comaroff, *Of Revelation and Revolution, Volume 2: The Dialectics of Modernity on a South African Frontier* (Chicago: University of Chicago Press, 1997), p. 65.

[103] Monica Wilson, "The Growth of Peasant Communities," in Wilson and Thompson, eds., *The Oxford History of South Africa, Volume II*, p. 72.

[104] Wilson, "The Growth of Peasant Communities," p. 74. Also of interest in this context is Lamin Sanneh, *Translating the Message: The Missionary Impact on Culture* (Maryknoll: Orbis, 1989), esp. pp. 146–208.

other, and from 1884 of independent African churches, groups which broke away from these missions under the leadership of some outstanding men. The characteristic of these groups was that they consisted solely of Africans, and in the initial splits the colour issue was dominant – Africans felt that they were not being treated as equals within the church."[105] Put differently, the independent church movement reacted to the missionary approach by secession. Ironically, "Nonconformists in Britain, it turns out, were conformists abroad. Hence their distress at the fact that, when most Tswana," for example, "finally entered the church, they either became 'nominal' Christians or remade Protestantism in their own image. Images, actually, since a multiplicity of Christianities was to emerge."[106]

The newly proselytizing churches, the most important of which was the Native Independent Congregational Church (NICC) formed at Manthe in 1885 by the breakaway prophet Kgantlapane Motlhabane, "proceeded to work out their own accommodation of the Word to their world. Although their theology and ritual bore the imprint of vernacular religious values, the mix was subtle, and free from bold, iconoclastic gestures. In fact, the style of worship and organization developed by such self-governing congregations within the Nonconformist mainstream remained closer than most to Victorian mission orthodoxy."[107] The independent church movement, in other words, practiced "mission Christianity *sans* missionaries."[108] Consequently, the London Missionary Society and Wesleyan Methodist Missionary Society largely failed at establishing their peculiar brands of Christianity.

It is important to understand in this context that "the belief that God is a righteous judge, and that Christ will return as a judge, played an important part in the development of the legal values of the Eastern as well as Western Church."[109] This belief also played an important part in the development of legal values in South Africa's independent churches, and, consequently, contributed to the development of a strong legal tradition among the country's black population. One characteristic of what I have termed the vernacular

[105] Wilson, "The Growth of Peasant Communities," p. 81. Allan Lea provides an early account in *The Native Separatist Church Movement in South Africa* (Cape Town: Juta, 1925). For comparative perspectives, see Bengt Sundkler and Christopher Steed, *A History of the Church in Africa* (Cambridge: Cambridge University Press, 2000); and, further afield, Vittorio Lanternari, *The Religions of the Oppressed: A Study of Modern Messianic Cults*, translated by Lisa Sergio (New York: Knopf, 1963). See also Lamin Sanneh and Joel A. Carpenter, eds., *The Changing Face of Christianity: Africa, the West, and the World* (Oxford: Oxford University Press, 2005).
[106] Comaroff and Comaroff, *Of Revelation and Revolution*, Volume 2, p. 7. For an ethnographic account of the structural transformation of the religious sphere in black South Africa, and the encounter between the spiritual colonizer and the spiritually colonized, see Jean Comaroff, *Body of Power, Spirit of Resistance: The Culture and History of a South African People* (Chicago: University of Chicago Press, 1985), esp. pp. 123–156.
[107] Comaroff and Comaroff, *Of Revelation and Revolution*, Volume 2, pp. 92; 93.
[108] Comaroff and Comaroff, *Of Revelation and Revolution*, Volume 2, p. 92.
[109] Berman, *Law and Revolution*, p. 167.

tradition of law was the strong emphasis that it laid on church constitutions.[110] These played a particular role in the business of naming and demarcation: there existed "a more or less holy competition between the leaders for acquiring the most truly Biblical name possible" for their churches, and it was the function of constitutions to enshrine this name, and to provide a charter for the resultant organization.[111] At a time when independent churches proliferated (and frequently fragmented), the constitutions served to demarcate contending organizations from one another.[112] Notice here the codification of appearances: "The function of the detailed codes, of the uniforms and the petty laws and taboos about behavior, is on the one hand to provide a standard with which to measure the loyalty of the members and to make sure whether they conform to the group or not, and on the other to ensure that all members of the group do feel at home in the Church."[113] The law, in other words, was constitutive *of* the collective and at the same time constituted *by* it. Isaac Schapera puts it thus for the Tswana of South Africa:

Christianity has brought much more to the Tswana than merely a set of religious beliefs. The missionaries built churches, introduced the vocations of preacher and catechist, established local Church councils, instituted new ceremonies (e.g., baptism, confirmation, and communion) and the observance of the Sabbath and other religious holidays, developed new forms of marriage and death ritual, and through their hymns provided a new and very popular form of music. They sought to impose a new system of morality conforming to Christian ideals, and to this end introduced sanctions of various kinds governing the lives of their members.[114]

As the codification of everyday life of the Tswana ("new Church councils," "new ceremonies," "new forms of marriage," "sanctions of various kinds") indicates, the constitutions of independent churches laid down what we might call the rules of religion, establishing, among other things, the levels and tasks of the organization, and the rights and responsibilities of the individuals

[110] I am grateful to John Comaroff for alerting me to the importance of the vernacular tradition, and for encouraging me to reconstruct its evolution.
[111] Bengt G. M. Sundkler, *Bantu Prophets in South Africa*, Second Edition (London: Oxford University Press, [1948] 1961), p. 59.
[112] The number of independent churches grew steadily, from 293 listed in 1932, to 511 in 1938, and 2,400 in 1966. These figures are reported in Wilson, "The Growth of Peasant Communities," p. 81.
[113] Sundkler, *Bantu Prophets in South Africa*, pp. 164–165. Noteworthy in this context is the fact that "[w]hile the codes and forms of group expression are manifold and varied [within the independent churches], the *sanctions* behind these codes can indeed be reduced to very few." Ibid., p. 165.
[114] Isaac Schapera, "Religion and Magic," in Isaac Schapera and John L. Comaroff, *The Tswana*, Revised Edition (London: Kegan Paul [1953] 1991), p. 52. For an extended treatment of the evangelical movement and the encounter between mission Christianity and Tswana religious sensibilities, see Comaroff and Comaroff, *Of Revelation and Revolution, Volume 2*, esp. pp. 63–118. On the latter, see also Jean Comaroff and John L. Comaroff, *Of Revelation and Revolution, Volume 1: Christianity, Colonialism and Consciousness in South Africa* (Chicago: University of Chicago Press, 1991).

operating within it.[115] The following is an example that revolves around the rules of term limits (especially for founding fathers) in one of the independent churches. Writes Bengt Sundkler, the doyen of African Christian studies,

When ... a Church is so intimately connected with a leader that his name is added to the name of the Church, it is only natural that his personal fate is of great importance to the organization he has founded. That is the reason why the bishop's or president's right to remain in office over a certain number of years, or even indefinitely, becomes an important issue in the independent Churches. Rev. L– learned that lesson to his dismay. In the Church originally founded by him, the president's term of office was five years, and after two such terms L– was ousted by a stronger man. L– had then of course to form a new Church, giving it his own clan's name. In the Constitution it is now expressly stated: "As the Rev. P. L– is the prime mover and founder of this church, he is appointed the first President of the Church and shall continue in office as such for all times, so long as he adheres to the Constitution."[116]

The foregoing evidences a clear penchant for *religious legalism* within the independent church movement. It exemplifies not only the importance of legal norms and institutions for clarifying roles ("shall remain in office for all times"), and thus a commitment to a legal way of doing things in the evangelical movement, but also the legitimacy that law enjoyed ("so long as he adheres to the Constitution"). This can be illustrated further by examining the checks and balances that many constitutions of independent churches in South Africa contained, for it was not uncommon that subleaders would try to restrain, by way of law, say, "the dangerous political radicalism" of a president."[117] The availability of such impeachment procedures – and Sundkler's finding that compliance was usually forthcoming – underscores the contribution of the vernacular tradition to the making of South African legal culture. In the church constitutions, rules of excommunication for the ordained are also elaborate. The Independent Methodist Church required the newly ordained to sign, upon admission to the ministry, the following document in order to protect the church in the event of an excommunication: "Once I am excommunicated, I will hand to the officer concerned all documents and properties of said church, repress myself and work no more with the name of the Independent Methodist Church of Africa."[118] Much more than a solemn oath, the document constituted a legal instrument. The use of

---

[115] The Tswana, of course, had displayed a sophisticated legal way of doing things, or "rule-centered paradigm," *prior* to the independent church movement. For a comprehensive analysis, see Isaac Schapera, *A Handbook of Tswana Law and Custom* (London: Oxford University Press, 1938). For an important response to Schapera, see John L. Comaroff and Simon Roberts, *Rules and Processes: The Cultural Logic of Dispute in an African Context* (Chicago: University of Chicago Press, 1981). It is significant, however, that prior to the independent church movement, Tswana law was not formally codified. Isaac Schapera, "Government and Law," in Schapera and Comaroff, *The Tswana*, p. 48. The vernacular tradition, in other words, gave the impetus to a *different* form of legalization.

[116] Sundkler, *Bantu Prophets in South Africa*, p. 117.

[117] Sundkler, *Bantu Prophets in South Africa*, p. 149.

[118] Sundkler, *Bantu Prophets in South Africa*, p. 146.

such documents was apparently widespread in the independent church movement. As one scholar observed, "It is characteristic of the situation that constitutions and ordination forms contain detailed instructions how the ordained should act if later excommunicated."[119]

Of course, there also was a problematic side to this constitutionalism: the proliferation of positions – and hierarchies – is one example that has its origins directly in the institutionalization of organizations. Recognizing the predicament, the Independent Methodist Church of Africa, at its 1940 synod, "protested against local tendencies within their congregation to create more than three classes of preachers (local preachers; local preachers on trial; and exhorters), and it was decided not to encourage such tendencies."[120] Interesting for our purposes is the observation that "whatever the local and denominational variations may be there is in this organization [of the independent churches] a definite system of rank, with well-defined tasks assigned to the subordinate in respect of his immediate superior, and of the higher ranks in the hierarchy."[121]

Consider also the experience of the Southern Tswana, which "are often said to have had a highly 'legalistic' worldview" prior to the deployment of "civilizing techniques" by European missionaries.[122] Because "the early Nonconformists were born of a world preoccupied with the nature and uses of the law, both sacred and secular," they "would tune their teaching to the language of legalism and rights."[123] Although, as John and Jean Comaroff write, "the whole issue of rights and legalities was to feature contradictorily in the civilizing mission, and in the colonial encounter at large," it demonstrated the utility of law – and the language of law – to the Southern Tswana.[124] The following depiction serves as a worthy coda:

Thus it was that, in 1884, Chief Montshiwa agreed to a treaty with the [British] Crown in the argot of *constitutional* nationhood; that he wrote, or had written, a string of letters in similar vein claiming *legal* entitlements and protections for his people; that, in 1903, his heir asked the Colonial Secretary, on behalf of the "Barolong *Nation*," to recognize "our *rights* and privileges as loyal citizens." In short, once the terms of this discourse [of law] were internalized, they became part of collective imaginings – and self assertion ...[125]

[119] Sundkler, *Bantu Prophets in South Africa*, p. 146.
[120] Sundkler, *Bantu Prophets in South Africa*, p. 138.
[121] Sundkler, *Bantu Prophets in South Africa*, pp. 138–139.
[122] Comaroff and Comaroff, *Of Revelation and Revolution*, Volume 2, p. 381.
[123] Comaroff and Comaroff, *Of Revelation and Revolution*, Volume 2, pp. 368; 369.
[124] The contradictions here refer to the fact that the language of law *both* laid "a practical basis for the material and political subordination of black South Africans" *and* "created the various spaces and the diverse terms in which the colonized peoples could refigure themselves, mobilize, and strike back." Comaroff and Comaroff, *Of Revelation and Revolution*, Volume 2, p. 370. This, once again, illustrates the workings of the dual state.
[125] Comaroff and Comaroff, *Of Revelation and Revolution*, Volume 2, pp. 392–393. Emphases added. This is not to deny the fact that law, particularly in the form of "customary law," also functioned as an instrument of "decentralized despotism," to use Mahmood Mamdani's memorable phrase, in South Africa, especially as far as the role of chiefs was concerned: "Together, segregation and customary law would create something more than just territorial segregation

Finally, there is the story of Ethiopianism. "Ethiopianism," according to Edward Roux, the first chronicler of black resistance in South Africa, "was an attempt on the part of Christian Africans to set up their own churches independent of the white ones. Though some of these churches were purely tribalistic affairs or confined to particular areas, others made a nation-wide appeal to all black Christians and tried to unite people of all tribes and nations. Though outwardly religious, they were also to a large extent political in their appeal."[126] Located somewhere between the orthodoxy of the independent church movement (mission *sans* missionaries) and self-directed *baperofeti* (missionaries *sans* mission), Ethiopianism constitutes the missing link between *religious* legalism and *secular* legalism in South Africa.[127] This is so because

between the colonizer and the colonized, the settler and the native; it would create an embryonic 'institutional segregation.' The agents administering customary law would be the chiefs, but with newly defined powers and accountability. So, ordinance 3 of 1849 defined the lieutenant governor as the 'supreme or paramount native chief, with full powers to appoint all subordinate chiefs, or other authorities among them' (clause 3). To codify customary law, the second leg of the policy of native control that came to be called native administration, a commission was appointed. The Code of Native Law it recommended was adopted as a set of guidelines in 1878 and then made legally binding in 1891." Mahmood Mamdani, *Citizen and Subject: Contemporary Africa and the Legacy of Late Colonialism* (Princeton: Princeton University Press, 1996), p. 63. See also Chanock, *The Making of South African Legal Culture, 1902–1936*, esp. pp. 243–272. Even though Mamdani's interpretation of South Africa has drawn criticism, it is worthwhile to contemplate how the discourse of law created incentives for chiefs to *strategically* embrace this discourse. "Conferred the power to enforce their notion of custom as law, chiefs were assured of backup support from colonial institutions – and direct force if need be – in the event they encountered opposition or defiance. Customary law," this legal way of doing things, "thus consolidated the non-customary power of colonial chiefs." Mamdani, *Citizen and Subject*, p. 122. It is for this reason that Mamdani denies the constraining power of law: "Liberal theory emphasized the double-sided character of law, that while it came from the state it also restrained power. Power was said to be grounded in consent. State command was presumed to be rule bound, not arbitrary. This was the meaning of the claim that civil society was framed by the rule of law. None of these claims, however, sounded sensible where power sought to secure order through conquest, not consent. In such a context, the triumph of techno-administration under the guise of indirect rule through customary law was nothing but retreat into legal administration." Ibid., p. 125. Concludes Mamdani: "Under colonial conditions, respect for the law was really respect for the law maker and the law enforcer, often the same person." Ibid., p. 125. While this argument has merit, it overlooks the plain fact that law structures not only state-society relations, but *intra-society* relations as well. And as the discussion of religious movements has hopefully shown, law was meaningful for a substantial portion of the members of three major societal groups in South Africa – and meaningful *irrespective* of the uses of law by the colonial state. On the latter, see the very interesting "The White Man's Burden: *Ersatz* Customary Law and Internal Pacification in South Africa" by Robert Gordon, published in the *Journal of Historical Sociology*, Vol. 2, No. 1 (March 1989), pp. 41–65, with its focus on the contribution of Afrikaner ethnography (*Volkekunde*) to the making of customary law in South Africa.

[126] Edward Roux, *Time Longer Than Rope: The Black Man's Struggle for Freedom in South Africa* (Madison: University of Wisconsin Press, [1948] 1964), p. 77.

[127] Beginning in the early twentieth century, the term *baperofeti* (the singular is *moperofeti*) signified prophets in Setswana. Comaroff and Comaroff, *Of Revelation and Revolution, Volume 2*, p. 96. Whence Ethiopianism? According to the Comaroffs, "The name of this movement derived originally from the Ethiopian Church, a secession from the Wesleyan

the social movement can be linked indirectly to the prevalence of law in the struggle against apartheid, from Mandela's drafting of a code of discipline for the "defiers" in the 1952 Defiance of Unjust Laws Campaign to the anti-apartheid lawyering of the 1970s and 1980s. Here is some evidence:

Unprecedented in the force of its challenge to white mission authority, Ethiopianism was the product of a particular phase in the rise of black consciousness in South Africa. This was the period that saw the emergence of an assertive African press and other supra-ethnic associations, and culminated in the formation of the South African Native National Congress (later ANC) in 1912. The connection between the independent Christian movement and African nationalism is usually said to have been limited. But the cultural content of both owed much to the long struggle with racism, both blatant and latent, within the Protestant churches.[128]

Of interest for this study is the underappreciated *legal* cultural content that was a feature of both the independent Christian movement *and* African nationalism. By instilling in the founding generation of the ANC – including R. W. Msimang and P. K. Seme – legal consciousness, the independent church movement contributed in no small measure to the legal consciousness of the ANC. For it was Msimang and Seme, both of whom had previously practiced law in Great Britain and worked as attorneys in Johannesburg, who were instrumental in the creation of the very liberation movement that would, nearly eighty years later, become the principal adversary of the National Party in apartheid's endgame. As Albie Sachs reminds us, "These early African lawyers became better known for their political activities than for their legal work. In particular they became remembered for having convened the first conference of the African National Congress (ANC) and for having drafted its constitution" in 1912.[129] Here religious legalism inspired secular legalism.

Society in Pretoria led, in 1892, by one of its first ordained African ministers, Rev. Mangena Mokone. Frustrated by the racism of the Methodist church, Mokone found a charter for ecclesiastical self-rule in a verse much favored by the British missionaries themselves: 'Ethiopia shall soon stretch out her hands unto God.' This evocative image reverberated rapidly through the dense networks that were coming to link black Christian communities across the country." Ibid., p. 100. For a somewhat dated, but nevertheless useful account, see George Shepperson, "Ethiopianism and African Nationalism," *Phylon*, Vol. 14, No. 1 (1953), pp. 9–18.

[128] Comaroff and Comaroff, *Of Revelation and Revolution, Volume* 2, p. 104. For a contrary perspective on the connection between the independent Christian movement and African nationalism, consult Leo Kuper, "African Nationalism in South Africa, 1910–1964," in Wilson and Thompson, eds., *The Oxford History of South Africa, Volume II*, esp. pp. 436–437. On the relationship between independent churches and mission churches, and the quest for a unified church movement, see Alan Gregor Cobley's interesting, "The 'African National Church': Self-Determination and Political Struggle among Black Christians in South Africa to 1948," *Church History*, Vol. 60, No. 3 (September 1991), pp. 356–371. Further discussion of the politics of theology can be found in Peter Walshe, "The Evolution of Liberation Theology in South Africa," *Journal of Law and Religion*, Vol. 5, No. 2 (1987), pp. 299–311; and idem., *Prophetic Christianity and the Liberation Movement in South Africa* (Pietermaritzburg: Cluster, 1995).

[129] Sachs, *Justice in South Africa*, p. 210. On the place of rights-based discourse in the ANC, see Kader Asmal, David Chidester, and Cassius Lubisi, *Legacy of Freedom: The ANC's Human Rights Tradition* (Cape Town: Jonathan Ball, 2005).

More generally, "the ANC has always stuck close to the ideology of liberal modernism first implanted by the Nonconformists; it grew out of the South African Native National Congress, formed in 1912 to protest the Land Act, and was led largely by mission school graduates. The SANNC spoke the language of civil and constitutional rights, relying heavily on rhetorical styles learned in the mainstream churches."[130] Fatima Meer adds the important point that the first generation of African leaders "were in the main mission-educated and mission-sponsored Christians who had gained impressive degrees abroad and who were greatly influenced by, and had infinite faith in, Christian democracy."[131] Their project was "fundamentally one of appealing to the Christian and liberal conscience inherent in white men."[132] It is therefore not altogether surprising that the vernacular tradition of law was inherited by the ANC, the successor organization of the SANNC.

Although important differences existed between the SANNC and the ANC, notably the latter's eventual commitment to armed struggle and the nationalization of certain industries, "the ANC, which has always had a substantial Tswana following, retains much of the disposition and ideology of its predecessor – albeit oriented energetically to the present."[133] It continued to deploy the language of rights in the decades to come, evincing a fundamental commitment to law. Drawn from the old guard, for instance, was Chief Albert Luthuli, who served from 1950 as one of two national Presidents of the ANC. It is remarkable that Luthuli, even though he was the nominal head of the Defiance Campaign, never deliberately violated the unjust pass laws against which his organization protested, thus remaining compliant – to the chagrin of some – with the law of apartheid.[134] Explains Richard Abel, "Opponents [of apartheid] honored the regime's pretensions by judging it in terms of legality. The ANC's Freedom Charter, adopted by the Congress of the People in 1955, contains an enumeration of rights that have furnished critical criteria and a blueprint for the post-apartheid society for nearly half a century."[135] Heinz Klug concurs, noting that the ANC's commitment to a bill of

---

[130] Comaroff and Comaroff, *Of Revelation and Revolution, Volume 2*, p. 401. Interestingly, the SANC drew inspiration from the 38 delegates to the 1909 Native Convention, which came together in Bloemfontein to deliberate the proposals for the 1910 constitution. The Convention subsequently established itself as a permanent body, "and its members later transformed the Native Convention by deliberation at the South African Native National Congress." Davenport, *South Africa*, p. 226. This is suggestive of another instance of legal consciousness that was present at the creation of the ANC.

[131] Fatima Meer, "African Nationalism – Some Inhibiting Factors," in Heribert Adam, *South Africa: Sociological Perspectives* (London: Oxford University Press, 1971), p. 126.

[132] Meer, "African Nationalism – Some Inhibiting Factors," p. 126.

[133] Comaroff and Comaroff, *Of Revelation and Revolution, Volume 2*, p. 401.

[134] Meer, "African Nationalism – Some Inhibiting Factors," p. 141.

[135] Abel, *Politics by Other Means*, p. 13; Raymond Suttner and Jeremy Cronin, eds., *30 Years of the Freedom Charter* (Johannesburg: Ravan, 1986); idem., *50 Years of the Freedom Charter* (London: Zed Books, 2007). Suttner and Cronin have been influential intellectuals of the ANC and South African Communist Party (SACP), respectively.

rights during the constitutional negotiations "was grounded in the movement's ability to draw on its own rights-based tradition. Implicit in both the African Claims document which was modeled on the Atlantic Charter, the expression of allied war aims in World War II, and the Freedom Charter were claims to rights. The existence of this rights-based tradition within the ANC facilitated the transition towards constitutionalism ..." in South Africa.[136] Although at times frustratingly vague and ambiguous – the ANC's Constitutional Guidelines, adopted in August 1988, but drafted by the organization's leadership and lawyers at a seminar in Lusaka in March 1988 (after initial deliberations at the 1985 Kabwe Consultative Conference) – embodied this rights tradition, representing, as they did, "a significant step by the ANC in the *process* of Constitution-making."[137] Inasmuch as disagreements immediately ensued over the nature of the substantive proposals contained in the document – the call for a centralized and unitary state, the rejection of group rights, the absence of any mention of due process rights, the inclusion of a right to strike – the ANC's commitment to effecting political transformation by way of legal means, rather than violent means, is striking. Although the organization's hyperbolic representation of the Constitutional Guidelines must be taken with a grain of salt, the adoption of the document (which was also meant to address international concerns about the ANC's prospective bargaining strategy in apartheid's endgame) is testament to the fact that "the seniority and legalistic frame of mind of many of the most influential contributors to the drafting process [won out] over [and held in check] the youthful mass militancy of the thousands of exiles who make up the bulk of the membership" of the ANC.[138] It is for this reason that Tom Lodge credits the Constitutional Guidelines for recapturing "the tradition of South African radical liberalism."[139]

---

[136] Klug, "Participating in the Design," p. 133. For a similar argument, see Asmal et al., *Legacy of Freedom*. For a broader treatment of the ANC, see, most recently, Saul Dubow's succinct *The African National Congress* (Cape Town: Jonathan Ball, 2000).

[137] Hugh Corder and Dennis Davis, "The Constitutional Guidelines of the African National Congress: A Preliminary Assessment," *South African Law Journal*, Vol. 106, No. 4 (November 1989), p. 637.

[138] Corder and Davis, "The Constitutional Guidelines of the African National Congress," p. 646. The mention of the "hyperbolic representation of the Constitutional Guidelines" is a reference to the remarks by Zole Skweyiya, the Head of the ANC's Constitutional and Legal Department, who maintained that "The guidelines lay down broad and general principles of government structures and powers and the fundamental rights and liberties of the people. They are framed in a broad pragmatic and flexible style. It is this flexibility that makes them a lethal weapon in the struggle against apartheid." See Zole Skweyiya's unpublished paper from the 1989 Harare Conference, "The ANC Constitutional Guidelines: A Vital Contribution to the Struggle Against Apartheid," as quoted in Corder and Davies, "The Constitutional Guidelines of the African National Congress," p. 647.

[139] Tom Lodge, "The Lusaka Amendments," *Leadership*, Vol. 7, No. 4 (1988), p. 20. For a less positive assessment of this liberalism, see Meer, "African Nationalism – Some Inhibiting Factors," esp. pp. 126–137.

In the preceding, we have encountered the two faces of black constitutionalism in South Africa – religious constitutionalism and secular constitutionalism – their subtle interconnections, and their complex origins, colonial and otherwise. As John and Jean Comaroff write toward the end of their magisterial *Of Revelation and Revolution*, "the European template for making the savage into a civilized citizen of empire, and of Christendom, was cut *imaginatively* from a culture of legalities."[140] From this template, the independent church movement constructed an *indigenized template*, incorporating the culture of legalities that colonialism had wrought.[141]

The preceding analysis of the religious foundations of legal tradition bears out the observation, made in a different context, that "[i]n any body of law there exist a plurality of autonomous but interacting conceptions of law which go to make up the legal system."[142] When considered in conjunction, the pieces of evidence offered here go a long way toward explaining the surprising confidence of black South Africans in the legal system under apartheid. Not least because of the constitution of religion was law "common knowledge" in South Africa. This knowledge, with its various sources, became a strategic resource that helped to overcome a coordination problem that stood in the way of tackling the larger problem of cooperation versus confrontation in apartheid's endgame. It is not particularly surprising therefore that "the new South African government," as one scholar remarked following its inception, "is a decidedly legalistic construct and that its legal institutions very much resemble those of the white-dominated government that it replaced."[143] This scholar, like I, believes that "the view South Africans had of the old order's legal system have played a part in the shaping of the new South Africa – that is, in the gathering process of choice by black and white South Africans of the sorts of laws and institutions with which they are prepared to comply in the future."[144] This instantiates my argument regarding law as common knowledge.

The common knowledge, however, was not uniform in the sense that democracy-demanding and democracy-resisting forces had an identical image

---

[140] Comaroff and Comaroff, *Of Revelation and Revolution*, Volume 2, p. 366.

[141] This conclusion is noteworthy, for it reminds us, once again in the words of John and Jean Comaroff, that "the way in which legal sensibilities and practices entered into colonizing processes, into their dramatic gestures and prosaic theaters, was a good deal more ambiguous, less audible, murkier than has typically been allowed. What is more, there has long been an *un*remarked rupture in the received narrative of the connection between colonialism and law in Africa." Comaroff and Comaroff, *Of Revelation and Revolution*, Volume 2, p. 367.

[142] Dennis M. Davis, "Competing Conceptions: Pro-Executive or Pro-Democratic – Judges Choose," *South African Journal on Human Rights*, Vol. 3, No. 1 (March 1987), p. 97. Davies' observation owes to the work of Peter Goodrich, in particular "Law and Modernity," *Modern Law Review*, Vol. 49, No. 5 (September 1986), pp. 545–559.

[143] Ellmann, "Law and Legitimacy in South Africa," p. 411.

[144] Ellmann, "Law and Legitimacy in South Africa," p. 411. For an insightful account of law's meaning in South Africa, see also Martin Chanock, "Reconstructing South African Law: Legal Formalism and Legal Culture in a New State," in Paul B. Rich, ed., *Reaction and Renewal in South Africa* (London: Macmillan, 1996), pp. 98–124.

of law. This was far from being the case. The prerogative state had been too invasive for the normative state to leave an undisputed mark.[145] The activities of the prerogative state regularly cut into the domain of the normative state. A notorious example is the case of the "Sharpeville Six" who were convicted on the basis of coerced confessions.[146] This notwithstanding, "[t]he colonial discourse of rights – its contradictions, paradoxes, and perversities intact – ... [made] itself felt as a new dawn [rose] on the South African postcolony."[147]

The knowledge of the language of law on one side of the political divide overlapped to an important extent with the knowledge on the other side. A reservoir of common knowledge developed, slowly and gradually (and not without fits and starts), into a reservoir of interpersonal trust, particularly among key elites. Further common knowledge was supplied by other, unconventional means. Consider this example.

Cyril Ramaphosa and Roelf Meyer, the young lieutenants of Mandela and de Klerk, who met some forty-three times between June and September 1992, first met over a trout-fishing trip in August 1991, organized by a Johannesburg stockbroker. Neither of the two men knew that the adversary would be there. Yet courtesy of the common knowledge, the ritual of trout fishing, both developed a bond that would prove lasting throughout the endgame.[148] Roelf Meyer observes that the creation and maintenance of credibility was an important factor in the resolution of apartheid's endgame. Meyer points out that "credibility can only be achieved by means of personal interaction with your opponent. The ANC was our chief opponent and it was imperative that we should achieve a high level of trust with them. Trust can only be developed between individuals and that is why it was a necessity that Cyril Ramaphosa and I should trust each other in full."[149] Or, as Jon Elster writes, "[b]argainers

---

[145] As Sachs reminds us, "While the higher courts from time to time delivered judgments which softened or delayed the impact of segregatory measures, the lower courts continuously and on a massive scale punished breaches of established race-statutes." Continues Sachs, "White lawyers and judges have generally directed their attention to the occasional superior court judgments which have had great constitutional interest but little practical impact, whereas black litigants have generally been more concerned with the extensive number of inferior court cases which have had slender constitutional import but considerable practical effect." Sachs, *Justice in South Africa*, p. 200. For a discussion of the limits of the normative state, based on select court proceedings, see also *No One to Blame? In Pursuit of Justice in South Africa* (Cape Town: David Philip, 1998) by George Bizos, the eminent human rights advocate who for decades was at the center of anti-apartheid litigation, representing defendants from Govan Mbeki, Nelson Mandela, and Walter Sisulu (in the Rivonia Trial, 1963–1964) to Patrick Lekota and Popo Molefe (in the Delmas Treason Trial, 1985–1989).

[146] Abel, *Politics by Other Means*, p. 539.

[147] Comaroff and Comaroff, *Of Revelation and Revolution, Volume 2*, p. 402.

[148] The story of the trout-fishing trip *itself* became common knowledge, in the sense defined above, in South Africa and drew the country closer together. I rely on Patti Waldmeir's telling of the story. See her *Anatomy of a Miracle*, pp. 208–209.

[149] Roelf Meyer as told to Hennie Marais, "From Parliamentary Sovereignty to Constitutionality: The Democratisation of South Africa, 1990 to 1994," in Penelope Andrews and Stephen

who meet each other over and over again usually end up learning a great about each other's preferences."[150]

Both of the aforementioned types of common knowledge solved coordination dilemmas – assurance games that aggravated the problem of the final game, the resolution of apartheid's endgame.[151] Meyer put it thus: "Together with a relationship of trust, a negotiator must be able to deliver whatever he undertakes because that in itself creates trust."[152]

The interactions between Meyer and Ramaphosa became more frequent and more durable in the course of the endgame. As Chapter 2 has shown, enlarging the shadow of the future is one valuable strategy of achieving cooperation under uncertainty.[153] The common knowledge of the law – and the common knowledge of its *value* and *utility* – helps explain why key agents honored the negotiated commitments reached between 1990 and 1996,

Ellmann, eds., *The Post-Apartheid Constitutions: Perspectives on South Africa's Basic Law* (Johannesburg: Witwatersrand University Press, 2001), p. 59.

[150] Elster, *The Cement of Society*, p. 83.

[151] Another example of common knowledge creation in apartheid's endgame, which helped solve a coordination problem at the *mass* level in South Africa, the importance of which is only slightly exaggerated, is Nelson Mandela's appearance at the Rugby World Cup final in Johannesburg in 1995 (a different endgame). Mandela's decision to don the national team uniform of the *Springboks* (as the national Rugby team is called in the vernacular) on this occasion not only surprised the team's captain, but the entire nation. Yet Mandela's surprising (while almost certainly calculated) move gripped the country's imagination like none had before. The "Rainbow nation" appeared within reach for months thereafter. The country was beaming, the mood clearly upbeat for the rest of the year. What exactly had Mandela accomplished? Mandela had stabilized expectations about expectations in an instance. Some background may be necessary: Rugby, long a symbol of apartheid, is to this day a predominantly white sport in South Africa (soccer, by contrast, is a predominantly black sport). By wearing the team uniform, Mandela reaffirmed the sport's value, and embraced parts of white culture. In so doing, Mandela reassured the white audiences at home and in the stadium that he would honor their rituals, and their way of life. By donning the team uniform, Mandela established common knowledge between blacks and whites, and simultaneously assured whites that in his eyes *their* common knowledge was worth preserving as well. In a bold move, Mandela essentially helped whites who were inclined to respect the figure "Nelson Mandela" and the fledgling democracy over which he presided, but may have been hesitant to admit this in front of their white friends and acquaintances, to do so openly. For Mandela's action established knowledge very publicly, thus ensuring that each and every spectator, whether in the stadium or in front of the television (this author chose the comfort of the latter), knew that others knew that respect was due. This episode nicely completes the circle of the origins and effects of common knowledge as a potential solution to coordination dilemmas. Here the coordination dilemma at the *mass* level was whether or not to support democracy openly in post-apartheid South Africa. Mandela single-handedly produced a tentative solution to this very important coordination problem.

[152] Meyer as told to Marais, "From Parliamentary Sovereignty to Constitutionality," p. 59. See also Cyril Ramaphosa, "Negotiating a New Nation: Reflections on the Development of South Africa's Constitution," in Penelope Andrews and Stephen Ellmann, eds., *The Post-Apartheid Constitutions: Perspectives on South Africa's Basic Law* (Johannesburg: Witwatersrand University Press, 2001), pp. 71–84.

[153] Axelrod, *The Evolution of Cooperation*, p. 126.

including commitments regarding federalism, proportional representation, and *de facto* power-sharing.[154] This argument finds support in the joint submission of Ismail Mahomed, then Chief Justice of South Africa; Arthur Chaskalson, then President of the Constitutional Court of South Africa; Michael Corbett, the former Chief Justice of South Africa; H.J.O. van Heerden, the then Deputy Chief Justice of South Africa; and Pius Langa, the then Deputy President of the Constitutional Court and current Chief Justice of South Africa, to the TRC. The eminent jurists, in what arguably constituted the most important contribution to the TRC's Legal Hearing, which was held between October 27 and October 29, 1997, maintained that, *despite* the contribution of law to injustice, "values central to the rule of law and a just legal system, were not entirely lost" in South Africa.[155] Bearing out the findings of this book, the justices argued that "[t]he maintenance of such values during the years of apartheid *facilitated* the transition to a constitutional democracy and provided an important *foundation* for the legal system in that democracy."[156] The preceding was devoted to specifying the mechanisms and processes of law's contribution.

But returning to the question concerning the salience of law in South African society, law's common knowledge was also instrumental in mobilizing Afrikaner support at the grassroots level of society. Significant in this context, for example, was the whites-only referendum that de Klerk, seeking a mandate to start constitutional negotiations with the ANC, called in March 1992. As Dan O'Meara remarks, "Afrikaners are a strongly legalistic people. After 2 February 1990, the KP [Conservative Party] had made some headway with the (technically legitimate) charge that De Klerk had no mandate from the white electorate to negotiate with yesteryear's 'terrorists'. The referendum changed that. With nearly seven out of ten whites endorsing the notion of a non-racial constitution, [d]e Klerk had a real mandate. Even the most obdurate Treurnichtite [Andries Treurnicht was the leader of the Conservative Party at the time] would have to concede the legitimacy of negotiations."[157]

South Africa's legal culture is very conservative in the sense that a strong faith in the precision and determinacy of words and texts exists. This has placed some strains on the transformation of law's role, but it also helped the immediate transition. As Karl Klare notes, there is reverence for law among South African lawyers *and* politicians. "Even through the long nightmare of apartheid, with its baroquely legalized system of oppression, many among the victims and within the opposition kept alive a distinct faith that law could somehow purify and

---

[154] Cf. my earlier discussion of meaningful legal action.

[155] Ismail Mahomed, Arthur Chaskalson, Michael Corbett, H J O van Heerden, and Pius Langa, "The Legal System in South Africa 1960–1994: Representations to the Truth and Reconciliation Commission," *South African Law Journal*, Vol. 115, No. 1 (1998), p. 29. Emphases added.

[156] Mahomed et al., "The Legal System in South Africa 1960–1994," p. 29. Emphases added.

[157] O'Meara, *Forty Lost Years*, p. 410.

cure the society's evils."[158] As discussed in the previous chapter, legal means were important in the struggle against apartheid. Here is another example.

When African workers were granted statutory trade union rights and black trade unions were recognized for the first time within the official industrial relations system of South Africa in the wake of the Wiehahn Commission of Inquiry, "the unions emphasized *legal* means of struggle."[159] South Africa's internal opposition achieved several victories in this struggle, as we have already seen, not least because many of the lawyers involved in these victories "took very seriously indeed what they saw as the highest aspirations of the legal system. Some of them, moreover, have been people who had manifestly gained the professional respect of their peers in that system. Those who had admired these lawyers may have found some ground for admiring what these lawyers valued as well, and for admiring a profession in which people could oppose injustice and fight against it."[160] The opposition's legal victories "strengthened the opposition's own commitment to legality and thus the prospect that the post-apartheid regime would respect the rule of law."[161] Both cause and consequence of this commitment, for example, was the popularity of the study of law among members of the resistance movement imprisoned on Robben Island. It is important to appreciate in this context just how pronounced this commitment to legality was within the higher echelons of the ANC:

Among the lawyers or legally trained activists who helped shape the ANC's positions or negotiate on its behalf (besides Nelson Mandela himself) were Kader Asmal, a legal scholar long in exile but by then returned to the University of the Western Cape (and now a cabinet minister); George Bizos, a leading anti-apartheid advocate; Arthur Chaskalson, another leading public interest lawyer (now President of the Constitutional Court); Nicholas Haysom, a scholar and practitioner involved in a wide range of anti-apartheid litigation (now counsel to President Mandela); Brigitte Mabandla, trained as a lawyer while in exile (now Deputy Minister of Culture); Penuel Meduna, a lawyer who went into exile during the years of apartheid (now Deputy Minister of the Interior); Abdullah Omar, a lawyer who had represented Nelson Mandela and who only a few years earlier had been a victim of emergency powers himself (see Omar v. Minister of Law and Order, 1987 (3) SA 859 (A))(now Minister of Justice); Matthew Posa, another lawyer who went into exile (now Premier of the Eastern Cape Province); Cyril Ramaphosa, a prominent union leader with law training (now the Chair of the Constitutional Assembly); Albie Sachs, a lawyer and scholar who suffered not only detention but also mutilation at the hands of the apartheid regime (now a judge of the

[158] Karl E. Klare, "Legal Culture and Transformative Constitutionalism," *South African Journal of Human Rights*, Vol. 14, Part 1 (1998), pp. 168–169.
[159] Glenn Adler and Eddie Webster, "Challenging Transition Theory: The Labor Movement, Radical Reform, and Transition to Democracy in South Africa," *Politics and Society*, Vol. 23, No. 1 (March 1995), p. 80.
[160] Ellmann, "Law and Legitimacy in South Africa," p. 467.
[161] Abel, "Legality Without a Constitution: South Africa," p. 80. See also Abel, *Politics by Other Means*.

Constitutional Court); and Joe Slovo, a lawyer and long-time leader of the South African Communist Party (Minister of Housing in the new government until his recent death).[162]

As impressive as this gallery is, "[e]ven this long list leaves out other distinguished lawyers who contributed" to the peaceful resolution of apartheid's endgame.[163]

The upshot of this extraordinary commitment to law was that important signaling in apartheid's endgame occurred. "[D]uring the negotiations that ended apartheid, the ANC as a whole embraced a process whose results bespeak at least a tolerance for legalism and a measure of confidence by the ANC in its ability to achieve power in such a framework."[164] The rule-by-law tradition signaled to the ANC-led opposition that cooperation, rather than confrontation, could end apartheid. It signaled to the government that negotiated commitments would be honored due to the opposition's commitment to law, also indicating the positive payoff of cooperation over confrontation. The law, in game theoretic terms, lengthened the shadow of the future for adversarial agents, and allowed for a rapprochement between them. The NP may have overplayed its hand, erroneously assuming that it could control the transition, but it upheld the commitments into which it entered, making them credible. For as Ellmann writes, "Adherence to law is not merely a matter of sophisticated calculation of self-interest. It is also a long-standing cultural tradition among South African whites."[165]

South Africa's rule-guided way of doing things – cherished by blacks and whites alike – made it possible for interacting adversaries to believe despite uncertainty. "South African whites continued, for a mixture of admirable and less-than-admirable reasons, to value and adhere to the law."[166] Aside from its origins in the religious foundations discussed earlier, the apartheid government embraced a rule-guided way of doing things – law – for three reasons: (1) law demonstrated its utility by serving as an effective method of control; (2) law promised to better the apartheid government's standing in the international community by providing a modicum of legitimacy; and (3) law embodied a sincere belief in its appropriateness. The first two are instances of what I have termed instrumental legal action (*law being useful*), the last of value-oriented legal action (*law being meaningful*).[167]

Triangulating these reasons, I propose, with Ellmann, that the uses of law by South African whites:

cannot be reduced to the overt or unconscious product of ... calculations of self-interest. On the contrary, belief in law is directly rooted in South African whites'

[162] Ellmann, "Law and Legitimacy in South Africa," p. 476, Fn. 218.
[163] Ellmann, "Law and Legitimacy in South Africa," p. 476, Fn. 218.
[164] Ellmann, "Law and Legitimacy in South Africa," p. 469.
[165] Stephen Ellmann, *In a Time of Trouble: Law and Liberty in South Africa's State of Emergency* (Oxford: Clarendon Press, 1992), p. 7.
[166] Mureinik, "Emerging from Emergency," p. 1980.
[167] For this tripartite explanation, see Ellmann, *In a Time of Trouble*, pp. 174–193.

broader traditions and values as well, and these historical and cultural factors *reinforce* the impact of considerations of utility and legitimation of South African thinking.[168]

The common knowledge of law, and actors' confidence in the instrumental value of law, created the conditions for the emergence of trust among them.[169] Iterative interaction expanded this reservoir of trust. Interacting adversaries found "faith in judicial decision-making as a source of legitimacy in the governance of a post-apartheid South Africa."[170] This led to the transformation of preferences on the part of these adversaries.

It is important to remember, however, that the law of apartheid was not readily embraced by *all* segments of South Africa's internal opposition. An intervening development occurred that turned law legitimate, keeping the county's transformation on track: the Truth and Reconciliation Commission, written into law in 1995.

THE LEGITIMACY OF LAW

"[I]f democratic institutions are to sustain themselves as legitimate," Ian Shapiro writes, "they cannot be detached from expectations that they operate to diminish injustice."[171] What are we to make of the legitimacy of law? This section continues the analysis begun earlier.

Weber defined legitimacy as the belief in the legality of enacted rules. Elaborating on my earlier discussion of legitimacy, however, I propose, *contra* Weber, that a belief in the legality of enacted rules is *insufficient* for law to be seen as legitimate *in the long run*. In the conceptualization employed here, *legitimacy* has two elements: *legality* and *morality*. I contend that, in South Africa, *backward legality* enhanced the chances of *forward legitimacy* by providing *forward legality*. The aforementioned survey data suggests that a properly constituted legal order, even if robbed of morality, may go a long way toward paving the way for the establishment of the rule of law. The formulation "favorable effective orientation" coined by Tom Tyler, perhaps the most influential scholar of law's legitimacy in the United States, is useful in this context, for it couches legitimacy's meaning in terms that are very straightforward. For example, for Tyler, law's legitimacy has to do with "attachment," "loyalty," and "allegiance." Ellmann, who sets the bar somewhat lower than Tyler but who has undoubtedly been influenced by the former, conceptualizes – and operationalizes – legitimacy in terms of "approval," "confidence," and "admiration." For him, "evidence of approval or confidence in the South African legal system is evidence of a measure of legitimacy

---

[168] Ellmann, *In a Time of Trouble*, p. 187. Emphases added.
[169] This refers to the collective memory of the normative state. The collective memory of the prerogative state complicated the endgame, of which more below.
[170] Klug, *Constituting Democracy*, p. 180.
[171] Shapiro, *Democracy's Place*, p. 108.

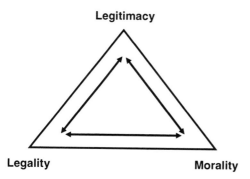

FIGURE 7.3. Dimensions of Legitimate Law

being accorded to that system."[172] Yet I believe that law is not inherently legitimate; it has to *turn* legitimate.

A Two-Step

Legitimate law, I believe, combines morality and legality. A triangular relationship exists among these elements (see Figure 7.3).

The three sides of the triangle are interdependent. Neither can legitimate law exist without legality, nor can it exist without morality. From this follows that two pathways toward legitimate law exist: (1) morality creates legality thus producing legitimacy; or (2) legality meets morality thus producing legitimacy. Law's legitimacy, I maintain, is what actors make of it. Legitimacy – like law itself – is a social construct.

I believe that the transition toward legitimate law in apartheid's endgame was one from legality to morality, the second of the ideal typical paths identified earlier. Before we turn to a comparative illustration of this mechanism in the next chapter, let us consider further apartheid's endgame, in particular the two-step toward legitimate law: the move from legality to morality (*Step 1*), and the subsequent move from morality to legitimacy (*Step 2*) (see Figure 7.4).

Whence the second step? In some instances, truth commissions may serve to marry morality to legality, thereby turning law legitimate. This is, I suggest, what happened in South Africa. Public opinion data confirm the point. A survey commissioned by South Africa's Institute for a Democratic South Africa (IDASA) in 1995 revealed that forty-one percent of the population was satisfied with democracy in South Africa. While the percentage of those dissatisfied with democracy was higher there (57 percent), the figures suggest that the population's confidence in the institutional structure of the state (which is necessary for democracy to function) was *generally* remarkable. The results

---

[172] Ellmann, "Law and Legitimacy in South Africa," p. 412.

FIGURE 7.4 A Path Toward Legitimate Law

compare favorably with those polled in other countries. After all, South Africa had been only in the fifth year of its democratic transition at the time of the poll (see Table 7.7).

Spain, which had begun its democratization twenty-one years earlier, achieved survey results very similar to South Africa. Forty-one percent of Spaniards were satisfied with democracy, 59 percent were not. Thus South Africa fared slightly *better* than Spain even though the achievement of democracy was more recent.[173] In comparison with Hungary and Belarus, the democratic achievements in South Africa stand out even more. The populations of both countries were extremely dissatisfied with democracy in 1995. The level of dissatisfaction amounted to 76 percent in Hungary, whereas 86 percent of Belarus was unhappy with the way democracy turned out. The survey results offer indirect support for the argument developed here. But it is important to bear in mind that in 1995 the Truth and Reconciliation Commission had not begun its work. At the time of the poll, it had only just been signed into law.

By marrying morality to legality the TRC became a reinforcing bridge in the transition from the rule *by* law to the rule *of* law. But the TRC served as a bridge in two further senses. First, it was poised between apartheid and the post-apartheid era; and, second, it was located in a liminal space between already existing institutions and organizations of the state. It was thus neither exclusively a legal institution (its hearings on human rights violations were not a court of law), nor was it exclusively a political institution (its amnesty hearings were constituted as court hearings with legal consequences).[174] It was a critical secondary institution in that it helped turn law legitimate. As Gibson explains, "The truth and reconciliation process succeeded in part due to its

---

[173] But it was not so recent that the euphoria, which often accompanies the achievement of democracy, would have clouded respondents' perceptions.

[174] See Wilson, *The Politics of Truth and Reconciliation in South Africa*, pp. 19–20.

TABLE 7.7. *Satisfaction with Democracy*

	South Africa	United States	Spain	Hungary	Belarus
Satisfied	41	72	41	23	14
Dissatisfied	57	28	59	76	86
Don't Know	2	0	3	2	23

Source: Institute for a Democratic South Africa (IDASA), "Honeymoon is Over, Poll Shows," *Opinion Poll*, Vol. 2, No. 1 (September 1996), p. 1, published by the Public Opinion Service of IDASA's Public Information Centre. The South Africa data came from a national opinion survey conducted by Market and Opinion Surveys (Pty) Ltd for IDASA, and were based on interviews with 2,674 individuals between September and November 1995. The results were weighted to reflect an electorate estimated at 24 million voters.

willingness to judge evenhandedly, applying the same standards to all parties, and that this practice was countenanced (and legitimized) by a fairly widespread commitment in the culture to the rule of law. ... This commitment reflects in part the European origins of South African whites and their continuing use of Europe as a reference group, as well as their desire to win the approval of Europeans and the rest of the Western world. Thus, in this sense, the success of the truth and reconciliation process may reflect a larger cultural commitment to the rule of law in South Africa."[175] The TRC, in this sense, was *both* legitimacy-receiving *and* legitimacy-conferring in apartheid's endgame.

By making possible the establishment of the TRC, the usable state was a *useful* state in apartheid's endgame. It is in this sense that it was necessary for making democracy work. It supplied legality (the legal foundation) and bureaucracy (the administrative backbone) without which the TRC in particular, and democracy in general, would have been impossible to establish. This notwithstanding, Johnny de Lange, the ANC Chair of the Select Committee on Justice of the National Assembly, bemoaned in 1995 that

[t]here is a deep crisis of legitimacy of our political institutions. The moral fabric of society has been torn. Expediency and principle have been blurred. Society is now held together by obstinacy, goodwill and good luck, instead of an inclusive moral base.[176]

What is not reflected in de Lange's assessment is the operation of the TRC. The TRC acted as an intervening variable in the period between 1995 and 1999. The TRC was the *missing link* between legality and legitimacy – a link that helped turn law legitimate.

---

[175] Gibson, "The Contributions of Truth to Reconciliation," pp. 423–424.
[176] Quoted in Wilson, *The Politics of Truth and Reconciliation in South Africa*, p. 17.

The Morality of Truth

A group of distinguished scholars recently devoted an entire volume to the morality of truth commissions. And yet, as important as morality is, absent legality, it will not suffice to constitute the legitimacy of law.

Backward legality, the surviving tradition of the normative state, created the conditions for achieving a reasonable degree of forward justice, a consensus on the moral foundations of democratic rule. It was considerably easier to construct a legitimate regime – by which I mean a regime that is based on the consent, tacit or otherwise, of the majority of its members – in apartheid's endgame from within the triangle depicted in Figure 7.3 than from outside it. Legality, backward and forward, was, in the final analysis, a most important – perhaps the most important – factor in the resolution of apartheid's endgame. One is reminded in this context of Sir Sydney Kentridge's remark, uttered in the early 1980s, that "the judicial system is the country's most valuable social institution."[177]

The usable state mattered, also its bureaucratic foundation, which has received slightly less attention here but the importance of which should have become clear if only by association.[178] Legality trumped the importance of international influence in the endgame (which is all too often exaggerated in the literature), and was at least as important as exceptional leadership in moving the endgame toward resolution.[179] Margaret Levi's remark applies: "Although a state able to produce interpersonal trust may be a just state in the sense that it enforces contracts made under its laws, it is not necessarily a democratic state."[180] The comment captures the conflicting imperatives inherent in the dual apartheid state.

Richard Wilson regrets that the truth commission process in South Africa was detached from a retributive understanding of justice. From a moral perspective this is indeed regrettable. From the perspective of sustainable democracy, by contrast, the neglect of retribution was desirable. The transition from retributive justice to restorative justice – orchestrated by elites within the ANC and partly the result of the compromise solution discussed above – cleared the way for iterated cooperation in the endgame. The absence of retribution created conditions for cooperation, and removed

[177] Sydney Kentridge, "Telling the Truth about Law," *South African Law Journal*, Vol. 99, No. 4 (November 1982), p. 649.
[178] See, once again, Lieberman's analysis in *Race and Regionalism in the Politics of Taxation in Brazil and South Africa*.
[179] Regarding the often-cited importance of international pressure in apartheid's endgame, Adam and Moodley respond dryly: "If all the changes were a result of mobilization from below, with the help of some hard-won external pressure, then there is no reason why the ruling class should be rewarded for reluctantly bowing to the inevitable." Adam and Moodley, *The Opening of the Apartheid Mind*, p. 48.
[180] Margaret Levi, "A State of Trust," in Valerie Braithwaite and Margaret Levi, eds., *Trust and Governance* (New York: Russell Sage Foundation, 1998), p. 94.

incentives for confrontation. Needless to say, satisfaction with this outcome was not universal.

Azanian People's Organization (AZAPO) and Others v. the President of the Republic of South Africa and Others

Steve Biko, Griffiths Mxenge, and Chris Ribeiro all had fallen victim to the prerogative state during apartheid. In April 1996, their families, together with the Azanian People's Organization (AZAPO), challenged the constitutionality of Section 20 (7) of the National Unity and Reconciliation Act, which regulated the amnesty provisions of the soon to be established TRC, before the Constitutional Court. The Court rejected the claims in a majority ruling.

Azanian People's Organization (AZAPO) and Others v. the President of the Republic of South Africa and Others is a landmark case in the brief history of the Constitutional Court of South Africa.[181] It may not be the most sophisticated and eloquent of the Court's decisions to date, but it was among the – if not *the* – most important ruling to come out of the court in Braamfontein, Johannesburg. Although Wilson vilifies the court ruling for having failed to (1) sufficiently take into account international law, and (2) give justice right of place, I consider it an important ingredient of law's legitimacy in South Africa. Three things in particular are remarkable about the case: the challenge, the decision, and the reactions to the decision.

The Challenge and the Decision

In the words of the TRC, AZAPO's challenge "struck at the heart of the Amnesty Committee's very existence."[182] The most remarkable aspect of the challenge is the simple fact that it was *made*. AZAPO's application for the initiation of legal proceedings before the Constitutional Court was, in many ways, an unlikely and unexpected outcome. AZAPO, founded in May 1978, has its origins in the Black Consciousness movement, as first articulated by Steve Biko. Located to the left of the PAC, AZAPO was the voice of militant discontent in the 1980s. Much emphasis was laid on race as a marker of identity. As Marx notes, "Activists turned to race as an immediately relevant form of social identity, which could again invigorate the opposition. Being

[181] *Azanian People's Organization (AZAPO) and others v. the President of the Republic of South Africa and others* 1996 (4) SA 671 (CC). Commentary on this judgment is available in Claudia Braude and Derek Spitz, "Memory and the Spectre of International Justice: A Comment on AZAPO," *South African Journal on Human Rights*, Vol. 13, No. 2 (1997), pp. 269–282; and John Dugard, "Is the Truth and Reconciliation Process Compatible with International Law? An Unanswered Question," *South African Journal on Human Rights*, Vol. 13, No. 2 (1997), pp. 258–268. For a competent history of constitutional jurisprudence since the inception of the Constitutional Court, see, most recently, Lynn Berat, "The Constitutional Court of South Africa and Jurisdictional Questions: In the Interest of Justice?," *International Journal of Constitutional Law*, Vol. 3, No. 1 (January 2005), pp. 39–76.
[182] *Truth and Reconciliation Commission of South Africa Report*, Volume 1, p. 174.

black was defined as a matter of malleable consciousness based on the experience of discrimination."[183]

Throughout apartheid's endgame, AZAPO had rejected *any* bargaining with National Party adversaries.[184] Described as a doctrinaire organization by some, it was "the most uncompromising of the actors in the liberation struggle, not only in its ideology, but also in its perceived role as the standard bearer of the goal of liberation in the tradition of Steve Biko. It spelled out the most revolutionary vision of change among major South African political actors."[185] Against this background, it is truly astonishing to see AZAPO challenge the constitutionality of a provision in the National Unity and Reconciliation Act. AZAPO claimed that Section 20 (7) violated the constitution, the making of which AZAPO had rejected on political grounds. Instead of resorting to means of mass mobilization to protest the impending truth commission process, AZAPO accorded supremacy to the law. Law became the continuation of the struggle by other means. By using the law to battle unwanted legislation, AZAPO's constitutional court challenge is an example, not a contradiction, of the legitimacy of law in post-apartheid South Africa.[186] In some ways this episode is a "most difficult" case for testing the legitimacy of law. For it shows a most recalcitrant actor in apartheid's endgame turn to law.[187]

Another "most difficult" case along the lines of *AZAPO and Others v. President of the Republic and Others* is the IFP challenge of the final constitution before the Constitutional Court in 1996, of which more later. AZAPO worked through the final constitution in the end because enough major agents in apartheid's endgame had worked within its confines (and within the confines of the Interim Constitution) long enough to get it established in other agents' expectations that there was no point in not working with the document. Russell Hardin has made the same argument with regard to the U.S. Constitution of 1787:

The agreement of certain people to it may have been important for those people to work within the Constitution, but agreement was not the only motivator. Many must have worked within the Constitution simply because it was the most useful thing for them to do in their own interests.[188]

---

[183] *Truth and Reconciliation Commission of South Africa Report*, Volume 1, p. 237.

[184] This decision was reached at AZAPO's first party conference in late 1990 after its unbanning in the same year. See Sisk, *Democratization in South Africa*, p. 97.

[185] Sisk, *Democratization in South Africa*, p. 195.

[186] For a slightly different finding, based on survey responses, see James L. Gibson and Gregory A. Caldeira, "Defenders of Democracy? Legitimacy, Popular Acceptance, and the South African Constitutional Court," *Journal of Politics*, Vol. 65, No. 1 (February 2003), pp. 1–30.

[187] It has been argued that AZAPO's constitutional challenge was motivated by an effort to reclaim a corner of the political stage from which the organization had been all but forced to retreat. While this argument has merit, it overlooks the fact that AZAPO was always – largely on account of its vociferous ideology – a comparatively marginal actor.

[188] Hardin, "Why a Constitution," p. 118.

AZAPO, like the IFP in the same year, worked *within* the constitution because it was in neither party's interest to renege on the document. It would have been too costly for both AZAPO and the IFP to recoordinate, mobilize against, or destroy, the constitution in 1996. There was no reason to believe that the costs of organizing collective action would be any less *after* the adoption of the document. Yet why did AZAPO and the IFP vest confidence in the constitution and the constitutional court? The answer goes back to this book's principal argument: the legacies of law. The *primary institution* of the state *qua* law (but also bureaucracy) was usable in apartheid's endgame. This made possible the negotiation of *secondary institutions*, including the constitution and the constitutional court. As demonstrated earlier, cooperation was required for making both institutions. These strategic games could be solved cooperatively because the usable state helped regulate these patterns of interactions.

The Reactions

The court's decision sparked no violent reaction, a remarkable achievement considering the historical issues at stake. Although the constitutional court decision did not cause violence, it caused a barrage of further litigation.[189] Remarkably, agents from all corners of the political spectrum took their case not to the streets, but again to the Braamfontein court. In *Truth and Reconciliation Commission v. Du Preez and Another* (1996), Brigadier Jan du Preez and Major General Nick van Rensburg objected to the procedure of the Truth Commission concerning its hearings, and the manner in which the plaintiffs were notified about the substance of the allegations against them. The hearing in question resolved around the murder of Siphiwe Mthimkulu in 1982.[190] In *National Party v. Desmond Mpilo Tutu and others* (1997), the National Party sought relief before the Cape Provincial Division of the High Court regarding statements made by Desmond Tutu, the Chairperson of the Truth Commission, and Alex Boraine, the Vice Chairperson, concerning the testimony of former State President F. W. de Klerk before the Commission on May 14, 1997. The matter was eventually settled out of court. The IFP as well as former members of the SADF took a different route. Each submitted complaints to the Office of the Public Protector, alleging prejudice and bias in the investigation of the Truth and Reconciliation Commission.[191] Finally, an important agent of the prerogative state turned to the new normative state for legal redress: Wouter Basson, alias "Dr. Death" (see Chapter 4). Basson feared that he might be prejudiced in his pending criminal trial if he appeared before the Truth and Reconciliation Commission. After the Commission ruled that the proceedings not be stayed, Basson unsuccessfully sought an injunction before the Cape High Court.

[189] For an overview of all legal challenges to the Truth and Reconciliation Commission, see *Truth and Reconciliation Commission of South Africa Report*, Volume 1, pp. 174–200.
[190] *Truth and Reconciliation Commission v. Du Preez and another* 1996 (3) SA 997.
[191] *Truth and Reconciliation Commission of South Africa Report*, Volume 1, pp. 196–197.

Truth commissions contribute to implement the rule of law "to the extent that they are public, investigate all sides in a conflict, recognize ways in which perpetrators can also be victims, and adopt measures to reduce bias."[192] The South African Truth and Reconciliation Commission did just that.[193] It connected law and legitimacy for the first time in the country's history. As such, the TRC might be said to have had a legitimacy-conferring capacity, an endowment that in the theoretical literature has typically been attributed to courts, notably the U.S. Supreme Court.[194] I consider a strength what Wilson has criticized as a weakness, namely the commission's "excessive legalism."[195]

Wilson claims that the ANC "when it inherited the battered shell of an authoritarian and illegitimate state, became motivated less by a vision of popular sovereignty than by bureaucratic imperatives. Nation-building allows other processes to be carried out, such as the legitimization of the apparatus of justice which still remains tainted by the authoritarian past. Legitimating the state's justice system in turn promotes a process of state-building, as the post-apartheid state has embarked upon a project of unifying the diversity of justice institutions in state and society."[196] Wilson claims that a legitimization of the law along these lines was not achieved by the TRC. The TRC, in his eyes, did not inaugurate a nation-building process, and thus failed. I beg to differ.

I submit that the TRC strengthened the foundation of what may be called (by paraphrasing Habermas's famous neologism) *institutional patriotism*, the beginnings of *civic nationalism* not unlike the nationalism that emerged in the Federal Republic of Germany in the aftermath of World War II. Justice Albie Sachs of the Constitutional Court of South Africa had this to say about the relationship between the TRC and nationhood: "The Commission of Truth and Reconciliation. It is the creation of a nation."[197] Michael Ignatieff's sensible argument bears resemblance to the principal argument of this book: "The only reliable antidote to ethnic nationalism turns out to be civic nationalism, because the only guarantee that ethnic groups will live side by side in peace is shared loyalty to a state, strong enough, fair enough, equitable enough to command their obedience."[198] Ignatieff, like I, emphasizes the utility of the state.

From the perspective of establishing civic nationalism, excessive legalism in the pursuit of truth and justice is, *pace* Wilson, a virtue, not a shortcoming. Indeed, Wilson's finding that a "program of legitimization which relied upon

[192] David A. Crocker, "Truth Commissions, Transitional Justice, and Civil Society," in Rotberg and Thompson, eds., *Truth v. Justice*, p. 105.
[193] For tentative quantitative evidence, see James L. Gibson, "Does Truth Lead to Reconciliation? Testing the Causal Assumptions of the South African Truth and Reconciliation Commission," Unpublished Paper, Washington University, October 2001.
[194] Dahl, "Decision Making in a Democracy," pp. 279–295.
[195] Wilson, *The Politics of Truth and Reconciliation in South Africa*, p. xix.
[196] Wilson, *The Politics of Truth and Reconciliation in South Africa*, p. 17.
[197] Quoted Alex Boraine, *The Healing of a Nation?* (Cape Town: Justice in Transition, 1995), p. 146.
[198] Michael Ignatieff, *Blood and Belonging: Journeys into the New Nationalism* (London: BBC Books/Chatto and Windus, 1993), p. 185.

formal rationality and a dry technocratic ethos" informed the operation of the TRC, is perfectly consistent with the twin arguments of this book. First, the reliance on formally rational law (legality) and technocratic ethos (bureaucracy) in the constitution and administration of the TRC confirms this book's argument that the usable state – a legacy of the dual state – was important for solving commitment problems. Second, the practical emphasis on legality (and the concomitant reliance on bureaucracy) provides support for the argument that legacies of the dual apartheid state spawned path-dependent outcomes. The surviving remnants of the apartheid state, notably its legal norms and institutions, structured strategic interactions, then and now.

A Final Look at the Truth

The return to the theme of transitional justice has underscored the principal argument of this chapter, further illustrating the relationship between legality, morality, and legitimacy in democratization.[199] Truth commissions on the whole differ. They come into existence for different reasons, by different ways, and have different missions.[200] In terms of their relationship to law, they "may presuppose, illustrate, and strengthen the rule of law."[201] They exist "to both transcend the limitations of the courts and restore the legitimacy of a tarnished legal system, which in turn can be directed to occupy the interstices created by the process of truth finding and indemnity for perpetrators."[202] In South Africa, the TRC, as a secondary institution, successfully linked morality and legality. It was a critical bridge in the country's two-step toward legitimate law. Backward legality, in other words, enabled the construction of forward legitimacy. That legitimacy was indeed achieved is underscored by the fact that no significant actor, or segment of society, has seriously, that is, violently, mobilized against the commission's work. As this chapter has shown, disputes over the TRC's mandate and reach did not go beyond ordinary levels of contention. Voice was strong, exit never occurred. Although the TRC was controversial throughout its tenure – and not entirely successful in its mission – it served as an important lifeline for the institution of law, infusing the latter with an extra dose of legitimacy.

Caveats

Yet the legitimacy of law, and of the state, was not absolute in South Africa. It is questionable whether it ever can be. Almost inevitably, human rights talk is

---

[199] South Africa's Truth and Reconciliation Commission, established by an Act of legislation in 1995, has become the most widely investigated topic in the country's transition.

[200] For a comparative discussion, see Priscilla B. Hayner, *Unspeakable Truths: Confronting State Terror and Atrocity* (New York: Routledge, 2001) and Mark Freeman, *Truth Commissions and Procedural Fairness* (Cambridge: Cambridge University Press, 2006). See also Minow, *Between Vengeance and Forgiveness*, chapter 4.

[201] Crocker, "Truth Commissions, Transitional Justice, and Civil Society," p. 105.

[202] Wilson, "Justice and Legitimacy in the South African Transition," p. 191.

a "contested discourse which draws popular legal consciousness closer to that of the state, while at the same time encountering resistance from localized organizations and moralities which assert the autonomous right to define and enforce justice."[203] Throughout the advanced stages of apartheid's endgame, "enclaves of revenge controlled by militarized youth and punitive elders continued to shape the character of justice in the townships of South Africa."[204] This is not surprising. As has been argued above, fears of victimhood reverberated throughout society. Moreover, the appreciation of law, whether legitimate or not, is never even in a society. Even advanced industrialized democracies including the United States (e.g., the Oklahoma City bombing), Germany (*Rote Armee Fraktion*), Italy (Red Brigades), Spain (*Euskadi Ta Askatasuna*), and Great Britain (*Irish Republican Army*) have faced violent challenges to what majorities in these countries have considered legitimate law.[205] It would be unreasonable to expect that society emerging from sustained authoritarianism, such as South Africa, burdened with deeply ingrained identities of group and countergroup membership, would *as a whole* converge on moral justifications within the span of a few years.

Wilson argues further that the "transfer of values from an elite to the masses was uneven and equivocal."[206] Inasmuch as the TRC did not reach as many South Africans as is often claimed, this critique seems disingenuous. Wilson criticizes the TRC for an overload of functions that it sought to serve but is himself guilty of an overload of expectations. That the transfer of values was uneven and equivocal is unsurprising considering what could have happened had apartheid's endgame gone awry. In the country's townships and squatter settlements, the prerogative state left a far deeper impression than the normative state ever could. Although black elites, like those working in law offices in downtown Johannesburg, had some access to the institutions of the normative state (and could thus remember the value of law), these institutions were all but inaccessible to the black masses on the ground. This notwithstanding, a surprising number of black South Africans vested confidence in the legal system under apartheid. Furthermore, the evidence that this legal system "could generate results that did not serve apartheid's interests, as well as the evidence that men and women devoted to the law could also be profoundly committed to the struggle against apartheid, could well have played a part in Africans' judgments about law's potential, and so in the legitimation not of the existing legal system but of the value of the rule of law in a future South Africa," which is precisely the argument advanced in this chapter.[207]

---

[203] Wilson, *The Politics of Truth and Reconciliation in South Africa*, p. xx.

[204] Wilson, *The Politics of Truth and Reconciliation in South Africa*, p. xx.

[205] See, for example, Donatella della Porta, *Social Movements, Political Violence, and the State: A Comparative Analysis of Italy and Germany* (Cambridge: Cambridge University Press, 1995); and Philip B. Heymann, *Terrorism and America: A Commonsense Strategy for a Democratic Society* (Cambridge, MA: MIT Press, 1998).

[206] Wilson, *The Politics of Truth and Reconciliation in South Africa*, p. 227.

[207] Ellmann, "Law and Legitimacy in South Africa," p. 477.

Put succinctly, legality brought about the transition to democracy and the transition to democracy brought about legitimacy.

The Idea of the State

This chapter has demonstrated how the state shaped, even reconstituted, preferences in apartheid's endgame, with particular reference to the surviving overhang of legal norms and institutions. In this section, it continues to explain why the state mattered. It turns from institutional explanation to explaining institutions, addressing the second part of what Peter Gourevitch has termed the "governance problem" in political science.[208] The governance problem arises when in strategic interactions both preferences and institutions are in flux. So far, the analysis in this chapter has held the state constant and has taken only a snapshot picture of its role. The necessary conditions for the state's role in apartheid's endgame, however, have their origins in the long-run development of the state (see Chapters 4 and 5).[209] What follows is a brief analysis of the transformation of the state, as perceived by interacting agents. It chronicles the state's transformation from *predator* to *prize* to *solution*, embedding the snapshot explanation in the moving reel of history.[210] As Timothy Mitchell has noted, the distinction "between abstract and real needs placing in historical question if we are to grasp how the modern state has appeared."[211] The following discussion links the analysis in this chapter with the content of earlier chapters.

The State as Problem

We have seen that the apartheid project was erected on the foundation of extraordinary state strength. The early stages of South Africa's strong-state path to democracy saw the early expansion of governmental capacity and the government's entry into the zone of authoritarianism under the auspices of a

---

[208] Gourevitch, "The Governance Problem in International Relations," pp. 137.

[209] As Margaret Levi writes, "The sources of present beliefs are past experiences and practices. Prior institutions, prior strategies, and prior actions delimit current options, and stories of yesteryears reveal what bargains have been broken and which kept." Levi, *Consent, Dissent, and Patriotism*, p. 3.

[210] Peter Evans's useful distinction of the state as problem and as solution is here amended with a third category: the state as prize. See Peter Evans, "The State as Problem and Solution: Predation, Embedded Autonomy, and Structural Change," in Stephan Haggard and Robert R. Kaufman, eds., *The Politics of Economic Adjustment: International Constraints, Distributive Conflicts, and the State* (Princeton: Princeton University Press, 1992), pp. 139–181; and idem., *Embedded Autonomy: States and Industrial Transformation* (Princeton: Princeton University Press, 1995).

[211] Timothy Mitchell, "The Limits of the State: Beyond Statist Approaches and their Critics," *American Political Science Review*, Vol. 85, No. 1 (March 1991), p. 95. For Robert Bates, the problem of institutional origins "stands at the very frontier of the field of political economy." See his "Macropolitical Economy in the Field of Development," in James E. Alt and Kenneth A. Shepsle, eds., *Perspectives on Positive Political Economy* (Cambridge: Cambridge University Press, 1990), p. 48.

predominantly prerogative state. The decline of the normative state in this period meant that the individuals and groups involved in the struggle against apartheid perceived the state primarily as a problem. In the eyes of the democracy-demanding forces, the state was synonymous with the regime and government.

The State as Prize

In the wake of the Soweto uprising, however, the state's strength declined. Organized civil disobedience and the defiance campaign of the 1980s further circumscribed its reach. Interestingly, the weakening of the state set in motion a paradigm shift in terms of perceptions regarding its utility as a social institution. Important planks of the apartheid state survived democratization almost entirely intact primarily because key agents in this period came to recognize their value. It is "important to look at whether actors who are initially on the periphery themselves become invested in the prevailing institutions and if so, in what ways. In such cases, shifts in the balance of power that go their way may result in institutional conversion rather than breakdown."[212] This important observation helps us to understand the state as a conceptual variable in apartheid's endgame. Consider also the remark that "institutions will be stable only if undergirded by organizations with a stake in their perpetuation."[213] This is precisely what transpired in apartheid's endgame.

Interacting agents preserved the state because they came to regard it as the prize to be won. The NP expected "apartheid to be replaced by a society in which existing institutions are stripped of their racial basis but are preserved – and in which 'First World' values and rights are entrenched."[214] As far as the ANC was concerned, the state was no longer a behemoth to be overthrown. "The fusion of state and regime," as one analyst put it, "was broken."[215] The regime, from the perspective of the ANC and its allies, needed changing, but the state needed preserving.[216] Both sides were aware "that continued

[212] Kathleen Thelen, "How Institutions Evolve: Insights from Comparative-Historical Analysis," in James Mahoney and Dietrich Rueschemeyer, eds., *Comparative Historical Analysis in the Social Sciences* (Cambridge: Cambridge University Press, 2003), p. 34.

[213] Douglass North, "Epilogue: Economic Performance through Time," in Lee J. Alston, Thráinn Eggertsson, and Douglass C. North, eds., *Empirical Studies in Institutional Change* (Cambridge: Cambridge University Press, 1996), p. 353.

[214] Steven Friedman, *The Shapers of Things to Come? National Party Choices in the South African Transition*, Research Report No. 22, Transition Series (Johannesburg: Centre for Policy Studies, 1992), p. 1.

[215] Hennie J. Kotzé, "South Africa: From Apartheid to Democracy," in Mattei Dogan and John Higley, eds., *Elites, Crises, and the Origins of Regimes* (Lanham, MD: Rowman and Littlefield, 1998), p. 223.

[216] For evidence, consult the controversial ANC document African National Congress, *The State and Social Transformation*, unpublished discussion document (November 1996). The document with its neoliberal bent caused a stir within the tripartite liberation alliance. For a discussion of the document's reception, see Hein Marais, "Leader of the Pack," *Leadership* (Johannesburg) (August 1997), pp. 52–63. SACP leaders Blade Nzimande and Jeremy Cronin in particular

stalemate will force the collapse of services. Civics know this could alienate residents – and make a new local government system impossible to run."[217] The state also needed preserving from the perspective of the NP. From the beginning, segregation and apartheid had been deeply intertwined with state formation.[218] Apartheid's endgame proved no different. It was the utility of the state, and its normative legacies, that served democracy. Thus in apartheid's endgame, members had an incentive to care about institutional preservation. As a result, the state had force. The usable state was useful: "Throughout the process [apartheid's endgame] both incumbent and challenging elites were guided by a strategic perspective which assigned a pivotal role to themselves. For the NP it was about retaining control of the state, and for the ANC in its 'war of position' it was about capturing these very positions albeit incrementally."[219]

The State as Solution

The claim that the surviving South African state bestowed on the regime a considerable capacity to govern relative to many democratizing states (especially most African states), however, should not distract from the reality that the post-apartheid state is not a perfect state.[220] The problem of crime stands out and undermines the positive externalities that both legality and bureaucracy, as the variables that underwrote the cooperative solution of apartheid's endgame, have produced.[221] In short, although the usable state helped solve various problems of democratic transition, it has not yet proved the solution to many problems of democratic consolidation. This, however, does not damage the principal argument of this book: that the apartheid state was, in an important respect, necessary for making democracy work in South Africa.

Consider in this context also the conviction of Colonel Eugene de Kock, the former commander of *Vlakplaas*, a leading covert unit operating under the

criticized the document for sliding "into a technocratic, 'class-neutral' approach to politics" and "promoting a passive, regulatory pragmatism." Marais, "Leader of the Pack," p. 58.

[217] Friedman, *The Shapers of Things to Come?*, p. 24.

[218] See Chapter 4. See also Price, "Apartheid and White Supremacy," p. 309.

[219] Pierre du Toit and Hennie Kotze, "The South African State in Transition, 1990–2000," Paper presented at the 18th International Political Science Association World Congress, Quebec, Canada, August 1–5, 2000, p. 7; and idem., "The State, Civil Society, and Democratic Transition in South Africa: A Survey of Elite Attitudes," *Journal of Conflict Resolution*, Vol. 39, No. 1 (March 1995), pp. 27–48.

[220] Khehla Shubane, "A Question of Balance," in Steven Friedman and Riaan de Villiers, eds., *The Right Thing: Two Perspectives on Public Order and Human Rights in South Africa's Emerging Democracy*, Research Report No. 64 (Johannesburg: Centre for Policy Studies, 1998), p. 13.

[221] For an incisive, anthropological perspective on the topic of crime – and the related topic of policing – in South Africa by the leading scholars on the subject, see John Comaroff and Jean Comaroff, "Policing Culture, Cultural Policing: Law and Social Order in Postcolonial South Africa," *Law and Society Review*, Vol. 29, No. 3 (Summer 2004), pp. 513–545. For a policy-oriented account, see Mark Shaw, *Crime and Policing in Post-Apartheid South Africa: Transforming under Fire* (Bloomington: Indiana University Press, 2002).

guises of the prerogative state. In late 1996, de Kock was sentenced to 212 years in prison. The proceeding, the most important criminal trial in the country's short democratic history, illustrated "the limits of the limits" of the post-apartheid state in the sense that it underlined the capacity and profes- sionalism that are inherent in the criminal justice system despite the many problems that have befallen the investigation and prosecution of ordinary crime in South Africa. The speedy conviction of de Kock was another important milestone on the path toward legitimate law. In sum, legality and bureaucracy, even if compromised by corruption and other ills, greatly improved the chances of democracy's constitution in apartheid's endgame. Consider this observation by Dennis Wrong, who sets the record straight on Max Weber:

Weber is quite frequently accused of overestimating the rationality and efficiency of bureaucracy and of ignoring the clogging effects of "red tape," the petty conservatism of officials, and the operation of such processes as "Parkinson's Law" that "work expands so as to fill the time available for its completion". These objections are irrel- evant to Weber's analysis. Of course individual bureaucracies are often top-heavy, inefficient, and slow-moving. The point remains that most of the activities of bureau- cracies could not under modern conditions even be carried out badly by nonbureau- cratic organizations.[222]

Following in the Weberian tradition, Wrong contends:

Without a bureaucratic organization it would be impossible to collect taxes from tens of millions of people according to a graduated scale prescribed in advance. Nor could a variety of highly complicated machines and specialized human skills be coordinated to manufacture large quantities of standardized product. These tasks may be carried out with varying degrees of efficiency by different bureaucratic organizations, but they could not be essayed at all except by an organization possessing the main structural features of bureaucracy: job specialization, a hierarchy of authority, detailed rules and regulations, and impersonal relations among co-workers.[223]

Wrong's exegesis is corroborated by Reinhard Bendix, the German refugee scholar and leading interpreter of Weber's writings: "[C]ontrary to many interpretations, Weber did not maintain that bureaucratic organizations operate as efficiently as 'slot machines.' He said, rather, that such organiza- tions operate more efficiently than alternative systems of administration and that they increase their efficiency to the extent that they 'depersonalize' the execution of official tasks."[224] It has been this book's principal argument that a relative high degree of formal legal rationalization proved beneficial to democratization in South Africa. There these attributes served as centripetal forces, pulling interacting agents closer together at the center of the political stage. In South Africa, the dual state, generated as a social institution by the

[222] Dennis H. Wrong, "Introduction: Max Weber," in idem., ed., *Max Weber* (New Jersey: Prentice-Hall, 1970), pp. 33–34.
[223] Wrong, "Introduction: Max Weber," pp. 33–34.
[224] Bendix, *Max Weber*, p. 422.

functional demands of "separate development," successfully perpetuated itself, *qua* law, into a future whose functional imperatives were radically changing.[225] Most important, the apartheid state, in the minds of key opposition agents, underwent a transformation from problem to prize to solution in the course of democratization. So much for the structural account, but what difference did agents make? How did leadership matter?

THE LIVES OF THE LAW

In what sense can leaders help solve endgame situations? In general, to solve problems of collective action – situations in which rational agents are unlikely to succeed in cooperating on mutual advantage – leaders "must change individual preferences (or more generally attitudes), or change beliefs (including expectations) or inject resources (very probably knowledge, or new technology like guns) into the group so as to make its members' efforts more productive."[226] What was the role of leadership in apartheid's endgame, and how did it affect the role of law?

Mandela's Law

The law firm of Mandela and Tambo opened in August 1952. It was located in Chancellor House, a picturesque old building near the magistrates' courts in the downtown area of Johannesburg. Mandela and Oliver Tambo are figures of historical proportions in the ANC. Near their office, in the same building, worked Walter Sisulu, another of the founding fathers of the struggle against apartheid. He ran the ANC headquarters from Chancellor House.[227] Mandela, Tambo, and Sisulu dominated apartheid's endgame. All three were trained as lawyers, practiced as lawyers, and reasoned like lawyers. All three honed their legal skills in the courts of Johannesburg. Mandela delivered one of the most memorable performances of his life as a lawyer in the notorious Rivonia Trial. This is how Albie Sachs, the Constitutional Court judge, estimates the significance of Mandela's performance:

When Mandela made his famous denunciation of South African justice at his first trial after his capture, he did so with an elegance that enriched the patrimony of English usage in South Africa and, utilizing the principles and procedures of South African law to the full, he turned RDL [Roman Dutch Law] into a weapon of attack. His basic critique of the legal system was *not* that it was Roman Dutch Law but that it was racist. Thus he did *not* object to having courts with trained judges, to written laws, to defence and prosecution lawyers doing battle with each other according to defined procedures, but to the fact that he felt he was a black person in a white person's court; the laws were

[225] Stephen D. Krasner, "Approaches to the State: Alternative Conceptions and Historical Dynamics," *Comparative Politics*, Vol. 16, No. 2 (January 1984), pp. 223–246.

[226] Michael Taylor, *The Possibility of Cooperation* (Cambridge: Cambridge University Press, 1987), p. 24.

[227] Sampson, *Mandela*, p. 78.

made by the whites and administered by the whites in a courtroom that breathed the atmosphere of white domination, and this should not be so.[228]

Tom Lodge, the doyen of resistance scholarship, like Sachs and I, emphasizes the critical – and largely overlooked – importance of Mandela's grounding in, and respect for, the law:

One especially significant instance of the continuities in his political beliefs was his conviction that reasoned discussion would eventually broker what he himself would eventually describe as a "legal revolution". Legal training and practice had a crucial impact upon Mandela's political development. In general, historians of anti-colonial movements have paid insufficient attention to the influence of colonial legal ideas on African nationalist leadership. Mandela's life is an especially striking demonstration of the ways in which ideas about human rights and civic obligations were shaped by his professional training. Most importantly, the structured world of courtroom procedure itself shaped Mandela's political practice, restraining it even in its most theatrically insurgent phases, and reinforcing his respect for institutions, traditions, and history.[229]

Mandela also understood the importance of bureaucracy. At Fort Hare, he professed interest in an administrative position: "I could not resist the glitter of a civil service career."[230]

This suggests that elements of the state *per se* were something for which key ANC leaders had respect, even admiration – even during apartheid. Although in apartheid's endgame there was "too little mutual familiarity with the style, culture and procedures of the opposing parties," and instead a pervasive tradition of "prescription and confrontation, of thesis and antithesis, of all or nothing," the legal education of the senior ANC elite, and their belief in the utility of *some* elements of the state, were crucial in different bargaining situations (recall the critique of the TRC as being excessively legal).[231]

Mandela's "rhetorical largesse" contributed significantly to his status as the indispensable elder statesman. No one would deny the extraordinary leadership that Mandela has provided throughout apartheid's endgame, and its prehistory as described in Chapters 4 and 5. Yet, it is important not to succumb to the personality cult surrounding the elder statesman. Inasmuch as Mandela moved bargaining forward, he also complicated strategic interaction at times. In the case of escalating violence in KwaZulu-Natal, Mandela hindered, rather than helped, the situation. But let us turn to another important point that warrants consideration.

It would be wrong to focus all the attention on Mandela, as he relied heavily on advisors in the wings. Once such confidant was current President Thabo Mbeki, whose political influence rose dramatically after the 1994 national

---

[228] Sachs, "The Future of Roman Dutch Law in a Non-Racial Democratic South Africa," pp. 218–219. Emphases added.
[229] Tom Lodge, *Mandela: A Critical Life* (Oxford: Oxford University Press, 2006), p. viii.
[230] Quoted in Sampson, *Mandela*, p. 27.
[231] Willem de Klerk, *F W de Klerk: The Man in His Time* (Johannesburg: Jonathan Ball, 1991), p. 166. The author, a liberal journalist, is the former President's brother.

democratic elections. Mbeki was Mandela's "Mr. Fix-It."[232] Mbeki was in charge of much government policy, and his appointment as Deputy President over Cyril Ramaphosa after the 1994 national democratic elections *de facto* decided who would succeed Mandela as leader of the fledgling democracy. As second in command, Mbeki moved economic planning into his office. Some suggest that he installed a weak labor minister in the first administration, Stella Sigcau, to keep control of the country's privatization agenda.[233] "Mbeki has effectively taken over the burden of governing," says van Zyl Slabbert. "The old man [Mandela] is still the boss, but he's delegated extraordinary powers to Thabo."[234] But other men mattered as well. In fact, Mandela likened his government role to that of a chairman of a company board. The "power barons within the ANC, such as Cyril Ramaphosa, Kader Asmal, and Mac Maharaj, shared a view of the presidency which downplayed the inherent powers of the office ... "[235] With this information, we are in a better position to understand the leadership dimension in apartheid's endgame. The discussion so far has revealed two things: first, Mandela was a more complicated leader than is often presumed; second, Mandela's leadership rested on many shoulders within the ANC. From this follows that it would be misleading to explain apartheid's endgame solely in terms of extraordinary leadership. As outlined at the beginning of this chapter, the literature on democratization in South Africa relies heavily on methodological individualism. Most scholars assume that it is both desirable and possible to explain apartheid's endgame in terms of the individuals that partook in it. This practice, however, is insufficient to come to explanation. It turns out that leadership was not always extraordinary in the ANC, and furthermore, it was not always a singular effort; more often it was a concerted one. And neither was the NP leadership alone responsible for the outcome explained here.

De Klerk's Law

The Afrikaner most frequently credited with moving interactions from confrontation to cooperation is Roelf Meyer, the NP's chief constitutional negotiator. De Klerk appointed Meyer secretary-general of the National Party apparently in recognition of Meyer's talents.[236] Bargaining at the second-level, between Meyer and his interlocutor Ramaphosa, proved critical in the endgame.[237] Although Meyer became regarded as a sellout within his own party (this later

---

[232] Joseph Contreras, "Mandela's Mr. Fix-It," *Newsweek*, March 20, 1995, p. 21.

[233] Ray Hartley, "Who's in Charge Anyway?," *Sunday Times* (Johannesburg), June 2, 1996, p. 23.

[234] Contreras, "Mandela's Mr. Fix-It," p. 21.

[235] Robert Schrire, "The Myth of the 'Mandela' Presidency," *Indicator South Africa*, Vol. 13, No. 2 (Autumn 1996), p. 16.

[236] This is the version of events as reported by de Klerk, *The Last Trek*, p. 358.

[237] On Meyer, see, for example, Waldmeir, *Anatomy of a Miracle*, pp. 206–218. For a portrait of another Afrikaner leader, P. W. Botha, see Deon Geldenhuys and Hennie Kotzé, "Man of Action," *Leadership*, Vol. 4, No. 2 (1985), pp. 30–47.

prompted him to leave the NP), his committed, unemotional leadership behind the scenes was on par with the skillful negotiators Mbeki and Ramaphosa.

De Klerk, in turn, like Mandela, was at times problem *and* solution. His hesitation to curb alleged "Third Force" activities under the auspices of the prerogative state almost derailed the endgame. In July 1991, the *Weekly Mail* reported a security police operation involved in the funding of Inkatha rallies and an Inkatha trade union, *Uwusa*, to rival the ANC and COSATU. "Inkathagate," as the scandal became known, illustrates the limits of Afrikaner leadership. De Klerk was reluctant to investigate covert activities of the security forces. This inaction certainly worsened de Klerk's relationship with Mandela. Mandela began to doubt de Klerk's motives and reconsidered the ANC's decision to abandon the armed struggle. "The ANC leader never forgave de Klerk for what he saw as an unpardonable sin: a callous indifference to the loss of black life, coupled with a willingness to play politics with death."[238]

From the start, the relationship between the two leaders was strained. On the first day of CODESA I, de Klerk publicly criticized the ANC for reneging on agreements, and for having violated the National Peace Accord by maintaining *Umkhonto we Sizwe* as a private army, and for stalling the demobilization of their cadres. Mandela retaliated in kind, accusing de Klerk and the government at a public press conference of a double agenda, of negotiating while funding covert organizations.[239] The exchange turned strategic interaction sour. Indeed, as Mandela writes, "much trust had been lost."[240] How was this trust recuperated in the endgame?

Voluntaristic explanations of apartheid's endgame gloss over a simple, yet consequential question: What explains the continuation of cooperation in the face of grave commitment problems and intense personal mistrust? Mandela repeatedly emphasized the strains, and the mistrust, in his relationship with de Klerk. "By the time CODESA 2 opened on 15 May 1992," he notes, "the prospects for agreement looked bleak. What we disagreed about was threatening all that we had agreed upon. Mr de Klerk and I had not managed to find a consensus on most of the outstanding issues."[241]

We know relatively little about de Klerk apart from his public persona.[242] His autobiography is largely elusive. His brother offers some insight: "FW's charisma lies in his rationality, logic, and balance. He has sincerity, persuasiveness, serenity and juristic preciseness, and these have undoubtedly contributed to his gravitas."[243] De Klerk was, interestingly, in many respects a

---

[238] Waldmeir, *Anatomy of a Miracle*, p. 187.

[239] Mandela, *Long Walk to Freedom*, p. 589.

[240] Mandela, *Long Walk to Freedom*, p. 589.

[241] Mandela, *Long Walk to Freedom*, p. 594.

[242] For a biographical essay, see Hennie Kotzé and Deon Geldenhuys, "Damascus Road," *Leadership*, Vol. 9, No. 6 (1990), pp. 12–28.

[243] De Klerk, *F W de Klerk*, p. 138.

mirror image of Mandela. Both men were lawyers and, as Mandela himself likes to emphasize, both men stem from families with power.[244]

A Truly Common Law

This is an opportune moment in which to consider, by way of an excursus, one question that I have not yet addressed head on: What role for the common law?[245] Was there anything intrinsic to this *particular* legal tradition, and South Africa's inheritance thereof, that can help further explain why things were "not all so much worse" in South Africa, to reprise Mureinik's provocative question?[246] One answer has to do with the country's legal tradition, for as one scholar points out, "South African common law [has] in many respects [been] decidedly supportive of human rights and South African statutory law has patently been directed at undercutting such rights."[247]

Although a comprehensive analysis is beyond the scope of this book, a number of features of South Africa's common law heritage (in this mixed legal system) come to mind that preserved a commitment to law, and contributed to containing the prerogative state.[248] I shall focus here on three of these features: (1) the doctrine of statutory interpretation; (2) the notion of fundamental rights; (3) and the principle of reasonableness.

Statutory Interpretation

First, the doctrine of statutory interpretation deserves a closer look. "Although apartheid was pervasive and affected all aspects of life," writes Chaskalson, "there were still areas of the law in which moral judges had an important role to play. This was particularly so in matters regulated by the common law."[249] What were these areas? We gain a quick answer from Mureinik, who thus provides a response to his own provocation:

[A]s the original module of apartheid statutes was augmented by more of the same, and as the cluster of statutes hardened into a substantial body of law, the argument that that body generated principles powerful enough to demand a place in the interpretive set

---

[244] Mandela apparently made much of this similar political genealogy. See Waldmeir, *Anatomy of a Miracle*, pp. 19–20.

[245] I am grateful to one of the anonymous reviewers for pushing me to elaborate on the *specific* contribution of South Africa's common law tradition to ensuring law's facilitative role in times of transition. On the argument that South Africa evolved "not one new system of common law but two," and the interaction of both with customary law, see Chanock, "Reconstructing South African Law," p. 105. For a fuller account, see idem., *The Making of South African Legal Culture.*

[246] Mureinik, "Emerging from Emergency," p. 1980.

[247] Ellmann, *In a Time of Trouble*, p. 49.

[248] I will sidestep herein the question as to the morality of South African jurists' participation in the apartheid legal system, which consumed – and partially divided – the country's legal profession in the 1980s.

[249] Chaskalson, "From Wickedness to Equality," p. 592.

might have been thought to have gained plausibility. But even when apartheid statutes were at their most abundant, they never constituted more than a small fraction of the materials in a South African law library. That, of course, is obviously a very crude measure of their significance. But it does suggest the point of substance: that there are immense tracts of South African law uncontaminated by the principles that apartheid statutes would generate, if they could.[250]

Mureinik proceeds to elucidate swiftly the real word consequences of these uncontaminated tracts of South African law:

South African judges almost always take it for granted that every racial distinction requires statutory justification, usually express. In the absence of such, they enforce contracts, and remedy delicts, and strike down administrative decisions, and administer companies, and protect property, and enforce statutory duties, and apply rules of court, on the unquestioned premise that the race of the parties before them is irrelevant. Routinely they affirm conceptions of the equal treatment of individuals which are quite discordant with the theory underlying apartheid statutes; whether consciously, such as when they strike down by-laws and regulations for partial or unequal treatment, or unconsciously, such, perhaps, as when they apply the doctrine of precedent.[251]

In a somewhat self-serving, but nevertheless accurate, way, Justice Corbett, whom we encountered earlier, elaborates on Mureinik's argument from the perspective of the bench in his submission to the TRC:

[The courts] were legitimately applying the principles of Roman-Dutch law relating to statutory interpretation, which included the presumption that the legislature did not intend to oust the jurisdiction of a court of law, or to interfere with the common law more than was plainly and unambiguously indicated; the presumption against retro-activity; the presumption that the legislature did not intend an inequitable, unjustifiable or unreasonable result; the restrictive interpretation given to penal provisions and the presumption *in favorem libertatis*; and so on. I could quote many examples illustrative of the application of this approach to statutory interpretation in the so-called "apartheid years", but this would unduly protract this presentation. Thus, generally speaking, our courts did by a process of interpretation ameliorate in many instances the effect of harsh laws.[252]

For case law bearing out this assessment, see my jurisprudential analysis in Chapter 6. Related is the proposition that South African lawyers have been

---

[250] Mureinik, "Dworkin and Apartheid," p. 207.

[251] Mureinik, "Dworkin and Apartheid," pp. 207–208. In his chapter, Mureinik engages Dworkin's philosophy of law, in particular the derivative argument that once it has become sufficiently entrenched in law, immorality (or iniquity) will continue to spread (what Mureinik terms Dworkin's "apartheid-as-cancer argument"). It is interesting to note, in an aside, that Dworkin actually played a minor role in apartheid's endgame. While still Professor of Jurisprudence at the University of Oxford, Dworkin convened, in June 1989, a conference for South African judges and lawyers and their counterparts at the ANC, which was still banned at the time. See Edwin Cameron, Gilbert Marcus, and Dirk Van Zyl Smit, "The Administration of Justice, Law Reform and Jurisprudence," *Annual Survey of South African Law* (1989), p. 556.

[252] M. M. Corbett, "Presentation to the Truth and Reconciliation Commission," reprinted in *South African Law Journal*, Vol. 115, No. 1 (1998), p. 18.

reared in a culture of justification, "where a principle is a justification, not merely an explanation."[253] Apartheid law, noted Mureinik, did not provide principles, which is why the common law was able to retain its influence in the twentieth century. The late legal scholar once again made his case eloquently: "[A]partheid statutes do not press themselves upon the interpreter consolidated; they come to him scattered amongst the content of the departments of law on which they trench, and diluted by that content. That is yet another impediment in the way of their generating interpretive principles fit for the best set," which for Mureinik was contained in the country's rich common law tradition.[254]

If we follow this argument, apartheid law (which I take in this context solely to be the body of discriminatory legislation passed by parliament) was "not all so much worse" for the country because, in a way, it did not shape up: it was incapable of producing legal principles. Apartheid statutes, on this view, lacked the *gravitas* that centuries of common law provided, and which generations of jurists studied in South Africa. Adds the renegade lawyer, apartheid statutes' "underlying principles, if such they be, are devoid of justifying power."[255]

Precisely because the doctrine of statutory interpretation loomed large in South Africa's common law tradition, it was possible for judges to use the discretionary power that was bestowed on them in the process of statutory interpretation to constrain the apartheid state. For as Dugard and others, with good reason, insisted, "a statute will often be ambiguous and thus not determine an answer to particular questions of interpretation. Judges have to answer those questions in accordance with their sense of justice and the common law supplies the values which should inform their decision."[256] Irrespective as to whether the majority, or merely a minority, of judges used these values to answer "those questions," and how much importance we want to accord to this argument in the first place, it is undeniable that in South Africa, "a country in which white

[253] For a critical, yet constructive appraisal of Mureinik's argument, and its implications for post-apartheid South Africa, see David Dyzenhaus, "Law as Justification: Etienne Mureinik's Conception of Legal Culture," *South African Journal on Human Rights*, Vol. 14, No. 1 (1998), pp. 11–37.
[254] Mureinik, "Dworkin and Apartheid," p. 209.
[255] Mureinik, "Dworkin and Apartheid," p. 208.
[256] Dyzenhaus, "Law as Justification," pp. 13–14. Of, course, as we have seen the power of discretion is a neutral resource: it can be deployed against, but also in support, of an authoritarian regime. See also Dyzenhaus, *Hard Cases in Wicked Legal Systems*. On the related debate over the ills of legal positivism in South Africa, which occupied legal scholars for two decades, see, for example, ibid.; as well as, most important, Dugard, *Human Rights and the South African Legal Order*, esp. 391–402; the latter's inaugural lecture at the University of the Witwatersrand, "Judicial Process, Positivism and Civil Liberty," *South African Law Journal*, Vol. 88, No. 2 (May 1971), pp. 181–200; a dissenting response ten years later by Christopher Forsyth and Johann Schiller, "Judicial Process, Positivism and Civil Liberty II," *South African Law Journal*, Vol. 98, No. 2 (May 1981), pp. 218–230; and a retort by John Dugard, "Some Realism about the Judicial Process and Positivism – A Reply," *South African Law Journal*, Vol. 98, No. 3 (August 1981), pp. 372–387.

oppression of blacks never ceased,"[257] it was the common law that made it, early and notably, in *Rex v. Abdurahman*,

the duty of the Courts to hold the scales evenly between the different classes of the community and to declare invalid any practice which, in the absence of the authority of an Act of Parliament, results in partial and unequal treatment to a substantial degree between different sections of the community.[258]

Fundamental Rights

Further illustrative of the fact that these common law values truly *did* inform the jurisprudence of South Africa's apartheid courts is, in addition to the cases already discussed, *Mandela v. Minister of Prisons*, in which the court held that government officials are *not* authorized to abolish, by subordinate legislation, such as regulations, fundamental common law rights unless the legislature bestowed this authority – "in the clearest language" – on the executive.[259] This ties in with the notion of fundamental rights that gradually calcified into doctrine in the jurisprudence of South Africa's Appellate Division.

The court's insistence in *Mandela* on the rule requiring specific authority is indicative of the recognition of a doctrine of fundamental rights by the highest court. "In other words, an inferior law that destroys a fundamental right is *intra vires* its empowering statute only if that statute, whether expressly or impliedly, specifically envisages the destruction of that fundamental right by an inferior law and, although this almost inevitably follows, acquiesces in that destruction. We might call this version of the doctrine that protects fundamental rights the rule requiring specific authority."[260] The content of the category of fundamental rights, and the boundaries of this category, was not always readily apparent in the common law of South Africa. Yet a growing pile of case law gradually carved out a niche – in spite of the notorious judgments in *Omar* and *Staatspresident* – for the right to counsel and the right to be heard, both longstanding common law rights. I will content myself with a brief inquiry into the position of the latter in South Africa's legal landscape.

---

[257] Ellmann, "Legal Text and Lawyers' Culture in South Africa," p. 401.
[258] *Rex v. Abdurahman* 1950 (3) SA 136 (A), at 145. *Abdurahman*, particularly in this passage, also shines light on another common law principle: that of equality, as well as on its cousin, liberty. On the latter, see the dissenting opinion by Judge Nestadt in *Tshwete v. Minister of Home Affairs* 1988 (4) SA 586 (A), at 612 (Nestadt JA, dissenting), proclaiming, "where a statute is reasonably capable of more than one meaning, a Court will give it the meaning which *least interferes* with the liberty of the individual;" that "a strict construction is placed on statutory provisions which interfere with elementary rights;" that "a statute is not presumed to take away prior existing rights;" and that "an interpretation which avoids harshness and injustice will, if possible be adopted." Emphased added.
[259] *Mandela v. Minister of Prisons* 1983 (1) SA 938 (A) at 959. For a subtle analysis of *Mandela*, which, he says, both fosters the doctrine of fundamental rights, *and* stunts it, see Etienne Mureinik, "Fundamental Rights and Delegated Legislation," *South African Journal of Human Rights*, Vol. 1, No. 2 (August 1985), pp. 111–123.
[260] Mureinik, "Fundamental Rights and Delegated Legislation," pp. 112. Emphases added.

It is an established principle of the common law that government officials taking judicial action must give the person at whom the action is directed an adequate opportunity of being heard. This right to be heard – expressed in the Latin maxim *audi alteram partem* – came to be affirmed as "a fundamental right" in the otherwise appalling appellate case of *Omar*.[261] Here we once more catch a glimpse of the dual-natured state: "So ... in a country where detention without trial has been widespread, common law principle obliges the state to give a hearing to those whose rights it proposes to impair."[262] This right derived from the principle *audi alteram partem* is interesting because it reflects a "core" common law protection (itself derived from natural law principles) that is also at play in the due process provisions in the constitutional law of the United States, as set out in the Fifth Amendment and the Fourteenth Amendment (the latter known as the "Due Process Clause").

Others concur with the overall argument, demonstrating the import of the notion of fundamental rights for the doctrine of statutory interpretation in South Africa. For example, Chaskalson reminds us that "principles of equality and liberty immanent in Roman-Dutch law formed part of South African common law. The common law doctrine of statutory interpretation required statutes to be interpreted, where possible, *consistently with such principles.* Thus, there was room for moral decisions in the development and application of the common law, in the interpretation and application of statutes not directly affected by apartheid, and even, though to a limited extent, in the interpretation and application of apartheid laws."[263] The continued (if not necessarily consistent) reliance by select judges on the common law regularly reequilibrated – and reinforced – the significance of law as common knowledge. Some of the judgments that accomplished this feat I showcased above. Let us finally consider a third feature of the common law that proved salient in South Africa, the principle of reasonableness.

Reasonableness

One prominent lawyer in the run-up to apartheid's endgame predicted that "we will come to appreciate that we owe much to our judges, and a great deal to some. For despite all the paradoxes they have somehow held to the infrastructure and have kept alive the principles of freedom and justice which permeate the common law."[264] The principle of reasonableness was one of the institutions of the common law that lived on under apartheid. In *Abdurahman*, for instance, the Appellate Division found that by-laws are unreasonable if "they are found to be partial and unequal in their operation as between

---

[261] See *Omar v. Minister of Law and Order* 1987 (3) SA 859 (A), at 893. On the pre-history of *audi alteram partem* in South Africa's appellate jurisprudence, and its contested standing, see C. S. Forsyth, *In Danger for Their Talents*, pp. 111–126.
[262] Ellmann, "Legal Text and Lawyers' Culture in South Africa," p. 401.
[263] Chaskalson, "From Wickedness to Equality," p. 594. Emphases added.
[264] Chaskalson, "Law in a Changing Society," p. 295.

different classes."[265] The appellate judges quickly extended the doctrine of
unreasonableness as a ground for review from the domain of legislative action to
that of administrative action, entrenching further this common law principle.[266]
Haysom and Plasket, too, have shown that apartheid courts were, by and large,
"testing regulations for reasonableness and certainty and determining that the
regulations complied with the implied restrictions on the exercise if administrative powers developed in our case law."[267] In other words, although the
principle in question, like the related principle of fairness, did not leave an
imprint on all judgments in every jurisdiction, it was "nonetheless acknowledged and reinforced in numerous judgments of the courts. That is an important
legacy and one which deserves neither to be diminished nor squandered."[268]
Neither Mandela nor de Klerk did.

This supplementary account of the meaning of the common law helps us to
understand how Mandela and de Klerk, and some of their brethren, overcame
the mistrust between them. It brings us back to the normative state, and the
legacies thereof, which were meaningful to *both* of our leading lawyers for the
reasons outlined a moment ago. For the common law was impressed upon
both Mandela and de Klerk in law school. For a practicing lawyer, there was
no escaping its internalization. It is these legacies that made the common law a
truly *common* law. What were the consequences of this – the institutional
structure of the apartheid state – for the creation and maintenance of trust in
apartheid's endgame?

Recent advances in game theory have shown that trust can arise between
nonaltruistic agents in iterated settings.[269] As per the theoretical model of this
book, confidence in institutions – namely, the state – generates trust in persons.
Trust in persons then generates more confidence in institutions, thereby
making democracy work. Put differently, the confidence to trust influences the
choice between confrontation and cooperation. These mechanisms represent
accurately the dynamics of contention in apartheid's endgame.

The normative overhang of the apartheid state inspired confidence in its
utility. Because "the South African state was based on structures that had legal
form," both de Klerk and Mandela were predisposed, and more inclined, to
place value on these structures, especially given their familial and professional
backgrounds.[270] The country's tradition of law, and the professionalism of
bureaucracy that undergirded the application of law, was appealing to these
agents – as lawyers with a tradition in common – and as heirs to powerful

---

[265] *Rex v. Abdurahman* 1950 (3) SA 136 (A), at 143.
[266] *Tayob v. Ermelo Local Transportation Board* 1951 (4) SA 440 (A); *R. v. Lusa* 1953 (2) SA
484 (A).
[267] Haysom and Plasket, "The War against Law," p. 308. On the intricacies of administrative law
in South Africa, see Davis and Corder, "A Long March," pp. 281–302.
[268] Chaskalson, "Law in a Changing Society," p. 295.
[269] More generally, see Andrew Kydd, "Overcoming Mistrust," *Rationality and Society*, Vol. 12,
No. 4 (November 2000), pp. 397–424.
[270] Chaskalson, "From Wickedness to Equality," p. 598.

family traditions. Confidence in the state then revived (or at least maintained) a necessary level of trust between them, making the cooperative resolution of apartheid's endgame first conceivable, then possible. As Giliomee writes, "It was above all Mandela and De Klerk who constructed the bridge, using as pillars the NP-ruled state and the ANC as the embodiment of the anti-apartheid struggle. Both showed great skill as leader-conciliators, able to deliver their respective constituencies."[271]

Analysts claiming that it was leadership that mattered "all the way" in apartheid's endgame usually focus on either Mandela, or de Klerk, or both. What the discussion in this chapter sought to show was that the interaction between these agents was more strained than harmonious, and that their leadership more than once was suboptimal. Conventional leadership accounts usually also underestimate the importance of inferior leadership levels in the endgame. On my analysis, leadership alone was insufficient for cutting through the veil of ignorance in the negotiations over South Africa's future. It were the remnants of the normative state that created the conditions allowing Mandela, de Klerk, and others to solve a series of assurance games, the successful resolution of which then contributed to the resolution of the endgame itself. Thus, to understand, with Polanyi, why that which happened, happened *at all* in apartheid's endgame, we must place agents in the strictures of structure. Among other structures, we must place Mandela and de Klerk in the structures of *law*. The legacies of law stacked the deck in favor of moderation. The shared mental model of law influenced what interacting agents wanted, and how they went about pursuing it. Moderating the demands among adversaries, the ideology of law lowered the threshold for cooperation.[272] Once cooperation was underway, the state helped turn commitments among these adversaries credible. It turns out that Ellmann was right, when he ventured, in the late 1980s, that "the law might cease to be a mere weapon of opposing social forces and, instead, become a vehicle for arguing over, and building, a new South Africa."[273] Yet it must not be forgotten that the possibility of this lineage of law owes to the legacies of law, and in no small way.

A Final Thought on Leadership

In methodological terms, the analysis of apartheid's endgame is somewhat similar to the analysis of the rise of Nazi dictatorship, as well as the demise of the Soviet Union. In all cases, scholars are confronted with making sense of an undeniable leadership factor. Hitler in Germany, Gorbachev in the Soviet Union, and Nelson Mandela and F. W. de Klerk in South Africa, wrote history. Their names and faces will forever define – and often be synonymous with – the

---

[271] Giliomee, *The Afrikaners*, p. 628.
[272] I am grateful to Stephen Walt for pointing out the connection between demands and institutions.
[273] Ellmann, "Legal Text and Lawyers' Culture in South Africa," p. 417.

larger processes and events in which they participated. Comparative historical scholarship on all three countries is ridden with cleavages. One of the deepest cleavages separates those indebted to methodological individualism from those committed to methodological structuralism.

In apartheid's endgame, Mandela and de Klerk, as well as Ramaphosa and Meyer, were critical, indispensable figures. The empirical data bear out the argument that even a usable state requires committed users to be useful in strategic interaction (see Chapter 2). It lends credence to the observation that "connecting the state apparatus, even a coherent one, to a fragmented set of powerholders with no interest of their own in transformation is unlikely to enhance its ability to enact change."[274] Yet the endgame did not hinge on these agents alone. In the preceding analysis, this chapter has integrated the roles of agents and of structure. In the final exposition of the argument, the chapter may have favored structure over agents. This relative deemphasis of agents is a corrective to the excessive individualism found in the academic literature on South Africa. As Geoffrey Hodgson remarks, "If individuals are affected by their circumstances, then why not in turn attempt to explain the causes acting upon individual 'goals and beliefs'? Why should the process of scientific inquiry be arrested as soon as the individual is reached?"[275]

A RECAPITULATION

The foregoing analysis has linked "structure and strategy, institutions and rationality, constraints and choices, collectivities and individuals, and the macro and the meso/micro."[276] The analytic narratives have gone beyond conventional approaches on the state and recent attempts to bring the state back in. They have done so by emphasizing that it was not so much the state *per se* that mattered in apartheid's endgame, but rather its past and presumed future – its value as a social institution, as perceived by interacting agents. The empirical evidence suggests that the idea of the state – and its relationship to formally rational law – may matter more in transitions from authoritarian rule than previously thought. "The idea of the state forms part of the considerations which groups have in mind when determining where their interests lie and what types of conduct will appeal to decision-makers and the public."[277] In the minds

[274] Evans, "The State as Problem and Solution," p. 179; Joel Migdal, *Strong Societies and Weak States: State-Society Relations and State Capabilities in the Third World* (Princeton: Princeton University Press, 1988).
[275] Geoffrey M. Hodgson, "The Return of Institutional Economics," in Neil J. Smelser and Richard Swedberg, eds., *The Handbook of Economic Sociology* (Princeton: Princeton University Press, 1994), p. 62.
[276] Mark I. Lichbach, "Contending Theories of Contentious Politics and the Structure-Action Problem of Social Order," *Annual Review of Political Science*, Vol. 1 (1998), p. 420.
[277] Dyson, *The State Tradition in Western Europe*, p. 3. However, the idea of the state is not synonymous with the structure of the state. As Dyson writes, we must avoid the "mistake of conflating the state with the idea of the state. ... Although they are inseparable in so far as the

of key democracy-demanding agents, the state underwent a transformation from problem to prize to solution in South Africa.

The chapter has shown that this transformation crucially influenced the dynamics of contention in apartheid's endgame. It made possible a convergence on mutual advantage among adversaries. It was this transformation in the perception of the state that paved the way for its important role. Thus the idea of the state and its institutional structure worked in unison. It did not hurt that the physical basis of the state was also relatively well developed in South Africa. The preserved apartheid state, albeit weakened, had force. Interacting agents deliberately chose to preserve key planks of its structure, not steal them. The idea of the state, its history and presumed future, mattered.

What is the relevance of this for the theory of democracy? Many scholars treat institutions "as incentive structures that merely define strategic opportunities for actors understood to have stable preferences and orientations."[278] By contrast, the analytic narratives in Chapter 6 *endogenized* the formation of preferences. They demonstrated how, and why, the preferences of key agents in apartheid's endgame *changed*. Existing accounts have overlooked the importance of this change, and even more important, the reasons that underlay it.

As I have sought to show in the preceding analysis, these reasons stem from the legacies of law. Having analyzed, for the first time, the preexisting forms of legal rule in South Africa, this and the preceding chapter have offered a *redescription* of apartheid's endgame.[279] The next chapter illustrates the significance of these findings – by way of a plausibility probe – for comparative historical analysis.

---

state is partly constituted by the beliefs that people hold about it, they are obviously different. For example, if anarchy broke out tomorrow, there would be no state apparatus, but the idea of the state would still be present. The danger of failing to make this distinction is a "superidealism," through which changes in the idea of the state are equated with changes in the state itself, nullifying questions about the causal effectiveness of ideas." Dyson, *The State Tradition in Western Europe*, p. 3. More generally, see Steinberger, *The Idea of the State.*

[278] Snyder and Mahoney, "The Missing Variable," p. 113.

[279] On the function of redescription in the methodology of the social sciences, see once again Shapiro, "Problems, Methods, and Theories in the Study of Politics," p. 39. On the importance of studying the preexisting forms of bureaucratic authoritarian rule, see, again, Bratton and Van de Walle, *Democratic Experiments in Africa*, p. 275.

PART III

A COMPARATIVE ANALYSIS

8

A Plausibility Probe

The preceding chapters have found a commitment to legality in *both* the transition to – and from – apartheid. I have demonstrated that this commitment not only facilitated South Africa's transition to democracy, but also provided an important foundation for the legal system in that democracy. It is important to appreciate, as Arthur Chaskalson reminds us, that "[s]ome unjust societies lack any semblance of such a commitment. There was, strangely, a commitment to legality in apartheid South Africa, and that is what makes it such an unusual case."[1] Or does it?

Do we possess comparative evidence that would further support my argument about path dependence and the law? Tentative evidence in support of the argument can be gleaned from the case of Chile, 1830–1990. What follows is an individualizing comparison of Pinochet's endgame, with particular reference to the legacies of law. The analysis, however, is tentative and should not be construed as an attempt at universal generalization. The individualizing comparison offered here is different from an all-encompassing comparison. This chapter does *not* compare the experiences of the countries under scrutiny – South Africa and Chile – in any systemic fashion. Nor does it offer a real "test" of the model advanced in the preceding chapters. Rather, the overall analysis concentrates on the singularities of each case in an effort to bring the revived concept of the dual state into sharper focus. The analysis focuses on "single nations taken singly; comparison with other national experiences serves mainly to bring out the special features of the national pattern."[2] In other words, the comparative analysis provides a *plausibility probe* for the theoretical model.

Plausibility probes are, by definition, insufficient for establishing the generality of a theoretical model. And yet, their significance should not be underestimated, for as one scholar writes, "Increasing the number of narratives does not in any way 'prove' the model, but in light of the temptation of inductivist

[1] Chaskalson, "From Wickedness to Equality," p. 598, Fn. 27.
[2] Charles Tilly, *Big Structures, Large Processes, and Huge Comparisons* (New York: Russell Sage Foundation, 1984), p. 90.

modifications of a given model, the ability of a model to withstand the difficult
test of application to different occurrences of the *explanandum* without ad hoc
alterations makes more plausible that it has captured the central, generalizable
dynamics rather than unique elements of a particular case."[3]

A DUAL STATE

Democratization meant *re*democratization in Chile. Chile had significant
experience with democracy before 1990, the year that marked the country's
return to democratic rule. As Ruth Berins Collier notes, "there is no question
that during the twentieth century Chile had a mass electorate and a large part
of the working class was enfranchised and electorally powerful, traits of Chilean
politics that have led country specialists to characterize Chile as a long-
standing democracy ... "[4] In the hundred years preceding the 1973 breakdown
of democracy, Chile enjoyed "a high level of party competition and popular
participation, open and fair elections, and strong respect for democratic freedoms."[5] Indeed, Kenneth A. Bollen, in a comparative, quantitative measurement
of levels of democracy, found that in 1965, Chile's democratic achievement was
greater than that of the United States, France, Italy, and West Germany.[6] The
long-standing tradition of democracy left a legacy with far-reaching effects.
Contrary to conventional wisdom, the Chilean dictatorship (1973–1990) was in
important respects institutionally constrained.[7] Consequently, Chile was *not* a
case of a personalized dictatorship, as the standard account would suggest, but
rather a form of bureaucratic constitutionalism. Like apartheid in South Africa,
nondemocratic rule was underpinned by a dual state in Chile.

THE PREROGATIVE STATE AND THE NORMATIVE STATE

The origins of the normative state date back to the nineteenth century when
Chile made significant headway in institutionalizing democracy. Under

[3] Tim Büthe, "Taking Temporality Seriously: Modeling History and the Use of Narratives as
Evidence," *American Political Science Review*, Vol. 96, No. 3 (September 2002), p. 489.
[4] Berins Collier, *Paths Toward Democracy*, p. 29.
[5] Arturo Valenzuela, "Chile: Origins, Consolidation, and Breakdown of a Democratic Regime,"
in Larry Diamond, Juan J. Linz, and Seymour Martin Lipset, eds., *Democracy in Developing
Countries: Latin America* (Boulder, CO: Lynne Rienner, 1989), p. 160.
[6] Kenneth A. Bollen, "Comparative Measurement of Political Democracy," *American
Sociological Review*, Vol. 45, No. 3 (June 1980), pp. 370–390. Chile was the first country in
South America to have a system of highly institutionalized contestation and a reasonable level
of participation, to use the Dahlian dimensions of democracy. The pervasive strength of
landlords in Chile, however, also meant "the continued exclusion of the peasantry and the
delay of the establishment of full democracy until the 1970s." Dietrich Rueschemeyer, Evelyne
Huber Stephens, and John D. Stephens, *Capitalist Development and Democracy* (Chicago:
University of Chicago Press, 1992), p. 176.
[7] Robert Barros, "Personalization and Institutional Constraints: Pinochet, the Military Junta, and the
1980 Constitution," *Latin American Politics and Society*, Vol. 43, No. 1 (Spring 2001), pp. 5–43.

General Manuel Bulnes, who won the presidential elections of 1840, Chile gained independent courts and an independent legislature. Bulnes also reduced the role of the military in politics, creating instead a civilian National Guard. Between 1830 and 1973, "Chile experienced only thirteen months of unconstitutional rule under some form of junta, and only four months under a junta dominated exclusively by the military."[8] And although citizenship and suffrage were severely restricted in the nineteenth century, Chile introduced secret voting earlier than Belgium, Denmark, France, Prussia, and Norway.[9]

Civilian Rule and the Establishment of Democracy in 1830

The development of a new, liberal class of government functionaries intensified the expansion of the Chilean state. This expansion was further backed by booming exports of wheat and minerals, which increased tax revenues. "From 1830 to 1860, customs revenues, which represented 60 percent of all revenues, increased sevenfold, enabling the Chilean state to undertake extensive public-works projects, including constructing Latin America's second railroad ..."[10] By 1860, more than twenty-five hundred Chileans were employed in state organizations. In this historical period "economic dependency contributed to strengthening, not weakening, the state."[11]

With the exception of a brief civil war, the country remained democratic until 1924, when a military junta of young officers temporarily took the reigns of power. When he was elected president in 1927, Colonel Carlos Ibañez, one of the members of the 1924 officers' movement, strengthened the bureaucracy of the Chilean state. He also expanded the foundations of the prerogative state that would later form the backdrop to the military junta of General Augusto Pinochet. In particular, Ibañez "sough to alter fundamentally Chilean politics by introducing 'efficient and modern' administrative practices, disdaining the role of Congress in cabinet appointments and resorting to emergency and executive measures, such as forced exile, in an attempt to crush labor and opposition political parties."[12] As the foregoing discussion of the history and prehistory of the apartheid state has shown, the use of emergency powers was a defining characteristic of the prerogative state.

In Chile, the prerogative state under Ibañez contained the seeds of the prerogative state under Pinochet. But Arturo Alessandri, Ibañez's successor and former President (1920–1924), initiated a resurgence of the normative state when he was elected President for a second time in 1932. He reaffirmed the value of democratic norms and institutions, thus reequilibrating democracy

---

[8] Valenzuela, "Chile," pp. 160; 179.
[9] Indeed, the Constitution of 1833 was strongly influenced by Anglo-American constitutional developments. Valenzuela, "Chile," pp. 161, 173.
[10] Ibid., p. 164.
[11] Ibid.
[12] Ibid., p. 167.

in Chile.[13] He emphasized the tradition of formally rational law that Chile's founding fathers had introduced with the 1833 Constitution. In this period, "the vast majority of political transactions were characterized by compromise, flexibility, and respect for the institutions and procedures of constitutional democracy," involving interparty agreements concerning government-sponsored industrialization, copper nationalization, agrarian reform, national health and welfare reform.[14] A legal way of doing things informed strategic interaction in Chile. "The legitimacy of public institutions was further reinforced by a strong commitment to public service, which extended from the presidential palace to the rural police station."[15] Valenzuela emphasizes that the sequence of institutional development benefited democracy in Chile. Contrary to Argentina and Brazil, the achievement of suffrage and the development of political parties preceded the growth of a centralized state bureaucracy in Chile. This, Valenzuela argues, reinforced the viability of representative institutions, and ultimately of the normative state.[16]

In 1948, President Gabriel González Videla oversaw a strengthening of the prerogative state, outlawing the Communist Party and sending its members to concentration camps, a precursor of things to come. After several decades of conservative governments, a rift between the Christian Democrats and the Right led to the election of Socialist presidential candidate Salvador Allende in 1970 with only 36 percent of the vote.

Military Rule and the Breakdown of Democracy in 1973

In a haphazard, rather than a coordinated move, elements within the military staged a coup d'état on September 11, 1973, causing the breakdown of democracy in Chile. The coup followed on the heels of a similar attempt just three months earlier. Although the successful coup in September was the culmination of a plot hatched among elements within the military to overthrow the regime even before Salvador Allende took office, the eventual removal of the Allende government was a contingent outcome. Contentious debate within the armed forces prolonged the lifespan of democracy. General Prats, Admiral Montero, and most commanding officers were "committed constitutionalists" who resisted a military solution to the regime crisis.[17] It was not until the removal or resignation of the constitutionalists that the antidemocratic elements

[13] Reequilibration refers here to a "political process that, after a crisis that has seriously threatened the continuity and stability of the basic democratic political mechanisms, results in their continued existence at the same or higher levels of democratic legitimacy, efficacy, and effectiveness." For this definition, see Juan J. Linz, *The Breakdown of Democratic Regimes: Crisis, Breakdown, and Reequilibration* (Baltimore: Johns Hopkins University Press, 1978), p. 87.

[14] Valenzuela, "Chile," p. 170.

[15] Ibid., p. 171.

[16] Ibid., pp. 181–182.

[17] Arturo Valenzuela, *The Breakdown of Democratic Regimes: Chile* (Baltimore: Johns Hopkins University Press, 1978), pp. 98–100.

within the armed forces, the so-called *golpistas*, were able to pursue a final military solution in Chile.

After Allende consented to the removal of key constitutionalists from their posts, the direct confrontation between the military and elements of the revolutionary Left paved the way for military dictatorship. Fear and uncertainty led the military to pursue a strategy of confrontation over cooperation. Militant rhetoric on the Left and the threat of working-class insurrection moved the country closer to dictatorship. Calls by the governing Popular Unity Coalition for the formation of a parallel army, an "Army of the People," in particular hastened the breakdown of democracy. Indeed, "the activities of the leftist leaders ... further reinforced the resolve of those intent on staging a coup and seriously undermined the position of those officers, particularly Admiral Montero, who continued to argue that the armed forces should remain neutral."[18] Fears of political and physical victimhood turned the military against democracy. "For a majority of officers, it was no longer a matter of objecting to erroneous government policies but a matter of defending themselves and their institutions from the possibility of destruction."[19] Not unlike Friedrich Ebert, Weimar Germany's president who lost control over a recalcitrant military supposed to uphold the fledgling democracy in the 1920s, Allende lost control over the *golpistas* in Chile half a century later. A key institution within the state turned against the state. As in Weimar, "the abdication of erstwhile supporters caught in the crossfire from both extremes" signified the end of democracy in Chile in 1973.[20] The breakdown of democracy was further facilitated by Chile's polarized party system, combined with a presidential constitutional framework, which increased incentives for confrontation rather than cooperation in adversarial interaction.[21] Valenzuela offers convincing counterfactual evidence that a parliamentary constitutional framework might have reduced these incentives, by inducing moderation and political accommodation.[22]

A general "inefficacy of the judicial branch in protecting civil liberties and rights" indicates the decline of the normative state in this period.[23] The inefficacy can be traced to "concerns for career and advancement in the court system, an initial disposition to believe the denials of government ministers and military officials, and, in some cases, an enthusiastic willingness to collaborate in the task

[18] Ibid., p. 103.
[19] Ibid.
[20] Ibid., p. 107. On the question of political abdication, in particular the abdication of the Social Democrat Party (SPD) in Weimar Germany, see Skach, *Borrowing Constitutional Designs*.
[21] On polarized pluralism in Chile, see Giovanni Sartori, *Parties and Party Systems: A Framework for Analysis* (Cambridge: Cambridge University Press, 1976).
[22] Arturo Valenzuela, "Party Politics and the Crisis of Presidentialism in Chile: A Proposal for a Parliamentary Form of Government," in Juan J. Linz and Arturo Valenzuela, eds., *The Failure of Presidential Democracy, Volume 2: The Case of Latin America* (Baltimore: Johns Hopkins University Press, 1994), pp. 91–150.
[23] Brian Loveman, *Chile: The Legacy of Hispanic Nationalism*, 3rd ed. (New York: Oxford University Press, 2001), p. 264.

of 'extirpating the Marxist cancer'" on the parts of Chilean legal officials.[24] Whereas the normative state was hollowed out, the prerogative state was expanded. The latter became a tool of repression in the hands of the military junta. Under the auspices of the prerogative state, the Junta committed widespread human rights violations, including the "neutralization" of regime opponents and suspension of political rights. The Report of the Chilean National Commission on Truth and Reconciliation lists over three hundred pages of violations that occurred between September and December 1973 alone.[25]

General Augusto Pinochet, who became president of the military Junta, Chief of the Nation, and President of Chile in 1974, ruled by way of emergency powers. A state of siege was declared from September 1973 until March 1978, from November 1984 until June 1985, and from September 1986 until January 1988, a total of more than six years.[26] In these periods of extraordinary rule, Pinochet and the Junta were exempt from accountability and beyond legal reproach. In June 1974, the *Dirección de Inteligencia Nacional* (National Intelligence Directorate, DINA) was created through Decree Law No. 521, making it the supreme organization within the expanding prerogative state until its replacement by the legally more circumscribed *Central Nacional de Informaciones* (CNI) in 1977.

Remnants of the Normative State

Although weakened in the construction of the Chilean dictatorship, remnants of the normative state that former President Bulnes had built in the nineteenth century survived the onslaught of the military. Whereas the Chilean National Commission on Truth and Reconciliation heavily criticized the behavior of the judiciary (not unlike the TRC's criticism of the judiciary in South Africa), especially the Chilean Supreme Court, during the junta regime, it is noteworthy that Pinochet and the other military leaders deemed it necessary to build a *dictatorship of law*. Between 1975 and 1976, the junta passed four constitutional acts in an attempt to legitimate the seizure of power in 1973. The acts also explicated a catalogue of rights and public freedoms. While many provisions were abrogated or circumscribed by other provisions in the same documents, it is noteworthy that the constitutional acts conferred broad powers to the courts; "if the judges had actually used them, they would have provided the most effective safeguard of human rights within the Chilean legal system."[27] We are

[24] Ibid.
[25] *Report of the Chilean National Commission on Truth and Reconciliation* (Notre Dame: University of Notre Dame Press, 1993), pp. 129–468.
[26] Alexandra Barahona de Brito, *Human Rights and Democratization in Latin America: Uruguay and Chile* (Oxford: Oxford University Press, 1997), p. 44.
[27] *Report of the Chilean National Commission on Truth and Reconciliation*, p. 85. Note, however, that the Commission was criticized for this statement. One line of criticism suggested that the judges would have been murdered by the junta had they attempted to use the powers conferred to them.

thus faced with the curious situation where a military junta *simultaneously* engaged in self-justification and self-binding. In particular, Act No. 3, in combination with Article 14 of Act No. 4, enshrined *habeas corpus* appeals and appeals for protection on the grounds of other constitutional rights. The Chilean National Commission on Truth and Reconciliation, whose work informed the recent investigations of Spanish magistrate Baltasar Garzón, noted the following about the constitutional acts in its report:

> The appeal for protection [*recurso de protección*] was an extremely important innovation. Any person or association could invoke it as a defense, for example, against unlawful mistreatment, against being judged by special commissions, against being prevented from assembling peacefully, and for preserving the inviolability of the home and of private communications, expressing opinion, and freely giving and receiving information.[28]

The Report went on to note that:

> The broadening of *habeas corpus* should also be emphasized. In principle from that point on it was possible to act on behalf of any person who might be prevented, disturbed, or threatened illegally from exercising his or her right to personal freedom and individual security. The respective appeals court was obliged to issue the rulings it judged conducive to establishing the rule of law and to assure that the individual in question was properly protected.[29]

Of course, the junta modified the constitutional acts shortly after their promulgation, declaring that the appeal for protection was inapplicable during states of emergency, and that Act No. 4 was suspended until corresponding legislation was passed. This, however, should not detract from the important fact that the normative state, while heavily curtailed, remained in operation during the dictatorship. This institutional trace left a legacy with unintended consequences.

PINOCHET'S ENDGAME

Conventional wisdom holds that the 1980 constitution complicated democratic transition and consolidation in Chile.[30] In this view, the document not only asserted the already existing dictatorship, but extended its reach by giving the president broad discretionary powers, and by inserting a number of so-called transitory dispositions into the text. Because the constitution was also drafted in secret, without any participation of the public, and ratified by plebiscite against the background of a state of emergency, in the context of severely circumscribed contestation, the democratic opposition deemed the document illegitimate. In this interpretation,

---

[28] Ibid., p. 85.
[29] Ibid., p. 85. Emphasis added.
[30] Linz and Stepan, *Problems of Democratic Transition and Consolidation*, p. 209.

The 1980 Constitution was merely a device to prolong military rule – and given the regime's proclivity towards organizing plebiscites, on its terms it appeared to promise at least sixteen more years of military rule. In academic analyses the illegitimacy argument melds with the interpretation of the regime as a personalized dictatorship. The constitution is functional to Pinochet's needs, corresponds to his preferences, and reflects Pinochet's hope of remaining in power "with popular legitimation, without modifying the authoritarian structure of the regime."[31]

This interpretation, no doubt, captures important considerations that influenced the decision to draft the 1980 Constitution. And yet, it misses important elements. First, the constitution was not the product of Pinochet alone. Although "Pinochet did seek to perpetuate himself in office, his bids for absolute power were blocked and only served to ignite the institutional debate."[32] New evidence suggests that the Chilean dictatorship was far less monistic than previously thought. The four members of the junta, which itself was established in the *Acta de Constitución de la Junta de Gobierno* on September 12, 1973, were contentious in their interactions with one another. Admiral José Toribio Merino, and Generals Gustavo Leigh, Mendoza, and Pinochet differed regarding the direction in which to lead the country.

Military Constitutionalism

Although Merino and Pinochet favored neoliberal economic reforms, the more senior Leigh was steadfastly opposed to such reforms. Leigh and Merino, by contrast, agreed on the question of constitutional reform, thwarting Pinochet's bid for absolute power. "In fact, much of the internal tension that emerged during 1977–78 arose precisely because the Junta had not established any procedure for resolving differences over the duration of the regime and the nature of the constitution."[33] Although all members of the Junta believed a return to civilian rule was premature, Pinochet's proposals for sustained, indefinite dictatorship were divisive. It is interesting that Admiral Merino seems to have *rejected* (1) a radical break with Chile's constitutional tradition, (2) the entrenchment of authoritarianism on a permanent basis, and (3) the extensive use of the prerogative state.[34] Second and related, the constitution

[31] Robert J. Barros, "By Reason and Force: Military Constitutionalism in Chile, 1973–1989," Ph.D. dissertation, University of Chicago, 1996, pp. 188–189.

[32] Ibid., p. 198.

[33] Ibid., p. 197.

[34] Ibid., pp. 203; 206–207. Note that Leigh, too, opposed permanent military rule. See especially his response to Pinochet's plan to unite the offices of the president, the office of the commander of the army, and the commander of the *carabineros* (police). Ibid., pp. 215–218. Consider in this context Stepan's finding that even though Chile had the second largest military establishment relative to population size in 1950s and 1960s Latin America, it also had one of the lowest military intervention scores. This finding is suggestive of the reach of the country's constitutional tradition among military officers like Leigh. See Alfred Stepan, *The Military in Politics: Changing Patterns in Brazil* (Princeton: Princeton University Press, 1971), p. 24.

was not merely a façade. Pinochet sowed constitutional seeds in the *Discurso de Chacarillas*, his 1977 blueprint for institutionalizing what he called "authoritarian democracy," but as the discussion already intimated above, he was really interested in achieving absolute power.[35] The 1980 Constitution contradicted this objective. Indeed, "the constitution was not Pinochet's preferred outcome but rather the expression of an interforce settlement agreed on only after the navy and the air force, in the face of international pressure, again rejected bids to institute a dictatorship of the army."[36]

A key advocate, and subsequent architect, of legal institutionalization that emerged in the late 1970s was Jaime Guzmán, a Senator and Pinochet confidante. A member of the *Unión Demócrata Independiente* (UDI), a major rightist party, Guzmán became the principal author of the 1980 constitution, advocating what may be called military constitutionalism. Indeed, Guzmán recognized the utility of formally rational law. He insisted that a self-binding constitution was a source of power for the junta, arguing that the stability of the regime "is strengthened to the extent that authority originates from and is framed within an impersonal, juridical order."[37] Guzmán's voice would ultimately prevail. It offered the military commanders in the junta a means with which to constrain Pinochet, carrying forward elements of constitutionalism in Chile while simultaneously strengthening the dictatorial power of the regime. Bringing the normative state back into the picture marked the return to a balanced dual state. "[A]lthough the constitution contained provisions that extended military rule, the main body set out the contours of a regime qualitatively distinct from a military government. It was not the constitution that would have emerged from an elected constituent assembly, but, at least in principle, the main body of the constitution did structure a democracy, albeit with protections and exclusions."[38]

A Limited Dictatorship

Based on the foregoing evidence, Barros describes Chile as a "limited dictatorship," noting that the "legal organization of military rule would stand through 1990 – the modifications affected in 1981 to the structure of the Junta would only perfect the separation of powers. General Pinochet would stand as President of the Republic, in charge of the executive, facing a legislative Junta until the final days of military rule in March 1990."[39] For the purposes of this

---

[35] Loveman, *Chile*, p. 265. In his infamous speech, Pinochet spelled out a plan for building a new democracy, involving the stages recuperation, transition, and consolidation. See Barros, "By Reason and Force," p. 219, Fn. 62.

[36] Barros, "Personalization and Institutional Constraints," p. 15.

[37] Jaime Guzmán, "Analisis sobre el proceso de institucionalización del país, y proposición de un possible plan o formula al respecto," Jaime Guzmán Papers (Santiago: Fundación Jaime Guzmán, 1977), p. 4, as quoted in Barros, "By Reason and Force," p. 223.

[38] Ibid., pp. 189–190.

[39] Ibid., p. 71.

study, it is important to emphasize the legal foundations of military rule in Chile. Inasmuch as the country's junta perpetrated some heinous crimes in international history, it also observed, even implemented, self-binding legal constraints. Table 8.1 provides an overview of the legal foundations of military rule in Chile, and of some of these constraints.[40]

As we have seen, law can be considered formally rational when it forms, or approximates, a gapless system of abstract rules. It is substantively rational if and when it is systematic in organization, yet driven by an extralegal ideology. In Chile, the ideology underpinning the country's dictatorship of law was, of course, "anti-Marxism," a loosely connected belief system grounded in fears of "Marxist totalitarianism."[41]

LONG-RUN CONSEQUENCES

The existence of a *reasonably* stable institutional structure within which the tasks of social regulation and integration could be carried out benefited the politics and economics of democratic transition in Chile.[42] Confidence in the state generated trust among adversaries; trust among persons, in turn, inspired further confidence in the state, as well as secondary institutions such as the 1980 constitution and other reform institutions. This facilitated the evolution of cooperation in Chile's endgame. Credible commitments were reached among democracy-demanding and democracy-resisting forces with respect to three fundamental issues: the political dispensation, the system of economic management, and relations between military and society. For the opposition, these commitments "meant trusting that the military would allow free elections and would transfer power in the event of an opposition victory; for the military and its supporters on the right, it meant trusting that an opposition victory would not result in populist economic chaos or in persecution of the military. This basic consensus represented a substantial moderation of the polarization that characterized Chilean society in the early 1970s."[43] This consensus echoes a convergence on the preservation of the state, as accepted by all sides. Law's survival, in particular reduced the uncertainty felt by

---

[40] See also Manuel Antonio Garretón, "Political Processes in an Authoritarian Regime: The Dynamics of Institutionalization and Opposition in Chile, 1973–1980," in J. Samuel Valenzuela and Arturo Valenzuela, eds., *Military Rule in Chile: Dictatorship and Oppositions* (Baltimore: Johns Hopkins University Press, 1986), pp. 159–160.

[41] Valenzuela, *The Breakdown of Democratic Regimes*, p. 107.

[42] The objective of this study is not to exonerate or in any way justify or legitimate the events that took place during Chile's military dictatorship. The atrocities committed under the military dictatorship have been widely documented.

[43] Genaro Arriagada Herrera and Carol Graham, "Chile: Sustaining Adjustment during Democratic Transition," in Stephan Haggard and Steven B. Webb, eds., *Voting for Reform: Democracy, Political Liberalization, and Economic Adjustment* (New York: Oxford University Press, 1994), p. 280.

TABLE 8.1. *Legal Foundations of Military Rule in Chile, 1973–1987*

Law	Date of Issuance	Provisions
Decree Laws		
DL 3	September 11, 1973	State of siege, defined initially as "state of internal war"
DL 4		
DL 5		State of emergency in provinces and regions
DL 8		Interpretive decree regarding Code of Military
DL 81		Justice, affirming the existence of a "state of war"
		Delegation to military authorities of power to rule through military edicts (*bandos militares*) and to exercise judicial authority over civilians (*jurisdicción militar*)
		Authority to expel (banish) persons from country during the state of siege (which lasted until 1978 and was reimposed several times thereafter)
DL 521	June 14, 1974	Official creation of the DINA (secret police, accountable to General Pinochet, which already functioned extraofficially in late 1973). This decree has "secret" provisions detailing the secret police's authority
DL 527	June 17, 1974	Charter of the military junta (*Estatuto de la Junta de Gobierno*)
DL 604	August 10, 1974	Prohibits entry into country of persons who spread or support doctrines that threaten national security or who are known to be "agitators of activists"
DL 640	September 2, 1974	Regulations defining the various "regimes of exception"
DL 788	December 4, 1974	Provides that the "decree laws" of the military junta have the effect of amending the 1925 constitution
DL 922	March 11, 1975	State of Siege Decree
DL 1.0008 *and* DL 1.009	May 8, 1975	Increases period during which detainees may be held "incommunicado" in cases involving crimes against the security of the state (arrestees cannot see lawyers or obtain habeas corpus writs)
DL 890 (M. Interior)	August 26, 1975	Modifies the Law of State Security, generally restricts civil rights and liberties (*garantías constitucionales*) and due process
DL 1.281	December 11, 1975	Authorizes Military Zone Commanders to censure or suspend publication of up to six editions of magazines, newspapers, and other media

(continued)

Table 8.1. (*continued*)

Law	Date of Issuance	Provisions
Constitutional Acts		
DL 1.319	January 9, 1975	
DL 1.551	September 11, 1976	"Essential Foundations of Chileanism"
DL 1.552		"Constitutional Rights and Duties"
DL 1.553		"On Regimes of Exception"
DL 1.877	1977	Modifies Law 12.927 (Internal Security Law), increased authority of the president during states of emergency
DL 1.878	August 13, 1977	Creates CNI (new secret police to replace DINA) and details its authority
	April 19, 1978	State of siege ends, country remains in "state of emergency"
DL 3.168	February 6, 1980	Authorizes internal exile (*relegación*) for persons who alter or seek to alter public order, for up to three months (Modification of DL 81 and DL 1.877, Internal Sec. of State)
Plebiscite for new Constitution	September 11, 1980	Occurs under "state of emergency," Constitution adds a new regime of exception, "state of perturbation of internal peace," with special powers for president when such a circumstance occurs
		Article 24 ("transitory article") provides that until full implementation of constitution (in practice, this would be after 1989), president has virtually unlimited authority to assure internal security by suspending civil liberties and rights; declaring appropriate regime of exception, etc.
DL 3.451	1980	Extends to twenty-five days the period during which detainees may be held in centers "other than jails" when certain crimes against internal security are being investigated
DL 3.645	1981	Clarifies the application of transitory Article 24, regarding expulsion of citizens and foreigners; also regulates labor unions
	1981–1984	Country under state of emergency (transitory Article 24)
Ley 18.015	July 27, 1981	Details infractions covered by Transitory Article 24, modified by Law 18.150, July 30 1982
	1984 (November)	Country declared under state of siege (seven months) and also state of emergency
Ley 18.313	1984	Law on "Abuse of the Media" (*Sobre abusos de la Publicidad*) amended; further restrictions on media

Law	Date of Issuance	Provisions
Ley 18.314	May 14, 1984	New "Antiterrorism Law" greatly broadens the definition of "terrorism" and increases penalties
Ley 18.415 DS 324	June 15, 1985	New Law and "States of Exception" New Law on press censorship and rules governing the mass Media Country declared in state of siege
Ley 18.667	November 27, 1987	Modifications of the Military Code allow maintaining secret documents that might affect the security of the state

Source: Brian Loveman, *Chile: The Legacy of Spanish Capitalism*, 3rd ed. (New York: Oxford University Press, 2001), pp. 273–274.

interacting adversaries, making possible the development of a modicum of trust among adversaries:

The law in Chile's transition clearly operated in a direction that was functional to reducing uncertainty for sectors that felt a democratic opening as threatening. That's clear. But the interesting thing is that the opposition at that time, the democratic opposition, recognized that the laws were there to be respected. And they did respect them.[44]

Law's tradition in other words made "a democratic opening feasible."[45] A critical juncture was the adoption of the 1980 Constitution, discussed earlier. In its aftermath, the Constitutional Court rediscovered its role as an institution of the normative state. Although the court had been subservient to the regime in the years after its inception in 1981, it struck down some nine legal decisions of the Junta in the mid-1980s. Through its ruling in the famous case of the special electoral court, the *Tribunal Calificador de Elecciones* (TRICEL), as well as subsequent decisions, "the constitutional court created the legal conditions for a fair electoral contest and structured incentives for the opposition to participate and eventually beat the military at its own game."[46]

The 1980 Constitution was of a dual character. It was a device that "both perpetuated military rule and provided a framework for a transition to a post-military constitutional order."[47] As in apartheid's endgame, legality in Chile reached backward and forward. The dual state became a usable state, making democracy possible, and work. "The concept of constitutional safeguards set into

[44] Carlos H. Acuña, Director, Maestría en Administración y Políticas Públicas, Universidad de San Andrés, Interview with the author, Victoria: May 15, 2001.
[45] Ibid.
[46] Barros, "Personalization and Institutional Constraints, " p. 20.
[47] Ibid., p. 22.

the 1980 charter was institutional – not tutelary – as Guzmán was wont to insist, the constitutional order was to be 'self-protected,' secured by organs internal to the political-institutional regime, and not protected by an external guardian, such as the armed forces."[48] It was this self-protection, and the shared belief in a legal way of doing things among members of democracy-demanding and democracy-resisting forces alike, that paved the path for democracy's return.

Perhaps the most crucial illustration of the continuation of the normative state in Chile is the fact that the end of the Pinochet dictatorship came in the form of a plebiscite. In the fall of 1988, millions of Chileans voted "No" to the question of whether General Pinochet should serve a second eight-year term as president, dealing a binding, electoral defeat to the military Junta. It is interesting to note that the armed forces had supplied the pencils and paper that ended their rule.[49] Although law's continuity made for a long transition to democracy, it arguably made for a safer transition. Although a number of "authoritarian enclaves" complicated democratic transition and consolidation, these golden parachutes have not unduly hindered the establishment of democracy in Chile.[50] Recent events have shown that even authoritarian enclaves have a limited half-life. Although Pinochet remained a powerful figure until 1998, the events surrounding his arrest in London on a Spanish warrant involving a series of charges of human rights abuses, gradually curtailed his standing in Chile. In subsequent years, a Chilean court stripped the former dictator of his immunity. He was indicted and (temporarily) put under house arrest on charges that he was linked to the notorious "caravan of death," a helicopter-borne death squad that is said to have killed seventy-five supporters of former president Salvador Allende in 1973.[51] The cooperative solution to Chile's endgame situation may ultimately have fostered, not stalled, democracy.[52]

---

[48] Barros, "By Reason and Force," p. 234.

[49] Ibid.

[50] On the notion of "authoritarian enclaves," see Manuel Antonio Garretón, *La posibilidad democrática en Chile* (Santiago: FLACSO Cuadernos de Difusión, 1989); and Stepan, *Rethinking Military Politics*, Chapter 7.

[51] In July 2001, a Chilean appeals court ruled, however, that General Pinochet was unfit to stand trial. See Clifford Krauss, "Chile Court Bars Trial of Pinochet," *New York Times*, July 10, 2001, pp. A1; A7. Legal defense and prosecution attorneys have since presented their cases as to whether the former dictator can be tried for human rights abuses before the Chilean Supreme Court. See "Pinochet 'Innocent' of Death Squad Crimes," *BBC News*, July 20, 2001, available at http://news.bbc.co.uk/hi/english/world/americas/newsid_843000/843863.stm, accessed on August 9, 2001. See also "Abnormal Events in an Increasingly Normal Chile," *The Economist*, December 7, 2000.

[52] Corroborating evidence is available from Argentina, where a confrontational, retributive approach to the question of transitional justice, for example, generated problems of democratic consolidation. See the remarks by former Solicitor General of Argentina, Jaime Malamud Goti, interview with the author, Buenos Aires: May 30, 2001. Malamud Goti, who was intimately involved in designing Argentina's response to the years of dictatorship, is very skeptical as to whether the country's criminal trials against the junta furthered the democratic cause. Writes Malamud Goti: "the trials, as they were designed, reinforced the very authoritarianism they were designed to eradicate." Idem., *Game Without End: State Terror and the Politics of Justice*

Furthermore, there is considerable evidence "that Chilean business trans-actions indeed benefit from legal simplicity and consistency of enforcement relative to their Brazilian counterparts."[53] The same study shows that "Brazilian businesses confront high transaction costs in regulation through more complex and resource-intensive regulatory processes and conflict reso-lution; and in orders, through greater uncertainty and frequent renegotiation. The net combination of these effects implies a somewhat inferior environment for business in Brazil."[54] The study shows that "Brazilian legal processes have the reputation of being expensive, slow, and unpredictable, whereas Chile's courts are reputed to be relatively swift and consistent in their judgments."[55] It illustrates that political uncertainty as a factor influencing enterprise decisions has been *less* significant in Chile than in Brazil. Chile's tax bureaucracy (just like South Africa's) was also considered *less* of an obstacle to economic development than the tax bureaucracy in Brazil.[56] This comparative empirical data, albeit tentative, lends further support to both of the principal arguments of this analysis. It shows (1) that the Chilean state was a dual state, and (2) that this dual state was a usable state in the sense here defined, and had the effects predicted by the theoretical model developed in Chapters 2 and 3.

"Le Echamos con un Lapis"

What the Chilean case shows is that "consensus on the fundamentals of public policy can be relatively low, while consensus on the rules and procedures for arriving at policy decisions can be high."[57] Although some of these institutional foundations were lost in the dictatorship of the 1970s and 1980s, others survived, turning the dual state into a usable state. A data point underwrites this finding: of the twenty-two presidents that governed between Bulnes and Pinochet, only two were career military officers. Most others began their careers as bureaucrats and congressmen, illustrating the long-standing tradition of civilian supremacy in

(Norman: University of Oklahoma Press, 1996), p. xiv. See also idem, "Dignity, Vengeance, and Fostering Democracy," *University of Miami Inter-American Law Review*, Vol. 29, No. 3 (Spring/Summer 1998), pp. 417–450; and idem., *Terror y justicia en al Argentina: Responsabilidad y democracia después de los juicos al terrorismo de Estado* (Buenos Aires: Ediciones de la Flor, 2000).
53 Andrew Stone, Brian Levy, and Ricardo Paredes, "Public Institutions and Private Transactions: A Comparative Analysis of the Legal and Regulatory Environment for Business Transactions in Brazil and Chile," in Lee J. Alston, Thráinn Eggertsson, and Douglass C. North, eds., *Empirical Studies in Institutional Change* (Cambridge: Cambridge University Press, 1996), p. 96.
54 Ibid.,
55 Ibid., p. 123.
56 Ibid. See also Lieberman, *Race and Regionalism in the Politics of Taxation in Brazil and South Africa*.
57 Valenzuela, "Chile," p. 176. "le Echamos con un Lapis" translates as "We threw him out with out a pencil." Thus read a curbside graffiti in the aftermath of Chile's 1988 plebiscite, the event that marked the end of the Pinochet dictatorship. As quoted in Barros, "By Reason and Force," p. 332.

Chile.[58] The Chilean case illustrates that the "institutionally unlimitable nature of authoritarian power implies neither that authoritarian regimes cannot be highly legalistic, with subordinate state agencies and actors subject to institutional constraints and rules, nor that authoritarian regimes necessarily rule arbitrarily, capriciously violating even their own rules."[59] Against the background of my analysis of apartheid's endgame (see Chapters 6–7), the evidence from Chile makes clear that a "legal organization of the state and a rule of law in which laws are publicly promulgated, prospective, general, and applied by a public authority; in which punishments are founded in law; can coexist with unconstrained power to make law."[60] I have outlined the origins and effects of this co-existence at great length, both theoretically and empirically, in this book. The discussion of the Chilean case offers additional, illustrative evidence in support of my overall argument.

From the perspective of the *longue durée*, the Chilean state underwent a double transformation: from usable state to dual state, and from dual state back to usable state. The country's long history of democratic rule and a normative state is responsible for the characterization of the state as a usable, possibly even a strong, state in the historical period preceding the dictatorship of the Junta. Throughout the dictatorship, the rise of a prerogative state turned the country's institutional structure into a dual state. Finally, the survival of important remnants of the normative state ensured that the state in Chile's transition to democracy was a usable state, thus underwriting credible commitments.

Patricio Aylwin's *Concertación de los Partidos por la Democracia*, a coalition government of seventeen political parties that had "placed strong emphasis on maintaining," was surprisingly successful at political and economic reform. Within years, Chile had become Latin America's overachiever in terms of macroeconomic management, restoring investor confidence at an unexpected speed. In 1991, Chile's rate of direct foreign investment averaged between 4 and 5 percent of GNP, among the highest in the world. Inflation was very low, especially in comparison with neighboring countries in transition (see Table 8.2). The Economist Intelligence Unit thus moved Chile into their category of low-risk countries – alongside Spain and South Korea.[61]

In Part Good, In Part Bad

In the early 1990s, Chileans were asked whether democracy was the best and most efficient political system for their country. In answer to this poll measuring the legitimacy and efficacy of the new regime, about 80 percent of the respondents answered in the affirmative. Linz and Stepan note that the attitudinal support for democracy found in Chile compared very favorably to that

---

[58] Ibid., p. 180.
[59] Barros, "Personalization and Institutional Constraints," p. 8.
[60] Ibid.
[61] Herrera and Graham, "Chile," pp. 252; 270–273.

TABLE 8.2. *Inflation in Chile and the Southern Cone, 1990*

Country	Inflation (Twelve months after Aylwin's election victory)	Inflation (Twelve months after Aylwin assumed the presidency)
Argentina	4,923.8	20,263.4
Brazil	1,783.6	6,233.8
Peru	2,775.3	2,068.4
Uruguay	89.2	95.4
Chile	21.4	23.9

Source: CEPAL, *Panorama económico de América Latina* (Santiago: CEPAL, 1991), adapted from Herrera and Graham, "Chile," p. 271.

in consolidated democracies such as Spain, Portugal, Greece, and Uruguay. In fact, citizens' perception of democratic performance in Chile and Spain was remarkably similar. Indeed, like Spaniards, Chileans felt that the previous authoritarian regime was "in part good, in part bad."[62] We see a distinct correlation between citizens' assessments of past and present regimes and the here developed characterization of the states of South Africa and Chile as dual states (see Figure 8.1). As Samuel Valenzuela writes,

Authoritarian regimes force opponents to organize themselves to pressure power holders in different ways. In some cases these are compatible with democracies, as when the regimes operate with electoral processes, though vitiated, and legislatures, though controlled and/or impotent. In such circumstances, democratization is easier and usually longer lasting.[63]

Empirical data corroborate this observation in the Chilean case. The aforementioned survey also revealed that Chile was "the only one of four Latin American cases whose citizens attested their belief in both the legitimacy and efficacy of democracy."[64] These data, especially the comparison between Chile and Spain, bring us back to apartheid's endgame.

The previous chapter discussed how the satisfaction with democracy in post-apartheid South Africa and Spain was nearly identical. This suggests that

---

[62] Linz and Stepan, *Problems of Democratic Transition and Consolidation*, p. 214.

[63] J. Samuel Valenzuela, "Class Relations and Democratization: A Reassessment of Barrington Moore's Model," in Miguel Angel Centeno and Fernando López-Alves, eds., *The Other Mirror: Grand Theory Through the Lens of Latin America* (Princeton: Princeton University Press, 2001), pp. 272–273. A decidedly institutionalist interpretation of Chilean politics, like the one advanced here, promises to advance on conventional, structuralist approaches that take classes and other large social categories as principal units of analysis. For a discussion, see ibid., pp. 266–277. For the opposite view as regards Chile, see Rueschemeyer et al., *Capitalist Development and Democracy*.

[64] Linz and Stepan, *Problems of Democratic Transition and Consolidation*, p. 214.

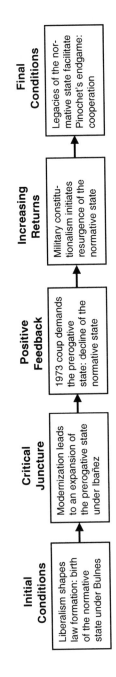

FIGURE 8.1. The Logic of Path-Dependent Explanation

Initial Conditions

Liberalism shapes law formation: birth of the normative state under Bulnes

Critical Juncture

Modernization leads to an expansion of the prerogative state under Ibañez

Positive Feedback

1973 coup demands the prerogative state: decline of the normative state

Increasing Returns

Military constitutionalism initiates resurgence of the normative state

Final Conditions

Legacies of the normative state facilitate Pinochet's endgame: cooperation

post-apartheid South Africa and post-authoritarian Chile have achieved similar levels of democratic development, at least in the perception of their citizens. In order to comprehend these outcomes fully, we must take seriously the legacies of law. Or, as one observer put it,

[W]e should not be content to assume that because unjust states manifestly find legal forms *useful*, the legalism of such countries is solely the product of calculations of *realpolitik* by the oppressors. The truth is that injustice and adherence to law can coexist. Self-interested calculations, moreover, can coalesce with other sources of support for law to maintain a culture that values law even as it practices or acquiesces in oppression. It is important to understand the multiple ways that law can take root, even in an unjust society, if we are to gauge the potential that law has to serve as a limit on rather than merely an instrument of injustice.[65]

Herein I have sought to do just that.

---

[65] Ellmann, *In a Time of Trouble*, p. 174.

9

Conclusion

> The rhetoric and the rules of a society are something a great deal more than sham. In the same moment they may modify, in profound ways, the behaviour of the powerful, and mystify the powerless. They may disguise the true realities of power, but, at the same time, they may curb that power and check its intrusions. And it is often from within that very rhetoric that a radical critique of the practice of the society is developed ...
>
> E. P. Thompson, Whigs and Hunters[1]

This chapter sums up. It briefly recapitulates the argument and evidence (*the legacies of law*). Then the chapter derives implications for the study of institutions, reflecting on the contending new institutionalisms in law and the social sciences, and elucidates the significance of my findings for the theory of democracy (*the lessons of law*). In this book I have argued, and tried to demonstrate, that

just as democratic legalism may be exploited to destroy democracies from within, authoritarian constitutionalism may be turned against dictatorships and may serve as a spring board for democratization, either by the incumbent regime or its democratic opponents.[2]

Or, to paraphrase E. P. Thompson, I believe that the rhetoric and rules of law are "something a great deal more than sham." In pursuit of this proposition I have revisited and reconfigured a theory of law developed by the German émigré Ernst Fraenkel for whom the United States, in the late 1930s, became a safe haven from the Nazi dictatorship. Soon after he arrived on the shores of New York, Fraenkel set about revising his unpublished manuscript, *Der Doppelstaat*, for Anglophone readers. The result was *The Dual State*, the hinge upon which this book turns. Against the background of Fraenkel's *magnum opus*, I introduced a mode of democratization, focusing on the law.

---

[1] E. P. Thompson, *Whigs and Hunters: The Origin of the Black Act* (New York: Pantheon, 1975), p. 265.
[2] Shain and Linz, "Part One," p. 16.

I maintained that law – especially formally rational law – will likely have value in democratization, and that this value – the ideology of law – has been neglected in the existing literature. It appears that ideologies of law, in the sense defined earlier, can assist individuals in the framing of complex and unfamiliar problems. Such framing can enable interacting adversaries to face strategic interaction with more ease. Law in democratization may work as a supplement to the formal and informal enforcement of commitments, or so I have argued. If agents have reasonable confidence in the law, they have more reason to believe despite uncertainty.

A habit of legality – not unlike "soft law" in the international realm – provides a reliable basis for the construction of credible commitments among adversaries. This is beneficial in democratization because humans *generally* long for reassurance:

Humans attempt to use their perceptions about the world to structure their environment in order to reduce uncertainty in human interaction. But whose perceptions matter and how they get translated into transforming the human environment are consequences of the institutional structure, which is a combination of formal rules, informal constraints, and their enforcement characteristics. This structure of human interaction determines who are the entrepreneurs whose choices matter and how such choices get implemented by the decision rules of that structure. Institutional constraints cumulate through time, and the culture of a society is the cumulative structure of rules and norms (and beliefs) that we inherit from the past that shape our present and influence our future.[3]

Law, like institutions more generally, is about the stabilization of expectations of those within its reach. Under the right conditions (specified earlier), law appears to be able to reduce uncertainty in democratization by invoking common cultural backgrounds and experiences. In instances in which interacting adversaries share *qua law* reasonably convergent mental models, the resolution of endgame situations appears to be less intractable.

THE LEGACIES OF LAW

I have marshaled empirical evidence in support of this theoretical argument, placing a comparative historical analysis of the evolution of law – and its effects – in South Africa during the period 1652–2000 alongside a short plausibility probe of the evolution of law – and its effects – in another case: Chile during the period 1830–1990. Let us review the "telling case" of South Africa.

A Telling Case

Telling cases, as we have seen, are those in which the particular circumstances surrounding a case serve to make previously obscure theoretical relationships

---

[3] North, *Understanding the Process of Economic Change*, p. 6.

sufficiently apparent. In the foregoing I hope to have demonstrated that from colonialism to apartheid, South Africa was ruled by an ever-changing dual state. I have reconstructed the institutional development of the two halves of this state, and elucidated the effects thereof, initially under segregation and apartheid.

The apartheid government embraced a rule-guided way of doing things – law – for three reasons: (1) law demonstrated its utility by serving as an effective method of control; (2) law promised to better the apartheid government's standing in the international community by providing a modicum of legitimacy; and (3) law embodied a sincere belief in its appropriateness.[4] The first two are instances of what I have termed instrumental legal action (*law being useful*), the last of value-oriented legal action (*law being meaningful*).

In apartheid's endgame, the common knowledge of law, and actors' confidence in the instrumental value of law, created the conditions for the emergence of trust among them. Iterative interaction expanded this reservoir of trust. Interacting adversaries found "faith in judicial decision-making as a source of legitimacy in the governance of a post-apartheid South Africa."[5] This, among other factors, led to the transformation of preferences on the part of these adversaries in deeply contested domains – from electoral to constitutional to justicial reform. Throughout my sole objective has been explanation and understanding. Achieving this objective required "telling the truth about the law," as Sir Sydney so cogently put it. Seeing that the achievement of "truth" is too elusive a goal, knowledge is what I was after. Unlike other studies, I have been intent on making sense of law also as a cultural phenomenon. This made it necessary to delve deeply into legal history, and to piece this history together where necessary. But a comprehensive and subtle grasp of history was not enough to shine light on the law, its evolution and effects. For the legal narrative to be useful, it had to be *analytic*.

On the occasion of the publication of Forsyth's *In Danger for Their Talents* and Corder's *Judges at Work* in the late 1980s, Dennis Davis, one of South Africa's foremost legal minds, remarked that although "these two careful studies have helped significantly to improve our understanding of the South African judiciary, neither work provides a clearly defined theoretical framework on which further analytical explanation can proceed."[6] It has been my ambition to provide such a framework. The one that I have constructed may not be the theoretical framework envisaged by Davis some twenty years ago, but I hope this analysis will contribute to improving our understanding of the South African judiciary nonetheless.

Sir Sydney's Advice
My findings about the role of law in South Africa, and its consequences, may invite criticism, perhaps even opposition. For as Sir Sydney Kentridge QC, one

[4] For this tripartite explanation, see Ellmann, *In a Time of Trouble*, pp. 174–193.
[5] Klug, *Constituting Democracy*, p. 180.
[6] Davis, "Competing Conceptions," p. 96.

of the world's most respected advocates, observed while reflecting on his long career of practicing law in South Africa,

[A]pproval of the South African legal system and the South African judiciary can ... bring wrath down on one. ... If one makes even so modest a statement as that the Supreme Court of South Africa is on the whole able and independent, and that in general accused persons appearing before that court get a fair trial, one runs the risk of being told that one is giving a veneer of legality and respectability to an oppressive system.[7]

I have made several such "modest statements" in the preceding chapters. Based on the empirical evidence, I have made even *less* modest statements than Sir Sydney. These statements might lead some to think mine a revisionist analysis. They should, for it is. I have sought to shed light on – but *not* to portray in any particular light – the multiple functions of law in South Africa's convoluted history. In revisiting this history, I have been preoccupied with *both* the instrumental function of law (which relates to ends and means) and the expressive function of law (which relates to norms and values). The available data, both qualitative and quantitative, show that for many South Africans "the law" has been useful *as well as* meaningful. This sets South Africa apart from countries where authoritarianism was justified by way of a sham legalism.

Like some of the scholars on whose shoulders I stand, I was struck by the *legality* and respectability of the apartheid system as much as I was struck by its *brutality*. Taking this observation as my starting point, I set out to do two things in this book: (1) to explain how the institutional structure of legality and brutality – this dual state – evolved in response to individual incentives, strategies, and choices; and (2) to understand how, once established, it influenced the responses of individuals in apartheid's endgame, and with what effects.

In South Africa, I have come to see, legalism was not just politics by other means – it also represented culture by other means. I have come to think of the country's uniquely developed legal tradition in terms of legacies of law; hence the book's title. If I had heeded Sir Sydney's advice, I would have titled the book thus: "Some Preliminary Observations on Certain Aspects of the South African Judicial System that are Seldom Openly Discussed."[8] It was a toss-up in the end.

A Plausible Case

I have argued that the case of Chile, 1830–1990, provides tentative evidence that further supports my argument about the legacies of law. Drawing on a sustained legal tradition (the year 1840 marked a critical juncture), Chile experienced only thirteen months of unconstitutional rule between 1830 and 1973. The normative state, although heavily curtailed, remained in operation

---

[7] Sydney Kentridge, "Telling the Truth about Law," *South African Law Journal*, Vol. 99, No. 4 (November 1982), p. 649.
[8] Kentridge, "Telling the Truth about Law," p. 650.

during the dictatorship (the leadership of which was far less homogenous than is commonly assumed). This institutional trace left, as in South Africa, a legacy with unintended consequences. The survival of a *reasonably* stable institutional structure within which the tasks of social regulation and integration could be carried out benefited the politics and economics of democratic transition in Chile. Confidence in the state generated trust among adversaries; trust among persons, in turn, inspired further confidence in the state, as well as secondary institutions such as the 1980 constitution and other reform institutions. This facilitated the evolution of cooperation in Chile's endgame. Credible commitments were reached – and sustained – among democracy-demanding and democracy-resisting forces.

THE LESSONS OF LAW

The objective of my comparative historical analysis of the South African case was to lay the foundation for a political economy of law, by which I mean the study of the role of both instrumental *and* expressive choice in the formation, deformation, and transformation of legal norms and institutions, and the long-run consequences of such choice.[9]

The *effects* of institutions have received by far the most attention in the study of institutional development. The analysis of the constraints that institutions exert on choice, be it the constraints of constitutions, legislatures, executives, courts, party systems, or electoral systems, is the hallmark of the new institutionalism. Much of this literature takes institutions as exogenous. As Barry Weingast writes,

Most studies of institutions, including those relying on approaches other than rational choice, assume institutions are fixed and study their effects. This begs the question of why institutions endure.[10]

I have attempted to answer this question in the context of large-scale social change. I have combined exogenous and endogenous approaches to the study of legal institutions. In both of the empirical analyses I therefore proceeded in two stages. I first took the state as the thing to be explained, and then analyzed its effects.

In the theoretical chapters I built a model of institutional stability. "A model of institutional stability," writes Weingast, "must meet two conditions: first, the model must allow institutions to be altered by particular actors, and second, it must show why these actors have no incentive to do so."[11] Through process tracing, I hope to have shown that both conditions held in the empirical application of my model. The individualizing comparison provided

---

[9] On the latter, see, for example, Alexander A. Schuessler, *A Logic of Expressive Choice* (Princeton: Princeton University Press, 2000).
[10] Weingast, "Political Institutions," p. 185.
[11] Ibid.

evidence of how actors in South Africa and Chile molded legal institutions in the quest for sustainable regimes, and how they have sustained – over the long run – a *general* commitment to a legal way of doing things. Inasmuch as this commitment was repeatedly honored in the breach, it remained surprisingly constant from the perspective of the *longue durée*.

Law of the Long Run

Like Fernand Braudel and the French *Annales* school, I have given priority to long-term historical structures – notably legal traditions – in my analysis of political order in changing societies.[12] Throughout this book, I have argued that choices about cooperation and confrontation in newly democratizing countries are crucially affected by the presence, or absence, as well as the nature of a legal tradition. I have suggested that legal traditions – or legal ideologies – provide shared mental models that *can*, under the conditions specified in this book, help overcome uncertainty and bargaining predicaments in transitions from authoritarian rule. Allow me to reprise Denzau and North:

Under conditions of uncertainty, individuals' interpretation of their environment will reflect their learning. Individuals with common cultural backgrounds and experiences will share reasonably convergent mental models, ideologies, and institutions; and individuals with different learning experiences (both cultural and environmental) will have different theories (models, ideologies) to interpret their environment.[13]

I maintain that South Africa's legal tradition, for the reasons explicated in the preceding chapters, served as a shared mental model in this sense, and with the effects described above. Confidence in these institutional traces was a path-dependent effect of the "self-binding" that the commitment to law of successive governments has affected over the span of several centuries. Mine, therefore, is an argument about the law of the long run. I believe that the long-run historical development of legal norms and institutions in both South Africa and Chile is causally related to democratic outcomes in the late twentieth century (see Figure 9.1).

I am *not* suggesting, however, that these initial conditions (which set in motion self-reproducing sequences) were the only causal factors that facilitated the – comparatively peaceful – resolution of both countries' endgames. As the preceding chapters have shown, factors *other* than these countries' legal traditions were necessary for making democracy work. And yet, it is imperative that we study more closely societies in which an historical commitment to law has, over the long run, induced further movement in the same direction. If and when such movement occurs, we may be faced with a structurally unique hybrid regime.

---

[12] Fernand Braudel, "History and the Social Sciences: The *Longue Durée*," in idem., ed., *On History* (Chicago: University of Chicago Press, 1980), pp. 25–54.
[13] Denzau and North, "Shared Mental Models," pp. 3–4.

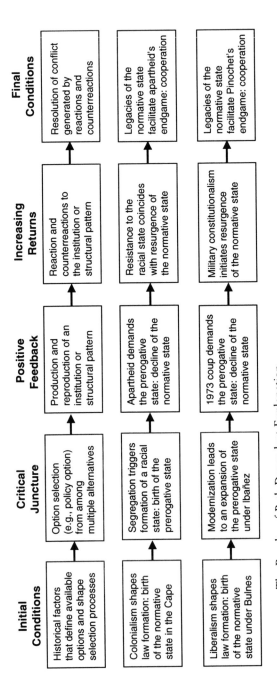

FIGURE 9.1. The Results of Path-Dependent Explanation

Initial Conditions

Historical factors that define available options and shape selection processes

Colonialism shapes law formation: birth of the normative state in the Cape

Liberalism shapes law formation: birth of the normative state under Bulnes

Critical Juncture

Option selection (e.g., policy option) from among multiple alternatives

Segregation triggers formation of a racial state: birth of the prerogative state

Modernization leads to an expansion of the prerogative state under Ibañez

Positive Feedback

Production and reproduction of an institution or structural pattern

Apartheid demands the prerogative state: decline of the normative state

1973 coup demands the prerogative state: decline of the normative state

Increasing Returns

Reaction and counterreactions to the institution or structural pattern

Resistance to the racial state coincides with resurgence of the normative state

Military constitutionalism initiates resurgence of the normative state

Final Conditions

Resolution of conflict generated by reactions and counterreactions

Legacies of the normative state facilitate apartheid's endgame: cooperation

Legacies of the normative state facilitate Pinochet's endgame: cooperation

Hybrid Regimes

So-called *hybrid regimes,* as theorized in the literature, represent one subtype of authoritarianism. What we might call *pure regimes,* that is, regimes essentially lacking contestation and participation, represent another. Examples of pure authoritarian regimes can be said to include neopatrimonial regimes such as that of Mobutu Sese Seko in the former Zaire and that of General Haji Mohammad Suharto in Indonesia. The defining characteristic of these regimes is the full-scale, untempered authoritarianism that they exhibit.[14]

The focus on hybridity as an institutional feature is part and parcel of "a new wave of scholarly attention to the varieties of nondemocratic regimes and to the rather astonishing frequency with which contemporary authoritarian regimes manifest, at least superficially, a number of democratic features."[15] Steve Levitsky and Lucan Way put it thus,

The post–Cold War world has been marked by the proliferation of hybrid political regimes. In different ways, and to varying degrees, polities across much of Africa (Ghana, Kenya, Mozambique, Zambia, Zimbabwe), postcommunist Eurasia (Albania, Croatia, Russia, Serbia, Ukraine), and Latin America (Haiti, Mexico, Paraguay, Peru) combined democratic rules with authoritarian governance during the 1990s.[16]

A New Subtype

Some authoritarian regimes might be deserving of the adjective "hybrid" because of the existence of some contestation in the country in question. We might call these, following Levitsky and Way, *competitive regimes*[17]: Other authoritarian regimes might be deserving of the "hybrid" moniker because of the existence of certain avenues of participation. We might call these, following Schedler, *electoral regimes* (see Figure 9.2).

I contend that dual states, as conceptualized herein, are different from *both* the competitive and electoral subtypes of authoritarianism, notably because they provide – albeit in heavily circumscribed form – for *both* competition *and* participation. The democratic features of dual states are not simply "superficial," but integral, to the governance of the polity.

To reiterate an earlier point, in contrast to much of the literature on hybrid regimes, I am *not* here concerned with instances of hybrid regimes that have erected "institutional façades of democracy, including regular multiparty elections for the chief executive, in order to conceal (and reproduce) harsh

---

[14] Larry Diamond, *Developing Democracy: Toward Consolidation* (Baltimore: Johns Hopkins University Press, 1999), pp. 15–16.

[15] Larry Diamond, "Thinking about Hybrid Regimes," *Journal of Democracy,* Vol. 13, No. 2 (April 2002), p. 23.

[16] Steven Levitsky and Lucan A. Way, "The Rise of Competitive Authoritarianism," *Journal of Democracy,* Vol. 13, No. 2 (April 2002), p. 51. For a related argument, see also Fareed Zakaria, "The Rise of Illiberal Democracy," *Foreign Affairs,* Vol. 76, No. 6 (November/ December 1997), pp. 22–43; and idem., *The Future of Freedom: Illiberal Democracy at Home and Abroad* (New York: Norton, 2003).

[17] Levitsky and Way, "The Rise of Competitive Authoritarianism."

322

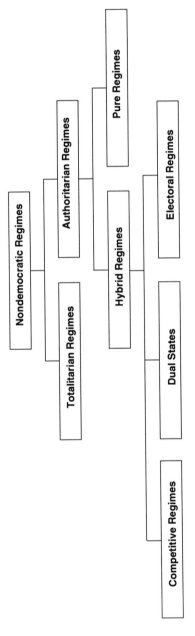

FIGURE 9.2. A Classification of Nondemocratic Regimes

realities of authoritarian governance."[18] The subtype of authoritarianism, or hybrid regime, with which I am concerned is *genuinely* comprised of two halves – a normative state and a prerogative state. Neither half serves to conceal the other. Although the influence of each half may be subject to fluctuation, the fundamental *structure* of this regime type, with its conflicting imperatives, will remain intact. This is the hallmark of the dual state, its defining characteristic. Dual states, as conceived herein, are *not* merely authoritarian regimes that use law. Dual states are authoritarian regimes that can look back on a tradition of liberalism, where commitment to law was an *expressive* pursuit, not just an instrumental one.

Are there lessons to be learned from this? According to one scholar, opposition legal victories in South Africa, this archetypical dual state,

demonstrated the [apartheid] regime's vulnerability and eroded its will to repress. They empowered the masses while offering activists protection from state retaliation. They strengthened the opposition's own commitment to legality and thus the prospect that the post-apartheid regime would respect the rule of law. This quixotic victory continues to offer a beacon to other struggles.[19]

Or does it?

THE LIMITS OF LAW

Inasmuch as the South African case, and insights from the Chilean case, may offer a beacon to other struggles, we must be careful not to exaggerate the beneficial role of law in times of transition.

The "Rule of Law" Sector

Interest in the promotion of so-called rule of law projects in changing societies came in the two waves. The first wave hit the newly independent countries in the 1960s and 1970s, the second the newly democratizing countries in the 1990s and 2000s. The first wave washed ashore under the banner "law and development" (L&D), the second under the "rule of law" (ROL) heading.

Then

The L&D movement, with its emphasis on the modernization of law, was led by a band of liberal lawyers who rejected the "formalism" of the legal cultures in the targeted societies. "By this the L&D planners meant rules were developed, interpreted, and applied without careful attention to policy goals."[20] Formalism

---

[18] Andreas Schedler, "The Logic of Electoral Authoritarianism," in idem., ed., *Electoral Authoritarianism: The Dynamics of Unfree Competition* (Boulder, CO: Lynne Rienner, 2006), p. 1.

[19] Abel, "Legality without a Constitution," p. 80.

[20] David M. Trubek, "The 'Rule of Law' in Development Assistance: Past, Present, and Future," in David M. Trubek and Alvaro Santos, eds., *The New Law and Economic Development: A Critical Appraisal* (Cambridge: Cambridge University Press, 2006), p. 76.

was thought to be the cause of inefficacy as well as illegitimacy; culturalism the answer. This antiformalist stance "led to the L&D programs that evolved in the 1960s. The primary goal of these programs was to transform legal culture and institutions through educational reform and selected transplants of 'modern' institutions. If formalism was the source of bad laws, weak enforcement, and ineffective or counterproductive lawyering, then the most important thing to do was to create a new, more instrumental *legal culture*. This culturalist approach led to a heavy emphasis on reform of legal education as the way to transform a formalist culture into an instrumental one."[21]

Although popular among donors, notably the Ford Foundation, the L&D wave of reform either left little mark on the societies that it hit (many of which were surprisingly resistant to institutional change) or had unintended consequences. "In some cases the 'transplants' did not take at all: some of the new laws promoted by the reformers remained on the books but were ignored in action. In others laws were captured by local elites and put to uses different from those the reformers intended."[22] The educational problems netted few results and "even when change did come about in the economic sphere, leading to more instrumental thinking, effective law making, purposive approaches to adjudication and pragmatic law-yering, the hoped-for spillover to democracy and protection of individual rights did not occur. This was a real shock to Western liberal legalists who had assumed that the legal system was a seamless whole and that reform in one sphere would nec-essarily lead to progressive change in other areas."[23] The L&D movement col-lapsed in the mid-1970s after a decade's worth of institutional design and export.

Now

In the late 1980s, international organizations such as the World Bank, and governmental organizations such as the U.S. Agency for International Devel-opment (USAID), began to emphasize once again the importance of a legal way of doings things for implementing political and economic reforms. Ever since then the World Bank estimates to have supported more than 330 ROL projects in over one hundred countries. In the decade from 1993 and 2003, according to World Bank Annual Reports, the international lending institution spent $3.8 million in furtherance of like projects. Driving this initiative, in the words of Ibrahim Shihata, general counsel and senior vice president of the World Bank between 1983 and 1998, was the assumption that

[r]eforms cannot be effective in the absence of a system, which translates them into workable rules and makes sure they are complied with. Such a system assumes that: a) there is a set of rules which are known in advance, b) such rules are actually in force, c) mechanisms exist to ensure the proper application of the rules and to allow for departure from them as needed according to established procedures, d) conflicts in the application of the rules can be resolved through binding decisions of an independent

[21] Ibid.
[22] Ibid., p. 79.
[23] Ibid.

judicial or arbitral body, and e) there are known procedures for amending the rules when they no longer serve their purpose.[24]

Elsewhere, Shihata elaborated further, citing the advantages of

a system based on abstract rules which are actually applied, and on functioning institutions which ensure the appropriate applications of such rules. This system of rules and institutions is reflected in the concept of the rule of law, generally known in different legal systems and often expressed in the familiar phrase of a "government of laws and not of men."[25]

On the face of it, the World Bank's insistence on taking seriously the law as an institutional structure is not dissimilar to the perspective that I adopted in this book. And yet the two perspectives generate *diametrically opposed* policy prescriptions. The World Bank model, at least until recently, centered on (1) the centrality of legal transplants; (2) a one-size-fits-all approach; (3) top-down methods; and (4) short-time horizons. The danger of the World Bank model, as even the World Bank is beginning to acknowledge, is that it leads to "an underestimation of the difficulty and complexity of legal development. If law can be seen as a set of neutral rules, or at most institutions, different national legal systems can be formally compared and modeled, and successful models can be transplanted into countries with failed systems, much as businesses adopt 'best practices' in manufacturing processes, inventory management, and so on."[26]

The problem with the World Bank model is that law "is seen as technology when it should be seen as sociology or politics."[27] As a corrective, I have emphasized the importance of understanding the law of the long run. The upshot is that legal traditions, like all traditions, develop very slowly. Neither formalism nor culturalism will ever be sufficient to create a legal culture. It is history that matters. Like state formation more generally, legal development is a macrohistorical process. As I have suggested elsewhere, "[c]ontrolling and concluding such a process is an improbable task."[28]

A TRUTH ABOUT LAW

This book has provided an account of the creation and maintenance, over centuries, of two sophisticated legal traditions – legal traditions akin to the ones that today's rule-of-law enthusiasts believe to be a prerequisite for

---

[24] As quoted in Frank Upham, "Mythmaking in the Rule-of-Law Othodoxy," in Thomas Carothers, ed., *Promoting the Rule of Law Abroad: In Search of Knowledge* (Washington, DC: Carnegie Endowment for International Peace, 2006), p. 77.

[25] As quoted in Alvaro Santos, "The World Bank's Uses of the 'Rule of Law' Promise in Economic Development," in David M. Trubek and Alvaro Santos, eds., *The New Law and Economic Development: A Critical Appraisal* (Cambridge: Cambridge University Press, 2006), p. 270.

[26] Upham, "Mythmaking in the Rule-of-Law Orthodoxy," pp. 75–76.

[27] Ibid., p. 76.

[28] Meierhenrich, "Forming States after Failure," p. 153.

political (e.g., USAID) and economic (e.g., World Bank) development, and therefore seek to create in changing societies.

Creating a Legal Tradition?

Unfortunately, "donors' faith in the rule-of-law orthodoxy reflects a 'build it and they will come' mentality that flows from a series of flawed assumptions."[29] The upshot of this book is that legal traditions are just that – traditions. They evolve and cannot be erected. Even well meaning, L&D-inspired efforts at "nurturing" rule of law cultures, whereas an improvement on the World Bank model, are unlikely to have a significant impact on legal development in changing societies. Where top-down reformers are blinded by universality, bottom-up reformers are regularly taken in by particularity. An example of this is the recent focus in the international donor community on support for ostensibly traditional mechanisms of dispute resolution – many of which are traditions solely invented for the purpose of extracting donor funds. The funding of "traditional institutions" by ROL advocates may be similarly inappropriate – and counterproductive – as the import of "modern institutions" by L&D advocates in the 1960s and 1970s. But this is a topic for another day.[30] Let me return to the argument of this book.

Lest I be misunderstood, I make no pretense to encompass all possible factors that influence changing societies' propensity for democracy. Variables other than the legacies of law invariably also shape democratization outcomes, including the depth of cleavages in a given society; the type of nondemocratic rule from which democracy emerges; the distribution of power between democracy-demanding and democracy-resisting forces; and developments at the international system level, to name but a few. This, however, thwarts *neither* the plausibility *nor* validity of my institutionalist account. For institutional analysis to be compelling, it is *not* necessary that it account for *all* of the variance in political, social, and economic outcomes and crowd out arguments that point to other explanatory factors.[31] Rather, it suffices that the causal mechanisms identified through institutional analysis are plausible and remain valid when applied empirically. Richard Abel, the eminent legal scholar, put it well for the principal case at hand:

Law was by no means the only or even the most important factor in the ultimate victory [of democracy over apartheid]. ... But the recognition that law was only one ingredient in the struggle should not diminish its value.[32]

[29] Stephen Golub, "A House without a Foundation," in Thomas Carothers, ed., *Promoting the Rule of Law Abroad: In Search of Knowledge* (Washington, DC: Carnegie Endowment for International Peace, 2006), p. 106.
[30] I take it up in my forthcoming book *The Invention of Law*, an analysis of legal responses to the 1994 genocide in Rwanda.
[31] Oran R. Young, *International Governance: Protecting the Environment in a Stateless Society* (Ithaca: Cornell University Press, 1994), p. 7.
[32] Abel, "Legality without a Constitution," p. 80.

Accordingly, the legacies of law command our respect as a conceptual variable and warrant further scholarly investigation. Having said this, this book, like any other, has its limits. My principal argument, although valid in the cases to which it was applied, remains a conjecture waiting to be tested more systematically across time and additional cases. Although the advantages of the single case study as a methodological device were evident, the small-*n* approach adopted here has some drawbacks. With the use of individualizing comparisons – comparisons that underscore first and foremost singularity, not similarity or variation – I have left myself open to criticism. Some readers might consider the comparison ungainly, others insufficient. Yet individualizing comparisons are the necessary first step toward grander, universalizing comparisons. They are the foundation for complex, encompassing comparisons like the "conceptual maps" that Stein Rokkan drew of Europe; simpler, more stylized comparisons such as Barrington Moore's historical search for principles of variation in processes and outcomes of modernization; or Theda Skocpol's comparative historical analysis of state effects in social revolutions.[33] We need to get historical particularities right before generalization can truly begin. This may necessitate redescription, as advocated by Ian Shapiro, one of the most astute critics of methodological unilateralism. He makes a persuasive case for thinking of redescription as a problem-driven enterprise:

> It is a two-step venture that starts when one shows that the accepted way of characterizing a piece of political reality fails to capture an important feature of what stands in need of explanation or justification. One then offers a recharacterization that speaks to the inadequacies in the prior account. When convincingly done, prior adherents to the old view will be unable to ignore it and remain credible.[34]

My redescription of apartheid's endgame was intended to draw attention to the insufficiently appreciated centrality of law. This missing variable stood in need of explanation (as well as understanding). In pursuit of this objective, the methodological approach adopted here – the pairing of an individualizing comparison with a longitudinal analysis of a telling case – has sought to integrate nomothetic and ideographic reasoning. To any critics of the single case methodology, I respond with Albert Hirschman who insisted that

> any theory is built on a limited number of observations; and that intimate acquaintance with an individual country has in fact produced many of our most useful generalizations about the social process.[35]

---

[33] Stein Rokkan, "Dimensions of State Formation and Nation-Building: A Possible Paradigm for Research on Variations Within Europe," in Charles Tilly, ed., *The Formation of National States in Western Europe* (Princeton: Princeton University Press, 1975), pp. 562–600; Moore, *Social Origins of Dictatorship and Democracy*. See Tilly, *Big Structures, Large Processes, and Huge Comparisons*, Chapters 6, 7, and 8; Theda Skocpol, *States and Social Revolutions: A Comparative Analysis of France, Russia, and China* (Cambridge: Cambridge University Press, 1979).

[34] Shapiro, "Problems, Methods, and Theories in the Study of Politics," p. 39.

[35] Albert O. Hirschman, *The Strategy of Economic Development* (Yale: Yale University Press, 1958), p. v.

Bibliography

Abbott, Kenneth W. and Duncan Snidal, "Hard Law and Soft Law in International Governance," *International Organization*, Vol. 54, No. 3 (Summer 2000), pp. 421–456.

Abel, Richard L., *Politics by Other Means: Law in the Struggle Against Apartheid, 1980–1994* (New York: Routledge, 1995).

"Legality Without a Constitution: South Africa," in David Dyzenhaus, ed., *Recrafting the Rule of Law: The Limits of Legal Order* (Oxford: Hart Publishing, 1999), pp. 66–80.

Abernethy, David B., *The Dynamics of Global Dominance: European Overseas Empires, 1415–1980* (New Haven: Yale University Press, 2000).

Adam, Heribert, *Modernizing Racial Domination: The Dynamics of South African Politics* (Berkeley: University of California Press, 1971).

"Perspectives in the Literature: A Critical Evaluation," in Heribert Adam and Hermann Giliomee, eds., *The Rise and Crisis of Afrikaner Power* (Cape Town: David Philip, [1979] 1983), pp. 16–60.

and Kogila Moodley, *South Africa Without Apartheid: Dismantling Racial Domination* (Berkeley: University of California Press, 1986).

and Kogila Moodley, *The Opening of the Apartheid Mind: Options for the New South Africa* (Berkeley: University of California Press, 1993).

and Kogila Moodley, *South Africa's Negotiated Revolution* (Johannesburg: Jonathan Ball, 1993).

Kogila Moodley, Frederik van Zyl Slabbert, *Comrades in Business: Post-Liberation Politics in South Africa* (Cape Town: Tafelberg, 1997).

Adler, Glenn and Eddie Webster, "Challenging Transition Theory: The Labor Movement, Radical Reform, and Transition to Democracy in South Africa," *Politics and Society*, Vol. 23, No. 1 (March 1995), pp. 75–106.

and Jonny Steinberg, eds., *From Comrades to Citizens: The South African Civics Movement and the Transition to Democracy* (London: Macmillan, 2000).

and Eddie Webster, eds., *Trade Unions and Democratization in South Africa, 1985–1997* (London: Macmillan, 2000).

African National Congress, *Documents of the Second National Consultative Conference of the African National Congress, Zambia, 16–23 June, 1985* (Lusaka: ANC, 1985).

The State and Social Transformation, Unpublished Discussion Document (November 1996).

Albertyn, Cathi, "Forced Removals and the Law: The Magopa Case," *South African Journal of Human Rights*, Vol. 2, No. 1 (March 1986), pp. 91–99.

"A Critical Analysis of Political Trials in South Africa, 1948–88," Ph.D. dissertation, University of Cambridge, 1991.

Alden, Chris, *Apartheid's Last Stand: The Rise and Fall of the South African Security State* (London: Macmillan, 1996).

Alexander, Gerard, "Institutionalized Uncertainty, the Rule of Law, and the Sources of Democratic Stability," *Comparative Political Studies*, Vol. 35, No. 10 (December 2002), pp. 1145–1170.

Allen, Francis A., *The Habits of Legality: Criminal Justice and the Rule of Law* (New York: Oxford University Press, 1996).

Allott, Philip, "The Concept of International Law," in Michael Byers, ed., *The Role of Law in International Politics: Essays in International Relations and International Law* (Oxford: Oxford University Press, 2000), pp. 69–89.

Aly, Götz and Karl Heinz Roth, *Die restlose Erfassung: Volkszählen, Identifizieren, Aussondern im Nationalsozialismus* (Frankfurt am Main: Fischer, 2000).

Anderson, Perry, *Lineages of the Absolutist State* (London: Verso, 1979).

Angermund, Ralph, *Deutsche Richterschaft 1919–1945: Krisenerfahrung, Illusion, politische Rechtsprechung* (Frankfurt am Main: Fischer, 1990).

Arthur, W. Brian, "Self-Reinforcing Mechanisms in Economics," in Philip W. Anderson, Kenneth J. Arrow, and David Pines, eds., *The Economy as an Evolving Complex System* (Redwood City: Addison-Wesley, 1988), pp. 9–31.

"Competing Technologies, Increasing Returns, and Lock-In by Historical Events," *Economic Journal*, Vol. 99, No. 394 (March 1989), pp. 116–131.

Increasing Returns and Path Dependence in the Economy (Ann Arbor: University of Michigan Press, 1994).

Asmal, Kader, "Truth, Reconciliation and Justice: The South African Experience in Perspective," *Modern Law Review*, Vol. 63, No. 1 (January 2000), pp. 1–24.

Louise Asmal, and Ronald Suresh Roberts, *Reconciliation Through Truth: A Reckoning of Apartheid's Criminal Governance*, 2nd ed. (Cape Town: David Philip, 1997).

David Chidester, and Cassius Lubisi, *Legacy of Freedom: The ANC's Human Rights Tradition* (Cape Town: Jonathan Ball, 2005).

Atiyah, P. S. and R. S. Summers, *Form and Substance in Anglo-American Law: A Comparative Study of Legal Reasoning, Legal Theory, and Legal Institutions* (Oxford: Clarendon Press, 1987).

Axelrod, Robert, *The Evolution of Cooperation* (New York: Basic Books, 1984).

The Complexity of Cooperation: Agent-Based Models of Competition and Collaboration (Princeton: Princeton University Press, 1997).

Badie, Bertrand, *The Sociology of the State*, translated by Arthur Goldhammer (Chicago: University of Chicago Press, 1983).

Barber, James, *Mandela's World: The International Dimension of South Africa's Political Revolution 1990–99* (Oxford: James Currey, 2004).

Bar-Gill, Oren and Chaim Fershtman, "Law and Preferences," *Journal of Law, Economics, and Organization*, Vol. 20, No. 2 (October 2004), pp. 331–352.

Barkey, Karen, *Bandits and Bureaucrats: The Ottoman Route to State Centralization* (Ithaca, NY: Cornell University Press, 1994).

Barros, Robert J., "By Reason and Force: Military Constitutionalism in Chile, 1973–1989," Ph.D. dissertation, University of Chicago, 1996.

"Personalization and Institutional Constraints: Pinochet, the Military Junta, and the 1980 Constitution," *Latin American Politics and Society*, Vol. 43, No. 1 (Spring 2001), pp. 5–43.

Constitutionalism and Dictatorship: Pinochet, the Junta, and the 1980 Constitution (Cambridge: Cambridge University Press, 2002).

Barry, Brian, "Review Article: Exit, Voice, and Loyalty," *British Journal of Political Science*, Vol. 4, No. 1 (January 1974), pp. 79–107.

Baskin, Jeremy, *Striking Back: A History of COSATU* (Johannesburg: Ravan, 1991).

Barzel, Yoram, *A Theory of the State: Economic Rights, Legal Rights, and the Scope of the State* (Cambridge: Cambridge University Press, 2002).

Basson, Dion, *South Africa's Interim Constitution: Text and Notes*, Revised Edition (Kenwyn: Juta, 1995).

Bates, Robert H., *Essays on the Political Economy of Africa* (Berkeley: University of California Press, 1983).

Beyond the Miracle of the Market: The Political Economy of Agrarian Development in Kenya (Cambridge: Cambridge University Press, 1989).

"Macropolitical Economy in the Field of Development," in James E. Alt and Kenneth A. Shepsle, eds., *Perspectives on Positive Political Economy* (Cambridge: Cambridge University Press, 1990), pp. 31–54.

Rui J. P. de Figueiredo, Jr., and Barry R. Weingast, "The Politics of Interpretation: Rationality, Culture, and Transition," *Politics and Society*, Vol. 26, No. 4 (December 1998), pp. 603–642.

Avner Greif, Margaret Levi, Jean-Laurent Rosenthal, and Barry R. Weingast, *Analytic Narratives* (Princeton: Princeton University Press, 1998).

Avner Greif, Margaret Levi, Jean-Laurent Rosenthal, and Barry R. Weingast, "Conclusion," in idem., *Analytic Narratives* (Princeton: Princeton University Press, 1998), pp. 231–241.

Baxter, Lawrence, "A Judicial Declaration of Martial Law," *South African Journal on Human Rights*," Vol. 3, No. 3 (November 1987), pp. 317–322.

Bebchuk, Lucian Arye, "A Theory of Path Dependence in Corporate Ownership and Governance," *Stanford Law Review*, Vol. 52, No. 1 (October 1999), pp. 127–170.

Becker, Charles M., "Economic Sanctions Against South Africa," *World Politics*, Vol. 33, No. 2 (January 1987), pp. 147–173.

Bendix, Reinhard, *Max Weber: An Intellectual Portrait* (New York: Doubleday, 1960).

Nation-Building and Citizenship, Enlarged Edition (Berkeley: University of California Press, 1977).

Beinart, William, *Twentieth-Century South Africa* (Cape Town: Oxford University Press, 1994).

Benedict, Philip, "The Historiography of Continental Calvinism," in Hartmut Lehmann and Guenther Roth, eds., *Weber's Protestant Ethic: Origins, Evidence, and Contexts* (Cambridge: Cambridge University Press, 1993), pp. 305–325.

Benton, Lauren, *Law and Colonial Cultures: Legal Regimes in World History, 1400–1900* (Cambridge: Cambridge University Press, 2002).

Benz, Wolfgang, *Dimension des Völkermords* (München: dtv, 1996).

Berat, Lynn, "The Constitutional Court of South Africa and Jurisdictional Questions: In the Interest of Justice?," *International Journal of Constitutional Law*, Vol. 3, No. 1 (January 2005), pp. 39–76.

Berins Collier, Ruth, *Regimes in Tropical Africa: Changing Forms Supremacy, 1945–1975* (Berkeley: University of California Press, 1982).

Paths Toward Democracy: The Working Class and Elites in Western Europe and South America (Cambridge: Cambridge University Press, 1999).

and David Collier, *Shaping the Political Arena: Critical Junctures, the Labor Movement, and Regime Dynamics in Latin America* (Princeton: Princeton University Press, 1991).

Berman, Harold J., *Law and Revolution: The Formation of the Western Legal Tradition* (Cambridge, MA: Harvard University Press, 1983).

and Charles J. Reid, Jr., "Max Weber as Legal Historian," in Stephen Turner, ed., *The Cambridge Companion to Weber* (Cambridge: Cambridge University Press, 2000), pp. 223–239.

Bernstein, Hilda, *No. 46: Steve Biko* (London: International Defence and Aid Fund, 1978).

Bhargava, Anurima, "Defining Political Crimes: A Case Study of the South African Truth and Reconciliation Commission," *Columbia Law Review*, Vol. 102, No. 5 (June 2002), pp. 1304–1339.

Bischop, W. R., "Sir James Rose Innes, K. C. M. G.," *Journal of the Society of Comparative Legislation*, New Series, Vol. 11, No. 1 (1910), pp. 9–12.

Bix, Brian H., "Natural Law: The Modern Tradition," in Jules Coleman and Scott Shapiro, eds., *The Oxford Handbook of Jurisprudence and Philosophy of Law* (Oxford: Oxford University Press, 2002), pp. 61–103.

Bizos, George, *No One to Blame? In Pursuit of Justice in South Africa* (Cape Town: David Philip, 1998).

Blau, Peter M., *Exchange and Power in Social Life* (New York: Wiley, 1964).

Blom-Cooper, J., "The South African Treason Trial: R. v. Adams and Others," *International and Comparative Law Quarterly*, Vol. 8, No. 1 (January 1959), pp. 59–72.

Blomeyer, Peter, *Der Nostand in den letzten Jahren von Weimar* (Berlin: Duncker und Humblot, 1999).

Böckenförde, Ernst-Wolfgang, *Staat, Gesellschaft, Freiheit: Studien zur Staatstheorie und zum Verfassungsrecht* (Frankfurt am Main: Suhrkamp, 1976).

"Entstehung und Wandel des Rechtsstaatsbegriffs," in idem., *Recht, Staat, Freiheit: Studien zur Rechtsphilosophie, Staatstheorie und Verfassungsgerichtsbarkeit* (Frankfurt am Main: Suhrkamp, 1991), pp. 143–169.

Bohannan, Paul, *Justice and Judgment Among the Tiv* (London: Oxford University Press, 1957).

Bohatec, Josef, *Calvin und das Recht* (Graz: Boehlaus, 1934).

Bollen, Kenneth A., "Comparative Measurement of Political Democracy," *American Sociological Review*, Vol. 45, No. 3 (June 1980), pp. 370–390.

Boraine, Alex, *The Healing of a Nation?* (Cape Town: Justice in Transition, 1995).

A Country Unmasked: Inside South Africa's Truth and Reconciliation Commission (Oxford: Oxford University Press, 2000).

Boulle, L. J., *South Africa and the Consociational Option: A Constitutional Analysis* (Cape Town: Juta, 1984).

Bowen, John R., *Islam, Law and Equality in Indonesia: An Anthropology of Public Reasoning* (Cambridge: Cambridge University Press, 2003).

Bracher, Karl Dietrich, "Stufen der Machtergreifung," in Karl Dietrich Bracher, Wolfgang Sauer, and Gerhard Schulz, eds., *Die Nationalsozialistische Machtergreifung: Studien zur Errichtung des totalitären Herrschaftssystems in Deutschland 1933/34* (Köln: Westdeutscher Verlag, 1960).

Braithwaite, Valerie and Margaret Levi, eds., *Trust and Governance* (New York: Russell Sage Foundation, 1998).

Bratton, Michael, "Beyond the State: Civil Society and Associational Life in Africa," *World Politics*, Vol. 41, No. 3 (April 1989), pp. 407–430.

and Nicolas Van de Walle, "Neopatrimonial Regimes and Political Transitions in Africa," *World Politics*, Vol. 46, No. 4 (July 1994), pp. 453–489.

and Nicolas Van de Walle, *Democratic Experiments in Africa: Regime Transitions in Comparative Perspective* (Cambridge: Cambridge University Press, 1997).

Braude, Claudia and Derek Spitz, "Memory and the Spectre of International Justice: A Comment on AZAPO," *South African Journal on Human Rights*, Vol. 13, No. 2 (1997), pp. 269–282.

Braudel, Fernand, "History and the Social Sciences: The *Longue Durée*," in idem., ed., *On History* (Chicago: University of Chicago Press, 1980), pp. 25–54.

Brennan, Geoffrey and Alan Hamlin, *Democratic Devices and Desires* (Cambridge: Cambridge University Press, 2000).

Brewer, John D., *Black and Blue: Policing in South Africa* (Oxford: Clarendon Press, 1994).

Bronstein, Victoria and Kim Robinson, "Constitutional Jurisprudence and the Bill of Rights: The Certification Judgments," *Annual Survey of South African Law* (1996), pp. 48–115.

Brooks, Alan and Jeremy Brickhill, *Whirlwind Before the Storm* (London: International Defence and Aid Fund for Southern Africa, 1980).

Broun, Kenneth S., *Black Layers, White Courts: The Soul of South African Law* (Athens: Ohio University Press, 2000).

Brubaker, Rogers, "Frontier Theses: Exit, Voice, and Loyalty in East Germany," *Migration World*, Vol. 18, No. 3/4 (1990), pp. 12–17.

Budlender, Geoff, "Law and Lawlessness in South Africa," *South African Journal on Human Rights*, Vol. 3, No. 2 (1988), pp. 139–152.

Büthe, Tim, "Taking Temporality Seriously: Modeling History and the Use of Narratives as Evidence," *American Political Science Review*, Vol. 96, No. 3 (September 2002), pp. 481–493.

Bunce, Valerie, *Subversive Institutions: The Design and the Destruction of Socialism and the State* (Cambridge: Cambridge University Press, 1999).

Burman, Sandra, "The Role of Street Committees Continuing South Africa's Practice of Alternative Justice," in Hugh Corder, ed., *Democracy and the Judiciary* (Cape Town: IDASA, 1988), pp. 151–166.

Butler, Jeffrey, Robert I. Rotberg, and John Adams, *The Black Homelands of South Africa: The Political and Economic Development of Bophuthatswana and KwaZulu* (Berkeley: University of California Press, 1977).

Buzan, Barry, *People, States, and Fear: An Agenda for International Security Studies in the Post-Cold War Era*, Second Edition (Hemel Hempstead: Harvester Wheatsheaf, 1991).

Calvert, Randall L., "Explaining Social Order: Internalization, External Enforcement, or Equilibrium?," in Karol Soltan, Eric M. Uslaner, and Virginia Haufler, eds., *Institutions and Social Order* (Ann Arbor: University of Michigan Press, 1998).

Cameron, Edwin, "Legal Chauvinism, Executive-Mindedness and Justice: L C Steyn's Impact on South African Law," *South African Law Journal*, Vol. 99, No. 1 (February 1982), pp. 38–75.

"Nude Monarchy: The Case of South Africa's Judges," *South African Journal of Human Rights*, Vol. 3, No. 3 (November 1987), pp. 338–346.

"Our Legal System – Precious and Precarious," *South African Law Journal*, Vol. 177, No. 2 (2000), pp. 371–376.

Gilbert Marcus, and Dirk Van Zyl Smit, "The Administration of Justice, Law Reform, and Jurisprudence," *Annual Survey of South African Law* (1988), pp. 500–556.

Gilbert Marcus, and Dirk Van Zyl Smit, "The Administration of Justice, Law Reform and Jurisprudence," *Annual Survey of South African Law* (1989), pp. 556–618.

Carey, John M. and Matthew Soberg Shugart, eds., *Executive Decree Authority* (Cambridge: Cambridge University Press, 1998).

Centre for Applied Legal Studies, *A Report on the Rabie Report: An Examination of Security Legislation in South Africa* (Johannesburg: Centre for Applied Legal Studies, 1982).

Centre for Policy Studies, "The Making of the Constitution," Special Report, *TransAct*, Vol. 2, No. 8 (September 1995).

Cerny, Philip G., *The Changing Architecture of Politics: Structure, Agency, and the Future of the State* (London: Sage, 1990).

Chanock, Martin, *Law, Custom and Social Order: The Colonial Experience in Malawi and Zambia* (Cambridge: Cambridge University Press, 1985).

"Reconstructing South African Law: Legal Formalism and Legal Culture in a New State," in Paul B. Rich, ed., *Reaction and Renewal in South Africa* (London: Macmillan, 1996), pp. 98–124.

The Making of South African Legal Culture 1902–1936: Fear, Favor, and Prejudice (Cambridge: Cambridge University Press, 2001).

Chaskalson, Arthur, "Law in a Changing Society: The Past Ten Years," *South African Journal on Human Rights*, Vol. 5, No. 3 (1989), pp. 293–300.

"The Transition to Democracy in South Africa," *New York University Journal of International Law and Politics*, Vol. 29, No. 3 (Spring 1997), pp. 285–298.

"From Wickedness to Equality: The Moral Transformation of South African Law," *International Journal of Constitutional Law*, Vol. 1, No. 4 (October 2003), pp. 590–609.

Chaskalson, Matthew and Glenda Fick, "Constitutional Law: Constitution of the Republic of South Africa Act 108 of 1996," *Annual Survey of South African Law* (1996), pp. 1–47.

Chaskalson, Matthew and Dennis Davis, "Constitutionalism, the Rule of Law, and the First Certification Judgment: *Ex parte Chairperson of the Constitutional Assembly in Re: Certification of the Constitution of the Republic of South Africa 1996* 1996 (4) SA 744 (CC)," *South African Journal on Human Rights*, Vol. 13, No. 3 (1997), pp. 430–445.

Chaudry, Kiren Aziz, *The Price of Wealth: Economies and Institutions in the Middle East* (Ithaca, NY: Cornell University Press, 1997).

Chong, Dennis, *Rational Lives: Norms and Values in Politics and Society* (Chicago: University of Chicago Press, 2000).

Chwe, Michael Suk-Young, *Rational Ritual: Culture, Coordination, and Common Knowledge* (Princeton: Princeton University Press, 2001).

Clapham, Christopher, *Africa and the International System: The Politics of State Survival* (Cambridge: Cambridge University Press, 1996).

Clark, William Roberts, "Agents and Structures: Two Views of Preferences, Two View of Institutions," *International Studies Quarterly*, Vol. 42, No. 2 (June 1998), pp. 245–270.

Cobley, Alan Gregor, "The 'African National Church': Self-Determination and Political Struggle among Black Christian in South Africa to 1948," *Church History*, Vol. 60, No. 3 (September 1991), pp. 356–371.

Cock, Jacklyn, "The Role of Violence in Current State Security Strategies," in Mark Swilling, ed., *Views on the South African State* (Pretoria: Human Sciences Research Council, 1990), pp. 85–108.

Coleman, James S., *Foundations of Social Theory* (Cambridge, MA: Belknap Press of Harvard University Press, 1990).

Coleman, Max, ed., *A Crime against Humanity: Analysing the Repression of the Apartheid State* (Claremont: David Philip, 1998).

Colomer, Josep M., *Strategic Transitions: Game Theory and Democratization* (Baltimore: Johns Hopkins University Press, 2000).

Comaroff, Jean, *Body of Power, Spirit of Resistance: The Culture and History of a South African People* (Chicago: University of Chicago Press, 1985).

and John L. Comaroff, *Of Revelation and Revolution, Volume 1: Christianity, Colonialism and Consciousness in South Africa* (Chicago: University of Chicago Press, 1991).

and John L. Comaroff, eds., *Law and Disorder in the Postcolony* (Chicago: University of Chicago Press, 2006).

Comaroff, John L. and Jean Comaroff, *Of Revelation and Revolution, Volume 2: The Dialectics of Modernity on a South African Frontier* (Chicago: University of Chicago Press, 1997).

and Jean Comaroff, "Policing Culture, Cultural Policing: Law and Social Order in Postcolonial South Africa," *Law and Society Review*, Vol. 29, No. 3 (Summer 2004), pp. 513–545.

Comaroff, John L. and Simon Roberts, *Rules and Processes: The Cultural Logic of Dispute in an African Context* (Chicago: University of Chicago Press, 1981).

Commission of Inquiry Regarding the Prevention of Public Violence and Intimidation, *Interim Report on the Violence in Hostels*, September 21, 1992.

Final Report into [sic] Train Violence, May 6, 1993.

Fifth Interim Report on Taxi Violence, July 26, 1993.

Interim Report on Criminal Political Violence by Elements within the South African Police, the KwaZulu Police and the Inkatha Freedom Party, March 18, 1994.

Coppedge, Michael, "Thickening Thin Concepts and Theories: Combining Large N and Small in Comparative Politics," *Comparative Politics*, Vol. 31, No. 4 (July 1999), pp. 465–476.

Corbett, M.M. "Presentation to the Truth and Reconciliation Commission," *South African Law Journal*, Vol. 115, No. 1 (1998), pp. 17–20.

Corder, Hugh, *Judges at Work: The Role and Attitudes of the South African Appellate Judiciary, 1910–50* (Cape Town: Juta, 1984).

"Crowbars and Cobwebs: Executive Autocracy and the Law in South Africa," *South African Journal on Human Rights*, Vol. 5, No. 1 (1989), pp. 1–25.

and Dennis Davis, "The Constitutional Guidelines of the African National Congress: A Preliminary Assessment," *South African Law Journal*, Vol. 106, No. 4 (November 1989), pp. 633–647.

Cotterrell, Roger, *Law's Community: Legal Theory in Sociological Perspective* (Oxford: Clarendon Press, 1995).

Crais, Clifton, *The Politics of Evil: Magic, State Power, and the Political Imagination in South Africa* (Cambridge: Cambridge University Press, 2002).

Crocker, David A., "Truth Commissions, Transitional Justice, and Civil Society," in Robert I. Rotberg and Dennis Thompson, eds., *Truth v. Justice: The Morality of Truth Commissions* (Princeton: Princeton University Press, 2000), pp. 91–121.

Dahl, Robert A., "Decision-Making in a Democracy: The Supreme Court as a National Policy Maker," *Journal of Public Law*, Vol. 6, No. 2 (1957), pp. 279–295.

Davenport, T. R. H., *South Africa: A Modern History*, 4th ed. (London: Macmillan, 1991).

David, Paul A., "Clio and the Economics of QWERTY," *American Economic Review*, Vol. 75, No. 2 (May 1985), pp. 332–337.

"Path Dependence, Its Critics, and the Quest for 'Historical Economics, '" in Pierre Garrouste and Stavros Ioannides, eds., *Evolution and Path Dependence in Economic Ideas: Past and Present* (Cheltenham: Edward Elgar, 2000).

David, René and Henry de Vries, *The French Legal System* (New York: Oceana, 1958). and John E. C. Brierley, *Major Legal Systems in the World Today: An Introduction to the Comparative Study of Law*, 2nd ed. (New York: The Free Press, 1978).

Davies, Rob, Dan O'Meara, and Sipho Dlamini, *The Struggle for South Africa: A Reference Guide to Movements, Organizations, and Institutions*, Two Vols. (London: Zed Books, 1984).

Davis, Dennis M., "Competing Conceptions: Pro-Executive or Pro-Democratic – Judges Choose," *South African Journal on Human Rights*, Vol. 3, No. 1 (March 1987), pp. 96–105.

"Judicial Endorsement of Apartheid Propaganda: An Enquiry into an Acute Case," *South African Journal on Human Rights*," Vol. 3, No. 2 (July 1987), pp. 223–233.

"*Omar*: A Retreat to the Sixties?," *South African Journal on Human Rights*, Vol. 3, No. 3 (November 1989), pp. 326–331.

"Remaking the South African Legal Order," *Social Justice*, Vol. 18, Nos. 1–2 (Spring/Summer 1991).

"Adjudication and Transformation: Out of the Heart of Darkness," *Cardozo Law Review*, Vol. 22, Nos. 3–4 (March 2001), pp. 817–835.

"Constitutional Borrowing: The Influence of Legal Culture and Local History in the Reconstitution of Comparative Influence: The South African Experience," *International Journal of Constitutional Law*, Vol. 1, No. 2 (April 2003), pp. 181–195.

and Hugh Corder, "A Long March: Administrative Law in the Appellate Division," *South African Journal on Human Rights*, Vol. 4, No. 3 (1988), pp. 281–302.

Gilbert J. Marcus, and Jonathan Klaaren, "The Administration of Justice, Law Reform and Jurisprudence," *Annual Survey of South African Law* (1996), pp. 882–914.

Davis, Stephen M., *Apartheid's Rebels: Inside South Africa's Hidden War* (New Haven: Yale University Press, 1987).

De Brito, Alexandra Barahona, *Human Rights and Democratization in Latin America: Uruguay and Chile* (Oxford: Oxford University Press, 1997).

De Figueiredo Jr., Rui J. P. and Barry Weingast, "The Rationality of Fear: Political Opportunism and Ethnic Conflict," in Barbara F. Walter and Jack Snyder, eds., *Civil Wars, Insecurity, and Intervention* (New York: Columbia University Press, 1999), pp. 261–302.

De Gruchy, John W., "Grappling with a Colonial Heritage: The English-speaking Churches under Imperialism and Apartheid," in Richard Elphick and Rodney Davenport, eds., *Christianity in South Africa: A Political, Social, and Cultural History* (Berkeley: University of California Press, 1997), pp. 155–172.

De Klerk, F. W. *The Last Trek – A New Beginning: The Autobiography* (New York: St. Martin's Press, 1998).

De Klerk, Willem, *F W de Klerk: The Man in His Time* (Johannesburg: Jonathan Ball, 1991).

De Villiers, Bertus, ed., *Birth of a Constitution* (Kenwyn: Juta 1994).

"Social and Economic Rights," in David van Wyk, John Dugard, Bertus de Villiers, and Dennis Davis, eds., *Rights and Constitutionalism: The New South African Legal Order* (Kenwyn: Juta, 1994), pp. 599–628.

De Villiers, René, "Afrikaner Nationalism," in Monica Wilson and Leonard Thompson, eds., *The Oxford History of South Africa, Volume II: South Africa 1870–1966* (Oxford: Clarendon Press, 1971), pp. 365–423.

De Vletter, Fion, "Recent Trends and Prospects of Black Migration to South Africa," *Journal of Modern African Studies*, Vol. 23, No. 4 (December 1985), pp. 667–702.

Della Porta, Donatella, *Social Movements, Political Violence, and the State: A Comparative Analysis of Italy and Germany* (Cambridge: Cambridge University Press, 1995).

Denzau, Arthur T. and Douglass C. North, "Shared Mental Models: Ideologies and Institutions," *Kyklos*, Vol. 47, No. 1 (1994), pp. 3–31.

Derrida, Jacques, "The Laws of Reflection: Nelson Mandela, In Admiration," in Jacques Derrida and Mustapha Tlili, eds., *For Nelson Mandela* (New York: Seaver, 1987), pp. 13–42.

De Villiers, Bertus, ed., *Birth of a Constitution* (Kenwyn: Juta 1994).

"Social and Economic Rights," in David van Wyk, John Dugard, Bertus de Villiers, and Dennis Davis, eds., *Rights and Constitutionalism: The New South African Legal Order* (Kenwyn: Juta, 1994), pp. 599–628.

Diamond, Larry, *Developing Democracy: Toward Consolidation* (Baltimore: Johns Hopkins University Press, 1999).

"Thinking about Hybrid Regimes," *Journal of Democracy*, Vol. 13, No. 2 (April 2002), pp. 21–35.

Dlamini, Charles, "The Influence of Race on the Administration of Justice in South Africa," *South African Journal on Human Rights*, Vol. 4, No. 1 (1988), pp. 37–54.

"Culture, Education, and Religion," in David van Wyk, John Dugard, Bertus de Villiers, and Dennis Davis, eds., *Rights and Constitutionalism: The New South African Legal Order* (Kenwyn: Juta, 1994), pp. 573–598.

Dowding, Keith, Robert E. Goodin, and Carole Pateman, eds., *Justice and Democracy: Essays for Brian Barry* (Cambridge: Cambridge University Press, 2004).

Dowding, Keith, Peter John, Thanos Mergoupis, and Mark van Vugt, "Exit, Voice and Loyalty: Analytic and Empirical Developments," *European Journal of Political Research*, Vol. 37 (2000), pp. 469–495.

Dreier, Ralf and Wolfgang Sellert, eds., *Recht und Justiz im "Dritten Reich"* (Frankfurt am Main: Suhrkamp, 1989).

Dubow, Saul, *The African National Congress* (Cape Town: Jonathan Ball, 2000).

Dugard, John, "Judicial Process, Positivism and Civil Liberty," *South African Law Journal*, Vol. 88, No. 2 (May 1971), pp. 181–200.

Human Rights and the South African Legal Order (Princeton: Princeton University Press, 1978).

"Some Realism about the Judicial Process and Positivism – A Reply," *South African Law Journal*, Vol. 98, No. 3 (August 1981), pp. 372–387.

"*Omar*: Support for Wacks's Ideas on the Judicial Process?," *South African Journal on Human Rights*, Vol. 3, No. 3 (November 1989), pp. 295–300.

"The Law of Apartheid," in John Dugard, Nicholas Haysom, Gilbert Marcus, eds., *The Years of Apartheid: Civil Liberties in South Africa* (New York: Ford Foundation, 1992), pp. 3–31.

"Blacks and the Administration of Justice," in John Dugard, Nicholas Haysom, Gilbert Marcus, eds., *The Years of Apartheid: Civil Liberties in South Africa* (New York: Ford Foundation, 1992), pp. 95–111.

"Human Rights and the Rule of Law in Postapartheid South Africa," in Robert A. Licht and Bertus de Villiers, eds., *South Africa's Crisis of Constitutional Democracy: Can the U.S. Constitution Help?* (Washington, DC: American Enterprise Institute, 1994), pp. 122–142.

"International Law and the South African Constitution," *European Journal of International Law*, Vol. 8, No. 1 (1997), pp. 77–92.

"Is the Truth and Reconciliation Process Compatible with International Law? An Unanswered Question," *South African Journal on Human Rights*, Vol. 13, No. 2 (1997), pp. 258–268.

Duncan, Sheena, "The Rikhoto Scandal," *Black Sash*, Vol. 26, No. 3 (November 1983), pp. 22–24.

Du Plessis, Lourens, *An Introduction to Law*, 3rd ed. (Kenwyn: Juta, 1999).

Du Toit, André and Hermann Giliomee, *Afrikaner Political Thought: Analysis and Documents, Vol. 1: 1780–1850* (Berkeley: University of California Press, 1983).

Du Toit, Pierre, *State Building and Democracy in Southern Africa: Botswana, Zimbabwe, and South Africa* (Washington, DC: United States Institute of Peace Press, 1995).

and Willie Esterhuyse, eds., *The Mythmakers: The Elusive Bargain for South Africa's Future* (Johannesburg: Southern Books, 1990).

and Hennie Kotze, "The State, Civil Society, and Democratic Transition in South Africa: A Survey of Elite Attitudes," *Journal of Conflict Resolution*, Vol. 39, No. 1 (March 1995), pp. 27–48.

and Hennie Kotzé, "The South African State in Transition, 1990–2000," Paper presented at the 18th International Political Science Association World Congress, Quebec, Canada, August 1–5, 2000.

Dyson, Kenneth, *The State Tradition in Western Europe* (Oxford: Martin Robertson, 1980).

Dyzenhaus, David, *Hard Cases in Wicked Legal Systems: South African Law in the Perspective of Legal Philosophy* (Oxford: Clarendon Press, 1991).

"The Legitimacy of Legality," *Archiv für Rechts- und Sozialphilosophie*, Vol. 82, No. 3 (1996), pp. 324–360.

Legality and Legitimacy: Carl Schmitt, Hans Kelsen and Hermann Heller in Weimar (Oxford: Oxford University Press, 1997).

"Law as Justification: Etienne Mureinik's Conception of Legal Culture," *South African Journal on Human Rights*, Vol. 14, No. 1 (1998), pp. 11–37.

Judging the Judges, Judging Ourselves: Truth, Reconciliation and the Apartheid Legal Order (Oxford: Hart, 1998).

Ebrahim, Hassen, *The Soul of the Nation: Constitution-Making in South Africa* (Cape Town: Oxford University Press, 1998).

"The Making of the South African Constitution: Some Influences," in Penelope Andrews and Stephen Ellmann, eds., *The Post-Apartheid Constitutions: Perspectives on South Africa's Basic Law* (Johannesburg: Witwatersrand University Press, 2001), pp. 85–102.

Eisenstadt, Shmuel and Bernhard Giesen, "The Construction of Collective Identity," *Archives Européennes de Sociologie*, Vol. 36, No. 1 (1995), pp. 72–102.

Ellis, Stephen, "The Historical Significance of South Africa's Third Force," *Journal of Southern African Studies*, Vol. 24, No. 2 (June 1998), pp. 261–299.

Ellis, Stephen and Tsepo Sechaba, *Comrades against Apartheid: The ANC and the South African Communist Party in Exile* (London: James Currey, 1992).

Ellmann, Stephen, "Legal Text and Lawyers' Culture in South Africa," *New York University Review of Law and Social Change*, Vol. 17, No. 3 (1989/1990), pp. 387–417.

"Lawyers against the Emergency," *South African Journal on Human Rights*, Vol. 6, No. 2 (1990), pp. 228–250.

In a Time of Trouble: Law and Liberty in South Africa's State of Emergency (Oxford: Clarendon Press, 1992).

"Law and Legitimacy in South Africa," *Law and Social Inquiry*, Vol. 20, No. 2 (Spring 1995), pp. 407–479.

Eloff, C. F., "The Role of the Judiciary," *South African Law Journal*, Vol. 115, No. 1 (1998), pp. 64–65.

Elphick, Richard and Rodney Davenport, eds., *Christianity in South Africa: A Political, Social, and Cultural History* (Berkeley: University of California Press, 1997).

Elphick, Richard and Hermann Giliomee, eds., *The Shaping of South African Society, 1652–1840* (Cape Town: Maskew Miller Longman, [1979] 1989).

and Hermann Giliomee, "The Origins and Entrenchment of European Dominance at the Cape, 1652–c.1840," in Richard Elphick and Hermann Giliomee, eds., *The Shaping of South African Society, 1652–1840* (Cape Town: Maskew Miller Longman, [1979] 1989), pp. 521–566.

Elster, Jon, *Explaining Technical Change* (Cambridge: Cambridge University Press, 1983).

"Introduction," in idem. ed., *Rational Choice* (New York: New York University Press, 1986), pp. 1–33.

The Cement of Society: A Study of Social Order (Cambridge: Cambridge University Press, 1989).

"On Doing What One Can," *East European Constitutional Review*, Vol. 1 (1992), pp. 15–17.

"Rational-Choice History: A Case of Excessive Ambition," *American Political Science Review*, Vol. 94, No. 3 (September 2000), pp. 685–695.

Emerson, Richard M., "Power-Dependence Relations," *American Sociological Review*, Vol. 27, No. 1 (February 1962), pp. 31–41.

"Social Exchange Theory," in Morris Rosenberg and Ralph H. Turner, eds., *Social Psychology: Sociological Perspectives* (New York: Basic Books, 1981), pp. 30–65.

Ensley, Michael J. and Michael C. Munger, "Ideological Competition and Institutions: Why 'Cultural' Explanations of Development Patterns Are Not Nonsense," in Ram Mudambi, Pietro Navarra, and Giuseppe Sobbrio, eds., *Rules and Reason: Perspectives on Constitutional Political Economy* (Cambridge: Cambridge University Press, 2001), pp. 114–115.

Etherington, Norman, "Recent Trends in the Historiography of Christianity in Southern Africa," *Journal of Southern African Studies*, Vol. 22, No. 2 (June 1996), pp. 201–219.

Evans, Graham, "South Africa in Remission: The Foreign Policy of an Altered State," *Journal of Modern African Studies*, Vol. 34, No. 2 (June 1996).

Evans, Ivan, *Bureaucracy and Race: Native Administration in South Africa* (Berkeley: University of California Press, 1997).

Evans, Peter, "The State as Problem and Solution: Predation, Embedded Autonomy, and Structural Change," in Stephan Haggard and Robert R. Kaufman, eds., *The Politics of Economic Adjustment: International Constraints, Distributive Conflicts, and the State* (Princeton: Princeton University Press, 1992), pp. 139–181.

Embedded Autonomy: States and Industrial Transformation (Princeton: Princeton University Press, 1995).

"The Eclipse of the State? Reflections on Stateness in an Era of Globalization," *World Politics*, Vol. 50, No. 1 (October 1997), pp. 62–87.

Fallon, Jr., Richard H., "'The Rule of Law' as a Concept in Constitutional Discourse," *Columbia Law Review*, Vol. 97, No. 1 (January 1997), pp. 1–56.

Farlam, Paul, Reinhard Zimmermann, C. G. van der Merwe, J. E. du Plessis, and M. J. de Waal, "The Republic of South Africa," in Vernon Valentine Palmer, ed., *Mixed Jurisdictions Worldwide: The Third Legal Family* (Cambridge: Cambridge University Press, 2001), pp. 83–200.

Fearon, James D., "Rationalist Explanations for War," *International Organization*, Vol. 49, No. 3 (Summer 1995), pp. 379–414.

"Commitment Problems and the Spread of Ethnic Conflict," in David A. Lake and Donald Rothchild, eds., *The International Spread of Ethnic Conflict: Fear, Diffussion, and Escalation* (Princeton: Princeton University Press, 1998), pp. 107–126.

Feinstein, Charles H., *An Economic History of South Africa: Conquest, Discrimination and Development* (Cambridge: Cambridge University Press, 2005).

Ferejohn, John and Pasquale Pasquino, "Rule of Democracy and Rule of Law," in José María Maravall and Adam Przeworski, eds., *Democracy and the Rule of Law* (Cambridge: Cambridge University Press, 2003), pp. 242–260.

Finnegan, William, "The Poison Keeper," *The New Yorker*, January 15, 2001, pp. 58–75.

Finnis, John, *Natural Law and Natural Rights* (Oxford: Clarendon Press, 1980).

"Natural Law: The Classical Tradition," in Jules Coleman and Scott Shapiro, eds., *The Oxford Handbook of Jurisprudence and Philosophy of Law* (Oxford: Oxford University Press, 2002), pp. 1–60.

Fischhoff, Baruch, "For Those Condemned to Study the Past: Heuristics and Biases in Hindsight," in Daniel Kahneman, Paul Slovic, and Amos Tversky, eds., *Judgment Under Uncertainty: Heuristics and Biases* (Cambridge: Cambridge University Press, 1982), pp. 335–351.

Fishman, Robert M., "Rethinking State and Regime: Southern Europe's Transition to Democracy," *World Politics*, Vol. 27, No. 3 (April 1990), pp. 422–440.

Forsyth, Christopher and Johann Schiller, "Judicial Process, Positivism and Civil Liberty II," *South African Law Journal*, Vol. 98, No. 2 (May 1981), pp. 218–230.

Forsyth, C. F., *In Danger for their Talents: A Study of the Appellate Division of the Supreme Court of South Africa 1950–80* (Cape Town: Juta, 1985).

Foster, Don and Dennis Davis, *Detention and Torture in South Africa: Psychological, Legal and Historical Studies* (New York: St. Martin's Press, 1987).

Foucault, Michel, "Nietzsche, Genealogy, History," in idem., *Language, Counter-Memory, Practice: Selected Essays and Interviews*, edited with an Introduction by Donald F. Bouchard, translated from the French by Donald F. Bouchard and Sherry Simon (Ithaca, NY: Cornell University Press, 1977), pp. 139–164.

Fox, Gregory H. and Brad R. Roth, eds., *Democratic Governance and International Law* (Cambridge: Cambridge University Press, 2000).

Fraenkel, Ernst, *The Dual State: A Contribution to the Theory of Dictatorship*, translated from the German by E. A. Shils, in collaboration with Edith Lowenstein and Klaus Knorr (New York: Oxford University Press, 1941).

"Anstatt einer Vorrede," in idem., *Reformismus und Pluralismus: Materialien zu einer ungeschriebenen politischen Autobiographie*, edited by Falk Esche and Frank Grube (Hamburg: Hoffmann und Campe, 1973).

"Das Dritte Reich als Doppelstaat," in idem., *Reformismus und Pluralismus: Materialien zu einer ungeschriebenen politischen Autobiographie*, edited by Falk Esche and Frank Grube (Hamburg: Hoffmann und Campe, 1973).

Reformismus und Pluralismus: Materialien zu einer ungeschriebenen politischen Autobiographie, edited by Falk Esche and Frank Grube (Hamburg: Hoffmann und Campe, 1973).

Der Doppelstaat (Frankfurt am Main: Europäische Verlagsanstalt, 1974).

Gesammelte Schriften, Volume 2: Nationalsozialismus und Widerstand, edited by Alexander v. Brünneck (Baden-Baden: Nomos Verlagsgesellschaft, 1999).

Franck, Thomas M., "The Emerging Right to Democratic Governance," *American Journal of International Law*, Vol. 86, No. 1 (January 1992), pp. 46–91.

Frank, Jerome, "Some Reflections on Judge Learned Hand," *University of Chicago Law Review*, Vol. 24, No. 4 (Summer 1957), pp. 666–705.

Frankel, Philip H., *Pretoria's Praetorians: Civil-Military Relations in South Africa* (Cambridge: Cambridge University Press, 1984).

An Ordinary Atrocity: Sharpeville and Its Massacre (New Haven: Yale University Press, 2001).

Fredrickson, George M., *White Supremacy: A Comparative Study in American and South African History* (Oxford: Oxford University Press, 1981).

The Comparative Imagination: On the History of Racism, Nationalism, and Social Movements (Berkeley: University of California Press, 1997).

Freeman, Mark, *Truth Commissions and Procedural Fairness* (Cambridge: Cambridge University Press, 2006).

Friedberg, Aaron L., *In the Shadow of the Garrison State: Amercia's Anti-Statism and its Cold War Grand Strategy* (Princeton: Princeton University Press, 2000).

Friedman, Steven, *Building Tomorrow Today: African Workers in Trade Unions, 1970–1984* (Johannesburg: Ravan, 1987).

The Shapers of Things to Come? National Party Choices in the South African Transition, Research Report No. 22, Transition Series (Johannesburg: Centre for Policy Studies, 1992).

"From Breakthrough to Breakdown," in idem., ed., *The Long Journey: South Africa's Quest for a Negotiated Settlement* (Johannesburg: Ravan Press, 1993), pp. 21–33.

ed., *The Long Journey: South Africa's Quest for a Negotiated Settlement* (Johannesburg: Ravan Press, 1993).

"South Africa: Divided in a Special Way," in Larry Diamond, Juan J. Linz, and Seymour Martin Lipset, eds., *Politics in Developing Countries: Comparing Experiences with Democracy*, Second Edition (Boulder: Lynne Rienner, 1995), pp. 531–581.

"Too Little Knowledge is a Dangerous Thing: South Africa's Bargained Transition, Democratic Prospects and John Rawls' 'Veil of Ignorance'," *Politikon*, Vol. 25, No. 2 (June 1998), pp. 57–80.

Friedrich, Carl J. and Zbigniew K. Brzezinski, *Totalitarian Dictatorship and Autocracy* (New York: Praeger, 1963).

Fukuyama, Francis, "'Stateness' First," *Journal of Democracy*, Vol. 16, No. 1 (January 2005), pp. 84–88.

Fuller, Lon L., "Positivism and Fidelity to Law: A Reply to Professor Hart," *Harvard Law Review*, Vol. 71, No. 4 (February 1958), pp. 630–672.

The Morality of Law, rev ed: (New Haven: Yale University Press, 1969).

Gambetta, Diego, "Can We Trust Trust?," in Idem., ed., *Trust: Making and Breaking Cooperative Relations* (Oxford: Basil Blackwell, 1988), pp. 213–237.

Garretón, Manuel Antonio, "Political Processes in an Authoritarian Regime: The Dynamics of Institutionalization and Opposition in Chile, 1973–1980," in J. Samuel Valenzuela and Arturo Valenzuela, eds., *Military Rule in Chile: Dictatorship and Oppositions* (Baltimore: Johns Hopkins University Press, 1986), pp. 144–183.

La posibilidad democrática en Chile (Santiago: FLACSO Cuadernos de Difusión, 1989).

Gautschi, Thomas, "History Effects in Social Dilemma Situations," *Rationality and Society*, Vol. 12, No. 2 (May 2000), pp. 131–162.

Geddes, Barbara, *Politician's Dilemma: Building State Capacity in Latin America* (Berkeley: University of California Press, 1994).

Geertz, Clifford, "Local Knowledge: Fact and Law in Comparative Perspective," in idem., *Local Knowledge: Further Essays in Interpretive Anthropology* (New York: Basic Books, 1983), pp. 167–234.

Geldenhuys, Deon, *Isolated States: A Comparative Analysis* (Johannesburg: Jonathan Ball Publishers, 1990).

and Hennie Kotzé, "Man of Action," *Leadership*, Vol. 4, No. 2 (1985), pp. 30–47.

Gerhart, Gail M., *Black Power in South Africa: The Evolution of an Ideology* (Berkeley: University of California Press, 1978).

Gerstner, Jonathan N., "A Christian Monopoly: The Reformed Church and Colonial Society under Dutch Rule," in Richard Elphick and Rodney Davenport, eds., *Christianity in South Africa: A Political, Social, and Cultural History* (Berkeley: University of California Press, 1997), pp. 16–30.

Gibson, James L., "Does Truth Lead to Reconciliation? Testing the Causal Assumptions of the South African Truth and Reconciliation Commission," Unpublished Paper, Washington University, October 2001.

Overcoming Apartheid: Can Truth Reconcile a Divided Nation? (New York: Russell Sage Foundation, 2004).

"The Contributions of Truth to Reconciliation: Lessons from South Africa," *Journal of Conflict Resolution*, Vol. 50, No. 3 (June 2006), pp. 409–432.

and Gregory A. Caldeira," Defenders of Democracy? Legitimacy, Popular Acceptance, and the South African Constitutional Court," *Journal of Politics*, Vol. 65, No. 1 (February 2003), pp. 1–30.

and Amanda Gouws, *Overcoming Intolerance in South Africa: Experiments in Democratic Persuasion* (Cambridge: Cambridge University Press, 2003).

Giddens, Anthony, *The Nation-State and Violence* (Berkeley: University of California Press, 1985).

Giliomee, Herman, "Surrender Without Defeat: Afrikaners and the South African 'Miracle,'" Unpublished Paper, University of Cape Town, n.d.

The Afrikaners: Biography of a People (Charlottesville: University of Virginia Press, 2003).

and Lawrence Schlemmer, *From Apartheid to Nation-Building* (Cape Town: Oxford University Press, 1989).

Ginsburg, Tom, *Judicial Review in New Democracies: Constitutional Courts in Asian Cases* (Oxford: Oxford University Press, 2003).

Gintis, Herbert, *Game Theory Evolving: A Problem-Centered Introduction to Modeling Strategic Interaction* (Princeton: Princeton University Press, 2000).

Glenn, H. Patrick, *Legal Traditions of the World: Sustainable Diversity in Law* (Oxford: Oxford University Press, 2000).

Gluckman, Max, *The Judicial Process among the Barotse of Northern Rhodesia* (Glencoe: Free Press, 1955).

Goldberg, David Theo, *The Racial State* (Oxford: Blackwell, 2001).

Goldstone, Jack A., "Initial Conditions, General Laws, Path Dependence, and Explanation in Historical Sociology," *American Journal of Sociology*, Vol. 104, No. 3 (November 1998), pp. 829–845.

González, Francisco E. and Desmond King, "The State and Democratization: The United States in Comparative Perspective," *British Journal of Political Science*, Vol. 34, No. 2 (April 2004), pp. 193–210.

Golub, Stephen, "Battling Apartheid, Building a New South Africa," in Mary McClymont and Stephen Golub, eds., *Many Roads to Justice: The Law-Related Work of Ford Foundation Grantees Around the World* (New York: Ford Foundation, 2000).

"A House without a Foundation," in Thomas Carothers, ed., *Promoting the Rule of Law Abroad: In Search of Knowledge*, (Washington, DC: Carnegie Endowment for International Peace, 2006),

Goodrich, Peter, "Law and Modernity," *Modern Law Review*, Vol. 49, No. 5 (September 1986), pp. 545–559.

Languages of Law: From Logics of Memory to Nomadic Masks (Cambridge: Cambridge University Press, 1990).

Gordon, Robter, The White Man's Burden: Ersatz Customary Law and Internal Pacification in South Africa," *Journal of Historical Sociology*, Vol. 2, No. 1 (March 1989), pp. 41–65.

Malamud Goti, Jaime, *Game Without End: State Terror and the Politics of Justice* (Norman: University of Oklahoma Press, 1996).

"Dignity, Vengeance, and Fostering Democracy," *University of Miami Inter-American Law Review*, Vol. 29, No. 3 (Spring/Summer 1998), pp. 417–450.

Terror y justicia en al Argentina: Responsabilidad y democracia después de los juicos al terrorismo de Estado (Buenos Aires: Ediciones de la Flor, 2000).

Gourevitch, Peter Alexis, "The Governance Problem in International Relations," in David A. Lake and Robert Powell, eds., *Strategic Choice and International Relations* (Princeton: Princeton University Press, 1999), pp. 137–164.

Grafstein, Robert, "Rational Choice: Theory and Institutions," in Kristen Renwick Monroe, ed., *The Economic Approach to Politics: A Critical Reassessment of the Theory of Rational Action* (New York: Harper Collins, 1991), pp. 259–278.

Gready, Paul and Lazarus Kgalema, "Magistrates under Apartheid: A Case Study of Professional Ethics and the Politicisation of Justice," Occasional Paper, Centre for the Study of Violence and Reconciliation, August 2000.

"Magistrates under Apartheid: A Case Study of the Politicisation of Justice and Complicity in Human Rights Abuse," *South African Journal on Human Rights*, Vol. 19, No. 2 (2003), pp. 141–188.

Greenberg, Stanley B., *Race and State in Capitalist Development: Comparative Perspectives* (New Haven: Yale University Press, 1980).

Legitimating the Illegitimate: State, Markets, and Resistance in South Africa (New Haven: Yale University Press, 1987).

Greif, Avner and David D. Laitin, "A Theory of Endogenous Institutional Change," *American Political Science Review*, Vol. 98, No. 4 (November 2004), pp. 633–652.

Grimm, Dieter, ed., *Staatsaufgaben* (Frankfurt am Main: Suhrkamp, 1996).

Grindlee, Merilee S., *Getting Good Government: Capacity Building in the Public Sectors of Developing Countries* (Cambridge, MA: Harvard Institute for International Development, 1997).

Griswold, Erwin N., "The 'Coloured Vote Case' in South Africa," *Harvard Law Review*, Vol. 65 (1952), pp. 1361–1374.

"The Demise of the High Court of Parliament in South Africa," *Harvard Law Review*, Vol. 66 (1952), pp. 864–875.

Grogan, John, "The Appellate Division and the Emergency: Another Step Backward," *South African Law Journal*, Vol. 106, No. 1 (February 1989).

Gruchmann, Lothar, "Die 'rechtsprechende Gewalt' im nationalsozialistischen Herschaftssytem: Eine rechtspolitisch–historische Betrachtung," in Wolfgang Benz, Hans Buchheim, and Hans Mommsen, eds., *Der Nationalsozialismus: Studien zur Ideologie und Herrschaft* (Frankfurt: Fischer, 1994), pp. 78–103.

Justiz im Dritten Reich 1933–1940: Anpassung und Unterwerfung in der Ära Gürtner, Third Edition (München: Oldenbourg, 2001).

Grundy, Kenneth W., *The Militarization of South African Politics* (Oxford: Oxford University Press, 1988).

Guelke, Adrian, "The Impact of the End of the Cold War on the South African Transition," *Journal of Contemporary African Studies*, Vol. 14, No. 1 (January 1996), pp. 87–104.

Haas, Guenther H., "Calvin's Ethics," in Donald K. McKim, ed., *The Cambridge Companion to John Calvin* (Cambridge: Cambridge University Press, 2004), pp. 93–105.

Habermas, Jürgen, *Faktizität und Geltung: Beiträge zur Diskurstheorie des Rechts und des demokratischen Rechtsstaats* (Frankfurt am Main: Suhrkamp, 1992).

Between Facts and Norms: Contributions to a Discourse Theory of Law and Democracy, translated by William Rehg (Cambridge, MA: MIT Press, [1992] 1996).

Haggard, Stephan, *Pathways from the Periphery: The Politics of Growth in the Newly Industrializing Countries* (Ithaca, NY: Cornell University Press, 1990).

Hahlo, H. R. and Ellison Kahn, *The South African Legal System and its Background* (Cape Town: Juta, 1968).

Hale, Matthew, *The History of the Common Law of England*, edited and with an Introduction by Charles M. Gray (Chicago: University of Chicago Press, [1713] 1971).

Hall, Peter, "Aligning Ontology and Methodology in Comparative Research," in James Mahoney and Dietrich Rueschemeyer, eds., *Comparative Historical Analysis in the Social Sciences* (Cambridge: Cambridge University Press, 2003), pp. 373–406.

Hallaq, Wael B., *The Origins and Evolution of Islamic Law* (Cambridge: Cambridge University Press, 2004).

Hancock, William Keith, *Smuts: The Fields of Force, 1919–1950* (Cambridge: Cambridge University Press, 1968).

Hardin, Russell, "Why a Constitution?," in Bernard Grofman and Donald Wittman, eds., *The Federalist Papers and the New Institutionalism* (New York: Agathon Press, 1989), pp. 100–120.

"The Social Evolution of Cooperation," in Karen Schweers Cook and Margaret Levi, eds., *The Limits of Rationality* (Chicago: University of Chicago Press, 1990), pp. 358–378.

One for All: The Logic of Group Conflict (Princeton: Princeton University Press, 1995).

Liberalism, Constitutionalism, and Democracy (Oxford: Oxford University Press, 1999).

"The Public Trust," in Susan J. Pharr and Robert D. Putnam, eds., *Disaffected Democracies: What's Troubling the Trilateral Countries?* (Princeton: Princeton University Press, 2000), pp. 31–51.

Trust and Trustworthiness (New York: Russell Sage Foundation, 2002).

"Law and Social Order," *Noûs*, Vol. 35, Supplement 1 (October 2001), pp. 61–85.

Hathaway, Oona A., "Path Dependence in the Law: The Course and Pattern of Legal Change in a Common Law System," *Iowa Law Review*, Vol. 86, No. 2 (January 2001), pp. 601–665.

Hayner, Priscilla B., *Unspeakable Truths: Confronting State Terror and Atrocity* (New York: Routledge, 2001).

Haynie, Stacia L., Idem., "Judicial Descision-Making and the Use of Panels in the South African Appellate Division, 1950–1990," *Politikon*, Vol. 29, No. 2 (November 2002), pp. 147–161.

Judging Black and White: Decision Making in the South African Appellate Division, 1950–1990 (New York: Lang, 2003).

Haysom, Nicholas, "Vigilantes and Militarization," in Jacklyn Cock and Laurie Nathan, eds., *War and Society: The Militarization of South Africa* (Cape Town: David Philip, 1989), pp. 188–199.

and Clive Pasket, "The War against Law: Judicial Activism and the Appellate Division," *South African Journal on Human Rights*, Vol. 4, No. 3 (1988), pp. 303–333.

Herbst, Jeffrey, *States and Power in Africa: Comparative Lessons in Authority and Control* (Princeton: Princeton University Press, 2000).

Herrera, Genaro Arriagada and Carol Graham, "Chile: Sustaining Adjustment during Democratic Transition," in Stephan Haggard and Steven B. Webb, eds., *Voting for Reform: Democracy, Political Liberalization, and Economic Adjustment* (New York: Oxford University Press, 1994), pp. 242–289.

Hesselink, I. John, *Calvin's Concept of the Law* (Allison Park: Pickwick Publications, 1992).

Heydebrand, Wolf, "Process Rationality as Legal Governance: A Comparative Perspective," *International Sociology*, Vol. 18, No. 2 (June 2003), pp. 325–349.

Heymann, Philip B., *Terrorism and America: A Commonsense Strategy for a Democratic Society* (Cambridge, MA: MIT Press, 1998).

Himma, Kenneth Einar, "Inclusive Legal Positivism," in Jules Coleman and Scott Shapiro, eds., *The Oxford Handbook of Jurisprudence and Philosophy of Law* (Oxford: Oxford University Press, 2002), pp. 125–165.

Hintze, Otto, "Preußens Entwicklung zum Rechtsstaat," in idem., *Regierung Verwaltung: Gesammelte Abhandlungen zur Staats-, Rechts- und Sozialgeschichte*, edited by Gerhard Oestreich (Göttingen: Vandenhock und Ruprecht, 1967), pp. 97–163.

"The Formation of States and Constitutional Development: A Study in History and Politics," in Felix Gilbert, ed., *The Historical Essays of Otto Hintze* (New York: Oxford University Press, 1975), pp. 157–177.

Hirschman, Albert O., *The Strategy of Economic Development* (New Haven: Yale University Press, 1958).

Exit, Voice, and Loyalty: Responses to Decline in Firms, Organizations, and States (Cambridge, MA: Harvard University Press, 1970).

"Exit, Voice, and the State," *World Politics*, Vol. 31, No. 1 (October 1978), pp. 90–107.

"Exit, Voice, and the Fate of the German Democratic Republic: An Essay in Conceptual History," *World Politics*, Vol. 45, No. 2 (January 1993), pp. 173–202.

Hobsbawm, Eric and Terence Ranger, eds., *The Invention of Tradition* (Cambridge: Cambridge University Press, 1983).

Hodgson, Geoffrey M., "The Return of Institutional Economics," in Neil J. Smelser and Richard Swedberg, eds., *The Handbook of Economic Sociology* (Princeton: Princeton University Press, 1994), pp. 58–76.

Hogue, Arthur R., *Origins of the Common Law* (Indianapolis: Liberty Fund, 1986).

Holder, R. Ward, "Calvin's Heritage," in Donald K. McKim, ed., *The Cambridge Companion to John Calvin* (Cambridge: Cambridge University Press, 2004), pp. 245–273.

Hollis, Martin, *Trust Within Reason* (Cambridge: Cambridge University Press, 1998).

Holmes, Stephen, "Precommitment and the Paradox of Democracy," in Jon Elster and Rune Slagstad, eds., *Constitutionalism and Democracy* (Cambridge: Cambridge University Press, 1988), pp. 195–240.

"Lineages of the Rule of Law," in José María Maravall and Adam Przeworski, eds., *Democracy and the Rule of Law* (Cambridge: Cambridge University Press, 2003), pp. 19–61.

and Cass R. Sunstein, *The Cost of Rights: Why Liberty Depends on Taxes* (New York: W. W. Norton, 1999).

Holsti, Kalevi J., *The State, War, and the State of War* (Cambridge: Cambridge University Press, 1996).

Homans, George C., *Social Behavior: Its Elementary Forms* (New York: Harcourt, Brace, 1961).

Horowitz, Donald L., *A Democratic South Africa? Constitutional Engineering in a Divided Society* (Berkeley: University of California Press, 1991).

Huang, Philip C., *Civil Justice in China* (Stanford: Stanford University Press, 1996).

Huck, Steffen, "Trust, Treason, and Trials: An Example of How the Evolution of Preferences Can Be Driven by Legal Institutions," *Journal of Law, Economics, and Organization*, Vol. 14, No. 1 (1998), pp. 44–60.

Hund, John and Hendrik W. van der Merwe, *Legal Ideology and Politics in South Africa: A Social Science Approach* (Cape Town: Centre for Intergroup Studies, 1986).

Huntington, Samuel P., *The Third Wave: Democratization in the Late Twentieth Century* (Norman: University of Oklahoma Press, 1991).

Allan C. Hutchinson, *Evolution and the Common Law* (Cambridge: Cambridge University Press, 2005).

and Patrick Monahan, eds., *The Rule of Law: Ideal or Ideology?* (Toronto: Carswell, 1987).

Ignatieff, Michael, *Blood and Belonging: Journeys into the New Nationalism* (London: BBC Books/Chatto and Windus, 1993).

International Commission of Jurists, *South Africa and the Rule of Law* (Geneva: International Commission of Jurists, 1960).

Jeffery, Anthea J., "The Rule of Law Since 1994," in R. W. Johnson and David Welsh, eds., *Ironic Victory: Liberalism in Post-Liberation South Africa* (Cape Town: Oxford University Press, 1998), pp. 73–141.

"Truth Commission Repudiated by Its Own Amnesty Committee," News Release, South African Institute of Race Relations, November 30, 2000, available at http://www.sairr.org.za/wsc/pstory.htx?storyID=195.

Jellinek, Georg, *Allgemeine Staatslehre* (Berlin: Häring, 1900).

Jervis, Robert, *Perception and Misperception in International Politics* (Princeton: Princeton University Press, 1976).

"Cooperation under the Security Dilemma," *World Politics*, Vol. 30, No. 2 (January 1978), pp. 167–214.

Johnson, Terry, Christopher Dandeker, and Clive Ashworth, *The Structure of Social Theory: Strategies, Dilemmas, and Projects* (New York: St. Martin's Press, 1984).

Jones Luong, Pauline, "The 'Use and Abuse' of Russia's Energy Resources: Implications for State-Society Relations," in Valerie Sperling, ed., *Building the Russian State: Institutional Crisis and the Quest for Democratic Governance* (Boulder, CO: Westview Press, 2000), pp. 27–45.

Jung, Courtney, *Then I Was Black: South African Political Identities in Transition* (New Haven: Yale University Press, 2000).

and Ian Shapiro, "South Africa's Negotiated Transition: Democracy, Opposition, and the New Constitutional Order," in Ian Shapiro, *Democracy's Place* (Ithaca, NY: Cornell University Press, 1996), pp. 175–219.

Jurgens, Richard, "The Civil War That Never Happened," *Leadership*, Vol. 17, No. 2 (1998), pp. 40–47.

Kaempfer, William H., James A. Lehman, and Anton D. Lowenberg, "Divestment, Investment Sanctions, and Disinvestment: An Evaluation of Anti-Apartheid Policy Instruments," *International Organization*, Vol. 41, No. 3 (Summer 1987), pp. 457–473.

Kahn, Paul W., *The Cultural Study of Law: Reconstructing Legal Scholarship* (Chicago: University of Chicago Press, 1999).

The Reign of Law: Marbury v. Madison and the Construction of America (New Haven: Yale University Press, 1997).

Kalberg, Stephen, *Max Weber's Comparative-Historical Sociology* (Cambridge: Polity Press, 1994).

Kalyvas, Stathis N., *The Rise of Christian Democracy in Europe* (Ithaca, NY: Cornell University Press, 1996).

"The Decay and Breakdown of Communist One-Party Systems," *Annual Review of Political Science*, Vol. 2 (1999), pp. 323–343.

Kapuscinski, Ryszard, *Another Day of Life* (San Diego: Harcourt Brace, 1987).

Karl, Terry Lynn, "Dilemmas of Democratization in Latin America," *Comparative Politics*, Vol. 23, No. 1 (October 1990), pp. 1–21.

The Paradox of Plenty: Oil Booms and Petro-States (Berkeley: University of California Press, 1997).

and Philippe C. Schmitter, "Modes of Transition in Latin America, Southern and Eastern Europe," *International Social Science Journal*, Vol. 43, No. 128 (1991), pp. 269–284.

Karis, Thomas G., "The South African Treason Trial," *Political Science Quarterly*, Vol. 76, No. 2 (June 1961), pp. 217–240.

and Gail M. Gerhart, *From Protest to Challenge: A Documentary History of African Politics in South Africa, 1882–1990, Volume 5: Nadir and Resurgence, 1964–1979* (Bloomington: Indiana University Press, 1997).

Kasrils, Ronnie, *"Armed and Dangerous": My Undercover Struggle against Apartheid* (London: Heinemann, 1993).

Katzenstein, Peter, "Analyzing Change in International Politics: The New Institutionalism and the Interpretative Approach," Discussion Paper, Max-Planck-Institut für Gesellschaftsforschung, Cologne, October 1990.

Keegan, Timothy, *Colonial South Africa and the Origins of the Racial Order* (Charlottesville: University Press of Virginia, 1996).

Kennedy, W. P. and H. J. Schlosberg, *The Law and Customs of the South African Constitution* (London: Oxford University Press, 1935).

Kentridge, Sydney, "Telling the Truth about Law," *South African Law Journal*, Vol. 99, No. 4 (November 1982), pp. 648–655.

Keohane, Robert, *After Hegemony: Cooperation and Discord in the World Political Economy* (Princeton: Princeton University Press, 1984).

"International Institutions: Two Approaches," in Friedrich Kratochwil and Edward D. Mansfield, eds., *International Organization: A Reader* (New York: Harper Collins, 1994), pp. 44–57.

Kinghorn, Johann, "Modernization and Apartheid: The Afrikaner Churches," in Richard Elphick and Rodney Davenport, eds., *Christianity in South Africa: A Political, Social, and Cultural History* (Berkeley: University of California Press, 1997), pp. 135–154.

Kirchheimer, Otto, "State Structure and Law in the Third Reich," in William E. Scheuerman, ed., *The Rule of Law under Siege: Selected Essays of Franz L. Neumann and Otto Kirchheimer* (Berkeley: University of California Press, 1996), pp. 142–171.

Kitschelt, Herbert, "Political Regime Change: Structure and Process-Driven Explanations," *American Political Science Review*, Vol. 86, No. 4 (December 1992), pp. 1028–1034.

and Zdenka Mansfeldova, Radoslaw Markowski, eds., *Post-Communist Party Systems: Competition, Representation, and Inter-Party Cooperation* (Cambridge: Cambridge University Press, 1999).

Klare, Karl E., "Legal Culture and Transformative Constitutionalism," *South African Journal of Human Rights*, Vol. 14, Part 1 (1998), pp. 146–188.

Klotz, Audie, "Norms Reconstituting Interests: Global Racial Equality and U.S. Sanctions Against South Africa," *International Organization*, Vol. 49, No. 3 (Summer 1995), pp. 451–478.

and Neta Crawford, eds., *How Sanctions Work* (London: Macmillan, 2000).

Klug, Heinz, "Constitutional Law: Constitutional Reform," *Annual Survey of South African Law* (1992), pp. 693–729.

"Constitutional Law: Towards a New Constitutional Order," *Annual Survey of South African Law* (1993), pp. 1–41.

"Constitutional Law," *Annual Survey of South African Law* (1994), pp. 1–23.

"Law Under and After Apartheid," *Law and Social Inquiry*, Vol. 25, No. 2 (Spring 2000), pp. 657–667.

Constituting Democracy: Law, Globalism and South Africa's Political Reconstruction (Cambridge: Cambridge University Press, 2000).

"Participating in the Design: Constitution-Making in South Africa," in Penelope Andrews and Stephen Ellmann, eds., *The Post-Apartheid Constitutions:*

Perspectives on South Africa's Basic Law (Johannesburg: Witwatersrand University Press, 2001), pp. 128–163.

Knight, Jack, *Institutions and Social Conflict* (Cambridge: Cambridge University Press, 1992).

Koelble, Thomas A., "The New Institutionalism in Political Science and Sociology," *Comparative Politics*, Vol. 27, No. 2 (January 1995), pp. 231–243.

Kohli, Atul *Democracy and Discontent: India's Growing Crisis of Governability* (Cambridge: Cambridge University Press, 1990).

Kotzé, Hennie J., "South Africa: From Apartheid to Democracy," in Mattei Dogan and John Higley, eds., *Elites, Crises, and the Origins of Regimes* (Lanham: Rowman and Littlefield, 1998), pp. 213–236.

Kotzé, Hennie and Deon Geldenhuys, "Damascus Road," *Leadership*, Vol. 9, No. 6 (1990), pp. 12–28.

Krasner, Stephen D., "Approaches to the State: Alternative Conceptions and Historical Dynamics," *Comparative Politics*, Vol. 16, No. 2 (January 1984), pp. 223–246.

Kratochwil, Friedrich, *Rules, Norms, and Decisions: On the Conditions of Practical and Legal Reasoning in International Relations and Domestic Affairs* (Cambridge: Cambridge University Press, 1989).

Kunig, Philip, "Rechtsstaat," in Neil J. Smelser and Paul B. Baltes, eds., *International Encyclopedia of the Social and Behavioral Sciences* (Amsterdam: Elsevier, 2001), p. 12824.

Kuper, Leo, "African Nationalism in South Africa, 1910–1964," in Monica Wilson and Leonard Thompson, eds., *The Oxford History of South Africa, Volume II: South Africa 1870–1966* (Oxford: Clarendon Press, 1971), pp. 424–476.

Kurz, Achim, *Demokratische Diktatur? Auslegung und Handhabung des Artikels 48 der Weimarer Verfassung 1919–25* (Berlin: Duncker und Humblot, 1992).

Kydd, Andrew, "Overcoming Mistrust," *Rationality and Society*, Vol. 12, No. 4 (November 2000), pp. 397–424.

Kuyper, Abraham, *Calvinism* (Amsterdam: Honeker and Wormser, 1899).

Lahno, Bernd, "Trust, Reputation, and Exit in Exchange Relationships," *Journal of Conflict Resolution*, Vol. 39, No. 3 (September 1995), pp. 495–510.

Laitin, David D., "South Africa: Violence, Myths, and Democratic Reform," *World Politics*, Vol. 39, No. 2 (January 1987), pp. 258–279.

Lake, David A. and Robert Powell, "International Relations: A Strategic-Choice Approach," in idem., eds., *Strategic Choice and International Relations* (Princeton: Princeton University Press, 1999), pp. 8–13.

Landsberg, Chris, "Directing from the Stalls? The International Community and the South African Negotiation Forum," in Steven Friedman and Doreen Atkinson, eds., *South African Review 7: The Small Miracle* (Johannesburg: Ravan Press, 1994), pp. 276–300.

Langa, Pius N., "Submission to the Truth and Reconciliation Commission on the Role of the Judiciary," *South African Law Journal*, Vol. 115, No. 1 (1998), pp. 36–41.

Lanternari, Vittorio, *The Religions of the Oppressed: A Study of Modern Messianic Cults*, Translated by Lisa Sergio (New York: Knopf, 1963).

Lasswell, Harold, "The Garrison State," *American Journal of Sociology*, Vol. 46, No. 4 (January 1941), pp. 455–468.

Lea, Allan, *The Native Separatist Church Movement in South Africa* (Cape Town: Juta, 1925).

Lebow, Richard Ned, "What's So Different about a Counterfactual?," *World Politics*, Vol. 52, No. 4 (July 2000), pp. 550–585.

Legal Aid in South Africa: Proceedings of a Conference held in the Faculty of Law, University of Natal, Durban, from 2nd-6th July, 1973 (Durban: University of Natal Faculty of Law, 1974).

Leman-Langlois, Stéphane, "Constructing a Common Language: The Function of Nuremberg in the Problematization of Postapartheid Justice," *Law and Society Review*, Vol. 27, No. 1 (Winter 2002), pp. 79–100.

Levi, Margaret, "A Model, a Method, and a Map: Rational Choice in Comparative and Historical Analysis," in Mark Irving Lichbach and Alan S. Zuckerman, eds., *Comparative Politics: Rationality, Culture, and Structure* (Cambridge: Cambridge University Press, 1997), pp. 19–41.

Consent, Dissent, and Patriotism (Cambridge: Cambridge University Press, 1997).

"A State of Trust," in Valerie Braithwaite and Margaret Levi, eds., *Trust and Governance* (New York: Russell Sage Foundation, 1998), pp. 77–101.

Levitsky, Steven and Lucan A. Way, "The Rise of Competitive Authoritarianism," *Journal of Democracy*, Vol. 13, No. 2 (April 2002), pp. 51–65.

Lichbach, Mark I., "Contending Theories of Contentious Politics and the Structure-Action Problem of Social Order," *Annual Review of Political Science*, Vol. 1 (1998), pp. 401–424.

Lieberman, Evan, "Payment for Privilege? The Politics of Taxation in Brazil and South Africa," Unpublished Paper, University of California, Berkeley, n.d.

Race and Regionalism in the Politics of Taxation in Brazil and South Africa (Cambridge: Cambridge University Press, 2003).

Lijphart, Arend, *Democracy in Plural Societies: A Comparative Exploration* (New Haven: Yale University Press, 1977).

Power-Sharing in South Africa (Berkeley: Institute of International Studies, University of California, Berkeley, 1985).

Lindner, Johannes and Berthold Rittberger, "The Creation, Interpretation and Contestation of Institutions – Revisiting Historical Institutionalism," *Journal of Common Market Studies*, Vol. 41, No. 3 (June 2003), pp. 445–473.

Linz, Juan J., "Totalitarian and Authoritarian Regimes," in Fred I. Greenstein and Nelson W. Polsby, eds., *Handbook of Political Science, Volume 3: Macropolitical Theory* (Reading, MA: Addison-Wesley, 1975), pp. 175–411.

The Breakdown of Democratic Regimes: Crisis, Breakdown, and Reequilibration (Baltimore: Johns Hopkins University Press, 1978).

and Alfred Stepan, *Problems of Democratic Transition and Consolidation. Southern Europe, South America, and Post-Communist Europe* (Baltimore: Johns Hopkins University Press, 1996).

Lipton, Merle, *Capitalism and Apartheid: South Africa, 1910–84* (Gower: Aldershot, 1985).

Little, David, *Religion, Order, and Law: A Study in Pre-Revolutionary England* (Chicago: University of Chicago Press, [1969] 1984).

Llewellyn, Karl N. and E. Adamson Hoebel, *The Cheyenne Way: Conflict and Case Law in Primitive Jurisprudence* (Norman: University of Oklahoma Press, 1941).

Lobban, Michael, *White Man's Justice: South African Political Trials in the Black Consciousness Era* (Oxford: Clarendon Press, 1996).

Locke, John, "The Second Treatise of Government," in idem., *Two Treatises of Government*, edited with an Introduction and Notes by Peter Laslett (Cambridge: Cambridge University Press, 1970), pp. 265–428.

Lodge, Tom, *Black Politics in South Africa since 1945* (Johannesburg: Ravan Press, 1983).

"The Lusaka Amendments," *Leadership*, Vol. 7, No. 4 (1988).

Mandela: A Critical Life (Oxford: Oxford University Press, 2006).

Loveman, Brian, *Chile: The Legacy of Hispanic Nationalism*, 3rd ed. (New York: Oxford University Press, 2001).

Lowenberg, Anton D. and Ben T. Yu, "Efficient Constitution Formation and Maintenance: The Role of 'Exit'," *Constitutional Political Economy*, Vol. 3, No. 1 (Winter 1992), pp. 51–72.

Lowenberg, Anton D. and William H. Kaempfer, *The Origins and Demise of South African Apartheid: A Public Choice Analysis* (Ann Arbor: University of Michigan Press, 1998).

Luhmann, Niklas, *Legitimation durch Verfahren* (Frankfurt am Main: Suhrkamp, [1969] 1983).

Vertrauen: Ein Mechanismus der Reduktion sozialer Komplexität (Stuttgart: Ferdinand Enke Verlag, 1973).

Ausdifferenzierung des Rechts: Beiträge zur Rechtssoziologie und Rechtstheorie (Frankfurt am Main: Suhrkamp, 1981).

Das Recht der Gesellschaft (Frankfurt am Main: Suhrkamp, 1993).

Lukes, Steven, ed., *Power* (Oxford: Blackwell, 1986).

Mahomed, Ismail, Arthur Chaskalson, Michael Corbett, H J O van Heerden, and Pius Langa, "The Legal System in South Africa 1960–1994: Representations to the Truth and Reconciliation Commission," *South African Law Journal*, Vol. 115, No. 1 (1998), pp. 21–35.

Mahoney, James, "Path Dependence in Historical Sociology," *Theory and Society*, Vol. 29, No. 4 (August 2000), pp. 507–548.

The Legacies of Liberalism: Path Dependence and Political Regimes in Central America (Baltimore: Johns Hopkins University Press, 2001).

"Long-Run Development and the Legacy of Colonialism in Spanish America," *American Journal of Sociology*, Vol. 109, No. 1 (July 2003), pp. 50–106.

Mainwaring, Scott and Timothy R. Scully, eds., *Building Democratic Institutions: Party Systems in Latin America* (Stanford: Stanford University Press, 1996).

Makropoulos, Michael, "Kontingenz: Aspekte einer theoretischen Semantik der Moderne," *Archives Européennes de Sociologie*, Vol. 45, No. 3 (December 2004), pp. 369–399.

Malamud Goti, Jaime, *Game Without End: State Terror and the Politics of Justice* (Norman: University of Oklahoma Press, 1996).

"Dignity, Vengeance, and Fostering Democracy," *University of Miami Inter-American Law Review*, Vol. 29, No. 3 (Spring/Summer 1998), pp. 417–450.

Terror y justicia en al Argentina: Responsabilidad y democracia después de los juicos al terrorismo de Estado (Buenos Aires: Ediciones de la Flor, 2000).

Mamdani, Mahmood, *Citizen and Subject: Contemporary Africa and the Legacy of Late Colonialism* (Princeton: Princeton University Press, 1996).

When Victims Become Killers: Colonialism, Nativism, and the Genocide in Rwanda (Princeton: Princeton University Press, 2001).

Mandela, Nelson, "Black Man in a White Man's Court" in Sheridan Johns and R. Hunt Davis, Jr., eds., *Mandela, Tambo, and the African National Congress: The Struggle Against Apartheid, 1948–1990* (New York: Oxford University Press, 1991), pp. 111–115.

Long Walk to Freedom: The Autobiography of Nelson Mandela (Randburg: Macdonald Purnell, 1994).

"Prosperity Will Prove that I was Innocent," reprinted in Kader Asmal, David Chidester, and Wilmot James, eds., *Nelson Mandela: In His Own Words* (New York: Little, Brown, 2003), pp. 18–26.

Mann, Michael, "Authoritarian and Liberal Militarism: A Contribution from Comparative and Historical Sociology," in Steve Smith, Ken Booth and Marysia Zalewski, eds., *International Theory: Positivism and Beyond* (Cambridge: Cambridge University Press, 1996), pp. 221–239.

Mansfield, Edward D. and Jack Snyder, "Democratization and War," *Foreign Affairs*, Vol. 74, No. 3 (May/June 1995), pp. 79–97.

"Democratization and the Danger of War," *International Security*, Vol. 20, No. 1 (Summer 1995), reprinted in Michael E. Brown, Sean M. Lynn-Jones, Steven E. Miller, eds., *Debating the Democratic Peace* (Cambridge, MA: MIT Press, 1996), pp. 301–334.

Mantzavinos, C., *Individuals, Institutions, and Markets* (Cambridge: Cambridge University Press, 2001).

Douglass C. North, and Syed Shariq, "Learning, Institutions, and Economic Performance," *Perspectives on Politics*, Vol. 2, No. 1 (March 2004), pp. 75–84.

Manzo, Kate and Pat McGowan, "Afrikaner Fears and the Politics of Despair," *International Studies Quarterly*, Vol. 36, No. 1 (March 1992), pp. 1–24.

Marais, Hein, "Leader of the Pack," *Leadership* (August 1997), pp. 52–63.

Marais, Hennie, "From Parliamentary Sovereignty to Constitutionality: The Democratisation of South Africa, 1990 to 1994," in Penelope Andrews and Stephen Ellmann, eds., *The Post-Apartheid Constitutions: Perspectives on South Africa's Basic Law* (Johannesburg: Witwatersrand University Press, 2001).

Maravall, José María, *Regimes, Politics, and Markets: Democratization and Economic Change in Southern and Eastern Europe* (Oxford: Oxford University Press, 1997).

and Adam Przeworski, eds., *Democracy and the Rule of Law* (Cambridge: Cambridge University Press, 2003).

March, James G. and Johan P. Olsen, *Rediscovering Institutions: The Organizational Basis of Politics* (New York: Free Press, 1989).

Marcus, Gilbert, "Civil Liberties Under Emergency Rule," in John Dugard, "The Law of Apartheid," in John Dugard, Nicholas Haysom, Gilbert Marcus, eds., *The Years of Apartheid: Civil Liberties in South Africa* (New York: Ford Foundation, 1992), pp. 32–54.

Maré, Gerhard, *African Population Relocation in South Africa* (Johannesburg: South African Institute of Race Relations, 1980).

Marmor, Andrei, "Exclusive Legal Positivism," in Jules Coleman and Scott Shapiro, eds., *The Oxford Handbook of Jurisprudence and Philosophy of Law* (Oxford: Oxford University Press, 2002), pp. 104–124.

"The Rule of Law and Its Limits," *Law and Philosophy*, Vol. 23, No. 1 (January 2004), pp. 1–43.

Marshall, Peter, "Smuts and the Preamble of the UN Charter," *The Round Table*, Vol. 358, No. 1 (January 2001), pp. 55–65.

Marks, Shula and Stanley Trapido, "The Politics of Race, Class and Nationalism," in idem., eds., *The Politics of Race, Class and Nationalism in Twentieth Century South Africa* (London: Longman, 1987), pp. 1–70.

Marsh, Robert, "Weber's Misunderstanding of Traditional Chinese Law," *American Journal of Sociology*, Vol. 106, No. 2 (September 2000), pp. 281–302.

Marx, Anthony W., *Lessons of Struggle: South African Internal Opposition, 1960–1990* (New York: Oxford University Press, 1992).

"Race-Making and the Nation-State," *World Politics*, Vol. 48, No. 2 (January 1996), pp. 180–208.

Making Race and Nation: A Comparison of the United States, South Africa, and Brazil (Cambridge: Cambridge University Press, 1998).

Marx, Christoph, " 'The Afrikaners': Disposal of History or a New Beginning," *Politikon*, Vol. 32, No. 1 (May 2005), pp. 139–147.

Mathews, Anthony S., "Security Laws and Social Change in the Republic of South Africa," in Heribert Adam, ed., *South Africa: Sociological Perspectives* (London: Oxford University Press, 1971), pp. 228–248.

Law, Order and Liberty in South Africa (Berkeley: University of California Press, 1972).

Freedom, State Security and the Rule of Law: Dilemmas of the Apartheid Society (Berkeley: University of California Press, 1986).

"Omar v. the Oumas," *South African Journal on Human Rights*, Vol. 3, No. 3 (November 1989), pp. 312–317.

and R. C. Albino, "The Permanence of the Temporary – An Examination of the 90- and 180-Day Detention Laws," *South African Law Journal*, Vol. 83, No. 1 (February 1966), pp. 16–43.

Mayekiso, Mzwanele, *Township Politics: Civic Struggles for a New South Africa* (New York: Monthly Review Press, 1996).

McAdam, Doug, Sidney Tarrow, and Charles Tilly, *Dynamics of Contention* (Cambridge: Cambridge University Press, 2001).

McAuley, Mary, *Russia's Politics of Uncertainty* (Cambridge: Cambridge University Press, 1997).

McCormick, John P., *Carl Schmitt's Critique of Liberalism: Against Politics as Technology* (Cambridge: Cambridge University Press, 1997).

McKeown, Timothy, "Why is a Single Case Important?," *Newsletter of the American Political Science Association Organized Section in Comparative Politics*, Vol. 9, No. 1 (Winter 1998), pp. 12–15.

"Case Studies and the Statistical Worldview," *International Organization*, Vol. 53, No. 1 (Winter 1999), pp. 161–190.

McQuoid-Mason, D. J., "Omar, Fani and Bill – Judicial Restraint Restrained: A New Dark Age?," *South African Journal on Human Rights*," Vol. 3, No. 3 (November 1987), pp. 323–326.

Meer, Fatima, "African Nationalism – Some Inhibiting Factors," in Heribert Adam, *South Africa: Sociological Perspectives* (London: Oxford University Press, 1971), pp. 121–157.

Meierhenrich, Jens, "Apartheid's Endgame and the State," D.Phil. thesis, University of Oxford, 2002.

"Forming States after Failure," in Robert I. Rotberg, ed., *When States Fail: Causes and Consequences* (Princeton: Princeton University Press, 2004), pp. 153–169.

"Varieties of Reconciliation," *Law and Social Inquiry*, Vol. 33, No. 1 (Winter 2008), pp. 195–231.

Merry, Sally Engle, *Colonizing Hawai'i: The Cultural Power of Law* (Princeton: Princeton University Press, 1999).

Merryman, John Henry, *The Civil Law Tradition: An Introduction to the Legal Systems of Western Europe and Latin America* (Stanford: Stanford University Press, 1969).

Mgoqi, Wallace, "The Work of the Legal Resources Centre in South Africa in the Area of Human Rights Promotion and Protection," *Journal of African Law*, Vol. 36, No. 1 (Spring 1992), pp. 1–10.

Migdal, Joel, *Strong Societies and Weak States: State-Society Relations and State Capabilities in the Third World* (Princeton: Princeton University Press, 1988).

"Studying the State," in Mark Irving Lichbach and Alan S. Zuckerman, eds., *Comparative Politics. Rationality, Culture, and Structure* (Cambridge: Cambridge University Press, 1997), pp. 208–235.

State in Society: Studying How States and Societies Transform and Constitute One Another (Cambridge: Cambridge University Press, 2001).

Milner, Helen, *Interests, Institutions, and Information: Domestic Politics and International Relations* (Princeton: Princeton University Press, 1997).

Minow, Martha, *Between Vengeance and Forgiveness: Facing History After Genocide and Mass Violence* (Boston: Beacon Press, 1998).

Misztal, Barbara A., *Trust in Modern Societies: The Search for the Bases of Social Order* (Cambridge: Polity Press, 1996).

Mitchell, Timothy, "The Limits of the State: Beyond Statist Approaches and their Critics," *American Political Science Review*, Vol. 85, No. 1 (March 1991), pp. 77–96.

"Society, Economy, and the State Effect," in George Steinmetz, ed., *State/Culture: State-Formation after the Cultural Turn* (Ithaca, NY: Cornell University Press, 1999), pp. 76–97.

Moe, Terry M., "Political Institutions: The Neglected Side of the Story," *Journal of Law, Economics, and Organization*, Vol. 6, Special Issue (April 1990), pp. 213–253.

Mokgatle, D.D., "The Exclusion of Blacks from the South African Judicial System," *South African Journal on Human Rights*, Vol. 3, No. 1 (March 1987), pp. 44–51.

Molm, Linda D., *Coercive Power in Social Exchange* (Cambridge: Cambridge University Press, 1997).

Moodie, T. Dunbar, *The Rise of Afrikanerdom: Power, Apartheid, and the Afrikaner Civil Religion* (Berkeley: University of California Press, 1975).

Moore, Sally Falk, *Social Facts and Fabrications: "Customary" Law on Kilimanjaro, 1880–1980* (Cambridge: Cambridge University Press, 1986).

Morgenstern, Scott and Benito Nacif, eds., *Legislative Politics in Latin America* (Cambridge: Cambridge University Press, 2002).

Morin, Richard, "Rainbow's End: Public Support for Democracy in the New South Africa," Working Paper 2000–10, Joan Shorenstein Center on the Press, Politics, and Public Policy, John F. Kennedy School of Government, Harvard University, 2000.

Moss, Glenn, *Political Trials: South Africa, 1976–1979* (Johannesburg: Development Studies Group, 1979).

Müller, Ingo, *Furchtbare Juristen: Die unbewältigte Vergangenheit unserer Justiz* (Munich: Kindler, 1987).

Hitler's Justice: The Courts of the Third Reich (Cambridge, MA: Harvard University Press, 1991).

Mureinik, Etienne, "Fundamental Rights and Delegated Legislation," *South African Journal of Human Rights*, Vol. 1, No. 2 (August 1985), pp. 111–123.

"Dworkin and Apartheid," in Hugh Corder, ed., *Essays on Law and Social Practice in South Africa* (Cape Town: Juta, 1988), pp. 181–217.

"Pursuing Principle: The Appellate Division and Review under the State of Emergency," *South African Journal of Human Rights*, Vol. 5, No. 1 (1989), pp. 60–72.

"Emerging from Emergency: Human Rights in South Africa," *Michigan Law Review*, Vol. 92, No. 6 (May 1994), pp. 1977–1988.

Murray, Christina and Catherine O'Regan, eds., *No Place to Rest: Forced Removals and the Law in South Africa* (Cape Town: Oxford University Press, 1990).

Murray, Martin, *The Revolution Deferred: The Painful Birth of Post-Apartheid South Africa* (London: Verso, 1994).

Nadel, Mark V. and Francis E. Rourke, "Bureaucracies," in Fred I. Greenstein and Nelson W. Polsby, eds., *Handbook of Political Science, Volume 5: Governmental Institutions and Processes* (Reading, MA: Addison-Wesley, 1975), pp. 373–440.

Nelson, Joan M., "Linkages between Politics and Economics," *Journal of Democracy*, Vol. 5, No. 4 (October 1994), pp. 49–62.

Nettl, J. P., "The State as a Conceptual Variable," *World Politics*, Vol. 20, No. 4 (July 1968), pp. 559–592.

Neumann, Franz, *Behemoth: The Structure and Practice of National Socialism* (New York: Oxford University Press, 1942).

"Der Funktionswandel des Gesetzes im Recht der bürgerlichen Gesellschaft," in idem., *Demokratischer und autoritärer Staat: Beiträge zur Soziologie der Politik* (Frankfurt am Main: Europäische Verlagsanstalt, [1957] 1967), pp. 7–57.

Die Herrschaft des Gesetzes: Eine Untersuchung zum Verhältnis von politischer Theorie und Rechtssystem in der Konkurrenzgesellschaft, übersetzt und mit einem Nachwort von Alfons Söllner (Frankfurt am Main: Suhrkamp, 1980).

North, Douglass C., "A Framework for Analyzing Economic Organization in History," in idem., *Structure and Change in Economic History* (New York: W. W. Norton, 1981), pp. 33–44.

Structure and Change in Economic History (New York: W. W. Norton, 1981).

Institutions, Institutional Change and Economic Performance (Cambridge: Cambridge University Press, 1990).

"Autobiographical Lecture," reprinted in William Breit and Roger W. Spencer, eds., *Lives of the Laureates: Thirteen Nobel Economists*, 3rd ed: (Cambridge, MA: MIT Press, 1995), pp. 251–267.

"Epilogue: Economic Performance through Time," in Lee J. Alston, Thráinn Eggertsson, and Douglass C. North, eds., *Empirical Studies in Institutional Change* (Cambridge: Cambridge University Press, 1996), pp. 342–355.

Understanding the Process of Economic Change (Princeton: Princeton University Press, 2005).

and Robert P. Thomas, *The Rise of the Western World: A New Economic History* (Cambridge: Cambridge University Press, 1973).

O'Donnell, Guillermo, "On the State, Democratization and Some Conceptual Problems: A Latin American View with Glances at Some Postcommunist Countries," *World Development*, Vol. 21, No. 8 (1993), pp. 1355–1369.

Philippe C. Schmitter, and Laurence Whitehead, eds., *Transitions from Authoritarian Rule: Prospects for Democracy*, Four Volumes (Baltimore: Johns Hopkins University Press, 1986).

O'Meara, Dan, *Volkskapitalisme: Class, Capital and Ideology in the Development of Afrikaner Nationalism* (Cambridge: Cambridge University Press, 1983).

Forty Lost Years: The Apartheid State and the Politics of the National Party, 1948–1994 (Johannesburg: Ravan Press, 1996).

Omar, Dullah, "An Overview of State Lawlessness in South Africa," in Desiree Hansson and Dirk van Zyl Smit, eds., *Towards Justice? Crime and State Control in South Africa* (Cape Town: Oxford University Press, 1990), pp. 17–27.

Ottaway, Marina, *South Africa: The Struggle for a New Order* (Washington, DC: The Brookings Institution, 1993).

Pakenham, Thomas, *The Boer War* (New York: Random House, 1979).

Parker, Peter and Joyce Mokhesi-Parker, *In the Shadow of Sharpeville: Apartheid and Criminal Justice* (New York: New York University Press, 1998).

Pasquino, Pasquale, "Locke on King's Prerogative," *Political Theory*, Vol. 26, No. 2 (April 1998), pp. 198–208.

Pauw, Jacques, *In the Heart of the Whore: The Story of Apartheid's Death Squads* (Halfway House: Southern Book Publishers, 1991).

Into the Heart of Darkness: Confessions of Apartheid's Assassins (Johannesburg: Jonathan Ball, 1997).

Pedriana, Nicholas "Rational Choice, Structural Context, and Increasing Returns: A Strategy for Analytic Narrative in Historical Sociology," *Sociological Methods and Research*, Vol. 33, No. 3 (February 2005), pp. 349–382.

Pierson, Paul, "Increasing Returns, Path Dependence, and the Study of Politics," *American Political Science Review*, Vol. 94, No. 2 (June 2000), pp. 251–267.

Politics in Time: History, Institutions, and Social Analysis (Princeton: Princeton University Press, 2004).

Platzky, Laurine and Cherryl Walker, *The Surplus People: Forced Removals in South Africa* (Johannesburg: Ravan Press, 1985).

Poggi, Gianfranco, *The Development of the Modern State: A Sociological Introduction* (Stanford: Stanford University Press, 1978).

Polanyi, Karl, *The Great Transformation: The Political and Economic Origins of Our Time* (Boston: Beacon Press, [1944] 2001).

Posel, Deborah, *The Making of Apartheid, 1948–1961: Conflict and Compromise* (Oxford: Clarendon Press, 1991).

"Whiteness and Power in the South African Civil Service: Paradoxes of the Apartheid State," *Journal of Southern African Studies*, Vol. 25, No. 1 (March 1999), pp. 99–119.

Graeme Simpson, eds., *Commissioning the Past: Understanding South Africa's Truth and Reconciliation Commission* (Johannesburg: Witwatersrand University Press, 2002).

Posen, Barry R., "The Security Dilemma and Ethnic Conflict," in Michael E. Brown, ed., *Ethnic Conflict and International Security* (Princeton: Princeton University Press, 1993), pp. 103–24.

Posner, Eric, *Law and Social Norms* (Cambridge, MA: Harvard University Press, 2000).

Posner, Richard A., *Frontier of Legal Theory* (Cambridge, MA: Harvard University Press, 2001), pp. 145–169.

Postema, Gerald J., *Bentham and the Common Law Tradition* (Oxford: Clarendon Press, 1986).

"Law's Autonomy and Public Practical Reason," in Robert P. George, ed., *The Autonomy of Law: Essays on Legal Positivism* (Oxford: Oxford University Press, 1996), pp. 79–118.

Pound, Roscoe, *Interpretations of Legal History* (New York: Macmillan, 1923).

Powell, Jr., G. Bingham, *Elections as Instruments of Democracy: Majoritarian and Proportional Visions* (New Haven: Yale University Press, 2000).

Price, Robert M., "Apartheid and White Supremacy: The Meaning of Government-Led Reform in the South African Context," in Robert M. Price and Carl G. Rosberg, eds., *The Apartheid Regime: Political Power and Racial Domination* (Berkeley: Institute of International Studies, University of California, Berkeley, 1980), pp. 297–331.

The Apartheid State In Crisis: Political Transformation in South Africa, 1975–1990 (New York: Oxford University Press, 1991).

Provine, Doris Marie, "Courts in the Political Process in France," in Herbert Jacob, Erhard Blankenburg, Herbert M. Kritzer, Doris Marie Provine, and Joseph Sanders, *Courts, Law, and Politics in Comparative Perspective* (New Haven: Yale University Press, 1996), pp. 177–248.

Przeworski, Adam, "Some Problems in the Study of the Transition to Democracy," in Guillermo O'Donnell, Philippe C. Schmitter and Laurence Whitehead, eds., *Transitions for Authoritarian Rule: Comparative Perspectives* (Baltimore: Johns Hopkins University Press, 1986), pp. 47–63.

Democracy and the Market: Political and Economic Reforms in Eastern Europe and Latin America (Cambridge: Cambridge University Press, 1991).

Sustainable Democracy (Cambridge: Cambridge University Press, 1995).

and Fernando Limongi, "Modernization: Theories and Facts," *World Politics*, Vol. 49, No. 2 (January 1997), pp. 155–183.

Rabie, André, "Failure of the Brakes of Justice: *Omar v. Minister of Law and Order* 1987 (3) SA 859 (A)," *South African Journal on Human Rights*, Vol. 3, No. 3 (November 1989), pp. 300–311.

Ramaphosa, Cyril, "Negotiating a New Nation: Reflections on the Development of South Africa's Constitution," in Penelope Andrews and Stephen Ellmann, eds., *The Post-Apartheid Constitutions: Perspectives on South Africa's Basic Law* (Johannesburg: Witwatersrand University Press, 2001), pp. 71–84.

Rawls, John, *A Theory of Justice* (Cambridge, MA: The Belknap Press of Harvard University Press, 1971).

Raz, Joseph, *The Concept of a Legal System: An Introduction to the Theory of Legal System* (Oxford: Clarendon Press, 1970).

"The Rule of Law and its Virtue," in idem., *The Authority of Law: Essays on Law and Morality* (Oxford: Clarendon Press, 1979), pp. 210–229.

The Morality of Freedom (Oxford: Oxford University Press, 1986).

Reno, William, "Shadow States and the Political Economy of Civil Wars," in Mats Berdal and David M. Malone, eds., *Greed and Grievance: Economic Agendas in Civil Wars* (Boulder, CO: Lynne Rienner, 2000), pp. 43–68.

Reisman, W. Michael, "Why Regime Change Is (Almost Always) a Bad Idea," *American Journal of International Law*, Vol. 98, No. 3 (July 2004), pp. 516–525.

Report of the Chilean National Commission on Truth and Reconciliation, two Vols. (Notre Dame: University of Notre Dame Press, 1993).

Reynolds, Andrew, *Electoral Systems and Democratization in Southern Africa* (Oxford: Oxford University Press, 1999).

Rigobon, Roberto and Dani Rodrik, "Rule of Law, Democracy, Openness, and Income: Estimating the Interrelationships," Working Paper No. 10750 (Cambridge, MA: National Bureau for Economic Research, September 2004).

Riker, William, "The Experience of Creating Institutions: The Framing of the United States Constitution," in Jack Knight and Itai Sened, eds., *Explaining Social Institutions* (Ann Arbor: University of Michigan Press, 1995), pp. 121–144.

Roe, Mark J., "Chaos and Evolution in Law and Economics," *Harvard Law Review*, Vol. 109, No. 3 (January 1996), pp. 641–668.

Rokkan, Stein, "Dimensions of State Formation and Nation-Building: A Possible Paradigm for Research on Variations Within Europe," in Charles Tilly, ed., *The Formation of National States in Western Europe* (Princeton: Princeton University Press, 1975), pp. 562–600

Rose-Ackerman, Susan, "Establishing the Rule of Law," in Robert I. Rotberg, ed., *When States Fail: Causes and Consequences* (Princeton: Princeton University Press, 2004), pp. 182–221.

Rosen, Lawrence, *The Justice of Islam* (Oxford: Oxford University Press, 2000).

The Anthropology of Justice: Law as Culture in Islamic Society (Cambridge: Cambridge University Press, 1989).

Ross, Fiona C., *Bearing Witness: Women and the Truth and Reconciliation Commission in South Africa* (London: Pluto Press, 2003).

Ross, Michael L., *Timber Booms and Institutional Breakdown in Southeast Asia* (Cambridge: Cambridge University Press, 2001).

Rotberg, Robert I. with Miles F. Shore, *The Founder: Cecil Rhodes and the Pursuit of Power* (New York: Oxford University Press, 1988).

and Dennis Thompson, eds., *Truth v. Justice: The Morality of Truth Commissions* (Princeton: Princeton University Press, 2000).

Rothchild, Donald and Caroline Hartzell, "Interstate and Intrastate Negotiations in Angola," in I. William Zartman, ed., *Elusive Peace. Negotiating an End to Civil Wars* (Washington, DC: Brookings, 1995).

Rothstein, Bo, "Trust, Social Dilemmas and Collective Memories," *Journal of Theoretical Politics*, Vol. 12, No. 4 (October 2000), pp. 477–501.

Roux, Edward, *Time Longer Than Rope: The Black Man's Struggle for Freedom in South Africa* (Madison: University of Wisconsin Press, [1948] 1964).

Rubin, Leslie, "The Adaptation of Customary Family Law in South Africa," in Hilda Kuper and Leo Kuper, eds., *African Law: Adaptation and Development* (Berkeley: University of California Press, 1965), pp. 149–164.

Rueschemeyer, Dietrich, Evelyne Huber Stephens, and John D. Stephens, *Capitalist Development and Democracy* (Chicago: University of Chicago Press, 1992).

Rüthers, Bernd, *Die Unbegrenzte Auslegung: Zum Wandel der Privatrechtsordnung im Nationalsozialismus*, 5th ed. (Heidelberg: C. F. Müller, [1967] 1997).

Entartetes Recht: Rechtslehren und Kronjuristen im Dritten Reich, 2nd ed. (München: C. H. Beck, 1989).

Sachs, Albie, *Justice in South Africa* (Berkeley: University of California Press, 1973).

"The Future of Roman Dutch Law in a Non-Racial Democratic South Africa: Some Preliminary Observations," *Social and Legal Studies*, Vol. 1, No. 2 (June 1992), pp. 217–227.

Sampson, Anthony, *Mandela: The Authorized Biography* (New York: Knopf, 1999).

Sarkin, Jeremy, "Judges in South Africa: Black Sheep or Albinos: An Examination of Judicial Responses in the 1980s to Law and Human Rights and the Options Available to Tempter the Effects of Apartheid," LL.M Thesis, Harvard Law School, 1988.

Sanneh, Lamin, *Translating the Message: The Missionary Impact on Culture* (Maryknoll, OH: Orbis, 1989).

and Joel A. Carpenter, eds., *The Changing Face of Christianity*, OH: *Africa, the West, and the World* (Oxford: Oxford University Press, 2005).

Santos, Alvaro, "The World Bank's Uses of the 'Rule of Law' Promise in Economic Development," in David M. Trubek and Alvaro Santos, eds., *The New Law and Economic Development: A Critical Appraisal* (Cambridge: Cambridge University Press, 2006), pp. 253–300.

Sartori, Giovanni, *Parties and Party Systems: A Framework for Analysis* (Cambridge: Cambridge University Press, 1976).

Saul, John S., "From Thaw to Flood: The End of the Cold War in Southern Africa," *Review of African Political Economy*, Vol. 18, No. 50 (1991), pp. 145–158.

Saul, John, "Globalism, Socialism, and Democracy in the South African Transition," *Socialist Register 1994* (London: Merlin Press, 1994).

Savage, Katharine, "Negotiating South Africa's New Constitution: An Overview of the Key Players and the Negotiation Process," in Penelope Andrews and Stephen Ellmann, eds., *The Post-Apartheid Constitutions: Perspectives on South Africa's Basic Law* (Johannesburg: Witwatersrand University Press, 2001), pp. 164–193.

Schärf, Winfried, "The Role of People's Courts in Transitions," in Hugh Corder, ed., *Democracy and the Judiciary* (Cape Town: IDASA, 1988), pp. 167–184.

Schapera, Isaac, *A Handbook of Tswana Law and Custom* (London: Oxford University Press, 1938).

"Religion and Magic," in Isaac Schapera and John L. Comaroff, *The Tswana*, rev. ed. (London: Kegan Paul [1953] 1991).

"Government and Law," in Isaac Schapera and John L. Comaroff, *The Tswana*, rev. ed. (London: Kegan Paul [1953] 1991).

Schauer, Frederick, *Playing by the Rules: A Philosophical Examination of Rule-Based Decision-Making in Law and in Life* (Oxford: Clarendon Press, 1991).

Schedler, Andreas, "The Logic of Electoral Authoritarianism," in idem., ed., *Electoral Authoritarianism: The Dynamics of Unfree Competition* (Boulder, CO: Lynne Rienner, 2006), pp. 1–23.

Schelling, Thomas, *The Strategy of Conflict* (Cambridge, MA: Harvard University Press, 1960).

Arms and Influence (New Haven: Yale University Press, 1966).

Scheppele, Kim Lane, *Legal Secrets: Equality and Efficiency in the Common Law* (Chicago: University of Chicago Press).

Schlemmer, Lawrence, "The Turn in the Road: Emerging Conditions in 1990," in Robin Lee and Lawrence Schlemmer, eds., *Transition to Democracy: Policy Perspectives 1991* (Cape Town: Oxford University Press, 1991).

Schmitt, Carl, "Die Diktatur des Reichspräsidenten nach Art. 48 der Reichsverfassung," *Veröffentlichungen der Vereinigung der deutschen Staatsrechtslehrer*, No. 1 (Berlin, 1924), reprinted in idem., *Die Diktatur: Von den Anfängen des modernen Souveränitätsgedankens* (Berlin: Duncker und Humblot, [1921] 1989).

Politische Theologie, 7th ed. (Berlin: Duncker and Humblot, [1922] 1996).

Verfassungslehre, 8th ed. (Berlin: Duncker und Humblot, [1928] 1993.

Schrire, Robert A., "The Context of South African Politics," in Anthony de Crespigny and Robert Schrire, eds., *The Government and Politics of South Africa* (Cape Town: Juta, 1978), pp. xiii–xxx.

Adapt or Die: The End of White Politics in South Africa (Johannesburg: The Ford Foundation, 1991).

"The Myth of the 'Mandela' Presidency," *Indicator South Africa*, Vol. 13, No. 2 (Autumn 1996), pp. 13–18.

Schofield, Norman, "Anarchy, Altruism, and Cooperation: A Review," *Social Choice and Welfare*, Vol. 2, No. 1 (November 1985), pp. 207–219.

Schuessler, Alexander A., *A Logic of Expressive Choice* (Princeton: Princeton University Press, 2000).

Schulz, Gerhard, "Die Anfänge des totalitären Maßnahmenstaates," in Karl Dietrich Bracher, Wolfgang Sauer, and Gerhard Schulz, *Die Nationalsozialistische Machtergreifung: Studien zur Errichtung des totalitären Herrschaftssystems in Deutschlanbd 1993/34* (Köln: Westdeutscher Verlag, 1960).

Schwartz, Herman, *The Struggle for Constitutional Justice in Post-Communist Europe* (Chicago: University of Chicago Press, 2000).

Seegers, Annette, "The Head of Government and the Executive," in Robert Schrire, ed., *Leadership in the Apartheid State: From Malan to de Klerk* (Cape Town: Oxford University Press, 1994), pp. 37–79.

The Military in the Making of Modern South Africa (London: I. B. Tauris, 1996).

Seekings, Jeremy, "People's Courts and Popular Politics," in Glenn Moss and Ingrid Obery, eds., *South African Review 5* (Johannesburg: Ravan Press, 1989), pp. 119–135.

"Visions of 'Community' in South Africa's Informal Township Courts," Paper presented at the International Sociological Association, Amsterdam, June 1991.

The UDF: A History of the United Democratic Front 1983–1991 (Cape Town: David Philip, 2000).

Sejersted, Francis, "Democracy and the Rule of Law: Some Historical Experiences of Contradictions in the Striving for Good Government," in Jon Elster and Rune Slagstad, eds., *Constitutionalism and Democracy* (Cambridge: Cambridge University Press, 1988), pp. 131–152.

Seidman, Gay W., *Manufacturing Militance: Workers' Movements in Brazil and South Africa, 1970–1985* (Berkeley: University of California Press, 1994).

Shain, Yossi and Juan J. Linz, "Part One: Theory," in ibid., eds., *Between States: Interim Governments and Democratic Transition* (Cambridge: Cambridge University Press, 1995), pp. 1–123.

Shapiro, Ian, *Democracy's Place* (Ithaca, NY: Cornell University Press, 1996).

"Problems, Methods, and Theories in the Study of Politics, or: What's Wrong with Political Science and What to Do About It," in Ian Shapiro, Rogers S. Smith, and Tarek E. Masoud, eds., *Problems and Methods in the Study of Politics* (Cambridge: Cambridge University Press, 2004), pp. 19–41.

and Russell Hardin, eds., *Political Order: NOMOS XXXVIII* (New York: New York University Press, 1996).

Shaw, Mark, *Crime and Policing in Post-Apartheid South Africa: Transforming under Fire* (Bloomington: Indiana University Press, 2002).

Shepperson, George, "Ethiopianism and African Nationalism," *Phylon*, Vol. 14, No. 1 (1953), pp. 9–18.

Shezi, Sipho, "South Africa: State Transition and the Management of Collapse," in I. William Zartman, ed., *Collapsed States: The Disintegration and Restoration of Legitimate Authority* (Boulder, CO: Lynne Rienner, 1995), pp. 191–204.

Shubane, Khehla, "A Question of Balance," in Steven Friedman and Riaan de Villiers, eds., *The Right Thing: Two Perspectives on Public Order and Human Rights in South Africa's Emerging Democracy*, Research Report No. 64 (Johannesburg: Centre for Policy Studies, 1998), pp. 8–28.

and Peter Madiba, *The Struggle Continues? Civic Associations in the Transition*, Research Report No. 25 (Johannesburg: Centre for Policy Studies, 1992).

Simkins, C. E. W., *The Economic Implications of the Rikhoto Judgement*, SALDRU Working Paper 52, Southern Africa Labour and Development Research Unit, January 1983.

Sisk, Timothy D., *Democratization in South Africa: The Elusive Social Contract* (Princeton: Princeton University Press, 1995).

Skach, Cindy, *Borrowing Constitutional Designs: Constitutional Law in Weimar Germany and the French Fifth Republic* (Princeton: Princeton University Press, 2005).

Skocpol, Theda, *States and Social Revolutions: A Comparative Analysis of France, Russia, and China* (Cambridge: Cambridge University Press, 1979).

Smith, Adam, *The Theory of Moral Sentiments*, edited by D. D. Raphael and A. L. Macfie (Indianapolis: Liberty Fund, [1759] 1979).

Smith, Steven S. and Thomas F. Remington, *The Politics of Institutional Choice: The Formation of the Russian Duma* (Princeton: Princeton University Press, 2001).

Snyder, Jack and Robert Jervis, "Civil War and the Security Dilemma," in Barbara F. Walter and Jack Snyder, eds., *Civil Wars, Insecurity, and Intervention* (New York: Columbia University Press, 1999), pp. 15–37.

Snyder, Richard and James Mahoney, "The Missing Variable: Institutions and the Study of Regime Change," *Comparative Politics*, Vol. 32, No. 1 (October 1999), pp. 103–122.

Solnick, Steven L., *Stealing the State: Control and Collapse in Soviet Institutions* (Cambridge: Harvard University Press, 1998).

Soltan, Karol, Eric M. Uslaner, and Virginia Haufler, eds., *Institutions and Social Order* (Ann Arbor: University of Michigan Press, 1998).

Sombart, Werner, *Das Wirtschaftsleben im Zeitalter des Hochkapitalismus* (München: Duncker und Humblot, 1928).

Sparks, Allister, *The Mind of South Africa* (New York: Knopf, 1990).
Tomorrow is Another Country: The Inside Story of South Africa's Negotiated Revolution (Johannesburg: Struik Book Distributors, 1994).

Spence, J. E., "Reflections of a First Time Voter," *African Affairs*, Vol. 93, No. 372 (July 1994), pp. 341–342.
"Opposition in South Africa," *Government and Opposition*, Vol. 32, No. 4 (Autumn 1997), pp. 522–540.

Stahl, Friedrich Julius, *Die Philosophie des Rechts*, Volume 2 (Heidelberg: J. B. C. Mohr, 1846).

Stark, David and László Bruszt, *Postsocialist Pathways: Transforming Politics and Property in East Central Europe* (Cambridge: Cambridge University Press, 1998).

Stedman, Stephen John, "Negotiation and Mediation in Internal Conflict," in Michael E. Brown, ed., *The International Dimensions of Internal Conflict* (Cambridge, MA: MIT Press, 1996), pp. 341–376.

Steinberger, Peter J., *The Idea of the State* (Cambridge: Cambridge University Press, 2004).

Steinmetz, George, "Introduction: Culture and the State," in idem., *State/Culture: State-Formation after the Cultural Turn* (Ithaca: Cornell University Press, 1999), pp. 1–49.

Stepan, Alfred, *The Military in Politics: Changing Patterns in Brazil* (Princeton: Princeton University Press, 1971).

and Cindy Skach, "Constitutional Frameworks and Democratic Consolidation: Parliamentarianism versus Presidentialism," *World Politics*, Vol. 46, No. 1 (October 1993), pp. 1–22.

Stiefel, Ernst C. and Frank Mecklenburg, *Deutsche Juristen im amerikanischen Exil (1933–1950)* (Tübingen: J. C. B. Mohr, 1991).

Stinchcombe, Arthur L., *When Formality Works: Authority and Abstraction in Law and Organizations* (Chicago: University of Chicago Press, 2001).

Stimson, Shannon, "Rethinking the State: Perspectives on the Legibility and Reproduction of Political Societies," *Political Theory*, Vol. 28, No. 6 (December 2000), pp. 822–834.

Stolleis, Michael, *Recht im Unrecht: Studien zur Rechtsgeschichte des Nationalsozialismus* (Frankfurt am Main: Suhrkamp, 1994).

Stone, Andrew, Brian Levy, and Ricardo Paredes, "Public Institutions and Private Transactions: A Comparative Analysis of the Legal and Regulatory Environment for Business Transactions in Brazil and Chile," in Lee J. Alston, Thráinn Eggertsson, and Douglass C. North, eds., *Empirical Studies in Institutional Change* (Cambridge: Cambridge University Press, 1996), pp. 95–128.

Strauss, Gerald, *Law, Resistance, and the State: The Opposition to Roman Law in Reformation Germany* (Princeton: Princeton University Press, 1986).

Strayer, Joseph R., *On the Medieval Origins of the Modern State* (Princeton: Princeton University Press, 1970).

Suleiman, Ezra, "Bureaucracy and Democratic Consolidation: Lessons from Eastern Europe," in Lisa Anderson, ed., *Transitions to Democracy* (New York: Columbia University Press, 1999), pp. 141–167.

Sundkler, Bengt G. M., *Bantu Prophets in South Africa*, 2nd ed. (London: Oxford University Press, [1948] 1961).

and Christopher Steed, *A History of the Church in Africa* (Cambridge: Cambridge University Press, 2000).

Sunstein, Cass R., "Constitutions and Democracies: An Epilogue," in Jon Elster and Rune Slagstad, eds., *Constitutionalism and Democracy* (Cambridge: Cambridge University Press, 1988), pp. 327–356.

Legal Reasoning and Political Conflict (New York: Oxford University Press, 1996).

Designing Democracy: What Constitutions Do (Oxford: Oxford University Press, 2001).

Suttner, Raymond and Jeremy Cronin, eds., *30 Years of the Freedom Charter* (Johannesburg: Ravan, 1986).

eds., *50 Years of the Freedom Charter* (London: Zed Books, 2007).

Tamanaha, Brian, *A General Jurisprudence of Law and Society* (New York: Oxford University Press, 2001).

On the Rule of Law: History, Politics, Theory (Cambridge: Cambridge University Press, 2004).

Taras, Raymond, ed., *Postcommunist Presidents* (Cambridge: Cambridge University Press, 1997).

Taylor, Michael, *The Possibility of Cooperation* (Cambridge: Cambridge University Press, 1987).

Taylor, Rupert and Mark Shaw, "The Dying Days of Apartheid," in David R. Howarth and Aletta J. Norval, eds., *South Africa in Transition: New Theoretical Perspectives* (London: Palgrave, 1998).

Teitel, Ruti G., *Transitional Justice* (Oxford: Oxford University Press, 2000).

Thelen, Kathleen, "How Institutions Evolve: Insights from Comparative-Historical Analysis," in James Mahoney and Dietrich Rueschemeyer, eds., *Comparative Historical Analysis in the Social Sciences* (Cambridge: Cambridge University Press, 2003).

and Sven Steinmo, "Historical Institutionalism in Comparative Politics," in Sven Steinmo, Kathleen Thelen, and Frank Longstreth, eds., *Structuring Politics: Historical Institutionalism in Comparative Analysis* (Cambridge: Cambridge University Press, 1992), pp. 1–32.

Thompson, Clive, "Trade Unions Using the Law," in Hugh Corder, ed., *Essays on Law and Social Practice in South Africa* (Cape Town: 1988), pp. 335–348.

Thompson, E. P., *Whigs and Hunters: The Origin of the Black Act* (New York: Pantheon, 1975).

Thompson, Leonard M., *The Unification of South Africa 1902–1910* (Oxford: Clarendon Press, 1960).

"The Subjection of the African Chiefdoms, 1870–1898," in Monica Wilson and Leonard Thompson, eds., *The Oxford History of South Africa, Volume II: South Africa, 1870–1966* (Oxford: Clarendon Press, 1971), pp. 245–286.

The Political Mythology of Apartheid (New Haven: Yale University Press, 1985).

A History of South Africa, rev. ed. (New Haven: Yale University Press, 1995).

Tilly, Charles, *Big Structures, Large Processes, and Huge Comparisons* (New York: Russell Sage Foundation, 1984).

Coercion, Capital, and European States: AD 990–1992 (Oxford: Basil Blackwell, 1990).

The Politics of Collective Violence (Cambridge: Cambridge University Press, 2003).

Contention and Democracy in Europe, 1650–2000 (Cambridge: Cambridge University Press, 2004).

Tyler, Tom R., *Why People Obey the Law* (Princeton: Princeton University Press, 2006).

Tlali, Miriam, *Muriel at Metropolitan* (Johannesburg: Ravan Press, 1975).

Tönnies, Ferdinand, *Gemeinschaft und Gesellschaft: Grundbegriffe der reinen Soziologie* (Berlin: Curtius, [1887] 1922).

Tohidipur, Mehdi, ed., *Der bürgerliche Rechtsstaat*, two vols. (Frankfurt am Main: Suhrkamp, 1978).

Trapido, Stanley, "Political Institutions and Afrikaner Social Structures in the Republic of South Africa," *American Political Science Review*, Vol. 57, No. 1 (March 1963), pp. 75–87.

Trubek, David M., "The 'Rule of Law' in Development Assistance: Past, Present, and Future," in David M. Trubek and Alvaro Santos, eds., *The New Law and Economic Development: A Critical Appraisal* (Cambridge: Cambridge University Press, 2006), pp. 74–94.

Truth and Reconciliation Commission of South Africa, *Truth and Reconciliation Commission of South Africa Report*, Five Volumes (London: Macmillan Reference Limited, 1999).

Truth and Reconciliation Commission of South Africa, *Truth and Reconciliation Commission of South Africa Report*, Volume 6 (Cape Town: Juta, 2003).

Turner, Stephen P. and Regis A. Factor, eds., *Max Weber: The Lawyer as Social Thinker* (London: Routledge, 1994).

Tutu, Desmond M., "Foreword," in Greg Marinovich and Joao Silva, *The Bang-Bang Club: Snapshots from a Hidden War*, (New York: Basic Books, 2000), pp. ix–xi.

Twining, William, "A Post-Westphalian Conception of Law," *Law and Society Review*, Vol. 37, No. 1 (March 2003), pp. 199–258.

Unger, Roberto M., *Law in Modern Society: Toward a Criticism of Social Theory* (New York: Free Press, 1976).

United Nations, *Maltreatment and Torture of Prisoners in South Africa: Report of the Special Committee on Apartheid* (New York: United Nations, 1973).

Upham, Frank, "Mythmaking in the Rule-of-Law Orthodoxy," in Thomas Carothers, ed., *Promoting the Rule of Law Abroad: In Search of Knowledge* (Washington, DC: Carnegie Endowment for International Peace, 2006), pp. 75–104.

Valenzuela, Arturo, *The Breakdown of Democratic Regimes: Chile* (Baltimore: Johns Hopkins University Press, 1978).

"Chile: Origins, Consolidation, and Breakdown of a Democratic Regime," in Larry Diamond, Juan J. Linz, and Seymour Martin Lipset, eds., *Democracy in Developing Countries: Latin America* (Boulder, CO: Lynne Rienner, 1989), pp. 159–206.

"Party Politics and the Crisis of Presidentialism in Chile: A Proposal for a Parliamentary Form of Government," in Juan J. Linz and Arturo Valenzuela, eds., *The Failure of Presidential Democracy, Volume 2: The Case of Latin America* (Baltimore: Johns Hopkins University Press, 1994), pp. 91–150.

Valenzuela, J. Samuel, "Class Relations and Democratization: A Reassessment of Barrington Moore's Model," in Miguel Angel Centeno and Fernando López-Alves, eds., *The Other Mirror: Grand Theory Through the Lens of Latin America* (Princeton: Princeton University Press, 2001), pp. 240–286.

Van Aggelen, Johannes, "The Preamble of the United Nations Declaration of Human Rights," *Denver Journal of International Law and Policy*, Vol. 28, No. 2 (2003), pp. 129–144.

Van Blerk, Adrienne, "The Record of the Judiciary (1)," in Hugh Corder, ed., *Democracy and the Judiciary* (Cape Town: IDASA, 1988), pp. 26–45.

Van der Leeuw, Graham, "The Audi Alteram Partem Rule and the Validity of Emergency Regulation 3(3)," *South African Journal on Human Rights*, Vol. 3, No. 3 (November 1989), pp. 331–334.

Van der Vyver, J. D., "Rigidity and Flexibility in Constitutions: The Judiciary, the Rule of Law and Constitutional Amendment," in John A. Benyon, ed., *Constitutional Change in South Africa* (Pietermaritzburg: University of Natal Press, 1978), pp. 52–84.

Van Onselen, Charles, *The Seed is Mine: The Life of Kas Maine, A South African Sharecropper 1894–1985* (New York: Hill and Wang, 1996).

Van Puymbroeck, Rudolf V., ed., *Comprehensive Legal and Judicial Development* (Washington, DC: The World Bank, 2001).

Van Rooyen, Johann, *Hard Right: The New White Power in South Africa* (London: I. B. Tauris, 1994).

Van Zyl Slabbert, Frederik, *The Quest for Democracy: South Africa in Transition* (London: Penguin, 1992).

Venter, Albert, *South African Government and Politics: An Introduction to its Institutions, Processes, and Policies* (Johannesburg: Southern Book Publishers, 1989).

"The Central Government: Legislative, Executive, Judicial and Administrative Institutions," in idem., ed., *South African Government and Politics: An Introduction to its Institutions, Processes, and Policies* (Johannesburg: Southern Book Publishers, 1989), pp. 45–98.

Von Brünneck, Alexander, "Die Justiz im deutschen Faschismus," *Kritische Justiz*, No. 1 (1970), reprinted in Redaktion Kritische Justiz, ed., *Der Unrechts-Staat: Recht und Justiz im Nationalsozialismus* (Frankfurt am Main: Europäische Verlagsanstalt, 1979), pp. 108–122.

"Vorwort zu diesem Band," in Ernst Fraenkel, *Gesammelte Schriften, Volume 2: Nationalsozialismus und Widerstand*, edited by Alexander v. Brünneck (Baden-Baden: Nomos Verlagsgesellschaft, 1999).

Wachsmann, Nikolaus, "'Annihilation through Labor': The Killing of State Prisoner's in the Third Reich," *Journal of Modern History*, Vol. 71, No. 3 (September 1999), pp. 624–659.

Waldmeir, Patti, *Anatomy of a Miracle: The End of Apartheid and the Birth of the New South Africa* (London: Viking, 1997).

Walshe, Peter, "The Evolution of Liberation Theology in South Africa," *Journal of Law and Religion*, Vol. 5, No. 2 (1987), pp. 299–311.

Prophetic Christianity and the Liberation Movement in South Africa (Pietermaritzburg: Cluster, 1995).

Walt, Stephen M., *Revolution and War* (Ithaca, NY: Cornell University Press, 1996).

Walter, Barbara F., "Conclusion," in Barbara F. Walter and Jack Snyder, eds., *Civil Wars, Insecurity, and Intervention* (New York: Columbia University Press, 1999), pp. 303–307.

Ward, Michael D. and Kristian S. Gleditsch, "Democratizing for Peace," *American Political Science Review*, Vol. 92, No. 1 (March 1998), pp. 51–61.

Warren, Mark E., ed., *Democracy and Trust* (Cambridge: Cambridge University Press, 1999).

Weber, Marianne, *Max Weber: Ein Lebensbild* (Tübingen: J. C. B. Mohr, [1926] 1984).

Weber, Max, *Wirtschaft und Gesellschaft: Grundriß der Verstehenden Soziologie*, 5th ed. (Tübingen: J. C. B. Mohr, [1921] 1972).

Economy and Society: An Outline of Interpretive Sociology, edited by Guenther Roth and Claus Wittich (Berkeley: University of California Press, [1921] 1978).

The Protestant Ethnic and the Spirit of Capitalism, Translated by Talcott Parsons with an Introduction by Anthony Giddens (London: Routledge, [1930] 1992.

The Theory of Social and Economic Organization, edited with an Introduction by Talcott Parsons (New York: The Free Press, [1947] 1964).

Max Weber on Law in Economics and Society, edited by Max Rheinstein (Cambridge, MA: Harvard University Press, 1954).

Rechtssoziologie, edited by Johannes Winckelmann (Neuwied: Luchterhand, 1960).

Weingast, Barry R., "Constitutions as Governance Structures: The Political Foundations of Secure Markets," *Journal of Institutional and Theoretical Economics*, Vol. 149, No. 1 (May 1993), pp. 286–311.

"Political Institutions: Rational-Choice Perspectives," in Robert E. Goodin and Hans-Dieter Klingemann, eds., *A New Handbook of Political Science* (Oxford: Oxford University Press, 1996), pp. 167–190.

"The Political Foundations of Democracy and the Rule of Law," *American Political Science Review*, Vol. 91, No. 2 (June 1997), pp. 245–263.

"Constructing Trust: The Political and Economic Roots of Ethnic and Regional Conflict," in Karol Soltan, Eric M. Uslaner, and Virginia Haufler, eds., *Institutions and Social Order* (Ann Arbor: University of Michigan Press, 1998), pp. 163–200.

"A Postscript to 'Political Foundations of Democracy and the Rule of Law, '" in José María Maravall and Adam Przeworski, eds., *Democracy and the Rule of Law* (Cambridge: Cambridge University Press, 2003), pp. 109–113.

Weiß, Hermann, ed., *Biographisches Lexikon zum Dritten Reich* (Frankfurt am Main: Fischer, 2002).

Welsh, David, "The Making of the Constitution," in Hermann Giliomee, Lawrence Schlemmer, and Sarita Hauptfleisch, eds., *The Bold Experiment: South Africa's New Democracy* (Halfway House: Southern Book Publishers, 1994), pp. 81–98.

Wendt, Alexander, "The Agent-Structure Problem in International Relations Theory," *International Organization*, Vol. 41, No. 3 (Summer 1987), pp. 335–370.

Wendt, Alexander and Daniel Friedheim, "Hierarchy under Anarchy: Informal Empire and the East German State," in Thomas J. Biersteker and Cynthia Weber, eds., *State Sovereignty as Social Construct* (Cambridge: Cambridge University Press, 1996), pp. 240–277.

Wessels, Leon, "The End of an Era: The Liberation and Confession of an Afrikaner," in Penelope Andrews and Stephen Ellmann, eds., *The Post-Apartheid Constitutions: Perspectives on South Africa's Basic Law* (Johannesburg: Witwatersrand University Press, 2001).

Westad, Odd Arne, *The Global Cold War: Third World Interventions and the Making of Our Times* (Cambridge: Cambridge University Press, 2007).

Western, John, *Outcast Cape Town* (Berkeley: University of California Press, 1996).

Whitehead, Laurence, "Three International Dimensions of Democratization," in idem., ed., *The International Dimensions of Democratization. Europe and the Americas* (Oxford: Oxford University Press, 1996).

Wilkins, Ivor and Hans Strydom, *The Super-Afrikaners: Inside the Afrikaner Broederbond* (Johannesburg: Jonathan Ball, 1978).

Williamson, Oliver E., *Markets and Hierarchies: Analysis and Antitrust Implications* (New York: The Free Press, 1975).

"Credible Commitments: Using Hostages to Support Exchange," *American Economic Review*, Vol. 73 (September 1983), pp. 519–540.

The Economic Institutions of Capitalism (New York: The Free Press, 1985).

Wilson, Francis and Mamphela Ramphele, *Uprooting Poverty: The South African Challenge* (Cape Town: David Philip, 1989).

Wilson, Monica, "The Growth of Peasant Communities," in Monica Wilson and Leonard Thompson, eds., *The Oxford History of South Africa, Volume II: South Africa 1870–1966* (Oxford: Clarendon Press, 1971), pp. 49–103.

and Leonard Thompson, eds., *The Oxford History of South Africa, Volume I: South Africa to 1870* (Oxford: Clarendon Press, 1971).

Wilson, Richard A., *The Politics of Truth and Reconciliation in South Africa: Legitimizing the Post-Apartheid State* (Cambridge: Cambridge University Press, 2001).

"Justice and Legitimacy in the South African Transition," in Alexandra Barahona de Brito, Carmen Gonzaléz-Enríquez, and Paloma Aguilar, eds., *The Politics of Memory: Transitional Justice in Democratizing Societies* (Oxford: Oxford University Press, 2001), pp. 190–217.

Wolff, Robert Paul, ed., *The Rule of Law* (New York: Simon and Schuster, 1971).

Understanding Rawls: A Reconstruction and Critique of "A Theory of Justice" (Princeton: Princeton University Press, 1977).

Wood, Elisabeth Jean, "The Stakes of the Game: The Politics of Redistribution in Democratic Transition," Paper presented at the Annual Meeting of the American Political Science Association, Atlanta, September 2–5, 1999.

Forging Democracy From Below: Insurgent Transitions in South Africa and El Salvador (Cambridge: Cambridge University Press, 2000).

World Bank, *World Development Report 1997: The State in a Changing World* (Washington, DC: The World Bank, 1997).

Wrong, Dennis H., "Introduction: Max Weber," in idem., ed., *Max Weber* (Eaglewood Cliffs, NJ: Prentice Hall, 1970), pp. 1–76.

Würtenberger, Thomas, "Legitimität, Legalität," in Otto Brunner, Werner Conze, and Reinhart Koselleck, eds., *Geschichtliche Grundbegriffe: Historisches Lexikon zur politisch-sozialen Sprache in Deutschland*, Volume 3 (Stuttgart: Klett-Cotta, 1982), pp. 677–740.

Young, Oran R. *International Governance: Protecting the Environment in a Stateless Society* (Ithaca, NY: Cornell University Press, 1994).

Young, H. Peyton, *Individual Strategy and Social Structure: An Evolutionary Theory of Institutions* (Princeton: Princeton University Press, 1998).

Zakaria, Fareed, "The Rise of Illiberal Democracy," *Foreign Affairs*, Vol. 76, No. 6 (November/December 1997), pp. 22–43.

  The Future of Freedom: Illiberal Democracy at Home and Abroad (New York: Norton, 2003).

Zimmermann, Reinhard and Daniel Visser, "Introduction: South African Law as a Mixed Legal System," in idem., eds., *Southern Cross: Civil Law and Common Law in South Africa* (Oxford: Clarendon Press, 1996), pp. 1–30.

Zulu, Paulus, "Durban Hostels and Political Violence: Case Studies in KwaMashu and Umlazi," *Transformation*, Vol. 21 (1993) pp. 1–23.

Index

Abel, Richard, 209, 256, 326
Ackerman, Laurie, Justice, 172
administrative law, 65, 75, 227
Administrator, Transvaal v. Traub
   (1989), 163
African customary law
   influence of on South African law, 92
African National Congress (ANC), 7, 8,
      9, 27, 117, 122, 138, 147, 150, 152,
      153, 169, 182, 183, 184, 196, 259,
      261, 267, 268, 272, 282, 289.
   See also South African Native
      National Congress (SANNC)
   and apartheid's endgame, 191–207,
      263, 276–277
   and constitutional design, 197–205
   and electoral design, 196–197
   and Ethiopianism, 255–258
   and National Front for the Liberation
      of Angola (FNLA), 176
   and National Union for the Total
      Independence of Angola
      (UNITA), 176
   and Nelson Mandela, 279–281
   and Pan Africanist Congress (PAC), 122
   and preference formation, 190–195
   and religious constitutionalism, 255–258
   and the "Third Force," 123–125
   and the end of the Cold War, 184–187
   and the independent church movement,
      255–258
   and the Rivonia Trial, 136–137
   and the Treason Trial, 136–137, 147

and the Truth and Reconciliation
   Commission of South Africa
   (TRC), 205–207
and township unrest, 179
and township youth, 179
leaders and the law, 226–231, 262–263
African nationalism, 248, 255
Afrikaner Weerstandsbeweging
   (AWB), 27
and constitutional design, 199
Afrikaners, 84, 86, 88, 95, 96, 97, 98,
   101, 103, 170, 177, 188, 227,
   238, 239, 241, 242, 243, 246, 247,
   248, 261
Alessandri, Arturo, 297
Allende, Salvador, 298, 308
Allott, Philip, 15
analytic narratives, 2, 9, 11, 195, 290,
   291, 310, 327
ANC. *See* African National Congress
   (ANC)
Anglican Church of the Province
   (CPSA), 248
apartheid, 3, 4, 10, 11, 12, 15, 47, 52, 79,
   83, 86, 87, 101, 112, 120, 151, 152,
   154, 187, 188, 192, 196, 197, 198,
   199, 211, 212, 215, 216, 217, 220,
   261, 266, 275, 276, 279, 280, 295,
   296, 316
and administration, 107–108
and anti-apartheid lawyering, 208–214,
   235, 238, 255
and bureaucracy, 103–104

apartheid *(cont.)*
  and constitutional tradition, 172
  and death sentences, 121
  and fundamental rights, 286–287
  and human rights violations, 113–129,
    205
  and job reservation laws, 133
  and law, 140, 168, 112, 208, 239, 255,
    261, 295, 316
  and state formation, 277
  and states of emergency, 105–106, 122,
    128, 140, 157, 161, 168, 179, 192,
    223, 229
  and the collapse of the Portuguese
    empire, 175–176
  and the dual state, 112
  and the end of the Cold War,
    184–187
  and the legal system, 170, 112,
    220–239, 258
  and the limits of the prerogative state,
    130, 215, 283–289
  and the normative state, 129–169, 276,
    283–289
  and the prerogative state, 113–129,
    269, 276, 278
  evolution of, 102–111
  legal struggle against, 208, 209
  legality of, 317
  opposition to, 195
  Rabie Commission and, 214–215
  repression under, 192
  resistance to, 179
  Riekert Commission and, 213
  transition from crisis to endgame,
    181–182
  Wiehahn Commission and, 213
apartheid law, 3, 4, 10, 107, 172, 208,
    256, 264, 285
  and democracy, 195
  and Nazi law, 170
  and racial domination, 172
  formally rational, 171
  legality of, 231
  morality of, 231
  opposition against, 102
  procedural understanding of, 172
  statutes of, 216, 284, 285
  structure of, 171

substantively irrational, 171, 172
survey data on perceptions of, 220–239
apartheid state, 11, 83, 84, 86, 112, 172,
    175, 183, 285
  and democracy, 175, 238, 277
  and democratization, 276
  and emergency powers, 297
  and racial domination, 171
  and taxation, 217–218
  as dual state, 112, 127, 191, 268, 273
  as normative state, 129–131, 139,
    129–140
  as prerogative state, 113–129
  as preserved state, 218, 291
  as usable state, 268
  confidence in institutions of, 223–226,
    229–230
  dual nature of, 152
  evolution of, 102–111
  structure of, 4, 288
  surviving remnants of, 272–273
  transformation of, 279
apartheid's crisis, 175–176, 182
  and international influence, 182
  and investment u-turn, 178–179
  economic downturn and, 177–178
  international dimensions of, 184–187
  Portuguese empire and, 175–176
  township resistance and, 179–181
apartheid's endgame, 2, 3, 4, 5, 6, 7, 9, 11,
    15, 27, 30, 47, 48, 52, 79, 83, 84, 87,
    109, 117, 123, 128, 131, 136, 139,
    169, 174, 184, 186, 187, 192, 196,
    207, 216, 255, 257, 268, 274, 279,
    280, 281, 289, 291, 307, 310, 311
  advanced stages of, 274
  agents and preferences in, 191–192, 195
  analytic narratives of, 9, 195
  and anti-apartheid lawyering, 208–218
  and behavioral cultures, 216
  and bill of rights, 202–205
  and confidence in the legal system, 221
  and law, 200, 205, 208, 231, 263, 270,
    316
  and legal tradition, 231, 258–264
  and the dual state, 83, 175, 317
  and the legal tradition, 219
  and the problem of outcome
    knowledge, 9

Kotze, J. G., Chief Justice, 95
Krohn v. Minister of Defence (1915), 169
Kruger, Paul, 96, 97, 239, 240, 241, 242,
     246, 247
Kuyper, Abraham, 241, 242
KwaNdebele, 162

Labor Relations Act (1979), 213
Labor Relations Act (1988), 214
Laitin, David, 2
Land Act (1913), 132, 256
Langa, Pius, Chief Justice, 108, 261
law, 15
  and apartheid, 316
  and apartheid's endgame, 175, 205,
     208
  and democracy, 175
  and legitimacy, 208
  and political and economic reform,
     324
  and resolution of endgames, 315
  and struggle against apartheid, 208
  and truth commissions, 273
  as common knowledge, 190, 258,
     264, 287
  as common knowledge in apartheid's
     endgame, 258–264
  behavioral effect of, 50
  bifurcated history of in South Africa,
     209
  command theory of, 64, 73, 75
  conception of, 56–57, 258
  constitutional, 287
  cultural study of, 62
  culture of, 78
  definition of, 15
  development of in South Africa, 92–95
  evolution of, 48, 174
  evolution of in Chile, 315
  evolution of in South Africa, 315
  expressive function of, 317
  formally irrational, 17
  formally rational, 20, 19–23, 207, 227,
     273, 290, 304, 315
  formally rational, in Chile, 298, 303
  function of, 237, 240
  function of in times of transition, 158
  gap between and justice, 213
  hermeneutic effect of, 50

  ideology of, 60, 219, 289, 315
  in apartheid's endgame, 231
  in democratization, 315
  inclusionary nature of in South Africa,
     142
  instrumental function of, 317
  language of, 259
  legacies of, 12, 44, 48, 50, 51, 59, 62,
     79, 174, 232, 271, 289, 291, 295,
     313, 314, 317, 326
  legality and legitimacy of, 23–25
  legality of, 208
  legitimacy of, 231, 264, 268, 270, 273
  legitimacy of in South Africa, 264–275
  legitimization of the, 272
  Max Weber's ideal types of, 15–23
  modernization of, 323
  multiple functions of in South Africa,
     317
  natural law theory, 73
  new institutionalism and path
     dependent effects of, 59–62
  Philip Allott on social function of, 15
  political economy of, 16, 50, 318
  principle of the inviolability of, 63, 75
  procedural theory of, 25, 73–74, 172
  rationalization of, 21
  rhetoric of, 314
  rule of, 12, 20, 23, 47, 65, 95, 133,
     138, 139, 140, 141, 158, 164,
     165, 169, 172, 211, 227,
     232, 245, 261, 262, 264, 266,
     267, 272, 273, 274, 301, 310,
     323, 325, 326
  rules of, 79, 314
  social function of in times of
     transition, 168
  South African, 284
  South African statutory, 283
  substantively irrational, 17–18
  substantively rational, 18–19
  theory of, 11, 15, 62, 73, 74, 75, 314
  transformation of in South Africa, 93
Le Grange, Louis, 111
*Lebowa, Government of the Republic of
     South Africa and another v.
     Government of KwaZulu and
     another* (1983), 162
Lederer, Emil, 44

Mendoza, Cesar, 302
mental models, 57, 59, 60, 219, 315, 319
Merino, José Toribio, 302
*Metal and Allied Workers' Union v. State
   President* (1986), 157, 159
methodological individualism, 6, 46, 281,
   290
methodological structuralism, 290
Meyer, Roelf, 259, 260, 281, 290
migrant workers, 141, 142, 143, 145
Mines and Works Act (1911), 133
Mines and Works Amendment Act
   (1926), 133
*Minister of Law and Order and another
   v. Swart* (1989), 165
*Minister of Law and Order and others v.
   Hurley and another* (1986), 156
Minister of Law and Order v. Dempsey
   (1988), 158, 163
*Minister of Posts and Telegraphs v.
   Rasool* (1934), 115
Minister of the Interior v. Harris (the
   High Court of Parliament case
   1952), 134, 135, 136, 154
Minister van Wet en Orde v. Matshoba
   (1990), 163
Mokoena v. Minister of Law and Order
   (1986), 153
Mokwena v. State President (1988),
   158
Moseneke, Dikgang, Justice, 226,
   227, 232
Msimang, R. W., 255
Mugabe, Robert, 176
Multiparty Negotiating Process (MPNP),
   198, 199, 201
Municipal Labour Officers (MLO), 143
Mureinik, Etienne, 166, 216, 283,
   284, 285

Napoleon I, 21
Natal, 88, 89, 90, 94, 212
   rebellion, 98
Natal Indian Congress v. State President
   (1988), 168
*Natal Newspapers (Pty) Limited v. State
   President* (1986), 157
National Association of Democratic
   Lawyers (NADEL), 146

National Association of Youth
   Organizations (NAYO), 148,
   149, 150
National Front for the Liberation of
   Angola (FNLA), 176
National Intelligence Service (NIS), 105,
   169
National Party (NP), 9, 101, 111, 134,
   135, 187, 281, 282, 289
   and apartheid's crisis, 263–264
   and apartheid's endgame, 263–264,
   276–277
   and constitutional design, 197–205
   and electoral design, 196–197
   and expansion of the apartheid state,
   86–87
   and preference formation, 190–195
   and racial domination, 101
   and the end of the Cold War,
   186–187
   and Truth and Reconciliation
   Commission of South Africa
   (TRC), 205–207
*National Party v. Desmond Mpilo Tutu
   and others* (1997), 271
National Peace Accord, 282
National Security Management System
   (NSMS), 109
National Socialism, 3, 42, 43, 65, 67
National Union for the Total
   Independence of Angola
   (UNITA), 176
National Unity and Reconciliation Act
   (1995), 269, 270
Native Affairs Department (NAD), 86
Native Independent Congregational
   Church (NICC), 250
Ndlwana v. Hofmeyr (1937), 134
Neumann, Franz, 42, 43, 67, 71
Ngqumba v. Staatspresident (1988),
   158, 165
*Nkondo and Gumede v. Minister
   of Law and Order* (1986), 153,
   156
*Nkwentsha v. Minister of Law and Order
   and another* (1988), 165
Nkwinti v. Commissioner of Police
   (1986), 158
nomothetic reasoning, 10, 327

CPSIA information can be obtained at www.ICGtesting.com
Printed in the USA
BVOW07s2210080114

341267BV00002B/158/P